P9-CAA-918

Withdrawn

THE BASEBALL MANIAC'S ALMANAC

4TH EDITION

Also by Bert Randolph Sugar

Bert Sugar's Baseball Hall of Fame

Baseball's 50 Greatest Games

Baseball Picture Quiz Book

The Baseball Trivia Book

The Baseball Trivia Book to End All Baseball Trivia Books, Promise!

The Great Baseball Players from McGraw to Mantle

Rain Delays

Who Was Harry Steinfeldt? & Other Baseball Trivia Questions

THE BASEBALL MANIAC'S ALMANAC

4TH EDITION

The ABSOLUTELY, POSITIVELY, and WITHOUT QUESTION GREATEST BOOK of FACTS, FIGURES, and ASTONISHING LISTS EVER COMPLIED

Edited by Bert Randolph Sugar
with Ken Samelson and Stuart Shea

Copyright © 2005, 2010, 2012, 2016 by Bert Randolph Sugar
New Material © 2012, 2016 by Skyhorse Publishing, Inc.

All Rights Reserved. No part of this book may be reproduced in any manner without the express written consent of the publisher, except in the case of brief excerpts in critical reviews or articles. All inquiries should be addressed to Sports Publishing, 307 West 36th Street, 11th Floor, New York, NY 10018.

Sports Publishing books may be purchased in bulk at special discounts for sales promotion, corporate gifts, fund-raising, or educational purposes. Special editions can also be created to specifications. For details, contact the Special Sales Department, Sports Publishing, 307 West 36th Street, 11th Floor, New York, NY 10018 or sportspubbooks@skyhorsepublishing.com.

Sports Publishing® is a registered trademark of Skyhorse Publishing, Inc.®, a Delaware corporation.

Visit our website at www.sportspubbooks.com

10 9 8 7 6 5 4 3 2 1

Library of Congress Cataloging-in-Publication Data available on file.

ISBN: 978-1-61321-805-1

Printed in the United States of America

CONTENTS

Foreword xxxi

Part 1 **Individual Statistics** 1

1 **Batting** 3

Base Hits 3

Most Hits by Decade 3–4
Evolution of Singles Record 4
Most Hits, Season 4
Base Hit Leaders by State of Birth 4–5
Players with 200 Hits and 40 Home Runs, Season 5
Players with 200 Base Hits and Fewer Than 40 Extra-Base Hits, Season (Post-1900) 6
Players with 3000 Hits, Career 6
Most Hits by Position, Season 7
Players Hitting for the Cycle Two or More Times (Post-1900) 7
Most Times at Bat Without a Hit, Season 7
Players with 200 Hits in Each of First Three Major League Seasons 7
Players with 600 Total Hits in First Three Major League Seasons 7–8
Players with 200-Hit Seasons in Each League 8
Players with 200 Hits in Five Consecutive Seasons 8

Rookies with 200 or More Hits 8
Teammates Finishing One-Two in Base Hits 8–9
Players Getting 1000 Hits Before Their 25th Birthday 9
Players with 10000 At Bats and Fewer Than 3000 Hits, Career 9
Players with 200 Hits, Batting Under .300, Season 9
Players with 2500 Hits and Career .300 Batting Average Never Winning Batting Title (Post-1900), 9
Former Negro Leaguers with 1500 Major League Hits 10
Players with 2500 Career Hits, Never Having a 200-Hit Season 10
Latino Players with 2500 Hits 11
3000 Hits, 500 Home Runs, and a .300 Batting Average, Career 11
Most Hits by Switch-Hitter, Career 11
Most Hits by Catcher, Career 11
Most Singles, Career 11
Fewest Singles, Season (Min. 150 Games) 12–13
Most Singles, Season 13
20 Triple Seasons (Since 1930) 14
Largest Differential Between League Leader in Hits and Runner-Up 14

Batting Average 14

Evolution of Batting Average Record 14
Highest Batting Average by Position, Season 15
Highest Batting Average by Decade (2000 At Bats) 15–16
Highest Batting Average for a Rookie 16
Top 10 Rookie Batting Averages, Each League (Min. 100 Games) 16
Lifetime Batting Averages of 20-Year Players (Not Including Pitchers) 16–17
Players Never Hitting Below .270 in Career (Min. 10 Years) 17
Players Batting .300 for 10 or More Consecutive Seasons From Start of Career 18
.400 Hitters and How Their Team Finished 18

.400 Hitters Versus League Batting Average (Post-1900) 18
Players Hitting .370 Since Ted Williams's .406 Season (1941) 18
Players Hitting .300 in Rookie *and* Final Seasons (Post-1900; Min. Five Years) 19
Players Hitting .300 in Their Only Major League Season (Post-1900; Min. 100 Games, 300 At Bats) 19
Players Batting .350 with 50 Home Runs 19
Players 40 or Older Hitting .300 (Min. 50 Games) 19
Players Hitting .325 for Two or More Different Clubs (Post-1945) 20–21

Batting Title 21

Closest Batting Races 21–22
Teammates Finishing One-Two in Batting Race 22
Switch-Hitting Batting Champions 22
Catchers Winning Batting Titles 23
Batting Champions on Last-Place Teams 23
Batting Title Winners Without a Home Run 23
Batting Champions Driving in Fewer Than 40 Runs 23
Batting Champions with 100 Strikeouts in Year They Led League 23
Lowest Batting Averages to Lead League 23–24
Highest Batting Average *Not* to Win Batting Title 24
Runners-Up for Batting Titles in Both Leagues 25
Players Winning Batting Title in Season *After* Joining New Club 25
Players Changing Team in Season *After* Winning Batting Title 25
Largest Margin Between Batting Champion and Runner-Up 26
Champions Whose Next Season's Batting Average Declined the Most 26–27
Lowest Lifetime Batting Averages for Players Who Led League 27
Two-Time Batting Champions with Lifetime Batting Averages Below .300 27
Years in Which Right-Handed Batters Won Batting Titles in Both Leagues 28
Fewest Strikeouts For Batting Champions 28

Home Runs 28

Evolution of Home Run Record 28
Most Home Runs by Decade 29
Career Home Run Leaders by Zodiac Sign 30
All-Time Home Run Leaders by First Letter of Last Name 30
Home Run Leaders by State of Birth 30–31
500th Home Run of 500 Home Run Hitters 31–32
Most Home Runs in First Three Seasons in Majors 32
Most Home Runs for One Club 32
Most Home Runs by Position, Career 33
Most Home Runs *Not* Leading League, Season 33
Most Home Runs, Never Leading League, Career 34
Most Inside-the-Park Home Runs, Career (Post-1898) 34
Players with 10 or More Letters in Last Name, Hitting 40 or More Home Runs in Season 34
Most Home Runs by Visiting Player, by Stadium, 34–36
Most Home Runs, Month by Month 36
Most Home Runs by Position, Season 37
Players Leading League in Home Runs for Different Teams 37–38
Players with 40 Home Run Seasons in Each League 38
Players Hitting a Total of 100 Home Runs in Two Consecutive Seasons 38–39
Players with First 20-Home Run Season After 35th Birthday 39
Shortstops with at Least Seven Consecutive 20-Home Run Seasons 39–40
Players Hitting Four Home Runs in One Game 40
Career Home Runs by Players Hitting Four Home Runs in One Game 40–41
Players with Three Home Runs in One Game, Fewer Than 10 in Season 41
Rookies Hitting 30 or More Home Runs 41
Former Negro Leaguers Who Led Major Leagues in Home Runs 41–42
Players with 50 Home Runs, Batting Under .300, Season 42
Players Hitting 49 Home Runs in Season, Never Hitting 50 42
Most Multi-Home Run Games 42

Most Grand Slams, Career 42–43
Players Hitting Two Grand Slams, Same Game 43
Most Home Runs by Age 43
Teenagers Hitting Grand Slams 43
Oldest Players to Hit Grand Slams 43–44
Oldest Home Run Champions 44
Most Career Home Runs by Players Hitting Home Run on First Pitch in Majors 44–45
Players Hitting Home Run in First Time At Bat, Never Hitting Another 45
Most At Bats, No Home Runs, Career 45
Most Consecutive At Bats Without a Home Run 45–46
Lowest Batting Average for Home Run Leaders, Season (Post-1900) 46
Players Hitting 30 or More Home Runs in First Three Seasons 46
Reverse 30–30 Club: Players with 30 Home Runs and 30 Errors, Season 46
Players Increasing Their Home Run Production in Seven Consecutive Seasons 47
Most Home Runs by Switch-Hitters, Career 47
Most Home Runs by Catcher, Season 47–48
Most Home Runs by Catcher, Career 48
300 Career Home Runs and 100 Home Runs, Both Leagues 48
Most Home Runs Hit in One Ballpark, Career 48–49
Players Whose Home Run in "Cycle" Was Grand Slam 49
Players with the Highest Percentage of Team's Total Home Runs, Season 49
Shortstops Leading League in Home Runs 49–50
Most Home Runs by Left-Handed Hitting Shortstops 50
Players Hitting Home Runs in 20 Consecutive Seasons Played 50
Players with 100 Home Runs, Three Different Teams 50
Players with 40-Home Run Seasons Before 25th Birthday 50–51
Players with More Home Runs Than Strikeouts, Season (Min. 10 Home Runs) 51–53
Largest Differential Between Leader in Home Runs and Runner-Up 53
Most Home Runs, Last Season in Majors 53–54
Fewest Career Home Runs for League Leader (Post-1920) 54

Runs Batted In 54

Evolution of RBI Record 54–55
Most RBIs by Decade 55–56
Career RBI Leaders by First Letter of Last Name 56
Teammates Finishing One-Two in RBIs 56–57
Largest Differential Between League Leader in RBIs and Runner-Up 57
Career RBI Totals, Players Hitting 500 Home Runs 58
Players Driving in 100 Runs in First Two Seasons in Majors 58
Players Driving in 500 Runs in First Four Years of Career 58
Catchers with 100 RBIs and 100 Runs Scored, Season 58
Catchers Hitting .300 with 30 Home Runs and 100 RBIs, Season 59
Players with 40 or More Home Runs and Fewer Than 100 RBIs, Season 59
Players with More Than 100 RBIs and Fewest Home Runs, Season 59–60
Players with Most Career RBIs, Never Leading League 60
Players with 1000 Career RBIs, Never Driving in 100 in One Season 60
Batters Driving in 100 Runs with Three Different Teams 60–61
Players Driving in 130 Teammates During Season 61
Players Driving in 100 Runs, Season, in Each League 62–64
Players with More RBIs Than Games Played, Season (Min. 100 Games) 64–65
Players Driving in 20 Percent of Their Team's Runs, Season 65
Players with Lowest Batting Average for 100-RBI Season 65–66
Players on Last-Place Teams Leading League in RBIs, Season 66
Players Driving in 95 or More Runs in Season Three Times, Never 100 66

Runs Scored 66

Evolution of Runs Scored Record 66
Most Runs Scored by Decade 66–67

Players with More Runs Scored Than Games Played, Season (Min. 100 Games) 67–68
Players Scoring 1000 Runs in Career, Never 100 in One Season 68
Most Runs Scored by Position, Season 68

Walks 69

Evolution of Batters' Walks Record 69
Players with 1000 Walks, 2000 Hits, and 300 Home Runs, Career 69–70
Players Leading League in Base Hits and Walks, Season 70
Players with 200 Base Hits and 100 Walks, Season 70–71
Players with More Walks Than Hits, Season (Min. 100 Walks) 71–72
Players Hitting 40 or More Home Runs, with More Home Runs Than Walks, Season 72
Players with 90 Walks in Each of First Two Seasons 72

Strikeouts 72

Average League Strikeouts (Minimum 300 At-Bats) 72–73
Players with 100 More Career Strikeouts Than Hits (Min. 375 strikeouts) 74–75
Players with 500 At Bats and Fewer Than 10 Strikeouts, Season 75
Players with 200 Hits and 100 Strikeouts, Season 76
Players with 40 Home Runs and Fewer Than 50 Strikeouts, Season 76–77
Players with 100 More Strikeouts Than RBIs, Season 77–78
Toughest Batters to Strike Out, Career 78

Pinch Hits 78

Highest Batting Average for Pinch Hitter, Season (Min. 25 At Bats) 78

Extra-Base Hits 78

Evolution of Total Bases Record 78–79
Players with 100 Extra-Base Hits, Season 79

Players with 400 Total Bases, Season 79–80
Evolution of Doubles Record 80
Players Hitting 40 Home Runs and 40 Doubles, Season 80–81
Evolution of Triples Record 81
Leaders in Doubles and Triples, Season 81–82
Leaders in Doubles and Home Runs, Season 82
Leaders in Triples and Home Runs, Season 82
Players Hitting 20 Home Runs, 20 Triples, and 20 Doubles, Season 83
Players Leading League in Doubles, Triples, and Home Runs During Career (Post-1900) 83
Players Since World War II with 100 Doubles, Triples, Home Runs, and Stolen Bases, Career 83–84
Players with 200 Hits and Fewer than 40 Extra-Base Hits, Season 84
Most Doubles by Position, Season 84
Most Triples by Position, Season 84–85
Most Total Bases by Position, Season 85

Stolen Bases 85

Evolution of Stolen Base Record 85
Most Stolen Bases by Position, Season 86
Most Stolen Bases by Decade 86–87
Teammates Combining for 125 Stolen Bases, Season 87
Players Stealing 30 Bases for 10 Consecutive Seasons 87
Players Leading League in Stolen Bases and Total Bases, Season 87–88
Players with 200 Home Runs and 200 Stolen Bases, Career 88
Players with 400 Home Runs and 10 Steals of Home, Career 88–89
Players with 200 Hits, 20 Home Runs, and 20 Stolen Bases, Season 89
Players with 10 Doubles, Triples, Home Runs, and Steals in Each of First Three Seasons in Majors 89
Players Who Have Stolen Second, Third, and Home in Same Inning 90
Most Stolen Bases by Catcher, Season 90
Most Stolen Bases by Catcher, Career 90

Players with 50 Stolen Bases and 100 RBIs, Season 91
Most Stolen Bases by Home Run Champion, Season 91
Players Stealing Bases in Four Decades 91
Best On-Base 92
Best On Base Plus Slugging 93

Batting Miscellany 94

Most Times Leading League in Offensive Category 94–95
Most Consecutive Seasons Leading League in Offensive Category 95–96
Players Leading in All Triple Crown Categories, but Not in Same Year 96
Highest Offensive Career Totals by Players Who Never Led League 96
Career Offensive Leaders by Players Under Six Feet Tall 96
Largest Margin Between League Leaders and Runners-Up 96–97
Evolution of Slugging Average Record 97
Players Hitting Safely in at Least 135 Games in Season 97
Players Hitting for the Cycle in Natural Order (Single, Double, Triple, Home Run) 98
Highest Slugging Average by Position, Season 98
Most Times Awarded First Base on Catcher's Interference or Obstruction 98
Winners of Two "Legs" of Triple Crown Since Last Winner 98

2 **Pitching** 99

Wins 99

Most Victories by Decade 99–100
Pitchers with the Most Career Wins by First Letter of Last Name 100
Pitchers with the Most Career Victories by Zodiac Sign 100
Pitchers with the Most Victories by State of Birth 100–101
Pitchers with Five or More Consecutive 20-Win Seasons (Post-1900) 101
100-Game Winners, Both Leagues 101
Pitchers with 500 Major League Decisions 102

Most Wins, Major and Minor Leagues Combined 102–103
Most Wins For One Team 103
Pitchers with 100 More Wins Than Losses, Career 103–104
Pitchers with Most Career Wins, Never Leading League in One Season 104
200-Game Winners, Never Winning 20 Games in Season 104
Pitchers with 100 Wins and 500 Hits, Career 104
Victories in Most Consecutive Seasons 105
Most Wins in a Season Without a Complete Game 105
Most Career Wins by Pitchers Six and a Half Feet Tall or Taller 105
Most Career Wins by Pitchers Under Six Feet Tall 105–106
Pitchers Winning 20 Games in Season Split Between Two Teams (Post-1900) 106
Pitchers Winning 20 Games with 3 Different Teams 106
Oldest Pitchers to Win 20 Games for First Time 107
Youngest Pitchers to Win 20 Games 107
Rookies Winning 20 Games 107
Most Seasons Logged Before First 20-Win Season 108
Rookie Pitchers with 20 Wins and 200 Strikeouts 108
Pitchers Winning 20 Games in Rookie Year, Fewer Than 20 Balance of Career 108
20-Game Winners Who Didn't Win 20 More Games in Career (Post-1900) 108
Pitchers Winning 20 Games in Last Season in Majors 109
Earliest 20-Game Winner During Season 109
Most Wins After Turning 40 109
Pitchers on Losing Teams, Leading League in Wins 109–110
20-Game Winners on Last-Place Teams 110
20-Game Winners with Worst Lifetime Winning Percentage (Post-1900) 110
"Pure" 20-Game Winners (Pitchers with 20 or More Wins Than Losses) 110–111

Lefties Winning 20 Games Twice Since World War II 111–112
Pitchers with 20-Win Seasons After Age 40 112
Pitchers Leading Both Leagues in Wins, Season 113
20-Game Winners One Season, 20-Game Losers the Next 113
20-Game Winners and Losers, Same Season 113
Pitchers Who Led League in Wins in Successive Seasons 114
Most Pitching Wins for One Season 114–115
Most Total Wins, Two Pitchers on Same Staff, Career Together as Teammates 115
Most Wins, Right-Hander and Left-Hander on Same Staff, Season 115
Largest Differential Between League Leader in Wins and Runner-Up 116–117
Highest Percentage of Team's Total Wins for Season 117
Pitchers Winning 300 Games, Never Striking Out 200 Batters, Season 117
Won-Loss Percentage of 300-Game Winners 118

Shutouts 118

Evolution of Shutout Record 118
20-Game Winners with No Complete Game Shutouts 119
Most Shutouts by a Rookie 119
Pitchers Leading League in Wins, No Complete Game Shutouts 119
Most Career Starts, No Shutouts 120
Most Career Shutouts, Never Led League 120
Pitchers with Shutouts in First Two Major League Starts 120
Most Hits Allowed by Pitcher Pitching Shutout 120
Players with Highest Percentage of Shutouts to Games Started, Career 121

Losses 121

Most Losses by Decade 121–122
Evolution of Pitchers' Losses Record 122

Pitchers with Seven or More Consecutive Losing Seasons 122–123
Pitchers with 150 Wins with More Losses Than Wins, Career 123
Pitchers on Winning Teams, Leading League in Losses, Season 123–124
Pitchers Winning 20 Games in Rookie Year, Losing 20 in Second Year 124
300-Game Winners with Fewer Than 200 Losses 124

Earned Run Average 124

Best ERA by Decade (Min. 1000 Innings) 124–125
Teammates Finishing One-Two in ERA, Season 125–126
Pitchers with 3000 Innings Pitched and an ERA Lower Than 3.00 (Post–1900) 126–127
Pitchers Leading League in ERA After Their 40th Birthday 127
ERA Under 2.00, Season (Since 1920) 127
Pitchers with Losing Record, Leading League in ERA 127–128
20-Game Winners with 4.00 ERA, Season 128
20-Game Losers with ERA Below 2.00 128
ERA Leaders with Fewer Than 10 Wins 128
Pitchers with Lowest ERA in Both Leagues 129
ERA Leaders with 25 or More Wins, Season 129–130
ERAs of 300-Game Winners 130

Strikeouts 130

Evolution of Strikeout Record 130–131
Most Strikeouts by Decade 131–132
Members of Same Pitching Staff Finishing One-Two in Strikeouts, Season 132
Pitchers Leading League with 100 More Strikeouts Than Runner-Up 132–133
Pitchers with 3000 Strikeouts, Never Leading League 133
Pitchers Striking Out 1000 Batters Before Their 24th Birthday 133
Most Times Striking Out 10 or More Batters in a Game, Career 133

Pitchers Averaging 10 Strikeouts per Nine Innings, Season 133–134
Pitchers with Combined Total of 500 Strikeouts and Walks, Season 134
Pitchers Striking Out the Side on Nine Pitches 135
Pitchers with 200 Strikeouts and Fewer Than 50 Walks, Season 135–136
Rookie Pitchers Striking Out 200 Batters 137
Rookies Leading League in Strikeouts 137
Pitchers Leading League in Strikeouts, 10 or More Years Apart 137
Oldest Pitchers to Lead League in Strikeouts 137
Strikeout Leaders on Last-Place Teams 138

Walks 138

Pitchers Walking 20 or Fewer Batters, Season (Min. 200 Innings) 138
Fewest Walks, Season (Min. One Inning Pitched Each Team Game) 138
Pitchers Walking Fewer Than One Batter Every Nine Innings, Season (Min. 160 IP) 138–139
Highest Percentage of Walks to Innings Pitched, Season 139–140

Low-Hit Games 140

Pitchers with a No-Hitter in First Major League Start 140
Pitchers with a One-Hitter in First Major League Game 140
Last Outs in Perfect Games 140–141
Perfect Game Pitchers, Career Wins 141
26-Batter Perfect Games (Spoiled by 27th Batter) 142
Most Walks Given Up by No-Hit Pitchers, Game 142
Pitchers Pitching No-Hitters in 20-Loss Season 142
Pitchers Hitting Home Runs in No-Hit Games 142
Pitchers Throwing No-Hitters in Consecutive Seasons 143
No-Hitters Pitched Against Pennant-Winning Teams 143
No-Hit Pitchers Going Winless the Next Season after Pitching a No-Hitter 143
Back-to-Back One-Hit Games (Post-1900) 143
Rookies Throwing No-Hitters 144

Saves/Relief Pitchers 144

Saves by Decade 144–145
Evolution of Saves Record 146
Pitchers with 100 Wins and 100 Saves, Career 146–147
Relief Pitchers with the Most Wins, Season 147
Most Games Won by Relief Pitcher, Career 147
Teams with Two Pitchers with 20 Saves, Season 147
Pitchers Having 20-Win Seasons and 20-Save Seasons, Career 147–148
Pitchers with 15 Saves and 15 Wins in Relief, Same Season 148

Pitching Miscellany 148

Best Winning Percentage by Decade (100 Decisions) 148–149
Best WHIP by Decade 149–150
Most Seasons Leading League in Pitching Category 150–151
Most Consecutive Seasons Leading League in Pitching Category 151
Most Consecutive Scoreless Innings Pitched 151
Highest Career Pitching Totals by Pitchers Who Never Led League 151–152
Career Pitching Leaders Under Six Feet Tall 152
Pitching's Triple Crown Winners (Led League in Wins, ERA, and Strikeouts, Same Season) 152–153
Most Home Runs Given Up, Season 153
Most Home Runs Given Up, Career 154
Pitchers Giving Up Most Grand Slams, Season 154
Pitchers with 2000 Innings Pitched, Allowing No Grand Slams 154
20-Game Winners Batting .300, Same Season 154
Pitchers with Two Seasons of 1.000 Batting Averages (Post-1900) 155
Complete Games by Decade 155–156
Evolution of Complete Games Record 156
Most Games Started By a Pitcher, Career 156
Highest Percentage of Complete Games to Games Started 156–157
Pitchers Starting 20 Games in 20 Consecutive Seasons 157
Evolution of Record for Most Games Pitched in a Season 157
Evolution of Innings Pitched Record 158

Most Wild Pitches, Season (Since 1900) 158
Last Legal Spitball Pitchers 158
Left-Handed Pitchers Appearing in More Than 700 Games, Career 158–159
Pitchers Who Pitched for Both Yankees and Mets and Threw No-Hitters 159
Pitchers Who Have Stolen Home 159

3 **Hall of Fame** 161

First Players Elected to Hall of Fame from Each Position 161
Highest Lifetime Batting Average for Hall of Fame Pitchers 161
Hall of Famers with Lifetime Batting Averages Below .265 (Excluding Pitchers) 161–162
Hall of Famers with Lowest Marks in Offensive Categories 162
Teams Fielding Most Future Hall of Fame Players 162
Infields Fielding Four Future Hall of Famers 162
Hall of Fame Pitchers Who Batted Right and Threw Left 162
Switch-Hitting Pitchers in Hall of Fame 162
Hall of Fame Pitchers Who Played Most Games at Other Positions 163
Hall of Fame Position Players Who Also Pitched 163
Hall of Fame Pitchers with Losing Records 163
Leading Career Pitching Marks by Those Not In Hall of Fame 163
Leading Career Batting Marks by Those Not In Hall of Fame 163–164
Most Career Hits by Players Not In Hall of Fame 164
Most Career Wins by Pitchers Not In Hall of Fame 164
Most Career Home Runs by Players Not In Hall of Fame 164
Hall of Fame Inductees Receiving 90 Percent of Vote 164–165
Won-Lost Percentage of Hall of Famers Elected as Players Who Managed in Majors 165–167
Hall of Famers Making Last Out in World Series 167
Hall of Famers Who Played for the Harlem Globetrotters 167
Hall of Famers Who Died on Their Birthday 167

4 **Awards** 169

Most Valuable Player 169

Unanimous Choice for MVP 169
Closest Winning Margins in MVP Voting 169
Widest Winning Margins in MVP Voting 170
Won MVP Award in Consecutive Years, by Position 170
Teammates Finishing One-Two in MVP Balloting 170–171
Triple Crown Winners *Not* Winning MVP 171
MVPs on Nonwinning Teams 171
MVPs *Not* Batting .300, Hitting 30 Home Runs, or Driving in 100 Runs (Not Including Pitchers) 171–172
Pitchers Winning MVP Award 172
Players Winning MVP Award First Season in League 172
MVPs Receiving Fewer First-Place Votes Than Runner-Up 172
Teams with Most Consecutive MVP Awards 172
Players Winning MVP Award with Two Different Teams 173
MVPs with Fewest Hits 173
Switch-Hitting MVPs 173

Cy Young Award 173

Pitchers Winning 25 Games, *Not* Winning Cy Young Award 173
Pitchers Winning 20 Games Only Once and Cy Young Award Same Season 174
Cy Young Winners *Not* in Top 10 in League in ERA, Season 174
Relief Pitchers Winning Cy Young Award 174
Cy Young Winners Increasing Their Number of Victories the Following Season 174
Won Both Cy Young and MVP Same Season 175
Cy Young Winners with Higher Batting Averages Than That Year's Home Run Leader 175

Rookie of the Year 175

Rookie of the Year Winners on Team Other Than the One First Played On 175
Relief Pitchers Winning Rookie of the Year 175
Rookie of the Year on Pennant-Winning Teams 175
Rookies of the Year Elected to Hall of Fame 176

Gold Gloves 176

Most Gold Gloves, by Position 176

5 **Managers** 177

Winningest Managers by First Letter of Last Name 177
Winningest Managers by Zodiac Sign 177–178
Managers During Most Presidential Administrations 178
Managers Winning 1000 Games with One Franchise 178
Managers with Over 1000 Career Wins and sub-.500 Winning Percentage 179
Managers with Most Career Victories for Each Franchise 180
Best Winning Percentage as Manager with One Team (Post-1900; Min. 150 Games) 181
Managers with 500 Wins in Each League 181
Played in 2000 Games, Managed in 2000 Games 181
Managers Managing 100-Loss Teams After 1000th Career Victory 181
Managers with Both 100 Wins and 100-Loss Seasons 181–182
Former Pitchers Winning Pennants as Managers (Post-1900) 182
Managers Taking Over World Series Teams in Midseason 182
Managers Replaced While Team Was in First Place 182
Managers Winning Pennant in First Year as Manager of Team 182
Managers Undefeated in World Series Play 183
Managers with Fewest Career Wins to Win World Series 183
Managers with Most Career Wins *Never* to Manage a World Series Team (Post-1903) 183

Pennant-Winning Managers with Fewest Career Games (Since 1900) 183
Most Times Managing the Same Club 184
Managers with Best Winning Percentage for First Five Full Years of Managing 184
Managers Never Experiencing a Losing Season (Post-1900; Min. Two Full Seasons) 184
Career One-Game Managers 184
Managers Managing in Civilian Clothes 185
Managers Who Were Lawyers 185
Pennant-Winning Managers Who Won Batting Titles 185
Managers with Same Initials as Team They Managed 185
Playing Managers After 1950 185–186
1000 Wins as Manager and 2000 Hits as Player 186

6 **Fielding** 187
Most Games Played by Position, Career 187
Most Consecutive Games Played at Each Position 187
Players Who Played 1000 Games at Two Positions, Career 187
Unassisted Triple Plays 188
Most No-Hitters Caught 188–189
Games Caught by Left-Handed Catchers 190
Players Pitching and Catching, Same Game 190

7 **Relatives** 191
Father-Son Combinations with 250 Home Runs, Career 191
Brother Batteries 191
Twins Who Played Major League Baseball 192
Hall of Famers Whose Sons Played in Majors 192
Players with Two Sons Who Played in Majors 192–193
Brother Double-Play Combinations 193
Most Home Runs, Brothers 193

Pitching Brothers Each Winning 20 Games in Same Season 194
Hall of Famers' Brothers Who Played 10 or More Seasons in Majors (Post-1900) 194
Father-Son Tandems Who Both Played for Same Manager 194
Sons Who Played for Their Fathers 194
Best Won-Lost Percentage for Pitching Brothers 194–196
Most Total Combined Career Wins for Pitching Brothers 196–197
Pitching Brothers Facing Each Other, Regular Season 197
Most Career Victories by Father-Son Combination (Post-1900) 197
Brothers Who Played Together on Three Major League Teams 198

8 **World Series** 199
Teams Never to Trail in a World Series 199
Highest Batting Average for a World Series Team 199
Lowest Batting Average for a World Series Team 199
Most Regular Season Losses, Reaching World Series 200
Teams Winning World Series a Year After Finishing with a Losing Record 200
Players Hitting .500 in World Series (Min. 10 At Bats) 200–201
0-for-the Series (10 or More At Bats) 201
Players on World Series–Winning Teams in Both Leagues 201–202
Pitchers in World Series with Highest Slugging Average 202
World Series–Ending Hits 203
Pitchers in World Series with 300 Career Wins 203
Players on World Series Teams in Three Decades 203–204
Players with World Series Home Runs in Three Decades 204
Player-Managers on World Series–Winning Teams 204
World Series-Winning Managers Who Never Played in Majors 204
Leaders in Offensive Categories, Never Appearing in World Series (Post-1903) 205
Most Seasons, Never Appearing in World Series (Post-1903) 205
Playing Most Games, Never Appearing in World Series (Post-1903) 205
Players with the Most Home Runs, Never Appearing in World Series 205–206
Players with Highest Lifetime Batting Average, Never Appearing in World Series (Post-1903; Min. 10 Seasons) 206

Players with Most Hits, Never Appearing in World Series (Post-1903) 206
Leaders in Pitching Categories, Never Pitching in World Series (Post-1903) 206–207
Pitchers with Most Wins, Never Appearing in World Series (Post-1903) 207
Pitchers with World Series Wins in Both Leagues 207
Pitchers with World Series Losses in Both Leagues 207
Players Whose Home Run Won World Series Game 1–0 207
Brothers Who Were World Series Teammates 207
Brothers Facing Each Other in World Series 207
Fathers and Sons in World Series Competition 208
Batting Average of .400 Hitters in World Series Play 208
Batting Averages of .400 in World Series Play 208
Players Hitting World Series Home Runs in Each League 208
World Series Inside-The-Park Home Runs 209
World Series Teams Using Six Different Starting Pitchers 209
Rookies Starting Seventh Game of World Series 209
Players Playing Four Different Positions in World Series Competition, Career 209
Players Stealing Home in World Series Game 210
Pitchers Hitting Home Runs in World Series Play 210
Cy Young Winners Facing Each Other in World Series Games 210
World Series in Which Neither Team Had a 20-Game Winner 210–211
Pitchers with Lowest ERA in Total World Series Play (Min. 25 Innings) 211
World Series Grand Slams 211
Players on Three Different World Series Clubs 212
Players Playing for Two Different World Series Champions in Successive Years 213
Players with Same Lifetime Batting Average as Their World Series Overall Average 213

Batting Champions Facing Each Other in World Series 213
Home Run Champions Facing Each Other in World Series 213
Players Hitting Home Run in First World Series At Bat 213
World Series Pitchers with Most Losses, Season 214
Teams Winning a World Series in First Year in New Ballpark 214
Pitchers on World Series Winning Teams, Both Winning 20 Games and *All* of Their Team's Series Victories 214
Teams' Overall Won-Lost Percentage in World Series Games Played 214–215
Oldest Players to Appear in World Series 215
Players with 3000 Hits Playing in World Series 216

9 **All-Star Game** 217

Players Who Made All-Star Roster After Starting Season in Minors 217
Pitchers Winning All-Star Game and World Series Game, Same Season 217
Pitchers Who Pitched More Than Three Innings in One All-Star Game 217
All-Star Game Managers Who Never Managed in World Series 217
Brothers Selected to Play in All-Star Game, Same Season 217
Players Hitting Home Runs in All-Star Game and World Series, Same Season 217–218
Fathers and Sons, Both of Whom Played in All-Star Games 218
Pitchers with No Victories, Named to All-Star Team 218
Oldest Players Named to All-Star Team 218

10 **Teams** 219

Teams' Won-Lost Percentage by Decade 219–223
Clubs Winning 100 Games, Not Winning Pennant 223
Pennant Winners One Year, Losing Record Next (Post-1900) 224
Pennant-Winning Season After Losing Record Year Before 224–225

Teams Winning 100 Games in a Season, Three Years in a Row 225
Largest Increase in Games Won by Team Next Season 225
Largest Decrease in Games Won Next Season 226
Teams with Worst Won-Lost Percentage 226
Teams Hitting .300 227
Teams with Three 20-Game Winners 227–228
Teams with 30-Game Winners, Not Winning Pennant 228
Teams Leading or Tied for First Place Entire Season 228
Teams Scoring in Every Inning 228–229
Most Lopsided Shutouts 229

11 **Miscellany** 231
Players with Both Little League and Major League World Series Teams 231
Olympians (in Sports Other Than Baseball) Who Played Major League Baseball 231
Babe Ruth's Yearly Salary 231
Players Leading N.Y. Yankees in Home Runs One Season, Playing Elsewhere Next Season 232
Billy Martin's Fights 232
Four-Decade Players 232–233
First Players Chosen in Draft by Expansion Teams 233
Last Active Player Once Playing for . . . 233
Last Players Born in Nineteenth Century to Play in Majors 234
First Players Born in Twentieth Century to Play in Majors 234
Second African American to Play for Each of 16 Original Major League Teams 234
Players and Mangers Same Number Retired on Two Different Clubs 234
Major Leaguers Who Played Pro Football in Same Year(s) 235
Performances by Oldest Players 235–236
Oldest Players, by Position 236

Youngest Players to Play in Majors 236
Youngest Players, by Position 236
Players Who Played During Most Presidential Administrations 237
Players Playing Most Seasons with One Address (One Club, One City in Majors) 237
Players Who Played 2500 Games in One Uniform (Post-1900) 238
Players Playing Most Seasons in City of Birth 238
Players with Same Surname as Town of Birth 238
Players with Longest Given Names 238
Players with Palindromic Surnames 238
Most Common Last Names in Baseball History 239
Number of Major League Players by First Letter of Last Name 239
Third Basemen on Tinker-to-Evers-to-Chance Chicago Cubs Teams 239
First Designated Hitter for Each Major League Team 239–240
Players Killed as Direct Result of Injuries Sustained in Major League Games 240
Players Who Played for Three New York Teams 240–241
Players Who Played for Both Original and Expansion Washington Senators 241
Players Who Played for Both Kansas City Athletics and Kansas City Royals 241
Players Who Played for Both Milwaukee Braves and Milwaukee Brewers 241
Pitchers Who Gave Up Most Hits to Pete Rose 241–242
Pitchers Who Gave Up Home Runs to Both Mark McGwire and Barry Bonds in Their Record-Breaking Seasons (1998 and 2001) 242
Major League Shortstops from San Pedro de Macoris, Dominican Republic 242
Players Born on Leap Year Day (February 29) 242
Players Who Played on Four of California's Five Major League Teams 242
Tallest Players in Major League History 243
Shortest Players in Major League History 243

Teammates the Longest 244
Teammates with 300 Wins and 500 Home Runs 244
New Baseball Stadiums Built Since 2005 244
Players Traded for Themselves 244
Players Wearing Numbers "0" and "00" 244

Part 2 **Team-by-Team Histories** 245

American League 247

Baltimore Orioles 247
Boston Red Sox 251
Chicago White Sox 257
Cleveland Indians 262
Detroit Tigers 268
Houston Astros 274
Kansas City Royals 277
Los Angeles Angels of Anaheim 280
Minnesota Twins 283
New York Yankees 286
Oakland Athletics 293
Seattle Mariners 297
Tampa Bay Rays 299
Texas Rangers 301
Toronto Blue Jays 303

National League 305

Arizona Diamondbacks 305
Atlanta Braves 307
Chicago Cubs 311

Cincinnati Reds 317
Colorado Rockies 323
Los Angeles Dodgers 325
Miami Marlins 329
Milwaukee Brewers 331
New York Mets 334
Philadelphia Phillies 337
Pittsburgh Pirates 343
St. Louis Cardinals 349
San Diego Padres 356
San Francisco Giants 359
Washington Nationals 362

Franchises No Longer in Existence 365

Boston Braves 365
Brooklyn Dodgers 369
New York Giants 373
Philadelphia Athletics 378
St. Louis Browns 382
Washington Senators 385

FOREWORD

Statistics (or as they are known in their circumcised, smaller version of the word, "stats") have been a part of baseball—indeed, the very mortar of the sport—since the dawn of the game, even if in the beginning their number was so few they could be entered on a postcard with more than enough room left for an oversized one-cent stamp and a generous message. And those few reduced to paper could be called statistics only in the same way raisins could be called fruit—technically and only in a manner of speaking.

Take, for example, one of the very first recorded: that of the number of miles traveled by the first professional baseball team, the Cincinnati Red Stockings, as they criss-crossed the country in 1869, their first year in existence. One of the early recordkeepers estimated that the Red Stockings had covered some 11,877 miles, playing in 57 games—of which they won 56 and tied one. However, one historian, ever Thomas the Doubter, doubling back on the historic breadcrumbs laid down by the Red Stockings, discovered that Harry Wright's team had played at least 80 games in their inaugural season and figured they had many a mile more to go than that originally estimated.

Many of those early records set down by recordkeepers were something of a hit-or-miss proposition—mostly miss. One of those came on the afternoon of Thursday, September 6, 1883, when Cap Anson's Chicago White Stockings set a record by scoring 18 runs in the seventh inning against the Detroit Wolverines. However, when the report of the game was wired to the ***Detroit Free Press,*** as well as other papers around the country, most of the details of the game were MIA. The sporting editor of the Free Press, taking note of the omissions, apologized to his readers, writing that the paper "would be pleased to submit the full score of this remarkable game to its readers, but the Western Union Telegraph Company, which has no excuse for its poor service, has furnished it bobtailed and in ludicrous deformity . . . the Company was requested to supply the missing links, but the head operator declined to do so."

There were several other instances of reporters or Western Union operatives exhibiting a polite fiction of the non-existence of such relevant statistics, several times omitting the names of batterymates. However, here it must be noted that many's the time in those early days of organized-and-disorganized-baseball, even the pitcher and the catcher didn't know the names of their batterymates. Such was the case in 1897 when the pitcher and the catcher of the Louisville team were as unfamiliar to one another as two shipwrecked survivors coming ashore on a wave-swept beach, neither knowing the name of the other. None of their teammates knew their names either, both having just joined the team—the pitcher the day before; the catcher being signed on a trial basis just before the game. When the pitcher was asked by writers who his catcher was, he answered, "Couldn't tell you, first time I ever saw him." The catcher's answer to the identity of the pitcher was ditto. Still at a loss as to the names of the two, the writers now approached manager Fred Clarke and asked the same question. As lost as Robinson Crusoe without a boat, all Clarke could do was point to the name "Weddel" on the scorecard and say, "This man will pitch." Then, pointing to the tall man putting on his catcher's gear, said, "And that tall fellow over there will catch." Calling over to his catcher, Clarke had him spell out his name for the writers, which he did: "S-c-h-r-e-c-k-e-n-g-o-s-t." Then, asked by the writers if the "Weddel" on the scorecard was the correct spelling, Clarke shrugged his shoulders and responded, "Don't know, you'll have to ask him." They did, discovering it was spelled "Waddell." (Ironically, after their dual Major League debut, Ossee Schreckengost and Rube Waddell's faces would become as recognizable to one another as those seen in the mirror every morning as they became batterymates for six seasons with the Philadelphia A's.)

The shoddy record keeping of the time also resulted in several other records being overlooked, there being no mention of the-then-record 11 RBIs in one game by Baltimore Oriole Wilbert Robinson nor the 27 home runs by Chicago White Stocking Ned Williamson in 1884, both records forgotten by the time they were broken—Robinson's by Jim Bottomley and Williamson's by Babe Ruth.

Ernest Lanigan, baseball's first great historian, noted that the omission of Williamson's season record of 27 home runs was occasioned by the fact that whenever Henry Chadwick—known as "The Father of Baseball," but whom Lanigan called "that human eliminator"—wrote on the subject of home runs, "which variety of hits he detested . . . (he) eliminated them from the guides."

Early records were thus cut and restitched to fit any pattern the recordkeeper wanted, many of their entries unable to stand up to the slightest investigation. In one classic case Wee Willie Keeler was credited by the Baltimore scorekeeper with four hits in a 1897 game versus St. Louis. However, St. Louis sportswriter Frank Houseman, pulling up the game to study its roots, wrote the following rundown of Keeler's run-up of hits: "Down in Baltimore, Keeler sent two flies to (Bud) Larry, who muffed both of them. Then he hit to (Fred) Hartman, who fumbled the ball and threw wild. Then Keeler made a good single. The next morning, four hits appeared to Keeler's credit in the Baltimore papers." Houseman couldn't resist adding, "Talk about stuffing records."

And, as if it wasn't enough that telegraphers or writers "stuffed" a player's performance, sometimes they even "stuffed" the line-up itself. In one of those moments that inspires a reference to A. Lincoln's sonnet about "fooling all the people . . . ," a St. Louis Western Union operative up in the press box named Lou Proctor, in a "Forgive us our Press Passes" moment, inserted his own name in a 1912 St. Louis Browns boxscore, fooling even the Macmillan Baseball Encyclopedia editors who included it in their first edition, giving him equal standing with "Moonlight" Graham before discovering the error and dropping Proctor from its later editions.

As sportswriters and fans voyaged, Columbus-like, into the new world of baseball statistics, commissions and omissions weren't the only problems they faced. One of those problems was the determinate criteria for stolen bases, there being no baseline (good word, that!) of agreed-upon standards. At given times over the years, runners were given credit for a stolen base when they scored from third on a fly out, when they took two bases on an infield out, when they were the successful half of a double-steal when the other half was thrown out, or even when they overslid a base and were tagged out.

Other statistics, like strikeouts, runs scored and batted in, and sacrifices, hitherto unaccountable in whole or in part, came late to the table and were incorporated into baseball's growing world of stats—soon to be joined by others.

Still, with annuals like the early day ***Reach*** and ***Spalding Guides*** and Balldom as well as ***The Sporting Life Base Ball Guide and Handbook*** and the while-you-get-your-haircut weeklies serving up heaping platefuls of statistics to satisfy the appetite of ever-increasingly hungry fans for such fare, statistics took on a life of their own, framing the game and providing a basis of comparison of the past and the present.

As baseball archaeologists like the aforementioned Lanigan began spackling the cracks by correcting some of the early statistics that had been recorded with all the innocence of Adam naming the animals on his first day in the Garden by early recordkeepers even they created problems of their own. One such error occurred when the ***Reach Guide*** of 1903, in a typographical error, credited Nap Lajoie with 43 triples in 1897 when the actual number of triples should have read 23. And so, when Pirate outfielder Owen Wilson, better known as "Chief," began belting the ball all over the lot, hitting seven triples against Chicago and Cincinnati pitching, five against St. Louis and New York, and three each versus Philadelphia and Brooklyn, sportswriters took little note of his feat, figuring his total of 36 still seven shy of Lajoie's "43." It would take some of baseball's best archaeologists to dig back through Lajoie's game-by-game record to exhume his real total and properly acknowledge Wilson's record.

By the 1920s, recordkeeping had approached the foothills of accuracy as statistical cryptographers resurrected and decoded the facts and figures of earlier historians, thus providing a correction to baseball's past. No longer random and haphazard, baseball statistics now had a relativism to earlier-day records and accomplishments, ensuring that no feat would vanish down the hole of history—for baseball records, like everything else, except maybe Eve telling Adam about all the men she could have married, are relative.

It was that thesis of baseball relativity that enabled Lanigan to compare Tip O'Neill's otherworldly .492 batting average in

1887 (later amended to .485) to Babe Ruth's .378 in his great offensive year of 1921 when he hit 59 home runs and drove in 171 runs. Pointing out that in 1887 batters received credit for base hits when they walked, producing helium-like averages, he calculated that Ruth would have an equally lofty .509 in '21 had his then-record of 145 bases on balls counted as hits.

In fact, it was the explosion of the long ball (as personified by The Babe, who held the original copyright) that changed the game. And along with it, its statistics. Suddenly, the trickle of records became a Niagara as statisticians wore a carload of pencils down to their stubs recording them as records lasting about as long as Hollywood bridegrooms.

As the game continued to evolve, so too did the statistics, growing with the game. And nothing proved that the body of statistics was growing at an exponential rate more than a quiz show back in the '50s called *The $64,000 Question*, where one contestant, a Georgian housewife named Myrtle Powers, was asked to name the seven players who "had a lifetime total of 3,000 or more hits." Ms. Powers correctly answered: "Ty Cobb, Honus Wagner, Nap Lajoie, Eddie Collins, Tris Speaker, Cap Anson, and Paul Waner," the number who had climbed that statistical mountain over the past 80- plus years. Now, a half-century later, a total of 29 players, over a fourfold number, have reached that magic mark.

But, even as baseball's "official" recordkeepers continue to collect each and every statistic from the obvious to the most minute, amateur historians who OD on baseball stats continue to find omissions and commissions—such as an extra run batted in by Hack Wilson in his record-setting 190 RBI season of 1930, an extra triple in the lifetime total of Lou Gehrig, and a double-counting of a two-for-three day by Ty Cobb in 1910, which would have cost him the batting title to Nap Lajoie by one point. (Such a finding of an error even occurred in that Holiest of Holy places, the Baseball Hall of Fame, when an eagle-eyed fan standing in front of the Babe Ruth plaque noted that the inscription for his playing days read "1915–1935" and pointed out to the powers-that-be that Ruth had first played for the Red Sox in 1914, not 1915.)

Now I had always considered myself as part of that amateur array of baseballogists, one of a large group of enthusiasts who accumulate lists of stats, especially those with more variations on the theme than even Mussorgsky had imagined.

But it wasn't until I met a fellow traveler in stats named Jack McClain that I realized that my variations were as nothing compared to those Jack had conceived—his lists defying normal categorization, like "Most Pitching Wins by Zodiac Sign," "Most Home Runs by State of Birth," et cetera, etc., etc., etc.—the et ceteras going on for about five pages or more. We decided on the spot to collaborate on a book of what we called "fun stats," a novel approach of combining our efforts into one volume that would be different from anything before.

Unfortunately, Jack passed away before we had finished our book, leaving me to carry on alone. But over the years, I have continued to develop list after list—so many, in fact, they are available at a discount. And now, with the able assistance of many others, including Bill Francis of the Baseball Hall of Fame, Cornell Richardson, the Office of the Baseball Commissioner, Mark Weinstein, Parker Bena, Frances J. Buonarota, Jason Katzman, and a cast of hundreds, if not thousands, it is my pleasure to give you a different perspective (call it a "different view from the same pew," if you will) on America's second most popular pastime: baseball statistics.

—Bert Randolph Sugar

THE BASEBALL MANIAC'S ALMANAC

4TH EDITION

PART 1
Individual Statistics

1

BATTING

Base Hits

Most Hits by Decade

Pre-1900

3012 ..... Cap Anson
2467 ..... Roger Connor
2303 ..... Jim O'Rourke
2296 ..... Dan Brouthers
2258 ..... Bid McPhee
2134 ..... Jimmy Ryan
2127 ..... Hugh Duffy
2107 ..... Monte Ward
2086 ..... George Van Haltren
2084 ..... Ed McKean

1900–09

1847 ..... Honus Wagner
1677 ..... Sam Crawford
1660 ..... Nap Lajoie
1566 ..... Willie Keeler
1559 ..... Ginger Beaumont
1460 ..... Cy Seymour
1431 ..... Elmer Flick
1396 ..... Fred Clarke
1387 ..... Fred Tenney
1373 ..... Bobby Wallace

1910–19

1948 ..... Ty Cobb
1821 ..... Tris Speaker
1682 ..... Eddie Collins
1556 ..... Clyde Milan
1548 ..... Joe Jackson
1535 ..... Jake Daubert
1516 ..... Zack Wheat
1502 ..... Home Run Baker
1481 ..... Heinie Zimmerman
1475 ..... Ed Konetchy

1920–29

2085 ..... Rogers Hornsby
2010 ..... Sam Rice
1924 ..... Harry Heilmann
1900 ..... George Sisler
1808 ..... Frankie Frisch
1734 ..... Babe Ruth
1698 ..... Joe Sewell
1623 ..... Charlie Jamieson
1570 ..... Charlie Grimm
1569 ..... George Kelly

1930–39

1959 ..... Paul Waner
1865 ..... Charlie Gehringer
1845 ..... Jimmie Foxx
1802 ..... Lou Gehrig
1786 ..... Earl Averill
1700 ..... Al Simmons
1697 ..... Ben Chapman
1676 ..... Chuck Klein
1673 ..... Mel Ott
1650 ..... Joe Cronin

1940–49

1578 ..... Lou Boudreau
1563 ..... Bob Elliott
1512 ..... Dixie Walker
1432 ..... Stan Musial
1407 ..... Bobby Doerr
1402 ..... Tommy Holmes
1376 ..... Luke Appling
1328 ..... Bill Nicholson
1310 ..... Marty Marion
1304 ..... Phil Cavarretta

1950–59

1875 ..... Richie Ashburn
1837 ..... Nellie Fox
1771 ..... Stan Musial
1675 ..... Alvin Dark
1605 ..... Duke Snider
1551 ..... Gus Bell
1526 ..... Minnie Minoso
1517 ..... Red Schoendienst
1499 ..... Yogi Berra
1491 ..... Gil Hodges

1960–69

1877 ..... Roberto Clemente
1819 ..... Hank Aaron
1776 ..... Vada Pinson
1744 ..... Maury Wills
1692 ..... Brooks Robinson
1690 ..... Curt Flood
1651 ..... Billy Williams
1635 ..... Willie Mays
1603 ..... Frank Robinson
1592 ..... Ron Santo

1970–79

2045 ..... Pete Rose
1787 ..... Rod Carew
1686 ..... Al Oliver
1617 ..... Lou Brock
1565 ..... Bobby Bonds
1560 ..... Tony Perez
1552 ..... Larry Bowa
1550 ..... Ted Simmons
1549 ..... Amos Otis
1548 ..... Bobby Murcer

1980–89

1731 ..... Robin Yount
1642 ..... Eddie Murray
1639 ..... Willie Wilson
1597 ..... Wade Boggs

1990–99

1754 ..... Mark Grace
1747 ..... Rafael Palmeiro
1728 ..... Craig Biggio
1713 ..... Tony Gwynn

2000–09

2030 ..... Ichiro Suzuki
1940 ..... Derek Jeter
1860 ..... Miguel Tejada
1756 ..... Todd Helton

continued on next page

1553 ..... Dale Murphy
1547 ..... Harold Baines
1539 ..... Andre Dawson
1507 ..... Rickey Henderson
1504 ..... Alan Trammell
1497 ..... Dwight Evans

1678 ..... Roberto Alomar
1622 ..... Ken Griffey Jr.
1589 ..... Cal Ripken Jr.
1584 ..... Dante Bichette
1573 ..... Fred McGriff
1568 ..... Paul Molitor

1751 ..... Vladimir Guerrero
1745 ..... Johnny Damon
1740 ..... Alex Rodriguez
1721 ..... Bobby Abreu
1717 ..... Albert Pujols
1674 ..... Carlos Lee

2010–15

1140 ..... Robinson Cano
1111 ..... Miguel Cabrera
1068 ..... Adrian Gonzalez
1067 ..... Adrian Beltre
1027 ..... Andrew McCutchen
1024 ..... Adam Jones
1024 ..... Nick Markakis
1007 ..... Billy Butler
991 ..... Starlin Castro
985 ..... Elvis Andrus

Evolution of Singles Record

American League

1901 Nap Lajoie, Phila. A's 154
1903 Patsy Dougherty, Bost. Red Sox 161
1904 Willie Keeler, N.Y. Yankees 164
1906 Willie Keeler, N.Y. Yankees 166
1911 Ty Cobb, Det. Tigers 169
1920 George Sisler, St.L. Browns 171
1921 Jack Tobin, St.L. Browns 179
1925 Sam Rice, Wash. Senators 182
1980 Willie Wilson, K.C. Royals 184
1985 Wade Boggs, Bost. Red Sox 187
2001 Ichiro Suzuki, Sea. Mariners 192
2004 Ichiro Suzuki, Sea. Mariners 225

National League (Post-1900)

1900 Willie Keeler, Bklyn. Dodgers 179
1901 Jesse Burkett, St.L. Cardinals 180
1927 Lloyd Waner, Pitt. Pirates 198

Most Hits, Season

American League

Ichiro Suzuki, Sea. Mariners, 2004 262
George Sisler, St.L. Browns, 1920 257
Al Simmons, Phila. A's, 1925 253
Ty Cobb, Det. Tigers, 1911 248
George Sisler, St.L. Browns, 1922 246
Ichiro Suzuki, Sea. Mariners, 2001 242
Heine Manush, St.L. Browns, 1928 241
Wade Boggs, Bost. Red Sox, 1985 240
Darin Erstad, Ana. Angels, 2000 240

National League (Post-1900)

Lefty O'Doul, Phila. Phillies, 1929 254
Bill Terry, N.Y. Giants, 1930 254
Rogers Hornsby, St.L. Cardinals, 1922 250
Chuck Klein, Phila. Phillies, 1930 250
Babe Herman, Bklyn. Dodgers, 1930 241

Base Hit Leaders by State of Birth

Alabama ..... Hank Aaron (Mobile) 3771
Alaska ..... Josh Phelps (Anchorage) 380
Arizona ..... Ian Kinsler (Tucson) 1518
Arkansas ..... Lou Brock (El Dorado) 3023
California ..... Eddie Murray (Los Angeles) 3255
Colorado ..... Roy Hartzell (Golden) 1146
Connecticut ..... Roger Connor (Waterbury) 2467
Delaware ..... Delino DeShields (Seaford) 1548
Florida ..... Andre Dawson (Miami) 2774
Georgia ..... Ty Cobb (Narrows) 4189
Hawaii ..... Shane Victorino (Wailuku) 1274
Idaho ..... Harmon Killebrew (Payette) 2086
Illinois ..... Robin Yount (Danville) 3142
Indiana ..... Sam Rice (Morocco) 2987

continued on next page

Iowa.....Cap Anson (Marshalltown) 3012
Kansas.....Johnny Damon (Fort Riley).....2769
Kentucky .....Pee Wee Reese (Ekron) 2170
Louisiana.....Mel Ott (Gretna) 2876
Maine.....George Gore (Saccarappa) 1612
Maryland .....Cal Ripken Jr. (Havre de Grace)...3184
Massachusetts.....Rabbit Maranville (Springfield) 2605
Michigan.....Charlie Gehringer (Fowlerville).....2839
Minnesota .....Paul Molitor (St. Paul) 3319
Mississippi.....Dave Parker (Grenada) 2712
Missouri .....Jake Beckley (Hannibal) 2934
Montana .....John Lowenstein (Wolf Point).....881
Nebraska .....Wade Boggs (Omaha) 3010
Nevada .....Marty Cordova (Las Vegas).....938
New Hampshire .....Arlie Latham (West Lebanon) 1836
New Jersey.....Derek Jeter (Pequannock).....3465
New Mexico.....Vern Stephens (McAllister) 1859
New York.....Carl Yastrzemski (Southampton)....3419
North Carolina.....Luke Appling (High Point) 2749
North Dakota.....Darin Erstad (Jamestown).....1697
Ohio.....Pete Rose (Cincinnati) 4256
Oklahoma .....Paul Waner (Harrah) 3152
Oregon.....Dale Murphy (Portland) 2111
Pennsylvania.....Stan Musial (Donora) 3630
Rhode Island.....Nap Lajoie (Woonsocket) 3242
South Carolina.....Jim Rice (Anderson) 2452
South Dakota.....Mark Ellis (Rapid City) 1343
Tennessee.....Vada Pinson (Memphis).....2757
Texas.....Tris Speaker (Lake Whitney).....3514
Utah .....Duke Sims (Salt Lake City) 580
Vermont .....Carlton Fisk (Bellows Falls).....2356
Virginia.....Willie Horton (Arno) 1993
Washington.....Ryne Sandberg (Spokane) 2386
West Virginia .....George Brett (Glen Dale).....3154
Wisconsin .....Al Simmons (Milwaukee) 2927
Wyoming .....Mike Lansing (Rawlings) 1124

American Samoa.....Tony Solaita (Nuuuli) 336
District of Columbia .Maury Wills.....2134
Puerto Rico .....Roberto Clemente (Carolina) 3000
Virgin Islands.....Horace Clarke (St. Croix) 1230

Players with 200 Hits and 40 Home Runs, Season

American League

	Hits	Home Runs
Babe Ruth, N.Y. Yankees, 1921	204	59
Babe Ruth, N.Y. Yankees, 1923	205	41
Babe Ruth, N.Y. Yankees, 1924	200	46
Lou Gehrig, N.Y. Yankees, 1927	218	47
Lou Gehrig, N.Y. Yankees, 1930	220	41
Lou Gehrig, N.Y. Yankees, 1931	211	46
Jimmie Foxx, Phila. A's, 1932	213	58
Jimmie Foxx, Phila. A's, 1933	204	48
Lou Gehrig, N.Y. Yankees, 1934	210	49
Lou Gehrig, N.Y. Yankees, 1936	205	49
Hal Trosky, Cle. Indians, 1936	216	42
Joe DiMaggio, N.Y. Yankees, 1937	215	46
Hank Greenberg, Det. Tigers, 1937	200	40
Al Rosen, Cle. Indians, 1953	201	43
Jim Rice, Bost. Red Sox, 1978	213	46
Mo Vaughn, Bost. Red Sox, 1996	207	44
Albert Belle, Chi. White Sox, 1998	200	49
Alex Rodriguez, Sea. Mariners, 1998	213	42
Mo Vaughn, Bost. Red Sox, 1998	205	40
Alex Rodriguez, Tex. Rangers, 2001	201	52
Miguel Cabrera, Det. Tigers, 2012	205	44

National League (Post-1900)

	Hits	Home Runs
Rogers Hornsby, St.L. Cardinals, 1922	250	42
Rogers Hornsby, Chi. Cubs, 1929	229	40
Chuck Klein, Phila. Phillies, 1929	219	43
Chuck Klein, Phila. Phillies, 1930	250	40
Hank Aaron, Milw. Braves, 1963	201	44
Billy Williams, Chi. Cubs, 1970	205	42
Ellis Burks, Colo. Rockies, 1996	211	40
Mike Piazza, L.A. Dodgers, 1997	201	40
Larry Walker, Colo. Rockies, 1997	208	49
Vinny Castilla, Colo. Rockies, 1998	206	46
Todd Helton, Colo. Rockies, 2000	216	42
Albert Pujols, St.L. Cardinals, 2003	212	43

Players with 200 Base Hits and Fewer Than 40 Extra-Base Hits, Season (Post-1900)

American League

	Hits	Extra-Base Hits
Doc Cramer, Bost. Red Sox, 1940	200	40
Johnny Pesky, Bost. Red Sox, 1942,	205	40
Nellie Fox, Chi. White Sox, 1954	201	34
Harvey Kuenn, Det. Tigers, 1954	201	393
Cesar Tovar, Min. Twins, 1971	204	33
Steve Sax, N.Y. Yankees, 1989	205	34
Ichiro Suzuki, Sea. Mariners, 2004	262	37
Ichiro Suzuki, Sea. Mariners, 2006	224	38
Ichiro Suzuki, Sea. Mariners, 2007	238	35
Ichiro Suzuki, Sea. Mariners, 2008	213	33
Ichiro Suzuki, Sea. Mariners, 2010	214	39

National League (Post-1900)

	Hits	Extra-Base Hits
Willie Keeler, Bklyn. Dodgers, 1900	204	29
Willie Keeler, Bklyn. Dodgers, 1901	202	32
Milt Stock, St.L. Cardinals, 1920	204	34
Milt Stock, Bklyn. Dodgers, 1925	202	38
Lance Richbourg, Bost. Braves, 1928	206	40
Chick Fullis, Phila. Phillies, 1933	200	38
Richie Ashburn, Phila. Phillies, 1953	205	36
Richie Ashburn, Phila. Phillies, 1958	215	39
Maury Wills, L.A. Dodgers, 1962	208	28
Curt Flood, St.L. Cardinals, 1964	211	33
Matty Alou, Pitt. Pirates, 1970	201	30
Ralph Garr, Atl. Braves, 1971	219	39
Dave Cash, Phila. Phillies, 1974	206	39
Tony Gwynn, S.D. Padres, 1989	203	38
Juan Pierre, Colo, Rockies, 2001	202	39
Juan Pierre, Fla. Marlins, 2003	204	36
Juan Pierre, Fla. Marlins, 2004	221	37
Dee Gordon, Mia. Marlins, 2015	205	36

Players with 3000 Hits, Career

	Hits	Date of 3000th Hit	Opposing Pitcher
Pete Rose	4256	May 5, 1978	Steve Rogers, Mont. Expos (NL)
Ty Cobb	4189	Aug. 19, 1921	Elmer Myers, Bost. Red Sox (AL)
Hank Aaron	3771	May 17, 1970	Wayne Simpson, Cin. Reds (NL)
Stan Musial	3630	May 13, 1958	Moe Drabowsky, Chi. Cubs (NL)
Tris Speaker	3514	May 17, 1925	Tom Zachary, Wash. Senators (AL)
Derek Jeter	3465	July 9, 2011	David Price, T.B. Rays (AL)
Honus Wagner	3420	June 9, 1914	Erskine Mayer, Phila. Phillies (NL)
Carl Yastrzemski	3419	Sept. 12, 1979	Jim Beattie, N.Y. Yankees (AL)
Paul Molitor	3319	Sept. 16, 1996	Jose Rosado, K.C. Royals (AL)
Eddie Collins	3315	June 3, 1925	Rip Collins, Det. Tigers (AL)
Willie Mays	3283	July 18, 1970	Mike Wegener, Mont. Expos (NL)
Eddie Murray	3255	June 30, 1995	Mike Trombley, Min. Twins (AL)
Nap Lajoie	3242	Sept. 27, 1914	Marty McHale, N.Y. Yankees (AL)
Cal Ripken Jr.	3184	Apr. 15, 2000	Hector Carrasco, Min. Twins (AL)
George Brett	3154	Sept. 30, 1992	Tim Fortugno, Cal. Angels (AL)
Paul Waner	3152	June 19, 1942	Rip Sewell, Pitt. Pirates (NL)
Robin Yount	3142	Sept. 9, 1992	Jose Mesa, Cle. Indians (AL)
Tony Gwynn	3141	Aug. 6, 1999	Dan Smith, Mont. Expos (NL)
Alex Rodriguez	3070	June 19, 2015	Justin Verlander, Det. Tigers (AL)
Dave Winfield	3110	Sept. 16, 1993	Dennis Eckersley, Oak. A's (AL)
Craig Biggio	3060	June 28, 2007	Aaron Cook, Colo. Rockies (NL)
Rickey Henderson	3055	Oct. 7, 2001	John Thomson, Colo. Rockies (NL)
Rod Carew	3053	Aug. 4, 1985	Frank Viola, Min. Twins (AL)
Lou Brock	3023	Aug. 13, 1979	Dennis Lamp, Chi. Cubs (NL)
Rafael Palmeiro	3020	July 15, 2005	Joel Piniero, Sea. Mariners (AL)
Cap Anson	3012	July 18, 1897	George Blackburn, Balt. Orioles (NL)
Wade Boggs	3010	Aug. 7, 1999	Chris Haney, Cle. Indians (AL)
Al Kaline	3007	Sept. 24, 1974	Dave McNally, Balt. Orioles (AL)
Roberto Clemente	3000	Sept. 30, 1972	Jon Matlack, N.Y. Mets (NL)

Most Hits by Position, Season

American League

First Base ..... 257 ..... George Sisler, St.L. Browns, 1920
Second Base ..... 232 ..... Nap Lajoie, Phila. A's, 1901
Third Base ..... 240 ..... Wade Boggs, Bost. Red Sox, 1985
Shortstop ..... 219 ..... Derek Jeter, N.Y. Yankees, 1999
Outfield ..... 262 ..... Ichiro Suzuki, Sea. Mariners, 2004
Catcher ..... 199 ..... Ivan Rodriguez, Tex. Rangers, 1999
Pitcher ..... 52 ..... George Uhle, Cle. Indians, 1923
Designated Hitter ... 216 ..... Paul Molitor, Milw. Brewers, 1991

National League (Post-1900)

First Base ..... 254 ..... Bill Terry, N.Y. Giants, 1930
Second Base ..... 250 .... Rogers Hornsby, St.L. Cardinals, 1922
Third Base ..... 231 ..... Fred Lindstrom, N.Y. Giants, 1928 and 1930
Shortstop ..... 211 ... Garry Templeton, St.L. Cardinals, 1978
Outfield ..... 254 ..... Lefty O'Doul, Phila. Phillies, 1929
Catcher ..... 201 ..... Mike Piazza, L.A. Dodgers, 1997
Pitcher ..... 47 ..... Red Lucas, Cin. Reds, 1927

Players Hitting for the Cycle Two or More Times (Post-1900)

Three Times

Babe Herman, Bklyn. Dodgers (NL), 1931 (2); Chi. Cubs (NL), 1933
Adrian Beltre, Sea. Mariners (AL), 2008; Tex. Rangers (AL), 2012, 2015
Bob Meusel, N.Y. Yankees (AL), 1921, 1922, 1928

Two Times

Ken Boyer, St.L. Cardinals (NL), 1961, 1964
Cesar Cedeno, Cin. Reds (NL), 1972, 1976
Fred Clarke, Pitt. Pirates (NL), 1901, 1903
Michael Cuddyer, Min. Twins, 2009; Colo. Rockies, 2014
Mickey Cochrane, Phila. A's (AL), 1932, 1933
Joe Cronin, Wash. Senators (AL), 1929; Bost. Red Sox (AL), 1940
Joe DiMaggio, N.Y. Yankees (AL), 1937, 1948
Bobby Doerr, Bost. Red Sox (AL), 1944, 1947
Jim Fregosi, L.A., Cal. Angels (AL), 1964, 1968
Lou Gehrig, N.Y. Yankees (AL), 1934, 1937
Aaron Hill, Ariz. D'backs, 2012 (2)
Chuck Klein, Phila. Phillies (NL), 1931, 1933
John Olerud, Sea. Mariners (AL) 2001, N.Y. Mets (NL) 1997
George Sisler, St.L. Browns (AL), 1920, 1921
Chris Speier Mont. Expos (NL) 1978, S.F. Giants (NL) 1988
Arky Vaughan, Pitt. Pirates (NL), 1933, 1939
Bob Watson, Hous. Astros (NL), 1977; Bost. Red Sox (AL), 1979
Wally Westlake, Pitt. Pirates (NL), 1948, 1949
Brad Wilkerson, Mont. Expos (NL) 2003, Wash. Nationals (NL) 2005

Most Times at Bat Without a Hit, Season

American League

61 ..... Bill Wight, Chi. White Sox, 1950
46 ..... Karl Drews, St.L. Browns, 1949
41 ..... Ernie Koob, St.L. Browns, 1916
39 ..... Ed Rakow, Det. Tigers, 1964
31 ..... Bob Miller, Min. Twins, 1969

National League (Post-1900)

70 ..... Bob Buhl, Milw. Braves–Chi. Cubs, 1962
47 ..... Ron Herbel, S.F. Giants, 1964
41 ..... Randy Tate, N.Y. Mets, 1975
40 ..... Jason Bergmann, Wash. Nationals, 2008
40 ..... Joey Hamilton, S.D. Padres, 1994
38 ..... Darryl Kile, Hous. Astros, 1991
37 ..... Eugenio Velez, S.F. Giants, 2011
36 ..... Harry Parker, N.Y. Mets, 1974

Players with 200 Hits in Each of First Three Major League Seasons

Willie Keeler, Balt. Orioles (NL) ..... 1894 (219), 1895 (221), and 1896 (214)
Johnny Pesky, Bost. Red Sox (AL) ..... 1942 (205), 1946 (208), and 1947 (207)
Ichiro Suzuki, Sea. Mariners (AL) ..... 2001 (242), 2002 (208), and 2003 (212)
Lloyd Waner, Pitt. Pirates (NL) ..... 1927 (223), 1928 (221), and 1929 (234)

Players with 600 Total Hits in First Three Major League Seasons

	Seasons–Hits	Total Hits
Lloyd Waner	1927: 223; 1928: 221; 1929: 234	678
Ichiro Suzuki	2001: 242; 2002: 202; 2003: 212	662
Willie Keeler	1894: 219; 1895: 221; 1896: 214	654
Paul Waner	1926: 180; 1927: 237; 1928: 223	640
Al Simmons	1924: 183; 1925: 253; 1926: 199	635

continued on next page

Johnny Pesky*	1942: 205; 1946: 208; 1947: 207	620
Earle Combs	1925: 203; 1926: 181; 1927: 231	615
Joe DiMaggio	1936: 206; 1937: 215; 1938: 194	615

* Was in the military in 1943.

Players with 200-Hit Seasons in Each League

Bill Buckner ..... Chi. Cubs (NL), 1982
Bost. Red Sox (AL), 1985

Vladimir Guerrero ..... Mont. Expos (NL), 1998, 2002,
Ana.–L.A. Angels (AL), 2004, 2006

Nap Lajoie ..... Phila. A's (AL), 1901
Cle. Naps (AL), 1904, 1906, and 1910
Phila. Phillies (NL), 1898

Al Oliver ..... Tex. Rangers (AL), 1980
Mont. Expos (NL), 1982

Steve Sax ..... L.A. Dodgers (NL), 1986
N.Y. Yankees (AL), 1989

George Sisler ..... St.L. Browns (AL), 1920–22, 1925, and 1927
Bost. Braves (NL), 1929

Players with 200 Hits in Five Consecutive Seasons

	Seasons
Ichiro Suzuki, Sea. Mariners (AL), 2001–10	10
Willie Keeler, Balt. Orioles (NL), 1894–98, and Bklyn. Dodgers (NL), 1899–1901	8
Wade Boggs, Bost. Red Sox (AL), 1983–89	7
Chuck Klein, Phila. Phillies (NL), 1929–33	5
Al Simmons, Phila. A's (AL), 1929–32, and Chi. White Sox (AL), 1933	5
Charlie Gehringer, Det. Tigers (AL), 1933–37	5

Rookies with 200 or More Hits

American League

Ichiro Suzuki, Sea. Mariners, 2001	242
Joe Jackson, Cle. Indians, 1911	233
Tony Oliva, Min. Twins, 1964	217
Dale Alexander, Det. Tigers, 1929	215
Harvey Kuenn, Det. Tigers, 1953	209
Kevin Seitzer, K.C. Royals, 1987	207
Hal Trosky, Cle. Indians, 1934	206
Joe DiMaggio, N.Y. Yankees, 1936	206
Johnny Pesky, Bost. Red Sox, 1942	205
Earle Combs, N.Y. Yankees, 1925	203
Roy Johnson, Det. Tigers, 1929	201
Dick Wakefield, Det. Tigers, 1943	200

National League (Post-1900)

Lloyd Waner, Pitt. Pirates, 1927	223
Johnny Frederick, Bklyn. Dodgers, 1929	209
Billy Herman, Chi. Cubs, 1932	206
Vada Pinson, Cin. Reds, 1959*	205
Juan Pierre, Colo. Rockies, 2001	202
Dick Allen, Phila. Phillies, 1964	201

*Not a rookie by present standards.

Teammates Finishing One-Two in Base Hits

American League

Season	Team	Leader	Hits	Runner-Up	Hits
1908	Det. Tigers	Ty Cobb	188	Sam Crawford	184
1915	Det. Tigers	Ty Cobb	208	Sam Crawford	183
1919	Det. Tigers (Tie)	Bobby Veach	191	Ty Cobb	191
1923	Cle. Indians	Charlie Jamieson	222	Tris Speaker	218
1927	N.Y. Yankees	Earl Combs	231	Lou Gehrig	218
1929	Det. Tigers (Tie)	Dale Alexander	215	Charlie Gehringer	215
1938	Bost. Red Sox	Joe Vosmik	201	Doc Cramer	198
1956	Det. Tigers	Harvey Kuenn	196	Al Kaline	194
1960	Chi. White Sox	Minnie Minoso	184	Nellie Fox	175
1965	Min. Twins	Tony Oliva	185	Zoilo Versalles	182
1982	Milw. Brewers	Robin Yount	210	Cecil Cooper	205
1993	Tor. Blue Jays	Paul Molitor	211	John Olerud	200
2001	Sea. Mariners	Ichiro Suzuki	242	Bret Boone	206
2011	Bost. Red Sox	Adrian Gonzalez	213	Jacoby Ellsbury	212

*Gonzalez tied for lead with Michael Young of Tex. Rangers

continued on next page

National League (Post-1900)

Season	Team	Leader	Hits	Runner-Up	Hits
1910	Pitt. Pirates (Tie)	Bobby Byrne	178	Honus Wagner	178
1920	St.L. Cardinals	Rogers Hornsby	218	Milt Stock	204
1927	Pitt. Pirates	Paul Waner	237	Lloyd Waner	223
1933	Phila. Phillies	Chuck Klein	223	Chick Fullis	200
1952	St.L. Cardinals	Stan Musial	194	Red Schoendienst	188
1957	Milw. Braves	Red Schoendienst	200*	Hank Aaron	198
1965	Cin. Reds	Pete Rose	209	Vada Pinson	204
1979	St.L. Cardinals	Garry Templeton	211	Keith Hernandez	210
2008	N.Y. Mets	Jose Reyes	204	David Wright	189

*Schoendienst had 78 with N.Y. Giants and 122 hits with Milw. Braves in 1957.

Players Getting 1000 Hits Before Their 25th Birthday

Ty Cobb, Det. Tigers (AL), 1911	24 years, 4 months
Mel Ott, N.Y. Giants (NL), 1933	24 years, 5 months
Al Kaline, Det. Tigers (AL), 1959	24 years, 7 months
Freddie Lindstrom, N.Y. Giants (NL), 1930	24 years, 8 months
Buddy Lewis, Wash. Senators (AL), 1941	24 years, 9 months
Robin Yount, Milw. Brewers (AL), 1980	24 years, 11 months

Players with 10,000 At Bats and Fewer Than 3000 Hits, Career

	At Bats	Hits
Brooks Robinson (1955–77)	10,654	2848
Omar Vizquel (1989–2011)	10,586	2877
Luis Aparicio (1956–73)	10,230	2677
Rabbit Maranville (1912–33, 1935)	10,078	2605
Frank Robinson (1956–76)	10,006	2943

Players with 200 Hits, Batting Under .300, Season

	Hits	Batting Average
Juan Pierre, Chi. Cubs (NL), 2006	204	.292
Jo-Jo Moore, N.Y. Giants (NL), 1935	201	.295
Maury Wills, L.A. Dodgers (NL), 1962	208	.299
Jimmy Rollins, Phila. Phillies (NL), 2007	212	.296
Jose Reyes, N.Y. Mets (NL), 2008	204	.297
Lou Brock, St.L. Cardinals (NL), 1967	206	.299
Matty Alou, Pitt. Pirates (NL), 1970	201	.297
Ralph Garr, Atl. Braves (NL), 1973	200	.299
Buddy Bell, Tex. Rangers (AL), 1979	200	.299
Bill Buckner, Bost. Red Sox (AL), 1985	201	.299

Players with 2500 Hits and Career .300 Batting Average, Never Winning Batting Title (Post-1900)

	Career Hits	Career Batting Average
Paul Molitor	3319	.306
Eddie Collins	3314	.333
Derek Jeter	3465	.310
Sam Rice	2987	.322
Sam Crawford	2925*	.309
Frankie Frisch	2880	.316
Mel Ott	2876	.304
Roberto Alomar	2724	.300
Vladimir Guerrero	2590	.318

*1899 totals not included.

Former Negro Leaguers with 1500 Major League Hits

3771—Hank Aaron, Milw. Braves (NL), 1954–65; Atl. Braves (NL), 1966–74; Milw. Brewers (AL), 1975–76. (Played in the Negro Leagues with Indianapolis Clowns.)

3283—Willie Mays, N.Y. Giants (NL), 1951–52, 1954–57; S.F. Giants (NL), 1958–71; N.Y. Mets (NL), 1972–73. (Played in the Negro Leagues with Chattanooga Choo-Choos, 1947; Birmingham Black Barons, 1948–50.)

2583—Ernie Banks, Chi. Cubs (NL), 1953–71. (Played in the Negro Leagues with Kansas City Monarchs, 1950–53.)

1963—Minnie Minoso, Cle. Indians (AL), 1949, 1951, 1958–59; Chi. White Sox (AL), 1951–57, 1960–61, 1964, 1976, 1980; St.L. Cardinals (NL), 1962; Wash. Senators (AL), 1963. (Played in the Negro Leagues with New York Cubans.)

1889—Jim "Junior" Gilliam, Bklyn. Dodgers (NL), 1953–57; L.A. Dodgers (NL), 1958–66. (Played in the Negro Leagues with Nashville Black Vols, 1946; Baltimore Elite Giants, 1946–51)

1518—Jackie Robinson, Bklyn. Dodgers (NL), 1947–56). (Played in the Negro Leagues with Kansas City Monarchs, 1944–45.)

1515—Larry Doby, Cle. Indians (AL), 1947–55; Chi. White Sox (AL), 1956–57, 1959. (Played in the Negro Leagues with Newark Eagles, 1942–43, 1946–47.)

Players with 2500 Career Hits, Never Having a 200-Hit Season

	Career Hits	Most in One Season
Carl Yastrzemski (1961–83)	3419	191 (1962)
Eddie Murray (1977–97)	3255	186 (1980)
Dave Winfield (1973–95)	3110	193 (1984)
Cap Anson (1871–97)	3081	187 (1886)
Rickey Henderson (1979–2003)	3055	179 (1980)
Jake Beckley (1888–1907)	2930	190 (1900)
Omar Vizquel (1989–2012)	2877	191 (1999)
Mel Ott (1926–47)	2876	191 (1935)
Harold Baines (1980–98)	2866	198 (1985)
Brooks Robinson (1955–77)	2848	194 (1964)
Ivan Rodriguez (1991–2011)	2844	199 (1999)
Ken Griffey Jr. (1989–2010)	2781	185 (1997)
Andre Dawson (1976–96)	2774	189 (1983)
Tony Perez (1964–86)	2732	186 (1970)
Barry Bonds (1987–2007)	2730	181 (1993)
Roberto Alomar (1988–2004)	2724	193 (1996)
Chipper Jones (1993, 1995–2012)	2726	189 (2001)
Rusty Staub (1963–85)	2716	186 (1971)
Gary Sheffield (1988–2009)	2689	190 (2003)
George Davis (1890–1909)	2683	195 (1893)
Luis Aparicio (1956–73)	2677	182 (1966)
Ted Williams (1939–42, 1946–60)	2654	194 (1949)
Rabbit Maranville (1912–33, 1935)	2605	198 (1922)
Tim Raines (1979–2002)	2605	194 (1986)
Reggie Jackson (1967–87)	2584	158 (1973)
Ernie Banks (1953–71)	2583	193 (1958)
Manny Ramirez (1993–2011)	2574	185 (2003)
Willie Davis (1960–76, 1979)	2561	198 (1971)
Steve Finley (1989–2007)	2548	195 (2006)
Joe Morgan (1963–84)	2517	167 (1973)
Jimmy Ryan (1885–1900, 1902–03)	2502	185 (1898)

Latino Players with 2500 Hits

3070 ..... Alex Rodriguez*
3053 ..... Rod Carew
3020 ..... Rafael Palmeiro
3000 ..... Roberto Clemente
2877 ..... Omar Vizquel
2844 ..... Ivan Rodriguez
2767 ..... Adrian Beltre*
2757 ..... Vada Pinson
2732 ..... Tony Perez
2724 ..... Roberto Alomar
2677 ..... Luis Aparicio
2666 ..... Albert Pujols*
2591 ..... Luis Gonzalez
2590 ..... Vladimir Guerrero
2586 ..... Julio Franco
2574 ..... Manny Ramirez

*Still active.

3000 Hits, 500 Home Runs, and a .300 Batting Average, Career

	Hits	Home Runs	Batting Average
Hank Aaron	3771	755	.305
Willie Mays	3283	660	.302

Most Hits by Switch-Hitter, Career

4256 ..... Pete Rose (1963–86)
3255 ..... Eddie Murray (1977–97)
2880 ..... Frankie Frisch (1919–37)
2877 ..... Omar Vizquel (1989–2012)
2726 ..... Chipper Jones (1993, 1995–2012)
2724 ..... Roberto Alomar (1988–2004)
2665 ..... Max Carey (1910–29)
2665 ..... George Davis (1890–1909)

Most Hits by Catcher, Career*

2844 ..... Ivan Rodriguez (1999–2011)
2472 ..... Ted Simmons (1968–88)
2356 ..... Carlton Fisk (1977–97)
2342 ..... Joe Torre (1960–77)
2195 ..... Jason Kendall (1996–2010)
2150 ..... Yogi Berra (1946–65)
2127 ..... Mike Piazza (1992–2007)
2092 ..... Gary Carter (1974–92)

*Played more than 50 percent of their games at catcher.

Most Singles, Career

3215 ..... Pete Rose (1963–86)
3053 ..... Ty Cobb (1905–28)
2643 ..... Eddie Collins (1906–30)
2614 ..... Cap Anson (1871–97)
2595 ..... Derek Jeter (1995–2014)
2513 ..... Willie Keeler (1892–1910)
2424 ..... Honus Wagner (1897–1917)
2404 ..... Rod Carew (1967–85)
2390 ..... Ichiro Suzuki (2001–)
2383 ..... Tris Speaker (1907–28)
2378 ..... Tony Gwynn (1982–2001)
2366 ..... Paul Molitor (1978–98)
2340 ..... Nap Lajoie (1896–1916)
2294 ..... Hank Aaron (1954–1976)
2273 ..... Jesse Burkett (1890–1905)
2271 ..... Sam Rice (1915–34)
2264 ..... Omar Vizquel (1989–2012)
2262 ..... Carl Yastrzemski (1961–83)
2253 ..... Stan Musial (1941–44, 1946–63)
2253 ..... Wade Boggs (1982–98)
2247 ..... Lou Brock (1961–79)
2243 ..... Paul Waner (1926–45)
2182 ..... Robin Yount (1974–93)
2182 ..... Rickey Henderson (1979–2003)
2171 ..... Frankie Frisch (1919–37)
2163 ..... Doc Cramer (1929–48)
2162 ..... Luke Appling (1930–50)
2161 ..... Nellie Fox (1947–65)
2156 ..... Eddie Murray (1977–97)
2154 ..... Roberto Clemente (1955–72)
2130 ..... Jake Beckley (1888–1907)
2121 ..... George Sisler (1915–22, 1924–30)
2119 ..... Richie Ashburn (1948–62)
2108 ..... Luis Aparicio (1956–73)
2106 ..... Cal Ripken Jr. (1981–98)
2104 ..... Zack Wheat (1909–27)
2097 ..... Sam Crawford (1899–1917)
2056 ..... Lave Cross (1887–1907)
2046 ..... Craig Biggio (1988–2007)
2035 ..... Al Kaline (1953–74)
2035 ..... George Brett (1973–93)
2033 ..... Lloyd Waner (1927–45)
2030 ..... Fred Clarke (1894–1911, 1913–15)
2030 ..... Brooks Robinson (1955–77)
2028 ..... George Van Haltren (1887–1903)
2020 ..... Rabbit Maranville (1912–33, 1935)
2017 ..... Max Carey (1910–29)
2017 ..... Dave Winfield (1973–95)

Fewest Singles, Season (Min. 150 Games)

American League

Singles		Games	Total Hits
50	Adam Dunn, Chi. White Sox, 2012	151	110
53	Mark McGwire, Oak. A's, 1991	154	97
53	Mark Reynolds, Balt. Orioles, 2011	155	118
56	Jose Bautista, Tor. Blue Jays, 2011	161	148
58	Gene Tenace, Oak. A's, 1974	158	102
59	Nick Swisher, N.Y. Yankees, 2009	150	124
60	Carlos Pena, T.B. Rays, 2012	160	98
61	Mike Pagliarulo, N.Y. Yankees, 1987	150	122
61	Carlos Delgado, Tor. Blue Jays, 1997	153	136
62	Ed Brinkman, Wash. Senators II, 1965	154	82
62	Gorman Thomas, Milw. Brewers, 1979	156	136
63	Mark McGwire*, Oak. A's–St.L. Cardinals, 1997	156	148
63	Nick Swisher, Chi. White Sox, 2008	153	109
64	Harmon Killebrew, Min. Twins, 1962	155	134
64	Jose Bautista, Tor. Blue Jays, 2015	153	136
64	Tom McCraw, Chi. White Sox, 1966	151	89
65	Reggie Jackson, Oak. A's, 1969	152	151
65	David Ortiz, Bost. Red Sox, 2009	150	129
66	Glenn Hoffman, Bost. Red Sox, 1982	150	98
66	Gorman Thomas, Milw. Brewers–Cle. Indians, 1983	152	112
66	Tom Brunansky, Min. Twins, 1983	151	123
66	Jose Canseco, Tor. Blue Jays, 1998	151	138
66	Troy Glaus, Ana. Angels, 2001	161	147
67	Monte Cross, Phila. A's, 1904	153	95
67	Tom Tresh, N.Y. Yankees, 1968	152	99
67	Mickey Tettleton, Det. Tigers, 1993	152	128
67	Jeromy Burnitz, Milw. Brewers, 1997	153	139
67	Melvin Upton, T.B. Rays, 2010	154	127
68	Harmon Killebrew, Wash. Senators, 1959	153	132
68	Tom Brookens, Det. Tigers, 1985	156	115
68	Darrell Evans, Det. Tigers, 1985	151	125
68	Carlton Fisk, Chi. White Sox, 1985	153	129
68	Mark McGwire, Oak. A's, 1990	156	123
68	Jason Giambi, N.Y. Yankees, 2003	156	134
68	Mickey Tettleton, Det. Tigers, 1992	157	125
68	Carlos Santana, Cle. Indians, 2011	155	132
69	Jesse Barfield, N.Y. Yankees, 1990	153	117
69	Frank Thomas, Chi. White Sox, 2003	153	146

* 46 with Oak. A's and 17 with St.L. Cardinals.

National League (Post-1900)

Singles		Games	Total Hits
49	Barry Bonds, S.F. Giants, 2001	153	156
53	Carlos Pena, Chi. Cubs, 2011	153	111
55	Joe Pederson, L.A. Dodgers, 2015	151	101
55	Andruw Jones, Atl. Braves, 1997	153	92
56	Jose Valentin, Milw. Brewers, 1998	151	96
57	Adam Dunn, Cin. Reds, 2005	160	134
58	Mark McGwire, St.L. Cardinals, 1999	153	145
59	Adam Dunn, Cin. Reds–Ariz. D'backs, 2008	158	122
60	Ike Davis, N.Y. Mets, 2012	156	118
61	Gary Matthews Jr., Chi. Cubs–Pitt. Pirates, 2001	152	92
61	Shane Andrews, Mont. Expos, 1998	150	117
61	Pedro Alvarez, Pitt. Pirates, 2015	150	106
61	Mark McGwire, St.L. Cardinals, 1998	155	152
63	Willie McCovey, S.F. Giants, 1970	152	143
63	Mike Schmidt, Phila. Phillies, 1979	160	137
65	Mike Schmidt, Phila. Phillies, 1975	158	140
65	Alex Gonzalez, Chi. Cubs, 2003	152	122

continued on next page

65	Pat Burrell, Phila. Phillies, 2007	155	121
65	Pat Burrell, Phila. Phillies, 2008	157	134
66	Todd Hundley, N.Y. Mets, 1996	153	140
66	Giancarlo Stanton, Fla. Marlins, 2011	150	135
66	Jay Bruce, Cin. Reds, 2015	157	131
67	Jeff Conine, Fla. Marlins, 1997	151	98
67	Jim Edmonds, St.L. Cardinals, 2004	153	150
67	Adam Dunn, Cin. Reds, 2006	160	131
67	Jay Bruce, Cin. Reds, 2012	155	141
67	Dan Uggla, Atl. Braves, 2012	154	115
68	Greg Vaughn, Cin. Reds, 1999	153	135
68	Brian Giles, Pitt. Pirates, 2002	153	148
69	Gil Hodges, Bklyn. Dodgers, 1952	153	129
69	Kevin Elster, N.Y. Mets, 1989	151	106
69	Jeromy Burnitz, Milw. Brewers, 2000	161	131
69	Jeromy Burnitz, N.Y. Mets, 2002	154	103
69	Adam Dunn, Cin. Reds, 2007	152	138
69	Adam Dunn, Wash. Nationals, 2010	158	145

Most Singles, Season

American League

Singles		Total Hits
225	Ichiro Suzuki, Sea. Mariners, 2004	262
203	Ichiro Suzuki, Sea. Mariners, 2007	238
192	Ichiro Suzuki, Sea. Mariners, 2001	242
187	Wade Boggs, Bost. Red Sox, 1985	240
186	Ichiro Suzuki, Sea. Mariners, 2006	224
184	Willie Wilson, K.C. Royals, 1980	230
182	Sam Rice, Wash. Senators, 1925	227
180	Rod Carew, Min. Twins, 1974	218
180	Ichiro Suzuki, Sea. Mariners, 2008	213
179	Jack Tobin, St.L. Browns, 1921	236
179	Ichiro Suzuki, Sea. Mariners, 2009	225
178	George Sisler, St.L. Browns, 1922	246
176	George Sisler, St.L. Browns, 1925	224

National League (Post-1900)

Singles		Total Hits
198	Lloyd Waner, Pitt. Pirates, 1927	223
184	Juan Pierre, Fla. Marlins, 2004	221
183	Matty Alou, Pitt. Pirates, 1969	231
181	Jesse Burkett, St.L. Cardinals, 1901	226
181	Lefty O'Doul, Phila. Phillies, 1929	254
181	Lloyd Waner, Pitt. Pirates, 1929	234
181	Richie Ashburn, Phila. Phillies, 1951	221
181	Pete Rose, Cin. Reds, 1973	230
180	Lloyd Waner, Pitt. Pirates, 1928	221
180	Ralph Garr, Atl. Braves, 1971	219
179	Maury Wills, L.A. Dodgers, 1962	208
178	Paul Waner, Pitt. Pirates, 1937	219
178	Curt Flood, St.L. Cardinals, 1964	211
177	Bill Terry, N.Y. Giants, 1930	254
177	Tony Gwynn, S.D. Padres, 1984	213
176	Richie Ashburn, Phila. Phillies, 1958	215
175	Willie Keeler, Bklyn. Dodgers, 1900	204

20 Triple Seasons (Since 1930)

American League

1930 Earle Combs, N.Y. Yankees 22
1935 Joe Vosmik, Cle. Indians 20
1941 Jeff Heath, Cle. Indians 20
1945 Snuffy Stirnweiss, N.Y. Yankees 22
1949 Dale Mitchell, Cle. Indians 23
1979 George Brett, K.C. Royals 20
1985 Willie Wilson, K.C. Royals 21
2000 Cristian Guzman, Min. Twins 20
2007 Curtis Granderson, Det. Tigers 23

National League (Post-1900)

1930 Adam Comorosky, Pitt. Pirates 23
1931 Bill Terry, N.Y. Giants 20
1943 Stan Musial, St.L. Cardinals 20
1946 Stan Musial, St.L. Cardinals 20
1957 Willie Mays, N.Y. Giants 20
1996 Lance Johnson, N.Y. Mets 21
2007 Jimmy Rollins, Phila. Phillies 20

Largest Differential Between League Leader in Hits and Runner-Up

American League

Differential	Season	Leader	Hits	Runner-Up	Hits
+46	2004	Ichiro Suzuki, Sea. Mariners	262	Michael Young, Tex. Rangers	216
+42	1901	Nap Lajoie, Phila. A's	232	John Anderson, Milw. Brewers	190
+37	1974	Rod Carew, Min. Twins	218	Tommy Davis, Balt. Orioles	181
+36	2001	Ichiro Suzuki, Sea. Mariners	242	Bret Boone, Sea. Mariners	206
+35	1917	Ty Cobb, Det. Tigers	225	George Sisler, St.L. Browns	190
+35	1922	George Sisler, St.L. Browns	246	Ty Cobb, Det. Tigers	211
+33	1910	Nap Lajoie, Cle. Indians	227	Ty Cobb, Det. Tigers	194
+33	1920	George Sisler, St.L. Browns	257	Eddie Collins, Chi. White Sox	224
+31	1928	Heinie Manush, St.L. Browns	241	Lou Gehrig, N.Y. Yankees	210
+29	1985	Wade Boggs, Bost. Red Sox	240	Don Mattingly, N.Y. Yankees	211
+27	1945	Snuffy Stirnweiss, N.Y. Yankees	195	Wally Moses, Chi. White Sox	168
+27	1977	Rod Carew, Min. Twins	239	Ron LeFlore, Det. Tigers	212
+26	1925	Al Simmons, Phila. A's	253	Sam Rice, Wash. Senators	227
+26	2000	Darin Erstad, Ana. Angels	240	Johnny Damon, K.C. Royals	214

National League (Post-1900)

Differential	Season	Leader	Hits	Runner-Up	Hits
+44	1946	Stan Musial, St.L. Cardinals	228	Dixie Walker, Bklyn. Dodgers	184
+40	1948	Stan Musial, St.L. Cardinals	230	Tommy Holmes, Bost. Braves	190
+35	1922	Rogers Hornsby, St.L. Cardinals	250	Carson Bigbee, Pitt. Pirates	215
+34	1987	Tony Gwynn, S.D. Padres	218	Pedro Guerrero, L.A. Dodgers	184
+30	1973	Pete Rose, Cin. Reds	230	Ralph Garr, Atl. Braves	200
+27	1945	Tommy Holmes, Bost. Braves	224	Goody Rosen, Bklyn. Dodgers	197

Batting Average

Evolution of Batting Average Record

American League

1901 Nap Lajoie, Phila. A's ..... .426

National League (Pre-1900)

1876 Ross Barnes, Chi. Cubs ..... .404
1879 Cap Anson, Chi. Cubs ..... .407
1887 Cap Anson, Chi. Cubs ..... .421
1887 Cap Anson, Chi. Cubs ..... .421
1894 Hugh Duffy, Bost. Beaneaters ..... .438

National League (Post-1899)

1900 Honus Wagner, Pitt. Pirates ..... .381
1901 Jesse Burkett, St.L. Cardinals ..... .382
1921 Rogers Hornsby, St.L. Cardinals ..... .397
1922 Rogers Hornsby, St.L. Cardinals ..... .401
1924 Rogers Hornsby, St.L. Cardinals ..... .424

Highest Batting Average by Position, Season

American League

First Base	.420	George Sisler, St.L. Browns, 1922
Second Base	.426	Nap Lajoie, Phila. A's, 1901
Third Base	.390	George Brett, K.C. Royals, 1980
Shortstop	.388	Luke Appling, Chi. White Sox, 1936
Outfield	.420	Ty Cobb, Det. Tigers, 1911
Catcher	.365	Joe Mauer, Min. Twins, 2009
Pitcher	.433	Walter Johnson, Wash. Senators, 1925
Designated Hitter	.356	Edgar Martinez, Sea. Mariners, 1995

National League (Post-1900)

First Base	.401	Bill Terry, N.Y. Giants, 1930
Second Base	.424	Rogers Hornsby, St. L. Cardinals, 1924
Third Base	.379	Fred Lindstrom, N.Y. Giants, 1930
Shortstop	.385	Arky Vaughan, Pitt. Pirates, 1935
Outfield	.398	Lefty O'Doul, Phila. Phillies, 1929
Catcher	.367	Babe Phelps, Bklyn. Dodgers, 1936
Pitcher	.427	Jack Bentley, N.Y. Giants, 1923

Highest Batting Average by Decade (2000 At Bats)

Pre-1900

.384	Willie Keeler
.356	Jesse Burkett
.349	Billy Hamilton
.345	Ed Delahanty
.342	Dan Brouthers
.342	Dave Orr
.341	Pete Browning
.340	Joe Kelley
.338	Jake Stenzel
.336	John McGraw

1900–09

.352	Honus Wagner
.346	Nap Lajoie
.338	Mike Donlin
.337	Ty Cobb
.312	Jesse Burkett
.312	Elmer Flick
.311	Willie Keeler
.311	Cy Seymour
.310	George Stone
.309	Ginger Beaumont

1910–19

.387	Ty Cobb
.354	Joe Jackson
.344	Tris Speaker
.331	George Sisler
.326	Eddie Collins
.321	Nap Lajoie
.314	Edd Roush
.313	Sam Crawford
.313	Benny Kauff
.310	Home Run Baker
.310	Vin Campbell
.310	Rogers Hornsby

1920–29

.382	Rogers Hornsby
.364	Harry Heilmann
.357	Ty Cobb
.356	Al Simmons
.356	Paul Waner
.355	Babe Ruth
.354	Tris Speaker
.347	George Sisler
.346	Eddie Collins
.342	Fats Fothergill

1930–39

.352	Bill Terry
.346	Johnny Mize
.345	Lefty O'Doul
.343	Lou Gehrig
.341	Joe DiMaggio
.338	Joe Medwick
.336	Jimmie Foxx
.336	Paul Waner
.331	Charlie Gehringer
.331	Babe Ruth

1940–49

.356	Ted Williams
.346	Stan Musial
.325	Joe DiMaggio
.321	Barney McCosky
.316	Johnny Pesky
.312	Enos Slaughter
.311	Luke Appling
.311	Dixie Walker
.308	Taffy Wright
.305	George Kell
.305	Joe Medwick

1950–59

.336	Ted Williams
.330	Stan Musial
.323	Hank Aaron
.317	Willie Mays
.314	Harvey Kuenn
.313	Richie Ashburn
.311	Al Kaline
.311	Mickey Mantle
.311	Jackie Robinson
.308	George Kell
.308	Duke Snider

1960–69

.328	Roberto Clemente
.312	Matty Alou
.309	Pete Rose
.308	Hank Aaron
.308	Tony Oliva
.304	Frank Robinson
.300	Dick Allen
.300	Willie Mays
.297	Curt Flood
.297	Manny Mota

1970–79

.343	Rod Carew
.320	Bill Madlock
.317	Dave Parker
.314	Pete Rose
.311	Lyman Bostock
.310	George Brett
.310	Ken Griffey Sr.
.310	Jim Rice
.307	Ralph Garr
.300	Fred Lynn

continued on next page

1980–89

.352 ..... Wade Boggs
.332 ..... Tony Gwynn
.323 ..... Don Mattingly
.323 ..... Kirby Puckett
.314 ..... Rod Carew
.311 ..... George Brett
.308 ..... Pedro Guerrero
.307 ..... Al Oliver
.305 ..... Robin Yount
.304 ..... Will Clark

1990–99

.344 ..... Tony Gwynn
.328 ..... Mike Piazza
.322 ..... Edgar Martinez
.320 ..... Frank Thomas
.318 ..... Derek Jeter
.313 ..... Paul Molitor
.313 ..... Larry Walker
.312 ..... Kirby Puckett
.310 ..... Mark Grace
.310 ..... Kenny Lofton

2000–09

.334 ..... Albert Pujols
.333 ..... Ichiro Suzuki
.331 ..... Todd Helton
.323 ..... Vladimir Guerrero
.322 ..... Barry Bonds
.317 ..... Derek Jeter
.317 ..... Manny Ramirez
.316 ..... Magglio Ordonez
.311 ..... Miguel Cabrera
.311 ..... Chipper Jones

2010–15

.333 ..... Miguel Cabrera
.312 ..... Buster Posey
.311 ..... Joey Votto
.311 ..... Adrian Beltre
.308 ..... Robinson Cano
.302 ..... Ryan Braun
.300 ..... Joe Mauer
.299 ..... Andrew McCutchen
.297 ..... Adrian Gonzalez
.296 ..... Carlos Gonzalez

Highest Batting Average for a Rookie

American League

.408 ..... Joe Jackson, Cle. Indians, 1911
.350 ..... Ichiro Suzuki, Sea. Mariners, 2001
.349 ..... Wade Boggs, Bost. Red Sox, 1982
.343 ..... Dale Alexander, Det. Tigers, 1929
.343 ..... Jeff Heath, Cle. Indians, 1938
.342 ..... Patsy Dougherty, Bost. Red Sox, 1902
.342 ..... Earle Combs, N.Y. Yankees, 1925
.337 ..... Ike Boone, Bost. Red Sox, 1924

National League (Post-1900)

.373 ..... George Watkins, St.L. Cardinals, 1930
.355 ..... Lloyd Waner, Pitt. Pirates, 1927
.354 ..... Kiki Cuyler, Pitt. Pirates, 1924
.352 ..... Hack Miller, Chi. Cubs, 1922
.350 ..... Cuckoo Christiansen, Cin. Reds, 1926
.336 ..... Paul Waner, Pitt. Pirates, 1926

Top 10 Rookie Batting Averages, Each League (Min. 100 Games)

American League

.408 ..... Joe Jackson, Cle. Indians, 1911
.350 ..... Ichiro Suzuki, Sea. Mariners, 2001
.349 ..... Wade Boggs, Bost. Red Sox, 1982
.343 ..... Dale Alexander, Det. Tigers, 1929
.343 ..... Jeff Heath, Cle. Indians, 1938
.342 ..... Patsy Dougherty, Bost. Red Sox, 1902
.342 ..... Earle Combs, N.Y. Yankees, 1925
.337 ..... Ike Boone, Bost. Red Sox, 1924
.334 ..... Heinie Manush, Det. Tigers, 1923
.334 ..... Charlie Keller, N.Y. Yankees, 1939
.331 ..... Mickey Cochrane, Phila. A's, 1925
.331 ..... Earl Averill, Cle. Indians, 1929
.331 ..... Johnny Pesky, Bost. Red Sox, 1942
.331 ..... Fred Lynn, Bost. Red Sox, 1975

National League (Post-1900)

.373 ..... George Watkins, St.L. Cardinals, 1930
.355 ..... Lloyd Waner, Pitt. Pirates, 1927
.354 ..... Kiki Cuyler, Pitt. Pirates, 1924
.352 ..... Hack Miller, Chi. Cubs, 1922
.350 ..... Cuckoo Christiansen, Cin. Reds, 1926
.339 ..... Lonnie Smith, Phila. Phillies, 1980
.336 ..... Paul Waner, Pitt. Pirates, 1926
.333 ..... Richie Ashburn, Phila. Phillies, 1948
.330 ..... Rico Carty, Milw. Braves, 1964
.329 ..... Johnny Mize, St.L. Cardinals, 1936
.329 ..... Albert Pujols, St.L. Cardinals, 2001
.328 ..... Johnny Frederick, Bklyn. Dodgers, 1929
.324 ..... Ryan Braun, Milw. Brewers, 2007

Lifetime Batting Averages of 20-Year Players (Not Including Pitchers)

.366 ..... Ty Cobb (24 years)
.359 ..... Rogers Hornsby (23 years)
.345 ..... Tris Speaker (22 years)
.342 ..... Babe Ruth (22 years)
.338 ..... Tony Gwynn (20 years)
.338 ..... Nap Lajoie (21 years)
.334 ..... Al Simmons (20 years)
.334 ..... Cap Anson (22 years)
.333 ..... Eddie Collins (25 years)
.333 ..... Paul Waner (20 years)
.331 ..... Stan Musial (22 years)
.328 ..... Honus Wagner (21 years)
.325 ..... Jimmie Foxx (20 years)
.322 ..... Sam Rice (20 years)
.312 ..... Fred Clarke (21 years)

continued on next page

.310 ..... Luke Appling (20 years)
.310 ..... Derek Jeter (20 years)
.308 ..... Jake Beckley (20 years)
.306 ..... Paul Molitor (21 years)
.305 ..... Hank Aaron (23 years)
.305 ..... George Brett (21 years)
.304 ..... Manny Mota (20 years)
.304 ..... Mel Ott (22 years)
.303 ..... Pete Rose (24 years)
.302 ..... Willie Mays (22 years)
.301 ..... Joe Cronin (20 years)
.298 ..... Barry Bonds (22 years)
.298 ..... Julio Franco (23 years)
.298 ..... Joe Judge (20 years)
.295 ..... George Davis (20 years)
.297 ..... Alex Rodriguez* (21 years)
.297 ..... Al Kaline (22 years)
.297 ..... Ivan Rodriguez (21 years)
.296 ..... Doc Cramer (20 years)
.294 ..... Tim Raines (23 years)
.294 ..... Frank Robinson (21 years)
.293 ..... Phil Cavarretta (22 years)
.292 ..... Lave Cross (21 years)
.292 ..... Gary Sheffield (22 years)
.290 ..... Charlie Grimm (20 years)
.289 ..... Harold Baines (22 years)
.289 ..... Bill Buckner (22 years)
.288 ..... Rafael Palmeiro (20 years)
.287 ..... Eddie Murray (21 years)
.286 ..... Johnny Cooney (20 years)
.286 ..... Mickey Vernon (20 years)
.285 ..... Max Carey (20 years)
.285 ..... Ted Simmons (21 years)
.285 ..... Alan Trammell (20 years)
.285 ..... Carl Yastrzemski (23 years)
.285 ..... Robin Yount (20 years)
.284 ..... Ken Griffey Jr. (22 years)
.283 ..... Dave Winfield (22 years)
.282 ..... Willie Stargell (21 years)
.282 ..... Elmer Valo (20 years)
.280 ..... Jimmy Dykes (22 years)
.279 ..... Andre Dawson (21 years)
.279 ..... Rickey Henderson (25 years)
.279 ..... Tony Perez (23 years)
.279 ..... Rusty Staub (23 years)
.278 ..... Deacon McGuire (26 years)
.277 ..... Harry Davis (22 years)
.277 ..... Jason Giambi (20 years)
.276 ..... Jim Thome (22 years)
.276 ..... Cal Ripken Jr. (21 years)
.273 ..... Bob O'Farrell (21 years)
.273 ..... Sandy Alomar (20 years)
.272 ..... Bill Dahlen (22 years)
.272 ..... Omar Vizquel (24 years)
.271 ..... Tim McCarver (21 years)
.271 ..... Joe Morgan (22 years)
.270 ..... Willie McCovey (22 years)
.269 ..... Carlton Fisk (24 years)
.268 ..... Bobby Wallace (25 years)
.267 ..... Brian Downing (20 years)
.267 ..... Jay Johnstone (20 years)
.267 ..... Brooks Robinson (23 years)
.266 ..... Ron Fairly (21 years)
.263 ..... Jack O'Connor (21 years)
.261 ..... Kid Gleason (22 years)
.259 ..... Luke Sewell (20 years)
.258 ..... Rabbit Maranville (23 years)
.256 ..... Harmon Killebrew (22 years)
.255 ..... Gary Gaetti (20 years)
.248 ..... Darrell Evans (21 years)
.248 ..... Graig Nettles (22 years)
.233 ..... Rick Dempsey (24 years)

*Still active.

Players Never Hitting Below .270 in Career (Min. 10 Years)

	Lifetime Batting Average	Lowest Batting Average	Seasons
Cap Anson (1876–97)	.334	.272 (1892)	22
Sam Rice (1915–34)	.322	.293 (1934)	20
Tony Gwynn (1982–2001)	.338	.289 (1982)	20
Rod Carew (1967–85)	.328	.273 (1968)	19
Vladimir Guerrero (1996–2011)	318	.290 (2011)	16
George Sisler (1915–22, 1924–30)	.340	.285 (1915)	15
Joe Sewell (1920–33)	.312	.272 (1932)	14
Mickey Cochrane (1925–37)	.320	.270 (1936)	13
Bruce Campbell (1930–42)	.290	.275 (1941)	13
Bibb Falk (1920–31)	.314	.285 (1921)	12
Fats Fothergill (1922–33)	.325	.281 (1930)	12
Earle Combs (1924–35)	.325	.282 (1935)	12
Matt Holliday (2004–)	.307	.272 (2014)	12
Dom DiMaggio (1940–42, 1946–53)	.298	.283 (1941, 1947)	11
Robinson Cano (2005–)	.307	.271 (2008)	11
Homer Summa (1920, 1922–30)	.302	.272 (1929)	10
Nick Markakis (2006–)	.291	.271 (2013)	10

Players Batting .300 for 10 or More Consecutive Seasons From Start of Career

17	Willie Keeler (1892–1906)	11	Al Simmons (1924–34)
17	Stan Musial (1941–44, 1946–58)	10	Wade Boggs (1982–91)
15	Ted Williams (1939–42, 1946–51, 1954–58)	10	Ichiro Suzuki (2001–10)
12	Paul Waner (1926–37)	10	Albert Pujols (2001–10)

.400 Hitters and How Their Team Finished

American League

	Batting Average	Team's Wins–Losses	Place	Games Behind
Nap Lajoie, Phila. A's, 1901	.427	74–62	4	9.5
Ty Cobb, Det. Tigers, 1911	.420	89–65	2	13.5
Joe Jackson, Cle. Indians, 1911	.408	80–73	3	22
Ty Cobb, Det. Tigers, 1912	.409	69–84	6	36.5
George Sisler, St.L. Browns, 1920	.407	76–77	4	21.5
George Sisler, St.L. Browns, 1922	.420	93–61	2	1
Ty Cobb, Det. Tigers, 1922	.401	79–75	3	15
Harry Heilmann, Det. Tigers, 1923	.403	83–71	2	16
Ted Williams, Bost. Red Sox, 1941	.406	84–70	2	17

National League (Post-1900)

	Batting Average	Team's Wins–Losses	Place	Games Behind
Rogers Hornsby, St.L. Cardinals, 1922	.401	85–69	3	8
Rogers Hornsby, St.L. Cardinals, 1924	.424	65–89	6	28.5
Rogers Hornsby, St.L. Cardinals, 1925	.403	77–76	4	18
Bill Terry, N.Y. Giants, 1930	.401	87–67	3	5

.400 Hitters Versus League Batting Average (Post-1900)

	Batting Average	League Batting Average	Differential
Nap Lajoie, Phila. A's (AL), 1901	.426	.277	+.149
Ty Cobb, Det. Tigers (AL), 1911	.420	.273	+.147
Ty Cobb, Det. Tigers (AL), 1912	.409	.265	+.144
Rogers Hornsby, St.L. Cardinals (NL), 1924	.424	.283	+.141
Ted Williams, Bost. Red Sox (AL), 1941	.406	.266	+.140
George Sisler, St.L. Browns (AL), 1922	.420	.284	+.136
Joe Jackson, Cle. Indians (AL), 1911	.408	.273	+.135
George Sisler, St.L. Browns (AL), 1920	.407	.283	+.124
Harry Heilmann, Det. Tigers (AL), 1923	.403	.282	+.121
Ty Cobb, Det. Tigers (AL), 1922	.401	.284	+.117
Rogers Hornsby, St.L. Cardinals (NL), 1925	.403	.292	+.111
Rogers Hornsby, St.L. Cardinals (NL), 1922	.401	.292	+.109
Bill Terry, N.Y. Giants (NL), 1930	.401	.303	+.098

Players Hitting .370 Since Ted Williams's .406 Season (1941)

American League

Ted Williams, Bost. Red Sox, 1957	.388
Rod Carew, Min. Twins, 1977	.388
George Brett, K.C. Royals, 1980	.390
Nomar Garciaparra, Bost. Red Sox, 2000	.372
Ichiro Suzuki, Sea. Mariners, 2004	.372

National League

Stan Musial, St.L. Cardinals, 1948	.376
Tony Gwynn, S.D. Padres, 1987	.370
Andres Galarraga, Colo. Rockies, 1993	.370
Tony Gwynn, S.D. Padres, 1994	.394
Tony Gwynn, S.D. Padres, 1997	.372
Larry Walker, Colo. Rockies, 1999	.379
Todd Helton, Colo. Rockies, 2000	.372

Players Hitting .300 in Rookie *and* Final Seasons (Post-1900; Min. Five Years)

First Year			Final Year	
Richie Ashburn	Phila. Phillies (NL), 1948	.333	N.Y. Mets (NL), 1962	.306
Wade Boggs	Bost. Red Sox (AL), 1982	.349	T.B. Devil Rays (AL), 1999	.301
Tony Cuccinello	Cin. Reds (NL), 1930	.312	Chi. White Sox (AL), 1945	.308
Fats Fothergill	Det. Tigers (AL), 1923	.315	Bost. Red Sox (AL), 1933	.344
Joe Jackson	Cle. Indians (AL), 1911	.408	Chi. White Sox (AL), 1920	.382
Del Pratt	St.L. Browns (AL), 1912	.302	Det. Tigers (AL), 1924	.303
Ted Williams	Bost. Red Sox (AL), 1939	.327	Bost. Red Sox (AL), 1960	.316

Players Hitting .300 in Their Only Major League Season (Post-1900; Min. 100 Games, 300 At Bats)

Irv Waldron, Milw. Brewers–Wash. Senators (AL), 1901	.311
Tex Vache, Bost. Red Sox (AL), 1925	.313
Buzz Arlett, Phila. Phillies (NL), 1931	.313

Players Batting .350 with 50 Home Runs

American League

	Batting Average	Home Runs
Babe Ruth, N.Y. Yankees, 1920	.356	54
Babe Ruth, N.Y. Yankees, 1921	.378	59
Babe Ruth, N.Y. Yankees, 1927	.356	60
Jimmie Foxx, Phila. A's, 1932	.364	58
Mickey Mantle, N.Y. Yankees, 1956	.353	52

National League

	Batting Average	Home Runs
Hack Wilson, Chi. Cubs, 1930	.356	56

Players 40 or Older* Hitting .300 (Min. 50 Games)

American League

	Age	Batting Average
Ty Cobb, Phila. A's, 1927	40	.357
Sam Rice, Wash. Senators, 1930	40	.349
Paul Molitor, Min. Twins, 1996	40	.341
Eddie Collins, Phila. A's, 1927	40	.338
Ted Williams, Bost. Red Sox, 1958	40	.328
Ty Cobb, Phila. A's, 1928	41	.323
Sam Rice, Wash. Senators, 1932	42	.323
Bert Campaneris, N.Y. Yankees, 1983	41	.322
Ted Williams, Bost. Red Sox, 1960	41	.316
Rickey Henderson, N.Y. Yankees, 1999	42	.315
Luke Appling, Chi. White Sox, 1948	41	.314
Harold Baines, Balt. Orioles–Cle. Indians	40	.312
Sam Rice, Wash. Senators, 1931	41	.310
Luke Appling, Chi. White Sox, 1949	42	.301
Wade Boggs, T.B. Devil Rays, 1999	40	.301
Paul Molitor, Min. Twins, 1997	41	.305
Bing Miller, Bost. Red Sox, 1935	41	.304
Enos Slaughter, N.Y. Yankees, 1958	42	.304
Wade Boggs, T.B. Devil Rays, 1999	40	.301
Luke Appling, Chi. White Sox, 1949	42	.301

*As of September of that year.

National League

	Age	Batting Average
Cap Anson, Chi. Colts, 1894	43	.388
Barry Bonds, S.F. Giants, 2004	40	.362
Moises Alou, N.Y. Mets 2007	40	.341
Cap Anson, Chi. Colts, 1895	44	.335
Cap Anson, Chi. Colts, 1896	45	.331
Stan Musial, St.L. Cardinals, 1962	41	.330
Tony Perez, Cin. Reds, 1985	43	.328
Jack Saltzgaver, Pitt. Pirates, 1945	40	.325
Pete Rose, Phila. Phillies, 1984	40	.325
Tony Gwynn, S.D. Padres, 2001	41	.324
Johnny Cooney, Bost. Braves, 1941	40	.319
Rickey Henderson, N.Y. Mets, 1999	40	.315
Cap Anson, Chi. Colts, 1893	42	.314
Al Nixon, Phila. Phillies, 1927	41	.312
Paul Waner, Bklyn. Dodgers, 1943	40	.311
Julio Franco, Atl. Braves, 2004	46	.309
Jim O'Rourke, N.Y. Giants, 1892	40	.304
Andres Galarraga, S.F. Giants, 2003	42	.301
Gabby Hartnett, N.Y. Giants, 1941	40	.300

Players Hitting .325 for Two or More Different Clubs (Post-1945)

Roberto Alomar	Tor. Blue Jays (AL)	1993	.326
	Balt. Orioles (AL)	1996	.328
		1997	.333
	Cle. Indians (AL)	2001	.336
Moises Alou	Mont. Expos (NL)	1994	.339
	Hous. Astros (NL)	2000	.355
		2001	.331
Albert Belle	Cle. Indians (AL)	1994	.357
	Chi. White Sox (AL)	1998	.328
Wade Boggs	Bost. Red Sox (AL)	1982	.349
		1983	.361
		1984	.325
		1985	.368
		1986	.357
		1987	.363
		1988	.366
		1989	.330
		1991	.332
	N.Y. Yankees (AL)	1994	.342
Ellis Burks	Colo. Rockies (NL)	1996	.344
	S.F. Giants (NL)	2000	.344
Miguel Cabrera	Fla. Marlins (NL)	2006	.339
	Det. Tigers (AL)	2010	.328
		2011	.344
		2012	.330
		2013	.348
		2015	.338
Rod Carew	Min. Twins (AL)	1969	.332
		1970	.366
		1973	.350
		1974	.364
		1975	.359
		1976	.331
		1977	.388
		1978	.333
	Cal. Angels (AL)	1980	.331
		1983	.339
Vladimir Guerrero	Mont. Expos (NL)	2000	.345
		2002	.336
	Ana.–L.A. Angels (AL)	2004	.337
		2006	.329
Carney Lansford	Bost. Red Sox (AL)	1981	.336
	Oak. A's (AL)	1989	.336
Kenny Lofton	Cle. Indians (AL)	1993	.325
		1994	.349
	Atl. Braves (NL)	1997	.333
	Phila. Phillies (NL)	2005	.335
Bill Madlock	Chi. Cubs (NL)	1975	.354
		1976	.339
	Pitt. Pirates (NL)	1981	.341
Paul Molitor	Milw. Brewers (AL)	1987	.353
	Tor. Blue Jays (AL)	1993	.332
		1994	.341
	Min. Twins (AL)	1996	.341
John Olerud	Tor. Blue Jays (AL)	1993	.363
	N.Y. Mets (NL)	1998	.354

continued on next page

Mike Piazza	L.A. Dodgers (NL)	1995	.346
		1996	.336
		1997	.362
	N.Y. Mets (NL)	1998	.348
Manny Ramirez	Cle. Indians (AL)	1997	.328
		1999	.333
		2000	.351
	Bost. Red Sox (AL)	2002	.349
		2003	.325
	L.A. Dodgers (AL)	2008	.332
Mickey Rivers	N.Y. Yankees (AL)	1977	.326
	Tex. Rangers (AL)	1980	.333
Ivan Rodriguez	Tex. Rangers (AL)	1999	.332
		2000	.347
	Det. Tigers (AL)	2004	.334
Pete Rose	Cin. Reds (NL)	1968	.335
		1969	.348
		1973	.338
	Phila. Phillies (NL)	1979	.331
		1981	.325
Gary Sheffield	S.D. Padres (NL)	1992	.330
	L.A. Dodgers (NL)	2000	.325
	Atl. Braves (NL)	2003	.330
Al Zarilla	St.L. Browns (AL)	1948	.329
	Bost. Red Sox (AL)	1950	.325

Batting Title

Closest Batting Races

American League

Spread	Season		Batting Average
.0001	1945	Snuffy Stirnweiss, N.Y. Yankees	.3085
		Tony Cuccinello, Chi. White Sox	.3084
.0001	1949	George Kell, Det. Tigers	.3429
		Ted Williams, Bost. Red Sox	.3428
.0004	1970	Alex Johnson, Cal. Angels	.3290
		Carl Yastrzemski, Bost. Red Sox	.3286
.0006	1935	Buddy Myer, Wash. Senators	.3490
		Joe Vosmik, Cle. Indians	.3484
.0009	1982	Willie Wilson, K.C. Royals	.3316
		Robin Yount, Milw. Brewers	.3307
.0010	1910	Ty Cobb, Det. Tigers	.3851
		Nap Lajoie, Cle. Indians	.3841
.0012	1976	George Brett, K.C. Royals	.3333
		Hal McRae, K.C. Royals	.3321
.0012	2003	Bill Mueller, Bost. Red Sox	.3263
		Manny Ramirez, Bost. Red Sox	.3251
.0016	1953	Mickey Vernon, Wash. Senators	.3372
		Al Rosen, Cle. Indians	.3356
.0017	1928	Goose Goslin, Wash. Senators	.3794
		Heinie Manush, St.L. Browns	.3777
.0022	1930	Al Simmons, Phila. A's	.3809
		Lou Gehrig, N.Y. Yankees	.3787
.0022	2008	Joe Mauer, Min. Twins	.3284
		Dustin Pedroia, Bost. Red Sox	.3262

continued on next page

National League (Post-1900)

Spread	Season		Batting Average
.0002	2003	Albert Pujols, St.L. Cardinals	.3587
		Todd Helton, Colo. Rockies	.3585
.0003	1931	Chick Hafey, St.L. Cardinals	.3489
		Bill Terry, N.Y. Giants	.3486
.0011	1991	Terry Pendleton, Atl. Braves	.3191
		Hal Morris, Cin. Reds	.3180
.0013	1911	Honus Wagner, Pitt. Pirates	.3340
		Doc Miller, Bost. Rustlers	.3327
.0016	1918	Zack Wheat, Bklyn. Dodgers	.3349
		Edd Roush, Cin. Reds	.3333
.0022	1976	Bill Madlock, Chi. Cubs	.3385
		Ken Griffey Sr., Cin. Reds	.3363

Teammates Finishing One-Two in Batting Race

American League

Season	Team	Leader	Batting Average	Runner-Up	Batting Average
1907	Det. Tigers	Ty Cobb	.350	Sam Crawford	.323
1908	Det. Tigers	Ty Cobb	.324	Sam Crawford	.311
1919	Det. Tigers	Ty Cobb	.384	Bobby Veach	.355
1921	Det. Tigers	Harry Heilmann	.394	Ty Cobb	.389
1942	Bost. Red Sox	Ted Williams	.356	Johnny Pesky	.331
1958	Bost. Red Sox	Ted Williams	.388	Pete Runnels	.322
1959	Det. Tigers	Harvey Kuenn	.353	Al Kaline	.327
1961	Det. Tigers	Norm Cash	.361	Al Kaline	.324
1976	K.C. Royals	George Brett	.333	Hal McRae	.332
1977	Min. Twins	Rod Carew	.388	Lyman Bostock	.336
1984	N.Y. Yankees	Don Mattingly	.343	Dave Winfield	.340
1993	Tor. Blue Jays	John Olerud	.363	Paul Molitor	.332
2003	Bost. Red Sox	Bill Mueller	.326	Manny Ramirez	.325

National League (Post-1900)

Season	Team	Leader	Batting Average	Runner-Up	Batting Average
1903	Pitt. Pirates	Honus Wagner	.355	Fred Clarke	.351
1923	St.L. Cardinals	Rogers Hornsby	.384	Jim Bottomley	.371
1925	St.L. Cardinals	Rogers Hornsby	.403	Jim Bottomley	.367
1926	Cin. Reds	Bubbles Hargrave	.353	Cuckoo Christenson	.350
1933	Phila. Phillies	Chuck Klein	.368	Spud Davis	.349
1937	St.L. Cardinals	Joe Medwick	.374	Johnny Mize	.364
1954	N.Y. Giants	Willie Mays	.354	Don Mueller	.342

Switch-Hitting Batting Champions

American League

Mickey Mantle, N.Y. Yankees, 1956 ..... .353
Willie Wilson, K.C. Royals, 1982 ..... .332
Bernie Williams, N.Y. Yankees, 1998 ..... .339
Bill Mueller, Bost. Red Sox, 2003 ..... .326

National League (Post-1900)

Pete Rose, Cin. Reds, 1968 ..... .335
Pete Rose, Cin. Reds, 1969 ..... .348
Pete Rose, Cin. Reds, 1973 ..... .338
Willie McGee, St.L. Cardinals, 1985 ..... .353
Tim Raines, Mont. Expos, 1986 ..... .334
Willie McGee*, St.L. Cardinals, 1990 ..... .335
Terry Pendleton, Atl. Braves, 1991 ..... .319
Chipper Jones, Atl. Braves, 2008 ..... .364
Jose Reyes, N.Y. Mets, 2011 ..... .337

*Also with Oak. A's (AL).

Catchers Winning Batting Titles

Bubbles Hargrave, Cin. Reds (NL), 1926	.353	(326 at bats, 115 hits)
Ernie Lombardi, Cin. Reds (NL), 1938	.342	(489 at bats, 167 hits)
Ernie Lombardi, Bost. Braves (NL), 1942	.330	(309 at bats, 102 hits)
Joe Mauer, Min. Twins (AL), 2006	.347	(521 at bats, 181 hits)
Joe Mauer, Min. Twins (AL), 2008	.328	(536 at bats, 176 hits)
Joe Mauer, Min. Twins (AL), 2009	.365	(523 at bats, 191 hits)
Buster Posey, S.F. Giants (NL), 2012	.336	(530 at bats, 178 hits)

Batting Champions on Last-Place Teams

American League

Dale Alexander*, Bost. Red Sox, 1932	.367
Edgar Martinez, Sea. Mariners, 1992	.343
Ichiro Suzuki, Sea. Mariners, 2004	.373

*Also with Det. Tigers (AL)
**Also with Oak. A's (AL)

National League (Post-1900)

Larry Doyle, N.Y. Giants, 1915	.320
Richie Ashburn, Phila. Phillies, 1958	.350
Tony Gwynn, S.D. Padres, 1987	.370
Willie McGee**, St.L. Cardinals, 1990	.335
Tony Gwynn, S.D. Padres, 1994	.394
Tony Gwynn, S.D. Padres, 1997	.372
Larry Walker, Colo. Rockies, 1999	.379
Larry Walker, Colo. Rockies, 2001	.350
Michael Cuddyer, Colo. Rockies, 2013	.331

Batting Title Winners Without a Home Run

Ginger Beaumont, Pitt. Pirates (NL), 1902	.357
Zack Wheat, Bklyn. Dodgers (NL), 1918	.335
Rod Carew, Min. Twins (AL), 1972	.318

Batting Champions Driving in Fewer Than 40 Runs

	Batting Average	RBIs
Richie Ashburn, Phila. Phillies (NL), 1958	.350	33
Pete Runnels, Bost. Red Sox (AL), 1960	.320	35
Matty Alou, Pitt. Pirates (NL), 1966	.342	27

Batting Champions with 100 Strikeouts in Year They Led League

Roberto Clemente, Pitt. Pirates (NL), 1967	.357	103 strikeouts
Dave Parker, Pitt. Pirates (NL), 1977	.338	107 strikeouts
Alex Rodriguez, Sea. Mariners (AL), 1996	.358	104 strikeouts
Larry Walker, Colo. Rockies (NL), 2001	.350	103 strikeouts
Derek Lee, Chi. Cubs (NL), 2005	.335	109 strikeouts
Matt Holliday, Colo. Rockies (NL), 2007	.340	126 strikeouts
Hanley Ramirez, Fla. Marlins (NL), 2009	.342	101 strikeouts
Carlos Gonzalez, Colo. Rockies (NL), 2010	.336	135 strikeouts
Michael Cuddyer, Colo. Rockies (NL), 2013	.331	100 strikeouts

Lowest Batting Averages to Lead League

American League

.301	Carl Yastrzemski, Bost. Red Sox, 1968
.306	Elmer Flick, Cle. Indians, 1905
.309	Snuffy Stirnweiss, N.Y. Yankees, 1945
.316	Frank Robinson, Balt. Orioles, 1966
.318	Rod Carew, Min. Twins, 1972
.320	Pete Runnels, Bost. Red Sox, 1960
.321	Carl Yastrzemski, Bost. Red Sox, 1963
.321	Tony Oliva, Min. Twins, 1965
.323	Tony Oliva, Min. Twins, 1964

National League (Post-1900)

.313	Tony Gwynn, S.D. Padres, 1988
.319	Terry Pendleton, Atl. Braves, 1991
.319	Justin Morneau, Colo. Rockies, 2014
.320	Larry Doyle, N.Y. Giants, 1915
.321	Edd Roush, Cin. Reds, 1919
.323	Bill Madlock, Pitt. Pirates, 1983
.324	Bill Buckner, Chi. Cubs, 1980
.325	Dick Groat, Pitt. Pirates, 1960
.326	Tommy Davis, L.A. Dodgers, 1962

continued on next page

.324 ..... Ty Cobb, Det. Tigers, 1908
.326 ..... Bill Mueller, Bost. Red Sox, 2003
.330 ..... Miguel Cabrera, Det. Tigers, 2012
.328 ..... Hank Aaron, Milw. Braves, 1956
.329 ..... Jake Daubert, Bklyn. Dodgers 1914
.329 ..... Roberto Clemente, Pitt. Pirates, 1965
.330 ..... Ernie Lombardi, Bost. Braves, 1942
.330 ..... Gary Sheffield, S.D. Padres, 1992

Highest Batting Average *Not* to Win Batting Title

American League

Batting Average	Season		Winner
.408	1911	Joe Jackson	Ty Cobb (.420)
.401	1922	Ty Cobb	George Sisler (.420)
.395	1912	Joe Jackson	Ty Cobb (.409)
.393	1923	Babe Ruth	Harry Heilmann (.403)
.392	1927	Al Simmons	Harry Heilmann (.398)
.389	1921	Ty Cobb	Harry Heilmann (.394)
.389	1925	Tris Speaker	Harry Heilmann (.393)
.388	1920	Tris Speaker	George Sisler (.407)
.387	1925	Al Simmons	Harry Heilmann (.393)
.383	1910	Ty Cobb	Nap Lajoie (.384)
.383	1912	Tris Speaker	Nap Lajoie (.384)
.382	1920	Joe Jackson	George Sisler (.407)
.379	1930	Lou Gehrig	Al Simmons (.381)
.378	1921	Babe Ruth	Harry Heilmann (.394)
.378	1928	Heinie Manush	Goose Goslin (.379)
.378	1922	Tris Speaker	George Sisler (.425)
.378	1936	Earl Averill	Luke Appling (.388)
.378	1911	Sam Crawford	Ty Cobb (.420)
.378	1925	Ty Cobb	Harry Heilmann (.393)
.376	1902	Ed Delahanty	Nap Lajoie (.378)
.376	1920	Babe Ruth	George Sisler (.407)

National League (Post-1900)

Batting Average	Season		Winner
.393	1930	Babe Herman	Billy Terry (.401)
.386	1930	Chuck Klein	Billy Terry (.401)
.383	1930	Lefty O'Doul	Billy Terry (.401)
.381	1929	Babe Herman	Lefty O'Doul (.398)
.380	1929	Rogers Hornsby	Lefty O'Doul (.398)
.379	1930	Fred Lindstrom	Bill Terry (.401)
.375	1924	Zack Wheat	Rogers Hornsby (.424)
.373	1930	George Watkins	Bill Terry (.401)
.372	1929	Bill Terry	Lefty O'Doul (.398)
.371	1923	Jim Bottomley	Rogers Hornsby (.384)
.370	1928	Paul Waner	Rogers Hornsby (.387)
.368	1994	Jeff Bagwell	Tony Gwynn (.394)
.368	1930	Paul Waner	Bill Terry (.401)
.367	1900	Elmer Flick	Honus Wagner (.381)
.367	1925	Jim Bottomley	Rogers Hornsby (.403)
.367	1936	Babe Phelps	Paul Waner (.373)
.366	1930	Pie Traynor	Bill Terry (.401)

Runners-Up for Batting Titles in Both Leagues

American League

Mike Donlin	Balt. Orioles, 1901	.341
Willie Keeler	N.Y. Yankees, 1904	.343
	N.Y. Yankees, 1905	.302
Al Oliver	Tex. Rangers, 1978	.324
Frank Robinson	Balt. Orioles, 1967	.311

National League

Cin. Reds, 1903	.351
Cin. Reds–N.Y. Giants, 1904	.329
N.Y. Giants, 1908	.334
Bklyn. Dodgers, 1901	.355
Bklyn. Dodgers, 1902	.338
Pitt. Pirates, 1974	.321
Cin. Reds, 1962	.342

Players Winning Batting Title in Season *After* Joining New Club

American League

Nap Lajoie (.426), Phila. A's, 1901	Jumped from Phila. Phillies (NL)
Ed Delahanty (.376), Wash. Senators, 1902	Jumped from Phila. Phillies (NL)
Tris Speaker (.386), Cle. Indians, 1916	Traded from Bost. Red Sox
Frank Robinson (.316), Balt. Orioles, 1966	Traded from Cin. Reds
Alex Johnson (.329), Cal. Angels, 1970	Traded from Cin. Reds
Carney Lansford (.336), Bost. Red Sox, 1981	Traded from Cal. Angels
Bill Mueller (.326), Bost. Red Sox, 2003	Free agent

National League (Post-1900)

Hal Chase (.339), Cin. Reds, 1916	Jumped from Federal League
Rogers Hornsby (.387), Bost. Braves, 1928	Traded from N.Y. Giants
Lefty O'Doul (.398), Phila. Phillies, 1929	Traded from N.Y. Giants
Debs Garms (.355), Pitt. Pirates, 1940	Traded from Bost. Braves
Ernie Lombardi (.330), Bost. Braves, 1942	Traded from Cin. Reds
Matty Alou (.342), Pitt. Pirates, 1966	Traded from S.F. Giants
Al Oliver (.331), Mont. Expos, 1982	Traded from Tex. Rangers (AL)
Terry Pendleton (.319), Atl. Braves, 1991	Traded from St.L. Cardinals
Gary Sheffield (.330), S.D. Padres, 1992	Traded from Milw. Brewers (AL)
Andres Galarraga (.370), Colo. Rockies, 1993	Free agent
Justin Morneau (.331), Colo. Rockies, 2014	Free agent
Dee Gordon (.333), Mia. Marlins, 2015	Traded from L.A. Dodgers

Players Changing Team in Season *After* Winning Batting Title

American League

Nap Lajoie (.426), Phila. A's, 1901	Sold to Cle. Indians, June 1902
Ferris Fain (.327), Phila. A's, 1952	Traded to Chi. White Sox, Jan. 1953
Harvey Kuenn (.353), Det. Tigers, 1959	Traded to Cle. Indians in off-season for Rocky Colavito
Pete Runnels (.326), Bost. Red Sox, 1962	Traded to Hous. Astros in off-season for Roman Mejias
Rod Carew (.333), Min. Twins, 1978	Traded to Cal. Angels in off-season for Ken Landreaux and 3 other players

National League (Post-1900)

Chick Hafey (.349), St.L. Cardinals, 1931	Traded to Cin. Reds, Apr. 1932
Chuck Klein (.368), Phila. Phillies, 1933	Traded to Chi. Cubs in off-season for 3 players and $65,000
Bill Madlock (.339), Chi. Cubs, 1976	Traded to S.F. Giants in off-season for Bobby Murcer and 2 other players
Willie McGee (.335), St.L. Cardinals, 1990	Traded to Oak. A's, end-of-season, 1990
Gary Sheffield (.330), S.D. Padres, 1992	Traded to Fla. Marlins, midseason, 1993
Jose Reyes (.337), N.Y. Mets, 2011	Signed as a free agent in off-season with Mia. Marlins

Largest Margin Between Batting Champion and Runner-Up

American League

Margin	Season	Winner	Batting Average	Runner-Up	Batting Average
+.086	1901	Nap Lajoie, Phila. A's	.426	Mike Donlin, Balt. Orioles	.340
+.052	1977	Rod Carew, Min. Twins	.388	Lyman Bostock, Min. Twins	.336
+.048	1974	Rod Carew, Min. Twins	.364	Jorge Orta, Chi. White Sox	.316
+.047	1941	Ted Williams, Bost. Red Sox	.406	Cecil Travis, Wash. Senators	.359
+.044	1973	Rod Carew, Min. Twins	.350	George Scott, Milw. Brewers	.306
+.038	1904	Nap Lajoie, Cle. Indians	.381	Willie Keeler, N.Y. Yankees	.343
+.038	1980	George Brett, K.C. Royals	.390	Cecil Cooper, Milw. Brewers	.352
+.037	1915	Ty Cobb, Det. Tigers	.369	Eddie Collins, Chi. White Sox	.332
+.037	1961	Norm Cash, Det. Tigers	.361	Al Kaline, Det. Tigers	.324
+.033	1904	Nap Lajoie, Cle. Indians	.376	Willie Keeler, N.Y. Yankees	.343
+.033	1985	Wade Boggs, Bost. Red Sox	.368	George Brett, K.C. Royals	.335
+.032	2004	Ichiro Suzuki, Sea. Mariners	.372	Melvin Mora, Balt. Orioles	.340
+.031	2010	Josh Hamilton, Tex. Rangers	.359	Miguel Cabrera, Det. Tigers	.328
+.031	1993	John Olerud, Tor. Blue Jays	.363	Paul Molitor, Tor. Blue Jays	.332
+.030	1909	Ty Cobb, Det. Tigers	.377	Eddie Collins, Phila. A's	.347
+.030	1917	Ty Cobb, Det. Tigers	.383	George Sisler, St.L. Browns	.353
+.030	1918	Ty Cobb, Det. Tigers	.382	George Burns, Phila. A's	.352

National League (Post-1900)

Margin	Season	Winner	Batting Average	Runner-Up	Batting Average
+.049	1924	Rogers Hornsby, St.L. Cardinals	.424	Zack Wheat, Bklyn. Dodgers	.375
+.047	1922	Rogers Hornsby, St.L. Cardinals	.401	Ray Grimes, Chi. Cubs	.354
+.046	1947	Harry Walker, St.L. Cardinals–Phila. Phillies	.363	Bob Elliott, Bost. Braves	.317
+.045	1921	Rogers Hornsby, St.L. Cardinals	.397	Edd Roush, Cin. Reds	.352
+.043	1948	Stan Musial, St.L. Cardinals	.376	Richie Ashburn, Phila. Phillies	.333
+.043	1999	Larry Walker, Colo. Rockies	.379	Luis Gonzalez, Ariz. D'backs	.336
+.041	1970	Rico Carty, Atl. Braves	.366	Joe Torre, St.L. Cardinals	.325
+.036	1925	Rogers Hornsby, St.L. Cardinals	.403	Jim Bottomley, St.L. Cardinals	.367
+.036	1940	Debs Garms, Pitt. Pirates	.355	Ernie Lombardi, Cin. Reds	.319
+.033	1985	Willie McGee, St.L. Cardinals	.353	Pedro Guerrero, L.A. Dodgers	.320
+.032	1935	Arky Vaughan, Pitt. Pirates	.385	Joe Medwick, St.L. Cardinals	.353
+.032	1946	Stan Musial, St.L. Cardinals	.365	Tommy Holmes, Bost. Braves	.333
+.032	1974	Ralph Garr, Atl. Braves	.353	Al Oliver, Pitt. Pirates	.321
+.032	1987	Tony Gwynn, S.D. Padres	.370	Pedro Guerrero, L.A. Dodgers	.338
+.032	2002	Barry Bonds, S.F. Giants	.370	Larry Walker, Colo. Rockies	.338

Champions Whose Next Season's Batting Average Declined the Most

American League

	Season (Batting Average)	Change
Norm Cash, Det. Tigers	1961 (.361), 1962 (.243)	–.118
George Sisler, St.L. Browns*	1922 (.420), 1924 (.305)	–.115
Julio Franco, Tex. Rangers	1991 (.341), 1992 (.234)	–.107
Goose Goslin, Wash. Senators	1928 (.379), 1929 (.288)	–.091
Lew Fonseca, Cle. Indians	1929 (.369), 1930 (.279)	–.090
Babe Ruth, N.Y. Yankees	1924 (.378), 1925 (.290)	–.088
Mickey Vernon, Wash. Senators	1946 (.353), 1947 (.265)	–.088
Dale Alexander, Det. Tigers–Bost. Red Sox	1932 (.367), 1933 (.281)	–.086

continued on next page

National League (Post-1900)

	Season (Batting Average)	Change
Willie McGee, St.L. Cardinals	1985 (.353), 1986 (.256)	–.097
Cy Seymour, Cin. Reds (N.Y. Giants)	1905 (.377), 1906 (.286)	–.091
Debs Garms, Pitt. Pirates	1940 (.355), 1941 (.264)	–.091
Rico Carty, Atl. Braves*	1970 (.366), 1972 (.277)	–.089
Rogers Hornsby, St.L. Cardinals	1925 (.403), 1926 (.317)	–.086
Richie Ashburn, Phila. Phillies	1958 (.350), 1959 (.266)	–.084
Lefty O'Doul, Bklyn. Dodgers (N.Y. Giants)	1932 (.368), 1933 (.284)	–.084

*Missed season after winning batting championship.

Lowest Lifetime Batting Averages for Players Who Led League

.268	Snuffy Stirnweiss (1943–52)	Led AL with .309 in 1945
.270	Terry Pendleton (1984–98)	Led NL with .319 in 1991
.277	Michael Cuddyer (2001–)	Led NL with .331 in 2013
.271	Norm Cash (1958–74)	Led AL with .361 in 1961
.281	Bobby Avila (1949–59)	Led AL with .341 in 1954
.281	Derrek Lee (1997–2011)	Led NL with .335 in 2005
.282	Justin Morneau (2003–)	Led NL with .319 in 2014
.284	Fred Lynn (1974–89)	Led AL with .333 in 1979
.285	Carl Yastrzemski (1961–83)	Led AL with .321 in 1963
		Led AL with .326 in 1967
		Led AL with .301 in 1968
.286	Mickey Vernon (1939–43, 1946–60)	Led AL with .353 in 1946
		Led AL with .337 in 1953
.286	Dick Groat (1952, 1955–67)	Led NL with .325 in 1960
.288	Alex Johnson (1964–76)	Led AL with .329 in 1970
.288	Paul O'Neill (1985–2001)	Led AL with .359 in 1994
.289	Bill Buckner (1969–90)	Led NL with .324 in 1980
.290	Larry Doyle (1907–20)	Led NL with .320 in 1915
.290	Ferris Fain (1947–55)	Led AL with .344 in 1951
		Led AL with .327 in 1952
.290	Billy Williams (1959–76)	Led NL with .333 in 1972
.290	Carney Lansford (1978–88)	Led AL with .336 in 1981
.290	Josh Hamilton (2007–)	Led AL with .359 in 2010
.290	Carlos Gonzalez (2008–)	Led NL with .336 in 2010
.290	Jose Reyes (2003–)	Led NL with .337 in 2011
.291	Sherry Magee (1904–19)	Led NL with .331 in 1910
.291	Hal Chase (1905–19)	Led NL with .339 in 1916
.291	Pete Runnels (1951–64)	Led AL with .320 in 1960
		Led AL with .326 in 1962
.291	Bill Mueller (1996–2006)	Led AL with .326 in 2003

Two-Time Batting Champions with Lifetime Batting Averages Below .300

Willie McGee (1982–99)	.295	Won NL batting titles in 1985 and 1990
Tommy Davis (1959–76)	.294	Won NL batting titles in 1962 and 1963
Ferris Fain (1947–55)	.290	Won AL batting titles in 1951 and 1952
Dave Parker (1973–91)	.290	Won NL batting titles in 1977 and 1978
Pete Runnels (1951–64)	.291	Won AL batting titles in 1960 and 1962
Mickey Vernon (1939–43, 1946–60)	.286	Won AL batting titles in 1946 and 1953
Carl Yastrzemski (1961–83)	.285	Won AL batting titles in 1963, 1967, and 1968

Years in Which Right-Handed Batters Won Batting Titles in Both Leagues

Season	American League	National League
1903	Nap Lajoie, Cle. Indians	Honus Wagner, Pitt. Pirates
1904	Nap Lajoie, Cle. Indians	Honus Wagner, Pitt. Pirates
1921	Harry Heilmann, Det. Tigers	Rogers Hornsby, St.L. Cardinals
1923	Harry Heilmann, Det. Tigers	Rogers Hornsby, St.L. Cardinals
1925	Harry Heilmann, Det. Tigers	Rogers Hornsby, St.L. Cardinals
1931	Al Simmons, Phila. A's	Chick Hafey, St.L. Cardinals
1938	Jimmie Foxx, Bost. Red Sox	Ernie Lombardi, Cin. Reds
1949	George Kell, Det. Tigers	Jackie Robinson, Bklyn. Dodgers
1954	Bobby Avila, Cle. Indians	Willie Mays, N.Y. Yankees
1959	Harvey Kuenn, Det. Tigers	Hank Aaron, Milw. Braves
1970	Alex Johnson, Cal. Angels	Rico Carty, Atl. Braves
1981	Carney Lansford, Bost. Red Sox	Bill Madlock, Pitt. Pirates
1992	Edgar Martinez, Sea. Mariners	Gary Sheffield, S.D. Padres
2005	Michael Young, Tex. Rangers	Derrek Lee, Chi. Cubs
2007	Magglio Ordonez, Chi. White Sox	Matt Holliday, Colo. Rockies
2012	Miguel Cabrera, Det. Tigers	Buster Posey, S.F. Giants
2013	Miguel Cabrera, Det. Tigers	Michael Cuddyer, Colo. Rockies

Fewest Strikeouts For Batting Champions

American League

Strikeouts		Batting Average
9	Nap Lajoie, Phila. A's, 1901	.426
13	George Kell, Det. Tigers, 1949	.343
14	George Sisler, St.L. Browns, 1922	.420
16	Harry Heilmann, Det. Tigers, 1927	.398
19	Nap Lajoie, Cle. Indians, 1904	.376
19	George Sisler, St.L. Browns, 1920	.407
19	Goose Goslin, Wash. Senators, 1928	.379
20	Tris Speaker, Cle. Indians, 1916	.386
20	Joe DiMaggio, N.Y. Yankees, 1939	.381
20	Ferris Fain, Phila. A's, 1951	.344

National League

Strikeouts		Batting Average
6	Debs Garms, Pitt. Pirates, 1940	.355
12	Ernie Lombardi, Bost. Braves, 1942	.330
14	Paul Waner, Pitt. Pirates, 1927	.380
14	Ernie Lombardi, Cin. Reds, 1938	.342
15	Tony Gwynn, S.D. Padres, 1995	.368
17	Honus Wagner, Pitt. Pirates, 1903	.355
17	Zack Wheat, Bklyn. Dodgers, 1918	.335
17	Bubbles Hargrove, Cin. Reds, 1926	.353
18	Arky Vaughan, Pitt. Pirates, 1935	.385
18	Stan Musial, St. L. Cardinals, 1943	.357
18	Bill Buckner, Chi. Cubs, 1980	.324
19	Edd Roush, Cin. Reds, 1919	.321
19	Lefty O'Doul, Phila. A's, 1926	.398
19	Tony Gwynn, S.D. Padres, 1994	.394
20	Lefty O'Doul, Bklyn. Dodgers, 1932	.368

Home Runs

Evolution of Home Run Record

American League

1901	Nap Lajoie, Phila. A's	14
1902	Socks Seybold, Phila. A's	16
1919	Babe Ruth, Bost. Red Sox	29
1920	Babe Ruth, N.Y. Yankees	54
1921	Babe Ruth, N.Y. Yankees	59
1927	Babe Ruth, N.Y. Yankees	60
1961	Roger Maris, N.Y. Yankees	61

National League (Pre-1900)

1876	George Hall, Phila. A's	5
1879	Charley Jones, Bost. Beaneaters	9
1883	Buck Ewing, N.Y. Gothams	10
1884	Ned Williamson, Chi. Colts	27

National League (Post-1900)

1900	Herman Long, Bost. Beaneaters	12
1901	Sam Crawford, Cin. Reds	16
1911	Frank Schulte, Chi. Cubs	21
1915	Gavvy Cravath, Phila. Phillies	24
1922	Rogers Hornsby, St.L. Cardinals	42
1929	Chuck Klein, Phila. Phillies	43
1930	Hack Wilson, Chi. Cubs	56
1998	Mark McGwire, St.L. Cardinals	70
2001	Barry Bonds, S.F. Giants	73

Most Home Runs by Decade

Pre-1900

138 Roger Connor
126 Sam Thompson
122 Harry Stovey
106 Mike Tiernan
106 Dan Brouthers
102 Hugh Duffy
100 Jimmy Ryan
97 Cap Anson
94 Fred Pfeffer
80 Ed Delahanty

1900–09

67 Harry Davis
58 Charlie Hickman
57 Sam Crawford
54 Buck Freeman
51 Socks Seybold
51 Honus Wagner
47 Nap Lajoie
43 Cy Seymour
40 Jimmy Williams
40 Hobe Ferris

1910–19

116 Gavvy Cravath
83 Fred Luderus
76 Home Run Baker
75 Frank Schulte
64 Larry Doyle
61 Sherry Magee
58 Heinie Zimmerman
57 Fred Merkle
55 Vic Saier
52 Owen Wilson

1920–29

467 Babe Ruth
250 Rogers Hornsby
202 Cy Williams
190 Ken Williams
146 Jim Bottomley
146 Lou Gehrig
146 Bob Meusel
142 Harry Heilmann
137 Hack Wilson
134 George Kelly

1930–39

415 Jimmie Foxx
347 Lou Gehrig
308 Mel Ott
241 Wally Berger
238 Chuck Klein
218 Earl Averill
206 Hank Greenberg
198 Babe Ruth
190 Al Simmons
186 Bob Johnson

1940–49

234 Ted Williams
217 Johnny Mize
211 Bill Nicholson
189 Rudy York
181 Joe Gordon
180 Joe DiMaggio
177 Vern Stephens
173 Charlie Keller
168 Ralph Kiner
164 Bobby Doerr

1950–59

326 Duke Snider
310 Gil Hodges
299 Eddie Mathews
280 Mickey Mantle
266 Stan Musial
256 Yogi Berra
250 Willie Mays
239 Ted Kluszewski
232 Gus Zernial
228 Ernie Banks

1960–69

393 Harmon Killebrew
375 Hank Aaron
350 Willie Mays
316 Frank Robinson
300 Willie McCovey
288 Frank Howard
278 Norm Cash
269 Ernie Banks
256 Mickey Mantle
254 Orlando Cepeda

1970–79

296 Willie Stargell
292 Reggie Jackson
290 Johnny Bench
280 Bobby Bonds
270 Lee May
252 Dave Kingman
252 Graig Nettles
235 Mike Schmidt
226 Tony Perez
225 Reggie Smith

1980–89

313 Mike Schmidt
308 Dale Murphy
274 Eddie Murray
256 Dwight Evans
250 Andre Dawson
230 Darrell Evans
225 Tony Armas
225 Lance Parrish
223 Dave Winfield
216 Jack Clark

1990–99

405 Mark McGwire
382 Ken Griffey Jr.
361 Barry Bonds
351 Albert Belle
339 Juan Gonzalez
332 Sammy Sosa
328 Rafael Palmeiro
303 Jose Canseco
301 Frank Thomas
300 Fred McGriff
300 Matt Williams

2000–09

435 Alex Rodriguez
368 Jim Thome
366 Albert Pujols
348 Manny Ramirez
324 Carlos Delgado
317 Barry Bonds
316 Adam Dunn
315 Vladimir Guerrero
309 Lance Berkman
308 Andruw Jones

2010–15

227 Jose Bautista
199 Miguel Cabrera
194 Albert Pujols
189 Edwin Encarnacion
186 Nelson Cruz
186 David Ortiz
165 Jay Bruce
165 Adam Jones
163 Adrian Beltre
161 Curtis Granderson

Career Home Run Leaders by Zodiac Sign

Aquarius (Jan. 20–Feb. 18)	Hank Aaron	755
Pisces (Feb. 19–Mar. 20)	Mel Ott	511
Aries (Mar. 21–Apr. 19)	Adrian Beltre*	413
Taurus (Apr. 20–May 20)	Willie Mays	660
Gemini (May 21–June 21)	Manny Ramirez	555
Cancer (June 22–July 22)	Harmon Killebrew	573
Leo (July 23–Aug. 22)	Barry Bonds	762
Virgo (Aug. 23–Sept. 22)	Jim Thome	612
Libra (Sept. 23–Oct. 23)	Mark McGwire	583
Scorpio (Oct. 24–Nov. 21)	Ken Griffey Jr.	630
Sagittarius (Nov. 22–Dec. 21)	Dave Kingman	442
Capricorn (Dec. 22–Jan. 19)	Albert Pujols*	560

*Still active.

All-Time Home Run Leaders by First Letter of Last Name

A	Hank Aaron (1954–76)	755
B	Barry Bonds (1986–2007)	762
C	Jose Canseco (1985–2001)	462
D	Carlos Delgado (1993–2009)	473
E	Darrell Evans (1969–89)	414
F	Jimmie Foxx (1925–42, 1944–45)	534
G	Ken Griffey Jr. (1989–2010)	630
H	Frank Howard (1958–73)	382
I	Raul Ibanez (1996– 2014)	305
J	Reggie Jackson (1967–87)	563
K	Harmon Killebrew (1954–75)	573
L	Carlos Lee (1999–2012)	358
M	Willie Mays (1951–52, 1954–73)	660
N	Graig Nettles (1967–88)	390
O	Mel Ott (1926–47)	511
P	Rafael Palmeiro (1986–2005)	569
Q	Carlos Quentin (2006–14)	130
R	Babe Ruth (1914–35)	714
S	Sammy Sosa (1989–2007)	609
T	Jim Thome (1991–2012)	612
U	Dan Uggla* (2006–)	235
V	Greg Vaughn (1989–2003)	355
W	Ted Williams (1939–42, 1946–60)	521
X	[No player]	
Y	Carl Yastrzemski (1961–83)	452
Z	Todd Zeile (1989–2004)	253

*Still active.

Home Run Leaders by State of Birth

Alabama	Hank Aaron (Mobile)	755
Alaska	Josh Phelps (Anchorage)	64
Arizona	Ian Kinsler* (Tucson)	184
Arkansas	Torii Hunter (Pine Bluff)	353
California	Barry Bonds (Riverside)	762
Colorado	Chase Headley* (Fountain)	104
Connecticut	Mo Vaughn (Norwalk)	328
Delaware	Paul Goldschmidt* (Wilmington)	116
Florida	Gary Sheffield (Tampa)	509
Georgia	Frank Thomas (Columbus)	521
Hawaii	Shane Victorino* (Wailuku)	108
Idaho	Harmon Killebrew (Payette)	573
Illinois	Jim Thome (Peoria)	612
Indiana	Gil Hodges (Princeton)	370
Iowa	Hal Trosky (Norway)	228
Kansas	Tony Clark (Newton)	251
Kentucky	Jay Buhner (Louisville)	310
Louisiana	Mel Ott (Gretna)	511

continued on next page

Maine	Del Bissonette (Winthrop)	66
Maryland	Babe Ruth (Baltimore)	714
Massachusetts	Jeff Bagwell (Boston)	449
Michigan	John Mayberry (Detroit) and Kirk Gibson (Pontiac)	255
Minnesota	Dave Winfield (St. Paul)	465
Mississippi	Ellis Burks (Vicksburg)	352
Missouri	Yogi Berra (St. Louis)	358
Montana	John Lowenstein (Wolf Point)	116
Nebraska	Alex Gordon* (Lincoln)	134
Nevada	Marty Cordova (Las Vegas)	122
New Hampshire	Phil Plantier (Manchester)	91
New Jersey	Eric Karros (Hackensack)	284
New Mexico	Ralph Kiner (Santa Rita)	369
New York	Alex Rodriguez* (Manhattan)	687
North Carolina	Josh Hamilton* (Raleigh), Ryan Zimmerman* (Washington)	200
North Dakota	Travis Hafner (Jamestown)	213
Ohio	Mike Schmidt (Dayton)	548
Oklahoma	Mickey Mantle (Spavinaw)	536
Oregon	Dave Kingman (Pendleton)	442
Pennsylvania	Ken Griffey Jr. (Donora)	630
Rhode Island	Paul Konerko (Providence)	439
South Carolina	Jim Rice (Anderson)	382
South Dakota	Jason Kubel (Belle Fourche)	140
Tennessee	Todd Helton (Knoxville)	369
Texas	Frank Robinson (Beaumont)	586
Utah	Duke Sims (Salt Lake City)	100
Vermont	Carlton Fisk (Bellows Falls)	376
Virginia	Willie Horton (Arno)	325
Washington	Ron Santo (Seattle)	342
West Virginia	George Brett (Glen Dale)	317
Wisconsin	Al Simmons (Milwaukee)	307
Wyoming	John Buck (Kemmerer)	134
American Samoa	Tony Solaita (Nuuuli)	50
District of Columbia	Don Money	176
Puerto Rico	Carlos Delgado (Aguadilla)	473
Virgin Islands	Elrod Hendricks (St. Thomas)	62

*Still active.

500th Home Run of 500 Home Run Hitters

Hitter	Career Home Runs	Date of 500th Home Run	Pitcher
Barry Bonds	762	Apr. 17, 2004	Terry Adams, L.A. Dodgers
Hank Aaron	755	July 14, 1968	Mike McCormick, S.F. Giants
Babe Ruth	714	Aug. 11, 1929	Willis Hudlin, Cle. Indians
Alex Rodriguez*	687	Aug. 4, 2007	Kyle Davies, K.C. Royals
Willie Mays	660	Sept. 13, 1965	Don Nottebart, Atl. Braves
Ken Griffey Jr.	630	June 6, 2004	Matt Morris, St.L. Cardinals
Jim Thome	612	Sept. 16, 2007	Dustin Mosley, L.A. Dodgers
Sammy Sosa	609	Apr. 4, 2004	Scott Sullivan, Cin. Reds
Frank Robinson	586	Sept. 13, 1971	Fred Scherman, Det. Tigers

continued on next page

Hitter	Career Home Runs	Date of 500th Home Run	Pitcher
Mark McGwire	583	Aug. 5, 1999	Andy Ashby S.D. Padres
Harmon Killebrew	573	Aug. 10, 1971	Mike Cuellar, Balt. Orioles
Rafael Palmeiro	569	May 11, 2003	Dave Elder, Cle. Indians
Reggie Jackson	563	Sept. 17, 1984	Bud Black, K.C. Royals
Albert Pujols*	560	Apr. 22, 2014	Taylor Jordan, Wash. Nationals
Manny Ramirez	555	May 31, 2008	Chad Bradford, Balt. Orioles
Mike Schmidt	548	Apr. 18, 1987	Don Robinson, Pitt. Pirates
Mickey Mantle	536	May 14, 1967	Stu Miller, Balt. Orioles
Jimmie Foxx	534	Sept. 24, 1940	George Caster, Phila. A's
Ted Williams	521	June 17, 1960	Wynn Hawkins, Cle. Indians
Willie McCovey	521	June 30, 1978	Jamie Easterly, Atl. Braves
Frank Thomas	521	June 28, 2007	Carlos Silva, Min. Twins
Eddie Mathews	512	July 14, 1967	Juan Marichal, S.F. Giants
Ernie Banks	512	May 12, 1970	Pat Jarvis, Atl. Braves
Mel Ott	511	Aug. 1, 1945	John Hutchings, Bost. Braves
Gary Sheffield	509	Apr. 17, 2009	Mitch Stetter, Milw. Brewers
Eddie Murray	504	Sept. 6, 1996	Felipe Lira, Det. Tigers
David Ortiz*	503	Sept. 12, 2015	Matt Moore, T.B. Rays

*Still active.

Most Home Runs in First Three Seasons in Majors

114	Ralph Kiner, Pitt. Pirates (NL)	1946 (23), 1947 (51), and 1948 (40)
114	Albert Pujols, St.L. Cardinals (NL)	2001 (37), 2002 (34), and 2003 (43)
112	Eddie Mathews, Bost.–Milw. Braves (NL)	1952 (25), 1953 (47), and 1954 (40)
107	Joe DiMaggio, N.Y. Yankees (AL)	1936 (29), 1937 (46), and 1938 (32)
107	Mark Teixeira, Tex. Rangers (AL)	2003 (26), 2004 (38), and 2005 (43)

Most Home Runs for One Club

733	Hank Aaron	Milw.–Atl. Braves* (NL) (1954–74)
659	Babe Ruth	N.Y. Yankees (AL) (1920–34)
646	Willie Mays	N.Y.–S.F. Giants* (NL) (1951–52, 1954–72)
586	Barry Bonds	S.F. Giants (NL) (1993–2007)
573	Sammy Sosa	Chi. Cubs (NL) (1989–2004)
565	Harmon Killebrew	Wash. Senators–Min. Twins* (AL) (1954–74)
548	Mike Schmidt	Phila. Phillies (NL) (1972–89)
536	Mickey Mantle	N.Y. Yankees (AL) (1951–68)
521	Ted Williams	Bost. Red Sox (AL) (1939–42, 1946–60)
512	Ernie Banks	Chi. Cubs (NL) (1953–71)
511	Mel Ott	N.Y. Giants (NL) (1926–47)
493	Lou Gehrig	N.Y. Yankees (AL) (1923–39)
493	Eddie Mathews	Bost.–Milw.–Atl. Braves* (NL) (1952–66)
475	Stan Musial	St.L. Cardinals (NL) (1941–44, 1946–63)
475	Willie Stargell	Pitt. Pirates (NL) (1962–82)
469	Willie McCovey	S.F. Giants (NL) (1959–80)
468	Chipper Jones	Atl. Braves (1993, 1995–2012)
452	Carl Yastrzemski	Bost. Red Sox (AL) (1961–83)
449	Jeff Bagwell	Hous. Astros (NL) (1991–2005)

*Franchises that moved.

Most Home Runs by Position*, Career

First Base	566	Mark McGwire
Second Base	351	Jeff Kent
Third Base	509	Mike Schmidt
Shortstop	345	Cal Ripken Jr.
Outfield	748	Barry Bonds
Catcher	396	Mike Piazza
Pitcher	36	Wes Ferrell
Designated Hitter	447	David Ortiz

*While in lineup at position indicated.

Most Home Runs *Not* Leading League, Season

American League

Home Runs	Season		Winner
54	1961	Mickey Mantle, N.Y. Yankees	Roger Maris (61), N.Y. Yankees
52	2002	Jim Thome, Cle. Indians	Alex Rodriguez (57), Tex. Rangers
50	1996	Brady Anderson, Balt. Orioles	Mark McGwire (52), Oak. A's
50	1938	Jimmie Foxx, Bost. Red Sox	Hank Greenberg (58), Det. Tigers
49	1998	Albert Belle, Chi. White Sox	Ken Griffey Jr. (56), Sea. Mariners
49	1996	Ken Griffey Jr., Sea. Mariners	Mark McGwire (52), Oak. A's
49	2001	Jim Thome, Cle. Indians	Alex Rodriguez (52), Tex. Rangers
48	1969	Frank Howard, Wash. Senators II	Harmon Killebrew (49), Min. Twins
48	1996	Albert Belle, Cle. Indians	Mark McGwire (52), Oak. A's
47	1999	Rafael Palmeiro, Tex. Rangers	Ken Griffey Jr. (48), Sea. Mariners
47	1969	Reggie Jackson, Oak. A's	Harmon Killebrew (49), Min. Twins
47	1996	Juan Gonzalez, Tex. Rangers	Mark McGwire (52), Oak. A's
47	1927	Lou Gehrig, N.Y. Yankees	Babe Ruth (60), N.Y. Yankees
47	2001	Rafael Palmeiro, Tex. Rangers	Alex Rodriguez (52), Tex. Rangers
47	1987	George Bell, Tor. Blue Jays	Mark McGwire (49), Oak. A's
47	2005	David Oritz, Bost. Red Sox	Alex Rodriguez (48), N.Y. Yankees
46	1961	Jim Gentile, Balt. Orioles	Roger Maris (61), N.Y. Yankees
46	1961	Harmon Killebrew, Min. Twins	Roger Maris (61), N.Y. Yankees

National League

66	1998	Sammy Sosa, Chi. Cubs	Mark McGwire (70), St.L. Cardinals
64	2001	Sammy Sosa, Chi. Cubs	Barry Bonds (73), S.F. Giants
63	1999	Sammy Sosa, Chi. Cubs	Mark McGwire (65), St.L. Cardinals
57	2001	Luis Gonzalez, Ariz. D'backs	Barry Bonds (73), S.F. Giants
50	1998	Greg Vaughn, S.D. Padres	Mark McGwire (70), St.L. Cardinals
49	2000	Barry Bonds, S.F. Giants	Sammy Sosa (50), Chi. Cubs
49	2001	Todd Helton, Colo. Rockies	Barry Bonds (73), S.F. Giants
49	2001	Shawn Green, L.A. Dodgers	Barry Bonds (73), S.F. Giants
49	2006	Albert Pujols, St.L. Cardinals	Ryan Howard (58), Phila. Phillies
49	1971	Hank Aaron, Atl. Braves	Willie Stargell (48), Pitt. Pirates
47	2000	Jeff Bagwell, Hous. Astros	Sammy Sosa (50), Chi. Cubs
47	1955	Ted Kluszewski, Cin. Reds	Willie Mays (51), N.Y. Giants
47	2007	Ryan Howard, Phila. Phillies	Prince Fielder (50), Milw. Brewers

Most Home Runs, Never Leading League, Career

569 ..... Rafael Palmeiro (1986–2005)
521 ..... Frank Thomas (1990–2008)
509 ..... Gary Sheffield (1988–2009)
475 ..... Stan Musial (1941–44, 1946–63)
473 ..... Carlos Delgado (1993–2009)
468 ..... Chipper Jones (1993, 1995–2012)
465 ..... Dave Winfield (1973–95)
449 ..... Jeff Bagwell (1991–2005)
449 ..... Vladimir Guerrero (1996–2011)
440 ..... Jason Giambi (1995–2014)
439 ..... Paul Konerko (1997–2011)
431 ..... Cal Ripken Jr. (1981–2001)
427 ..... Mike Piazza (1992–2007)
426 ..... Billy Williams (1959–76)
412 ..... Alfonso Soriano (1999–2014)
399 ..... Al Kaline (1953–74)
396 ..... Joe Carter (1983–98)

Most Inside-the-Park Home Runs, Career (Post-1898)

51 ..... Sam Crawford (1899–1917)
48 ..... Tommy Leach (1898–1918)
47 ..... Ty Cobb (1905–28)
29 ..... Edd Roush (1913–29, 1931)
22 ..... Rabbit Maranville (1912–35)
21 ..... Sam Rice (1915–34)
16 ..... Kiki Cuyler (1920–37)
15 ..... Ben Chapman (1930–48)
14 ..... Tris Speaker (1907–28)
14 ..... Honus Wagner (1897–1917)

Players with 10 or More Letters in Last Name, Hitting 40 or More Home Runs in Season

	Season	Home Runs
Roy Campanella, Bklyn. Dodgers (NL)	1953	41
Edwin Encarnacion, Tor. Blue Jays (AL)	2012	42
Curtis Granderson, N.Y. Yankees (AL)	2011	41
	2012	43
Ted Kluszewski, Cin. Reds (NL)	1953	40
	1954	49
	1955	47
Rico Petrocelli, Bost. Red Sox (AL)	1969	40
Carl Yastrzemski, Bost. Red Sox (AL)	1967	44
	1969	40
	1970	40

Most Home Runs by Visiting Player by Stadium

Stadium	Team	Years Open	Player	Home Runs
Sportsman's Park (Busch Stadium)	St.L. (NL)	1875–77 (Brown Stockings)	Babe Ruth	58
		1882–93 (Brown Stockings)		
		1902–53 (Browns)		
		1920–66 (Cardinals)		
Baker Bowl	Phila. (NL)	1887–1938	Mel Ott	40
League Park	Cle. (AL)	1891–99, 1901–32, 1934–46	Babe Ruth	46
Polo Grounds	N.Y. (NL)	1891–1957 (Giants)	Stan Musial	49
		1913–22 (Yankees)		
		1962–63 (Mets)		
Shibe Park	Phila. (AL)	1909–54 (A's)	Babe Ruth	68
		1938–70 (Phillies)		
Forbes Field	Pitt. (NL)	1909–70	Eddie Mathews	38
Comiskey Park I	Chi. (AL)	1910–90	Babe Ruth	45
Griffith Stadium	Wash. (AL)	1911–60 (Senators I)	Babe Ruth	34
		1961 (Senators II)		

continued on next page

Crosley Field	Cin. (NL)	1912–70	Eddie Mathews	50
Tiger Stadium	Det. (AL)	1912–99	Babe Ruth	60
Fenway Park	Bost. (AL)	1912–present (Red Sox) 1914–15 (Braves)	Mickey Mantle/Babe Ruth	38
Ebbets Field	Bklyn. (NL)	1913–57	Stan Musial	37
Braves Field	Bost. (NL)	1915–52	Bill Nicholson	20
Wrigley Field	Chi. (NL)	1916–present	Willie Mays	54
Yankee Stadium	N.Y. (AL)	1923–73, 1976–2008	Goose Goslin	32
Cleveland Stadium	Cle. (AL)	1932–33, 1936–93	Mickey Mantle	36
Milwaukee County Stadium	Milw. (NL) (Braves–Brewers)	1953–65, 1970–2000	Frank Robinson	35
Memorial Stadium	Balt. (AL)	1954–91	Harmon Killebrew	30
Municipal Stadium	K.C. (AL) (A's–Royals)	1955–67, 1969–72	Harmon Killebrew	33
Los Angeles Memorial Coliseum	L.A. (NL)	1958–61	Ken Boyer/Frank Thomas	17
Candlestick Park	S.F. (NL)	1960–99	Dale Murphy/Willie Stargell	25
Metropolitan Stadium	Min. (AL)	1961–81	Reggie Jackson	20
Robert F. Kennedy Memorial Stadium	Wash. (AL/NL)	1962–71 (Senators II) 2005–07 (Nationals)	Harmon Killebrew	25
Dodger Stadium	L.A. (NL)	1962–present (Dodgers) 1962–65 (Angels)	Barry Bonds	29
Shea Stadium	N.Y. (NL)	1964–2008 (Mets) 1974–75 (Yankees)	Willie Stargell/Mike Schmidt	26
Astrodome	Hous. (NL)	1965–99	Tony Perez	19
Atlanta-Fulton County Stadium	Atl. (NL)	1966–96	Johnny Bench/Willie McCovey	32
Busch Memorial Stadium (Busch Stadium II)	St.L. (NL)	1966–2005	Mike Schmidt	27
Angel Stadium of Anaheim	L.A. (AL)	1966–present	Alex Rodriguez	38
O.co Coliseum	Oak. (AL)	1968–present	Alex Rodriguez	21
Jarry Park Stadium	Mont. (NL)	1969–76	Willie Stargell	17
Qualcomm Stadium	S.D. (NL)	1969–2003	Barry Bonds	39
Three Rivers Stadium	Pitt. (NL)	1970–2000	Mike Schmidt	25
Cinergy Field	Cin. (NL)	1970–2002	Barry Bonds	31
Veterans Stadium	Phila. (NL)	1971–2003	Barry Bonds	27
Arlington Stadium	Tex. (AL)	1972–93	Reggie Jackson	23
Kauffman Stadium	K.C. (AL)	1973–present	Juan Gonzalez	22
Exhibition Stadium	Tor. (AL)	1977–89	Jim Rice	18
Kingdome	Sea. (AL)	1977–99	Brian Downing	19
Olympic Stadium	Mont. (NL)	1977–2004	Barry Bonds	30
Hubert H. Humphrey Metrodome	Min. (AL)	1982–2009	Jim Thome	28
Rogers Centre	Tor. (AL)	1989–present	David Ortiz	39
U.S. Cellular Field	Chi. (AL)	1991–present	Torii Hunter	20
Camden Yards	Balt. (AL)	1992–present	Alex Rodriguez	33
Sun Life Stadium	Fla. (NL)	1993–2011	Chipper Jones	16
Progressive Field	Cle. (AL)	1994–present	Miguel Cabrera	23
Globe Life Park in Arlington	Tex. (AL)	1994–present	Jason Giambi	20
Coors Field	Colo. (NL)	1995–present	Barry Bonds	26

continued on next page

Turner Field	Atl. (NL)	1997–present	Ryan Howard	21
Chase Field	Ariz. (NL)	1998–present	Adrian Gonzalez	21
Tropicana Field	T.B. (AL)	1998–present	David Ortiz	33
Safeco Field	Sea. (AL)	1999–present	Rafael Palmeiro	40
Comerica Park	Det. (AL)	2000–present	David Ortiz	21
Minute Maid Park	Hous. (NL–AL)	2000–present	Albert Pujols	27
AT&T Park	S.F. (NL)	2000–present	Troy Tulowitzki/Dan Uggla	9
Miller Park	Milw. (AL–NL)	2001–present	Albert Pujols	19
PNC Park	Pitt. (NL)	2001–present	Albert Pujols	29
Great American Ball Park	Cin. (NL)	2003–present	Lance Berkman	23
Citizens Bank Park	Phila. (NL)	2004–present	David Wright	20
Petco Park	S.D. (NL)	2004–present	Todd Helton/Justin Upton/Pablo Sandoval/Adam LaRoche	10
Busch Stadium (Busch Stadium III)	St.L. (NL)	2006–present	Aramis Ramirez	12
Nationals Park	Wash. (NL)	2008–present	Giancarlo Stanton	15
Yankee Stadium	N.Y. (AL)	2009–present	Jose Bautista	17
Citi Field	N.Y. (NL)	2009–present	Adam LaRoche	13
Target Field	Min. (AL)	2010–present	Carlos Santana/Jose Bautista	11
Marlins Park	Mia. (NL)	2012–present	Ryan Zimmerman	7

Most Home Runs, Month by Month

	American League		National League	
Mar.	2	Jorge Posada, N.Y. Yankees, 2004	2	Vinny Castilla, Colo. Rockies, 1998
	2	Jim Thome, Chi. White Sox, 2008	2	Corey Patterson, Chi Cubs, 2003
	2	Alejandro De Aza, Chi. White Sox, 2014	2	Xavier Nady, Pitt. Pirates, 2008
Apr.	14	Alex Rodriguez, N.Y. Yankees, 2007	14	Albert Pujols, St.L. Cardinals, 2006
May	16	Mickey Mantle, N.Y. Yankees, 1956	17	Barry Bonds, S.F. Giants, 2001
	16	Edwin Encarnacion, Tor. Blue Jays, 2014		
June	15	Babe Ruth, N.Y. Yankees, 1930	20	Sammy Sosa, Chi. Cubs, 1998
		Bob Johnson, Phila. A's, 1934		
		Roger Maris, N.Y. Yankees, 1961		
July	16	Albert Belle, Chi. White Sox, 1998	16	Mark McGwire, St.L. Cardinals, 1999
Aug.	18	Rudy York, Det. Tigers, 1937	17	Willie Mays, S.F. Giants, 1965
				Sammy Sosa, Chi. Cubs, 2001
Sept.	17	Babe Ruth, N.Y. Yankees, 1927	16	Ralph Kiner, Pitt. Pirates, 1949
		Albert Belle, Cle. Indians, 1995		
Oct.	4	Gus Zernial, Chi. White Sox, 1950	5	Richie Sexson, Milw. Brewers, 2001
		George Brett, K.C. Royals, 1985		Sammy Sosa, Chi. Cubs, 2001
		Ron Kittle, Chi. White Sox, 1985		
		Wally Joyner, Cal. Angels, 1987		
		Jose Cruz Jr., Tor. Blue Jays, 2001		

Most Home Runs by Position, Season*

	American League	National League
First Base	58.....Hank Greenberg, Det. Tigers, 1938	69.....Mark McGwire, St.L. Cardinals, 1998
Second Base	39.....Alfonso Soriano, N.Y. Yankees, 2002	42....Rogers Hornsby, St.L. Cardinals, 1922
		42.....Davey Johnson, Atl. Braves, 1973
Third Base	52.....Alex Rodriguez, N.Y. Yankees, 2007	48.....Mike Schmidt, Phila. Phillies, 1980
		48.....Adrian Beltre, L.A. Dodgers, 2004
Shortstop	57.....Alex Rodriguez, Tex. Rangers, 2002	47.....Ernie Banks, Chi. Cubs, 1958
Outfield	61.....Roger Maris, N.Y. Yankees, 1961	71.....Barry Bonds, S.F. Giants, 2001
Catcher	35.....Ivan Rodriguez, Tex. Rangers, 1999	42.....Javy Lopez, Atl. Braves, 2003
Pitcher	9 .....Wes Ferrell, Cle. Indians, 1931	7.....Don Newcombe, Bklyn. Dodgers, 1955
		7.....Don Drysdale, L.A. Dodgers, 1958
		L.A. Dodgers, 1965
		Mike Hampton, Colo. Rockies, 2001
Designated Hitter	47.....David Ortiz, Bost. Red Sox, 2006	

*While in lineup at position indicated.

Players Leading League in Home Runs for Different Teams

Tony Armas	Oak. A's (AL)	1981	22
	Bost. Red Sox (AL)	1984	43
Sam Crawford	Cin. Reds (NL)	1901	16
	Det. Tigers (AL)	1908	7
		1914	8
Jimmie Foxx	Phila. A's (AL)	1932	58
		1933	48
		1935	36
	Bost. Red Sox (AL)	1939	35
Reggie Jackson	Oak. A's (AL)	1973	32
		1975	36
	N.Y. Yankees (AL)	1980	41
	Cal. Angels (AL)	1982	39
Dave Kingman	Chi. Cubs (NL)	1979	48
	N.Y. Mets (NL)	1982	37
Fred McGriff	Tor. Blue Jays (AL)	1989	36
	S.D. Padres (NL)	1992	35
Mark McGwire	Oak. A's (AL)	1987	49
		1996	52
	St.L. Cardinals (NL)	1998	70
		1999	65
Johnny Mize	St.L. Cardinals (NL)	1939	28
		1940	43
	N.Y. Giants (NL)	1947	51 (Tie)
		1948	40 (Tie)
Alex Rodriguez	Tex. Rangers (AL)	2001	52
		2002	57
		2003	47
	N.Y. Yankees (AL)	2005	48
		2007	54
Babe Ruth	Bost. Red Sox (AL)	1918	11
		1919	29
	N.Y. Yankees (AL)	1920	54
		1921	59
		1923	41
		1924	46
		1926	47
		1927	60
		1928	54

continued on next page

		1929	46
		1930	49
		1931	46 (Tie)
Cy Williams	Chi. Cubs (NL)	1916	12
	Phila. Phillies (NL)	1920	15
		1923	41

Players with 40 Home Run Seasons in Each League

Adam Dunn	Cin. Reds (NL)	2004	46
		2005	40
		2006	40
		2007	40
	Cin. Reds–Ariz. D'backs (NL)	2008	40
	Chi. White Sox (AL)	2012	41
Albert Pujols	St.L. Cardinals (NL)	2003	43
		2004	46
		2005	41
		2006	49
		2009	47
		2010	42
	L.A. Angels (AL)	2015	40
Mark McGwire	Oak. A's (AL)	1987	49
		1992	42
		1996	52
		1997	58*
	St.L. Cardinals (NL)	1998	70
		1999	65
Jim Thome	Cle. Indians (AL)	1997	40
		2001	49
		2002	52
	Phila. Philles (NL)	2003	47
		2004	42
	Chi. White Sox (AL)	2006	42
Ken Griffey Jr.	Sea. Mariners (AL)	1993	45
		1994	40
		1996	49
		1997	56
		1998	56
		1999	48
	Cin. Reds (NL)	2000	40
Darrell Evans	Det. Tigers (AL)	1958	40
	Atl. Braves (NL)	1973	41

*34 with Oak. A's (AL) and 24 with St.L. Cardinals (NL).

Players Hitting a Total of 100 Home Runs in Two Consecutive Seasons

	Total Home Runs
Mark McGwire, St.L. Cardinals (NL), 1998 (70) and 1999 (65)	135
Sammy Sosa, Chi. Cubs (NL), 1998 (66) and 1999 (63)	129
Barry Bonds, S.F. Giants (NL), 2000 (49) and 2001 (73)	122
Barry Bonds, S.F. Giants (NL), 2001 (73) and 2002 (46)	119
Babe Ruth, N.Y. Yankees (AL), 1927 (60) and 1928 (54)	114
Sammy Sosa, Chi. Cubs (NL), 2000 (50) and 2001 (64)	114
Babe Ruth, N.Y. Yankees (AL), 1920 (54) and 1921 (59)	113
Sammy Sosa, Chi. Cubs (NL), 1999 (63) and 2000 (50)	113
Sammy Sosa, Chi. Cubs (NL), 2001 (64) and 2002 (49)	113
Ken Griffey Jr., Sea. Mariners (AL), 1997 (56) and 1998 (56)	112
Alex Rodriguez, Tex. Rangers (AL), 2001 (52) and 2002 (57)	109
Babe Ruth, N.Y. Yankees (AL), 1926 (47) and 1927 (60)	107
Jimmie Foxx, Phila. A's (AL), 1932 (58) and 1933 (48)	106
Ken Griffey Jr., Sea. Mariners (AL), 1996 (49) and 1997 (56)	105
Ryan Howard, Phila. Phillies (NL) 2006 (58) and 2007 (47)	105
Ken Griffey Jr., Sea. Mariners (AL), 1998 (56) and 1999 (48)	104

continued on next page

Alex Rodriguez, Tex. Rangers (AL), 2002 (57) and 2003 (47)	104
Ralph Kiner, Pitt. Pirates (NL), 1949 (54) and 1950 (47)	101
David Ortiz, Bost. Red Sox (AL) 2005 (47) and 2006 (54)	101
Roger Maris, N.Y. Yankees (AL), 1960 (39) and 1961 (61)	100

Players with First 20-Home Run Season After 35th Birthday

	Season	Home Runs	35th Birthday
Cy Williams, Phila. Phillies (NL)	1922	26	Dec. 21, 1921
Charlie Gehringer, Det. Tigers (AL)	1938	20	May 11, 1938
Luke Easter, Cle. Indians (AL)	1950	28	Aug. 4, 1949
Mickey Vernon, Wash. Senators (AL)	1954	20	Apr. 22, 1953
John Lowenstein, Balt. Orioles (AL)	1982	24	Jan. 27, 1982
Frank White, K.C. Royals (AL)	1985	20	Sept. 4, 1985
Buddy Bell, Cin. Reds (NL)	1986	20	Aug. 27, 1986

Shortstops with at Least Seven Consecutive 20-Home Run Seasons

		Season	Home Runs
Cal Ripken Jr., Balt. Orioles (AL) (10 seasons)		1982	28
		1983	27
		1984	27
		1985	26
		1986	25
		1987	27
		1988	23
		1989	21
		1990	21
		1991	34
Alex Rodriguez, Tex. Rangers (AL) (8 seasons)		1996	36
		1997	23
		1998	44
		1999	42
		2000	41
		2001	52
		2002	57
		2003	47
Miguel Tejada (8 seasons)	Oak. A's (AL) (5 seasons)	1999	21
		2000	30
		2001	31
		2002	34
		2003	27
	Balt. Orioles (AL) (3 seasons)	2004	34
		2005	26
		2006	24
Ernie Banks, Chi. Cubs (NL) (7 seasons)		1955	44
		1956	28
		1957	43*
		1958	47
		1959	45
		1960	41
		1961	29**

*Played 58 games at third base.
**Played 28 games in outfield, 76 at first.

Players Hitting Four Home Runs in One Game

American League

Batter	Date	Opposing Pitcher(s)
Lou Gehrig, N.Y. Yankees	June 3, 1932	George Earnshaw (3 home runs) and Roy Mahaffey (1 home run), Phila. A's
Pat Seerey, Chi. White Sox	July 18, 1948	Carl Scheib (2 home runs), Bob Savage (1 home run), and Lou Brissie (1 home run), Phila. A's
Rocky Colavito, Cle. Indians	June 10, 1959	Jerry Walker (2 home runs), Arnold Portocarrero (1 home run), and Ernie Johnson (1 home run), Balt. Orioles
Mike Cameron, Sea. Mariners	May 2, 2002	Jon Rauch (1 home run) and Jim Parque (3 home runs), Chi. White Sox
Carlos Delgado, Tor. Blue Jays	Sept. 25, 2003	Jorge Sosa (2 home runs), Joe Kennedy (1 home run), and Lance Carter (1 home run), T.B. Devil Rays
Josh Hamilton, Tex Rangers	May 8, 2012	Jake Arietta (2 home runs), Zach Phillips (1 home run), Darren O'Day (1 home run), Balt. Orioles

National League

Batter	Date	Opposing Pitcher(s)
Bobby Lowe, Bost. Beaneaters	May 30, 1894	Icebox Chamberlain (4 home runs), Cin. Reds
Ed Delahanty, Phila. Phillies	July 13, 1896	Adonis Bill Terry (4 home runs), Chi. Cubs
Chuck Klein, Phila. Phillies	July 10, 1936	Jim Weaver (1 home run), Mace Brown (2 home runs), and Bill Swift (1 home run), Pitt. Pirates
Gil Hodges, Bklyn. Dodgers	Aug. 31, 1950	Warren Spahn (1 home run), Normie Roy (1 home run), Bob Hall (1 home run), and Johnny Antonelli (1 home run), Bost. Braves
Joe Adcock, Milw. Braves	July 31, 1954	Don Newcombe (1 home run), Erv Palica (1 home run), Pete Wojey (1 home run), and Johnny Podres (1 home run), Bklyn. Dodgers
Willie Mays, S.F. Giants	Apr. 30, 1961	Lew Burdette (2 home runs), Seth Morehead (1 home run), and Don McMahon (1 home run), Milw. Braves
Mike Schmidt, Phila. Phillies	Apr. 17, 1976	Rick Reuschel (2 home runs), Mike Garman (1 home run), and Paul Reuschel (1 home run), Chi. Cubs
Bob Horner, Atl. Braves	July 6, 1986	Andy McGaffigan (3 home runs) and Jeff Reardon (1 home run), Mont. Expos
Mark Whiten, St.L. Cardinals	Sept. 7, 1993	Larry Luebbers (1 home run), Mike Anderson (2 home runs), and Rob Dibble (1 home run), Cin. Reds
Shawn Green, L.A. Dodgers	May 23, 2002	Glendon Rusch (1 home runs), Brian Mallette (2 home runs), and Jose Cabrera (1 home run), Milw. Brewers

Career Home Runs by Players Hitting Four Home Runs in One Game

American League

Batter	Date	Result	Career Home Runs
Lou Gehrig, N.Y. Yankees	June 3, 1932	N.Y. Yankees 20, Phila. A's 13	493
Carlos Delgado, Tor. Blue Jays	Sept. 25, 2003	Tor. Blue Jays 10, T.B. Devil Rays 8	473
Rocky Colavito, Cle. Indians	June 10, 1959	Cle. Indians 11, Balt. Orioles 8	374
Mike Cameron, Sea. Mariners	May 2, 2002	Sea. Mariners 15, Chi. White Sox 4	278
Josh Hamilton, Tex. Rangers	May 8, 2012	Tex. Rangers 10, Balt. Orioles 3	200
Pat Seerey, Chi. White Sox	July 18, 1948	Chi. White Sox 12, Phila. A's 11	86

National League

Batter	Date	Result	Career Home Runs
Willie Mays, S.F. Giants	Apr. 30, 1961	S.F. Giants 14, Milw. Brewers 4	660
Mike Schmidt, Phila. Phillies	Apr. 17, 1976	Phila. Phillies 18, Chi. Cubs 16	548
Gil Hodges, Bklyn. Dodgers	Aug. 31, 1950	Blyn. Dodgers 19, Bost. Braves 3	370
Joe Adcock, Milw. Brewers	July 31, 1954	Milw. Brewers 15, Bklyn. Dodgers 7	336
Shawn Green, L.A. Dodgers	May 23, 2002	L.A. Dodgers 16, Milw. Brewers 3	328

continued on next page

Chuck Klein, Phila. Phillies.....July 10, 1936..... Phila. Phillies 9, Pitt. Pirates 6 300
Bob Horner, Atl. Braves.....July 6, 1986..... Mont. Expos 11, Atl. Braves 8.....218
Mark Whiten, St.L. Cardinals....Sept. 7, 1993..... St.L. Cardinals 15, Cin. Reds 2 105
Ed Delahanty, Phila. Phillies.....July 13, 1896..... Chi. Cubs 9, Phila. Phillies 8.....101
Bobby Lowe, Bost. Beaneaters...May 30, 1894..... Bost. Beaneaters 20, Cin. Reds 11.....71

Players with Three Home Runs in One Game, Fewer Than 10 in Season

American League

	Home Runs
Mickey Cochrane, Phila. A's, 1925	6
Merv Connors, Chi. White Sox, 1938	6
Billy Glynn, Cle. Indians, 1954	5
Preston Ward, K.C. A's, 1958	6
Don Leppert, Wash. Senators II, 1963	6
Joe Lahoud, Bost. Red Sox, 1969	9
Fred Patek, Cal. Angels, 1980	5
Juan Beniquez, Balt. Orioles, 1986	6
Dan Johnson, Chi. White Sox, 2012	3

National League (Post-1900)

	Home Runs
Hal Lee, Bost. Braves, 1934	8
Babe Ruth, Bost. Braves, 1935	6
Clyde McCullough, Chi. Cubs, 1942	5
Jim Tobin, Bost. Braves, 1942	6
Tommy Brown, Bklyn. Dodgers, 1950	8
Del Wilber, Phila. Phillies, 1951	8
Jim Pendleton, Milw. Braves, 1953	7
Bob Thurman, Cin. Reds, 1956	8
Roman Mejias, Pitt. Pirates, 1958	5
Gene Oliver, Atl. Braves, 1966	8
Mike Lum, Atl. Braves, 1970	7
George Mitterwald, Chi. Cubs, 1974	7
Pete Rose, Cin. Reds, 1978	7
Karl Rhodes, Chi. Cubs, 1994	8
Cory Snyder, L.A. Dodgers, 1994	6
Bobby Estalella, Phila. Phillies, 1999	4
Todd Hollandsworth, Colo. Rockies, 2001	6
Damion Easley, Ariz. D'backs, 2006	9
Jarrett Parker, S.F. Giants, 2015	6
Kirk Nieuwenhuis, N.Y. Mets, 2015	4

Rookies Hitting 30 or More Home Runs

Mark McGwire, Oak. A's (AL), 1987	49
Wally Berger, Bost. Braves (NL), 1930	38
Frank Robinson, Cin. Reds (NL), 1956	38
Al Rosen, Cle. Indians (AL), 1950	37
Albert Pujols, St.L. Cardinals (NL), 2001	37
Hal Trosky, Cle. Indians (AL), 1934	35
Jose Abreu. Chi. White Sox (AL), 2014	36
Rudy York, Det. Tigers (AL), 1937	35
Walt Dropo, Bost. Red Sox (AL), 1950	34
Ryan Braun, Milw. Brewers (NL), 2007	34
Jimmie Hall, Min. Twins (AL), 1963	33
Earl Williams, Atl. Braves (NL), 1971	33
Jose Canseco, Oak. A's (AL), 1986	33
Tony Oliva, Min. Twins (AL), 1964	32
Chris Young, Ariz. D'backs (NL), 2007	32
Ted Williams, Bost. Red Sox (AL), 1939	31
Jim Hart, S.F. Giants (NL), 1964	31
Bob Allison, Wash. Senators (AL), 1959	30
Willie Montanez, Phila. Phillies (NL), 1971	30
Pete Incaviglia, Tex. Rangers (AL), 1986	30
Matt Nokes, Det. Tigers (AL), 1987	30
Mike Trout, L.A. Angels (AL), 2012	30

Former Negro Leaguers Who Led Major Leagues in Home Runs

Hank Aaron	Milw. Brewers (NL)	1957	44
	Milw. Brewers (NL)	1963	44
	Atl. Braves (NL)	1966	44
	Atl. Braves (NL)	1967	39
	(Played in Negro Leagues with Indianapolis Clowns, 1952.)		
Willie Mays	N.Y. Giants (NL)	1955	51
	S.F. Giants (NL)	1962	49
	S.F. Giants (NL)	1964	47
	S.F. Giants (NL)	1965	52
	(Played in Negro Leagues with Chattanooga Choo-Choos, 1947; Birmingham Black Barons, 1948–50.)		

continued on next page

Ernie Banks	Chi. Cubs (NL)	1958	47
	Chi. Cubs (NL)	1960	41
	(Played in Negro Leagues with Kansas City Monarchs, 1950–53.)		
Larry Doby	Cle. Indians (AL)	1952	32
	Cle. Indians (AL)	1954	32
	(Played in Negro Leagues with Newark Eagles, 1942–43, 1946–47.)		

Players with 50 Home Runs, Batting Under .300, Season

	Home Runs	Batting Average
Mark McGwire, St.L. Cardinals (NL), 1998	70	.299
Brady Anderson, Balt. Orioles (AL), 1996	50	.297
Prince Fielder, Milw. Brewers (NL), 2007	50	.297
Sammy Sosa, Chi. Cubs (NL), 1999	63	.288
David Ortiz, Bost. Red Sox (AL), 2006	54	.287
Chris Davis, Balt. Orioles (AL), 2013	53	.286
Ken Griffey Jr., Sea. Mariners (AL), 1998	56	.284
Mark McGwire, St.L. Cardinals (NL), 1999	65	.278
Cecil Fielder, Det. Tigers (AL), 1990	51	.277
Mark McGwire, Oak. A's (AL)–St.L. Cardinals (NL), 1997	58	.274
Greg Vaughn, S.D. Padres (NL), 1998	50	.272
Roger Maris, N.Y. Yankees (AL), 1961	61	.269
Andruw Jones, Atl. Braves (NL), 2005	51	.263
Jose Bautista, Tor. Blue Jays (AL) 2010	54	.260

Players Hitting 49 Home Runs in Season, Never Hitting 50

American League

Lou Gehrig, N.Y. Yankees, 1934 and 1936
Harmon Killebrew, Min. Twins, 1964 and 1969
Frank Robinson, Balt. Orioles, 1966

National League

Ted Kluszewski, Cin. Reds, 1954
Andre Dawson, Chi. Cubs, 1987
Larry Walker, Colo. Rockies, 1997
Shawn Green, L.A. Dodgers, 2001
Todd Helton, Colo. Rockies, 2001
Albert Pujols, St.L. Cardinals, 2006*
*Still active.

Most Multi-Home Run Games, Career

72	Babe Ruth (1914–35)
71	Barry Bonds (1986–2007)
69	Sammy Sosa (1989–2007)
67	Mark McGwire (1914–35)
63	Willie Mays (1951–52, 1954–73)
62	Hank Aaron (1954–76)
62	Alex Rodriguez* (1994–2013, 2015–)
55	Jimmie Foxx (1925–42, 1944–45)
55	Ken Griffey Jr. (1989–2010)
54	Frank Robinson (1956–76)
54	Manny Ramirez (1993–2011)

* Still active.

Most Grand Slams, Career

25	Alex Rodriguez* (1994–2013, 2015–)
23	Lou Gehrig (1923–39)
21	Manny Ramirez (1993–2011)
19	Eddie Murray (1977–97)
18	Willie McCovey (1959–80)
18	Robin Ventura (1989–2004)

continued on next page

17 ..... Jimmie Foxx (1925–42, 1944–45)
17 ..... Carlos Lee (1999–2012)
17 ..... Ted Williams (1939–42, 1946–60)
16 ..... Hank Aaron (1954–76)
16 ..... Dave Kingman (1971–86)
16 ..... Babe Ruth (1914–35)
15 ..... Ken Griffey Jr. (1989–2010)
15 ..... Richie Sexson (1997–2008)

Players Hitting Two Grand Slams, Same Game

American League

Tony Lazzeri, N.Y. Yankees, May 24, 1936
Jim Tabor, Bost. Red Sox, July 4, 1939
Rudy York, Bost. Red Sox, July 27, 1946
Jim Gentile, Balt. Orioles, May 9, 1961
Jim Northrup, Det. Tigers, June 24, 1968
Frank Robinson, Balt. Orioles, June 26, 1970
Robin Ventura, Chi. White Sox, Sept. 4, 1995
Chris Hoiles, Balt. Orioles, Aug. 14, 1998
Nomar Garciaparra, Bost. Red Sox, May 10, 1999
Bill Mueller, Bost. Red Sox, July 29, 2003

National League

Tony Cloninger, Atl. Braves, July 3, 1966
Fernando Tatis, St.L. Cardinals, Apr. 23, 1999*
Josh Willingham, Wash. Nationals, July 17, 2009
*Same inning.

Most Home Runs by Age

Teens

24 ..... Tony Conigliaro
22 ..... Bryce Harper
19 ..... Mel Ott
18 ..... Phil Cavarretta
16 ..... Ken Griffey Jr.
13 ..... Mickey Mantle

Twenties

424 ..... Alex Rodriguez
382 ..... Ken Griffey Jr.
376 ..... Jimmie Foxx
370 ..... Eddie Mathews
366 ..... Albert Pujols
361 ..... Mickey Mantle
342 ..... Hank Aaron

Thirties

444 ..... Barry Bonds
424 ..... Babe Ruth
396 ..... Rafael Palmeiro
371 ..... Hank Aaron
356 ..... Jim Thome
354 ..... Mark McGwire
349 ..... Willie Mays

Forties

72 ..... Carlton Fisk
67 ..... Darrell Evans
59 ..... Dave Winfield
59 ..... Barry Bonds
53 ..... Raul Ibanez
48 ..... Carl Yastrzemski

Teenagers Hitting Grand Slams

Scott Stratton, Lou. Colonels (AA), May 27, 1889 ..... 19 years, 7 months
George S. Davis, Cle. Spiders (NL), May 30, 1890 ..... 19 years, 9 months
Eddie Onslow, Det. Tigers (AL), Aug. 22, 1912 ..... 19 years, 6 months
Phil Cavarretta, Chi. Cubs (NL), May 16, 1936 ..... 19 years, 10 months
Al Kaline, Det. Tigers (AL), June 11, 1954 ..... 19 years, 6 months
Harmon Killebrew, Wash. Senators (AL), June 11, 1954 ..... 19 years, 11 months
Vada Pinson, Cin. Reds (NL), Apr. 18, 1958 ..... 19 years, 8 months
Tony Conigliaro, Bost. Red Sox (AL), June 3, 1964 ..... 19 years, 5 months

Oldest Players to Hit Grand Slams

American League

Henry Blanco, Sea. Mariners, Aug. 1, 2013 ..... 41 years, 11 months
Henry Blanco, Sea. Mariners, June 15, 2013 ..... 41 years, 9 months
Minnie Minoso, Wash. Senators II, July 24, 1963 ..... 41 years, 5 months
Raul Ibanez, Sea. Mariners, May 15, 2013 ..... 40 years, 11 months
Rafael Palmeiro, Balt. Orioles, June 4, 2005 ..... 40 years, 9 months
Darrell Evans, Det. Tigers, Sept. 5, 1987 ..... 40 years, 3 months

continued on next page

Matt Stairs, Tor. Blue Jays, May 14, 2008 ..... 40 years, 3 months
Mickey Vernon, Cle. Indians, Apr. 25, 1958 ..... 40 years, 0 months
Raul Ibanez, N.Y. Yankees, July 16, 2012 ..... 40 years, 1 month
Alex Rodriguez, N.Y. Yankees, Aug. 18, 2015 ..... 40 years, 0 months

National League

Julio Franco, Atl. Braves, June 25, 2005 ..... 46 years, 10 months
Julio Franco, Atl. Braves, June 3, 2004 ..... 45 years, 10 months
Cap Anson, Chi. Cubs, Aug. 1, 1894 ..... 42 years, 3 months
Craig Biggio, Hous. Astros, July 29, 2007 ..... 41 years, 8 months
Matt Stairs, Phila. Phillies, Sept. 10, 2009 ..... 41 years, 7 months
Honus Wagner, Pitt. Pirates, July 29, 1915 ..... 41 years, 5 months
Craig Biggio, Hous. Astros, Apr. 20, 2007 ..... 41 years, 5 months
Stan Musial, St.L. Cardinals, June 23, 1961 ..... 40 years, 7 months
Hank Aaron, Atl. Braves, June 4, 1974 ..... 40 years, 3 months
Hank Aaron, Atl. Braves, Apr. 26, 1974 ..... 40 years, 2 months

Oldest Home Run Champions*

American League

	Age	Home Runs
Darrell Evans, Det. Tigers, 1985	38 years, 5 months	40
Babe Ruth, N.Y. Yankees, 1931	36 years, 8 months	46
Reggie Jackson, Cal. Angels, 1982	36 years, 5 months	39
Hank Greenberg, Det. Tigers, 1946	35 years, 9 months	44
Babe Ruth, N.Y. Yankees, 1930	35 years, 8 months	49

National League (Post-1900)

	Age	Home Runs
Cy Williams, Phila. Phillies, 1927	39 years, 10 months	30
Gavvy Cravath, Phila. Phillies, 1919	38 years, 7 months	12
Gavvy Cravath, Phila. Phillies, 1918	37 years, 7 months	8
Barry Bonds, S.F. Giants, 2001	37 years, 3 months	73
Mike Schmidt, Phila. Phillies, 1986	37 years, 1 month	37
Gavvy Cravath, Phila. Phillies, 1917	36 years, 7 months	12
Mark McGwire, St.L. Cardinals, 1999	36 years, 0 months	65
Cy Williams, Phila. Phillies, 1923	35 years, 10 months	41
Johnny Mize, N.Y. Giants, 1948	35 years, 9 months	40
Sam Thompson, Phila. Phillies, 1895	35 years, 7 months	18
Hank Sauer, Chi. Cubs, 1952	35 years, 7 months	37
Andres Galarraga, Colo. Rockies, 1996	35 years, 4 months	47
Jack Fournier, Bklyn. Dodgers, 1924	35 years, 1 month	27
Mike Schmidt, Phila. Phillies, 1984	35 years, 1 month	35
Mark McGwire, St.L. Cardinals, 1998	35 years, 0 months	70

*As of October that year.

Most Career Home Runs by Players Hitting Home Run on First Pitch in Majors

360 ..... Gary Gaetti, Min. Twins (AL), Sept. 20, 1981
284 ..... Will Clark, S.F. Giants (NL), Apr. 8, 1986
260 ..... Tim Wallach, Mont. Expos (NL), Sept. 6, 1980
238 ..... Earl Averill, Cle. Indians (AL), Apr. 16, 1929
202 ..... Bill White, N.Y. Giants (NL), May 7, 1956
195 ..... Jay Bell, Cle. Indians (AL), Sept. 29, 1986
182 ..... Terry Steinbach, Oak. A's (AL), Sept. 12, 1986
142 ..... Wally Moon, St.L. Cardinals (NL), Apr. 13, 1954
125 ..... Bob Nieman, St.L. Browns (AL), Sept. 13, 1951
115 ..... Marcus Thames, N.Y. Yankees (AL), June 10, 2002
114 ..... Whitey Lockman, N.Y. Giants (NL), July 5, 1945
87 ..... Kevin Kouzmanoff, Cle. Indians (AL), Sept. 2, 2006

continued on next page

80.....J.P. Arencibia, Tor. Blue Jays (AL), Aug. 7, 2010
79.....Bert Campaneris, K.C. A's (AL), July 23, 1964
69..... Clyde Vollmer, Cin. Reds (NL), May 31, 1942
55.....Junior Felix, Tor. Blue Jays (AL), May 14, 1989
49..... Starling Marte, Pitt. Pirates (NL), July 26, 2012
38.....Brant Alyea, Wash. Senators II (AL), Sept. 12, 1965
35..... Al Woods, Tor. Blue Jays (AL), Apr. 7, 1977
34..... Chris Richard, St.L. Cardinals (NL), July 17, 2000
32.....Kazuo Matsui, N.Y. Mets (NL), Apr. 6, 2004
24.....Daniel Nava, Bost. Red Sox (AL), June 12, 2010
21..... Chuck Tanner, Milw. Braves (NL), Apr. 12, 1955
14.....Andy Phillips, N.Y. Yankees (AL), Sept. 26, 2004
13..... Eddie Rosario, Min. Twins (AL), May 6, 2015
12.....George Vico, Det. Tigers (AL), Apr. 20, 1948
8.....Jim Bullinger, Chi. Cubs (NL), June 8, 1992
6..... Adam Wainwright, St.L. Cardinals (NL), May 24, 2006
3..... Clise Dudley, Bklyn. Dodgers (NL), Apr. 27, 1929
3.....Jay Gainer, Colo. Rockies (NL), May 14, 1993
2.....Frank Ernaga, Chi. Cubs (NL), May 24, 1957
1..... Don Rose, Cal. Angels (AL), May 24, 1972
1..... Eddie Morgan, St.L. Cardinals (NL), Apr. 14, 1936
1..... Estéban Yan, T.B. Devil Rays, June 4, 2000
1..... Gene Stechschulte, St.L. Cardinals, Apr. 27, 2001
1..... Mark Saccomanno, Hous. Astros, Sept. 8, 2008
1..... Tom Milone, Wash. Nationals, Sept. 3, 2011

Players Hitting Home Run in First Time At Bat, Never Hitting Another

American League

Luke Stuart, St.L. Browns, Aug. 8, 1921 (Career: 1921)
Bill Lefebvre, Bost. Red Sox, June 10, 1938 (Career: 1938–39, 1943–44)
Hack Miller, Det. Tigers, Apr. 23, 1944 (Career: 1944–45)
Bill Roman, Det. Tigers, Sept. 30, 1964 (Career: 1964–65)
Don Rose, Cal. Angels, May 24, 1972 (Career: 1971–72, 1974)
Dave Machemer, Cal. Angels, June 21, 1978 (Career: 1978–79)
Andre David, Min. Twins, June 29, 1984 (Career: 1984, 1986)
Esteban Yan, T.B. Devil Rays, June 4, 2000 (Career: 1996–2006)

National League (Post-1900)

Eddie Morgan, St.L. Cardinals, Apr. 14, 1936 (Career: 1936–37)
Dan Bankhead, Bklyn. Dodgers, Aug. 26, 1947 (Career: 1947, 1950–51)
Hoyt Wilhelm, N.Y. Giants, Apr. 23, 1952 (Career: 1952–72)
Cuno Barragan, Chi. Cubs, Sept. 1, 1961 (Career: 1961–63)
Jose Sosa, Hous. Astros, July 30, 1975 (Career: 1975–76)
Dave Eiland, S.D. Padres, Apr. 10, 1992 (Career: 1988–93, 1995, 1998–2000)
Mitch Lyden, Fla. Marlins, June 6, 1993 (Career: 1993)
Gene Stechschulte, St.L. Cardinals, Apr. 17, 2001 (Career: 2000–02)
David Matranga, Hous. Astros, June 27, 2003 (Career: 2003)
Mark Worrell, St.L. Cardinals, June 5, 2008 (Career: 2008–11)
Mark Saccomanno, Hous. Astros, Sept. 8, 2008 (Career: 2008)

Most At Bats, No Home Runs, Career

2335.....Bill Holbert (1876–88)
1931.....Tom Oliver (1930–33)
1904.....Irv Hall (1943–46)
1466.....Pat Deasley (1881–88)
1441..... Tommy Bond (1876–84)
1426..... Roxy Walters (1915–25)
1364.....Paul Cook (1884–91)
1354.....Don Sutton (1966–89)
1297.....Joe McGinnity (1899–1908)
1287.....Waite Hoyt (1918–38)

Most Consecutive At Bats Without a Home Run

3347..... Tommy Thevenow ..... Sept. 22, 1926–end of career, 1938
3278..... Eddie Foster..... Apr. 20, 1916–end of career, 1923
3246..... Al Bridwell..... Start of career, 1905–Apr. 30, 1913
3186..... Terry Turner ..... July 16, 1906–June 30, 1914
3104..... Sparky Adams..... July 26, 1925–June 30, 1931
3021..... Jack McCarthy ..... June 28, 1899–end of career, 1907
2701..... Lee Tannehill..... Sept. 2, 1903–July 31, 1910
2663..... Doc Cramer..... Sept. 8, 1935–May 21, 1940
2617..... Donie Bush ..... Aug. 29, 1915–Aug. 21, 1920
2568..... Mike Tresh..... May 19, 1940–Apr. 20, 1948

continued on next page

2480	Bill Bergen	June 3, 1901–Sept. 6, 1909
2426	Joe Sugden	May 31, 1895–end of career, 1912
2423	Emil Verban	Start of career, 1944–Sept. 6, 1948
2401	Everett Scott	Aug. 1, 1914–Apr. 26, 1920

Lowest Batting Average for Home Run Leaders, Season (Post-1900)

Batting Average		Home Runs
.204	Dave Kingman, N.Y. Mets (NL), 1982	37
.227	Carlos Pena, T.B. Rays (AL), 2009	39
.232	Gavvy Cravath, Phila. Phillies (NL), 1918	8
.233	Pedro Alvarez, Pitt. Pirates (NL), 2013	36
.241	Fred Odwell, Cin. Reds (NL), 1905	9
.242	Harmon Killebrew, Min. Twins (AL), 1959	42
.243	Harmon Killebrew, Min. Twins (AL), 1962	48
.244	Wally Pipp, N.Y. Yankees (AL), 1917	9
.244	Ralph Kiner, Pitt. Pirates (NL), 1952	37
.244	Gorman Thomas, Milw. Brewers (AL), 1979	45
.245	Gorman Thomas, Milw. Brewers (AL), 1982	39
.247	Tim Jordan, Bklyn. Dodgers (NL), 1908	12
.247	Ralph Kiner, Pitt. Pirates (NL), 1946	23
.248	Darrell Evans, Det. Tigers (AL), 1985	40
.249	Mike Schmidt, Phila. Phillies (NL), 1975	38

Players Hitting 30 or More Home Runs in First Three Seasons

Jose Canseco, Oak. A's (AL)	1986 (33), 1987 (31), and 1988 (42*)
Mark McGwire, Oak. A's (AL)	1987 (49*), 1988 (32), and 1989 (33)
Albert Pujols, St.L. Cardinals (NL)	2001 (37), 2002 (34), and 2003 (43)
Ryan Braun, Milw. Brewers (NL)	2007 (34), 2008 (37), and 2009 (32)

*Led the league.

Reverse 30–30 Club: Players with 30 Home Runs and 30 Errors, Season

American League (Post-1900)

	Home Runs	Errors
Harmon Killebrew, Wash Senators, 1959	42	30
Mark Reynolds, Balt. Orioles, 2011	37	31

National League (Post-1900)

	Home Runs	Errors
Rogers Hornsby, St.L. Cardinals, 1922	42	30
Davey Johnson, Atl. Braves, 1973	43	30
Pedro Guerrero, L.A. Dodgers, 1983	32	30
Howard Johnson, N.Y. Mets, 1991	38	31
Ernie Banks, Chi. Cubs, 1958	47	32
Tony Perez, Cin. Reds, 1969	37	32
Rogers Hornsby, St.L. Cardinals, 1924	39	34
Tony Perez, Cin. Reds, 1970	40	35

Players Increasing Their Home Run Production in Seven Consecutive Seasons

Tim McCarver	St.L. Cardinals (NL), 1960	0
	St.L. Cardinals (NL), 1961	1
	St.L. Cardinals (NL), 1963	4
	St.L. Cardinals (NL), 1964	9
	St.L. Cardinals (NL), 1965	11
	St.L. Cardinals (NL), 1966	12
	St.L. Cardinals (NL), 1967	14
Jimmy Piersall	Bost. Red Sox (AL), 1950	0
	Bost. Red Sox (AL), 1952	1
	Bost. Red Sox (AL), 1953	3
	Bost. Red Sox (AL), 1954	8
	Bost. Red Sox (AL), 1955	13
	Bost. Red Sox (AL), 1956	14
	Bost. Red Sox (AL), 1957	19
Eddie Robinson	Cle. Indians (AL), 1942	0
	Cle. Indians (AL), 1946	3
	Cle. Indians (AL), 1947	14
	Cle. Indians (AL), 1948	16
	Wash. Senators (AL), 1949	18
	Wash. Senators–Chi. White Sox (AL), 1950	21
	Chi. White Sox (AL), 1951	29
John Shelby	Balt. Orioles (AL), 1981	0
	Balt. Orioles (AL), 1982	1
	Balt. Orioles (AL), 1983	5
	Balt. Orioles (AL), 1984	6
	Balt. Orioles (AL), 1985	7
	Balt. Orioles (AL), 1986	11
	L.A. Dodgers (NL), 1987	22
Cy Williams	Chi. Cubs (NL), 1917	5
	Phila. Phillies (NL), 1918	6
	Phila. Phillies (NL), 1919	9
	Phila. Phillies (NL), 1920	15
	Phila. Phillies (NL), 1921	18
	Phila. Phillies (NL), 1922	26
	Phila. Phillies (NL), 1923	41

Most Home Runs by Switch-Hitters, Career

536	Mickey Mantle (1951–68)
504	Eddie Murray (1977–97)
468	Chipper Jones (1993, 1995–2012)
394	Mark Teixeira (2003–)
392	Carlos Beltran (1998–)

Most Home Runs by Catcher, Season*

42	Javy Lopez, Atl. Braves (NL), 2003
41	Todd Hundley, N.Y. Mets (NL), 1996
40	Roy Campanella, Bklyn. Dodgers (NL), 1953
40	Mike Piazza, L.A. Dodgers (NL), 1997
40	Mike Piazza, N.Y. Mets (NL), 1999

continued on next page

38 ..... Johnny Bench, Cin. Reds (NL), 1970
36 ..... Gabby Hartnett, Chi. Cubs (NL), 1930
36 ..... Mike Piazza, L.A. Dodgers (NL), 1996

*While in lineup as catcher.

Most Home Runs by Catcher, Career*

396 ..... Mike Piazza (1992–2007)
351 ..... Carlton Fisk (1969, 1971–93)
327 ..... Johnny Bench (1967–83)
306 ..... Yogi Berra (1946–65)
304 ..... Ivan Rodriguez (1991–2011)
299 ..... Lance Parrish (1977–95)
298 ..... Gary Carter (1974–92)

*While in lineup as catcher.

300 Career Home Runs and 100 Home Runs, Both Leagues

	American League	National League	Total
Adrian Beltre*	266	147	413
Carlos Beltran*	157	235	392
Bobby Bonds	135	197	332
Ellis Burks	177	175	352
Miguel Cabrera*	270	138	408
Chili Davis	249	101	350
Adam Dunn	108	354	462
Carlos Delgado	336	137	473
Jim Edmonds	121	272	393
Darrell Evans	141	273	414
Shawn Green	119	209	328
Ken Griffey Jr.	420	210	630
Vladimir Guerrero	215	234	449
Frank Howard	259	123	382
David Justice	145	160	305
Carlos Lee	161	197	358
Lee May	126	228	354
Fred McGriff	224	269	493
Mark McGwire	363	220	583
Eddie Murray	396	108	504
Albert Pujols*	115	445	560
Frank Robinson	262	324	586
Richie Sexson	164	142	306
Gary Sheffield	141	368	509
Reggie Smith	149	165	314
Alfonso Soriano	185	227	412
Jim Thome	511	101	511
Greg Vaughn	229	126	355

*Still active.

Most Home Runs Hit in One Ballpark, Career

323 ..... Mel Ott ..... Polo Grounds
293 ..... Sammy Sosa ..... Wrigley Field
290 ..... Ernie Banks ..... Wrigley Field
266 ..... Mickey Mantle ..... Yankee Stadium
265 ..... Mike Schmidt ..... Veterans Stadium
263 ..... Frank Thomas ..... U.S. Cellular Field
259 ..... Babe Ruth ..... Yankee Stadium
252 ..... Stan Musial ..... Sportsman's Park
251 ..... Lou Gehrig ..... Yankee Stadium
248 ..... Ted Williams ..... Fenway Park
246 ..... Harmon Killebrew ..... Metropolitan Stadium
237 ..... Carl Yastrzemski ..... Fenway Park
236 ..... Willie McCovey ..... Candlestick Park

continued on next page

231	Billy Williams	Wrigley Field
227	Todd Helton	Coors Field
226	Chipper Jones	Turner Field
212	Ron Santo	Wrigley Field
212	Norm Cash	Tiger Stadium

Players Whose Home Run in "Cycle" Was Grand Slam

American League

Nap Lajoie, Phila. A's, July 30, 1901
Tony Lazzeri, N.Y. Yankees, June 3, 1932
Jimmie Foxx, Phila. A's, Aug. 14, 1933
Jay Buhner, Sea. Mariners, July 23, 1993
Miguel Tejada, Oak. A's, Sept. 29, 2001
Jason Kubel, Min. Twins, Apr. 17, 2009
Bengie Molina, Tex. Rangers, July 16, 2010

National League

Bill Terry, N.Y. Giants, May 29, 1928

Players with the Highest Percentage of Team's Total Home Runs, Season

American League

88%	Babe Ruth, Bost. Red Sox, 1919	29 of team's 33
73%	Babe Ruth, Bost. Red Sox, 1918	11 of team's 15
56%	Smoky Joe Wood, Cle. Indians, 1918	5 of team's 9
55%	Goose Goslin, Wash. Senators, 1924	12 of team's 22
55%	Stan Spence, Wash. Senators, 1944	18 of team's 33
51%	Jimmie Foxx, Bost. Red Sox, 1938	50 of team's 98
50%	Erve Beck, Cle. Blues, 1901	6 of team's 12
50%	Tilly Walker, Phila. A's, 1918	11 of team's 22
50%	Joe Judge, Wash. Senators, 1917	2 of team's 4
50%	Sam Chapman, Phila. A's, 1946	20 of team's 40

National League (Post-1900)

60%	Shad Barry, Phila. Phillies, 1902	3 of team's 5
60%	Jimmy Seckard, Bklyn. Dodgers, 1903	9 of team's 15
60%	Harry Lumley, Bklyn. Dodgers, 1904	9 of team's 15
58%	Wally Berger, Bost. Braves, 1930	38 of team's 66
56%	Wally Berger, Bost. Braves, 1931	19 of team's 34
56%	Bill Nicholson, Chi. Cubs, 1943	29 of team's 52
53%	Ed Konetchy, St.L. Cardinals, 1913	8 of team's 15
53%	Cy Williams, Phila. Phillies, 1927	30 of team's 57
52%	Dick Hoblitzel, Cin. Reds, 1911	11 of team's 21
50%	Homer Smoot, St.L. Cardinals, 1903	4 of team's 8
50%	Sherry Magee, Phila. Phillies, 1906	6 of team's 12
50%	Harry Lumley, Bklyn. Dodgers, 1907	9 of team's 18
50%	Wally Berger, Bost. Braves, 1933	27 of team's 54

Federal League

50%	Ed Konetchy, Pitt. Pirates, 1915	10 of team's 20

Shortstops Leading League in Home Runs

American League

Vern Stephens, St.L. Browns, 1945	24
Alex Rodriguez, Tex. Rangers, 2001	52

National League

Ernie Banks, Chi. Cubs, 1958	47
Ernie Banks, Chi. Cubs, 1959	45

continued on next page

Alex Rodriguez, Tex. Rangers, 2002 57
Alex Rodriguez, Tex. Rangers, 2003 47

Most Home Runs by Left-Handed Hitting Shortstops

Home Runs		Games at Short
114	Stephen Drew (2006–)	968
96	Arky Vaughan (1932–43, 1947–48)	1485
57	Tony Kubek (1957–65)	882
49	Joe Sewell (1920–33)	1216
46	Brandon Crawford (2011–)	614
42	Craig Reynolds (1975–89)	1240
40	Billy Klaus (1952–53, 1955–63)	426
28	Ozzie Guillen (1985–2000)	1896

Players Hitting Home Runs in 20 Consecutive Seasons Played

Rickey Henderson (1979–2003)	25
Ty Cobb (1905–28)	24
Hank Aaron (1954–76)	23
Carl Yastrzemski (1961–83)	23
Rusty Staub (1963–85)	23
Carlton Fisk (1971–93)	23
Stan Musial (1941–44, 1946–63)	22
Willie Mays (1951–52, 1954–73)	22
Al Kaline (1953–74)	22
Brooks Robinson (1956–77)	22
Willie McCovey (1959–80)	22
Tony Perez (1965–86)	22
Dave Winfield (1973–88, 1990–95)	22
Gary Sheffield (1988–2009)	22
Barry Bonds (1986–2007)	22
Jim Thome (1991–2012)	22
Babe Ruth (1915–35)	21
Frank Robinson (1956–76)	21
Ken Griffey Jr. (1989–2009)	21
Ron Fairly (1958–78)	21
Reggie Jackson (1967–87)	21
Graig Nettles (1968–88)	21
Eddie Murray (1977–97)	21
Harold Baines (1980–2000)	21
Tim Raines (1981–99, 2001–02)	21
Cal Ripken Jr. (1981–2001)	21
Ivan Rodriguez (1991–2011)	21
Mel Ott (1927–46)	20
Dwight Evans (1972–91)	20
Brian Downing (1973–92)	20
George Brett (1974–93)	20
Robin Yount (1974–93)	20
Andre Dawson (1977–96)	20
Tony Gwynn (1982–2001)	20
Alex Rodriguez (1995–2013, 2015)	20
Jason Giambi (1995–2014)	20
Rafael Palmiero (1986–2005)	20

Players with 100 Home Runs, Three Different Teams

Adrian Beltre*	L.A. Dodgers (NL), 1998–2004	147
	Sea. Mariners (AL), 2005–09	103
	Tex Rangers (AL), 2011–	135
Darrell Evans	Atl. Braves (NL), 1969–76, 1989	131
	S.F. Giants (NL), 1976–83	142
	Det. Tigers (AL), 1984–88	141
Reggie Jackson	K.C.–Oak. A's (AL), 1967–75, 1987	269
	N.Y. Yankees (AL), 1977–81	144
	Cal. Angels (AL), 1982–86	123
Jim Thome	Cle. Indians (AL), 1991–2002, 2011	337
	Phi. Phillies (NL), 2003–2005, 2012	101
	Chi. White Sox (AL), 2006–09	134
Alex Rodriguez*	Sea. Mariners (AL), 1994–2000	189
	Tex. Rangers (AL), 2001–03	156
	N.Y. Yankees (AL), 2004–13, 2015	342

*Still active.

Players with 40-Home Run Seasons Before 25th Birthday

		Home Runs	Age
Hank Aaron	Milw. Braves (NL), 1957	44	23
Richie Allen	Phila. Phillies (NL), 1966	40	24
Ernie Banks	Chi. Cubs (NL), 1955	44	24
Johnny Bench	Cin. Reds (NL), 1970	45	22
	Cin. Reds (NL), 1972	40	24

continued on next page

Joe DiMaggio	N.Y. Yankees (AL), 1937	46	22
Adam Dunn	Cin. Reds (NL), 2004	46	24
Prince Fielder	Milw. Brewers (NL), 2007	50	23
Jimmie Foxx	Phila. A's (AL), 1932	58	24*
Lou Gehrig	N.Y. Yankees (AL), 1927	47	24
Troy Glaus	Ana. Angels (AL), 2000	47	23
Ken Griffey Jr.	Sea. Mariners (AL), 1993	45	23
	Sea. Mariners (AL), 1994	40	24
Bryce Harper	Wash. Nationals (NL), 2015	42	22
Reggie Jackson	Oak. A's (AL), 1969	47	23
Harmon Killebrew	Wash. Senators (AL), 1959	42	23
Ralph Kiner	Pitt. Pirates (NL), 1947	51	24*
Chuck Klein	Phila. Phillies (NL), 1929	43	24*
Mickey Mantle	N.Y. Yankees (AL), 1956	52	24*
Eddie Mathews	Milw. Braves (NL), 1953	47	21
Willie Mays	N.Y. Giants (NL), 1954	41	23
	N.Y. Giants (NL), 1955	51	24
Mark McGwire	Oak. A's (AL), 1987	49	23
Mel Ott	N.Y. Giants (NL), 1929	42	20
Albert Pujols	St.L. Cardinals (NL), 2003	43	23
	St.L. Cardinals (NL), 2004	46	24
Alex Rodriguez	Sea. Mariners (AL), 1998	42	23
	Sea. Mariners (AL), 1999	42	24
	Sea. Mariners (AL), 2000	41	25
Hal Trosky	Cle. Indians (AL), 1936	42	23

*Turned 25 during season.

Players with More Home Runs Than Strikeouts, Season (Min. 10 Home Runs)

American League

	Home Runs	Strikeouts	Differential
Lou Gehrig, N.Y. Yankees, 1934	49	31	+18
Joe DiMaggio, N.Y. Yankees, 1941	30	13	+17
Yogi Berra, N.Y. Yankees, 1950	28	12	+16
Ken Williams, St.L. Browns, 1925	25	14	+11
Joe DiMaggio, N.Y. Yankees, 1938	32	21	+11
Joe DiMaggio, N.Y. Yankees, 1939	30	20	+10
Ted Williams, Bost. Red Sox, 1941	37	27	+10
Joe DiMaggio, N.Y. Yankees, 1937	46	37	+9
Joe DiMaggio, N.Y. Yankees, 1948	39	30	+9
Lou Boudreau, Cle. Indians, 1948	18	9	+9
Ken Williams, St.L. Browns, 1922	39	31	+8
Joe Sewell, N.Y. Yankees, 1932	11	3	+8
Bill Dickey, N.Y. Yankees, 1937	29	22	+7
Ted Williams, Bost. Red Sox, 1950	28	21	+7
Yogi Berra, N.Y. Yankees, 1951	27	20	+7
Yogi Berra, N.Y. Yankees, 1955	27	20	+7
Bill Dickey, N.Y. Yankees, 1936	22	16	+6
Yogi Berra, N.Y. Yankees, 1952	30	24	+6
Mickey Cochrane, Phila. A's, 1927	12	7	+5
Bill Dickey, N.Y. Yankees, 1938	27	22	+5
Ted Williams, Bost. Red Sox, 1955	28	24	+4
Charlie Gehringer, Det. Tigers, 1935	19	16	+3

continued on next page

American League

	Home Runs	Strikeouts	Differential
Bill Dickey, N.Y. Yankees, 1935	14	11	+3
Lou Gehrig, N.Y. Yankees, 1936	49	46	+3
Ted Williams, Bost. Red Sox, 1953	13	10	+3
Lou Skizas, K.C. A's, 1957	18	15	+3
Tris Speaker, Cle. Indians, 1923	17	15	+2
Al Simmons, Phila. A's, 1930	36	34	+2
Bill Dickey, N.Y. Yankees, 1932	15	13	+2
Charlie Gehringer, Det. Tigers, 1936	15	13	+2
Vic Power, K.C. A's–Cle. Indians, 1958	16	14	+2
George Brett, K.C. Royals, 1980	24	22	+2
Ken Williams, St.L. Browns, 1924	18	17	+1
Mickey Cochrane, Phila. A's, 1932	23	22	+1
Joe DiMaggio, N.Y. Yankees, 1940	31	30	+1
Joe DiMaggio, N.Y. Yankees, 1946	25	24	+1
Johnny Mize, N.Y. Yankees, 1950	25	24	+1
Yogi Berra, N.Y. Yankees, 1956	30	29	+1

National League

	Home Runs	Strikeouts	Differential
Tommy Holmes, Bost. Braves, 1945	28	9	+19
Ted Kluszewski, Cin. Reds, 1954	49	35	+14
Lefty O'Doul, Phila. Phillies, 1929	32	19	+13
Johnny Mize, N.Y. Giants, 1947	51	42	+9
Cap Anson, Chi. Colts, 1884	21	13	+8
Ernie Lombardi, N.Y. Giants, 1945	19	11	+8
Sam Thompson, Phila. Phillies, 1895	18	11	+7
Ted Kluszewski, Cin. Reds, 1955	47	40	+7
Jack Clements, Phila. Phillies, 1895	13	7	+6
Billy Southworth, St.L. Cardinals, 1926	16	10	+6
Ernie Lombardi, Cin. Reds, 1935	12	6	+6
Willard Marshall, N.Y. Giants, 1947	36	30	+6
Ted Kluszewski, Cin. Reds, 1953	40	34	+6
Bill Terry, N.Y. Giants, 1932	28	23	+5
Ernie Lombardi, Cin. Reds, 1938	19	14	+5
Stan Musial, St.L. Cardinals, 1948	39	34	+5
Mel Ott, N.Y. Giants, 1929	42	38	+4
Frank McCormick, Cin. Reds, 1941	17	13	+4
Andy Pafko, Chi. Cubs, 1950	36	32	+4
Ted Kluszewski, Cin. Reds, 1956	35	31	+4
Barry Bonds, S.F. Giants, 2004	45	41	+4
Dan Brouthers, Det. Wolverines, 1887	12	9	+3
Hugh Duffy, Bost. Beaneaters, 1894	18	15	+3
Irish Meusel, N.Y. Giants, 1923	19	16	+3
Frank McCormick, Cin. Reds, 1944	20	17	+3
Johnny Mize, N.Y. Giants, 1948	40	37	+3
Don Mueller, N.Y. Giants, 1951	16	13	+3
Billy O'Brien, Wash. Statesmen, 1887	19	17	+2
Irish Meusel, N.Y. Giants, 1925	21	19	+2
Frank McCormick, Cin. Reds, 1939	18	16	+2
Tommy Holmes, Bost. Braves, 1944	13	11	+2
Lefty O'Doul, Phila. Phillies, 1930	22	21	+1

continued on next page

Lefty O'Doul, Bklyn. Dodgers, 1932	21	20	+1
Arky Vaughan, Pitt. Pirates, 1935	19	18	+1
Ernie Lombardi, Cin. Reds, 1939	20	19	+1

Largest Differential Between Leader in Home Runs and Runner-Up

American League

Differential	Season	Leader	Home Runs	Runner-Up	Home Runs
+35	1920	Babe Ruth, N.Y. Yankees	54	George Sisler, St.L. Browns	19
+35	1921	Babe Ruth, N.Y. Yankees	59	Ken Williams, St.L. Browns, and Bob Meusel, N.Y. Yankees	24
+28	1926	Babe Ruth, N.Y. Yankees	47	Al Simmons, Phila. A's	19
+27	1928	Babe Ruth, N.Y. Yankees	54	Lou Gehrig, N.Y. Yankees	27
+20	1956	Mickey Mantle, N.Y. Yankees	52	Vic Wertz, Cle. Indians	32
+19	1919	Babe Ruth, Bost. Red Sox	29	Home Run Baker, N.Y. Yankees, George Sisler, St.L. Browns, and Tilly Walker, Phila. A's	10
+19	1924	Babe Ruth, N.Y. Yankees	46	Joe Hauser, Phila. A's	27
+17	1932	Jimmie Foxx, Phila. A's	58	Babe Ruth, N.Y. Yankees	41
+15	2010	Jose Bautista, Tor. Blue Jays	54	Paul Konerko, Chi. White Sox	39
+14	1933	Jimmie Foxx, Phila. A's	48	Babe Ruth, N.Y. Yankees	34
+13	1927	Babe Ruth, N.Y. Yankees	60	Lou Gehrig, N.Y. Yankees	47
+12	1923	Babe Ruth, N.Y. Yankees	41	Ken Williams, St.L. Browns	29
+12	1978	Jim Rice, Bost. Red Sox	46	Don Baylor, Cal. Angels, and Larry Hisle, Milw. Brewers	34
+12	1990	Cecil Fielder, Det. Tigers	51	Mark McGwire, Oak. A's	39
+12	1997	Ken Griffey Jr., Sea. Mariners	56	Tino Martinez, N.Y. Yankees	44
+11	1929	Babe Ruth, N.Y. Yankees	46	Lou Gehrig, N.Y. Yankees	35

National League

Differential	Season	Leader	Home Runs	Runner-Up	Home Runs
+19	1923	Cy Williams, Phila. Phillies	41	Jake Fournier, Bklyn. Dodgers	22
+18	1940	Johnny Mize, St.L. Cardinals	43	Bill Nicholson, Chi. Cubs	25
+18	1949	Ralph Kiner, Pitt. Pirates	54	Stan Musial, St.L. Cardinals	36
+16	1922	Rogers Hornsby, St.L. Cardinals	42	Cy Williams, Phila. Phillies	26
+16	1930	Hack Wilson, Chi. Cubs	56	Chuck Klein, Phila. Phillies	40
+15	1925	Rogers Hornsby, St.L. Cardinals	39	Gabby Hartnett, Chi. Cubs	24
+14	1964	Willie Mays, S.F. Giants	47	Billy Williams, Chi. Cubs	33
+13	1899	Buck Freeman, Wash. Senators	25	Bobby Wallace, St.L. Cardinals	12
+13	1965	Willie Mays, S.F. Giants	52	Willie McCovey, S.F. Giants	39
+13	1980	Mike Schmidt, Phila. Phillies	48	Bob Horner, Atl. Braves	35
+12	1958	Ernie Banks, Chi. Cubs	47	Frank Thomas, Pitt. Pirates	35
+11	1915	Gavvy Cravath, Phila. Phillies	24	Cy Williams, Chi. Cubs	13
+11	1943	Bill Nicholson, Chi. Cubs	29	Mel Ott, N.Y. Giants	18
+11	1950	Ralph Kiner, Pitt. Pirates	47	Andy Pafko, Chi. Cubs	36
+11	1977	George Foster, Cin. Reds	52	Jeff Burroughs, Atl. Braves	41
+11	1989	Kevin Mitchell, S.F. Giants	47	Howard Johnson, N.Y. Mets	36

Most Home Runs, Last Season in Majors

35 ..... Dave Kingman, Oak. A's (AL), 1986
29 ..... Ted Williams, Bost. Red Sox (AL), 1960
29 ..... Mark McGwire, St.L. Cardinals (NL), 2001
28 ..... Barry Bonds, S.F. Giants (NL), 2007
27 ..... Jermaine Dye, Chi. White Sox (AL), 2009
25 ..... Hank Greenberg, Pitt. Pirates (NL), 1947
24 ..... Roy Cullenbine, Det. Tigers (AL), 1947
24 ..... Jack Graham, St.L. Browns (AL), 1949
23 ..... Kirby Puckett, Min. Twins (AL), 1995
23 ..... Albert Belle, Balt. Orioles (AL), 2000
22 ..... Phil Nevin, Tex. Rangers (AL)–Chi. Cubs (NL) Min. Twins (AL), 2006
21 ..... Dave Nilsson, Milw. Brewers (NL), 1999

continued on next page

21 .....Paul O'Neill, N.Y. Yankees (AL), 2001
21 .....Sammy Sosa, Tex. Rangers (AL), 2007
19 .....Joe Gordon, Cle. Indians (AL), 1950
19 .....Chili Davis, N.Y. Yankees (AL), 1999
19 .....George Brett, K.C. Royals (AL), 1993
19 ....Derrek Lee, Balt. Orioles (AL)–Pitt. Pirates (NL), 2011
19 ...Jose Guillen, K.C. Royals (AL)–S.F. Giants (NL), 2010
19 .....George Brett, K.C. Royals (AL), 1993
18 .....Buzz Arlett, Phila. Phillies (NL), 1931
18 .....Ralph Kiner, Cle. Indians (AL), 1955
18 .....Joe Adcock, Cal. Angels (AL), 1966
18 .....Mickey Mantle, N.Y. Yankees (AL), 1968
18 .....Reggie Smith, S.F. Giants (NL), 1982
18 .....Rafael Palmeiro, Balt. Orioles (AL), 2005

Fewest Career Home Runs for League Leader (Post-1920)

American League

89 .....Nick Etten (N.Y. Yankees), led league in 1944 with 22
156.....Bob Meusel (N.Y. Yankees), led league in 1925 with 33
160.....Bill Melton (Chi. White Sox), led league in 1971 with 33
166.....Tony Conigliaro (Bost. Red Sox), led league in 1965 with 32
192.....Al Rosen (Cle. Indians), led league in 1950 with 37 and in 1953 with 43
196.....Ken Williams (St.L. Browns), led league in 1922 with 39
203.....Chris Davis (Balt. Orioles), led league in 2013 with 53, and in 2015 with 47
224.....Bobby Grich (Cal. Angels), led league in 1981 with 22
228.....Troy Glaus (Ana. Angels), led league in 2000 with 47
235.....Ben Oglivie (Milw. Brewers), led league in 1980 with 41
237.....Gus Zernial (Phila. A's), led league in 1951 with 33
241.....Jesse Barfield (Tor. Blue Jays), led league in 1986 with 40
241.....Nelson Cruz (Balt. Orioles) led league in 2014 with 40
247.....Vern Stephens (St.L. Browns), led league in 1945 with 24

National League

70 .....Nolan Arenado* (Colo. Rockies), led league in 2015 with 42
88 .....Tommy Holmes (Bost. Braves), led league in 1945 with 28
97 .....Bryce Harper* (Wash. Nationals), led league in 2015 with 42
116 .....Paul Goldschmidt* (Ariz. D'backs), led league in 2013 with 36
131.....Pedro Alvarez* (Pitt. Pirates), led league in 2013 with 36
135.....Ripper Collins (St.L. Cardinals), led league in 1934 with 35
136.....Jack Fournier (Bklyn. Dodgers), led league in 1924 with 27
148.....George Kelly (N.Y. Giants), led league in 1921 with 23
181.....Giancarlo Standon* (Mia. Marlins), led league in 2014 with 37
205.....Joe Medwick (St.L. Cardinals), led league in 1937 with 31
205.....Matt Kemp* (L.A. Dodgers), led league in 2011 with 39
219.....Jim Bottomley (St.L. Cardinals), led league in 1928 with 31
228.....Howard Johnson (N.Y. Mets), led league in 1991 with 38
234.....Kevin Mitchell (S.F. Giants), led league in 1989 with 47
235.....Bill Nicholson (Chi. Cubs), led league in 1943 with 29 and in 1944 with 33
239.....Dolph Camilli (Bklyn. Dodgers), led league in 1941 with 34
242.....Wally Berger (Bost. Braves), led league in 1935 with 34
244.....Hack Wilson (Chi. Cubs), led league in 1926 with 21, in 1927 with 30, in 1928 with 31, and in 1930 with 56

* Still active.

Runs Batted In

Evolution of RBI Record

American League

1901.....Nap Lajoie, Phila. A's.....125
1911.....Ty Cobb, Det. Tigers.....127
1912.....Home Run Baker, Phila. A's.....130
1920.....Babe Ruth, N.Y. Yankees.....137
1921.....Babe Ruth, N.Y. Yankees.....170
1927.....Lou Gehrig, N.Y. Yankees.....175
1931.....Lou Gehrig, N.Y. Yankees.....184

continued on next page

National League (Pre-1900)

1876	Deacon White, Chi. White Stockings	60
1879	Charley Jones, Bost. Beaneaters	62
	John O'Rourke, Bost. Beaneaters	62
1880	Cap Anson, Chi. White Stockings	74
1881	Cap Anson, Chi. White Stockings	82
1882	Cap Anson, Chi. White Stockings	83
1883	Dan Brouthers, Buf. Bisons	97
1884	Cap Anson, Chi. White Stockings	102
1885	Cap Anson, Chi. White Stockings	108
1886	Cap Anson, Chi. White Stockings	147
1887	Sam Thompson, Det. Wolverines	166

National League (Post-1899)

1900	Elmer Flick, Phila. Phillies	110
1901	Honus Wagner, Pitt. Pirates	126
1910	Sherry Magee, Phila. Phillies	123
1913	Gavvy Cravath, Phila. Phillies	128
1922	Rogers Hornsby, St.L. Cardinals	152
1929	Hack Wilson, Chi. Cubs	159
1930	Hack Wilson, Chi. Cubs	191

Most RBIs by Decade

Pre-1900

1880	Cap Anson
1323	Roger Connor
1302	Sam Thompson
1296	Dan Brouthers
1218	Hugh Duffy
1135	Ed Delahanty
1124	Ed McKean
1080	Jake Beckley
1072	Bid McPhee
1021	Fred Pfeffer

1900–09

956	Honus Wagner
808	Sam Crawford
793	Nap Lajoie
688	Harry Davis
685	Cy Seymour
680	Jimmy Williams
638	Bobby Wallace
610	Harry Steinfeldt
597	Bill Dahlen
590	Charlie Hickman

1910–19

828	Ty Cobb
793	Home Run Baker
765	Heinie Zimmerman
746	Sherry Magee
718	Tris Speaker
718	Duffy Lewis
697	Sam Crawford
687	Ed Konetchy
682	Eddie Collins
665	Gavvy Cravath

1920–29

1331	Babe Ruth
1153	Rogers Hornsby
1133	Harry Heilmann
1005	Bob Meusel
923	George Kelly
885	Jim Bottomley
860	Ken Williams
827	George Sisler
821	Goose Goslin
821	Joe Sewell

1930–39

1403	Jimmie Foxx
1358	Lou Gehrig
1135	Mel Ott
1081	Al Simmons
1046	Earl Averill
1036	Joe Cronin
1003	Charlie Gehringer
979	Chuck Klein
937	Bill Dickey
893	Wally Berger

1940–49

903	Bob Elliott
893	Ted Williams
887	Bobby Doerr
854	Rudy York
835	Bill Nicholson
824	Vern Stephens
786	Joe DiMaggio
759	Dixie Walker
744	Johnny Mize
710	Joe Gordon

1950–59

1031	Duke Snider
1001	Gil Hodges
997	Yogi Berra
972	Stan Musial
925	Del Ennis
863	Jackie Jensen
841	Mickey Mantle
823	Ted Kluszewski

1960–69

1107	Hank Aaron
1013	Harmon Killebrew
1011	Frank Robinson
1003	Willie Mays
937	Ron Santo
925	Ernie Banks
896	Orlando Cepeda
862	Roberto Clemente

1970–79

1013	Johnny Bench
954	Tony Perez
936	Lee May
922	Reggie Jackson
906	Willie Stargell
860	Rusty Staub
856	Bobby Bonds
846	Carl Yastrzemski

continued on next page

817 ..... Gus Bell
816 ..... Larry Doby

1980–89

996 ..... Eddie Murray
929 ..... Dale Murphy
929 ..... Mike Schmidt
900 ..... Dwight Evans
899 ..... Dave Winfield
895 ..... Andre Dawson
868 ..... Jim Rice
851 ..... George Brett
835 ..... Harold Baines
821 ..... Robin Yount

853 ..... Billy Williams
836 ..... Brooks Robinson

1990–99

1099 ..... Albert Belle
1091 ..... Ken Griffey Jr.
1076 ..... Barry Bonds
1068 ..... Juan Gonzalez
1068 ..... Rafael Palmeiro
1040 ..... Frank Thomas
979 ..... Dante Bichette
975 ..... Fred McGriff
961 ..... Jeff Bagwell
960 ..... Matt Williams

840 ..... Bobby Murcer
832 ..... Bob Watson

2000–09

1243 ..... Alex Rodriguez
1112 ..... Albert Pujols
1106 ..... Manny Ramirez
1046 ..... Miguel Tejada
1045 ..... Carlos Delgado
1037 ..... Vladimir Guerrero
1026 ..... Lance Berkman
1019 ..... Carlos Lee
1016 ..... David Ortiz
993 ..... Bobby Abreu

2010–15

692 ..... Miguel Cabrera
632 ..... Adrian Gonzalez
589 ..... Robinson Cano
586 ..... Albert Pujols
582 ..... Jose Bautista
529 ..... Ryan Braun
573 ..... David Ortiz
561 ..... Adrian Beltre
532 ..... Nelson Cruz
531 ..... Prince Fielder

Career RBI Leaders by First Letter of Last Name

A	Hank Aaron (1954–76)	2297
B	Barry Bonds (1986–2007)	1996
C	Ty Cobb (1905–28)	1938
D	Andre Dawson (1976–96)	1591
E	Dwight Evans (1972–91)	1384
F	Jimmie Foxx (1925–42, 1944–45)	1922
G	Lou Gehrig (1923–39)	1995
H	Rogers Hornsby (1915–37)	1584
I	Raul Ibanez (1996–2014)	1207
J	Reggie Jackson (1967–87)	1702
K	Harmon Killebrew (1954–75)	1584
L	Nap Lajoie (1896–1916)	1599
M	Stan Musial (1941–44, 1946–63)	1951
N	Graig Nettles (1967–88)	1314
O	Mel Ott (1926–47)	1860
P	Rafael Palmeiro (1986–2005)	1835
Q	Joe Quinn (1884–86, 1888–1901)	795
R	Babe Ruth (1914–35)	2213
S	Al Simmons (1924–41, 1943–44)	1827
T	Frank Thomas (1990–2008)	1704
U	Chase Utley* (2003–)	925
V	Mickey Vernon (1939–43, 1946–60)	1311
W	Ted Williams (1939–42, 1946–60)	1839
X	[No player]	
Y	Carl Yastrzemski (1961–83)	1844
Z	Todd Zeile (1989–2004)	1110

*Still active.

Teammates Finishing One-Two in RBIs

American League

Season	Team	Leader	RBIs	Runner-Up	RBIs
1902	Bost. Americans	Buck Freeman	121	Charlie Hickman*	110
1905	Phila. A's	Harry Davis	83	Lave Cross	77
1908	Det. Tigers	Ty Cobb	108	Sam Crawford	80
1909	Det. Tigers	Ty Cobb	107	Sam Crawford	97
1910	Det. Tigers	Sam Crawford	120	Ty Cobb	91
1913	Phila. A's	Home Run Baker	126	Stuffy McInnis	90
1915	Det. Tigers	Bobby Veach	112 (Tie)	Sam Crawford	112
1917	Det. Tigers	Bobby Veach	103	Ty Cobb	102
1926	N.Y. Yankees	Babe Ruth	146	Tony Lazzeri	114 (Tie)
1927	N.Y. Yankees	Lou Gehrig	175	Babe Ruth	164
1928	N.Y. Yankees	Lou Gehrig	142 (Tie)	Babe Ruth	142
1931	N.Y. Yankees	Lou Gehrig	184	Babe Ruth	163

continued on next page

American League

Season	Team	Leader	RBIs	Runner-Up	RBIs
1932	Phila. A's	Jimmie Foxx	169	Al Simmons	151
1940	Det. Tigers	Hank Greenberg	150	Rudy York	134
1949	Bost. Red Sox	Vern Stephens	159 (Tie)	Ted Williams	159
1950	Bost. Red Sox	Vern Stephens	144 (Tie)	Walt Dropo	144
1952	Cle. Indians	Al Rosen	105	Larry Doby	104 (Tie)
1980	Milw. Brewers	Cecil Cooper	122	Ben Oglivie	118
1984	Bost. Red Sox	Tony Armas	123	Jim Rice	122
2011	N.Y. Yankees	Curtis Granderson	119	Robinson Cano	118

*161 with Cle. Bronchos and 32 with Bost. Americans.

National League (Post-1900)

Season	Team	Leader	RBIs	Runner-Up	RBIs
1900	Phila. Phillies	Elmer Flick	110	Ed Delahanty	109
1902	Pitt. Pirates	Honus Wagner	91	Tommy Leach	85
1904	N.Y. Giants	Bill Dahlen	80	Sam Mertes	78
1914	Phila. Phillies	Sherry Magee	103	Gavvy Cravath	100
1932	Phila. Phillies	Don Hurst	143	Chuck Klein	137
1960	Milw. Braves	Hank Aaron	126	Eddie Mathews	124
1965	Cin. Reds	Deron Johnson	130	Frank Robinson	113
1970	Cin. Reds	Johnny Bench	148	Tony Perez	129
1976	Cin. Reds	George Foster	121	Joe Morgan	111
1996	Colo. Rockies	Andres Galarraga	150	Dante Bichette	141

Largest Differential Between League Leader in RBIs and Runner-Up

American League

Differential	Season	Leader	RBIs	Runner-Up	RBIs
+51	1935	Hank Greenberg, Det. Tigers	170	Lou Gehrig, N.Y. Yankees	119
+36	1913	Home Run Baker, Phila. A's	126	Stuffy McInnis, Phila. A's, and Duffy Lewis, Bost. Red Sox	90
+32	1921	Babe Ruth, N.Y. Yankees	171	Harry Heilmann, Det. Tigers	139
+31	1926	Babe Ruth, N.Y. Yankees	145	George H. Bums, Cle. Indians, and Tony Lazzeri, N.Y. Yankees	114
+30	1953	Al Rosen, Cle. Indians	145	Mickey Vernon, Wash. Senators	115
+29	1910	Sam Crawford, Det. Tigers	120	Ty Cobb, Det. Tigers	91
+29	1911	Ty Cobb, Det. Tigers	144	Sam Crawford, Det. Tigers, and Home Run Baker, Phila A's	115
+29	1922	Ken Williams,. St.L. Browns	155	Bobby Veach, Det. Tigers	126
+29	1938	Jimmie Foxx, Bost. Red Sox	175	Hank Greenberg, Det. Tigers	146
+28	1908	Ty Cobb, Det. Tigers	108	Sam Crawford, Det. Tigers	80

National League (Post-1900)

Differential	Season	Leader	RBIs	Runner-Up	RBIs
+39	1937	Joe Medwick, St.L. Cardinals	154	Frank Demaree, Chi. Cubs	115
+35	1910	Sherry Magee, Phila. Phillies	123	Mike Mitchell, Cin. Reds	88
+33	1913	Gavvy Cravath, Phila. Phillies	128	Heinie Zimmerman, Chi. Cubs	95
+28	1915	Gavvy Cravath, Phila. Phillies	115	Sherry Magee, Phila. Phillies	87
+27	1943	Bill Nicholson, Chi. Cubs	128	Bob Elliott, Pitt. Pirates	101
+27	1957	Hank Aaron, Milw. Braves	132	Del Ennis, St.L. Cardinals	105

Career RBI Totals, Players Hitting 500 Home Runs

	HRs	RBIs
Hank Aaron	755	2297
Babe Ruth	714	2213
Alex Rodriguez*	687	2055
Barry Bonds	762	1996
Jimmie Foxx	534	1922
Eddie Murray	504	1917
Willie Mays	660	1903
Mel Ott	511	1860
Ted Williams	521	1839
Ken Griffey Jr.	630	1836
Rafael Palmeiro	569	1835
Manny Ramirez	555	1831
Frank Robinson	586	1812
Frank Thomas	521	1704
Reggie Jackson	563	1702
Jim Thome	612	1699
Gary Sheffield	509	1676
Sammy Sosa	609	1667
David Ortiz*	503	1641
Ernie Banks	512	1636
Mike Schmidt	548	1595
Harmon Killebrew	573	1584
Willie McCovey	521	1555
Mickey Mantle	536	1509
Eddie Mathews	512	1453
Mark McGwire	583	1414

*Still active.

Players Driving in 100 Runs in First Two Seasons in Majors

American League

Al Simmons, Phila. A's	1924 (102) and 1925 (129)
Tony Lazzeri, N.Y. Yankees	1926 (114) and 1927 (102)
Dale Alexander, Det. Tigers	1929 (137) and 1930 (135)
Hal Trosky, Cle. Indians	1934 (142) and 1935 (113)
Joe DiMaggio, N.Y. Yankees	1936 (125) and 1937 (167)
Rudy York, Det. Tigers	1937 (103) and 1938 (127)
Ted Williams, Bost. Red Sox	1939 (145) and 1940 (113)
Jose Canseco, Oak. A's	1986 (117) and 1987 (113)
Wally Joyner, Cal. Angels	1986 (100) and 1987 (117)
Frank Thomas, Chi. White Sox	1991 (109) and 1992 (115)
Hideki Matsui, N.Y. Yankees	2003 (106) and 2004 (108)
Jose Abreu, Chi. White Sox	2014 (107) and 2015 (101)

National League (Post-1900)

Glenn Wright, Pitt. Pirates	1924 (111) and 1925 (121)
Pinky Whitney, Phila. Phillies	1928 (103) and 1929 (115)
Ray Jablonski, St.L. Cardinals	1953 (112) and 1954 (104)
Albert Pujols, St.L. Cardinals	2001 (130) and 2002 (127)

Players Driving in 500 Runs in First Four Years of Career

558	Joe DiMaggio, 1936–39, N.Y. Yankees (AL)
545	Hal Troksy, 1934–37, Cle. Indians (AL)
515	Ted Williams, 1939–42, Bost. Red Sox (AL)
504	Albert Pujols, 2001–04, St.L. Cardinals (NL)

Catchers with 100 RBIs and 100 Runs Scored, Season

American League

	RBIs	Runs
Mickey Cochrane, Phila. A's, 1932	112	118
Yogi Berra, N.Y. Yankees, 1950	124	116
Carlton Fisk, Bost. Red Sox, 1977	102	106
Darrell Porter, K.C. Royals, 1979	112	101
Ivan Rodriguez, Tex. Rangers, 1999	113	116

National League (Post-1900)

	RBIs	Runs
Roy Campanella, Bklyn. Dodgers, 1953	142	103
Johnny Bench, Cin. Reds, 1974	129	108
Mike Piazza, L.A. Dodgers, 1997	124	104
Mike Piazza, N.Y. Mets, 1999	124	100

Catchers Hitting .300 with 30 Home Runs and 100 RBIs, Season

American League

	Home Runs	RBIs	Batting Average
Rudy York*, Det. Tigers, 1937	35	103	.307
Ivan Rodriguez, Tex. Rangers, 1999	35	113	.332

National League (Post-1900)

	Home Runs	RBIs	Batting Average
Gabby Hartnett, Chi.Cubs, 1930	37	122	.339
Walker Cooper, N.Y. Giants, 1947	35	122	.305
Roy Campanella, Bklyn. Dodgers, 1951	33	108	.325
Roy Campanella, Bklyn. Dodgers, 1953	41	142	.312
Roy Campanella, Bklyn. Dodgers, 1955	32	107	.318
Joe Torre,** Atl. Braves, 1966	36	101	.315
Mike Piazza, L.A. Dodgers, 1993	35	112	.318
Mike Piazza, L.A. Dodgers, 1996	36	105	.336
Mike Piazza, L.A. Dodgers, 1997	40	124	.362
Mike Piazza, L.A. Dodgers–Fla. Marlins–N.Y. Mets, 1998	32	111	.328
Mike Piazza, N.Y. Mets, 1999	40	124	.303
Mike Piazza, N.Y. Mets, 2000	38	113	.324
Javy Lopez, Atl. Braves, 2003	43	109	.328

*54 at catcher, 43 at other positions

**114 at catcher, 36 at other positions

Players with 40 or More Home Runs and Fewer Than 100 RBIs, Season

American League

	Home Runs	RBIs
Mickey Mantle, N.Y. Yankees, 1958	42	97
Mickey Mantle, N.Y. Yankees, 1960	40	94
Harmon Killebrew, Min. Twins, 1963	45	96
Rico Petrocelli, Bost. Red Sox, 1969	40	97
Darrell Evans, Det. Tigers, 1985	40	94
Ken Griffey Jr., Sea. Mariners, 1994	40	90
Adam Dunn, Chi. White Sox, 2012	41	96
Nelson Cruz, Sea. Mariners, 2015	44	93
Albert Pujols, L.A. Angels, 2015	40	95
Mike Trout, L.A. Angels, 2015	41	90

National League (Post-1900)

	Home Runs	RBIs
Duke Snider, Bklyn. Dodgers, 1957	40	92
Hank Aaron, Atl. Braves, 1969	44	97
Hank Aaron, Atl. Braves, 1973	40	96
Davey Johnson, Atl. Braves, 1973	43	99
Matt Williams, S.F. Giants, 1994	43	96
Barry Bonds, S.F. Giants, 2003	45	90
Adam Dunn, Cin. Reds, 2006	40	92
Alfonso Soriano, Wash. Nationals, 2006	46	95
Adrian Gonzalez, S.D. Padres, 2009	40	99
Carlos Gonzalez, Colo. Rockies, 2015	40	97
Bryce Harper, Wash. Nationals, 2015	42	99

Players with More Than 100 RBIs and Fewest Home Runs, Season

American League

	RBIs	Home Runs
Lave Cross, Phila. A's, 1902	108	0
Larry Gardner, Cle. Indians, 1920	118	3
Larry Gardner, Cle. Indians, 1921	115	3
Joe Sewell, Cle. Indians, 1923	109	3

continued on next page

Joe Sheely, Chi. White Sox, 1924	103	3
Billy Rogell, Det. Tigers, 1934	100	3

National League (Post-1900)

	RBIs	Home Runs
Ross Youngs, N.Y. Giants, 1921	102	3
Pie Traynor, Pitt. Pirates, 1928	124	3
Pie Traynor, Pitt. Pirates, 1931	103	2

Players with Most Career RBIs, Never Leading League

Willie Mays (1951–52, 1954–73)	1903	Tony Perez (1964–86)	1652
Rafael Palmeiro (1986–2005)	1835	Harold Baines (1980–2000)	1628
Frank Thomas (1990–2008)	1704	Chipper Jones (1993, 1995–2012)	1623
Jim Thome (1991–2012)	1699	Jake Beckley (1888–1907)	1575
Cal Ripken Jr. (1981–2001)	1695	George Brett (1973–93)	1595
Gary Sheffield (1988–2009)	1676	Al Kaline (1953–74)	1583

Players with 1000 Career RBIs, Never Driving in 100 in One Season

Pete Rose (1963–86)	1314	Jose Cruz (1970–88)	1077
Julio Franco (1982–94, 1996–97, 1999, 2001–07)	1194	Jimmy Dykes (1918–39)	1071
Craig Biggio (1988–2007)	1175	Willie Davis (1960–79)	1053
Mark Grace (1988–2003)	1146	Ron Fairly (1958–78)	1044
Johnny Damon (1995–2012)	1139	Bobby Murcer (1965–83)	1043
Tommy Corcoran (1890–1907)	1135	Joe Judge (1915–34)	1037
Rickey Henderson (1979–2003)	1115	Dusty Baker (1968–86)	1013
Charlie Grimm (1916, 1918–36)	1078	Amos Otis (1967–84)	1007

Batters Driving in 100 Runs with Three Different Teams

Richie Allen	Phila. Phillies (NL)	1966	110
	St.L. Cardinals (NL)	1970	101
	Chi. White Sox (AL)	1972	113
Adrian Beltre	L.A. Dodgers (NL)	2004	121
	Bost. Red Sox (AL)	2010	102
	Tex. Rangers (AL)	2011	105
		2012	102
Orlando Cepeda	S.F. Giants (NL)	1959	105
		1961	142
		1962	114
	St.L. Cardinals (NL)	1967	111
	Atl. Braves (NL)	1970	111
Rocky Colavito	Cle. Indians (AL)	1958	113
		1959	111
		1965	108
	Det. Tigers (AL)	1961	140
		1962	112
	K.C. A's (AL)	1964	102
Adrian Gonzalez	S.D. Padres (NL)	2007	100
		2008	119
		2010	101
	Bost. Red Sox (AL)	2011	117
	Bost. Red Sox (AL)–L.A. Dodgers (NL)	2012	108
	L.A. Dodgers (NL)	2013	100
		2014	116
Vladimir Guerrero	Mont. Expos (NL)	1998	109
		1999	131
		2000	123
		2004	108

continued on next page

	L.A. Angels (AL)	2009	126
		2005	108
		2006	116
		2007	125
	Tex. Rangers (AL)	2010	115
Lee May	Cin. Reds (NL)	1969	110
	Hous. Astros (NL)	1973	105
	Balt. Orioles (AL)	1976	109
Alex Rodriguez	Sea. Mariners (AL)	1996	123
		1998	124
		1999	111
		2000	132
	Tex. Rangers (AL)	2001	135
		2002	142
		2003	118
	N.Y. Yankees (AL)	2004	106
		2005	130
		2006	121
		2007	156
		2008	103
		2009	100
Alfonso Soriano	N.Y. Yankees (AL)	2002	102
	Tex. Rangers (AL)	2005	104
	Chi. Cubs. (NL)	2012	108
	Chi Cubs (NL)–N.Y. Yankees (AL)	2013	101
Gary Sheffield	S.D. Padres (NL)	1992	100
	Fla. Marlins (NL)	1996	120
	L.A. Dodgers (NL)	1999	116
		2000	100
		2001	101
	Atl. Braves (NL)	2003	132
	N.Y. Yankees (AL)	2004	121
		2005	123
Dave Winfield	S.D. Padres (NL)	1979	118
	N.Y. Yankees (AL)	1982	106
		1983	116
		1984	100
		1985	114
		1985	104
		1988	107
	Tor. Blue Jays (AL)	1992	108

Players Driving in 130 Teammates During Season

American League

	Teammates	Home Runs	RBIs
Hank Greenberg, Det. Tigers, 1937	143	40	183
Lou Gehrig, N.Y. Yankees, 1935	138	46	184
Ty Cobb, Det. Tigers, 1911	136	8	144
Lou Gehrig, N.Y. Yankees, 1930	133	41	174
Hank Greenberg, Det. Tigers, 1935	134	36	170

National League (Post-1900)

	Teammates	Home Runs	RBIs
Hack Wilson, Chi. Cubs, 1930	135	56	191
Chuck Klein, Phila. Phillies, 1930	130	40	170

Players Driving in 100 Runs, Season, in Each League

Bobby Abreu	National League	Phila. Phillies, 2001	110
		Phila. Phillies, 2003	101
		Phila. Phillies, 2004	105
		Phila. Phillies, 2005	102
	American League	N.Y. Yankees, 2007	101
		N.Y. Yankees, 2008	100
		L.A. Angels, 2009	103
Dick Allen	National League	Phila. Phillies, 1966	110
		St.L. Cardinals, 1970	101
	American League	Chi. White Sox, 1972	113
Adrian Beltre	National League	L.A. Dodgers, 2004	121
	American League	Bost. Red Sox, 2010	102
		Tex Rangers, 2011	105
		Tex Rangers, 2012	102
Carlos Beltran	American League	K.C. Royals, 1999	108
		K.C. Royals, 2001	101
		K.C. Royals, 2002	105
		K.C. Royals, 2003	100
	National League	N.Y. Mets, 2006	116
		N.Y. Mets, 2007	112
		N.Y. Mets, 2008	112
Jason Bay	National League	Pitt. Pirates, 2005	101
		Pitt. Pirates, 2006	104
	American League	Bost. Red Sox, 2009	119
Bobby Bonds	National League	S.F. Giants, 1971	102
	American League	Cal. Angels, 1977	115
Bill Buckner	National League	Chi. Cubs, 1982	105
	American League	Bost. Red Sox, 1985	110
		Bost. Red Sox, 1986	102
Jeff Burroughs	American League	Tex. Rangers, 1974	118
	National League	Atl. Braves, 1977	114
Miguel Cabrera	National League	Fla. Marlins, 2004	112
		Fla. Marlins, 2005	116
		Fla. Marlins, 2006	114
		Fla. Marlins, 2007	119
	American League	Det. Tigers, 2008	127
		Det. Tigers, 2009	103
		Det. Tigers, 2010	126
		Det. Tigers, 2011	105
		Det. Tigers, 2012	139
		Det. Tigers, 2013	137
		Det. Tigers, 2014	109
Prince Fielder	National League	Mil. Brewers, 2007	119
		Mil. Brewers, 2008	102
		Mil. Brewers, 2009	141
		Mil. Brewers, 2011	120
	American League	Det. Tigers, 2012	108
		Det. Tigers, 2013	106
Sam Crawford	National League	Cin. Reds, 1901	104
	American League	Det. Tigers, 1910	120
		Det. Tigers, 1911	115
		Det. Tigers, 1912	109
		Det. Tigers, 1914	104
		Det. Tigers, 1915	112
Adrian Gonzalez	National League	S.D. Padres, 2007	100
		S.D. Padres, 2008	119
		S.D. Padres, 2010	101
		L.A. Dodgers, 2013	100
		L.A. Dodgers, 2014	116
	American League	Bost. Red Sox, 2011	117
Ken Griffey Jr.	American League	Sea. Mariners, 1991	100
		Sea. Mariners, 1992	103
		Sea. Mariners, 1993	109
		Sea. Mariners, 1996	140
		Sea. Mariners, 1997	147
		Sea. Mariners, 1998	146
		Sea. Mariners, 1999	134
	National League	Cin. Reds, 2000	118

continued on next page

Vladimir Guerrero	National League	Mont. Expos, 1998	104
		Mont. Expos, 1999	131
		Mont. Expos, 2000	123
		Mont. Expos, 2001	108
		Mont. Expos, 2002	111
	American League	Ana. Angels, 2004	126
		L.A. Angels, 2005	108
		L.A. Angels, 2006	116
		L.A. Angels, 2007	125
		Tex. Rangers, 2010	115
Frank Howard	National League	L.A. Dodgers, 1962	119
	American League	Wash. Senators II, 1968	106
		Wash. Senators II, 1969	111
		Wash. Senators II, 1970	126
Nap Lajoie	National League	Phila. Phillies, 1897	127
		Phila. Phillies, 1898	127
	American League	Phila. A's, 1901	125
		Cle. Blues, 1904	102
Carlos Lee	American League	Chi. White Sox, 2003	113
	National League	Milw. Brewers, 2005	114
		Hous. Astros, 2007	119
		Hous. Astros, 2008	100
		Hous. Astros, 2009	102
Mike Lowell	National League	Fla. Marlins, 2001	100
		Fla. Marlins, 2003	105
	American League	Bost. Red Sox, 2007	120
Lee May	National League	Cin. Reds, 1969	110
		Hous. Astros, 1973	105
	American League	Balt. Orioles, 1976	109
Fred McGriff	National League	S.D. Padres, 1991	106
		S.D. Padres–Atl. Braves, 1993	101
		Chi. Cubs, 2002	103
	American League	T.B. Devil Rays, 1999	104
		T.B. Devil Rays, 2000	106
Mark McGwire	American League	Oak. A's, 1987	118
		Oak. A's, 1990	108
		Oak. A's, 1992	104
		Oak. A's, 1995	113
	National League	St.L. Cardinals, 1998	147
		St.L. Cardinals, 1999	147
Albert Pujols	National League	St.L. Cardinals, 2001	130
		St.L. Cardinals, 2002	127
		St.L. Cardinals, 2003	124
		St.L. Cardinals, 2004	123
		St.L. Cardinals, 2005	117
		St.L. Cardinals, 2006	137
		St.L. Cardinals, 2007	103
		St.L. Cardinals, 2008	116
		St.L. Cardinals, 2009	135
		St.L. Cardinals, 2010	118
	American League	L.A. Angels, 2012	105
		L.A. Angels, 2014	105
Tony Perez	National League	Cin. Reds, 1967	102
		Cin. Reds, 1969	122
		Cin. Reds, 1970	129
		Cin. Reds, 1973	101
		CIn. Reds, 1974	101
		Cin. Reds, 1975	109
	American League	Bost. Red Sox, 1980	105
Frank Robinson	National League	Cin. Reds, 1959	125
		Cin. Reds, 1961	124
		Cin. Reds, 1962	136
		Cin. Reds, 1965	113
	American League	Balt. Orioles, 1966	122
		Balt. Orioles, 1969	100
Alfonso Soriano	American League	N.Y. Yankees, 2002	102
		Tex Rangers, 2005	104
	National League	Chi Cubs, 2012	108

continued on next page

Gary Sheffield	National League	S.D. Padres, 1992	100
		Fla. Marlins, 1996	120
		L.A. Dodgers, 1999	101
		L.A. Dodgers, 2000	109
		L.A. Dodgers, 2001	100
		Atl. Braves, 2003	132
	American League	N.Y. Yankees, 2004	121
		N.Y. Yankees, 2005	123
Richie Sexson	American League	Cle. Indians, 1999	116
		Sea. Mariners, 2005	121
		Sea. Mariners, 2006	107
	National League	Milw. Brewers, 2001	125
		Milw. Brewers, 2002	102
		Milw. Brewers, 2003	124
Ken Singleton	National League	Mont. Expos, 1973	103
	American League	Balt. Orioles, 1979	111
		Balt. Orioles, 1980	104
Rusty Staub	National League	N.Y. Mets, 1975	105
	American League	Det. Tigers, 1977	101
		Det. Tigers, 1978	121
Dick Stuart	National League	Pitt. Pirates, 1961	117
	American League	Bost. Red Sox, 1963	118
		Bost. Red Sox, 1964	114
Jim Thome	American League	Cle. Indians, 1996	116
		Cle. Indians, 1997	102
		Cle. Indians, 1999	108
		Cle. Indians, 2000	106
		Cle. Indians, 2001	124
		Cle. Indians, 2002	118
		Chi. White Sox, 2006	109
	National League	Phila. Phillies, 2003	131
		Phila. Phillies, 2004	105
Richie Zisk	National League	Pitt. Pirates, 1974	100
	American League	Chi. White Sox, 1977	101

Players with More RBIs Than Games Played, Season (Min. 100 Games)

American League

	RBIs	Games	Differential
Lou Gehrig, N.Y. Yankees, 1931	184	155	+29
Hank Greenberg, Det. Tigers, 1937	183	154	+29
Al Simmons, Phila. A's, 1930	165	138	+27
Jimmie Foxx, Bost. Red Sox, 1938	175	149	+26
Lou Gehrig, N.Y. Yankees, 1927	175	155	+20
Lou Gehrig, N.Y. Yankees, 1930	174	154	+20
Babe Ruth, N.Y. Yankees, 1921	171	152	+19
Babe Ruth, N.Y. Yankees, 1929	154	135	+19
Babe Ruth, N.Y. Yankees, 1931	163	145	+18
Hank Greenberg, Det. Tigers, 1935	170	152	+18
Manny Ramirez, Cle. Indians, 1999	165	147	+18
Joe DiMaggio, N.Y. Yankees, 1937	167	151	+16
Jimmie Foxx, Phila. A's, 1932	169	154	+15

continued on next page

Al Simmons, Phila. A's, 1929	157	143	+14
Jimmie Foxx, Phila. A's, 1933	163	149	+14
Babe Ruth, N.Y. Yankees, 1927	164	151	+13
Lou Gehrig, N.Y. Yankees, 1934	165	154	+11
Hal Trosky, Cle. Indians, 1936	162	151	+11
Juan Gonzalez, Tex. Rangers, 1996	144	134	+10
Babe Ruth, N.Y. Yankees, 1930	153	145	+8
Walt Dropo, Bost. Red Sox, 1950	144	136	+8
Joe DiMaggio, N.Y. Yankees, 1939	126	120	+6
Babe Ruth, N.Y. Yankees, 1932	137	133	+4
Vern Stephens, Bost. Red Sox, 1949	159	155	+4
Ted Williams, Bost. Red Sox, 1949	159	155	+4
Kirby Puckett, Min. Twins, 1994	112	108	+4
Manny Ramirez, Cle. Indians, 2000	122	118	+4
Ken Williams, St.L. Browns, 1925	105	102	+3
Jimmie Foxx, Phila. A's, 1930	156	153	+3
Juan Gonzalez, Tex. Rangers, 1998	157	154	+3
Ken Williams, St.L. Browns, 1922	155	153	+2
Al Simmons, Phila. A's, 1927	108	106	+2
Lou Gehrig, N.Y. Yankees, 1937	159	157	+2
Hank Greenberg, Det. Tigers, 1940	150	148	+2
Joe DiMaggio, N.Y. Yankees, 1948	155	153	+2
Joe DiMaggio, N.Y. Yankees, 1940	133	132	+1
George Brett, K.C. Royals, 1980	118	117	+1

National League (Post-1900)

	RBIs	Games	Differential
Hack Wilson, Chi. Cubs, 1930	190	155	+35
Chuck Klein, Phila. Phillies, 1930	170	156	+14
Hack Wilson, Chi. Cubs, 1929	159	150	+9
Jeff Bagwell, Hous. Astros, 1994	116	110	+6
Rogers Hornsby, St.L. Cardinals, 1925	143	138	+5
Met Ott, N.Y. Giants, 1929	151	150	+1

Players Driving in 20 Percent of Their Team's Runs, Season

Nate Colbert, S.D. Padres (NL), 1972	111 of 488	22.75%
Wally Berger, Bost. Braves (NL), 1935	130 of 575	22.61%
Ernie Banks, Chi. Cubs (NL), 1959	143 of 673	21.25%
Sammy Sosa, Chi. Cubs (NL), 2001	160 of 777	20.59%
Jim Gentile, Balt. Orioles (AL), 1961	141 of 691	20.40%
Bill Buckner, Chi. Cubs (NL), 1981	75 of 370	20.27%
Bill Nicholson, Chi. Cubs (NL), 1943	128 of 632	20.25%
Frank Howard, Wash. Senators II (AL), 1968	106 of 524	20.23%
Babe Ruth, Bost. Red Sox (AL), 1919	114 of 565	20.18%
Frank Howard, Wash. Senators II (AL), 1970	126 of 626	20.13%

Players with Lowest Batting Average for 100-RBI Season

	RBIs	Batting Average
Tony Armas, Bost. Red Sox (AL), 1983	107	.218
Carlos Peña, T.B. Rays (AL), 2009	100	.227
Roy Sievers, Wash. Senators (AL), 1954	102	.232
Joe Carter, S.D. Padres (NL), 1990	115	.232
Curtis Granderson, N.Y. Yankees (AL), 2012	106	.232
Ruben Sierra, Oak. A's (AL), 1993	101	.233
Pedro Alvarez, Pitt. Pirates (NL), 2013	100	.233
Joe Carter, Tor. Blue Jays (AL) ,1997	102	.234
Mark Trumbo, L.A. Angels (AL), 2013	100	.234

continued on next page

	RBIs	Batting Average
Mark McGwire, Oak. A's (AL), 1990	108	.235
Adam Dunn, Cin. Reds (NL)–Ariz. D'backs (NL), 2008	100	.236
Jose Canseco, Tor. Blue Jays (AL), 1998	107	.237
Jeff King, K.C. Royals (AL), 1997	112	.238
Carlton Fisk, Chi. White Sox (AL), 1985	107	.238
Gorman Thomas, Milw. Brewers (AL), 1980	105	.239
Phil Plantier, S.D. Padres (NL), 1993	100	.240
Jose Canseco, Oak. A's (AL), 1986	117	.240
Tony Batista. Mont. Expos (NL), 2004	110	.241
Ron Cey, L.A. Dodgers (NL), 1977	110	.241
Harmon Killebrew, Min. Twins (AL), 1959	105	.242

Players on Last-Place Teams Leading League in RBIs, Season

	RBIs
Wally Berger, Bost. Braves (NL), 1935	130
Roy Sievers, Wash. Senators (AL), 1957	114
Frank Howard, Wash. Senators II (AL), 1970	126
Andre Dawson, Chi. Cubs (NL), 1987	137
Alex Rodriguez, Tex. Rangers (AL), 2002	142

Players Driving in 95 or More Runs in Season Three Times, Never 100

Donn Clendenon (1961–72)	1965	96
	1966	98
	1970	97
Kevin McReynolds (1983–94)	1986	96
	1987	95
	1988	99
Arky Vaughan (1932–43, 1947–48)	1933	97
	1935	99
	1940	95

Runs Scored

Evolution of Runs Scored Record

American League

1901	Nap Lajoie, Phila. A's	145
1911	Ty Cobb, Det. Tigers	147
1920	Babe Ruth, N.Y. Yankees	158
1921	Babe Ruth, N.Y. Yankees	177

National League (Pre-1900)

1876	Ross Barnes, Chi. White Stockings	126
1886	King Kelly, Chi. White Stockings	155
1894	Billy Hamilton, Phila. Phillies	198

National League (Post-1899)

1900	Roy Thomas, Phila. Phillies	132
1901	Jesse Burkett, St.L. Cardinals	142
1925	Kiki Cuyler, Pitt. Pirates	144
1929	Rogers Hornsby, Chi. Cubs	156
1930	Chuck Klein, Phila. Phillies	158

Most Runs Scored by Decade

Pre-1900

1722	Cap Anson
1684	Bid McPhee
1620	Roger Connor
1523	Dan Brouthers
1523	Tom Brown
1523	Billy Hamilton
1492	Harry Stovey
1480	Arlie Latham
1470	Hugh Duffy
1445	Jim O'Rourke

1900–09

1014	Honus Wagner
885	Fred Clarke
862	Roy Thomas
835	Ginger Beaumont
828	Tommy Leach
813	Sam Crawford
807	Jimmy Sheckard
806	Nap Lajoie
799	Fielder Jones
797	Willie Keeler

1910–19

1051	Ty Cobb
991	Eddie Collins
967	Tris Speaker
958	Donie Bush
868	Harry Hooper
765	Joe Jackson
758	Clyde Milan
745	Larry Doyle
733	Home Run Baker
727	Max Carey
727	Jake Daubert

continued on next page

1920–29

1365 Babe Ruth
1195 Rogers Hornsby
1001 Sam Rice
992 Frankie Frisch
962 Harry Heilmann
896 Lu Blue
894 George Sisler
868 Charlie Jamieson
830 Ty Cobb
830 Tris Speaker

1930–39

1257 Lou Gehrig
1244 Jimmie Foxx
1179 Charlie Gehringer
1102 Earl Averill
1095 Mel Ott
1009 Ben Chapman
973 Paul Waner
955 Chuck Klein
930 Al Simmons
885 Joe Cronin

1940–49

951 Ted Williams
815 Stan Musial
803 Bob Elliott
764 Bobby Doerr
758 Lou Boudreau
743 Bill Nicholson
721 Dom DiMaggio
708 Vern Stephens
704 Dixie Walker
684 Joe DiMaggio

1950–59

994 Mickey Mantle
970 Duke Snider
952 Richie Ashburn
948 Stan Musial
902 Nellie Fox
898 Minnie Minoso
898 Eddie Yost
890 Gil Hodges
860 Alvin Dark
848 Yogi Berra

1960–69

1091 Hank Aaron
1050 Willie Mays
1013 Frank Robinson
916 Roberto Clemente
885 Vada Pinson
874 Maury Wills
864 Harmon Killebrew
861 Billy Williams
816 Ron Santo
811 Al Kaline

1970–79

1068 Pete Rose
1020 Bobby Bonds
1005 Joe Morgan
861 Amos Otis
845 Carl Yastrzemski
843 Lou Brock
837 Rod Carew
833 Reggie Jackson
816 Bobby Murcer
792 Johnny Bench

1980–89

1122 Keith Hernandez
957 Robin Yount
956 Dwight Evans
938 Dale Murphy
866 Tim Raines
858 Eddie Murray
845 Willie Wilson
832 Mike Schmidt
828 Paul Molitor
823 Wade Boggs

1990–99

1091 Barry Bonds
1042 Craig Biggio
1002 Ken Griffey Jr.
968 Frank Thomas
965 Rafael Palmeiro
951 Roberto Alomar
950 Chuck Knoblauch
946 Tony Phillips
932 Rickey Henderson
921 Jeff Bagwell

2000–09

1190 Alex Rodriguez
1115 Johnny Damon
1088 Derek Jeter
1071 Albert Pujols
1061 Bobby Abreu
1017 Todd Helton
973 Ichiro Suzuki
961 Carlos Beltran
960 Miguel Tejada
959 Lance Berkman

2010–15

599 Miguel Cabrera
578 Ian Kinsler
569 Jose Bautista
565 Andrew McCutchen
552 Robinson Cano
541 Justin Upton
528 Albert Pujols
522 Austin Jackson
516 Curtis Granderson
511 Adrian Beltre

Players with More Runs Scored Than Games Played, Season (Min. 100 Games)

American League

	Runs	Games	Differential
Babe Ruth, N.Y. Yankees, 1921	177	152	+25
Babe Ruth, N.Y. Yankees, 1920	158	142	+16
Nap Lajoie, Phila. A's, 1901	145	131	+14
Al Simmons, Phila. A's, 1930	152	138	+14
Lou Gehrig, N.Y. Yankees, 1936	167	155	+12
Babe Ruth, N.Y. Yankees, 1928	163	154	+9
Lou Gehrig, N.Y. Yankees, 1932	163	155	+8
Babe Ruth, N.Y. Yankees, 1927	158	151	+7

continued on next page

Jimmie Foxx, Bost. Red Sox, 1939	130	124	+6
Babe Ruth, N.Y. Yankees, 1930	150	145	+5
Babe Ruth, N.Y. Yankees, 1931	149	145	+4
Rickey Henderson, N.Y. Yankees, 1985	146	143	+3
Ty Cobb, Det. Tigers, 1911	147	146	+1

National League (Post-1900)

	Runs	Games	Differential
Chuck Klein, Phila. Phillies, 1930	158	156	+2

Players Scoring 1000 Runs in Career, Never 100 in One Season

	Career Runs	Most in One Season
Torii Hunter (1997–2015)	1391	94 (2007)
Luis Aparicio (1956–73)	1335	98 (1959)
Harold Baines (1980–2001)	1299	89 (1982)
Chili Davis (1981–99)	1240	87 (1984)
Willie Randolph (1975–92)	1239	99 (1980)
Brooks Robinson (1955–77)	1232	91 (1966)
Graig Nettles (1967–88)	1193	99 (1977)
Rusty Staub (1963–85)	1189	98 (1970)
Al Oliver (1968–85)	1189	96 (1974)
Bert Campaneris (1964–81, 1983)	1181	97 (1970)
Paul Konerko (1997–2014)	1162	98 (2005)
Buddy Bell (1972–89)	1151	89 (1979, 1988)
Steve Garvey (1969–87)	1143	95 (1974)
Deacon White (1871–90)	1140	82 (1884)
Gary Gaetti (1981–2000)	1130	95 (1987)
Jack Clark (1975–92)	1118	93 (1987)
Jimmy Dykes (1918–39)	1108	93 (1925)
Edd Roush (1913–29, 1931)	1099	95 (1926)
Aramis Ramirez (1998–2015)	1098	99 (2004)
Garret Anderson (1994–2010)	1084	93 (2002)
Paul Hines (1872–91)	1083	94 (1884)
Bill Buckner (1969–90)	1077	93 (1982)
Ted Simmons (1968–88)	1074	84 (1980)
Mike Cameron (1995–2011)	1064	99 (2001)
Bob Elliott (1939–53)	1064	99 (1948)
Bobby Wallace (1894–1918)	1057	99 (1897)
Tony Fernandez (1983–2000)	1057	91 (1986)
Paul O'Neill (1985–2001)	1041	95 (1998)
Jose Cruz (1970–88)	1036	96 (1984)
Bobby Grich (1970–86)	1033	93 (1976)
Gary Carter (1974–92)	1025	91 (1982)
Kid Gleason (1888–1908, 1912)	1020	95 (1905)
Tino Martinez (1990–2005)	1009	96 (1997)
Robin Ventura (1989–2004)	1006	96 (1996)
Harry Davis (1895–1917)	1001	94 (1906)

Most Runs Scored by Position, Season

American League

First Base	167	Lou Gehrig, N.Y. Yankees, 1936
Second Base	145	Nap Lajoie, Phila. A's, 1901
Third Base	141	Harlond Clift, St.L. Browns, 1936
Shortstop	141	Alex Rodriguez, Sea. Mariners, 1996
Outfield	177	Babe Ruth, N.Y. Yankees, 1921
Catcher	118	Mickey Cochrane, Phila. A's, 1932
Pitcher	31	Jack Coombs, Phila. A's, 1911
Designated Hitter	133	Paul Molitor, Milw. Brewers, 1991

National League

First Base	152	Jeff Bagwell, Hous. Astros, 2000
Second Base	156	Rogers Hornsby, Chi. Cubs, 1929
Third Base	130	Pete Rose, Cin. Reds, 1976
Shortstop	139	Jimmy Rollins, Phila. Phillies, 2008
Outfield	158	Chuck Klein, Phila. Phillies, 1930
Catcher	112	Jason Kendall, Pitt. Pirates, 2000
Pitcher	25	Claude Hendrix, Pitt. Pirates, 1912

Walks

Evolution of Batters' Walks Record

American League

1901	Dummy Hoy, Chi. White Sox	86
1902	Topsy Hartsel, Phila. A's	87
1905	Topsy Hartsel, Phila. A's	121
1920	Babe Ruth, N.Y. Yankees	150
1923	Babe Ruth, N.Y. Yankees	170

National League (Pre-1900)

1876	Ross Barnes, Chi. Cubs	20
1879	Charley Jones, Bost. Beaneaters	29
1881	John Clapp, Cle. Spiders	35
1883	Tom York, Cle. Spiders	37
1884	George Gore, Chi. Cubs	61
1885	Ned Williamson, Chi. Cubs	75
1886	George Gore, Chi. Cubs	102
1890	Cap Anson, Chi. Cubs	113
1892	John Crooks, St.L. Cardinals	136

National League (Post-1900)

1900	Roy Thomas, Phila. Phillies	115
1910	Miller Huggins, St.L. Cardinals	116
1911	Jimmy Sheckard, Chi. Cubs	147
1945	Eddie Stanky, Bklyn. Dodgers	148
1996	Barry Bonds, S.F. Giants	151
1998	Mark McGwire, St.L. Cardinals	162
2001	Barry Bonds, S.F. Giants	177
2002	Barry Bonds, S.F. Giants	198
2004	Barry Bonds, S.F. Giants	232

Players with 1000 Walks, 2000 Hits, and 300 Home Runs, Career

	Walks	Hits	Home Runs
Hank Aaron (1954–76)	1402	3771	755
Jeff Bagwell (1991–2005)	1401	2314	449
Harold Baines (1980–2000)	1054	2855	384
Lance Berkman (1999–2013)	1201	1905	366
Barry Bonds (1986–2007)	2558	2935	762
George Brett (1973–93)	1096	3154	317
Chili Davis (1981–99)	1194	2380	350
Carlos Delgado (1993–2009)	1109	2038	473
Darrell Evans (1969–89)	1605	2223	414
Dwight Evans (1972–91)	1391	2446	385
Jimmie Foxx (1925–42, 1944–45)	1452	2646	534
Lou Gehrig (1923–39)	1508	2721	493
Jason Giambi (1995–2014)	1366	2010	440
Luis Gonzalez (1990–2008)	1155	2591	354
Ken Griffey Jr. (1989–2010)	1312	2781	630
Todd Helton (1997–2013)	1335	2519	369
Rogers Hornsby (1915–37)	1038	2930	301
Reggie Jackson (1967–87)	1375	2584	563
Chipper Jones (1993, 1995–2012)	1512	2726	468
Al Kaline (1953–74)	1277	3007	399

continued on next page

Harmon Killebrew (1954–75)	1559	2086	573
Mickey Mantle (1951–68)	1733	2415	536
Edgar Martinez (1987–2004)	1283	2247	309
Eddie Mathews (1952–68)	1444	2315	512
Willie Mays (1951–52, 1954–73)	1464	3283	660
Willie McCovey (1959–80)	1345	2211	521
Fred McGriff (1986–2004)	1305	2484	493
Eddie Murray (1977–97)	1333	3255	504
Stan Musial (1941–44, 1946–63)	1599	3630	475
Graig Nettles (1967–88)	1088	2225	390
David Ortiz* (1997–)	1239	2303	503
Rafael Palmeiro (1986–2005)	1353	3020	569
Albert Pujols* (2001–)	1165	2666	560
Mel Ott (1926–47)	1708	2876	511
Manny Ramirez (1993–2011)	1329	2574	555
Cal Ripken Jr. (1981–2001)	1129	3164	431
Frank Robinson (1956–76)	1420	2943	586
Alex Rodriguez* (1994–2013, 2015–)	1324	3070	687
Babe Ruth (1914–35)	2062	2873	714
Ron Santo (1960–74)	1108	2254	342
Mike Schmidt (1972–89)	1507	2234	548
Gary Sheffield (1988–2009)	1475	2689	509
Frank Thomas (1990–2008)	1667	2468	521
Jim Thome (1991–2012)	1747	2328	612
Ted Williams (1939–42, 1946–60)	2021	2654	521
Billy Williams (1959–76)	1045	2711	426
Dave Winfield (1973–95)	1216	3110	465
Carl Yastrzemski (1961–83)	1845	3419	452

*Still active.

Players Leading League in Base Hits and Walks, Season

American League

	Hits	Walks
Carl Yastrzemski, Bost. Red Sox, 1963	183	95

National League (Post-1900)

	Hits	Walks
Rogers Hornsby, St.L. Cardinals, 1924	227	89
Richie Ashburn, Phila. Phillies, 1958	215	97
Lenny Dykstra, Phila. Phillies, 1993	194	129

Players with 200 Base Hits and 100 Walks, Season

American League

	Hits	Walks
Ty Cobb, Det. Tigers, 1915	208	118
Babe Ruth, N.Y. Yankees, 1921	204	145
Babe Ruth, N.Y. Yankees, 1923	205	170
Babe Ruth, N.Y. Yankees, 1924	200	142
Lou Gehrig, N.Y. Yankees, 1927	218	109
Lou Gehrig, N.Y. Yankees, 1930	220	101
Lou Gehrig, N.Y. Yankees, 1931	211	117
Jimmie Foxx, Phila. A's, 1932	213	116
Lou Gehrig, N.Y. Yankees, 1932	208	138
Lou Gehrig, N.Y. Yankees, 1934	210	109
Lou Gehrig, N.Y. Yankees, 1936	205	130

National League (Post-1900)

	Hits	Walks
Woody English, Chi. Cubs, 1930	214	100
Hack Wilson, Chi. Cubs, 1930	208	105
Stan Musial, St.L. Cardinals, 1949	207	107
Stan Musial, St.L. Cardinals, 1953	200	105
Todd Helton, Colo. Rockies, 2000	216	103
Todd Helton, Colo. Rockies, 2003	209	111

continued on next page

Lou Gehrig, N.Y. Yankees, 1937	200	127
Hank Greenberg, Det. Tigers, 1937	200	102
Wade Boggs, Bost. Red Sox, 1986	207	105
Wade Boggs, Bost. Red Sox, 1987	200	105
Wade Boggs, Bost. Red Sox, 1988	214	125
Wade Boggs, Bost. Red Sox, 1989	205	107
John Olerud, Tor. Blue Jays, 1993	200	114
Bernie Williams, N.Y. Yankees, 1999	202	100

Players with More Walks Than Hits, Season (Min. 100 Walks)

American League

	Walks	Hits	Differential
Roy Cullenbine, Det. Tigers, 1947	137	104	+33
Eddie Yost, Wash. Senators, 1956	151	119	+32
Max Bishop, Phila. A's, 1929	128	110	+18
Max Bishop, Phila. A's, 1930	128	111	+17
Eddie Joost, Phila. A's, 1949	149	138	+11
Max Bishop, Phila. A's, 1926	116	106	+10
Gene Tenace, Oak. A's, 1974	110	102	+8
Mickey Tettleton, Balt. Orioles, 1990	106	99	+7
Max Bishop, Phila. A's, 1932	110	104	+6
Toby Harrah, Tex. Rangers, 1985	113	107	+6
Mickey Tettleton, Tex. Rangers, 1995	107	102	+5
Jack Cust, Oak. A's, 2007	105	101	+4
Eddie Joost, Phila. A's, 1947	114	111	+3
Ted Williams, Bost. Red Sox, 1954	136	133	+3
Mickey Mantle, N.Y. Yankees, 1968	106	103	+3
Max Bishop, Phila. A's, 1927	105	103	+2
Mickey Mantle, N.Y. Yankees, 1962	122	121	+1

National League (Post-1900)

	Walks	Hits	Differential
Barry Bonds, S.F. Giants, 2004	232	135	+97
Barry Bonds, S.F. Giants, 2002	198	149	+49
Barry Bonds, S.F. Giants, 2007	132	94	+38
Jim Wynn, Atl. Braves, 1976	127	93	+34
Wes Westrum, N.Y. Giants, 1951	104	79	+25
Gene Tenace, S.D. Padres, 1977	125	102	+23
Jack Clark, S.D. Padres, 1989	132	110	+22
Barry Bonds, S.F. Giants, 2001	177	156	+21
Jack Clark, St.L. Cardinals, 1987	136	120	+16
Barry Bonds, S.F. Giants, 2006	115	99	+16
Jim Wynn, Hous. Astros, 1969	148	133	+15
Barry Bonds, S.F. Giants, 2003	148	133	+15
Jack Clark, S.D. Padres, 1990	104	89	+15
Rickey Henderson, S.D. Padres, 1996	125	112	+13
Gene Tenace, S.D. Padres, 1978	101	90	+11
Mark McGwire, St.L. Cardinals, 1998	162	152	+10
Gary Sheffield, Fla. Marlins, 1997	121	111	+10

continued on next page

Morgan Ensberg, Hous. Astros, 2006	101	91	+10
Jim Wynn, L.A. Dodgers, 1975	110	102	+8
Eddie Stanky, Bklyn. Dodgers, 1945	148	143	+5
Eddie Stanky, Bklyn. Dodgers, 1946	137	132	+5
Hank Greenberg, Pitt. Pirates, 1947	104	100	+4
Willie McCovery, S.F. Giants, 1973	105	102	+3

Players Hitting 40 or More Home Runs, with More Home Runs Than Walks, Season

American League

	Home Runs	Walks	Differential
Tony Armas, Bost. Red Sox, 1984	43	32	+11
Juan Gonzalez, Tex. Rangers, 1993	46	37	+9
Juan Gonzalez, Tex. Rangers, 1997	42	33	+9
George Bell, Tor. Blue Jays, 1987	47	39	+8
Juan Gonzalez, Tex. Rangers, 1992	43	35	+8
Hal Trosky, Cle. Indians, 1936	42	36	+6
Tony Batista, Tor. Blue Jays, 2000	41	35	+6
Juan Gonzalez, Tex. Rangers, 1996	47	45	+2

National League (Post-1900)

	Home Runs	Walks	Differential
Dante Bichette, Colo. Rockies, 1995	40	22	+18
Andre Dawson, Chi. Cubs, 1987	49	32	+17
Matt Williams, S.F. Giants, 1994	43	33	+10
Javy Lopez, Atl. Braves, 2003	43	33	+10
Nolan Arenado, Colo. Rockies, 2015	42	34	+8
Orlando Cepeda, S.F. Giants, 1961	46	39	+7
Andres Galarraga, Colo. Rockies, 1996	47	40	+7
Sammy Sosa, Chi. Cubs, 1996	40	34	+6
Vinny Castilla, Colo. Rockies, 1998	46	40	+6
Vinny Castilla, Colo. Rockies, 1996	40	35	+5
Dave Kingman, Chi. Cubs, 1979	48	45	+3

Players with 90 Walks in Each of First Two Seasons

Jack Crooks, Col. Solons (AA)	1890 (96) and 1891 (103)
Alvin Davis, Sea. Mariners (AL)	1984 (97) and 1985 (90)
Ferris Fain, Phila. A's (AL)	1947 (95) and 1948 (113)
Roy Thomas, Phila. Phillies (NL)	1899 (115) and 1900 (115)
Ted Williams, Bost. Red Sox (AL)	1939 (107) and 1940 (96)

Strikeouts

Average League Strikeouts (Minimum 300 At-Bats)

Year	American League	National League	Year	American League	National League
1920	27.51	27.14	1930	31.55	30.82
1921	27.88	24.97	1931	30.26	28.63
1922	25.25	25.19	1932	32.96	30.46
1923	27.29	25.73	1933	31.32	27.60
1924	23.89	25.18	1934	33.30	32.99
1925	23.51	24.85	1935	32.96	33.74
1926	25.54	24.59	1936	33.47	32.04
1927	21.66	24.86	1937	34.35	34.43
1928	25.75	25.70	1938	33.50	32.33
1929	27.87	27.21	1939	32.48	29.37

continued on next page

Year	American League	National League
1940	39.55	32.82
1941	40.66	41.13
1942	32.98	30.98
1943	32.72	32.20
1944	31.60	29.37
1945	31.70	29.79
1946	37.03	31.50
1947	36.98	34.48
1948	33.00	34.83
1949	33.88	32.55

Year	American League	National League
1950	35.92	40.34
1951	35.52	36.22
1952	40.87	39.17
1953	38.61	42.77
1954	38.87	41.62
1955	41.28	41.90
1956	45.62	46.83
1957	42.60	47.12
1958	44.61	44.38
1959	44.90	50.40

Year	American League	National League
1960	47.58	51.60
1961	53.56	51.78
1962	55.89	57.75
1963	60.61	51.88
1964	62.80	58.01
1965	58.71	65.28
1966	60.57	62.76
1967	64.60	59.79
1968	62.32	60.11
1969	58.26	63.79

Year	American League	National League
1970	61.53	63.90
1971	55.34	56.28
1972	55.67	56.07
1973	58.64	59.38
1974	58.11	56.72
1975	58.41	55.90
1976	58.12	52.43
1977	63.05	62.16
1978	57.15	59.10
1979	54.95	57.95

Year	American League	National League
1980	54.09	53.29
1981	38.67	37.63
1982	61.15	60.28
1983	59.00	61.44
1984	61.07	63.53
1985	65.95	60.88
1986	72.93	63.08
1987	72.66	67.55
1988	66.58	64.19
1989	64.31	64.62

Year	American League	National League
1990	64.76	63.97
1991	69.33	65.38
1992	66.04	61.04
1993	69.39	68.12
1994	53.01	54.14
1995	66.45	63.48
1996	77.99	74.92
1997	78.23	76.00
1998	79.09	77.54
1999	75.94	76.91

Year	American League	National League
2000	76.39	75.54
2001	78.22	78.98
2002	75.93	73.33
2003	73.01	74.45
2004	78.03	69.93
2005	75.49	70.66
2006	76.97	76.54
2007	78.87	79.28
2008	75.72	84.49
2009	81.02	82.37

Year	American League	National League
2010	80.47	87.73
2011	81.12	78.55
2012	91.43	87.07
2013	90.09	86.11
2014	89.76	89.96
2015	88.73	84.98

Players with 100 More Career Strikeouts Than Hits (Min. 375 strikeouts)

	Strikeouts	Hits	Differential
Adam Dunn (2001–14)	2379	1631	+748
Mark Reynolds* (2007–)	959	1519	+560
Rob Deer (1984–96)	1409	853	+556
Russell Branyan (1998–2011)	1118	682	+436
Carlos Pena (2001–14)	1577	1146	+431
Ryan Howard* (2004–)	1729	1410	+319
Jack Cust (2001–11)	819	510	+309
Chris Davis* (2008–)	1090	797	+293
Chris Carter* (2010–)	669	377	+292
Gorman Thomas (1973–86)	1339	1051	+288
Dave Nicholson (1960–67)	573	301	+272
Melvin Upton* (2004, 2006–)	1406	1143	+263
Kelly Shoppach (2005–13)	624	361	+263
Drew Stubbs* (2009–)	925	667	+258
Jonny Gomes* (2003–)	1088	835	+253
Bo Jackson (1986–94)	841	598	+243
Dave Kingman (1971–86)	1816	1575	+241
Jarrod Saltalamacchia* (2007–)	860	619	+241
Mark Bellhorn (1997–2007)	723	484	+239
Pete Incaviglia (1986–98)	1277	1043	+234
Jose Hernandez (1991–2006)	1391	1166	+225
Jeff Mathis* (2005–)	593	371	+222
Jim Thome (1991–2012)	2548	2328	+220
Pedro Alvarez* (2010–)	809	590	+219
Mike Cameron (1995–2011)	1901	1700	+201
Mike Napoli* (2006–)	1111	910	+201
Melvin Nieves (1992–98)	483	284	+199
David Ross* (2002–)	681	483	+198
Dan Uggla* (2006–)	1341	1149	+192
Tyler Flowers* (2009–)	464	283	+181
Mickey Tettleton (1984–97)	1307	1132	+175
Ron Karkovice (1986–97)	749	574	+175
Pat Burrell (2000–11)	1564	1393	+171
Danny Espinosa* (2010–)	660	490	+170
Ruben Rivera (1995–2003)	510	343	+167
Brad Wilkerson (2001–08)	947	788	+159
Miguel Olivo (2002–14)	1060	905	+155
J.P. Arencibia* (2010–15)	484	353	+151
Alex Avila* (2009–)	653	504	+149
Greg Maddux (1986–2008)	419	272	+147
Colby Rasmus* (2009–)	921	775	+146
Bill Hall (2002–12)	971	827	+144
Giancarlo Stanton* (2010–)	837	693	+144
Steve Balboni (1981–93)	856	714	+142
Bob Gibson (1959–75)	415	274	+141
Shane Andrews (1995–2002)	515	375	+140
Tom Egan (1965–75)	336	196	+140
Juan Francisco (2009–14)	375	235	+140
Ray Oyler (1965–70)	359	221	+138
Brandon Inge (2001–13)	1306	1166	+140

continued on next page

Don Lock (1962–69)	776	642	+134
Wily Mo Pena (2002–11)	559	425	+134
Jay Buhner (1987–2001)	1406	1273	+133
Jason LaRue (1999–2010)	760	628	+132
Ian Stewart (2007–12, 2014)	473	341	+132
Brandon Moss* (2007–)	699	574	+125
Warren Spahn (1947–65)	487	363	+124
Chris Iannetta* (2006–)	713	590	+123
Craig Wilson (2001–07)	643	527	+116
John Buck (2004–14)	959	844	+115
Todd Hundley (1990–2003)	988	883	+105
Ryan Langerhans (2002, 2005–13)	283	283	+105
Rickie Weeks* (2003, 2005–)	1127	1023	+104
Dean Palmer (1989–2003)	1332	1229	+103
Gary Pettis (1982–92)	958	855	+103

*Still active.

Players with 500 At Bats and Fewer Than 10 Strikeouts, Season

American League (Post-1913)*

	At Bats	Strikeouts
Sam Rice, Wash. Senators, 1929	616	9
Joe Sewell, Cle. Indians, 1925	608	4
Joe Sewell, Cle. Indians, 1928	588	9
Stuffy McInnis, Bost. Red Sox, 1921	584	9
Homer Summa, Cle. Indians, 1926	581	9
Joe Sewell, Cle. Indians, 1926	578	7
Joe Sewell, Cle. Indians, 1929	578	4
Joe Sewell, Cle. Indians, 1927	569	7
Lou Boudreau, Cle. Indians, 1948	560	9
Stuffy McInnis, Cle. Indians, 1922	537	5
Joe Sewell, N.Y. Yankees, 1933	524	4
Tris Speaker, Wash. Senators, 1927	523	8
Mickey Cochrane, Phila. A's, 1929	514	8
Dale Mitchell, Cle. Indians, 1952	511	9
Eddie Collins, Chi. White Sox, 1923	505	8
Joe Sewell, N.Y. Yankees, 1932	503	3

National League (Post-1910)*

	At Bats	Strikeouts
Tommy Holmes, Bost. Braves, 1945	636	9
Charlie Hollocher, Chi. Cubs, 1922	592	5
Stuffy McInnis, Bost. Braves, 1924	581	6
Emil Verban, Phila. Phillies, 1947	540	8
Pie Traynor, Pitt. Pirates, 1929	540	7
Freddy Leach, N.Y. Giants, 1931	515	9
Lloyd Waner, Pitt. Pirates, 1933	500	8

*Official strikeouts first recorded by American League in 1913 and National League in 1910.

Players with 200 Hits and 100 Strikeouts, Season

American League

	Hits	Strikeouts
Hank Greenberg, Det. Tigers, 1937	200	101
Ron LeFlore, Det. Tigers, 1977	212	121
Jim Rice, Bost. Red Sox, 1977	206	120
Jim Rice, Bost. Red Sox, 1978	213	126
Alex Rodriguez, Sea. Mariners, 1996	215	104
Mo Vaughn, Bost. Red Sox, 1996	207	154
Derek Jeter, N.Y. Yankees, 1998	203	119
Alex Rodriguez, Sea. Mariners, 1998	213	121
Mo Vaughn, Bost. Red Sox, 1998	205	144
Derek Jeter, N.Y. Yankees, 1999	219	116
Alex Rodriguez, Tex. Rangers, 2001	201	131
Bret Boone, Sea. Mariners, 2001	206	110
Alfonso Soriano, N.Y. Yankees, 2002	209	157
Michael Young, Tex. Rangers, 2003	204	103
Derek Jeter, N.Y. Yankees, 2005	202	117
Derek Jeter, N.Y. Yankees, 2006	214	102
Derek Jeter, N.Y. Yankees, 2007	206	100
Michael Young, Tex. Rangers, 2007	201	107
Adrian Gonzalez, Bost. Red Sox, 2011	213	119

National League (Post-1900)

	Hits	Strikeouts
Bill White, St.L. Cardinals, 1963	200	100
Dick Allen, Phila. Phillies, 1964	201	138
Lou Brock, Chi. Cubs–St.L. Cardinals, 1964	200	127
Roberto Clemente, Pitt. Pirates, 1966	202	109
Lou Brock, St.L. Cardinals, 1967	206	109
Roberto Clemente, Pitt. Pirates, 1967	209	103
Bobby Bonds, S.F. Giants, 1970	200	189
Lou Brock, St.L. Cardinals, 1971	200	107
Dave Parker, Pitt. Pirates, 1977	215	107
Ryne Sandberg, Chi. Cubs, 1984	200	101
Ellis Burks, Colo. Rockies, 1996	211	114
Craig Biggio, Hous. Astros, 1998	210	113
Chase Utley, Phila. Phillies, 2006	203	132
Matt Holliday, Colo. Rockies, 2007	216	126
Ryan Braun, Milw. Brewers, 2009	203	121

Players with 40 Home Runs and Fewer Than 50 Strikeouts, Season

American League

	Home Runs	Strikeouts
Lou Gehrig, N.Y. Yankees, 1934	49	31

National League

	Home Runs	Strikeouts
Mel Ott, N.Y. Giants, 1929	42	38

continued on next page

Lou Gehrig, N.Y. Yankees, 1936 ..... 49 46
Joe DiMaggio, N.Y. Yankees, 1937 ..... 46 37
Ted Williams, Bost. Red Sox, 1949 ..... 43 48
Al Rosen, Cle. Indians, 1953 ..... 43 48
Johnny Mize, St.L. Cardinals, 1940 ..... 43 49
Johnny Mize, N.Y. Giants, 1947 ..... 51 42
Johnny Mize, N.Y. Giants, 1948 ..... 40 37
Ted Kluszewski, Cin. Reds, 1953 ..... 40 34
Ted Kluszewski, Cin. Reds, 1954 ..... 49 35
Ted Kluszewski, Cin. Reds, 1955 ..... 47 40
Hank Aaron, Atl. Braves, 1969 ..... 44 47
Barry Bonds, S.F. Giants, 2002 ..... 46 47
Barry Bonds, S.F. Giants, 2004 ..... 45 41

Players with 100 More Strikeouts Than RBIs, Season

American League

	Strikeouts	RBIs	Differential
Austin Jackson, Det. Tigers, 2011	181	45	+136
Adam Dunn, Chi. White Sox, 2011	177	42	+135
Austin Jackson, Det. Tigers, 2010	170	41	+129
Adam Dunn, Chi. White Sox, 2012	222	96	+126
Carlos Pena, T.B. Rays, 2012	182	61	+121
Jack Cust, Oak. A's, 2008	197	77	+120
Anthony Gose, Det. Tigers, 2015	145	26	+119
Jack Cust, Oak. A's, 2009	185	70	+115
Mark Reynolds, Balt. Orioles, 2011	196	86	+110
Tyler Flowers, Chi. White Sox, 2014	159	50	+109
Rob Deer, Milw. Brewers, 1987	186	80	+106
Curtis Granderson, Det. Tigers, 2006	174	68	+106
Dave Nicholson, Chi. White Sox, 1963	175	70	+105
Kelly Johnson, Tor. Blue Jays, 2012	159	55	+104
Al Avila, Det. Tigers, 2014	151	47	+104
Steven Souza, T.B. Rays, 2015	144	40	+104
Mike Zunino, Sea. Mariners, 2015	132	28	+104
Adam Dunn, Chi. White Sox, 2013	189	86	+103
Melvin Upton, T.B. Rays, 2010	164	62	+102
Ron LeFlore, Det. Tigers, 1975	139	37	+102
Chris Davis, Balt. Orioles, 2014	173	72	+101

National League

	Strikeouts	RBIs	Differential
Drew Stubbs, Cin. Reds, 2011	205	44	+161
Melvin Upton, Atl. Braves, 2014	173	35	+138
Danny Espinosa, Wash. Nationals, 2012	189	56	+133
Mark Reynolds, Ariz. D'backs, 2010	211	85	+126
Drew Stubbs, Cin. Reds, 2012	166	40	+126
Ian Desmond, Wash. Nationals, 2015	187	62	+125
Melvin Upton, Atl. Braves, 2013	151	26	+125
Mark Reynolds, Ariz. D'backs, 2009	223	102	+121
Dan Uggla, Atl. Braves, 2013	171	55	+116
Joe Pederson, L.A. Dodgers, 2015	170	54	+116
Jose Hernandez, Milw. Brewers, 2002	188	73	+115
Bobby Bonds, S.F. Giants, 1970	189	78	+111
Mark Reynolds, Ariz. D'backs, 2011	196	86	+110
Dexter Fowler, Chi. Cubs, 2015	154	46	+108
Mark Reynolds, Ariz. D'backs, 2008	204	97	+107
Jose Hernandez, Milw. Brewers, 2001	185	78	+107

continued on next page

Rickie Weeks, Milw. Brewers, 2012	169	63	+106
Starling Marte, Pitt. Pirates, 2013	138	35	+103
Adam Dunn, Cin. Reds, 2006	194	92	+102
Jayson Werth, Wash. Nationals, 2011	160	58	+102
Rickie Weeks, Milw. Brewers, 2010	184	83	+101
Chris Johnson, Atl. Braves, 2014	159	58	+101
Chris Owings, Ariz. D'backs, 2015	144	43	+101
Kris Bryant., Chi. Cubs, 2015	199	99	+100
Marlon Byrd, Phila. Phillies, 2014	185	85	+100

Toughest Batters to Strike Out, Career*

	At Bats	Strikeouts
Joe Sewell (1920–33)	7132	113 (1 every 63 at bats)
Lloyd Waner (1927–45)	7772	173 (1 every 45 at bats)
Nellie Fox (1947–65)	9232	216 (1 every 43 at bats)
Tommy Holmes (1942–52)	4992	122 (1 every 41 at bats)
Tris Speaker (1913–28)	7899	220 (1 every 36 at bats)
Stuffy McInnis (1913–27)	6667	189 (1 every 35 at bats)
Frankie Frisch (1919–37)	9112	272 (1 every 34 at bats)
Homer Summa (1920–30)	3001	88 (1 every 34 at bats)
Andy High (1922–34)	4440	130 (1 every 34 at bats)
Dale Mitchell (1946–56)	3984	119 (1 every 34 at bats)
Sam Rice (1915–34)	9269	276 (1 every 33 at bats)
Johnny Cooney (1921–44)	3372	107 (1 every 32 at bats)
Jimmy Brown (1937–46)	3512	110 (1 every 32 at bats)

*Batter strikeouts not recorded until 1913 in American League and 1910 in National League.

Pinch Hits

Highest Batting Average for Pinch Hitter, Season (Min. 25 At Bats)

American League

.467	Smead Jolley, Chi. White Sox, 1931	14-for-30
.457	Rick Miller, Bost. Red Sox, 1983	16-for-35
.452	Elmer Valo, K.C. A's, 1955	14-for-31
.450	Gates Brown, Det. Tigers, 1968	18-for-40
.433	Ted Easterly, Cle. Indians–Chi. White Sox, 1912	13-for-30
.433	Randy Bush, Min. Twins, 1986	13-for-30
.429	Joe Cronin, Bost. Red Sox, 1943	18-for-42
.429	Don Dillard, Cle. Indians, 1961	15-for-35
.419	Dick Williams, Balt. Orioles, 1962	13-for-31
.414	Jose Offerman, Min. Twins, 2004	12-for-29
.412	Bob Hansen, Milw. Brewers, 1974	14-for-34

National League (Post-1900)

.486	Ed Kranepool, N.Y. Mets, 1974	17-for-35
.472	Seth Smith, Colo. Rockies, 2009	17-for-36
.465	Frenchy Bordagaray, St.L. Cardinals, 1938	20-for-43
.455	Bill Spiers, Hous. Astros, 1997	15-for-33
.455	Jorge Piedra, Colo. Rockies, 2005	15-for-33
.452	Jose Pagan, Pitt. Pirates, 1969	19-for-42
.452	Mark Johnson, Pitt. Pirates, 1996	19-for-31
.433	Milt Thompson, Atl. Braves, 1985	13-for-30
.419	Bob Bowman, Phila. Phillies, 1958	13-for-31
.425	Candy Maldonado, S.F. Giants, 1986	17-for-40
.419	Reed Johnson, Chi. Cubs–Atl. Braves, 2012	18-for-43
.419	Richie Ashburn, N.Y. Mets, 1962	13-for-31
.415	Merritt Ranew, Chi. Cubs, 1963	17-for-41

Extra-Base Hits

Evolution of Total Bases Record

American League

1901	Nap Lajoie, Phila. A's	350

continued on next page

1911	Ty Cobb, Det. Tigers	367
1920	George Sisler, St.L. Browns	399
1921	Babe Ruth, N.Y. Yankees	457

National League (Pre-1900)

1876	Ross Barnes, Chi. White Stockings	190
1879	Paul Hines, Pro. Grays	197
1883	Dan Brouthers, Buff. Bisons	243
1884	Abner Dalrymple, Chi. Cubs	263
1886	Dan Brouthers, Det. Wolverines	284
1887	Sam Thompson, Det. Wolverines	308
1893	Ed Delahanty, Phila. Phillies	347
1894	Hugh Duffy, Bost. Beaneaters	374

National League (Post-1900)

1921	Rogers Hornsby, St.L. Cardinals	378
1922	Rogers Hornsby, St.L. Cardinals	450

Players with 100 Extra-Base Hits, Season

	Doubles	Triples	Home Runs	Total
Babe Ruth, N.Y. Yankees (AL), 1921	44	16	59	119
Lou Gehrig, N.Y. Yankees (AL), 1927	52	18	47	117
Chuck Klein, Phila. Phillies (NL), 1930	59	8	40	107
Barry Bonds, S.F. Giants (NL), 2001	32	2	73	107
Todd Helton, Colo. Rockies (NL), 2001	54	2	49	105
Chuck Klein, Phila. Phillies (NL), 1932	50	15	38	103
Hank Greenberg, Det. Tigers (AL), 1937	49	14	40	103
Stan Musial, St.L. Cardinals (NL), 1948	46	18	39	103
Albert Belle, Cle. Indians (AL), 1995	52	1	50	103
Todd Helton, Colo. Rockies (NL), 2000	59	2	42	103
Sammy Sosa, Chi. Cubs (NL), 2001	34	5	64	103
Rogers Hornsby, St.L. Cardinals (NL), 1922	46	14	42	102
Lou Gehrig, N.Y. Yankees (AL), 1930	42	17	41	100
Jimmie Foxx, Phila. A's (AL), 1932	33	9	58	100
Luis Gonzalez, Ariz. D'backs (NL), 2001	36	7	57	100

Players with 400 Total Bases, Season

American League

Babe Ruth, N.Y. Yankees, 1921	457
Lou Gehrig, N.Y. Yankees, 1927	447
Jimmie Foxx, Phila. A's, 1932	438
Lou Gehrig, N.Y. Yankees, 1930	419
Joe DiMaggio, N.Y. Yankees, 1937	418
Babe Ruth, N.Y. Yankees, 1927	417
Lou Gehrig, N.Y. Yankees, 1931	410
Lou Gehrig, N.Y. Yankees, 1934	409
Jim Rice, Bost. Red Sox, 1978	406
Hal Trosky, Cle. Indians, 1936	405
Jimmie Foxx, Phila. A's, 1933	403
Lou Gehrig, N.Y. Yankees, 1936	403

National League (Post-1900)

Rogers Hornsby, St.L. Cardinals, 1922	450
Chuck Klein, Phila. Phillies, 1930	445
Stan Musial, St.L. Cardinals, 1948	429
Sammy Sosa, Chi. Cubs, 2001	425
Hack Wilson, Chi. Cubs, 1930	423
Chuck Klein, Phila. Phillies, 1932	420
Luis Gonzalez, Ariz. D'backs, 2001	419
Babe Herman, Bklyn. Dodgers, 1930	416
Sammy Sosa, Chi. Cubs, 1998	416
Barry Bonds, S.F. Giants, 2001	411
Rogers Hornsby, Chi. Cubs, 1929	409
Larry Walker, Colo. Rockies, 1997	409
Joe Medwick, St.L. Cardinals, 1937	406
Chuck Klein, Phila. Phillies, 1929	405

continued on next page

Todd Helton, Colo. Rockies, 2000 405
Todd Helton, Colo. Rockies, 2001 402
Hank Aaron, Milw. Braves, 1959 400

Evolution of Doubles Record

American League

1901 ..... Nap Lajoie, Phila. A's 48
1904 ..... Nap Lajoie, Cle. Blues 49
1910 ..... Nap Lajoie, Cle. Naps 51
1912 ..... Tris Speaker, Bost. Red Sox 53
1923 ..... Tris Speaker, Cle. Indians 59
1926 ..... George H. Burns, Cle. Indians 64
1931 ..... Earl Webb, Bost. Red Sox 67

National League (Pre-1900)

1876 ..... Ross Barnes, Chi. White Stockings 21
Dick Higham, Har. Dark Blues 21
Paul Hines, Chi. White Stockings 21
1878 ..... Dick Higham, Pro. Grays 22
1879 ..... Charlie Eden, Cle. Spiders 31
1882 ..... King Kelly, Chi. White Stockings 37
1883 ..... Ned Williamson, Chi. White Stockings 49
1894 ..... Hugh Duffy, Bost. Beaneaters 51
1899 ..... Ed Delahanty, Phila. Phillies 55

National League (Post-1899)

1900 ..... Honus Wagner, Pitt. Pirates 45
1922 ..... Rogers Hornsby, St.L. Cardinals 46
1928 ..... Paul Waner, Pitt. Pirates 50
1929 ..... Johnny Frederick, Bklyn. Dodgers 52
1930 ..... Chuck Klein, Pitt. Pirates 59
1932 ..... Paul Waner, Pitt. Pirates 62
1936 ..... Joe Medwick, St.L. Cardinals 64

Players Hitting 40 Home Runs and 40 Doubles, Season

American League

	Home Runs	Doubles
Babe Ruth, N.Y. Yankees, 1921	59	44
Babe Ruth, N.Y. Yankees, 1923	41	45
Lou Gehrig, N.Y. Yankees, 1927	47	52
Lou Gehrig, N.Y. Yankees, 1930	41	42
Lou Gehrig, N.Y. Yankees 1934	49	40
Hal Trosky, Cle. Indians, 1936	42	45
Hank Greenberg, Det. Tigers, 1937	40	49
Hank Greenberg, Det. Tigers, 1940	41	50
Albert Belle, Cle. Indians, 1995	50	52
Albert Belle, Chi. White Sox, 1998	49	48
Juan Gonzalez, Tex. Rangers, 1998	45	50
Shawn Green, Tor. Blue Jays, 1999	42	45
Frank Thomas, Chi. White Sox, 2000	43	44
Carlos Delgado, Tor. Blue Jays, 2000	41	57
Manny Ramirez, Bost. Red Sox, 2004	43	44
David Ortiz, Bost. Red Sox, 2004	41	47
David Ortiz, Bost. Red Sox, 2005	47	40

continued on next page

Mark Teixeira, Tex. Rangers, 2005	43	41
Miguel Cabrera, Det. Tigers, 2012	44	40
Chris Davis, Balt. Orioles, 2013	53	42
Josh Donaldson, Tor. Blue Jays, 2015	41	41

National League (Post-1900)

	Home Runs	Doubles
Rogers Hornsby, St.L. Cardinals, 1922	42	46
Chuck Klein, Phila. Phillies, 1929	43	45
Chuck Klein, Phila. Phillies, 1930	40	59
Willie Stargell, Pitt. Pirates, 1973	44	43
Ellis Burks, Colo. Rockies, 1996	40	45
Larry Walker, Colo. Rockies, 1997	49	46
Jeff Bagwell, Hous. Astros, 1997	43	40
Chipper Jones, Atl. Braves, 1999	45	41
Todd Helton, Colo. Rockies, 2000	42	59
Richard Hidalgo, Hous. Astros, 2000	44	42
Todd Helton, Colo. Rockies, 2001	49	54
Albert Pujols, St.L. Cardinals, 2003	43	51
Albert Pujols, St.L. Cardinals, 2004	46	51
Derrek Lee, Chi. Cubs, 2005	46	50
Alfonso Soriano, Wash. Nationals, 2006	46	41
Albert Pujols, St.L. Cardinals, 2009	47	45
Nolan Arenado, Colo. Rockies, 2015	42	43

Evolution of Triples Record

American League

1901	Jimmy Williams, Balt. Orioles	21
1903	Sam Crawford, Det. Tigers	25
1912	Joe Jackson, Cle. Indians	26

National League (Pre-1900)

1876	Ross Barnes, Chi. White Stockings	14
1882	Roger Connor, Troy Haymakers	18
1884	Buck Ewing, N.Y. Gothams	20
1887	Sam Thompson, Det. Wolverines	23
1890	Long John Reilly, Cin. Reds	26
1893	Perry Werden, St.L. Cardinals	29
1894	Heinie Reitz, Balt. Orioles	31

National League (Post-1899)

1900	Honus Wagner, Pitt. Pirates	22
1911	Larry Doyle, N.Y. Giants	25
1912	Owen Wilson, Pitt. Pirates	36

Leaders in Doubles and Triples, Season

American League

	Doubles	Triples
Ty Cobb, Det. Tigers, 1908	36	20
Ty Cobb, Det. Tigers, 1911	47	24
Ty Cobb, Det. Tigers, 1917	44	23

continued on next page

Bobby Veach, Det. Tigers, 1919	45	17
Charlie Gehringer, Det. Tigers, 1929	45	19
Joe Vosmik, Cle. Indians, 1935	47	20
Zoilo Versalles, Min. Twins, 1964	45	12
Cesar Tovar, Min. Twins, 1970	36	13

National League (Post-1900)

	Doubles	Triples
Honus Wagner, Pitt. Pirates, 1900	45	22
Honus Wagner, Pitt. Pirates, 1908	39	19
Rogers Hornsby, St.L. Cardinals, 1921	44	18
Stan Musial, St.L. Cardinals, 1943	48	20
Stan Musial, St.L. Cardinals, 1946	50	20
Stan Musial, St.L. Cardinals, 1948	46	18
Stan Musial, St.L. Cardinals, 1949	41	13
Lou Brock, St.L. Cardinals, 1968	46	14

Leaders in Doubles and Home Runs, Season

American League

	Doubles	Home Runs
Nap Lajoie, Phila. A's, 1901	48	14
Tris Speaker, Bost. Red Sox, 1912	53	10 (Tie)
Hank Greenberg, Det. Tigers, 1940	50	41
Ted Williams, Bost. Red Sox, 1949	39	43
Albert Belle, Cle. Indians, 1995	52	50

National League (Post-1900)

	Doubles	Home Runs
Heinie Zimmerman, Chi. Cubs, 1912	41	14
Rogers Hornsby, St.L. Cardinals, 1922	46	42
Chuck Klein, Phila. Phillies, 1933	44	28
Joe Medwick, St.L. Cardinals, 1937	56	31 (Tie)
Willie Stargell, Pitt. Pirates, 1973	43	44

Leaders in Triples and Home Runs, Season

American League

	Triples	Home Runs
Mickey Mantle, N.Y. Yankees, 1955	11 (Tie)	37
Jim Rice, Bost. Red Sox, 1978	15	46

National League (Post-1900)

	Triples	Home Runs
Tommy Leach, Pitt. Pirates, 1902	22	6
Harry Lumley, Bklyn. Dodgers, 1904	18	9
Jim Bottomley, St.L. Cardinals, 1928	20	31 (Tie)
Willie Mays, N.Y. Giants, 1955	15 (Tie)	51

Players Hitting 20 Home Runs, 20 Triples, and 20 Doubles, Season

American League

	Doubles	Triples	Home Runs
Jeff Heath, Cle. Indians, 1941	32	20	24
George Brett, K.C. Royals, 1979	42	20	23

National League (Post-1900)

	Doubles	Triples	Home Runs
Curtis Granderson, Det. Tigers, 2007	38	23	23
Frank Schulte, Chi. Cubs, 1911	30	21	21
Jim Bottomley, St.L. Cardinals, 1928	42	20	31
Willie Mays, N.Y. Giants, 1957	26	20	35
Jimmy Rollins, Phila. Phillies, 2007	38	20	30

Players Leading League in Doubles, Triples, and Home Runs During Career (Post-1900)

Jim Bottomley	Doubles: 1925 (44) and 1926 (40) Triples: 1928 (20) Home Runs: 1928 (31)
Ty Cobb	Doubles: 1908 (36), 1911 (47), and 1917 (44) Triples: 1908 (20), 1911 (24), 1917 (24), and 1918 (14) Home Runs: 1909 (9)
Sam Crawford	Doubles: 1909 (35) Triples: 1902 (23), 1903 (25), 1910 (19), 1913 (23), 1914 (26), and 1915 (19) Home Runs: 1908 (7)
Lou Gehrig	Doubles: 1927 (52) Triples: 1926 (20) Home Runs: 1931 (46), 1934 (49), and 1936 (49)
Rogers Hornsby	Doubles: 1920 (44), 1921 (44), and 1922 (46) Triples: 1917 (17) and 1921 (18) Home Runs: 1922 (42) and 1925 (39)
Johnny Mize	Doubles: 1941 (39) Triples: 1938 (16) Home Runs: 1939 (28), 1940 (43), 1947 (51-Tie), and 1948 (40-Tie)

Players Since World War II with 100 Doubles, Triples, Home Runs, and Stolen Bases, Career

	Doubles	Triples	Home Runs	Stolen Bases
George Brett (1973–93)	665	137	317	201
Lou Brock (1961–79)	486	141	149	938
Carl Crawford* (2002–)	307	122	136	480
Johnny Damon (1995–2012)	307	122	136	480
Willie Davis (1960–79)	395	138	182	398
Steve Finley (1989–2007)	449	124	304	320
Kenny Lofton (1991–2007)	383	116	130	622
Willie Mays (1951–73)	523	140	660	338
Paul Molitor (1978–98)	605	114	234	504
Vada Pinson (1958–75)	485	127	256	305
Tim Raines (1979–2002)	430	113	170	808
Jose Reyes* (2003–)	337	117	118	479

continued on next page

Jimmy Rollins* (2000–)	503	114	229	465
Pete Rose (1963–86)	746	135	160	198
Juan Samuel (1983–98)	287	102	161	396
Mickey Vernon (1939–60)	490	120	172	137
Robin Yount (1974–93)	583	126	251	271

* Still active.

Players with 200 Hits and Fewer than 40 Extra-Base Hits, Season

American League

	Hits	Extra-Base Hits
Cesar Tovar, Min. Twins, 1971	204	33
Ichiro Suzuki, Sea. Mariners, 2008	213	33
Nellie Fox, Chi. White Sox, 1954	201	34
Steve Sax, N.Y. Yankees, 1989	205	34
Johnny Pesky, Bost. Red Sox, 1947	207	35
Ichiro Suzuki, Sea. Mariners, 2007	238	35
Ichiro Suzuki, Sea. Mariners, 2004	262	37
Rod Carew, Min. Twins, 1974	218	38
Ichiro Suzuki, Sea. Mariners, 2006	224	38
Harvey Kuenn, Det. Tigers, 1954	201	39
Ichiro Suzuki, Sea. Mariners, 2010	214	39

National League (Post-1900)

	Hits	Extra-Base Hits
Lloyd Waner, Pitt. Pirates, 1927	223	25
Maury Wills, L.A. Dodgers, 1962	208	29
Matty Alou, Pitt. Pirates, 1970	201	30
Willie Keeler, Bklyn. Dodgers, 1901	202	33
Curt Flood, St.L. Cardinals, 1964	211	33
Milt Stock, St.L. Cardinals, 1920	204	34
Richie Ashburn, Phila. Phillies, 1953	205	36
Tony Gwynn, S.D. Padres, 1984	213	36
Juan Pierre, Fla. Marlins, 2003	204	36
Juan Pierre, Fla. Marlins, 2004	221	37
Milt Stock, Bklyn. Dodgers, 1925	202	38
Chick Fullis, Phila. Phillies, 1933	200	38
Tony Gwynn, S.D. Padres, 1989	203	38
Richie Ashburn, Phila. Phillies, 1958	215	39
Ralph Garr, Atl. Braves, 1971	219	39
Dave Cash, Phila. Phillies, 1974	213	39
Juan Pierre, Colo. Rockies, 2001	202	39
Dee Gordon, Mia. Marlins, 2015	205	36

Most Doubles by Position, Season

American League

First Base	64	George H. Burns, Cle. Indians, 1926
Second Base	60	Charlie Gehringer, Det. Tigers, 1936
Third Base	56	George Kell, Det. Tigers, 1950
Shortstop	56	Nomar Garciaparra, Bost. Red Sox, 2002
Outfield	67	Earl Webb, Bost. Red Sox, 1931
Catcher	47	Ivan Rodriguez, Tex. Rangers, 1996
Pitcher	13	Smoky Joe Wood, Bost. Red Sox, 1912
	13	Red Ruffing, Bost. Red Sox, 1928
Designated Hitter	52	Edgar Martinez, Sea. Mariners, 1995
	52	Edgar Martinez, Sea. Mariners, 1996
	52	David Ortiz, Bost. Red Sox, 2007

National League (Post-1900)

First Base	59	Todd Helton, Colo. Rockies, 2000
Second Base	57	Billy Herman, Chi. Cubs, 1935 and 1936
Third Base	53	Jeff Cirillo, Colo. Rockies, 2000
	53	Freddie Sanchez, Pitt. Pirates, 2006
Shortstop	54	Mark Grudzielanek, Mont. Expos, 1997
Outfield	64	Joe Medwick, St.L. Cardinals, 1936
Catcher	46	Jonathan Lucroy, Milw. Brewers, 2014
Pitcher	11	Red Lucas, Cin. Reds, 1932

Most Triples by Position, Season

American League

First Base	20	Lou Gehrig, N.Y. Yankees, 1926
Second Base	22	Snuffy Stirnweiss, N.Y. Yankees, 1945
Third Base	22	Bill Bradley, Cle. Indians, 1903
Shortstop	21	Bill Keister, Balt. Orioles, 1901
Outfield	26	Joe Jackson, Cle. Indians, 1912
	26	Sam Crawford, Det. Tigers, 1914

National League (Post-1900)

First Base	22	Jake Daubert, Cin. Reds, 1922
Second Base	25	Larry Doyle, N.Y. Giants, 1911
Third Base	22	Tommy Leach, Pitt. Pirates, 1902
Shortstop	20	Honus Wagner, Pitt. Pirates, 1912
	20	Jimmy Rollins, Phila. Phillies, 2007
Outfield	36	Owen Wilson, Pitt. Pirates, 1912

continued on next page

Catcher.....12.....Mickey Cochrane, Phila. A's, 1928
12.....Eddie Ainsmith, Det. Tigers, 1919
Pitcher.....6.....Jesse Tannehill, N.Y. Yankees, 1904
6.....Walter Johnson, Wash. Senators, 1913
Designated Hitter.....13.....Paul Molitor, Milw. Brewers, 1991

Catcher.....13.....Johnny Kling, Chi. Cubs, 1903
13.....Tim McCarver, St.L. Cardinals, 1966
Pitcher.....6.....Claude Hendrix, Pitt. Pirates, 1912

Most Total Bases by Position, Season

American League

First Base.....447.....Lou Gehrig, N.Y. Yankees, 1927
Second Base..381...Alfonso Soriano, N.Y. Yankees, 2002
Third Base.....376....Alex Rodriguez, N.Y. Yankees, 2007
Shortstop.....393.....Alex Rodriguez, Tex. Rangers, 2001
Outfield.....457.....Babe Ruth, N.Y. Yankees, 1921
Catcher.....335.....Ivan Rodriguez, Tex. Rangers, 1999
Pitcher.....80.....Wes Ferrell, Cle. Indians, 1931
Designated Hitter.....363.....David Ortiz, Bost. Red Sox, 2005

National League (Post-1900)

First Base.....405.....Todd Helton, Colo. Rockies, 2000
Second Base...450.Rogers Hornsby, St.L. Cardinals, 1922
Third Base.....380.....Vinny Castilla, Colo. Rockies, 1998
Shortstop.....380.....Jimmy Rollins, Phila. Phillies, 2007
Outfield.....445.....Chuck Klein, Phila. Phillies, 1930
Catcher.....355.....Mike Piazza, L.A. Dodgers, 1997
355.....Johnny Bench, Cin. Reds, 1970
Pitcher.....74..Don Newcombe, Bklyn. Dodgers, 1955

Stolen Bases

Evolution of Stolen Base Record

American League

1901.....Frank Isbell, Chi. White Sox.....52
1907.....Ty Cobb, Det. Tigers.....53
1909.....Ty Cobb, Det. Tigers.....76
1910.....Eddie Collins, Phila. A's.....81
1911.....Ty Cobb, Det. Tigers.....83
1912.....Clyde Milan, Wash. Senators.....88
1915.....Ty Cobb, Det. Tigers.....96
1980.....Rickey Henderson, Oak. A's.....100
1982.....Rickey Henderson, Oak. A's.....130

National League (Pre-1900)

1886.....Ed Andrews, Phila. Phillies.....56
1887.....Monte Ward, N.Y. Gothams.....111

National League (Post-1899)

1900.....George Van Haltren, N.Y. Giants.....45
Patsy Donovan, St.L. Cardinals
1901.....Honus Wagner, Pitt. Pirates.....49
1903.....Jimmy Sheckard, Bklyn. Dodgers.....67
Frank Chance, Chi. Cubs.....67
1910.....Bob Bescher, Cin. Reds.....70
1911.....Bob Bescher, Cin. Reds.....81
1962.....Maury Wills, L.A. Dodgers.....104
1974.....Lou Brock, St.L. Cardinals.....118

Most Stolen Bases by Position, Season

American League

First Base ..... 52 ..... Frank Isbell, Chi. White Sox, 1901
Second Base .. 81 ..... Eddie Collins, Phila. A's, 1910
Third Base ..... 74 ..... Fritz Maisel, N.Y. Yankees, 1914
Shortstop ..... 62 ..... Bert Campaneris, Oak. A's, 1968
Outfield ..... 130 ..... Rickey Henderson, Oak. A's, 1982
Catcher ..... 36 ..... John Wathan, K.C. Royals, 1982
Pitcher ..... 10 ... Nixey Callahan, Chi. White Sox, 1901
Designated Hitter ..... 22 ..... Hal McRae, K.C. Royals, 1976
22 ..... Paul Molitor, Tor. Blue Jays, 1993
22 ..... Gary Sheffield, Det. Tigers, 2007

National League (Post-1900)

First Base ..... 67 ..... Frank Chance, Chi. Cubs, 1903
Second Base ... 77 ..... Davey Lopes, L.A. Dodgers, 1975
Third Base ..... 59 ..... Art Devlin, N.Y. Giants, 1905
Shortstop ..... 104 ..... Maury Wills, L.A. Dodgers, 1962
Outfield ..... 118 ..... Lou Brock, St.L. Cardinals, 1974
Catcher ..... 26 ..... Jason Kendall, Pitt. Pirates, 1998
Pitcher ..... 8 ..... Bill Dinneen, Bost. Beaneaters, 1901

Most Stolen Bases by Decade

Pre-1900

862 ..... Billy Hamilton
741 ..... Arlie Latham
657 ..... Tom Brown
568 ..... Bid McPhee
558 ..... Dummy Hoy
548 ..... Hugh Duffy
540 ..... Monte Ward
509 ..... Harry Stovey
494 ..... George Van Haltren
473 ..... Mike Griffin

1900–09

487 ..... Honus Wagner
359 ..... Frank Chance
305 ..... Sam Mertes
295 ..... Jimmy Sheckard
275 ..... Elmer Flick
252 ..... Jimmy Slagle
250 ..... Frank Isbell
239 ..... Fred Clarke
239 ..... Wid Conroy
239 ..... Fielder Jones

1910–19

576 ..... Ty Cobb
489 ..... Eddie Collins
434 ..... Clyde Milan
392 ..... Max Carey
364 ..... Bob Bescher
340 ..... Tris Speaker
324 ..... Donie Bush
293 ..... George J. Burns
286 ..... Buck Herzog
285 ..... Burt Shotton

1920–29

346 ..... Max Carey
310 ..... Frankie Frisch
254 ..... Sam Rice
214 ..... George Sisler
210 ..... Kiki Cuyler
180 ..... Eddie Collins
175 ..... Johnny Mostil
167 ..... Bucky Harris
145 ..... Cliff Heathcote
144 ..... Jack Smith

1930–39

269 ..... Ben Chapman
176 ..... Bill Werber
158 ..... Lyn Lary
158 ..... Gee Walker
136 ..... Pepper Martin
118 ..... Kiki Cuyler
115 ..... Roy Johnson
101 ..... Charlie Gehringer
100 ..... Pete Fox
100 ..... Stan Hack

1940–49

285 ..... George Case
130 ..... Snuffy Stirnweiss
126 ..... Wally Moses
117 ..... Johnny Hopp
108 ..... Pee Wee Reese
108 ..... Mickey Vernon
93 ..... Joe Kuhel
91 ..... Luke Appling
90 ..... Bob Dillinger
88 ..... Jackie Robinson

1950–59

179 ..... Willie Mays
167 ..... Minnie Minoso
158 ..... Richie Ashburn
150 ..... Jim Rivera
134 ..... Luis Aparicio
134 ..... Jackie Jensen
132 ..... Jim Gilliam
124 ..... Pee Wee Reese
121 ..... Billy Bruton
109 ..... Jackie Robinson

1960–69

535 ..... Maury Wills
387 ..... Lou Brock
342 ..... Luis Aparicio
292 ..... Bert Campaneris
240 ..... Willie Davis
208 ..... Tommy Harper
204 ..... Hank Aaron
202 ..... Vada Pinson
161 ..... Don Buford
157 ..... Tony Taylor

1970–79

551 ..... Lou Brock
488 ..... Joe Morgan
427 ..... Cesar Cedeno
380 ..... Bobby Bonds
375 ..... Davey Lopes
344 ..... Fred Patek
336 ..... Bert Campaneris
324 ..... Billy North
294 ..... Ron LeFlore
294 ..... Amos Otis

1980–89

838 ..... Rickey Henderson
583 ..... Tim Raines
472 ..... Vince Coleman
451 ..... Willie Wilson
364 ..... Ozzie Smith

1990–99

478 ..... Otis Nixon
463 ..... Rickey Henderson
433 ..... Kenny Lofton
393 ..... Delino DeShields
381 ..... Marquis Grissom

2000–09

459 ..... Juan Pierre
362 ..... Carl Crawford
341 ..... Ichiro Suzuki
326 ..... Jimmy Rollins
301 ..... Jose Reyes

continued on next page

333 ..... Steve Sax
331 ..... Lonnie Smith
307 ..... Brett Butler
293 ..... Mookie Wilson
284 ..... Dave Collins
343 ..... Barry Bonds
335 ..... Chuck Knoblauch
319 ..... Craig Biggio
311 ..... Roberto Alomar
297 ..... Lance Johnson
295 ..... Bobby Abreu
280 ..... Chone Figgins
276 ..... Luis Castillo
271 ..... Rafael Furcal
266 ..... Scott Podsednik

2010–15

229 ..... Rajai Davis
205 ..... Michael Bourn
188 ..... Dee Gordon
184 ..... Elvis Andrus
178 ..... Jose Reyes
176 ..... Ben Revere
172 ..... Jacoby Ellsbury
169 ..... Jose Altuve
163 ..... Brett Gardner
162 ..... Coco Crisp
162 ..... Carlos Gomez

Teammates Combining for 125 Stolen Bases, Season

American League

Rickey Henderson (130) and Davey Lopes (28), Oak. A's, 1982 158
Rickey Henderson (108) and Mike Davis (33), Oak. A's, 1983 141
Clyde Milan (75) and Danny Moeller (62), Wash. Senators, 1913 137
Ty Cobb (96) and Donie Bush (35), Det. Tigers, 1915 131
Ty Cobb (76) and Donie Bush (53), Det. Tigers, 1909 129
Bill North (75) and Bert Campaneris (54), Oak. A's, 1976 129
Rickey Henderson (100) and Dwayne Murphy (26), Oak. A's, 1980 126

National League (Post-1900)

Vince Coleman (110) and Willie McGee (56), St.L. Cardinals, 1985 166
Ron LeFlore (96) and Rodney Scott (63), Mont. Expos, 1980 159
Vince Coleman (109) and Ozzie Smith (43), St.L. Cardinals, 1987 152
Lou Brock (118) and Bake McBride (30), St.L. Cardinals, 1974 148
Vince Coleman (107) and Ozzie Smith (31), St.L. Cardinals, 1986 138
Vince Coleman (81) and Ozzie Smith (57), St.L. Cardinals, 1988 138
Maury Wills (104) and Willie Davis (32), L.A. Dodgers, 1962 136

Players Stealing 30 Bases for 10 Consecutive Seasons

	Seasons
Rickey Henderson, 1979–93	15
Lou Brock, 1964–77	14
Ty Cobb, 1907–18	12
Tim Raines, 1981–92	12
Honus Wagner, 1899–1909	11
Willie Wilson, 1978–88	11
Brett Butler, 1983–93	11
Bert Campaneris, 1965–74	10
Otis Nixon, 1988–97	10
Juan Pierre, 2001–10	10

Players Leading League in Stolen Bases and Total Bases, Season

American League

	Stolen Bases	Total Bases
Ty Cobb, Det. Tigers, 1907	49	286
Ty Cobb, Det. Tigers, 1909	76	296
Ty Cobb, Det. Tigers, 1911	83	367
Ty Cobb, Det. Tigers, 1915	96	274
Ty Cobb, Det. Tigers, 1917	55	336
Snuffy Stirnweiss, N.Y. Yankees, 1945	33	301

continued on next page

National League (Post-1900)

	Stolen Bases	Total Bases
Honus Wagner, Pitt. Pirates, 1904	53	255
Honus Wagner, Pitt. Pirates, 1907	61	264
Honus Wagner, Pitt. Pirates, 1908	53	308
Chuck Klein, Phila. Phillies, 1932	20	420

Players with 200 Home Runs and 200 Stolen Bases, Career

	Home Runs	Stolen Bases
Hank Aaron (1954–76)	755	240
Bobby Abreu (1996–2014)	288	400
Roberto Alomar (1988–2004)	210	474
Brady Anderson (1988–2002)	210	315
Jeff Bagwell (1991–2005)	449	202
Don Baylor (1970–88)	338	285
Carlos Beltran* (1998–)	392	311
Craig Biggio (1988–2007)	291	414
Barry Bonds (1986–2007)	762	514
Bobby Bonds (1968–81)	332	461
George Brett (1973–93)	317	201
Mike Cameron (1995–2011)	278	297
Jose Canseco (1985–2001)	462	200
Joe Carter (1983–98)	396	231
Johnny Damon (1995–2012)	235	408
Eric Davis (1984–94, 1996–2001)	282	349
Andre Dawson (1976–96)	438	314
Steve Finley (1989–2007)	304	320
Ron Gant (1987–2003)	321	243
Kirk Gibson (1979–95)	255	284
Marquis Grissom (1989–2005)	227	429
Rickey Henderson (1979–2003)	297	1406
Reggie Jackson (1967–87)	563	228
Derek Jeter (1996–2014)	260	358
Howard Johnson (1982–95)	228	231
Ray Lankford (1990–2002, 2004)	238	258
Willie Mays (1951–52, 1954–73)	660	338
Paul Molitor (1978–98)	234	504
Raul Mondesi (1993–2005)	271	229
Joe Morgan (1963–84)	268	689
Vada Pinson (1958–75)	256	305
Hanley Ramirez* (2005–)	210	267
Frank Robinson (1956–76)	586	204
Alex Rodriguez* (1994–2013, 2015–)	687	326
Jimmy Rollins* (2000–)	229	465
Ryne Sandberg (1981–97)	282	344
Reggie Sanders (1991–2007)	305	304
Gary Sheffield (1988–2009)	509	253
Alfonso Soriano (1999–2014)	412	289
Sammy Sosa (1989–2005, 2007)	609	234
Darryl Strawberry (1983–99)	335	221
Larry Walker (1989–2005)	383	230
Devon White (1985–2001)	208	346
Dave Winfield (1973–88, 1990–95)	465	223
Jimmy Wynn (1963–77)	291	225
Robin Yount (1974–93)	251	271

*Still active.

Players with 400 Home Runs and 10 Steals of Home, Career

	Home Runs	Steals of Home
Lou Gehrig	493	15
Babe Ruth	714	10

Players with 200 Hits, 20 Home Runs, and 20 Stolen Bases, Season

American League

	Hits	Home Runs	Stolen Bases
Joe Carter, Cle. Indians, 1986	200	29	29
Kirby Puckett, Min. Twins, 1986	223	31	20
Alan Trammell, Det. Tigers, 1987	205	28	21
Paul Molitor, Tor. Blue Jays, 1993	211	22	22
Nomar Garciaparra, Bost. Red Sox, 1997	209	30	22
Alex Rodriguez, Sea. Mariners, 1998	213	42	46
Darin Erstad, Ana. Angels, 2000	240	25	28
Alfonso Soriano, N.Y. Yankees, 2002	209	39	41
Jacoby Ellsbury, Bost. Red Sox, 2011	212	32	39
Michael Brantley, Cle. Indians, 2014	200	20	23

National League

	Hits	Home Runs	Stolen Bases
Babe Herman, Bklyn. Dodgers, 1929	217	21	21
Chuck Klein, Phila. Phillies, 1932	226	38	20
Willie Mays, S.F. Giants, 1958	208	29	31
Vada Pinson, Cin. Reds, 1959	205	20	21
Hank Aaron, Milw. Braves, 1963	201	44	31
Vada Pinson, Cin. Reds, 1963	204	22	27
Vada Pinson, Cin. Reds, 1965	205	22	21
Lou Brock, St.L. Cardinals, 1967	206	21	52
Bobby Bonds, S.F. Giants, 1970	200	26	48
Marquis Grissom, Atl. Braves, 1996	207	23	28
Ellis Burks, Colo. Rockies, 1996	211	40	32
Larry Walker, Colo. Rockies, 1997	208	49	33
Craig Biggio, Hous. Astros, 1998	210	20	50
Vladimir Guerrero, Mont. Expos, 2002	206	39	40
Hanley Ramirez, Fla. Marlins, 2007	212	29	51
Ryan Braun, Milw. Brewers, 2009	203	32	20

Players with 10 Doubles, Triples, Home Runs, and Steals in Each of First Three Seasons in Majors

		Doubles	Triples	Home Runs	Steals
Ben Chapman	N.Y. Yankees (AL), 1930	31	10	10	14
	N.Y. Yankees (AL), 1931	28	11	17	61
	N.Y. Yankees (AL), 1932	41	15	10	38
Juan Samuel	Phila. Phillies (NL), 1984	36	19	15	72
	Phila. Phillies (NL), 1985	31	13	19	53
	Phila. Phillies (NL), 1986	36	12	16	42
	Phila. Phillies (NL), 1987	37	15	28	35

Players Who Have Stolen Second, Third, and Home in Same Inning

American League

Dave Fultz, Phila. A's, Sept. 4, 1902
Wild Bill Donovan, Det. Tigers, May 7, 1906
Bill Coughlin, Det. Tigers, June 4, 1906
Ty Cobb, Det. Tigers, July 22, 1909
Ty Cobb, Det. Tigers, July 12, 1911
Ty Cobb, Det. Tigers, July 4, 1912
Joe Jackson, Cle. Indians, Aug. 11, 1912
Eddie Collins, Phila. A's, Sept. 22, 1912
Eddie Ainsmith, Wash. Senators, June 26, 1913
Red Faber, Chi. White Sox, July 14, 1915
Don Moeller, Wash. Senators, July 19, 1915
Fritz Maisel, N.Y. Yankees, Aug. 17, 1915
Buck Weaver, Chi. White Sox, Sept. 6, 1919
Bobby Roth, Wash. Senators, May 31, 1920
Bob Meusel, N.Y. Yankees, May 16, 1927
Jack Tavener, Det. Tigers, July 10, 1927
Jack Tavener, Det. Tigers, July 25, 1928
Don Kolloway, Chi. White Sox, June 28, 1941
Rod Carew, Min. Twins, May 18, 1969
Dave Nelson, Tex. Rangers, Aug. 30, 1974
Paul Molitor, Milw. Brewers, July 26, 1987
Devon White, Cal. Angels, Sept. 9, 1989
Chris Stynes, K.C. Royals, May 12, 1996

National League (Post-1900)

Honus Wagner, Pitt. Pirates, Sept. 25, 1907
Hans Lobert, Cin. Reds, Sept. 27, 1908
Honus Wagner, Pitt. Pirates, May 2, 1909
Dode Paskert, Cin. Reds, May 23, 1910
Wilbur Good, Chi. Cubs, Aug. 18, 1915
Jim Johnstone, Bklyn. Dodgers, Sept. 22, 1916
Greasy Neale, Cin. Reds, Aug. 15, 1919
Max Carey, Pitt. Pirates, Aug. 13, 1923
Max Carey, Pitt. Pirates, May 26, 1925
Harvey Hendrick, Bklyn. Dodgers, June 12, 1928
Pete Rose, Phila. Phillies, May 11, 1980
Dusty Baker, S.F. Giants, June 27, 1984
Eric Young, Colo. Rockies, June 30, 1996
Jayson Werth, Phila. Phillies, May 12, 2009
Dee Gordon, L.A. Dodgers, July 1, 2011

Most Stolen Bases by Catcher, Season

36 ..... John Wathan, K.C. Royals (AL), 1982
30 ..... Ray Schalk, Chi. White Sox (AL), 1916
28 ..... John Wathan, K.C. Royals (AL), 1983*
26 ..... Jason Kendall, Pitt. Pirates (NL), 1998
25 ..... Johnny Kling Chi. Cubs (NL), 1902
25 ..... Roger Bresnahan, N.Y. Giants (NL), 1906*
25 ..... John Stearns, N.Y. Mets (NL), 1978
25 ..... Ivan Rodriguez, Tex. Rangers (AL), 1999
25 ..... Craig Biggio, Hous. Astros (NL), 1990
24 ..... Ray Schalk, Chi. White Sox (AL), 1914
23 ..... Johnny Kling, Chi. Cubs (NL), 1903
22 ..... Jason Kendall, Pitt. Pirates (NL), 1999
22 ..... Jason Kendall, Pitt. Pirates (NL), 2000
21 ..... Benito Santiago, S.D. Padres (NL), 1987
21 ..... B.J. Surhoff, Milw. Brewers (AL), 1988
21 ..... Craig Biggio, Hous. Astros (NL), 1989
21 ..... Russell Martin, L.A. Dodgers (NL), 2007
20 ..... Red Dooin, Phila. Phillies (NL), 1908

*Caught in majority of games played during season.

Most Stolen Bases by Catcher, Career

212 ..... Roger Bresnahan* (1900–15)
189 ..... Jason Kendall (1996–2010)
177 ..... Ray Schalk (1912–29)
133 ..... Red Dooin (1902–16)
128 ..... Carlton Fisk (1969–93)
127 ..... Ivan Rodriguez (1991–2011)
124 ..... Johnny Kling (1900–13)
121 ..... Wally Schang (1913–31)
105 ..... John Wathan* (1976–85)
102 ..... Brad Ausmus (1993–2010)
97 ..... Russell Martin (2006–)
92 ..... Billy Sullivan (1899–14)
91 ..... Benito Santiago (1986–2005)
91 ..... John Stearns (1975–84)
87 ..... Ivy Wingo (1911–29)
86 ..... Eddie Ainsmith (1910–24)
86 ..... Jimmie Wilson (1923–40)
80 ..... Tony Pena (1980–1997)

*Caught in majority of games played during career.

Players with 50 Stolen Bases and 100 RBIs, Season

	Stolen Bases	RBIs
Sam Mertes, N.Y. Giants (NL), 1905	52	108
Honus Wagner, Pitt. Pirates (NL), 1905	57	101
Ty Cobb, Det. Tigers (AL), 1908	53	119
Honus Wagner, Pitt. Pirates (NL), 1908	53	109
Ty Cobb, Det. Tigers (AL), 1909	76	107
Ty Cobb, Det. Tigers (AL), 1911	83	127
Ty Cobb, Det. Tigers (AL), 1917	55	102
George Sisler, St.L. Browns (AL), 1922	51	105
Ben Chapman, N.Y. Yankees (AL), 1931	61	122
Cesar Cedeno, Hous. Astros (NL), 1974	57	102
Joe Morgan, Cin. Reds (NL), 1976	60	111
Eric Davis, Cin. Reds (NL), 1987	50	100
Barry Bonds, S.F. Giants (NL), 1990	52	114

Most Stolen Bases by Home Run Champion, Season

American League

76	Ty Cobb, Det. Tigers, 1909 (9 home runs)
52	Tris Speaker, Bost. Red Sox, 1912 (10 home runs) (Tie)
40	Home Run Baker, Phila. A's, 1912 (10 home runs) (Tie)
40	Jose Canseco, Oak. A's, 1988 (42 home runs)
38	Home Run Baker, Phila. A's, 1911 (11 home runs)
37	Ken Williams, St.L. Browns, 1922 (39 home runs)
36	Harry Davis, Phila. A's, 1905 (8 home runs)
34	Home Run Baker, Phila. A's, 1913 (12 home runs)
27	Nap Lajoie, Phila. A's, 1901 (14 home runs)
26	Jose Canseco, Oak. A's, 1991 (44 home runs)

National League (Post-1900)

67	Jimmy Sheckard, Bklyn. Dodgers, 1903 (9 home runs)
48	Red Murray, N.Y. Giants, 1909 (7 home runs)
40	Matt Kemp L.A. Dodgers, 2011 (39 home runs)
33	Larry Walker, Colo. Rockies, 1997 (49 home runs)
31	Hank Aaron, Atl. Braves, 1963 (44 home runs)
30	Harry Lumley, Bklyn. Dodgers, 1904 (9 home runs)
30	Ryan Braun, Milw. Brewers, 2012 (41 home runs)
30	Howard Johnson, N.Y. Mets, 1991 (38 home runs)
29	Mike Schmidt, Phila. Phillies, 1975 (38 home runs)
29	Darryl Strawberry, N.Y. Mets, 1988 (39 home runs)
29	Barry Bonds, S.F. Giants, 1993 (26 home runs)
25	Tommy Leach, Pitt. Pirates, 1902 (6 home runs)
25	Ryne Sandberg, Chi. Cubs, 1990 (40 home runs)

Players Stealing Bases in Four Decades

	Decades	Total
Rickey Henderson (1979–2003)	1970s (33), 1980s (838), 1990s (463), 2000s (72)	1406
Tim Raines (1979–99, 2001–02)	1970s (2), 1980s (583), 1990s (222), 2000s (1)	808
Omar Vizquel (1989–2012)	1980s (1) 1990s (237), 2000s (151), 2010s (15)	404
Ted Williams (1939–42, 1946–60)	1930s (2), 1940s (14), 1950s (7), 1960s (1)	24

Best On-Base Percentage (OBP) by Decade

Pre-1900

.461 John McGraw
.459 Billy Hamilton
.435 Bill Joyce
.433 Jesse Burkett
.432 Joe Kelley
.430 Willie Keeler
.428 Cupid Childs
.424 Dan Brouthers
.410 Ed Delahanty
.408 Jake Stenze

1900–09

.417 Honus Wagner
.411 Roy Thomas
.397 Frank Chance
.391 Mike Donlin
.389 Roger Bresnahan
.388 Nap Lajoie
.388 Jesse Burkett
.386 Topsy Hartsel
.383 Elmer Flick
.380 Fred Clarke
.380 Ty Cobb

1910–19

.457 Ty Cobb
.428 Tris Speaker
.424 Eddie Collins
.422 Joe Jackson
.402 Miller Huggins
.399 Johnny Bates
.395 Jimmy Sheckard
.389 Benny Kauff
.384 Wally Schang
.382 Johnny Evers

1920–29

.488 Babe Ruth
.460 Rogers Hornsby
.441 Tris Speaker
.436 Eddie Collins
.436 Lou Gehrig
.433 Harry Heilmann
.431 Paul Waner
.431 Ty Cobb
.420 Max Bishop
.420 Johnny Bassler

1930–39

.472 Babe Ruth
.453 Lou Gehrig
.440 Jimmie Foxx
.434 Mickey Cochrane
.427 Max Bishop
.425 Johnny Mize
.420 Mel Ott
.420 Arky Vaughan
.415 Hank Greenberg
.414 Charlie Gehringer

1940–49

.496 Ted Williams
.428 Stan Musial
.414 Augie Galan
.411 Roy Cullenbine
.406 Charlie Keller
.404 Joe DiMaggio
.404 Elbie Fletcher
.403 Luke Appling
.403 Eddie Stanky
.403 Mel Ott

1950–59

.476 Ted Williams
.431 Ferris Fain
.425 Mickey Mantle
.421 Stan Musial
.416 Jackie Robinson
.406 Eddie Yost
.403 Elmer Valo
.400 Minnie Minoso
.399 Richie Ashburn
.398 Ralph Kiner

1960–69

.415 Mickey Mantle
.402 Frank Robinson
.387 Harmon Killebrew
.383 Carl Yastrzemski
.381 Al Kaline
.380 Dick Allen
.380 Norm Cash
.379 Joe Morgan
.379 Albie Pearson
.378 Willie McCovey

1970–79

.408 Rod Carew
.404 Joe Morgan
.400 Mike Hargrove
.398 Ken Singleton
.390 Ron Hunt
.389 Pete Rose
.388 Bernie Carbo
.386 Gene Tenace
.384 Carl Yastrzemski
.383 Fred Lynn

1980–89

.443 Wade Boggs
.403 Rickey Henderson
.392 George Brett
.392 Alvin Davis
.391 Tim Raines
.391 Mike Hargrove
.390 Keith Hernandez
.389 Jack Clark
.389 Tony Gwynn
.388 Rod Carew

1990–99

.440 Frank Thomas
.434 Barry Bonds
.430 Edgar Martinez
.416 Jeff Bagwell
.412 Rickey Henderson
.412 Jim Thome
.411 Mark McGwire
.406 John Olerud
.402 John Kruk
.401 Garry Sheffield

2000–09

.517 Barry Bonds
.436 Todd Helton
.427 Albert Pujols
.421 Larry Walker
.419 Manny Ramirez
.418 Jason Giambi
.413 Lance Berkman
.413 Chipper Jones
.408 Joe Mauer
.402 Bobby Abreu
.402 Nick Johnson

2010–15

.436 Joey Votto
.418 Miguel Cabrera
.397 Mike Trout
.395 Paul Goldschmidt
.392 Prince Fielder
.391 Andrew McCutchen
.390 Jose Bautista
.384 Matt Holiday
.381 Shin-Soo Choo
.381 Joe Mauer

Best On-Base Plus Slugging (OPS) by Decade

Pre-1900

.943	Dan Brouthers
.925	Joe Kelley
.915	Ed Delahanty
.912	Willie Keeler
.902	Jesse Burkett
.902	Bill Joyce
.900	Billy Hamilton
.891	Sam Thompson
.887	Jake Stenzel
.883	Roger Connor

1900–09

.925	Honus Wagner
.876	Nap Lajoie
.865	Mike Donlin
.839	Ty Cobb
.829	Elmer Flick
.802	Sam Crawford
.799	Jesse Burkett
.797	Fred Clarke
.795	Frank Chance
.785	Buck Freeman

1910–19

.998	Ty Cobb
.933	Joe Jackson
.913	Tris Speaker
.871	Gavvy Cravath
.844	Eddie Collins
.839	Benny Kauff
.831	Sam Crawford
.819	George Sisler
.811	Rogers Hornsby
.810	Home Run Baker

1920–29

1.228	Babe Ruth
1.096	Rogers Hornsby
1.058	Lou Gehrig
.991	Harry Heilmann
.976	Tris Speaker
.970	Paul Waner
.966	Al Simmons
.954	Hack Wilson
.945	Ken Williams
.938	Jim Bottomley

1930–39

1.116	Babe Ruth
1.091	Jimmie Foxx
1.091	Lou Gehrig
1.032	Hank Greenberg
1.030	Johnny Mize
1.019	Joe DiMaggio
.980	Mel Ott
.939	Hal Trosky
.938	Bob Johnson
.937	Lefty O'Doul

1940–49

1.143	Ted Williams
1.005	Stan Musial
.989	Hank Greenberg
.972	Joe DiMaggio
.966	Ralph Kiner
.954	Johnny Mize
.926	Charlie Keller
.879	Mel Ott
.846	Enos Slaughter
.871	Jeff Heath
.871	Tommy Henrich

1950–59

1.098	Ted Williams
.994	Mickey Mantle
.989	Stan Musial
.981	Willie Mays
.959	Duke Snider
.931	Hank Aaron
.931	Eddie Mathews
.931	Ralph Kiner
.917	Frank Robinson
.913	Ernie Banks

1960–69

.962	Frank Robinson
.957	Mickey Mantle
.941	Hank Aaron
.935	Willie Mays
.933	Dick Allen
.933	Harmon Killebrew
.923	Willie McCovey
.878	Norm Cash
.875	Roberto Clemente
.875	Al Kaline

1970–79

.928	Willie Stargell
.910	Jim Rice
.909	Fred Lynn
.899	Hank Aaron
.891	Dave Parker
.889	Dick Allen
.885	Mike Schmidt
.881	Reggie Smith
.870	Reggie Jackson
.869	George Foster

1980–89

.925	Mike Schmidt
.922	Wade Boggs
.913	George Brett
.905	Will Clark
.879	Eric Davis
.889	Don Mattingly
.888	Pedro Guerrero
.882	Dwight Evans
.880	Ken Phelps
.878	Darryl Strawberry

1990–99

1.036	Barry Bonds
1.025	Mark McGwire
1.013	Frank Thomas
.975	Manny Ramirez
.966	Mike Piazza
.965	Ken Griffey Jr.
.962	Edgar Martinez
.961	Jeff Bagwell
.961	Larry Walker
.959	Jim Thome

2000–09

1.241	Barry Bonds
1.055	Albert Pujols
1.018	Manny Ramirez
1.006	Todd Helton
.988	Alex Rodriguez
.983	Larry Walker
.972	Lance Berkman
.962	Jim Thome
.961	Jason Giambi
.961	Ryan Howard

2010–15

1.004	Miguel Cabrera
.969	Joey Votto
.956	Mike Trout
.945	Jose Bautista
.931	David Ortiz
.930	Paul Goldschmidt
.909	Giancarlo Stanton
.908	Troy Tulowitzki
.902	Bryce Harper
.897	Ryan Braun

Batting Miscellany

Most Times Leading League in Offensive Category

American League

	Seasons	
Base Hits	8	Ty Cobb, 1907–09, 1911–12, 1915, 1917, and 1919
Singles	10	Ichiro Suzuki, 2001–10
Doubles	8	Tris Speaker, 1912, 1914, 1916, 1918, and 1920–23
Triples	5	Sam Crawford, 1903, 1910, and 1913–15
Home Runs	12	Babe Ruth, 1918–21, 1923–24, and 1926–31
Total Bases	6	Ty Cobb, 1907–09, 1911, 1915, and 1917
	6	Babe Ruth, 1919, 1921, 1923–24, 1926, and 1928
	6	Ted Williams, 1939, 1942, 1946–47, 1949, and 1951
Slugging Percentage	13	Babe Ruth, 1918–24 and 1926–31
Batting Average	12	Ty Cobb, 1907–15 and 1917–19
Runs	8	Babe Ruth, 1919–21, 1923–24, and 1926–28
RBIs	6	Babe Ruth, 1919–21, 1923, 1926, and 1928
Walks	11	Babe Ruth, 1920–21, 1923–24, 1926–28, and 1930–33
Strikeouts	7	Jimmie Foxx, 1929–31, 1933, 1935–36, and 1941
Stolen Bases	12	Rickey Henderson, 1980–86, 1988–91, 1998

National League (Post-1900)

Base Hits	7	Pete Rose, 1965, 1968, 1970, 1972–73, 1976, and 1981
Singles	4	Ginger Beaumont, 1902–04 and 1907
	4	Lloyd Waner, 1927–29 and 1931
	4	Richie Ashburn, 1951, 1953, and 1957–58
	4	Maury Wills, 1961–62, 1965, and 1967
Doubles	8	Stan Musial, 1943–44, 1946, 1948–49, and 1952–54
Triples	5	Stan Musial, 1943, 1946, 1948–49, and 1951
Home Runs	8	Mike Schmidt, 1974–76, 1980–81, 1983–84, and 1986
Total Bases	8	Hank Aaron, 1956–57, 1959–61, 1963, 1967, and 1969
Slugging Percentage	11	Rogers Hornsby, 1917–25 and 1928–29
Batting Average	8	Honus Wagner, 1900, 1903–04, 1906–09, and 1911
Runs	5	Rogers Hornsby, 1921–22, 1924, 1927, and 1929
	5	Stan Musial, 1946, 1948, 1951–52, and 1954
RBIs	4	Honus Wagner, 1901–02 and 1908–09
	4	Rogers Hornsby, 1920–22 and 1925
	4	Hank Aaron, 1957, 1960, 1963, and 1966
	4	Mike Schmidt, 1980–81, 1984, and 1986
Walks	12	Barry Bonds, 1992, 1994–97, 2000–2004, 2006–07
Strikeouts	6	Vince DiMaggio, 1937–38 and 1942–45
Stolen Bases	10	Max Carey, 1913, 1915–18, 1920, and 1922–25

Most Consecutive Seasons Leading League in Offensive Category

	American League		National League (Post-1900)	
	Seasons		Seasons	
Batting Average	9	Ty Cobb, 1907–15	6	Rogers Hornsby, 1920–25
Slugging Percentage	7	Babe Ruth, 1918–24	6	Rogers Hornsby, 1920–25
Runs	3	Ty Cobb, 1909–11	3	Chuck Klein, 1930–32
	3	Eddie Collins, 1912–14	3	Duke Snider, 1953–55

continued on next page

	3	Babe Ruth, 1919–21 and 1926–28	3	Pete Rose, 1974–76
	3	Ted Williams, 1940–42	3	Albert Pujols, 2003–05
	3	Mickey Mantle, 1956–58		
	3	Mike Trout, 2012–14		
Base Hits	5	Ichiro Suzuki, 2006–10	3	Ginger Beaumont, 1902–04
			3	Rogers Hornsby, 1920–22
			3	Frank McCormick, 1938–40
Singles	10	Ichiro Suzuki, 2001–10	3	Ginger Beaumont, 1902–04
			3	Lloyd Waner, 1927–29
				Ryan Theriot, 2008–10
Doubles	4	Tris Speaker, 1920–23	4	Honus Wagner, 1906–09
Triples	3	Elmer Flick, 1905–07	3	Garry Templeton, 1977–79
	3	Sam Crawford, 1913–15		
	3	Zoilo Versalles, 1963–65		
	3	Carl Crawford, 2004–06		
Home Runs	6	Babe Ruth, 1926–31	7	Ralph Kiner, 1946–52
Total Bases	3	Ty Cobb, 1907–09	4	Honus Wagner, 1906–09
	3	Jim Rice, 1977–79	4	Chuck Klein, 1930–33
RBIs	3	Ty Cobb, 1907–09	3	Rogers Hornsby, 1920–22
	3	Babe Ruth, 1919–21	3	Joe Medwick, 1936–38
			3	George Foster, 1976–78
Walks	4	Babe Ruth, 1930–33	5	Barry Bonds, 2000–2004
	4	Ted Williams, 1946–49		
Strikeouts	4	Vince DiMaggio, 1942–45	4	Hack Wilson, 1927–30
	4	Reggie Jackson, 1968–71		
Stolen Bases	9	Luis Aparicio, 1956–64	6	Maury Wills, 1960–65

Players Leading in All Triple Crown Categories, but Not in Same Year*

Hank Aaron.....Batting: 1956 (.328) and 1959 (.355)
Home Runs: 1957 (44), 1963 (44 Tie), 1966 (44), and 1967 (39)
RBIs: 1957 (132), 1960 (126), 1963 (130), and 1966 (127)

Barry Bonds.....Batting: 2002 (.370) and 2004 (.363)
Home Runs: 1993 (46) and 2001 (73)
RBIs: 1993 (123)

Dan Brouthers.....Batting: 1882 (.368), 1883 (.374), 1889 (.373), 1891 (.350), and 1892 (.335)
Home Runs: 1881 (8) and 1886 (11)
RBIs: 1892 (97)

Ed Delahanty.....Batting: 1899 (.410) and 1902 (.376)
Home Runs: 1893 (19) and 1896 (13)
RBIs: 1893 (146), 1896 (126), and 1899 (137)

Joe DiMaggio.....Batting: 1939 (.381) and 1940 (.352)
Home Runs: 1937 (46) and 1948 (39)
RBIs: 1941 (125) and 1948 (155)

Johnny Mize.....Batting: 1939 (.349)
Home Runs: 1939 (28), 1940 (43), 1947 (51 Tie), and 1948 (40 Tie)
RBIs: 1940 (137), 1942 (110), and 1947 (138)

Manny Ramirez.....Batting: 2002 (.349)
Home Runs: 2004 (43)
RBIs: 1999 (155)

Albert Pujols.....Batting: 2003 (.348)
Home Runs: 2009 (41) and 2010 (42)
RBIs: 2010 (118)

continued on next page

Babe Ruth ..... Batting: 1924 (.378)
Home Runs: 1918 (11), 1919 (29), 1920 (54), 1921 (59), 1923 (41), 1924 (46), 1926 (47), 1927 (60), 1928 (54), 1929 (46), 1930 (49), and 1931 (46 Tie)
RBIs: 1919 (114), 1920 (137), 1921 (171), 1923 (131), 1926 (146), and 1928 (142 Tie)

*Includes only players who *never* won triple crown.

Highest Offensive Career Totals by Players Who Never Led League

American League

Base Hits	3315	Eddie Collins
Singles	2262	Carl Yastrzemski
Doubles	539	Al Simmons
Triples	223	Tris Speaker
Home Runs	544	Rafael Palmeiro
Total Bases	4921	Derek Jeter
Batting Avg.	.356	Joe Jackson
Slugging %	.556	Carlos Delgado
Runs	1882	Tris Speaker
RBIs	1740	Rafael Palmeiro
Walks	1381	Tris Speaker
Strikeouts	2220	Alex Rodriguez
Stolen Bases	504	Paul Molitor

National League (Post-1900)

Base Hits	3060	Craig Biggio
Singles	2424	Honus Wagner
Doubles	601	Barry Bonds
Triples	177	Rabbit Maranville
Home Runs	475	Stan Musial
Total Bases	5752	Pete Rose
Batting Avg.	.336	Riggs Stephenson
Slugging %	.588	Vladimir Guerrero
Runs	1619	Chipper Jones
RBIs	1903	Willie Mays
Walks	1566	Pete Rose
Strikeouts	1753	Craig Biggio
Stolen Bases	550	Cesar Cedeno

Career Offensive Leaders by Players Under Six Feet Tall

Games Played	3562	Pete Rose (5'11")
At Bats	14,053	Pete Rose (5'11")
Base Hits	4256	Pete Rose (5'11")
Singles	3115	Pete Rose (5'11")
Doubles	793	Tris Speaker (5'11½")
Triples	222	Tris Speaker (5'11")
Home Runs	660	Willie Mays (5'10½")
Extra-Base Hits	1323	Willie Mays (5'10½")
Total Bases	6066	Willie Mays (5'10½")
Runs	2295	Rickey Henderson (5'10")
RBIs	1903	Willie Mays (5'10½")
Walks	2190	Rickey Henderson (5'10")
Strikeouts	1753	Craig Biggio (5'11")
Batting Average	.358	Rogers Hornsby (5'11")
Slugging Average	.577	Rogers Hornsby (5'11")
Stolen Bases	1406	Rickey Henderson (5'10")

Largest Margin Between League Leaders and Runners-Up

American League

	Margin	Season	Leader		Runner-Up	
Batting Average	.086	1901	Nap Lajoie, Phila A's	.426	Mike Donlin, Balt. Orioles	.340
Hits	46	2004	Ichiro Suzuki, Sea. Mariners	262	Michael Young, Tex. Rangers	216
Doubles	15	1910	Nap Lajoie, Cle. Indians	51	Ty Cobb, Det. Tigers	36
Triples	10	1949	Dale Mitchell, Cle. Indians	23	Bob Dillinger, St.L. Browns	13
Home Runs	35	1920	Babe Ruth, N.Y. Yankees	54	George Sisler, St.L. Browns	19
Runs Scored	45	1921	Babe Ruth, N.Y. Yankees	177	Jack Tobin, St.L. Browns	132
RBIs	51	1935	Hank Greenberg, Det. Tigers	170	Lou Gehrig, N.Y. Yankees	119

continued on next page

Total Bases	92	1921	Babe Ruth, N.Y. Yankees	457	Harry Heilmann, Det. Tigers	365
Slugging Average	.240	1921	Babe Ruth, N.Y. Yankees	.846	Harry Heilmann, Det. Tigers	.606
Stolen Bases	76	1982	Rickey Henderson, Oak. A's	130	Damaso Garcia, Tor. Blue Jays	54
Walks	72	1923	Babe Ruth, N.Y. Yankees	170	Joe Sewell, Cle. Indians	98

National League

	Margin	Season	Leader		Runner-Up	
Batting Average	.049	1924	Rogers Hornsby, St.L. Cardinals	.424	Zack Wheat, Bklyn. Dodgers	.375
Hits	44	1946	Stan Musial, St.L. Cardinals	228	Dixie Walker, Bklyn. Dodgers	184
Doubles	16	1904	Honus Wagner, Pitt. Pirates	44	Sam Mertes, N.Y. Giants	28
Triples	16	1912	Owen Wilson, Pitt. Pirates	36	Honus Wagner, Pitt. Pirates	20
Home Runs	19	1923	Cy Williams, Phila. Phillies	41	Jack Fournier, Bklyn. Dodgers	22
Runs Scored	29	1909	Tommy Leach, Pitt. Pirates	126	Fred Charles, Pitt. Pirates	97
RBIs	39	1937	Joe Medwick, St.L. Cardinals	154	Frank Demaree, Chi. Cubs	115
Total Bases	136	1922	Rogers Hornsby, St.L. Cardinals	450	Irish Meusel, N.Y. Giants	314
Slugging Average	.177	2002	Barry Bonds, S.F. Giants	.799	Brian Giles, Pitt. Pirates	.622
Stolen Bases	72	1962	Maury Wills, L.A. Dodgers	104	Willie Davis, L.A. Dodgers	32
Walks	105	2004	Barry Bonds, S.F. Giants	232	Bobby Abreu, Phila. Phillies	127
					Lance Berkman, Hous. Astros	127
					Todd Helton, Colo. Rockies	127

Evolution of Slugging Percentage Record

American League

1901	Nap Lajoie, Phila. A's	.643
1919	Babe Ruth, Bost. Red Sox	.657
1920	Babe Ruth, N.Y. Yankees	.847

National League (Pre-1900)

1876	Ross Barnes, Chi. White Stockings	.590
1894	Sam Thompson, Phila. Phillies	.696

National League (Post-1899)

1922	Rogers Hornsby, St.L. Cardinals	.722
1925	Rogers Hornsby, St.L. Cardinals	.756
2001	Barry Bonds, S.F. Giants	.863

Players Hitting Safely in at Least 135 Games in Season

American League

Wade Boggs, Bost. Red Sox, 1985 (240 hits in 161 games, .368 batting average)

Derek Jeter, N.Y. Yankees, 1999 (219 hits in 158 games, .349 batting average)

Ichiro Suzuki, Sea. Mariners, 2001 (242 hits in 157 games, .350 batting average)

National League (Post-1900)

Rogers Hornsby, St.L. Cardinals, 1922 (250 hits in 154 games, .401 batting average)

Chuck Klein, Phila. Phillies, 1930 (250 hits in 156 games, .386 batting average)

Players Hitting for the Cycle in Natural Order (Single, Double, Triple, Home Run)

American League

Fats Fothergill, Det. Tigers, Sept. 26, 1926

Tony Lazzeri, N.Y. Yankees, June 3, 1932

Charlie Gehringer, Det. Tigers, May 27, 1939

National League (Post-1900)

Bill Collins, Bost. Doves, Oct. 6, 1910

Jim Hickman, N.Y. Mets, Aug. 7, 1963

Ken Boyer, St.L. Cardinals, June 16, 1964

continued on next page

Leon Culberson, Bost. Red Sox, July 3, 1943
Bob Watson, Bost. Red Sox, Sept. 15, 1979
Jose Valentin, Chi. White Sox, Apr. 27, 2000
Gary Matthews Jr., Tex. Rangers, Sept. 13, 2006
Billy Williams, Chi. Cubs, July 17, 1966
Tim Foli, Mont. Expos, Apr. 22, 1976
John Mabry, St.L. Cardinals, May 18, 1996
Brad Wilkerson, Mont. Expos, June 24, 2003

Highest Slugging Percentage by Position, Season

American League

First Base ..... .765 ..... Lou Gehrig, N.Y. Yankees, 1927
Second Base ..... .643 ..... Nap Lajoie, Phila. A's, 1901
Third Base ... .664 ..... George Brett, K.C. Royals, 1980
Shortstop ..... .631 ... Alex Rodriguez, Sea. Mariners, 1996
Outfield ..... .847 ..... Babe Ruth, N.Y. Yankees, 1920
Catcher ..... .617 ..... Bill Dickey, N.Y. Yankees, 1936
Pitcher ..... .621 ..... Wes Ferrell, Cle. Indians, 1931
Designated Hitter ..... .628 .. Edgar Martinez, Sea. Mariners, 1995

National League (Post-1900)

First Base .... .752... Mark McGwire, St.L. Cardinals, 1998
Second Base ..... .756.. Rogers Hornsby, St.L. Cardinals, 1925
Third Base ... .644..... Mike Schmidt, Phila. Phillies, 1981
Shortstop .... .614..... Ernie Banks, Chi. Cubs, 1958
Outfield ..... .863..... Barry Bonds, S.F. Giants, 2001
Catcher ..... .638..... Mike Piazza, L.A. Dodgers, 1997
Pitcher ..... .632. Don Newcombe, Bklyn. Dodgers, 1955

Most Times Awarded First Base on Catcher's Interference or Obstruction

29 ..... Pete Rose (1963–86)
18 ..... Julian Javier (1960–72)
18 ..... Dale Berra (1977–87)
17 ..... Roberto Kelly (1988–2000)
17 ..... Andy Van Slyke (1983–95)
17 ..... Carl Crawford (2002–)
16 ..... Bob Stinson (1969–80)
14 ..... Jacoby Ellsbury (2007–)
13 ..... Phil Nakso (1954–87)
13 ..... Darin Erstad (1996–2009)
13 ..... Ryan Ludwick (2002–05, 2007–14)
12 ..... Hector Torres (1968–77)
12 ..... Craig Counsell (1995–2011)

Winners of Two "Legs" of Triple Crown Since Last Winner*

American League

Chris Davis, Balt. Orioles, 2013 ..... 53 home runs, 138 RBIs (batting avg. .286, twenty-first behind Miguel Cabrera's .348)

National League

Paul Goldschmidt, Ariz. D'backs, 2013 ... 36 home runs, 125 RBIs (batting avg. .302, eleventh behind Michael Cuddyer's .331)
Nolan Arenado, Colo. Rockies, 2015..... 42 home runs, 130 RBIs (batting avg. .287, twentieth behind Dee Gordon's .333)

*Miguel Cabrera, 2012

2

PITCHING

Wins

Most Victories by Decade

Pre-1900

361 ..... Pud Galvin
342 ..... Tim Keefe
328 ..... John Clarkson
309 ..... Old Hoss Radbourn
307 ..... Mickey Welch
297 ..... Kid Nichols
284 ..... Tony Mullane
267 ..... Cy Young
265 ..... Jim McCormick
258 ..... Gus Weyhing

1900–09

236 ..... Christy Mathewson
230 ..... Cy Young
218 ..... Joe McGinnity
192 ..... Jack Chesbro
188 ..... Vic Willis
186 ..... Eddie Plank
183 ..... Rube Waddell
166 ..... Sam Leever
160 ..... Jack Powell
157 ..... George Mullin

1910–19

265 ..... Walter Johnson
208 ..... Grover C. Alexander
162 ..... Eddie Cicotte
156 ..... Hippo Vaughn
149 ..... Slim Sallee
144 ..... Rube Marquard
140 ..... Eddie Plank
137 ..... Christy Mathewson
135 ..... Claude Hendrix
126 ..... Hooks Dauss

1920–29

190 ..... Burleigh Grimes
166 ..... Eppa Rixley
165 ..... Grover C. Alexander
163 ..... Herb Pennock
161 ..... Waite Hoyt
156 ..... Urban Shocker
154 ..... Eddie Rommel
153 ..... Jesse Haines
152 ..... George Uhle
149 ..... Red Faber

1930–39

199 ..... Lefty Grove
188 ..... Carl Hubbell
175 ..... Red Ruffing
170 ..... Wes Ferrell
165 ..... Lefty Gomez
158 ..... Mel Harder
156 ..... Larry French
150 ..... Tommy Bridges
148 ..... Paul Derringer
147 ..... Dizzy Dean

1940–49

170 ..... Hal Newhouser
137 ..... Bob Feller
133 ..... Rip Sewell
129 ..... Dizzy Trout
122 ..... Dutch Leonard
122 ..... Bucky Walters
114 ..... Mort Cooper
111 ..... Claude Passeau
105 ..... Kirby Higbe
105 ..... Bobo Newsom
105 ..... Harry Brecheen

1950–59

202 ..... Warren Spahn
199 ..... Robin Roberts
188 ..... Early Wynn
155 ..... Billy Pierce
150 ..... Bob Lemon
128 ..... Mike Garcia
126 ..... Lew Burdette
126 ..... Don Newcombe
121 ..... Whitey Ford
116 ..... Johnny Antonelli

1960–69

191 ..... Juan Marichal
164 ..... Bob Gibson
158 ..... Don Drysdale
150 ..... Jim Bunning
142 ..... Jim Kaat
141 ..... Larry Jackson
137 ..... Sandy Koufax
134 ..... Jim Maloney
131 ..... Milt Pappas
127 ..... Camilo Pascual

1970–79

186 ..... Jim Palmer
184 ..... Gaylord Perry
178 ..... Steve Carlton
178 ..... Ferguson Jenkins
178 ..... Tom Seaver
169 ..... Catfish Hunter
166 ..... Don Sutton
164 ..... Phil Niekro
155 ..... Vida Blue
155 ..... Nolan Ryan

continued on next page

1980–89

162 ..... Jack Morris
140 ..... Dave Steib
137 ..... Bob Welch
128 ..... Charlie Hough
128 ..... Fernando Valenzuela
123 ..... Bert Blyleven
122 ..... Nolan Ryan
119 ..... Jim Clancy
117 ..... Frank Viola
116 ..... Rick Sutcliffe

1990–99

176 ..... Greg Maddux
164 ..... Tom Glavine
152 ..... Roger Clemens
150 ..... Randy Johnson
143 ..... Kevin Brown
143 ..... John Smoltz
141 ..... David Cone
136 ..... Mike Mussina
135 ..... Chuck Finley
130 ..... Scott Erickson

2000–09

148 ..... Andy Pettitte
143 ..... Randy Johnson
140 ..... Jamie Moyer
139 ..... Roy Halladay
137 ..... Tim Hudson
137 ..... Roy Oswalt
136 ..... CC Sabathia
135 ..... Mark Buehrle
134 ..... Greg Maddux
134 ..... Mike Mussina

2010–15

101 ..... Clayton Kershaw
96 ..... Max Scherzer
94 ..... David Price
92 ..... Zack Greinke
92 ..... Justin Verlander
87 ..... Jered Weaver
85 ..... Madison Bumgarner
85 ..... Felix Hernandez
85 ..... Jon Lester
84 ..... Gio Gonzalez
84 ..... James Shields

Pitchers with the Most Career Wins by First Letter of Last Name

A	Grover C. Alexander	373
B	Bert Blyleven	287
C	Roger Clemens	354
D	Hooks Dauss, Paul Derringer	223
E	Dennis Eckersley	197
F	Bob Feller	266
G	Pud Galvin	361
H	Carl Hubbell	253
I	Jason Isringhausen	51
J	Walter Johnson	417
K	Tim Keefe	341
L	Ted Lyons	260
M	Christy Mathewson	373
N	Kid Nichols	361
O	Al Orth	204
P	Eddie Plank	326
Q	Jack Quinn	247
R	Nolan Ryan	324
S	Warren Spahn	363
T	Frank Tanana	240
U	George Uhle	200
V	Dazzy Vance	197
W	Mickey Welch	307
X	[No pitcher]	
Y	Cy Young	511
Z	Tom Zachary	186

Pitchers with the Most Career Victories by Zodiac Sign

Aquarius (Jan. 20–Feb. 18)	Nolan Ryan	324
Pisces (Feb. 19–Mar. 20)	Grover C. Alexander	373
Aries (Mar. 21–Apr. 19)	Cy Young	511
Taurus (Apr. 20–May 20)	Warren Spahn	363
Gemini (May 21–June 21)	Tommy John	288
Cancer (June 22–July 22)	John Clarkson	328
Leo (July 23–Aug. 22)	Christy Mathewson	373
Virgo (Aug. 23–Sept. 22)	Kid Nichols	361
Libra (Sept. 23–Oct. 23)	Robin Roberts	286
Scorpio (Oct. 24–Nov. 21)	Walter Johnson	417
Sagittarius (Nov. 22–Dec. 21)	Old Hoss Radbourn	309
Capricorn (Dec. 22–Jan. 19)	Pud Galvin	361

Pitchers with the Most Victories by State of Birth

Alabama	Don Sutton (Clio)	324
Alaska	Curt Schilling (Anchorage)	216
Arizona	John Denny (Prescott)	123
Arkansas	Lon Warneke (Mount Ida)	192
California	Tom Seaver (Fresno)	311
Colorado	Roy Halladay (Denver)	203
Connecticut	Bill Hutchinson (New Haven)	182
Delaware	Sadie McMahon (Wilmington)	177
Florida	Steve Carlton (Miami)	329
Georgia	Tim Hudson (Columbus)	222
Hawaii	Charlie Hough (Honolulu)	216
Idaho	Larry Jackson (Nampa)	194
Illinois	Robin Roberts (Springfield)	286
Indiana	Tommy John (Terre Haute)	288

continued on next page

Iowa	Bob Feller (Van Meter)	266
Kansas	Walter Johnson (Humboldt)	417
Kentucky	Gus Weyhing (Louisville)	264
Louisiana	Ted Lyons (Sulphur)	260
Maine	Bob Stanley (Portland)	115
Maryland	Lefty Grove (Lonaconing)	300
Massachusetts	Tim Keefe (Cambridge)	341
Michigan	Jim Kaat (Zeeland)	283
Minnesota	Jack Morris (St.Paul)	254
Mississippi	Guy Bush (Aberdeen)	176
Missouri	Pud Galvin (St. Louis)	361
Montana	Dave McNally (Billings)	184
Nebraska	Grover C. Alexander (Elba)	373
Nevada	Barry Zito (Las Vegas)	165
New Hampshire	Mike Flanagan (Manchester)	167
New Jersey	Al Leiter (Toms River)	162
New Mexico	Wade Blasingame (Deming)	46
New York	Warren Spahn (Buffalo)	363
North Carolina	Gaylord Perry (Williamston)	314
North Dakota	Rick Helling (Devils Lake)	93
Ohio	Cy Young (Gilmore)	511
Oklahoma	Allie Reynolds (Bethany)	182
Oregon	Mickey Lolich (Portland)	217
Pennsylvania	Christy Mathewson (Factoryville)	373
Rhode Island	Tom Lovett (Providence)	88
South Carolina	Bobo Newsom (Hartsville)	211
South Dakota	Floyd Bannister (Pierre)	134
Tennessee	Bob Caruthers (Memphis)	218
Texas	Greg Maddux (San Angelo)	355
Utah	Bruce Hurst (St. George)	145
Vermont	Ray Fisher (Middlebury)	100
Virginia	Eppa Rixey (Culpepper)	266
Washington	Todd Stottlemyre (Sunnyside)	138
West Virginia	Wilbur Cooper (Bearsville)	216
Wisconsin	Kid Nichols (Madison)	361
Wyoming	Tom Browning (Casper)	123
District of Columbia	Doc White	189
Puerto Rico	Javier Vazquez (Ponce)	165
Virgin Islands	Al McBean (Charlotte Amalie)	67

Pitchers with Five or More Consecutive 20-Win Seasons (Post-1900)

	Seasons
Christy Mathewson, N.Y. Giants (NL), 1903–14	12
Walter Johnson, Wash. Senators (AL), 1910–19	10
Lefty Grove, Phila. A's (AL), 1927–33	7
Three Finger Brown, Chi. Cubs (NL), 1906–11	6
Robin Roberts, Phila. Phillies (NL), 1950–55	6
Warren Spahn, Milw. Braves (NL), 1956–61	6
Ferguson Jenkins, Chi. Cubs (NL), 1967–72	6
Grover C. Alexander, Phila. Phillies (NL), 1913–17	5
Carl Hubbell, N.Y. Giants (NL), 1933–37	5
Catfish Hunter, Oak. A's (AL), 1971–74, and N.Y. Yankees (AL), 1975	5

100-Game Winners, Both Leagues

	American League	National League	Total Wins
Cy Young	221 (1901–11)	290 (1890–1900, 1911)	511
Nolan Ryan	189 (1972–79, 1989–93)	135 (1966–71, 1980–88)	324
Gaylord Perry	139 (1972–77, 1980, 1982–83)	175 (1962–71, 1978–79, 1981)	314
Randy Johnson	164 (1989–98, 2005–06)	139 (1988–89, 1998–2004, 2007–09)	303
Ferguson Jenkins	115 (1974–81)	169 (1965–73, 1982–83)	284
Dennis Martinez	141 (1976–86, 1994–98)	104 (1986–93)	245
Jim Bunning	118 (1955–63)	106 (1964–71)	224
Pedro Martinez	117 (1998–2004)	102 (1992–97, 2005–09)	219
Kevin Brown	102 (1986–95, 2004–05)	109 (1996–2003)	211
Al Orth	104 (1902–09)	100 (1895–1901)	204

Pitchers with 500 Major League Decisions

	Wins–Losses	Total
Cy Young (1890–1911)	511–316	827
Walter Johnson (1907–27)	417–279	696
Pud Galvin (1879–92)	361–308	669
Nolan Ryan (1966–93)	324–292	616
Warren Spahn (1942, 1946–65)	363–245	608
Phil Niekro (1964–87)	318–274	592
Greg Maddux (1986–2008)	355–277	582
Grover C. Alexander (1911–30)	373–208	581
Don Sutton (1966–88)	324–256	580
Gaylord Perry (1962–83)	314–265	579
Steve Carlton (1965–88)	329–244	573
Kid Nichols (1890–1901, 1904–06)	361–208	569
Tim Keefe (1880–93)	342–225	567
Christy Mathewson (1900–16)	373–188	561
Early Wynn (1939, 1941–44, 1946–63)	300–244	544
Roger Clemens (1984–2007)	354–184	538
Bert Blyleven (1970–92)	287–250	537
Robin Roberts (1948–66)	286–245	531
Jim Kaat (1959–83)	283–237	520
Eddie Plank (1901–17)	326–194	520
Tommy John (1963–74, 1976–89)	288–231	519
Mickey Welch (1880–92)	307–210	517
Eppa Rixey (1912–17, 1919–33)	266–251	517
Tom Seaver (1967–86)	311–205	516
Ferguson Jenkins (1965–83)	284–226	510
Tom Glavine (1987–2008)	305–203	508
John Clarkson (1882, 1884–94)	328–178	506
Tony Mullane (1881–94)	284–220	504
Old Hoss Radbourn (1880–91)	309–194	503

Most Wins, Major and Minor Leagues Combined

Total		Majors	Minors
526	Cy Young	511	15
481	Joe McGinnity	246	235
445	Kid Nichols	361	84
418	Grover C. Alexander	373	45
417	Walter Johnson	417	0
415	Warren Spahn	363	52
412	Lefty Grove	300	112
398	Christy Mathewson	373	25
391	Greg Maddux	355	36
369	Gaylord Perry	314	55
366	Early Wynn	300	66
364	Roger Clemens	354	10
361	Pud Galvin	361	0
361	Phil Niekro	318	43
360	Tony Freitas	25	335
355	Joe Martina	6	349
353	Steve Carlton	329	24
350	Bobo Newsom	211	139

continued on next page

348	Stan Coveleski	215	133
348	Don Sutton	324	24
348	Bill Thomas	0	348
347	Jack Quinn	247	100
345	Nolan Ryan	324	21
342	Burleigh Grimes	270	72
341	Tim Keefe	341	0
338	Gus Weyhing	264	74
334	Tom Glavine	305	29
332	Red Faber	254	78
332	Dazzy Vance	197	135
331	Randy Johnson	303	28
331	Alex McColl	4	327

Most Wins For One Team

American League

417 Walter Johnson, Wash. Senators (1907–27)
284 Eddie Plank, Phila. A's (1900–14)
268 Jim Palmer, Balt. Orioles (1965–84)
266 Bob Feller, Cle. Indians (1936–41, 1945–56)
260 Ted Lyons, Chi. White Sox (1923–42, 1946)
254 Red Faber, Chi. White Sox (1914–33)
236 Whitey Ford, N.Y. Yankees (1950, 1953–67)
231 Red Ruffing, N.Y. Yankees (1930–42, 1945–46)
223 Mel Harder, Cle. Indians (1928–47)
222 Hooks Dauss, Det. Tigers (1912–26)
219 Andy Pettitte, N.Y. Yankees (1995–2003, 2007–10, 2012–13)
209 George Mullin, Det. Tigers (1902–13)
207 Bob Lemon, Cle. Indians (1946–58)
207 Mickey Lolich, Det. Tigers (1963–75)
200 Hal Newhouser, Det. Tigers (1939–53)

National League

372 Christy Mathewson, N.Y. Giants (1900–16)
356 Warren Spahn, Bost.–Milw. Braves (1942, 1946–64)
329 Kid Nichols, Bost. Beaneaters (1899–1901)
266 Phil Niekro, Atl. Braves (1966–83)
253 Carl Hubbell, N.Y. Giants (1928–43)
251 Bob Gibson, St.L. Cardinals (1959–75)
244 Tom Glavine, Atl. Braves (1987–2002, 2008)
241 Steve Carlton, Phila. Phillies (1972–86)
241 Cy Young, Cle. Spiders (1890–98)
238 Juan Marichal, S.F. Giants (1960–73)
238 Mickey Welch, N.Y. Giants (1885–92)
234 Robin Roberts, Phila. Phillies (1948–61)
233 Amos Rusie, N.Y. Giants (1890–95, 1897–98)
233 Don Sutton, L.A. Dodgers (1966–80, 1988)
218 Pud Galvin, Buff. Bisons (1879–85)
210 John Smoltz, Atl. Braves (1988–99, 2001–08)
210 Jesse Haines, St.L. Cardinals (1920–37)
202 Wilbur Cooper, Pitt. Pirates (1912–24)
201 Charlie Root, Chi. Cubs (1926–41)

Pitchers with 100 More Wins Than Losses, Career

	Wins	Losses	Differential
Cy Young (1890–1911)	511	315	+196
Christy Mathewson (1900–16)	373	188	+185
Roger Clemens (1984–2007)	354	184	+170
Grover C. Alexander (1911–30)	373	208	+165
Lefty Grove (1925–41)	300	141	+159
Kid Nichols (1890–1901, 1904–06)	361	208	+153
John Clarkson (1882, 1884–94)	328	178	+150
Walter Johnson (1907–27)	417	279	+138
Randy Johnson (1988–2009)	303	166	+137
Eddie Plank (1901–17)	326	194	+132
Whitey Ford (1950, 1953–67)	236	106	+130
Greg Maddux (1986–2008)	355	227	+128
Bob Caruthers (1884–92)	218	97	+121
Pedro Martinez (1992–2009)	219	100	+119

continued on next page

Tim Keefe (1880–93)	341	223	+118
Warren Spahn (1942, 1946–65)	363	245	+118
Jim Palmer (1965–84)	268	152	+116
Old Hoss Radbourn (1880–91)	309	194	+115
Tom Seaver (1967–86)	311	205	+106
Joe McGinnity (1899–1908)	246	142	+104
Bob Feller (1936–41, 1945–56)	266	162	+104
Andy Pettitte (1995–2010, 2012–13)	256	153	+103
Tom Glavine (1987–2008)	305	203	+102
Juan Marichal (1960–75)	243	142	+101

Pitchers with Most Career Wins, Never Leading League in One Season

Pud Galvin (1879–92)	361	Tony Mullane (1881–84, 1886–94)	284
Eddie Plank (1901–17)	326	Jamie Moyer (1986–91, 1993–2010, 2012)	269
Nolan Ryan (1966–88)	324	Gus Weyhing (1887–1901)	264
Don Sutton (1966–88)	324	Red Faber (1914–33)	254
Mickey Welch (1880–92)	307	Vic Willis (1898–1910)	249
Tommy John (1963–74, 1976–89)	288	Jack Quinn (1909–15, 1918–33)	247
Bert Blyleven (1970–92)	287	Jack Powell (1897–1912)	246

200-Game Winners, Never Winning 20 Games in Season

	Career Wins	Most in One Season
Dennis Martinez (1976–98)	245	16 (1978, 1982, 1989, and 1992)
Frank Tanana (1973–93)	240	19 (1976)
Jerry Reuss (1969–90)	220	18 (1975, 1980)
Kenny Rogers (1989–2008)	219	18 (2004)
Charlie Hough (1970–94)	216	18 (1987)
Mark Buehrle (2000–)	214	19 (2002)
Milt Pappas (1957–73)	209	17 (1971, 1972)
Chuck Finley (1986–2002)	200	18 (1990, 1991)
Tim Wakefield (1991–93, 1995–2011)	200	17 (1998)

Pitchers with 100 Wins and 500 Hits, Career

	Wins	Hits
Charlie Buffinton (1882–93)	231	543
Bob Caruthers (1884–96)	218	694
Dave Foutz (1884–96)	147	1254
Pud Galvin (1875, 1879–92)	361	554
Kid Gleason (1888–1908, 1912)	134	1944
Guy Hecker (1882–90)	177	822
Walter Johnson (1907–27)	417	549
Bobby Mathews (1871–87)	298	505
Win Mercer (1894–1902)	131	502
Tony Mullane (1881–84, 1886–94)	285	661
Old Hoss Radbourn (1880–91)	309	585
Red Ruffing (1924–42, 1945–47)	273	521
Jack Stivetts (1889–99)	207	592
Adonis Terry (1884–97)	197	594
Monte Ward (1878–84)	161	2123
Jim Whitney (1881–90)	192	559
Smoky Joe Wood (1908–15, 1917–22)	116	553
Cy Young (1890–1911)	511	623

Victories in Most Consecutive Seasons

Seasons	
26	Nolan Ryan, 1968–93
24	Roger Clemens, 1984–2007
24	Don Sutton, 1966–1988
23	Greg Maddux, 1986–2008
23	Jim Kaat, 1960–82
23	Dennis Martinez, 1976–98
23	Phil Niekro, 1965–87
22	Steve Carlton, 1966–87
22	Charlie Hough, 1973–94
22	Randy Johnson, 1989–2009
22	Tom Glavine, 1987–2008
22	Gaylord Perry, 1962–83
22	Early Wynn, 1941–44, 1946–63*
22	Cy Young, 1890–1911
21	Bert Blyleven, 1970–90
21	Walter Johnson, 1907–27
21	Joe Niekro, 1967–87
21	Jerry Reuss, 1969–89
21	Eppa Rixey, 1912–17, 1919–33
21	Red Ruffing, 1925–42, 1945–47*
21	Frank Tanana, 1973–93
21	David Wells, 1987–2007
20	Red Faber, 1914–33
20	Lindy McDaniel, 1956–75
20	Tom Seaver, 1967–86
20	Warren Spahn, 1946–65
20	Kenny Rogers, 1989–2008

*Missing years were spent in military service.

Most Wins in a Season Without a Complete Game

American League	
21	Max Scherzer, Det. Tigers, 2013
20	Roger Clemens, N.Y. Yankees, 2001
20	Mike Mussina, N.Y. Yankees, 2008
19	Collin McHugh, Hous. Astros, 2015
18	Roger Clemens, N.Y. Yankees, 2004
18	Bartolo Colon, Cle. Indians, 2004
18	Daisuke Matsuzaka, Bost. Red Sox, 2008
18	Phil Hughes, N.Y. Yankees, 2010
17	John Hiller, Det. Tigers, 1974
17	Bill Campbell, Min. Twins, 1976
17	Milt Wilcox, Det. Tigers, 1984
17	CC Sabathia, Cle. Indians, 2001
17	Kenny Rogers, Det. Tigers, 2006
17	Tim Wakefield, Bost. Red Sox, 2007
17	Scott Feldman, Tex. Rangers, 2009
17	C.J. Wilson, L.A. Angels, 2013

National League	
19	Roy Oswalt, Hous. Astros, 2002
19	Jake Peavy, S.D. Padres, 2007
19	Gerrit Cole, Pitt. Pirates, 2015
18	Roy Face, Pitt. Pirates, 1959
18	Kent Bottenfield, St.L. Cardinals, 1999
18	Woody Williams, St.L. Cardinals, 2003
18	Chris Capuano, Milw. Brewers, 2005
18	Lance Lynn, St.L. Cardinals, 2013
17	Andy Pettitte, Hous. Astros, 2005
17	Ted Lilly, Chi. Cubs, 2008
17	Edison Volquez, Cin. Reds, 2008
17	Wily Peralta, Milw. Brewers, 2014
17	Zack Greinke, L.A. Dodgers, 2014
17	Michael Wacha, St.L. Cardinals, 2015

Most Career Wins by Pitchers Six and a Half Feet Tall or Taller

303	Randy Johnson (1988–2009)	6'10"
214	CC Sabathia* (2001–)	6'7"
206	Roy Halladay (1998–2013)	6'6'
200	Chuck Finley (1986–2002)	6'6"
177	John Candelaria (1975–93)	6'7"
176	Derek Lowe (1997–2013)	6'6"
171	Rick Sutcliffe (1976, 1978–94)	6'7"
165	John Lackey* (2002–)	6'6"
155	Andy Benes (1989–2002)	6'6"
146	Ron Reed (1966–84)	6'6"
144	Chris Carpenter (1997–2012)	6'6"

* Still active.

Most Career Wins by Pitchers Under Six Feet Tall

Wins		Height
361	Pud Galvin (1875, 1879–92)	5'8"
361	Kid Nichols (1890–1901, 1904–06)	5'10½"
341	Tim Keefe (1880–93)	5'10½"
328	John Clarkson (1882, 1884–94)	5'10"
326	Eddie Plank (1901–17)	5'11½"
309	Old Hoss Radbourn (1881–91)	5'9"
307	Mickey Welch (1880–92)	5'8"
284	Tony Mullane (1881–84, 1886–94)	5'10½"
270	Burleigh Grimes (1916–34)	5'10"
265	Jim McCormick (1878–87)	5'10½'

continued on next page

264	Gus Weyhing (1887–96, 1899–1901)	5'10"
260	Ted Lyons (1923–42, 1946)	5'11"
246	Joe McGinnity (1899–1908)	5'11"
245	Jack Powell (1897–1912)	5'11"
239	Three Finger Brown (1903–16)	5'10
237	Clark Griffith (1891–1914)	5'6"
236	Whitey Ford (1950, 1953–67)	5'10"
229	Will White (1877–86)	5'9½'
228	George Mullin (1902–15)	5'11"
223	Hooks Dauss (1912–26)	5'10½'
219	Pedro Martinez (1992–2009)	5'11"
218	Bob Caruthers (1884–92)	5'7"
218	Bartolo Colon (1997–2009, 2011–)	5'11"
218	Earl Whitehill (1923–39)	5'9½"
217	Freddie Fitzsimmons (1925–43)	5'11"
216	Wilbur Cooper (1912–26)	5'11½"
215	Stan Coveleski (1912, 1916–28)	5'11"
211	Billy Pierce (1945, 1948–64)	5'10"
209	Eddie Cicotte (1905, 1908–20)	5'9"
208	Carl Mays (1915–29)	5'11½"
201	Charlie Root (1923, 1926–41)	5'10½"

Pitchers Winning 20 Games in Season Split Between Two Teams (Post-1900)

Joe McGinnity, 21–18	1902	Balt. Orioles (AL), 13–10	N.Y. Giants (NL), 8–8
Bob Wicker, 20–9	1903	St.L. Cardinals (NL), 0–0	Chi. Cubs (NL), 20–9
Patsy Flaherty, 20–11	1904	Chi. White Sox (AL), 1–2	Pitt. Pirates (NL), 19–9
John Taylor, 20–12	1906	St.L. Cardinals (NL), 8–9	Chi. Cubs (NL), 12–3
Bobo Newsom, 20–11	1939	St.L. Browns (AL), 3–1	Det. Tigers (AL), 17–10
Red Barrett, 23–12	1945	Bost. Braves (NL), 2–3	St.L. Cardinals (NL), 21–9
Hank Borowy, 21–7	1945	N.Y. Yankees (AL), 10–5	Chi. Cubs (NL), 11–2
Virgil Trucks, 20–10	1953	St.L. Browns (AL), 5–4	Chi. White Sox (AL), 15–6
Tom Seaver, 21–6	1977	N.Y. Mets (NL), 7–3	Cin. Reds (NL), 14–3
Rick Sutcliffe, 20–6	1984	Cle. Indians (AL), 4–5	Chi. Cubs (NL), 16–1
Bartolo Colon, 20–8	2002	Cle. Indians (AL), 10–4	Mont. Expos (NL), 10–4

Pitchers Winning 20 Games with 3 Different Teams

Grover C. Alexander	Phila. Phillies	1911, 1913, 1914, 1915, 1916, 1917
	Chi. Cubs	1920, 1923
	St.L. Cardinals	1927
Roger Clemens	Bost. Red Sox	1986, 1987, 1990
	Tor. Blue Jays	1997, 1998
	N.Y. Yankees	2001
Claude Hendrix	Pitt. Pirates	1912
	Chi. Whales (FL)	1914
	Chi. Cubs	1918
Carl Mays	Bost. Red Sox	1917, 1918
	N.Y. Yankees	1920, 1921
	Cin. Reds	1924
Joe McGinnity	Balt. Orioles (NL)	1899
	Bklyn. Dodgers	1900
	Balt. Orioles (AL)	1901
	N.Y. Giants	1903, 1904, 1905, 1906
Gaylord Perry	S.F. Giants	1966, 1970
	Cle. Indians	1972, 1974
	S.D. Padres	1978
Cy Young	Cle. Spiders	1891–98
	St.L. Cardinals	1899
	Bost. Red Sox	1901–04, 1907

Oldest Pitchers to Win 20 Games for First Time

American League

	Age	Wins–Losses
Mike Mussina, N.Y. Yankees, 2008	39	20–9
Jamie Moyer, Sea. Mariners, 2001	38	20–6
Allie Reynolds, N.Y. Yankees, 1952	37	20–8
David Wells, Tor. Blue Jays, 2000	37	20–8
Spud Chandler, N.Y. Yankees, 1943	36	20–4
Thornton Lee, Chi. White Sox, 1941	35	22–11
Dick Donovan, Cle. Indians, 1962	35	20–10
Earl Whitehill, Wash. Senators, 1933	34	22–8
Roger Wolff, Wash. Senators, 1945	34	20–10
Rube Walberg, Phila. A's, 1931	34	20–12

National League (Post-1899)

	Age	Wins–Losses
R.A. Dickey, N.Y. Mets, 2012	37	20–6
Curt Davis, St.L. Cardinals, 1939	36	22–16
Rip Sewell, Pitt. Pirates, 1943	36	21–9
Preacher Roe, Bklyn. Dodgers, 1951	36	22–3
Murry Dickson, Pitt. Pirates, 1951	35	20–16
Slim Sallee, Cin. Reds, 1919	34	21–7
Jim Turner, Bost. Braves, 1937	34	20–11
Whit Wyatt, Bklyn. Dodgers, 1941	34	22–10
Sal Maglie, N.Y. Giants, 1951	34	23–6
Sal Maglie, N.Y. Giants, 1951	34	23–6
Sam Jones, S.F. Giants, 1959	34	21–15
Tommy John, L.A. Dodgers, 1977	34	20–7
Joe Niekro, Hous. Astros, 1979	34	21–11
Mike Krukow, S.F. Giants, 1986	34	20–9

Youngest Pitchers to Win 20 Games

American League

	Age	Wins–Losses
Bob Feller, Cle. Indians, 1939	20 years, 10 months	24–9
Bret Saberhagen, K.C. Royals, 1985	21 years, 5 months	20–6
Babe Ruth, Bost. Red Sox, 1916	21 years, 7 months	23–12
Wes Ferrell, Cle. Indians, 1929	21 years, 8 months	21–10
Bob Feller, Cle. Indians, 1940	21 years, 10 months	27–11

National League (Post-1900)

	Age	Wins–Losses
Christy Mathewson, N. Y. Giants, 1901	20 years, 1 month	20–17
Dwight Gooden, N.Y. Mets, 1985	20 years, 10 months	24–4
Al Mamaux, Pitt. Pirates, 1915	21 years, 4 months	21–8
Ralph Branca, Bklyn. Dodgers, 1947	21 years, 9 months	21–12
Nick Maddox, Pitt. Pirates, 1908	21 years, 10 months	23–8

Rookies Winning 20 Games

American League

Roscoe Miller, Det. Tigers, 1901	23–13
Roy Patterson, Chi. White Sox, 1901	20–16
Ed Summers, Det. Tigers, 1908	24–12
Russ Ford, N.Y. Yankees, 1910	26–6
Vean Gregg, Cle. Indians, 1911	23–7
Reb Russell, Chi. White Sox, 1913	21–17
Scott Perry, Phila. A's, 1918	21–19
Wes Ferrell, Cle. Indians, 1929	21–10
Monte Weaver, Wash. Senators, 1932	22–10
Dave Ferriss, Bost. Red Sox, 1945	21–10
Gene Bearden, Cle. Indians, 1948	20–7
Alex Kellner, Phila. A's, 1949	20–12
Bob Grim, N.Y. Yankees, 1954	20–6

National League (Post-1900)

Christy Mathewson, N.Y. Giants, 1901	20–17
Henry Schmidt, Bklyn. Bridegrooms, 1903	21–13
Jake Weimer, Chi. Cubs, 1903	21–9
Irv Young, Bost. Beaneaters, 1905	20–21
George McQuillan, Phila. Phillies, 1908	23–17
King Cole, Chi. Cubs, 1910	20–4
Grover C. Alexander, Phila. Phillies, 1911	28–13
Larry Cheney, Chi. Cubs, 1912	26–10
Jeff Pfeffer, Bklyn. Dodgers, 1914	23–12
Lou Fette, Bost. Braves, 1937	20–10
Cliff Melton, N.Y. Giants, 1937	20–9
Jim Turner, Bost. Braves, 1937	20–11
Johnny Beazley, St.L. Cardinals, 1942	21–6
Bill Voiselle, N.Y. Giants, 1944	21–16
Larry Jansen, N.Y. Giants, 1947	21–5
Harvey Haddix, St.L. Cardinals, 1953	20–9
Tom Browning, Cin. Reds, 1985	20–9

Most Seasons Logged Before First 20-Win Season

Seasons		20-Win Season
18	Mike Mussina (1991–2008)	20–9 in 2008
14	Tommy John (1963–74, 1976–89)	20–7 in 1977
14	Jamie Moyer (1986–91, 1993–10, 2012)	20–6 in 2001
13	Red Ruffing (1924–42, 1945–47)	20–12 in 1936
13	David Wells (1987–2007)	20–8 in 2000
12	Slim Sallee (1908–21)	21–7 in 1919
12	Lee Meadows (1915–29)	20–9 in 1926
12	Whit Wyatt (1929–45)	22–10 in 1941
11	Wee Willie Sherdel (1918–32)	21–10 in 1928
11	Earl Whitehill (1923–39)	22–8 in 1933
11	Early Wynn (1939, 1941–44, 1946–63)	20–13 in 1951
11	Allie Reynolds (1942–54)	20–8 in 1952
10	Mike Krukow (1976–89)	20–9 in 1986
9	Rube Walberg (1923–37)	20–12 in 1931
9	Preacher Roe (1938, 1944–54)	22–3 in 1951
9	R.A. Dickey (2001, 2003–06, 2008–)	20–6 in 2012

Rookie Pitchers with 20 Wins and 200 Strikeouts

	Wins–Losses	Strikeouts
Christy Mathewson, N.Y. Giants (NL), 1901	20–17	221
Russ Ford, N.Y. Yankees (AL), 1910	26–6	209
Grover C. Alexander, Phila. Phillies (NL), 1911	28–13	227

Pitchers Winning 20 Games in Rookie Year, Fewer Than 20 Balance of Career

	Rookie Year	Career
Roscoe Miller, Det. Tigers (AL) (1901–04)	23–13 (1901)	39–46
Henry Schmidt, Bklyn. Bridegrooms (NL) (1903)	21–13 (1903)	21–13
Johnny Beazley, St.L. Cardinals (NL) (1941–42, 1946–49)	21–6 (1942)	31–12

20-Game Winners Who Didn't Win 20 More Games in Career (Post-1900)

Sandy Koufax, Bklyn. Dodgers (NL) (1955–57), L.A. Dodgers (1958–66)*	27 wins (1966)	0 rest of career
Steve Stone, S.F. Giants (NL) (1971–72), Chi. White Sox (AL) (1973, 1977–78), Chi. Cubs (NL) (1974–76), Balt. Orioles (AL) (1978–80)	25 wins (1980)	4 rest of career
Denny McLain, Det. Tigers (AL) (1963–70), Wash. Senators II (AL) (1971), Oak. A's (AL) (1972), Atl. Braves (NL) (1972)	24 wins (1969)	17 rest of career
Ron Bryant, S.F. Giants (NL) (1967, 1969–75)	24 wins (1973)	3 rest of career
Roscoe Miller, Det. Tigers (AL) (1901–04)	23 wins (1901)	16 rest of career
Lefty Williams, Det. Tigers (AL) (1913–14), Chi. White Sox (AL) (1916–20)*	22 wins (1920)	0 rest of career
Eddie Cicotte, Det. Tigers (AL) (1905), Bost. Red Sox (AL) (1908–12), Chi. White Sox (AL) (1912–1920)**	21 wins (1920)	0 rest of career
Henry Schmidt, Bklyn. Bridegrooms (NL) (1903)	21 wins (1903)	0 rest of career
Buck O'Brien, Bost. Red Sox (AL) (1911–13)	20 wins (1912)	9 rest of career
Bill James, Bost. Braves (NL) (1913–15, 1919)	26 wins (1914)	11 rest of career
Brandon Webb, Ariz. D'backs (NL) (2003–09)	22 wins (2008)	0 rest of career
George McConnell, Chi. Whales (FL) (1909, 1912–16)	25 wins (1915)	16 rest of career
Jack Morris, Det. Tigers (AL) (1977–90), Min. Twins (AL) (1991), Tor. Blue Jays (AL) (1992–93), Cle. Indians (AL) (1994)	21 wins (1992)	17 rest of career
Joaquin Andujar, Hous. Astros (NL) (1976–81, 1988), St.L. Cardinals (NL) (1981–85), Oak. A's (AL) (1986–87)	21 wins (1985)	17 rest of career
Johnny Beazley, St.L. Cardinals (NL) (1941–42, 1946–49)	21 wins (1942)	10 rest of career
Mike Mussina, Balt. Orioles (AL) (1991–2000), N.Y. Yankees (AL) (2001–08)*	20 wins (2008)	0 rest of career

* Retired after season.

** Banned from baseball for gambling after season.

Pitchers Winning 20 Games in Last Season in Majors

Mike Mussina, N.Y. Yankees (AL), 2008 20–9
Eddie Cicotte, Chi. White Sox (AL), 1920 21–10
Sandy Koufax, L.A. Dodgers (NL), 1966 27–9
Henry Schmidt, Bklyn. Dodgers (NL), 1903 21–13
Lefty Williams, Chi. White Sox (AL), 1920 22–14

Earliest 20-Game Winner During Season

American League

		Final Record
July 25, 1931	Lefty Grove, Phila. A's	31–4
July 27, 1968	Denny McLain, Det. Tigers	31–6

National League

		Final Record
July 19, 1912	Rube Marquard, N.Y. Giants	26–11

Most Wins After Turning 40

Wins After 40		Total Career Wins
121	Phil Niekro	318
105	Jamie Moyer	269
96	Jack Quinn	247
75	Cy Young	511
75	Warren Spahn	363
73	Randy Johnson	303
71	Nolan Ryan	324
67	Charlie Hough	216
61	Roger Clemens	354
54	David Wells	239
54	Hoyt Wilhelm	143

Pitchers on Losing Teams, Leading League in Wins

American League

Pitcher	Wins–Losses	Team Record
Walter Johnson, Wash. Senators, 1916	25–20	76–77
Eddie Rommel, Phila. A's, 1922	27–13	65–89
Ted Lyons, Chi. White Sox, 1927	22–14	70–83
Bob Feller, Cle. Indians, 1941	25–13	75–79
Bob Feller, Cle. Indians, 1946	26–15	68–86
Jim Perry, Cle. Indians, 1960	18–10	76–78
Gaylord Perry, Cle. Indians, 1972	24–16	72–84
Wilbur Wood, Chi. White Sox, 1973	24–20	77–85
Roger Clemens, Bost. Red Sox, 1987	20–9	78–84
Kevin Brown, Tex. Rangers, 1992	21–11	77–85
Roger Clemens, Tor. Blue Jays, 1997	21–7	76–86

National League (Post-1900)

Pitcher	Wins–Losses	Team Record
Grover C. Alexander, Phila. Phillies, 1914	27–15	74–80
Grover C. Alexander, Chi. Cubs, 1920	27–14	75–79
Dazzy Vance, Bklyn. Dodgers, 1925	22–9	68–85
Jumbo Elliott, Phila. Phillies, 1931	19–14 (Tie)	66–88
Heine Meine, Pitt. Pirates, 1931	19–13 (Tie)	75–79
Ewell Blackwell, Cin. Reds, 1947	22–8	73–81
Warren Spahn, Bost. Braves, 1949	21–14	75–79
Robin Roberts, Phila. Phillies, 1954	23–15	75–79
Larry Jackson, Chi. Cubs, 1964	24–11	76–86
Bob Gibson, St.L. Cardinals, 1970	23–7	76–86
Steve Carlton, Phila. Phillies, 1972	27–10	59–97
Randy Jones, S.D. Padres, 1976	22–14	73–89
Phil Niekro, Atl. Braves, 1979	21–20	66–94

continued on next page

Fernando Valenzuela, L.A. Dodgers, 1986	21–11	73–89
Rick Sutcliffe, Chi. Cubs, 1987	18–10	76–85
Greg Maddux, Chi. Cubs, 1992	20–11	78–84
Brandon Webb, Ariz. D'backs, 2006	16–8	76–86

20-Game Winners on Last-Place Teams

American League

Pitcher	Wins–Losses	Team Record
Scott Perry, Phila. A's, 1918	20–19	52–76
Howard Ehmke, Bost. Red Sox, 1923	20–17	61–91
Sloppy Thurston, Chi. White Sox, 1924	20–14	66–87
Ned Garver, St.L. Browns, 1951	20–12	52–102
Nolan Ryan, Cal. Angels, 1974	22–16	68–94
Roger Clemens, Tor. Blue Jays, 1997	21–7	76–86

National League (Post-1900)

Pitcher	Wins–Losses	Team Record
Noodles Hahn, Cin. Reds, 1901	22–19	52–87
Steve Carlton, Phila. Phillies, 1972	27–10	59–97
Phil Niekro, Atl. Braves, 1979	21–20	66–94

20-Game Winners with Worst Lifetime Winning Percentage (Post-1900)

	Percentage	Lifetime	20-Win Season(s)
Scott Perry	.376	41–68	1918
Irv Young	.397	62–94	1905
Pete Schneider	.399	57–86	1917
Ben Cantwell	.413	76–108	1933
Joe Oeschger	.417	83–116	1921
Tom Hughes	.427	128–172	1903
Willie Sudhoff	.430	102–135	1903
Roger Wolff	.430	52–69	1945
Frank Allen	.431	50–66	1915
Otto Hess	.434	69–90	1906
Bob Harmon	.436	103–133	1911
Al Schulz	.440	48–61	1915
Vem Kennedy	.441	104–132	1936
Patsy Flaherty	.443	66–83	1904
Bob Groom	.446	121–150	1912
Oscar Jones	.446	45–56	1903
Randy Jones	.448	100–123	1975, 1976
Ned Garver	.451	129–157	1951
George McConnell	.452	42–51	1915
Chick Fraser	.454	176–212	1901

"Pure" 20-Game Winners (Pitchers with 20 or More Wins Than Losses)

American League

Cy Young, Bost. Americans, 1901	33–10
Cy Young, Bost. Americans, 1902	32–11
Jack Chesbro, N.Y. Highlanders, 1904	41–12
Ed Walsh, Chi. White Sox, 1908	40–15
George Mullin, Det. Tigers, 1909	29–8
Jack Coombs, Phila. A's, 1910	31–9

National League (Post-1900)

Joe McGinnity, Bklyn. Bridegrooms, 1900	29–9
Jack Chesbro, Pitt. Pirates, 1902	28–6
Joe McGinnity, N.Y. Giants, 1904	35–8
Christy Mathewson, N.Y. Giants, 1904	33–12
Christy Mathewson, N.Y. Giants, 1905	31–8
Three Finger Brown, Chi. Cubs, 1906	26–6

continued on next page

Russ Ford, N.Y. Highlanders, 1910 26–6
Smoky Joe Wood, Bost. Red Sox, 1912 34–5
Walter Johnson, Wash. Senators, 1912 32–12
Eddie Plank, Phila. A's, 1912 26–6
Walter Johnson, Wash. Senators, 1913 36–7
Eddie Cicotte, Chi. White Sox, 1919 29–7
Lefty Grove, Phila. A's, 1930 28–5
Lefty Grove, Phila. A's, 1931 31–4
Lefty Gomez, N.Y. Yankees, 1934 26–5
Hal Newhouser, Det. Tigers, 1944 29–9
Whitey Ford, N.Y. Yankees, 1961 25–4
Denny McLain, Det. Tigers, 1968 31–6
Ron Guidry, N.Y. Yankees, 1978 25–3
Roger Clemens, Bost. Red Sox, 1986 24–4

Three Finger Brown, Chi. Cubs, 1908 29–9
Christy Mathewson, N.Y. Giants, 1908 37–11
Grover C. Alexander, Phila. Phillies, 1914 31–10
Grover C. Alexander, Phila. Phillies, 1916 33–12
Dazzy Vance, Bklyn. Dodgers, 1923 28–6
Dizzy Dean, St.L. Cardinals, 1934 30–7
Carl Hubbell, N.Y. Giants, 1935 26–6
Robin Roberts, Phila. Phillies, 1951 28–7
Don Newcombe, Bklyn. Dodgers, 1955 27–7
Sandy Koufax, L.A. Dodgers, 1962 25–5
Dwight Gooden, N.Y. Mets, 1985 24–4

Lefties Winning 20 Games Twice Since World War II

American League

Vida Blue	Oak. A's	1971	24
	Oak. A's	1973	20
	Oak. A's	1975	22
Mike Cuellar	Balt. Orioles	1969	23
	Balt. Orioles	1970	24
	Balt. Orioles	1974	22
Whitey Ford	N.Y. Yankees	1961	25
	N.Y. Yankees	1963	24
Ron Guidry	N.Y. Yankees	1978	25
	N.Y. Yankees	1983	21
	N.Y. Yankees	1985	22
Tommy John*	N.Y. Yankees	1979	21
	N.Y. Yankees	1980	22
Jim Kaat	Min. Twins	1966	25
	Chi. White Sox	1974	21
	Chi. White Sox	1975	20
Mickey Lolich	Det. Tigers	1971	25
	Det. Tigers	1972	22
Dave McNally	Balt. Orioles	1968	22
	Balt. Orioles	1969	20
	Balt. Orioles	1970	24
	Balt. Orioles	1971	21
Jamie Moyer	Sea. Mariners	2001	21
	Sea. Mariners	2003	21
Hal Newhouser	Det. Tigers	1946	26
	Det. Tigers	1948	21
Mel Parnell	Bost. Red Sox	1949	25
	Bost. Red Sox	1953	21
Andy Pettitte	N.Y. Yankees	1996	21
	N.Y. Yankees	2003	21
Billy Pierce	Chi. White Sox	1956	20
	Chi. White Sox	1957	20
Wilbur Wood	Chi. White Sox	1971	22
	Chi. White Sox	1972	24
	Chi. White Sox	1973	24
	Chi. White Sox	1974	20

continued on next page

National League

Johnny Antonelli	N.Y. Giants	1954	21
	N.Y. Giants	1956	20
Steve Carlton	St.L. Cardinals	1971	20
	Phila. Phillies	1972	27
	Phila. Phillies	1976	20
	Phila. Phillies	1977	23
	Phila. Phillies	1980	24
	Phila. Phillies	1982	23
Tom Glavine	Atl. Braves	1991	20
	Atl. Braves	1992	20
	Atl. Braves	1993	22
	Atl. Braves	1998	20
	Atl. Braves	2000	21
Randy Johnson**	Ariz. D'backs	2001	21
	Ariz. D'backs	2002	24
Randy Jones	S.D. Padres	1975	20
	S.D. Padres	1976	22
Clayton Kershaw	L.A. Dodgers	2011	21
	L.A. Dodgers	2014	21
Sandy Koufax	L.A. Dodgers	1963	25
	L.A. Dodgers	1965	26
	L.A. Dodgers	1966	27
Claude Osteen	L.A. Dodgers	1969	20
	L.A. Dodgers	1972	20
Howie Pollet	St.L. Cardinals	1946	21
	St.L. Cardinals	1949	20
Warren Spahn	Bost. Braves	1947	21
	Bost. Braves	1949	21
	Bost. Braves	1950	21
	Bost. Braves	1951	22
	Milw. Braves	1953	23
	Milw. Braves	1954	21
	Milw. Braves	1956	20
	Milw. Braves	1957	21
	Milw. Braves	1958	22
	Milw. Braves	1959	21
	Milw. Braves	1960	21
	Milw. Braves	1961	21
	Milw. Braves	1963	23

*Also won 20 games in 1977 with the L.A. Dodgers.
**Also won 20 games in 1997 with the Sea. Mariners

Pitchers with 20-Win Seasons After Age 40

		Age	Season	Wins–Losses
Grover C. Alexander	St.L. Cardinals (NL)	40	1927	21–10
Jamie Moyer	Sea. Mariners (AL)	40	2003	21–7
Phil Niekro	Atl. Braves (NL)	40	1979	21–20
Gaylord Perry	S.D. Padres (NL)	40	1978	21–6
Eddie Plank	St.L. Terriers (FL)	40	1915	21–11
Warren Spahn	Milw. Braves (NL)	40	1961	21–13
	Milw. Braves (NL)	42	1963	23–7
Cy Young	Bost. Americans (AL)	40	1907	21–15
	Bost. Americans (AL)	41	1908	21–11

Pitchers Leading Both Leagues in Wins, Season

American League			National League		
Jack Chesbro	N.Y. Highlanders, 1904	41–13	Pitt. Pirates, 1902	28–6	
Roy Halladay	Tor. Blue Jays, 2003	22–7	Phila. Phillies, 2010	21–10	
Ferguson Jenkins	Tex. Rangers, 1974	25–12 (Tie)	Chi. Cubs, 1971	24–13	
Gaylord Perry	Cle. Indians, 1972	24–16 (Tie)	S.F. Giants, 1970	23–13 (Tie)	
			S.D. Padres, 1978	21–6	
Curt Schilling	Bost. Red Sox, 2004	21–6	Ariz. D'backs, 2001	22–6	
Cy Young	Bost. Americans, 1901	33–10	Cle. Spiders, 1892	36–12 (Tie)	
	Bost. Americans, 1902	32–11	Cle. Spiders, 1895	35–10	
	Bost. Americans, 1903	28–9			

20-Game Winners One Season, 20-Game Losers the Next

American League

George Mullin, Det. Tigers	21–18 (1906)	20–20 (1907)
Al Orth, N.Y. Highlanders	27–17 (1906)	27–21 (1907)
Russ Ford, N.Y. Highlanders	22–11 (1911)	13–21 (1912)
Walter Johnson, Wash. Senators	27–13 (1915)	25–20 (1916)
Hooks Dauss, Det. Tigers	21–9 (1919)	13–21 (1920)
Bobo Newsom, Det. Tigers	21–5 (1940)	12–20 (1941)
Alex Kellner, Phila. A's	20–12 (1949)	8–20 (1950)
Mel Stottlemyre, N.Y. Yankees	20–9 (1965)	12–20 (1966)
Luis Tiant, Cle. Indians	21–9 (1968)	9–20 (1969)
Stan Bahnsen, Chi. White Sox	21–16 (1972)	18–21 (1973)
Wilbur Wood, Chi. White Sox	24–17 (1972)	24–20 (1973)
Wilbur Wood, Chi. White Sox	20–19 (1974)	16–20 (1975)

National League (Post-1900)

Joe McGinnity, Bklyn. Bridegrooms (NL), Balt. Orioles (AL)	28–8 (1900)	26–20 (1901)
Vic Willis, Bost. Beaneaters	20–17 (1901)	27–20 (1902)
Togie Pittinger, Bost. Beaneaters	27–16 (1902)	18–22 (1903)
Jack Taylor, St.L. Cardinals	20–19 (1904)	15–21 (1905)
Irv Young, Bost. Beaneaters	20–21 (1905)	16–25 (1906)
Nap Rucker, Bklyn. Dodgers	22–18 (1911)	18–21 (1912)
Rube Marquard, N.Y. Giants	23–10 (1913)	12–22 (1914)
Eppa Rixey, Phila. Phillies	22–10 (1916)	16–21 (1917)
Joe Oeschger, Bost. Braves	20–14 (1921)	6–21 (1922)
Murry Dickson, Pitt. Pirates	20–16 (1951)	14–21 (1952)
Larry Jackson, Chi. Cubs	24–11 (1964)	14–21 (1965)
Steve Carlton, Phila. Phillies	27–10 (1972)	13–20 (1973)
Jerry Koosman, N.Y. Mets	21–10 (1976)	8–20 (1977)

20-Game Winners and Losers, Same Season

American League

Joe McGinnity, Balt. Orioles, 1901	26–20
Bill Dinneen, Bost. Americans, 1902	21–21
George Mullin, Det. Tigers, 1905	21–21
George Mullin, Det. Tigers, 1907	20–20
Jim Scott, Chi. White Sox, 1913	20–20
Walter Johnson, Wash. Senators, 1916	25–20
Wilbur Wood, Chi. White Sox, 1973	24–20

National League (Post-1900)

Vic Willis, Bost. Beaneaters, 1902	27–20
Joe McGinnity, N.Y. Giants, 1903	31–20
Irv Young, Bost. Beaneaters, 1905	20–21
Phil Niekro, Atl. Braves, 1979	21–20

Pitchers Who Led League in Wins in Successive Seasons

American League

Seasons	
4	Walter Johnson, Wash, Senators, 1913–16
3	Cy Young, Bost. Americans, 1901–03
3	Bob Feller, Cle. Indians, 1939–41
3	Hal Newhouser, Det. Tigers, 1944–46
3	Jim Palmer, Balt. Orioles, 1975–77
2	Jack Coombs, Phila A's, 1910–11
2	Lefty Grove, Phila A's, 1930–31
2	General Crowder, Wash. Senators, 1932–33
2	Bob Feller, Cle. Indians, 1946–47
2	Bob Lemon, Cle. Indians, 1954–55
2	Denny McLain, Det. Tigers, 1968–69
2	Wilbur Wood, Chi. White Sox, 1972–73
2	Catfish Hunter, Oak. A's, 1974–75
2	LaMarr Hoyt, Chi. White Sox, 1982–83
2	Roger Clemens, Bost. Red Sox, 1986–87
2	Roger Clemens, Tor. Blue Jays, 1997–98
2	CC Sabathia, N.Y. Yankees, 2009–10
2	Max Scherzer, Det. Tigers, 2013–14

National League

Seasons	
5	Warren Spahn, Milw. Braves, 1957–61
4	Grover C. Alexander, Phila. Phillies, 1914–17
4	Robin Roberts, Phila. Phillies, 1952–55
3	Bill Hutchison, Chi. Colts, 1890–92
3	Kid Nichols, Bost. Beaneaters, 1896–98
3	Tom Glavine, Atl. Braves, 1991–93
2	Tommy Bond, Bost. Red Caps, 1877–78
2	Old Hoss Radbourn, Pro. Grays, 1883–84
2	Joe McGinnity, Balt. Orioles, 1899–1900
2	Joe McGinnity, N.Y. Giants, 1903–04
2	Christy Mathewson, N.Y. Giants, 1907–08
2	Dazzy Vance, Bklyn. Dodgers, 1924–25
2	Pat Malone, Chi. Cubs, 1929–30
2	Dizzy Dean, St.L. Cardinals, 1934–35
2	Carl Hubbell, N.Y. Giants, 1936–37
2	Bucky Walters, Cin. Reds, 1939–40
2	Mort Cooper, St.L. Cardinals, 1942–43
2	Warren Spahn, Bost. Braves, 1949–50
2	Sandy Koufax, L.A. Dodgers, 1965–66
2	Greg Maddux, Atl. Braves, 1994–95

Most Pitching Wins for One Season

Pitcher	Wins	Year	Team
Old Hoss Radbourn	59	1884	Pro. Grays (NL)
John Clarkson	53	1885	Chi. White Stockings (NL)
Guy Hecker	52	1884	Lou. Colonels (AA)
John Clarkson	49	1889	Bost. Beaneaters (NL)
Old Hoss Radbourn	48	1883	Pro. Grays (NL)
Charlie Buffinton	48	1884	Bost. Beaneaters (NL)
Al Spalding	47	1876	Chi. White Stockings (NL)
Monte Ward	47	1879	Pro. Grays (NL)
Pud Galvin	46	1883	Buff. Bisons (NL)
Pud Galvin	46	1884	Buff. Bisons (NL)
Matt Kilroy	46	1887	Balt. Orioles (AA)
George Bradley	45	1876	St.L. Brown Stockings (NL)
Jim McCormick	45	1880	Cle. Blues (NL)
Silver King	45	1888	St.L. Browns (AA)
Mickey Welch	44	1885	N.Y. Giants (NL)
Bill Hutchinson	44	1891	Chi. Colts (NL)
Will White	43	1879	Cin. Reds (NL)
Larry Corcoran	43	1880	Chi. White Stockings (NL)
Will White	43	1883	Cin. Red Stockings (AA)
Billy Taylor	43	1884	Phila. A's (AA)–St.L. Maroons (UA)
Tommy Bond	43	1897	Bost. Red Caps (NL)

continued on next page

Lady Baldwin	42	1886	Det. Wolverines (NL)
Tim Keefe	42	1886	N.Y. Giants (NL)
Bill Hutchinson	42	1890	Chi. Colts (NL)
Tim Keefe	41	1883	N.Y. Metropolitans (AA)
Charlie Sweeney	41	1884	Pro. Grays (NL)–St.L. Maroons (UA)
Dave Foutz	41	1886	St.L. Browns (AA)
Ed Morris	41	1886	Pitt. Alleghenys (AA)
Jack Chesbro	41	1904	N.Y. Highlanders (AL)
Tommy Bond	40	1877	Bost. Red Caps (NL)
Tommy Bond	40	1878	Bost. Red Caps (NL)
Will White	40	1882	Cin. Red Stockings (AA)
Jim McCormick	40	1884	Cle. Blues (NL)–Cin. Outlaw Reds (UA)
Bill Sweeney	40	1884	Balt. Monumentals (UA)
Bob Caruthers	40	1885	St.L. Browns (AA)
Bob Caruthers	40	1889	Bklyn. Bridegrooms (AA)
Ed Walsh	40	1908	Chi. White Sox (AL)

Most Total Wins, Two Pitchers on Same Staff, Career Together as Teammates

American League

440 ..... Eddie Plank (247) and Chief Bender (193), Phila. A's (1903–14)
408 ..... Lefty Grove (257) and Rube Walberg (151), Phila. A's (1925–33) and Bost. Red Sox (1934–37)
408 ..... Red Ruffing (219) and Lefty Gomez (189), N.Y. Yankees (1930–42)
361 ..... Hal Newhouser (200) and Dizzy Trout (161), Det. Tigers (1939–52)
355 ..... Bob Lemon (201) and Bob Feller (154), Cle. Indians (1946–56)
349 ..... Early Wynn (177) and Bob Lemon (172), Cle. Indians (1949–58)
332 ..... Ed Walsh (190) and Doc White (142), Chi. White Sox (1904–13)
331 ..... Bob Lemon (192) and Mike Garcia (139), Cle. Indians (1948–58)

National League

443 ..... Warren Spahn (264) and Lew Burdette (179), Bost.–Milw. Braves (1951–63)
433 ..... Christy Mathewson (297) and Hooks Wiltse (136), N.Y. Giants (1904–14)
408 ..... Tom Glavine (242) and John Smoltz (166), Atl. Braves (1988–2002, 2008)
358 ..... Carl Hubbell (204) and Hal Schumacher (154), N.Y. Giants (1931–42)
347 ..... Greg Maddux (178) and Tom Glavine (169), Atl. Braves (1993–2002)
342 ..... Christy Mathewson (191) and Joe McGinnity (151), N.Y. Giants (1902–08)
340 ..... Sam Leever (172) and Deacon Phillippe (168), Pitt. Pirates (1900–10)
340 ..... Don Drysdale (177) and Sandy Koufax (163), Bklyn.–L.A. Dodgers (1956–66)
336 ..... Juan Marichal (202) and Gaylord Perry (134), S.F. Giants (1962–71)
326 ..... Robin Roberts (212) and Curt Simmons (114), Phila. Phillies (1948–50, 1952–60)
318 ..... Three Finger Brown (182) and Ed Reulbach (136), Chi. Cubs (1905–13)
317 ..... Bob Friend (176) and Vern Law (141), Pitt. Pirates (1951, 1954–65)

Most Wins, Right-Hander and Left-Hander on Same Staff, Season

American League

58 ..... Ed Walsh (RH, 40) and Doc White (LH, 18), Chi. White Sox, 1908
56 ..... Hal Newhouser (LH, 29) and Dizzy Trout (RH, 27), Det. Tigers, 1944
53 ..... Walter Johnson (RH, 36) and Joe Boehling (LH, 17), Wash. Senators, 1913

continued on next page

52 ..... Eddie Cicotte (RH, 29) and Lefty Williams (LH, 23), Chi. White Sox, 1919
52 ..... Lefty Grove (LH, 31) and George Earnshaw (RH, 21), Phila. A's, 1931
51 ..... Doc White (LH, 27) and Ed Walsh (RH, 24), Chi. White Sox, 1907
51 ..... Jack Coombs (RH, 28) and Eddie Plank (LH, 23), Phila. A's, 1911
50 ..... Ed Killian (LH, 25) and Bill Donovan (RH, 25), Det. Tigers, 1907
50 ..... Lefty Grove (LH, 28) and George Earnshaw (RH, 22), Phila. A's, 1930
48 ..... Mel Parnell (LH, 25) and Ellis Kinder (RH, 23), Bost. Red Sox, 1949
48 ..... Denny McLain (RH, 31) and Mickey Lolich (LH, 17), Det. Tigers, 1968
47 ..... Cy Young (RH, 26) and Jesse Tannehill (LH, 21), Bost. Red Sox, 1904
47 ..... Jack Coombs (RH, 31) and Eddie Plank (LH, 16), Phila. A's, 1910
47 ..... Smoky Joe Wood (RH, 34) and Ray Collins, (LH, 13), Bost. Red Sox, 1912
47 ..... Eddie Plank (LH, 26) and Jack Coombs (RH, 21), Phila. A's, 1912
46 ..... Babe Ruth (LH, 24) and Carl Mays (RH, 22), Bost. Red Sox, 1917
46 ..... General Crowder (RH, 24) and Earl Whitehill (LH, 22), Wash. Senators, 1933
46 ..... Hooks Dauss (RH, 24) and Harry Coveleski (LH, 22), Det. Tigers, 1915

National League (Post-1900)

60 ..... Christy Mathewson (RH, 37) and Hooks Wiltse (LH, 23), N.Y. Giants, 1908
55 ..... Grover C. Alexander (RH, 33) and Eppa Rixey (LH, 22), Phila. Phillies, 1916
50 ..... Christy Mathewson (RH, 26) and Rube Marquard (LH, 24), N.Y. Giants, 1911
49 ..... Rube Marquard (LH, 26) and Christy Mathewson (RH, 23), N.Y. Giants, 1912
49 ..... Sandy Koufax (LH, 26) and Don Drysdale (RH, 23), L.A. Dodgers, 1965
48 ..... Jack Chesbro (RH, 28) and Jesse Tannehill (LH, 20), Pitt. Pirates, 1902
48 ..... Joe McGinnity (RH, 35) and Hooks Wiltse (LH, 13), N.Y. Giants, 1904
48 ..... Christy Mathewson (RH, 25) and Rube Marquard (LH, 23), N.Y. Giants, 1913
47 ..... Randy Johnson (LH, 24) and Curt Schilling (RH, 23), Ariz. D'backs, 2002
47 ..... Dolf Luque (RH, 27) and Eppa Rixey (LH, 20), Cin. Reds, 1923
46 ..... Christy Mathewson (RH, 31) and Hooks Wiltse (LH, 15), N.Y. Giants, 1905
46 ..... Three Finger Brown (RH, 26) and Jack Pfiester (LH, 20), Chi. Cubs, 1906
46 ..... Grover C. Alexander (RH, 30) and Eppa Rixey (LH, 16), Phila. Phillies, 1917
46 ..... Grover C. Alexander (RH, 27) and Hippo Vaughn (LH, 19), Chi. Cubs, 1920

Largest Differential Between League Leader in Wins and Runner-Up

American League

Differential		Leader	Runner(s)-Up
+16	1908	Ed Walsh, Chi. White Sox (40)	Addie Joss, Cle. Indians (24)
			Ed Summers, Det. Tigers (24)
+15	1904	Jack Chesbro, N.Y. Yankees (41)	Eddie Plank, Phila. A's (26)
			Cy Young, Bost. Americans (26)
+13	1913	Walter Johnson, Wash. Senators (36)	Cy Falkenberg, Cle. Indians (23)
+9	1931	Lefty Grove, Phila. A's (31)	Wes Ferrell, Cle. Indians (22)
+9	1968	Denny McLain, Det. Tigers (31)	Dave McNally, Balt. Orioles (22)
+8	1902	Cy Young, Bost. Americans (32)	Rube Waddell, Phila. A's (24)

National League (Post-1900)

+10	1952	Robin Roberts, Phila. Phillies (28)	Sal Maglie, N.Y. Giants (18)
+9	1915	Grover C. Alexander, Phila. Phillies (31)	Dick Rudolph, Bost. Braves (22)
+8	1900	Joe McGinnity, Bklyn. Bridegrooms (28)	Bill Dinneen, Bost. Beaneaters (20)
			Brickyard Kennedy, Bklyn. Dodgers (20)
			Deacon Phillippe, Pitt. Pirates (20)
			Jesse Tannehill, Pitt. Pirates (20)

continued on next page

+8 ..... 1905 ..... Christy Mathewson, N.Y. Giants (31) ..... Togie Pittinger, Phila. Phillies (23)
+8 ..... 1908 ..... Christy Mathewson, N.Y. Giants (37) ..... Three Finger Brown, Chi. Cubs (29)
+8 ..... 1916 ..... Grover C. Alexander, Phila. Phillies (33) ..... Jeff Pfeffer, Bklyn. Dodgers (25)

Highest Percentage of Team's Total Wins for Season

American League

45.6% ..... Jack Chesbro (N.Y. Highlanders, 1904) ..... 41 of team's 92 wins
45.5% ..... Ed Walsh (Chi. White Sox, 1908) ..... 40 of team's 88 wins
41.8% ..... Cy Young (Bost. Americans, 1901) ..... 33 of team's 79 wins
41.7% ..... Joe Bush (Phila. A's, 1916) ..... 15 of team's 36 wins
41.6% ..... Cy Young (Bost. Red Sox, 1902) ..... 32 of team's 77 wins
41.5% ..... Eddie Rommel (Phila. A's, 1922) ..... 27 of team's 65 wins
40.3% ..... Red Faber (Chi. White Sox, 1921) ..... 25 of team's 62 wins
40.0% ..... Walter Johnson (Wash. Senators, 1913) ..... 36 of team's 90 wins
39.1% ..... Walter Johnson (Wash. Senators, 1911) ..... 25 of team's 64 wins
38.9% ..... Elmer Myers (Phila. A's, 1916) ..... 14 of team's 36 wins
38.5% ..... Ned Garver (St.L. Browns, 1951) ..... 20 of team's 52 wins
38.5% ..... Scott Perry (Phila. A's, 1918) ..... 20 of team's 52 wins
38.2% ..... Joe McGinnity, (Balt. Orioles, 1901) ..... 26 of team's 68 wins
38.2% ..... Bob Feller (Cle. Indians, 1946) ..... 26 of team's 68 wins
37.9% ..... Walter Johnson (Wash. Senators, 1910) ..... 25 of team's 66 wins

National League (Post-1900)

45.8% ..... Steve Carlton (Phila. Phillies, 1972) ..... 27 of team's 59 wins
42.3% ..... Noodles Hahn (Cin. Reds, 1901) ..... 22 of team's 52 wins
39.2% ..... Irv Young (Bost. Beaneaters, 1905) ..... 20 of team's 51 wins
38.5% ..... Christy Mathewson (N.Y. Giants, 1901) ..... 20 of team's 52 wins
37.8% ..... Christy Mathewson (N.Y. Giants, 1908) ..... 37 of team's 98 wins
37.3% ..... Slim Sallee (St.L. Cardinals, 1913) ..... 19 of team's 51 wins
37.0% ..... Togie Pittinger (Bost. Beaneaters, 1902) ..... 27 of team's 73 wins
37.0% ..... Vic Willis (Bost. Beaneaters, 1902) ..... 27 of team's 73 wins
36.9% ..... Joe McGinnity (N.Y. Giants, 1903) ..... 31 of team's 84 wins

Pitchers Winning 300 Games, Never Striking Out 200 Batters, Season

Pitcher	Wins	Most Strikeouts (Season)
Tom Glavine	305	192 (1991)
Warren Spahn	363	191 (1950)
Early Wynn	300	184 (1957)

Won-Loss Percentage of 300-Game Winners

Won-Loss Percentage	Player	Years	Record
.680	Lefty Grove	(1925–41)	300–141
.665	Christy Mathewson	(1900–16)	373–188
.658	Roger Clemens	(1984–2007)	354–184
.648	John Clarkson	(1882–94)	328–178
.646	Randy Johnson	(1988–2009)	303–166
.642	Grover C. Alexander	(1911–30)	373–208
.634	Kid Nichols	(1890–1906)	361–208
.627	Eddie Plank	(1901–17)	326–194
.619	Cy Young	(1890–1911)	511–316
.614	Old Hoss Radbourn	(1880–91)	309–194
.610	Greg Maddux	(1986–2008)	355–227
.603	Tim Keefe	(1880–93)	341–225
.603	Tom Seaver	(1967–86)	311–205
.600	Tom Glavine	(1987–2008)	305–203
.599	Walter Johnson	(1907–27)	417–279
.597	Warren Spahn	(1946–65)	363–245
.594	Mickey Welch	(1880–92)	307–210
.574	Steve Carlton	(1965–88)	329–244
.559	Don Sutton	(1966–88)	324–256
.551	Early Wynn	(1939, 1941–44, 1946–63)	300–244
.542	Gaylord Perry	(1962–83)	314–265
.540	Pud Galvin	(1879–92)	361–308
.537	Phil Niekro	(1964–87)	318–274
.526	Nolan Ryan	(1966, 1968–93)	324–292

Shutouts

Evolution of Shutout Record

American League

1901	Clark Griffith, Chi. White Sox	5
	Cy Young, Bost. Americans	5
1903	Cy Young, Bost. Americans	7
1904	Cy Young, Bost. Americans	10
1908	Ed Walsh, Chi. White Sox	11
1910	Jack Coombs, Phila. A's	13

National League (Pre-1900)

1876	George Bradley, St.L. Brown Stockings	16

National League (Post-1899)

1900	Clark Griffith, Chi. Cubs	4
	Noodles Hahn, Cin. Reds	4
	Kid Nichols, Bost. Beaneaters	4
	Cy Young, St.L. Cardinals	4
1901	Jack Chesbro, Pitt. Pirates	6
	Al Orth, Phila. Phillies	6
	Vic Willis, Bost. Beaneaters	6
1902	Jack Chesbro, Pitt. Pirates	8
	Christy Mathewson, N.Y. Giants	8
	Jack Taylor, Chi. Cubs	8
1904	Joe McGinnity, N.Y. Giants	9
1908	Christy Mathewson, N.Y. Giants	11
1915	Grover C. Alexander, Phila. Phillies	12
1916	Grover C. Alexander, Phila. Phillies	16

20-Game Winners with No Complete Game Shutouts

American League

Wins	Losses	
26	7	Joe Bush, N.Y. Yankees, 1922
24	15	General Crowder, Wash. Senators, 1933
23	5	Barry Zito, Oak. A's, 2002
22	14	Lefty Williams, Chi. White Sox, 1920
22	11	Earl Wilson, Det. Tigers, 1967
21	9	Esteban Loaiza, Chi. White Sox, 2003
21	9	Dave Stewart, Oak. A's, 1989
21	8	Andy Pettitte, N.Y. Yankees, 1996
21	8	Andy Pettitte, N.Y. Yankees, 2003
21	8	Bartolo Colon, L.A. Angels, 2005
21	7	Jamie Moyer, Sea. Mariners, 2003
21	7	CC Sabathia, N.Y. Yankees, 2010
21	6	Curt Schilling, Bost. Red Sox, 2004
21	3	Max Scherzer, Det. Tigers, 2013
20	16	Bobo Newsom, St.L. Browns, 1938
20	13	Luis Tiant, Bost. Red Sox, 1973
20	12	Alex Kellner, Phila. A's, 1949
20	12	Dave Boswell, Min. Twins, 1969
20	9	Mike Mussina, N.Y. Yankees, 2008
20	9	Bill Gullickson, Det. Tigers, 1991
20	9	Hugh Bedient, Bost. Red Sox, 1912
20	7	Josh Beckett, Bost. Red Sox, 2007
20	7	David Cone, N.Y. Yankees, 1998
20	6	Jamie Moyer, Sea. Mariners, 2001
20	4	Pedro Martinez, Bost. Red Sox, 2002
20	3	Roger Clemens, N.Y. Yankees, 2001

National League (Post-1900)

Wins	Losses	
24	12	Ron Bryant, S.F. Giants, 1973
23	12	Christy Mathewson, N.Y. Giants, 1912
21	12	Three Finger Brown, Chi. Cubs, 1911
21	10	Jose Lima, Hous. Astros, 1999
21	10	Willie Sherdel, St.L. Cardinals, 1928
20	19	Pete Schneider, Cin. Reds, 1917

Most Shutouts by a Rookie

American League

8 ..... Russ Ford, 1910 N.Y. Yankees
Reb Russell, 1913 Chi. White Sox
7 ..... Harry Krause, 1909 Phila. A's
6 ..... Fred Glade, 1904 St.L. Browns
Gene Bearden, 1948 Cle. Indians

National League

8 ..... Fernando Valenzuela, 1981 L.A. Dodgers
7 ..... Irv Young, 1905 Bost. Beaneaters
George McQuillan, 1908 Phila. Phillies
Grover C. Alexander, 1911 Phila. Phillies
Jerry Koosman, 1968 N.Y. Mets
6 ..... Harvey Haddix, 1953 St.L. Cardinals
Ewell Blackwell, 1946 Cin. Reds

Pitchers Leading League in Wins, No Complete Game Shutouts

American League

Wins	Losses	
24	15	General Crowder, Wash. Senators, 1933
23	5	Barry Zito, Oak. A's, 2002
22	11	Earl Wilson, Det. Tigers, 1967
22	6	Tex Hughson, Bost. Red Sox, 1942
21	8	Andy Pettitte, N.Y. Yankees, 1996
21	8	Bartolo Colon, L.A. Angels, 2005
21	7	CC Sabathia, N.Y. Yankees, 2010
21	6	Curt Schilling, Bost. Red Sox, 2004
21	3	Max Scherzer, Det. Tigers, 2013
20	9	Bill Gullickson, Det. Tigers, 1991
20	7	David Cone, N.Y. Yankees, 1998
20	7	Josh Beckett, Bost. Red Sox, 2007
19	6	Johan Santana, Min. Twins, 2006
18	10	Bob Lemon, Cle. Indians, 1955
18	9	Jered Weaver, L.A. Angels, 2014

National League (Post-1900)

Wins	Losses	
24	12	Ron Bryant, S.F. Giants, 1973
19	8	Adam Wainwright, St.L. Cardinals, 2009
19	6	Jake Peavy, S.D. Padres, 2007
16	9	Brad Penny, L.A. Dodgers, 2006
16	8	Derek Lowe, L.A. Dodgers, 2006
16	7	Carlos Zambrano, Chi. Cubs, 2006

Most Career Starts, No Shutouts

Starts		Wins–Losses
217	Jorge De La Rosa (2004–)	93–75
213	Mike Pelfrey (2006–)	61–81
206	Chris Young (2004–12, 2014–)	76–58
203	Jason Bere (1993–2003)	71–65
201	Adam Eaton (2000–09)	71–68
187	Nate Robertson (2002–10)	57–77
167	Tony Armas (1999–2008)	53–65
167	Shaun Marcum (2005–08, 2010–13, 2015–)	61–48
166	Bud Norris (2009–)	56–68
160	Josh Johnson (2005–13)	58–45
153	Paul Wilson (1996–2005)	40–58

Most Career Shutouts, Never Led League

Starts		Overall Record
50	Rube Waddell (1897, 1899–1910)	191–145
49	Ferguson Jenkins (1965–83)	284–226
46	Doc White (1901–13)	190–157
45	Phil Niekro (1964–87)	318–274
42	Catfish Hunter (1965–79)	224–166
41	Chief Bender (1903–17, 1925)	210–127
40	Mickey Welch (1880–92)	311–207
40	Ed Reulbach (1905–17)	181–105
40	Claude Osteen (1957, 1959–75)	196–195
40	Mel Stottlemyre (1964–74)	164–139

Pitchers with Shutouts in First Two Major League Starts

American League

	Season Record	Shutouts
Joe Doyle, N.Y. Highlanders, 1906	2–2	2
Johnny Marcum, Phila. A's, 1933	3–2	2
Hal White, Det. Tigers, 1941	12–12	4
Dave Ferriss, Bost. Red Sox, 1945	21–10	5
Tom Phoebus, Balt. Orioles, 1966	2–1	2

National League (Post-1900)

	Season Record	Shutouts
Al Worthington, N.Y. Giants, 1953	4–8	2
Karl Spooner, Bklyn. Dodgers, 1954	2–0	2

Most Hits Allowed by Pitcher Pitching Shutout

American League

14 ..... Milt Gaston, Wash. Senators, July 10, 1928
13 ..... Mudcat Grant, Min. Twins, July 15, 1964
12 ..... Bob Shawkey, N.Y. Yankees, June 13, 1920
12 ..... Duster Mails, Cle. Indians, July 10, 1926
12 ..... Stan Bahnsen, Chi. White Sox, June 21, 1973

National League (Post-1900)

14 ..... Larry Cheney, Chi. Cubs, Sept. 14, 1913
13 ..... Dizzy Dean, St.L. Cardinals, Apr. 20, 1937
13 ..... Bill Lee, Chi. Cubs, Sept. 17, 1938
12 ..... Pol Perritt, N.Y. Giants, Sept. 14, 1917
Rube Benton, N.Y. Giants, Aug. 28, 1920
Leon Cadore, Bklyn. Dodgers, Sept. 4, 1920
George Smith, Phila. Phillies, Aug. 12, 1921
Hal Schumacher, N.Y. Giants, July 19, 1934
Fritz Ostermueller, Pitt. Pirates, May 17, 1947
Lew Burdette, Milw. Braves, May 26, 1959
Bob Friend, Pitt. Pirates, Sept. 24, 1959
Rick Reuschel , Chi. Cubs, June 20, 1974
Dennis Martinez, Mont. Expos, June 2, 1998

Players with Highest Percentage of Shutouts to Games Started, Career

	Games Started	Shutouts	Percentage
Ed Walsh (1904–17)	315	57	18.10
Smoky Joe Wood (1908–15, 1917–20)	158	28	17.72
Addie Joss (1902–10)	260	46	17.69
Three Finger Brown (1903–16)	332	57	17.17
Walter Johnson (1907–27)	666	110	16.52
Grover C. Alexander (1911–30)	598	90	15.05
Lefty Leifield (1905–13, 1918–20)	217	32	14.75
Rube Waddell (1897, 1899–1910)	340	50	14.71
Christy Mathewson (1900–16)	552	80	14.49
Spud Chandler (1937–47)	184	26	14.13
Nap Rucker (1907–16)	273	38	13.92
Mort Cooper (1938–47, 1949)	239	33	13.81
Ed Reulbach (1905–17)	299	40	13.38
Babe Adams (1906–07, 1909–26)	355	47	13.24
Eddie Plank (1901–17)	527	69	13.09
Sam Leever (1898–1910)	299	39	13.04

Losses

Most Losses by Decade

Pre-1900

308 Pud Galvin
225 Gus Weyhing
225 Tim Keefe
220 Tony Mullane
214 Jim McCormick
210 Mickey Welch
204 Jim Whitney
194 Adonis Terry
194 Old Hoss Radbourn
178 John Clarkson

1900–09

172 Vic Willis
163 Jack Powell
146 Cy Young
143 Al Orth
141 Bill Dinneen
139 Rube Waddell
138 Harry Howell
135 Long Tom Hughes
134 Chick Fraser
134 George Mullin

1910–19

143 Walter Johnson
124 Bob Groom
122 Bob Harmon
120 Eddie Cicotte
117 Red Ames
114 Slim Sallee
110 Hippo Vaughn
104 Claude Hendrix
104 Ray Caldwell
103 Rube Marquard
103 Pet Ragan

1920–29

146 Dolf Luque
142 Eppa Rixey
137 Howard Ehmke
135 Slim Harriss
130 Burleigh Grimes
128 Jimmy Ring
124 George Uhle
122 Tom Zachary
119 Jesse Haines
118 Sad Sam Jones

1930–39

137 Paul Derringer
134 Larry French
123 Mel Harder
119 Bump Hadley
115 Wes Ferrell
115 Ted Lyons
112 Ed Brandt
111 Danny MacFayden
107 Earl Whitehill
106 Willis Hudlin

1940–49

123 Dutch Leonard
120 Bobo Newsom
119 Dizzy Trout
118 Hal Newhouser
100 Sid Hudson
92 Johnny Vander Meer
92 Early Wynn
90 Bucky Walters
89 Ken Raffensberger
88 Jim Tobin

1950–59

149 Robin Roberts
131 Warren Spahn
127 Bob Friend
124 Murry Dickson
123 Bob Rush
121 Billy Pierce
119 Early Wynn

1960–69

133 Jack Fisher
132 Dick Ellsworth
132 Larry Jackson
126 Don Drysdale
121 Claude Osteen
119 Jim Kaat
118 Jim Bunning

1970–79

151 Phil Niekro
146 Nolan Ryan
133 Gaylord Perry
130 Ferguson Jenkins
128 Bert Blyleven
127 Jerry Koosman
126 Steve Carlton

continued on next page

117 ..... Ned Garver
113 ..... Chuck Stobbs
100 ..... Alex Kellner

111 ..... Don Cardwell
105 ..... Bob Gibson
105 ..... Ken Johnson

123 ..... Wilbur Wood
117 ..... Mickey Lolich
117 ..... Rick Wise

1980–89

126 ..... Jim Clancy
122 ..... Frank Tanana
119 ..... Jack Morris
118 ..... Bob Knepper
114 ..... Charlie Hough
109 ..... Floyd Bannister
109 ..... Rich Dotson
109 ..... Dave Steib
107 ..... Mike Moore
104 ..... Nolan Ryan

1990–99

116 ..... Andy Benes
115 ..... Tim Belcher
113 ..... Bobby Witt
112 ..... Jaime Navarro
110 ..... Tom Candiotti
108 ..... Scott Erickson
108 ..... Chuck Finley
101 ..... John Burkett
101 ..... Mike Morgan
100 ..... Terry Mulholland

2000–09

124 ..... Livan Hernandez
116 ..... Javier Vasquez
110 ..... Jeff Suppan
106 ..... Jeff Weaver
106 ..... Barry Zito
103 ..... Kevin Millwood
102 ..... Jon Garland
101 ..... Greg Maddux
101 ..... Jarrod Washburn
99 ..... Derek Lowe

2010–15

74 ..... Jeremy Guthrie
72 ..... A.J. Burnett
69 ..... Dan Haren
69 ..... Rick Porcello
68 ..... Edwin Jackson
67 ..... John Danks
67 ..... Kyle Kendrick
66 ..... Ubaldo Jimenez
66 ..... Tim Lincecum
65 ..... Kevin Correia
65 ..... R.A. Dickey
65 ..... Bud Norris

Evolution of Pitchers' Losses Record

American League

1901 ..... Pete Dowling, Milw. Brewers–Cle. Blues 25
1904 ..... Happy Townsend, Wash. Senators 25

National League (Pre-1900)

1876 ..... Jim Devlin, Lou. Colonels 35
1879 ..... George Bradley, Troy Trojans 40
Jim McCormick, Cle. Spiders 40
1880 ..... Will White, Cin. Reds 42
1883 ..... John Coleman, Phila. Quakers 48

National League (Post-1899)

1900 ..... Bill Carrick, N.Y. Giants 22
1901 ..... Dummy Taylor, N.Y. Giants 27
1905 ..... Vic Willis, Bost. Beaneaters 29

Pitchers with Seven or More Consecutive Losing Seasons

Seasons

10 ..... Bill Bailey, St.L. Browns (AL), 1908–12; Balt. (FL), 1913; Balt.–Chi. (FL), 1914; Det. Tigers (AL), 1918; and St.L. Cardinals (NL), 1921–22

10 ..... Ron Kline, Pitt. Pirates (NL), 1952, 1955–59; St.L. Cardinals (NL), 1960; L.A. Angels–Det. Tigers (AL), 1961; Det. Tigers (AL), 1962; and Wash. Senators II (AL), 1963

9 ..... Milt Gaston, St.L. Browns (AL), 1926–27; Wash. Senators (AL), 1928; Bost. Red Sox (AL), 1929–31; and Chi. White Sox (AL), 1932–34

8 ..... Pete Broberg, Wash. Senators II (AL), 1971; Tex. Rangers (AL), 1972–74; Milw. Brewers (AL), 1975–76; Chi. Cubs (NL), 1977; and Oak. A's (AL), 1978

8 ..... Jack Fisher, Balt. Orioles (AL), 1961–62; S.F. Giants (NL), 1963; N.Y. Mets (NL), 1964–67; and Chi. White Sox (AL), 1968

8 ..... Bill Hart, Phila. A's (AA), 1886–87; Bklyn. Trolley Dodgers (NL), 1892; Pitt. Pirates (NL), 1895; St.L. Cardinals (NL), 1896–97; Pitt. Pirates (NL), 1898; and Cle. Blues (AL), 1901

continued on next page

8 .....Ken Raffensberger, Cin. Reds (NL), 1940–41; Phila. Phillies (NL), 1943–46; Phila. Phillies–Cin. Reds (NL), 1947; and Cin. Reds (NL), 1948
8 .....Charlie Robertson, Chi. White Sox (AL), 1919 and 1922–25; St.L. Browns (AL), 1926; and Bost. Braves (NL), 1927–28
8 .....Socks Seibold, Phila. A's (AL), 1916–17 and 1919; and Bost. Braves (NL), 1929–33
7 .....Boom Boom Beck, St.L. Browns (AL), 1928; Bklyn. Dodgers (NL), 1933–34; and Phila. Phillies (NL), 1939–42
7 .....Bert Cunningham, Bklyn. Bridegrooms (AA), 1887; Balt. Orioles (AA), 1888–89; Phila. Quakers–Buffalo Bisons (Players), 1890; Balt. Orioles (AA), 1891; and Lou. Colonels (NL), 1895–96
7 .....Bill Dietrich, Phila. A's (AL), 1933–35; Phila. A's–Wash. Senators–Chi. White Sox (AL), 1936; and Chi. White Sox (AL), 1937–39
7 .....Jeff Francis, Colo. Rockies (NL), 2008, 2010; K.C. Royals (AL), 2011; Colo. Rockies (NL), 2012–13; Cin. Reds (NL)–Oak. A's–N.Y. Yankees (AL), 2014; and Tor. Blue Jays (AL), 2015
7 .....Roberto Hernandez, Cle. Indians (AL), 2009–12; T.B. Rays (AL), 2013; Phila. Phillies–L.A. Dodgers (NL), 2014; and Hous. Astros (AL), 2015
7 .....Kevin Gregg, L.A. Angels (AL), 2005–06; Fla. Marlins (NL), 2007–08; Chi. Cubs (NL), 2009; Tor. Blue Jays (AL), 2010; and Balt. Orioles (AL), 2011
7 .....Jesse Jefferson, Balt. Orioles–Chi. White Sox (AL), 1975; Chi. White Sox (AL), 1976; Tor. Blue Jays (AL), 1977–79; Tor. Blue Jays (AL)–Pitt. Pirates (NL), 1980; and Cal. Angels (AL), 1981
7 .....Howie Judson, Chi. White Sox (AL), 1948–52; and Cin. Reds (NL), 1953–54
7 .....Dick Littlefield, Det. Tigers–St.L. Browns (AL), 1952; St.L. Browns (AL), 1953; Balt. Orioles (AL)–Pitt. Pirates (NL), 1954; Pitt. Pirates (NL), 1955; Pitt. Pirates–St.L. Cardinals–N.Y. Giants (NL), 1956; Chi. Cubs (NL), 1957; and Milw. Braves (NL), 1958
7 .....Eric Rasmussen, St.L. Cardinals (NL), 1976–77; St.L. Cardinals–S.D. Padres (NL), 1978; S.D. Padres (NL), 1979–80; St.L. Cardinals (NL), 1982; and St.L. Cardinals (NL)–K.C. Royals (AL), 1983
7 .....Skip Lockwood, Sea. Pilots (AL), 1969; Milw. Brewers (AL), 1970–73; Cal. Angels (AL), 1974; and N.Y. Mets (NL), 1975
7.....Tim Redding, Hous. Astros (2002–04); S.D. Padres–N.Y. Yankees (2005); Wash. Nationals (2007–08); and N.Y. Mets (2009)
7 .....Buck Ross, Phila. A's (AL), 1936–40; Phila. A's–Chi. White Sox (AL), 1941; and Chi. White Sox (AL), 1942
7 .....Jack Russell, Bost. Red Sox (AL), 1926–31; and Bost. Red Sox–Cle. Indians (AL), 1932
7 .....Herm Wehmeier, Cin. Reds (NL), 1949–53; Cin. Reds–Phila. Phillies (NL), 1954; and Phila. Phillies (NL), 1955
7 .....Bob Weiland, Chi. White Sox (AL), 1929–31; Bost. Red Sox (AL), 1932–33; Bost. Red Sox–Cle. Indians (AL), 1934; and St.L. Browns (AL), 1935
7 .....Kip Wells, Chi. White Sox , AL, 1999–2001; Pitt. Pirates (NL), 2002–05; Pitt. Pirates (NL)–Tex Rangers (AL), 2006; St.L. Cardinals (NL), 2007, Colo. Rockies–K.C. Royals (AL), 2008; Wash. Nationals–Cin. Reds, 2009; and S.D. Padres, 2012
7 .....Carlton Willey, Milw. Braves (NL), 1959–62; and N.Y. Mets (NL), 1963–65

Pitchers with 150 Wins with More Losses Than Wins, Career

	Career Record	Winning Percentage
Jack Powell (1897–1912)	245–254	.491
Bobo Newsom (1929–30, 1932, 1934–48, 1952–53)	211–222	.487
Bob Friend (1951–66)	197–230	.461
Jim Whitney (1881–90)	191–204	.484
Tom Zachary (1918–36)	186–191	.493
Chick Fraser (1896–1909)	175–212	.452
Murry Dickson (1939–40, 1942–43, 1946–59)	172–181	.487
Danny Darwin (1978–98)	171–182	.484
Bill Dinneen (1898–1909)	170–177	.490
Pink Hawley (1892–1901)	167–179	.483
Red Donahue (1893, 1895–1906)	164–175	.484
Mike Moore (1982–95)	161–176	.478
Bump Hadley (1926–41)	161–165	.494
Ted Breitenstein (1891–1901)	160–170	.485
Mark Baldwin (1887–93)	154–165	.483
Rudy May (1965–83)	152–156	.494
Tom Candiotti (1983–99)	151–164	.479
Jim Slaton (1971–86)	151–158	.489

Pitchers on Winning Teams, Leading League in Losses, Season

American League

Pitcher	Wins–Losses	Team Wins–Losses
Bill Dinneen, Bost. Americans, 1902	21–21	77–60
Herman Pillette, Det. Tigers, 1923	14–19 (Tie)	83–71

continued on next page

Hal Newhouser, Det. Tigers, 1947	17–17	85–69
Brian Kingman, Oak. A's, 1980	8–20	83–79
Bert Blyleven, Min. Twins, 1988	10–17	91–71
Corey Kluber, Cle. Indians, 2015	9–16	81–80

National League (Post-1900)

Pitcher	Wins–Losses	Team Wins–Losses
Dick Rudolph, Bost. Braves, 1915	22–19 (Tie)	83–69
Dolf Luque, Cin. Reds, 1922	13–23	86–68
Wilbur Cooper, Pitt. Pirates, 1923	17–19	87–67
Charlie Root, Chi. Cubs, 1926	18–17 (Tie)	82–72
Rip Sewell, Pitt. Pirates, 1941	14–17	81–73
Ron Kline, Pitt. Pirates, 1958	13–16	84–70
Bob Friend, Pitt. Pirates, 1959	8–19	78–76
Phil Niekro, Atl. Braves, 1980	15–18	81–80
Ken Hill, St.L. Cardinals, 1989	7–15	86–76
Doug Drabek, Hous. Astros, 1993	9–18	85–7
Livan Hernandez, S.F. Giants, 2002	12–16	95–66
Jason Marquis, St.L. Cardinals, 2006	14–16	83–78
Derek Lowe, Atl. Braves, 2011	9–17	89–73
Tim Lincecum, S.F. Giants, 2012	10–15	94–68

Pitchers Winning 20 Games in Rookie Year, Losing 20 in Second Year

Roscoe Miller, Det. Tigers (AL), 1901 (23–13), 1902 (7–20) Alex Kellner, Phila. A's (AL), 1949 (20–12), 1950 (8–20)

300-Game Winners with Fewer Than 200 Losses

Differential		Wins	Losses
+185	Christy Mathewson (1900–16)	373	188
+170	Roger Clemens (1984–2007)	354	184
+154	Lefty Grove (1925–41)	300	141
+150	John Clarkson (1882, 1884–94)	328	178
+137	Randy Johnson (1988–2009)	303	166
+132	Eddie Plank (1901–17)	326	194
+115	Old Hoss Radbourn (1880–91)	309	194

Earned Run Average

Best ERA by Decade (Min. 1000 Innings)

Pre-1900		1900–09		1910–19	
1.89	Jim Devlin	1.63	Three Finger Brown	1.59	Walter Johnson
2.10	Monte Ward	1.68	Ed Walsh	1.97	Smoky Joe Wood
2.25	Tommy Bond	1.72	Ed Reulbach	1.98	Ed Walsh
2.28	Will White	1.87	Addie Joss	2.09	Grover C. Alexander
2.36	Larry Corcoran	1.98	Christy Mathewson	2.15	Carl Mays
2.43	Terry Larkin	2.11	Rube Waddell	2.19	Babe Ruth
2.43	Jim McCormick	2.12	Cy Young	2.20	Jeff Pfeffer
2.50	George Bradley	2.13	Orval Overall	2.22	Dutch Leonard
2.62	Tim Keefe	2.19	Frank Smith	2.25	Eddie Plank
2.67	Charlie Ferguson	2.20	Lefty Leifield	2.28	Fred Toney
		2.20	Doc White		

1920–29		1930–39		1940–49	
3.04	Grover C. Alexander	2.71	Carl Hubbell	2.67	Spud Chandler
3.09	Lefty Grove	2.91	Lefty Grove	2.68	Max Lanier
3.09	Dolf Luque	2.96	Dizzy Dean	2.74	Harry Brecheen
3.10	Dazzy Vance	3.21	Bill Lee	2.84	Hal Newhouser

continued on next page

3.20 Stan Coveleski
3.24 Eppa Rixey
3.24 Tommy Thomas
3.33 Urban Shocker
3.33 Walter Johnson
3.34 Red Faber
3.36 Wilbur Cooper
3.23 Lon Warneke
3.24 Lefty Gomez
3.38 Hal Schumacher
3.42 Larry French
3.42 Van Lingle Mungo
3.50 Curt Davis
3.50 Paul Derringer
3.50 Charlie Root
2.90 Bob Feller
2.93 Mort Cooper
2.94 Tex Hughson
2.94 Claude Passeau
2.97 Bucky Walters
2.99 Howie Pollet

1950–59

2.66 Whitey Ford
2.79 Hoyt Wilhelm
2.92 Warren Spahn
3.06 Billy Pierce
3.07 Allie Reynolds
3.12 Eddie Lopat
3.14 Bob Buhl
3.18 Johnny Antonelli
3.19 Sal Maglie
3.28 Early Wynn

1960–69

2.16 Hoyt Wilhelm
2.36 Sandy Koufax
2.57 Juan Marichal
2.74 Bob Gibson
2.76 Mike Cuellar
2.77 Dean Chance
2.81 Tommy John
2.83 Don Drysdale
2.83 Whitey Ford
2.83 Joe Horlen
2.83 Bob Veale

1970–79

2.58 Jim Palmer
2.61 Tom Seaver
2.88 Bert Blyleven
2.89 Rollie Fingers
2.92 Gaylord Perry
2.93 Andy Messersmith
2.93 Frank Tanana
2.97 Jon Matlack
2.98 Mike Marshall
3.01 Don Wilson

1980–89

2.64 Dwight Gooden
2.69 Orel Hershiser
3.06 Roger Clemens
3.08 Dave Righetti
3.13 Dave Dravecky
3.13 John Tudor
3.14 Nolan Ryan
3.19 Fernando Valenzuela
3.21 Bob Welch
3.22 Sid Fernandez

1990–99

2.54 Greg Maddux
2.74 Jose Rijo
2.83 Pedro Martinez
3.02 Roger Clemens
3.14 Randy Johnson
3.21 David Cone
3.21 Tom Glavine
3.25 Kevin Brown
3.31 Curt Schilling
3.32 John Smoltz

2000–09

3.01 Pedro Martinez
3.12 Johan Santana
3.23 Roy Oswalt
3.26 Jake Peavy
3.27 Brandon Webb
3.28 John Smoltz
3.34 Roger Clemens
3.34 Randy Johnson
3.40 Roy Halladay
3.50 Tim Hudson

2010–15

2.24 Clayton Kershaw
2.85 Adam Wainwright
2.87 Johnny Cueto
2.89 Felix Hernandez
2.91 Chris Sale
2.95 Cliff Lee
2.97 David Price
3.05 Madison Bumgarner
3.07 Zack Greinke
3.09 Stephen Strasburg

Teammates Finishing One-Two in ERA, Season

American League

Season	Team	Leader	ERA	Runner-Up	ERA
1914	Bost. Red Sox	Dutch Leonard	1.01	Rube Foster	1.65
1924	Wash. Senators	Walter Johnson	2.72	Tom Zachary	2.75
1927	N.Y. Yankees	Wilcy Moore	2.28	Waite Hoyt	2.63
1933	Cle. Indians	Monte Pearson	2.33	Mel Harder	2.95
1943	N.Y. Yankees	Spud Chandler	1.64	Tiny Bonham	2.27
1944	Det. Tigers	Dizzy Trout	2.12	Hal Newhouser	2.22
1945	Det. Tigers	Hal Newhouser	1.81	Al Benton	2.02
1948	Cle. Indians	Gene Bearden	2.43	Bob Lemon	2.82 (Tie)
1957	N.Y. Yankees	Bobby Shantz	2.45	Tom Sturdivant	2.54
1963	Chi. White Sox	Gary Peters	2.33	Juan Pizarro	2.39

continued on next page

1966	Chi. White Sox	Gary Peters	1.98	Joe Horlen	2.43
1967	Chi. White Sox	Joe Horlen	2.06	Gary Peters	2.28
1968	Cle. Indians	Luis Tiant	1.60	Sam McDowell	1.81
1979	N.Y. Yankees	Ron Guidry	2.78	Tommy John	2.97
1996	Tor. Blue Jays	Juan Guzman	2.93	Pat Hentgen	3.22
2002	Bost. Red Sox	Pedro Martinez	2.26	Derek Lowe	2.58

National League

Season	Team	Leader	ERA	Runner-Up	ERA
1901	Pitt. Pirates	Jesse Tannehill	2.18	Deacon Phillippe	2.22
1906	Chi. Cubs	Three Finger Brown	1.04	Jack Pfiester	1.56
1907	Chi. Cubs	Jack Pfiester	1.15	Carl Lundgren	1.17
1912	N.Y. Giants	Jeff Tesreau	1.96	Christy Mathewson	2.12
1918	Chi. Cubs	Hippo Vaughn	1.74	Lefty Tyler	2.00
1919	Chi. Cubs	Grover C. Alexander	1.72	Hippo Vaughn	1.79
1923	Cin. Reds	Dolf Luque	1.93	Eppa Rixey	2.80
1925	Cin. Reds	Dolf Luque	2.63	Eppa Rixey	2.88
1931	N.Y. Giants	Bill Walker	2.26	Carl Hubbell	2.66
1935	Pitt. Pirates	Cy Blanton	2.58	Bill Swift	2.70
1942	St.L. Cardinals	Mort Cooper	1.78	Johnny Beazley	2.13
1943	St.L. Cardinals	Howie Pollet	1.75	Max Lanier	1.90
1944	Cin. Reds	Ed Heusser	2.38	Bucky Walters	2.40
1945	Chi. Cubs	Hank Borowy*	2.13	Ray Prim	2.40
1956	Milw. Braves	Lew Burdette	2.70	Warren Spahn	2.78
1957	Bklyn. Dodgers	Johnny Podres	2.66	Don Drysdale	2.69
1959	S.F. Giants	Sam Jones	2.83	Stu Miller	2.84
1964	L.A. Dodgers	Sandy Koufax	1.74	Don Drysdale	2.18
1974	Atl. Braves	Buzz Capra	2.28	Phil Niekro	2.38
1981	Hous. Astros	Nolan Ryan	1.69	Bob Knepper	2.18
2001	Ariz. D'backs	Randy Johnson	2.49	Curt Schilling	2.98
2005	Hous. Astros	Roger Clemens	1.87	Andy Pettitte	2.39

*Also with N.Y. Yankees (3.13 ERA).

Pitchers with 3000 Innings Pitched and an ERA Lower Than 3.00 (Post-1900)

	Innings	ERA
Three Finger Brown (1903–16)	3172	2.06
Christy Mathewson (1901–16)	4755	2.11
Cy Young (1901–11)	3312	2.12
Walter Johnson (1907–27)	5914	2.17
Eddie Plank (1905–17)	4496	2.35
Eddie Cicotte (1905–20)	3226	2.38
Doc White (1901–13)	3041	2.39
Chief Bender (1903–25)	3017	2.46
Vic Willis (1901–10)	3106	2.50
Grover C. Alexander (1911–30)	5190	2.56
Red Ames (1905–19)	3069	2.65
Whitey Ford (1950, 1953–67)	3170	2.75
Jack Powell (1901–12)	3161	2.75
George Mullin (1902–13)	3687	2.82
Jim Palmer (1965–84)	3948	2.86
Tom Seaver (1967–86)	4782	2.86
Juan Marichal (1960–75)	3507	2.89
Stanley Coveleski (1912, 1916–28)	3082	2.89

continued on next page

Wilbur Cooper (1912–26)	3480	2.89
Bob Gibson (1959–75)	3884	2.91
Carl Mays (1915–29)	3020	2.92
Don Drysdale (1956–69)	3432	2.95
Carl Hubbell (1928–43)	3589	2.97

Pitchers Leading League in ERA After Their 40th Birthday

	Age	ERA
Ted Lyons, Chi. White Sox (AL), 1942	42	2.10
Spud Chandler, N.Y. Yankees (AL), 1947	40	2.46
Nolan Ryan, Hous. Astros (NL), 1987	40	2.76

ERA Under 2.00, Season (Since 1920, Min. 162 IP)

American League

1.60	Luis Tiant, Cle. Indians, 1968
1.64	Spud Chandler, N.Y. Yankees, 1943
1.65	Dean Chance, L.A. Angels, 1964
1.74	Ron Guidry, N.Y. Yankees, 1978
1.74	Pedro Martinez, Bost. Red Sox, 2000
1.81	Sam McDowell, Cle. Indians, 1968
1.81	Hal Newhouser, Det. Tigers, 1945
1.82	Vida Blue, Oak. A's, 1971
1.88	Joe Horlen, Chi. White Sox, 1964
1.91	Luis Tiant, Bost. Red Sox, 1972
1.91	Wilbur Wood, Chi. White Sox, 1971
1.92	Gaylord Perry, Cle. Indians, 1972
1.93	Roger Clemens, Bost. Red Sox, 1990
1.94	Hal Newhouser, Det. Tigers, 1946
1.95	Dave McNally, Bal. Orioles, 1968
1.96	Denny McLain, Det. Tigers, 1968
1.97	Billy Pierce, Chi. White Sox, 1955
1.98	Tommy John, Chi. White Sox, 1968
1.98	Gary Peters, Chi. White Sox, 1966

National League

1.12	Bob Gibson, St.L. Cardinals, 1968
1.53	Dwight Gooden, N.Y. Mets, 1986
1.56	Greg Maddux, Atl. Braves, 1994
1.63	Greg Maddux, Atl. Braves, 1995
1.66	Carl Hubbell, N.Y. Giants, 1933
1.66	Zack Greinke, L.A. Dodgers, 2015
1.69	Nolan Ryan, Hous. Astros, 1981*
1.73	Sandy Koufax, L.A. Dodgers, 1966
1.74	Sandy Koufax, L.A. Dodgers, 1964
1.76	Tom Seaver, N.Y. Mets, 1971
1.77	Clayton Kershaw, L.A. Dodgers, 2014
1.77	Jake Arietta, Chi. Cubs, 2015
1.78	Mort Cooper, St.L. Cardinals, 1942
1.83	Clayton Kershaw, L.A. Dodgers, 2013
1.87	Roger Clemens, Hous. Astros, 2005
1.87	Phil Niekro, Atl. Braves, 1967
1.88	Sandy Koufax, L.A. Dodgers, 1963
1.89	Kevin Brown, Fla. Marlins, 1996
1.90	Pedro Martinez, Mon. Expos, 1997
1.90	Max Lanier, St.L. Cardinals, 1943
1.91	Grover C. Alexander, Chi. Cubs, 1920
1.93	John Tudor, St.L. Cardinals, 1985
1.93	Dolph Luque, Cin. Reds, 1923
1.97	Steve Carlton, Phil. Phillies, 1972
1.99	Gary Nolan, Cin. Reds, 1972
1.99	Bobby Bolin, S.F. Giants, 1968

*Strike-shortened season.

Pitchers with Losing Record, Leading League in ERA

American League

	ERA	Wins–Losses
Ed Siever, Det. Tigers, 1902	1.91	8–11
Ed Walsh, Chi. White Sox, 1910	1.27	18–20
Stan Coveleski, Cle. Indians, 1923	2.76	13–14
Kevin Millwood, Cle. Indians, 2005	2.86	9–11

National League (Post-1900)

	ERA	Wins–Losses
Rube Waddell, Pitt. Pirates, 1900	2.37	8–13
Dolf Luque, Cin. Reds, 1925	2.63	16–18
Dave Koslo, N.Y. Giants, 1949	2.50	11–14
Stu Miller, S.F. Giants, 1958	2.47	6–9

continued on next page

Nolan Ryan, Hous. Astros, 1987	2.76	8–16
Joe Magrane, St.L. Cardinals, 1988	2.18	5–9

20-Game Winners with 4.00 ERA, Season

American League

	ERA	Wins–Losses
Bobo Newsom, St.L. Browns, 1938	5.08	20–16
Vern Kennedy, Chi. White Sox, 1936	4.63	21–9
George Earnshaw, Phila. A's, 1930	4.44	22–13
Rick Helling, Tex. Rangers, 1998	4.41	20–7
Lefty Gomez, N.Y. Yankees, 1932	4.21	24–7
Wes Ferrell, Bost. Red Sox, 1936	4.19	20–15
Tim Hudson, Oak. A's, 2000	4.14	20–6
David Wells, Tor. Blue Jays, 2000	4.11	20–8
Monte Weaver, Wash. Senators, 1932	4.08	22–10
George Uhle, Cle. Indians, 1922	4.07	22–16
Billy Hoeft, Det. Tigers, 1956	4.06	20–14
Jack Morris, Tor. Blue Jays, 1992	4.04	21–6
Andy Pettitte, N.Y. Yankees, 2003	4.02	21–8
Vic Raschi, N.Y. Yankees, 1950	4.00	21–8

National League (Post-1899)

	ERA	Wins–Losses
Ray Kremer, Pitt. Pirates, 1930	5.02	20–12
Jim Merritt, Cin. Reds, 1970	4.08	20–12
Lew Burdette, Milw. Braves, 1959	4.07	21–15
Murry Dickson, Pitt. Pirates, 1951	4.02	20–16

20-Game Losers with ERA Below 2.00

American League

	ERA	Wins–Losses
Ed Walsh, Chi. White Sox, 1910	1.27	18–20
Walter Johnson, Wash. Senators, 1916	1.90	25–20
Jim Scott, Chi. White Sox, 1913	1.90	20–20
Harry Howell, St.L. Browns, 1905	1.98	15–22

National League

	ERA	Wins–Losses
Kaiser Wilhelm, Bklyn. Dodgers, 1908	1.87	16–22

ERA Leaders with Fewer Than 10 Wins

American League

Wins		ERA
6	Steve Ontiveros, Oak. A's, 1994*	2.65
8	Ed Siever, Det. Tigers, 1902	1.91
9	Kevin Millwood, Cle. Indians, 2005	2.86

National League

Wins		ERA
5	Joe Magrane, St.L. Cardinals, 1988	2.18
6	Stu Miller, S.F. Giants, 1958	2.47
8	Rube Waddell, Pitt. Pirates, 1900	2.37
	Fred Anderson, N.Y. Giants, 1917	1.44
	Nolan Ryan, Hous. Astros, 1987	2.76
9	Craig Swan, N.Y. Mets, 1978	2.43

*Strike-shortened season.

Pitchers with Lowest ERA in Both Leagues

Roger Clemens	1986 Bost. Red Sox (AL)	2.48
	1990 Bost. Red Sox (AL)	1.93
	1991 Bost. Red Sox (AL)	2.62
	1992 Bost. Red Sox (AL)	2.41
	1997 Tor. Blue Jays (AL)	2.05
	1998 Tor. Blue Jays (AL)	2.65
	2005 Hous. Astros (NL)	1.87
Zack Greinke	2009 K.C. Royals (AL)	2.16
	2015 L.A. Dodgers (NL)	1.66
Randy Johnson	1995 Sea. Mariners (AL)	2.48
	1999 Ariz. D'backs (NL)	2.49
	2001 Ariz. D'backs (NL)	2.49
	2002 Ariz. D'backs (NL)	2.32
Pedro Martinez	1997 Mont. Expos (NL)	1.90
	1999 Bost. Red Sox (AL)	2.07
	2000 Bost. Red Sox (AL)	1.74
	2002 Bost. Red Sox (AL)	2.26
	2003 Bost. Red Sox (AL)	2.22
Johan Santana	2004 Min. Twins (AL)	2.61
	2006 Min. Twins (AL)	2.77
	2008 N.Y. Mets (NL)	2.54
Rube Waddell	1900 Pitt. Pirates (NL)	2.37
	1905 Phila. A's (AL)	1.48
Hoyt Wilhelm	1952 N.Y. Giants (NL)	2.43
	1959 Balt. Orioles (AL)	2.19
Cy Young	1892 Cle. Spiders (NL)	1.93
	1901 Bost. Red Sox (AL)	1.62

ERA Leaders with 25 or More Wins, Season

American League

	ERA	Wins
Cy Young, Bost. Americans, 1901	1.62	33
Rube Waddell, Phila. A's, 1905	1.48	26
Walter Johnson, Wash. Senators, 1912	1.39	32
Walter Johnson, Wash. Senators, 1913	1.14	36
Eddie Cicotte, Chi. White Sox, 1917	1.53	28
Red Faber, Chi. White Sox, 1921	2.48	25
Lefty Grove, Phila. A's, 1930	2.54	28
Lefty Grove, Phila. A's, 1931	2.06	31
Lefty Grove, Phila. A's, 1932	2.84	25
Lefty Gomez, N.Y. Yankees, 1934	2.33	26
Bob Feller, Cle. Indians, 1940	2.61	27
Dizzy Trout, Det. Tigers, 1944	2.12	27
Hal Newhouser, Det. Tigers, 1945	1.81	25
Hal Newhouser, Det. Tigers, 1946	1.94	26
Mel Parnell, Bost. Red Sox, 1949	2.77	25
Catfish Hunter, Oak. A's, 1974	2.49	25
Ron Guidry, N.Y. Yankees, 1978	1.74	25

National League (Post-1900)

	ERA	Wins
Sam Leever, Pitt. Pirates, 1903	2.06	25
Joe McGinnity, N.Y. Giants, 1904	1.61	35
Christy Mathewson, N.Y. Giants, 1905	1.28	31

continued on next page

Three Finger Brown, Chi. Cubs, 1906	1.04	26
Christy Mathewson, N.Y. Giants, 1908	1.43	37
Christy Mathewson, N.Y. Giants, 1909	1.14	25
Christy Mathewson, N.Y. Giants, 1911	1.99	26
Christy Mathewson, N.Y. Giants, 1913	2.06	25
Grover C. Alexander, Phila. Phillies, 1915	1.22	31
Grover C. Alexander, Phila. Phillies, 1916	1.55	33
Grover C. Alexander, Chi. Cubs, 1920	1.91	27
Dolf Luque, Cin. Reds, 1923	1.93	27
Dazzy Vance, Bklyn. Dodgers, 1924	2.16	28
Carl Hubbell, N.Y. Giants, 1936	2.31	26
Bucky Walters, Cin. Reds, 1939	2.29	27
Sandy Koufax, L.A. Dodgers, 1963	1.88	25
Sandy Koufax, L.A. Dodgers, 1965	2.04	26
Sandy Koufax, L.A. Dodgers, 1966	1.73	27
Steve Carlton, Phila. Phillies, 1972	1.97	27

ERAs of 300-Game Winners

	ERA	Wins
Christy Mathewson (1900–16)	2.13	373
Walter Johnson (1907–27)	2.17	417
Eddie Plank (1901–17)	2.35	326
Grover C. Alexander (1911–30)	2.56	373
Cy Young (1890–1911)	2.63	511
Tim Keefe (1880–93)	2.63	342
Old Hoss Radbourn (1880–91)	2.68	309
Mickey Welch (1880–92)	2.71	307
John Clarkson (1882, 1884–94)	2.81	328
Tom Seaver (1967–86)	2.86	311
Pud Galvin (1879–92)	2.87	361
Kid Nichols (1890–1901, 1904–06)	2.96	361
Lefty Grove (1925–41)	3.06	300
Warren Spahn (1942, 1946–65)	3.09	363
Gaylord Perry (1962–83)	3.11	314
Roger Clemens (1984–2007)	3.12	354
Greg Maddux (1986–2008)	3.16	355
Nolan Ryan (1966, 1968–93)	3.19	324
Steve Carlton (1965–88)	3.22	329
Don Sutton (1966–88)	3.26	324
Randy Johnson (1988–2009)	3.29	303
Phil Niekro (1967–87)	3.35	318
Tom Glavine (1987–2008)	3.54	305
Early Wynn (1939, 1941–44, 1946–63)	3.54	300

Strikeouts

Evolution of Strikeout Record

American League

1901	Cy Young, Bost. Americans	158
1902	Rube Waddell, Phila. A's	210
1903	Rube Waddell, Phila. A's	302
1904	Rube Waddell, Phila. A's	349
1973	Nolan Ryan, Cal. Angels	383

continued on next page

National League (Pre-1900)

1876	Jim Devlin, Lou. Grays	122
1877	Tommy Bond, Bost. Red Caps	170
1878	Tommy Bond, Bost. Red Caps	182
1879	Monte Ward, Pro. Grays	239
1880	Larry Corcoran, Chi. White Stockings	268
1883	Jim Whitney, Bost. Red Caps	345
1884	Old Hoss Radbourn, Pro. Grays	441

National League (Post-1899)

1900	Noodles Hahn, Cin. Reds	132
1901	Noodles Hahn, Cin. Reds	239
1903	Christy Mathewson, N.Y. Giants	267
1961	Sandy Koufax, L.A. Dodgers	269
1963	Sandy Koufax, L.A. Dodgers	306
1965	Sandy Koufax, L.A. Dodgers	382

Most Strikeouts by Decade

Pre-1900

2564	Tim Keefe
1978	John Clarkson
1944	Amos Rusie
1850	Mickey Welch
1830	Old Hoss Radbourn
1803	Tony Mullane
1799	Pud Galvin
1704	Jim McCormick
1700	Charlie Buffinton
1650	Gus Weyhing

1900–09

2251	Rube Waddell
1799	Christy Mathewson
1565	Cy Young
1342	Eddie Plank
1304	Vic Willis
1293	Wild Bill Donovan
1237	Jack Chesbro
1209	Jack Powell
1115	Long Tom Hughes
1105	Doc White

1910–19

2219	Walter Johnson
1539	Grover C. Alexander
1253	Hippo Vaughn
1141	Rube Marquard
1104	Eddie Cicotte
1028	Bob Groom
1020	Claude Hendrix
938	Lefty Tyler
926	Larry Cheney
913	Willie Mitchell

1920–29

1464	Dazzy Vance
1018	Burleigh Grimes
904	Dolf Luque
895	Walter Johnson
837	Lefty Grove
824	Howard Ehmke
808	George Uhle
804	Red Faber
788	Bob Shawkey
753	Urban Shocker

1930–39

1337	Lefty Gomez
1313	Lefty Grove
1281	Carl Hubbell
1260	Red Ruffing
1207	Tommy Bridges
1144	Dizzy Dean
1022	Van Lingle Mungo
1018	Paul Derringer
1006	Bump Hadley
963	Bobo Newsom

1940–49

1579	Hal Newhouser
1396	Bob Feller
1070	Bobo Newsom
972	Johnny Vander Meer
930	Dizzy Trout
853	Kirby Higbe
791	Allie Reynolds
779	Dutch Leonard
772	Mort Cooper
760	Virgil Trucks

1950–59

1544	Early Wynn
1516	Robin Roberts
1487	Billy Pierce
1464	Warren Spahn
1093	Harvey Haddix
1072	Bob Rush
1026	Johnny Antonelli
1000	Mike Garcia
994	Sam Jones
983	Bob Turley

1960–69

2071	Bob Gibson
2019	Jim Bunning
1910	Don Drysdale
1910	Sandy Koufax
1840	Juan Marichal
1663	Sam McDowell
1585	Jim Maloney
1435	Jim Kaat
1428	Bob Veale
1391	Camilo Pascual

1970–79

2678	Nolan Ryan
2304	Tom Seaver
2097	Steve Carlton
2082	Bert Blyleven
1907	Gaylord Perry
1866	Phil Niekro
1841	Ferguson Jenkins
1767	Don Sutton
1600	Vida Blue
1587	Jerry Koosman

1980–89

2167	Nolan Ryan
1644	Fernando Valenzuela
1629	Jack Morris
1480	Bert Blyleven
1457	Bob Welch
1453	Steve Carlton
1380	Dave Stieb
1363	Charlie Hough
1360	Mario Soto
1356	Floyd Bannister

1990–99

2538	Randy Johnson
2101	Roger Clemens
1928	David Cone
1893	John Smoltz
1784	Chuck Finley
1764	Greg Maddux
1655	Andy Benes
1581	Kevin Brown
1561	Curt Schilling
1534	Pedro Martinez

2000–09

2182	Randy Johnson
2001	Javier Vazquez
1733	Johan Santana
1620	Pedro Martinez
1590	CC Sabathia
1545	Curt Schilling
1501	Barry Zito
1488	Mike Mussina
1473	Roy Oswalt
1441	Andy Pettitte

continued on next page

2010–15

1461 ..... Clayton Kershaw
1357 ..... Max Scherzer
1332 ..... Felix Hernandez
1258 ..... David Price
1236 ..... Cole Hamels
1227 ..... James Shields
1197 ..... Justin Verlander
1177 ..... Jon Lester
1137 ..... Zack Greinke
1120 ..... Madison Bumgarner

Members of Same Pitching Staff Finishing One-Two in Strikeouts, Season

American League

Season	Team	Leader	Strikeouts	Runner-Up	Strikeouts
1905	Phila. A's	Rube Waddell	287	Eddie Plank	210
1918	Wash. Senators	Walter Johnson	162	Jim Shaw	129
1919	Wash. Senators	Walter Johnson	147	Jim Shaw	128
1927	Phila. A's	Lefty Grove	174	Rube Walberg	136
1929	Phila. A's	Lefty Grove	170	George Earnshaw	149
1930	Phila. A's	Lefty Grove	209	George Earnshaw	193
1931	Phila. A's	Lefty Grove	175	George Earnshaw	152
1935	Det. Tigers	Tommy Bridges	163	Schoolboy Rowe	140
1944	Det. Tigers	Hal Newhouser	187	Dizzy Trout	144
1948	Cle. Indians	Bob Feller	164	Bob Lemon	147
1949	Det. Tigers	Virgil Trucks	153	Hal Newhouser	144
1953	Chi. White Sox	Billy Pierce	186	Virgil Trucks	149*
1976	Cal. Angels	Nolan Ryan	327	Frank Tanana	261
1990	Tex. Rangers	Nolan Ryan	232	Bobby Witt	221
2012	Det. Tigers	Justin Verlander	239	Max Scherzer	231

National League (Post-1900)

Season	Team	Leader	Strikeouts	Runner-Up	Strikeouts
1903	N.Y. Giants	Christy Mathewson	267	Joe McGinnity	171
1905	N.Y. Giants	Christy Mathewson	206	Red Ames	198
1920	Chi. Cubs	Grover C. Alexander	173	Hippo Vaughn	131 (Tie)
1924	Bklyn. Dodgers	Dazzy Vance	262	Burleigh Grimes	135
1960	L.A. Dodgers	Don Drysdale	246	Sandy Koufax	197
1961	L.A. Dodgers	Sandy Koufax	269	Stan Williams	205
1962	L.A. Dodgers	Don Drysdale	232	Sandy Koufax	216
1987	Hous. Astros	Nolan Ryan	270	Mike Scott	233
1990	N.Y. Mets	David Cone	233	Dwight Gooden	223
2001	Ariz. D'backs	Randy Johnson	372	Curt Schilling	293
2002	Ariz. D'backs	Randy Johnson	334	Curt Schilling	316
2003	Chi. Cubs	Kerry Wood	266	Mark Prior	245

Federal League

Season	Team	Leader	Strikeouts	Runner-Up	Strikeouts
1914	Ind. Hoosiers	Cy Falkenberg	236	Earl Moseley	205

*Trucks also pitched 16 games with St.L. Browns, striking out 47; 102 strikeouts with Chi. White Sox.

Pitchers Leading League with 100 More Strikeouts Than Runner-Up

American League

Season	Leader	Strikeouts	Runner-Up	Strikeouts
1903	Rube Waddell, Phila. A's	302	Wild Bill Donovan, Det. Tigers	187
1904	Rube Waddell, Phila. A's	349	Jack Chesbro, N.Y. Highlanders	239

continued on next page

1973	Nolan Ryan, Cal. Angels	383	Bert Blyleven, Min. Twins	258
1974	Nolan Ryan, Cal. Angels	367	Bert Blyleven, Min. Twins	249
1993	Randy Johnson, Sea. Mariners	308	Mark Langston, Cal. Angels	196
1999	Pedro Martinez, Bost. Red Sox	313	Chuck Finley, Ana. Angels	200

National League (Post-1900)

Season	Leader	Strikeouts	Runner-Up	Strikeouts
1924	Dazzy Vance, Bklyn. Dodgers	262	Burleigh Grimes, Bklyn. Dodgers	135
1965	Sandy Koufax, L.A. Dodgers	382	Bob Veale, Pitt. Pirates	276
1979	J.R. Richard, Hous. Astros	313	Steve Carlton, Phila. Phillies	213
1999	Randy Johnson, Ariz. D'backs	364	Kevin Brown, L.A. Dodgers	221
2000	Randy Johnson, Ariz. D'backs	347	Chan Ho Park, L.A. Dodgers	217

Pitchers with 3000 Strikeouts, Never Leading League

Don Sutton (1966–88)	3574
Gaylord Perry (1962–83)	3534
Greg Maddux (1986–2008)	3371

Pitchers Striking Out 1000 Batters Before Their 24th Birthday

	Number of Strikeouts on 24th Birthday	Date of Birth
Bob Feller (1936–41)	1233	Nov. 3, 1918
Bert Blyleven (1970–74)	1094	Apr. 6, 1951
Dwight Gooden (1984–88)	1067	Nov. 16, 1964

Most Times Striking Out 10 or More Batters in a Game, Career

215	Nolan Ryan
212	Randy Johnson
110	Roger Clemens
108	Pedro Martinez
97	Sandy Koufax
93	Curt Schilling
84	Steve Carlton
74	Sam McDowell
74	Bob Gibson
70	Tom Seaver
70	Rube Waddell

Pitchers Averaging 10 Strikeouts per Nine Innings, Season

American League

	Average	Strikeouts	Innings
Pedro Martinez, Bost. Red Sox, 1999	13.20	313	213
Randy Johnson, Sea. Mariners, 1995	12.35	294	214
Randy Johnson, Sea. Mariners, 1997	12.30	291	213
Yu Darvish, Tex. Rangers, 2013	11.89	277	210
Chris Sale, Chi. White Sox, 2015	11.82	274	209
Pedro Martinez, Bost. Red Sox, 2000	11.78	284	217
Nolan Ryan, Tex. Rangers, 1989	11.32	301	239
Max Scherzer, Det. Tigers, 2012	11.08	240	214
Erik Bedard, Balt. Orioles, 2007	10.93	221	182
Randy Johnson, Sea. Mariners, 1993	10.86	308	255
Pedro Martinez, Bost. Red Sox, 2002	10.79	239	199
Chris Sale, Chi. White Sox, 2014	10.76	208	174
Sam McDowell, Cle. Indians, 1965	10.71	325	273
Chris Archer, T.B. Rays, 2015	10.70	252	212
Randy Johnson, Sea. Mariners, 1994	10.67	204	172
Carlos Carrasco, Cle. Indians, 2015	10.59	216	184
Nolan Ryan, Cal. Angels, 1973	10.57	383	326

continued on next page

Nolan Ryan, Tex. Rangers, 1991	10.56	203	173
Johan Santana, Min. Twins, 2004	10.46	265	228
Nolan Ryan, Cal. Angels, 1972	10.43	329	284
Sam McDowell, Cle. Indians, 1966	10.42	225	194
Yu Darvish, Tex. Rangers, 2012	10.40	221	191
Scott Kazmir, T.B. Devil Rays, 2007	10.41	239	207
Roger Clemens, Tor. Blue Jays, 1998	10.39	271	234
Nolan Ryan, Cal. Angels, 1976	10.35	327	284
Randy Johnson, Sea. Mariners, 1992	10.31	241	210
Max Scherzer, Det. Tigers, 2014	10.29	252	220
Corey Kluber, Cle. Indians, 2014	10.27	269	236
Nolan Ryan, Cal. Angels, 1977	10.26	341	299
David Cone, N.Y. Yankees, 1997	10.25	222	195
Nolan Ryan, Tex. Rangers, 1990	10.24	232	204

National League

	Average	Strikeouts	Innings
Randy Johnson, Ariz. D'backs, 2001	13.41	372	249
Kerry Wood, Chi. Cubs, 1998	12.58	233	166
Randy Johnson, Ariz. D'backs, 2000	12.56	347	248
Randy Johnson, Ariz. D'backs, 1999	12.06	364	271
Clayton Kershaw, L.A. Dodgers, 2015	11.64	301	233
Randy Johnson, Ariz. D'backs, 2002	11.56	334	260
Nolan Ryan, Hous. Astros, 1987	11.48	270	211
Dwight Gooden, N.Y. Mets, 1984	11.39	276	218
Pedro Martinez, Mont. Expos, 1997	11.37	305	241
Kerry Wood, Chi. Cubs, 2003	11.35	266	211
Curt Schilling, Phila. Phillies, 1997	11.29	319	254
Kerry Wood, Chi. Cubs, 2001	11.20	217	174
Hideo Nomo, L.A. Dodgers, 1995	11.10	236	191
Oliver Perez, Pitt. Pirates, 2004	10.97	239	196
Curt Schilling, Ariz. D'backs, 2002	10.97	316	259
Max Scherzer, Wash. Nationals, 2015	10.86	276	229
Clayton Kershaw, L.A. Dodgers, 2014	10.85	239	198
Randy Johnson, Ariz. D'backs, 2004	10.62	290	246
Sandy Koufax, L.A. Dodgers, 1962	10.55	216	184
Zack Greinke, Milw. Brewers, 2011	10.54	201	172
Tim Lincecum, S.F. Giants, 2008	10.51	265	227
Mark Prior, Chi. Cubs, 2003	10.43	245	211
Tim Lincecum, S.F. Giants, 2009	10.42	261	225

Pitchers with Combined Total of 500 Strikeouts and Walks, Season

American League

	Strikeouts	Walks	Total
Bob Feller, Cle. Indians, 1946	348	153	501
Nolan Ryan, Cal. Angels, 1973	383	162	545
Nolan Ryan, Cal. Angels, 1974	367	202	569
Nolan Ryan, Cal. Angels, 1976	327	183	510
Nolan Ryan, Cal. Angels, 1977	341	204	545

National League

[None]

Pitchers Striking Out the Side on Nine Pitches

American League

Rube Waddell, Phila. A's, July 1, 1902 (3rd inning)
Sloppy Thurston, Chi. White Sox, Aug. 22, 1923 (12th inning)
Lefty Grove, Phila. A's, Aug. 23, 1928 (2nd inning)
Lefty Grove, Phila. A's, Sept. 27, 1928 (7th inning)
Billy Hoeft, Det. Tigers, Sept. 7, 1953 (7th inning, 2nd game)
Jim Bunning, Det. Tigers, Aug. 2, 1959 (9th inning)
Al Downing, N.Y. Yankees, Aug. 11, 1967 (2nd inning, 1st game)
Nolan Ryan, Cal. Angels, July 9, 1972 (2nd inning)
Ron Guidry, N.Y. Yankees, Aug. 7, 1984 (9th inning, 2nd game)
Jeff Montgomery, K.C. Royals, Apr. 29, 1990 (8th inning)
Stan Belinda, K.C. Royals, Aug. 6, 1994 (9th inning)
Roger Clemens, Tor. Blue Jays. Sept. 18, 1997 (1st inning)
Doug Jones, Milw. Brewers, Sept. 23, 1997 (9th inning)
Jimmy Key, Balt. Orioles, Apr. 14, 1998 (4th inning)
Mike Mussina, Balt. Orioles, May 9, 1998 (9th inning)
B.J. Ryan, Balt. Orioles, Sept. 5, 1999 (6th inning)
Pedro Martinez, Bost. Red Sox, May 18, 2002 (1st inning)
Rich Harden, Oak. A's, June 8, 2008 (1st inning)
Felix Hernandez, Sea. Mariners, June 17, 2008 (4th inning)
A. J. Burnett, N. Y. Yankees, June 20, 2009 (3rd inning)
Rafael Soriano, T. B Rays, Aug. 23, 2010 (9th inning)
Clay Buchholz, Bost. Red Sox, Aug. 16, 2012 (6th inning)
Ivan Nova, N.Y. Yankees, May 29, 2013 (8th inning)
Steve Delabar, Tor. Blue Jays, July 30, 2013 (8th inning)
Brad Boxberger, T.B. Rays, May 8, 2014 (6th inning)
Justin Masterson, Cle. Indians, June 2, 2014 (4th inning)
Garrett Richards, L.A. Angels, June 4, 2014 (2nd inning)
Brandon McCarthy, N.Y. Yankees, Sept. 17, 2014 (7th inning)

National League (Post-1900)

Pat Ragan, Bklyn. Dodgers, Oct. 5, 1914
(8th inning, 2nd game)
Hod Eller, Cin. Reds, Aug. 21, 1917 (9th inning)
Joe Oeschger, Bost. Braves, Sept. 8, 1921
(4th inning, 1st game)
Dazzy Vance, Bklyn. Dodgers, Sept. 14, 1924 (3rd inning)
Warren Spahn, Bost. Braves, July 2, 1949 (2nd inning)
Robin Roberts, Phila. Phillies, Aug. 17, 1956 (2nd inning)
Sandy Koufax, L.A. Dodgers, June 30, 1962 (1st inning)
Tony Cloninger, Milw. Braves, June 15, 1963 (8th inning)
Sandy Koufax, L.A. Dodgers, Apr. 18, 1964 (3rd inning)
Bob Bruce, Hous. Astros, Apr. 19, 1964 (8th inning)
Nolan Ryan, N.Y. Mets, Apr. 19, 1968 (3rd inning)
Bob Gibson, St.L. Cardinals, May 12, 1969 (7th inning)
Billy Wilson, Phila. Phillies, July 6, 1971 (6th inning)
John Strohmayer, Mont. Expos, July 10, 1971 (5th inning)
Milt Pappas, Chi. Cubs, Sept. 24, 1971 (4th inning)
Bruce Sutter, Chi. Cubs, Sept. 8, 1977 (9th inning)
Pedro Borbon, Cin. Reds, June 23, 1979 (9th inning)
Lynn McGlothen, Chi. Cubs, Aug. 25, 1979 (3rd inning)
Joey McLaughlin, At. Braves, Sept. 11, 1979 (7th inning)
Jeff Robinson, Pitt. Pirates, Sept. 7, 1987 (8th inning)
Rob Dibble, Cin. Reds, June 4, 1989 (8th inning)
Andy Ashby, Phila. Phillies, June 15, 1991 (4th inning)
David Cone, N.Y. Mets, Aug. 30, 1991 (5th inning)
Pete Harnisch, Hous. Astros, Sept. 6, 1991 (7th inning)
Trevor Wilson, S.F. Giants, June 7, 1992 (9th inning)
Mel Rojas, Mont. Expos, May 11, 1994 (9th inning)
Todd Worrell, L.A. Dodgers, Aug. 13, 1995 (9th inning)
Mike Magnante, Hous. Astros, Aug. 22, 1997 (9th inning)
Orel Hershiser, S.F. Giants, June 16, 1998 (4th inning)
Randy Johnson, Hous. Astros, Sept. 2, 1998 (6th inning)
Jesus Sanchez, Fla. Marlins, Sept. 13, 1998 (3rd inning)
Shane Reynolds, Hous. Astros, June 15, 1999 (1st inning)
Ugueth Urbina, Mont. Expos, Apr. 4, 2000 (9th inning)
Randy Johnson, Ariz. D'backs, Aug. 23, 2001 (6th inning)
Jason Isringhausen, St.L. Cardinals, Apr. 13, 2002 (9th inning)
Byung-Hyun Kim, Ariz. D'backs, May 11, 2002 (8th inning)
Brian Lawrence, S.D. Padres, June 12, 2002 (3rd inning)
Brandon Backe, Hous. Astros, Apr. 15, 2004 (8th inning)
Ben Sheets, Milw. Brewers, June 13, 2004 (3rd inning)
LaTroy Hawkins, Chi. Cubs, Sept. 11, 2004 (9th inning)
Rick Helling, Milw. Brewers, June 20, 2006 (1st inning)
Buddy Carlyle, Atl. Braves, July 6, 2007 (4th inning)
Ross Ohlendorf, Pitt. Pirates, Sept. 5, 2009 (7th inning)
Jordan Zimmermann, Wash. Nationals, May 6, 2011 (2nd inning)
Juan Perez, Phila. Phillies, July 8, 2011 (10th inning)
Wade Miley, Ariz. D'backs, Oct. 1, 2012 (3rd inning)
Cole Hamels, Phila. Phillies, May 17, 2014 (3rd inning)
Rex Brothers, Colo. Rockies, June 14, 2014 (8th inning)
Carlos Contreras, Cin. Reds, July 11, 2014 (7th inning)
Mike Fiers, Milw. Brewers, May 7, 2015 (4th inning)
Santiago Casilla, S.F. Giants, May 17, 2015 (9th inning)

Pitchers with 200 Strikeouts and Fewer Than 50 Walks, Season

American League

	Strikeouts	Walks
Cy Young, Bost. Americans, 1904	200	29
Cy Young, Bost. Americans, 1905	210	30
Walter Johnson, Wash. Senators, 1913	243	38
Jim Kaat, Min. Twins, 1967	211	42
Ferguson Jenkins, Tex. Rangers, 1974	225	45
Pedro Martinez, Bost. Red Sox, 1999	313	37
Pedro Martinez, Bost. Red Sox, 2000	284	32
Mike Mussina, Balt. Orioles, 2000	210	46
Mike Mussina, N.Y. Yankees, 2001	214	42
Pedro Martinez, Bost. Red Sox, 2002	239	40
Pedro Martinez, Bost. Red Sox, 2003	206	47
Roy Halladay, Tor. Blue Jays, 2003	204	32

continued on next page

American League

	Strikeouts	Walks
Curt Schilling, Bost. Red Sox, 2004	203	35
Randy Johnson, N.Y. Yankees, 2005	211	47
Johan Santana, Min. Twins, 2005	238	45
Johan Santana, Min. Twins, 2006	245	47
CC Sabathia, Cle. Indians, 2007	209	37
Ervin Santana, L.A. Angels, 2008	214	47
Roy Halladay, Tor. Blue Jays, 2008	206	39
Roy Halladay, Tor. Blue Jays, 2009	208	35
Chris Sale, Chi. White Sox, 2013	226	46
Felix Hernandez, Sea. Mariners, 2013	216	46
David Price, T.B. Rays–Det. Tigers, 2014	271	38
Felix Hernandez, Sea. Mariners, 2014	248	46
Jon Lester, Bost. Red Sox–Oak. A's, 2014	220	48
Chris Sale, Chi. White Sox, 2015	274	42
Corey Kluber, Cle. Indians, 2015	245	45
David Price, Det. Tigers–Tor. Blue Jays, 2015	225	47
Carlos Carrasco, Cle. Indians, 2015	216	43

National League (Post-1900)

	Strikeouts	Walks
Christy Mathewson, N.Y. Giants, 1908	259	42
Jim Bunning, Phila. Phillies, 1964	219	46
Juan Marichal, S.F. Giants, 1965	240	46
Juan Marichal, S.F. Giants, 1966	222	36
Gaylord Perry, S.F. Giants, 1966	201	40
Juan Marichal, S.F. Giants, 1968	218	46
Tom Seaver, N.Y. Mets, 1968	205	48
Ferguson Jenkins, Chi. Cubs, 1971	263	37
Shane Reynolds, Hous. Astros, 1996	204	44
Greg Maddux, Atl. Braves, 1998	204	45
Kevin Brown, S.D. Padres, 1998	257	49
Kevin Brown, L.A. Dodgers, 2000	216	47
Curt Schilling, Ariz. D'backs, 2001	293	39
Javier Vazquez, Mont. Expos, 2001	208	44
Curt Schilling, Ariz. D'backs, 2002	316	33
Jason Schmidt, S.F. Giants, 2003	208	46
Randy Johnson, Ariz. D'backs, 2004	290	44
Ben Sheets, Milw. Brewers, 2004	264	32
Pedro Martinez, N.Y. Mets, 2005	208	47
Dan Haren, Ariz. D'backs, 2008	206	40
Javier Vazquez, Atl. Braves, 2008	238	44
Dan Haren, Ariz. D'backs, 2009	223	38
Roy Halladay, Phila. Phillies, 2010	219	30
Zack Greinke, Milw. Brewers, 2011	201	45
Roy Halladay, Phila. Phillies, 2011	220	35
Cliff Lee, Phila. Phillies, 2011	238	42
Cliff Lee, Phila. Phillies, 2012	238	42
Cliff Lee, Phila. Phillies, 2013	222	32
Adam Wainwright, St.L. Cardinals, 2013	219	35
Stephen Strasburg, Wash. Nationals, 2014	242	43
Clayton Kershaw, L.A. Dodgers, 2014	239	31
Madison Bumgarner, S.F. Giants, 2014	219	43
Zack Greinke, L.A. Dodgers, 2014	207	43
Clayton Kershaw, L.A. Dodgers, 2015	301	42
Max Scherzer, Wash. Nationals, 2015	276	34
Jake Arietta, Chi. Cubs, 2015	236	48
Madison Bumgarner, S.F. Giants, 2015	234	39
Jon Lester, Chi. Cubs, 2015	207	47
Jacob deGrom, N.Y. Mets, 2015	205	38
Gerrit Cole, Pitt. Pirates, 2015	202	44
Zack Greinke, L.A. Dodgers, 2015	200	40

Rookie Pitchers Striking Out 200 Batters

American League

Herb Score, Cle. Indians, 1955 245
Yu Darvish, Tex. Rangers, 2012 221
Russ Ford, N.Y. Highlanders, 1910 209
Bob Johnson, K.C. Royals, 1970 206
Mark Langston, Sea. Mariners, 1984 204
Daisuke Matsuzaka, Bost. Red Sox, 2007 201

National League (Post-1900)

Dwight Gooden, N.Y. Mets, 1984 276
Hideo Nomo, L.A. Dodgers, 1995 236
Kerry Wood, Chi. Cubs, 1998 233
Grover C. Alexander, Phila. Phillies, 1911 227
Tom Hughes, Chi. Cubs, 1901 225
Christy Mathewson, N.Y. Giants, 1901 221
John Montefusco, S.F. Giants, 1975 215
Don Sutton, L.A. Dodgers, 1966 209
Gary Nolan, Cin. Reds, 1966 206
Tom Griffin, Hous. Astros, 1969 200

Rookies Leading League in Strikeouts

American League

Lefty Grove, Phila. A's, 1925 116
Allie Reynolds, Cle. Indians, 1943 151
Herb Score, Cle. Indians, 1955 245
Mark Langston, Sea. Mariners, 1984 204

National League (Post-1900)

Dazzy Vance, Bklyn. Dodgers, 1922 134
Dizzy Dean, St.L. Cardinals, 1932 191
Bill Voiselle, N.Y. Giants, 1944 161
Sam Jones, Chi. Cubs, 1955 198
Jack Sanford, S.F. Giants, 1957 188
Fernando Valenzuela, L.A. Dodgers, 1981 180
Dwight Gooden, N.Y. Mets, 1984 276
Hideo Nomo, L.A. Dodgers, 1995 236

Pitchers Leading League in Strikeouts, 10 or More Years Apart

Steve Carlton ..... Phila. Phillies (NL), 1972 ..... Phila. Phillies (NL), 1982 and 1983
Roger Clemens ..... Bost. Red Sox (AL), 1988 ..... Tor. Blue Jays (AL), 1998
Bob Feller ..... Cle. Indians (AL), 1938 ..... Cle. Indians (AL), 1948
Randy Johnson ..... Sea. Mariners (AL), 1992 ..... Ariz. D'backs (NL), 2002 and 2004
Walter Johnson ..... Wash. Senators (AL), 1910 ..... Wash. Senators (AL), 1924
Nolan Ryan ..... Cal. Angels (AL), 1972 ..... Hous. Astros (NL), 1987 and 1988

Oldest Pitchers to Lead League in Strikeouts

American League

Age		Strikeouts
43	Nolan Ryan, Tex. Rangers, 1990	232
42	Nolan Ryan, Tex. Rangers, 1989	301
38	Early Wynn, Chi. White Sox, 1958	184
37	Early Wynn, Chi. White Sox, 1957	154
36	Walter Johnson, Wash. Senators, 1924	158
36	Roger Clemens, Tor. Blue Jays, 1998	271
35	Walter Johnson, Wash. Senators, 1923	130
35	Allie Reynolds, N.Y. Yankees, 1952	160
35	Roger Clemens, Tor. Blue Jays, 1997	257

National League

Age		Strikeouts
41	Nolan Ryan, Hous. Astros, 1988	228
41	Randy Johnson, Ariz. D'backs, 2004	290
40	Nolan Ryan, Hous. Astros, 1987	270
39	Randy Johnson, Ariz. D'backs, 2002	334
38	Phil Niekro, Atl. Braves, 1977	262
38	Steve Carlton, Phila. Phillies, 1983	275
38	Randy Johnson, Ariz. D'backs, 2001	372
37	Dazzy Vance, Bklyn. Dodgers, 1928	200
37	Steve Carlton, Phila. Phillies, 1982	286
37	Randy Johnson, Ariz. D'backs, 2000	347
36	Dazzy Vance, Bklyn. Dodgers, 1927	184
36	Randy Johnson, Ariz. D'backs, 1999	364
35	Dazzy Vance, Bklyn. Dodgers, 1926	140
35	Jim Bunning, Phila. Phillies, 1967	253
35	Steve Carlton, Phila. Phillies, 1980	286
35	Randy Johnson, Ariz. D'backs, 1999	364

Strikeout Leaders on Last-Place Teams

American League

Sam McDowell, 1969 Cle. Indians 279
Nolan Ryan, 1974 Cal. Angels 367
Frank Tanana, 1975 Cal. Angels 269
Scott Kazmir, 2007 T.B. Devil Rays 239

National League

Kirby Higbe, 1940 Phila. Phillies 134
Sam Jones, 1956 Chi. Cubs 176
Steve Carlton, 1972 Phila. Phillies 310
Phil Niekro, 1977 Atl. Braves 262
Randy Johnson, 2004 Ariz. D'backs 290

Walks

Pitchers Walking 20 or Fewer Batters, Season (Min. 200 Innings)

	Walks	Pitcher's Record
Phil Hughes, Min. Twins (AL)	16 (in 209⅔ innings)	16–10
Babe Adams, Pitt. Pirates (NL), 1920	18 (in 263 innings)	17–13
Red Lucas, Cin. Reds (NL), 1933	18 (in 219⅔ innings)	10–16
Cliff Lee, Sea. Mariners–Tex. Rangers, 2010	18 (in 212⅓ innings)	12–9
Bob Tewksbury, St.L. Cardinals (NL), 1992	20 (in 233 innings)	16–5
Greg Maddux, Atl. Braves (NL), 1997	20 (in 232⅔ innings)	19–4
Slim Sallee, Cin. Reds (NL), 1919	20 (in 227⅔ innings)	21–7
Bob Tewksbury, St.L. Cardinals (NL), 1993	20 (in 213⅔ innings)	17–10
David Wells, N.Y. Yankees (AL), 2003	20 (in 213 innings)	15–7
LaMarr Hoyt, S.D. Padres (NL), 1985	20 (in 210⅓ innings)	16–8

Fewest Walks, Season (Min. One Inning Pitched Each Team Game)

American League

	Innings
9.....Carlos Silva, Min. Twins, 2005	188⅓
18.....John Lieber, N.Y. Yankees, 2004	176⅔
18.....Cliff Lee, Sea. Mariners–Tex. Rangers, 2010	212⅓

National League

	Innings
13.....Bret Saberhagen, N.Y. Mets, 1994	177⅓
15.....Babe Adams, Pitt. Pirates, 1922	171⅓
18.....Babe Adams, Pitt. Pirates, 1920	263
18.....Red Lucas, Cin. Reds, 1993	219⅔
18.....Bill Burns, Pitt. Pirates, 1908	165
18.....Babe Adams, Pitt. Pirates, 1921	160
19.....Dennis Eckersley, Chi. Cubs, 1985	169⅓

Pitchers Walking Fewer Than One Batter Every Nine Innings, Season (Min. 160 IP)

American League

	Walks	Innings
Cy Young, Bost. Americans, 1901	37	371
Cy Young, Bost. Americans, 1903	37	342
Cy Young, Bost. Americans, 1904	29	380
Cy Young, Bost. Americans, 1905	30	321
Cy Young, Bost. Americans, 1906	25	288
Addie Joss, Cle. Indians, 1908	30	325
Bill Burns, Wash. Senators, 1908	18	164
Walter Johnson, Wash. Senators, 1913	38	346
Tiny Bonham, N.Y. Yankees, 1942	24	226
David Wells, N.Y. Yankees, 2003	20	213

continued on next page

Jon Lieber, N.Y. Yankees, 2004	18	177
Carlos Silva, Min. Twins, 2005	9	188
Cliff Lee, Sea. Mariners–Tex. Rangers, 2010	18	212
Phil Hughes, Min. Twins, 2014	16	210

National League (Post-1900)

	Walks	Innings
Deacon Phillippe, Pitt. Pirates, 1902	26	272
Jesse Tannehill, Pitt. Pirates, 1902	25	231
Deacon Phillippe, Pitt. Pirates, 1903	29	289
Christy Mathewson, N.Y. Giants, 1913	21	306
Christy Mathewson, N.Y. Giants, 1914	23	312
Babe Adams, Pitt. Pirates, 1919	23	263
Slim Sallee, Cin. Reds, 1919	20	228
Babe Adams, Pitt. Pirates, 1920	18	263
Grover C. Alexander, Chi. Cubs, 1923	30	305
Red Lucas, Cin. Reds, 1933	18	220
LaMarr Hoyt, S.D. Padres, 1985	20	210
Bob Tewksbury, St.L. Cardinals, 1992	20	233
Bob Tewksbury, St.L. Cardinals, 1993	20	213
Bret Saberhagen, N.Y. Mets, 1994	13	177
Greg Maddux, Atl. Braves, 1995	23	210
Greg Maddux, Atl. Braves, 1997	20	232
David Wells, S.D. Padres, 2004	20	196

Highest Percentage of Walks to Innings Pitched, Season

American League

	Walks	Innings	Percentage
Tommy Byrne, N.Y. Yankees–St.L. Browns, 1951	150	143⅔	1.044
Bobby Witt, Tex. Rangers, 1987	140	143	.979
Mickey McDermott, Bost. Red Sox, 1950	124	130	.954
Tommy Byrne, N.Y. Yankees, 1949	179	196	.913
Bob Wiesler, Wash. Senators, 1956	112	123	.911
Bobby Witt, Tex. Rangers, 1986	143	157⅔	.907
Eric Plunk, Oak. A's, 1986	102	120⅓	.848
Emmett O'Neill, Bost, Red Sox, 1945	117	141⅔	.826
Bill Kennedy, Cle. Indians–St.L Browns, 1948	117	143⅓	.816
Hal Newhouser, Det. Tigers, 1941	137	173	.792
Tommy Byrne, N.Y. Yankees, 1950	160	203⅓	.787
Lefty Mills, St.L. Browns, 1939	113	144⅓	.783
Bob Turley, N.Y. Yankees, 1956	103	132	.780
Jason Bere, Chi. White Sox, 1995	106	137⅔	.770
Tommy Byrne, N.Y. Yankees, 1948	101	133⅔	.756
Randy Johnson, Sea. Mariners, 1991	152	201⅓	.755
Ken Chase, Wash. Senators, 1938	113	150⅔	.753
Tex Shirley, St.L. Browns, 1946	105	139	.752
Bob Feller, Cle. Indians, 1938	208	277⅔	.749
Bob Turley, Balt. Orioles, 1954	181	247⅓	.732
Bill Burbach, N.Y. Yankees, 1969	102	140⅔	.725
Bob Turley, N.Y. Yankees, 1955	177	246⅔	.718
Herb Score, Cle. Indians, 1959	115	160⅔	.716
Bob Feller, Cle. Indians, 1937	106	148⅔	.713

continued on next page

Sam McDowell, Cle. Indians, 1971	153	214 2/3	.713
Daniel Cabrera, Balt. Orioles, 2006	104	148	.703
Bump Hadley, Chi. White Sox–St.L. Browns, 1932	171	248 1/3	.689
Randy Johnson, Sea. Mariners, 1992	144	210 1/3	.685
Bobo Newsom, Wash. Senators–Bost. Red Sox, 1937	167	275 1/3	.607
Nolan Ryan, Cal. Angels, 1974	202	332 2/3	.607
Weldon Wycoff, Phila. A's, 1915	165	276	.598
Bobo Newsom, St.L. Browns, 1938	192	329 2/3	.582

National League (Post-1900)

	Walks	Innings	Percentage
Roy Golden, St.L. Cardinals, 1911	129	148 2/3	.868
Sam Jones, Chi. Cubs, 1955	185	241 2/3	.766
Nolan Ryan, N.Y. Mets, 1971	116	152	.763
Victor Zambrano, T.B Devil Rays–N.Y. Mets, 2004	102	142	.718
Jose de Jesus, Phila. Phillies, 1991	128	181 2/3	.705

Low-Hit Games

Pitchers with a No-Hitter in First Major League Start

Ted Breitenstein, St.L. Browns (vs. Lou. Colonels) (AA), Oct. 4, 1891 (final score: 8–0)
Bumpus Jones, Cin. Reds (vs. Pitt. Pirates) (NL), Oct. 15, 1892 (final score: 7–1)
Bobo Holloman, St.L. Browns (vs. Phila. A's) (AL), May 6, 1953 (final score: 6–0)

Pitchers with a One-Hitter in First Major League Game

Addie Joss, Cle. Indians (AL), Apr. 26, 1902
Ed Albrecht, St.L. Browns (AL), Oct. 2, 1949
Mike Fornieles, Wash. Senators (AL), Sept. 2, 1952
Juan Marichal, S.F. Giants (NL), July 19, 1960
Bill Rohr, Bost. Red Sox (AL), Apr. 14, 1967
Jimmy Jones, S.D. Padres (NL), Sept. 21, 1986

Last Outs in Perfect Games*

Lee Richmond, Worc. Brown Stockings (NL) (vs. Cle. Spiders, NL), June 12, 1880 (final: 1–0) ..... Last out: second baseman George Creamer
John M. Ward, Pro. Grays (NL) (vs. Buff. Bisons, NL), June 17, 1880 (final: 5–0) ..... Last out: pitcher Pud Galvin
Cy Young, Bost. Red Sox (AL) (vs. Phila. A's, AL), May 5, 1904 (final: 3–0) ..... Last out: pitcher Rube Waddell (fly out to center)
Addie Joss, Cle. Indians (AL) (vs. Chi. White Sox, AL), Oct. 2, 1908 (final: 1–0) ..... Last out: pinch hitter John Anderson (ground out to third)
Charley Robertson, Chi. White Sox (AL) (vs. Det. Tigers, AL), Apr. 30, 1922 (final: 2–0) ..... Last out: pinch hitter John Bassler (fly out to left)
Don Larsen, N.Y. Yankees (AL) (vs. Bklyn. Dodgers, NL) (World Series), Oct. 8, 1956 (final: 2–0) ..... Last out: pinch hitter Dale Mitchell (strikeout)
Jim Bunning, Phila. Phillies (NL) (vs. N.Y. Mets, NL), June 21, 1964 (final: 6–0) ..... Last out: pinch hitter John Stephenson (strikeout)
Sandy Koufax, L.A. Dodgers (NL) (vs. Chi. Cubs, NL), Sept. 9, 1965 (final: 1–0) ..... Last out: pinch hitter Harvey Kuenn (strikeout)
Catfish Hunter, Oak. A's (AL) (vs. Min. Twins, AL), May 8, 1968 (final: 4–0) ..... Last out: pinch hitter Rich Reese (strikeout)
Len Barker, Cle. Indians (AL) (vs. Tor. Blue Jays, AL), May 15, 1981 (final: 3–0) ..... Last out: pinch hitter Ernie Whitt (fly out to center)

continued on next page

Mike Witt, Cal. Angels (AL) (vs. Tex. Rangers, AL),
Sept. 30, 1984 (final: 1–0) ..... Last out: pinch hitter Marv Foley (ground out to second)
Tom Browning, Cin. Reds (NL) (vs. L.A. Dodgers, NL),
Sept. 16, 1988 (final: 1–0) ..... Last out: pinch hitter Tracy Woodson (strikeout)
Dennis Martinez, Mont. Expos (NL) (vs. L.A. Dodgers, NL),
July 28, 1991 (final: 2–0) ..... Last out: pinch hitter Chris Gwynn (fly out to center)
Kenny Rogers, Tex. Rangers (AL) (vs. Cal. Angels, AL),
July 28, 1994 (final: 4–0) ..... Last out: shortstop Gary DiSarcina (fly out to center)
David Wells, N.Y. Yankees (AL) (vs. Min. Twins, AL),
May 17, 1998 (final: 4–0) ..... Last out: shortstop Pat Meares (fly out to center)
David Cone, N.Y. Yankees (AL) (vs. Mont. Expos, NL),
July 18, 1999 (final: 5–0) ..... Last out: shortstop Orlando Cabrera (foul pop to third)
Randy Johnson, Ariz. D'backs (NL) (vs. Atl. Braves, NL),
May 18, 2004 (final: 2–0) ..... Last out: pinch hitter Eddie Perez (strikeout)
Mark Buehrle, Chi. White Sox (AL) (vs. T.B. Rays, AL),
July 23, 2009 (final: 5–0) ..... Last out: shortstop Jason Bartlett (ground out to shortstop)
Dallas Braden, Oak. A's (AL) (vs. T.B. Rays, AL),
May 9, 2010 (final: 4–0) ..... Last out: right fielder Gabe Kapler (ground out to shortstop)
Roy Halladay, Phila. Phillies (NL) (vs Fla. Marlins, NL),
May 29, 2010 (final: 1–0) ..... Last out: pinch hitter Ronny Paulino (ground out to third)
Philip Humber, Chi. White Sox (AL) (vs. Sea. Mariners, AL),
Apr. 21, 2012 (final: 4–0) ..... Last out: pinch hitter Brendan Ryan (strikeout)
Matt Cain, S.F. Giants (NL) (vs. Hous. Astros, NL),
June 13, 2012 (final: 10–0) ..... Last out: pinch hitter Jason Castro (ground out to third)
Felix Hernandez, Sea. Mariners (AL) (vs. T.B. Rays, AL),
Aug. 15, 2012 (final: 1–0) ..... Last out: third baseman Sean Rodriguez (strikeout)

*27 batters up, 27 out.

Perfect Game Pitchers, Career Wins

Cy Young (1890–1911)	511
Randy Johnson (1988–2009)	303
Dennis Martinez (1976–98)	245
David Wells (1988–2007)	239
Jim Bunning (1955–71)	224
Catfish Hunter (1965–79)	224
Kenny Rogers (1989–2008)	219
Roy Halladay (1998–2013)	203
David Cone (1986–2001, 2003)	194
Sandy Koufax (1955–66)	165
Monte Ward (1878–84)	161
Mark Buehrle* (2000–)	161
Felix Hernandez* (2005–)	143
Addie Joss (1902–10)	160
Tom Browning (1984–95)	123
Mike Witt (1981–91, 1993)	117
Matt Cain* (2005–)	97
Don Larsen (1953–65, 1967)	81
Lee Richmond (1879–83, 1886)	75
Len Barker (1976–85, 1987)	74
Charlie Robertson (1919, 1922–28)	49
Dallas Braden (2007–2011)	26
Philip Humber (2006–13)	16

*Still active.

26-Batter Perfect Games (Spoiled by 27th Batter)

	Spoiler
Hooks Wiltse, N.Y. Giants (vs. Phila. Phillies) (NL), July 4, 1908	George McQuillan, hit by pitch
Tommy Bridges, Det. Tigers (vs. Wash. Senators) (AL), Aug. 5, 1932	Dave Harris, singled
Billy Pierce, Chi. White Sox (vs. Wash. Senators) (AL), June 28, 1958	Ed FitzGerald, doubled
Milt Pappas, Chi. Cubs (vs. S.D. Padres) (NL), Sept. 2, 1972	Larry Stahl, walked
Milt Wilcox, Det. Tigers (vs. Chi. White Sox) (AL), Apr. 15, 1983	Jerry Hairston, singled
Ron Robinson, Cin. Reds (vs. Mont. Expos) (NL), May 2, 1988	Wallace Johnson, singled
Dave Stieb, Tor. Blue Jays (vs. N.Y. Yankees) (AL), Aug. 4, 1989	Roberto Kelly, doubled
Brian Holman, Sea. Mariners (vs. Oak. A's) (AL), Apr. 20, 1990	Ken Phelps, home run
Mike Mussina, N.Y. Yankees (vs. Bost. Red Sox) (AL), Sept. 2, 2001	Carl Everett, singled
Armando Gallaraga, Det. Tigers (vs. Cle. Indians) (AL), June 2 2010	Jason Donald, infield hit
Yu Darvish, Tex. Rangers (vs. Hous. Astros) (AL), Apr. 2, 2013	Marwin Gonzalez, singled
Yusmeiro Petit, S.F. Giants (vs. Ariz. D'backs) (NL), Sept. 6, 2013	Eric Chavez, singled
Max Scherzer, Wash. Nationals (vs. Pitt. Pirates) (NL), June 20, 2015	Jose Tabata, hit by pitch

Most Walks Given Up by No-Hit Pitchers, Game

11 ..... Blue Moon Odom (9 in 5 innings) and Francisco Barrios (2 in 4 innings), Chi. White Sox (vs. Oak. A's) (AL), July 28, 1976, won 6–0

10 ..... Jim Maloney, Cin. Reds (vs. Chi. Cubs) (NL), Aug. 19, 1965, won 1–0

10 ..... Steve Barber (10 in 8⅔ innings) and Stu Miller (0 in ⅓ inning), Balt. Orioles (vs. Det. Tigers) (AL), Apr. 30, 1967, lost 1–2

9 ..... John Klippstein (7 in 7 innings), Hersh Freeman (0 in 1 inning), and Joe Black (2 in 1 inning), Cin. Reds (vs. Milw. Braves) (NL), May 26, 1956, lost 1–2

9 ..... A.J. Burnett, Fla. Marlins (vs.S.D. Padres) (NL), May 12, 2001, won 3–0

8 ..... Amos Rusie, N.Y. Giants (vs. Bklyn. Bridegrooms) (NL), July 31, 1891, won 6–0

8 ..... Johnny Vander Meer, Cin. Reds (vs. Bklyn. Dodgers) (NL), June 15, 1938, won 6–0

8 ..... Cliff Chambers, Pitt. Pirates (vs. Bost. Braves) (NL), May 6, 1951, won 3–0

8 ..... Dock Ellis, Pitt. Pirates (vs. S.D. Padres) (NL), June 12, 1970, won 2–0

8 ..... Nolan Ryan, Cal. Angels (vs. Min. Twins) (AL), Sept. 28, 1974, won 4–0

8 ..... Edwin Jackson, Ariz. D'backs (vs.T.B. Rays) (AL), June 25, 2010, won 1–0

7 ..... Bobo Newsom, St.L. Browns (vs. Bost. Red Sox) (AL), Sept. 18, 1934, lost 1–2

7 ..... Sam Jones, Chi. Cubs (vs. Pitt. Pirates) (NL), May 12, 1955, won 4–0

7 ..... Burt Hooton, Chi. Cubs (vs. Phila. Phillies) (NL), Apr. 16, 1972, won 4–0

7 ..... Bill Stoneman, Mont. Expos (vs. N.Y. Mets) (NL), Oct. 2, 1972, won 7–0

7 ..... Joe Cowley, Chi. White Sox (vs. Cal. Angels) (AL), Sept. 19, 1986, won 7–1

7 ..... Tommy Greene, Phila. Phillies (vs. Mont. Expos) (NL), May 23, 1991, won 2–0

7 ..... Matt Young, Bost. Red Sox (vs. Cle. Indians) (AL), Apr. 12, 1992, lost 1–2

Pitchers Pitching No-Hitters in 20-Loss Season

	Wins	Losses
Joe Bush, Phila. A's (vs. Cle. Indians), Aug. 26, 1916	15	22
Sam Jones, Chi. Cubs (vs. Pitt. Pirates), May 12, 1955	14	20
Bobo Newsom, St.L. Browns (vs. Bost. Red Sox), Sept. 18, 1934	16	20
Nap Rucker, Bklyn. Dodgers (vs. Bost. Doves), Sept. 5, 1908	18	20

Pitchers Hitting Home Runs in No-Hit Games

	Opposing Pitcher(s)
Wes Ferrell, Cle. Indians (vs. St.L. Cardinals) (NL), Apr. 29, 1931	Sam Gray
Jim Tobin, Bost. Braves (vs. Bklyn. Dodgers) (NL), Apr. 27, 1944	Fritz Ostermueller
Earl Wilson, Bost. Red Sox (vs. L.A. Angels) (AL), June 26, 1962	Bo Belinsky
Rick Wise, Phila. Phillies (vs. Cin. Reds) (NL), June 23, 1971	Ross Grimsley and Clay Carroll (2)

Pitchers Throwing No-Hitters in Consecutive Seasons

4 .....Sandy Koufax, L.A. Dodgers, 1962–65
3 .....Nolan Ryan, Cal. Angels, 1973–75
2 .....Warren Spahn, Milw. Braves, 1960–61
2 .....Steve Busby, K.C. Royals, 1973–74
2 .....Homer Bailey, Cin. Reds, 2012–13
2 .....Tim Lincecum, S.F. Giants, 2013–14

No-Hitters Pitched Against Pennant-Winning Teams

American League

Ernie Koob, St.L. Browns (vs. Chi. White Sox), May 5, 1917
Bob Groom, St.L. Browns (vs. Chi. White Sox), May 6, 1917
Virgil Trucks, Det. Tigers (vs. N.Y. Yankees), Aug. 25, 1952
Hoyt Wilhelm, Balt. Orioles (vs. N.Y. Yankees), Sept. 20, 1958
Jim Bibby, Tex. Rangers (vs. Oak. A's), July 30, 1973
Dick Bosman, Cle. Indians (vs. Oak. A's), July 19, 1974
Nolan Ryan, Tex. Rangers (vs. Oak. A's), June 11, 1990

National League (Post-1900)

Tex Carleton, Bklyn. Dodgers (vs. Cin. Reds), Apr. 30, 1940
Bob Moose, Pitt. Pirates (vs. N.Y. Mets), Sept. 20, 1969
Bob Gibson, St.L. Cardinals (vs. Pitt. Pirates), Aug. 14, 1971
Nolan Ryan, Hous. Astros (vs. L.A. Dodgers), Sept. 26, 1981
Tom Browning, Cin. Reds (vs. L.A. Dodgers), Sept. 16, 1988 (perfect game)
Roy Oswalt, Pete Munro, Kirk Saarloos, Brad Lidge, Octavio Dotel, and Billy Wagner, Hous. Astros (vs. N.Y. Yankees), June 11, 2003
Chris Heston, S.F. Giants (vs. N.Y. Mets), June 9, 2015
Max Scherzer, Wash. Nationals (vs. N.Y. Mets), Oct. 3, 2015

No-Hit Pitchers Going Winless the Next Season After Pitching No-Hitter

American League

Weldon Henley, Phila. A's (vs. St.L. Browns), July 22, 1905
Tom Hughes, N.Y. Highlanders (vs. Cle. Indians), Aug. 30 1910
Addie Joss, Cle. Indians (vs. Chi. White Sox), Apr. 20, 1910*
Ernie Koob, St.L. Browns (vs. Chi. White Sox), May 5, 1917
Ernie Shore, Bost. Red Sox (vs. Wash. Senators), June 23, 1917
Bobo Holloman, St.L. Browns (vs. Phila. A's), May 6, 1953**
Mel Parnell, Bost. Red Sox (vs. Chi. White Sox), July 14, 1956*
Bob Keegan, Chi. White Sox (vs. Wash. Senators), Aug. 20, 1957
Joe Cowley, Chi. White Sox (vs. Cal. Angels), Sept. 19, 1986
Mike Witt, Cal. Angels (vs. Sea. Mariners), Apr. 11, 1990***
Mike Flanagan, Balt. Orioles (vs. Oak. A's), July 13, 1991***
Philip Humber, Chi. White Sox (vs. Sea. Mariners), Apr. 21, 2012
Kevin Milwood, Sea. Mariners (vs. L.A. Dodgers), June 8, 2012*, ***
Mark Williamson, Balt. Orioles (vs. Oak. A's), July 13, 1991***

*Last Major League season.
**Only Major League season.
***Pitched no-hitter in tandem with other pitcher(s).

National League (Post-1900)

Mal Eason, Bklyn. Dodgers (vs. St.L. Cardinals), July 20, 1906*
Jeff Pfeffer, Bost. Doves (vs. Cin. Reds), May 8, 1907
Tex Carleton, Bklyn. Dodgers (vs. Cin. Reds), Apr. 30, 1940*
Clyde Shoun, Cin. Reds (vs. Bost. Braves), May 15, 1944
Ed Head, Bklyn. Dodgers (vs. Bost. Braves), Apr. 23, 1946*
Jim Maloney, Cin. Reds (vs. Hous. Astros), Apr. 30, 1969
Fernando Valenzuela, L.A. Dodgers (vs. St.L. Cardinals), June 29, 1990
Ricardo Rincon, Pitt. Pirates (vs. Hous. Astros), July 12, 1997***
Johan Santana, N.Y. Mets (vs. St.L. Cardinals), June 1, 2012*

Back-to-Back One-Hit Games (Post-1900)

Rube Marquard, N.Y. Giants (NL) ..... Aug. 28 and Sept. 1, 1911
Lon Warneke, Chi. Cubs (NL) ..... Apr. 17 and Apr. 22, 1934
Mort Cooper, St.L. Cardinals (NL) ..... May 31 and June 4, 1943
Whitey Ford, N.Y. Yankees (AL) ..... Sept. 2 and Sept. 7, 1955
Sam McDowell, Cle. Indians (AL) ..... Apr. 25 and May 1, 1966
Dave Steib, Tor. Blue Jays (AL) ..... Sept. 24 and Oct. 1, 1988
R.A. Dickey, N.Y. Mets (NL) ..... June 13 and June 18, 2012

Rookies Throwing No-Hitters

American League

Pitcher	Date	Result
Charlie Robertson	Apr. 30, 1922	Chi. White Sox vs. Cle. Indians, 2–0 (PG)
Vern Kennedy	Aug. 31, 1935	Chi. White Sox vs. Cle. Indians, 5–0
Bill McCahan	Sept. 3, 1947	Phila. A's vs. Wash. Senators, 3–0
Bobo Holloman*	May 6, 1953	St.L. Browns vs. Phila. A's, 6–0
Bo Belinsky	May 5, 1962	L.A. Angels vs. Balt. Orioles, 2–0
Vida Ble	Sept. 21, 1970	Oak. A's vs. Min. Twins, 6–0
Steve Busby	Apr. 27, 1973	K.C. Royals at Det. Tigers, 3–0
Jim Bibby	July 30, 1973	Tex. Rangers at Oak. A's, 6–0
Mike Warren	Sept. 29, 1983	Oak. A's vs. Chi. White Sox, 3–0
Wilson Alvarez**	Aug. 11, 1991	Chi. White Sox at Balt. Orioles, 7–0
Clay Buchholz**	Sept. 1, 2007	Bost. Red Sox vs. Balt. Orioles, 10–0

*First Major League Start.

**Second Major League Start.

National League

Pitcher	Date	Result
Christy Mathewson	July 15, 1901	N.Y. Dodgers vs. St.L. Cardinals, 5–0
Nick Maddox	Sept. 20, 1907	Pitt. Pirates vs. Bklyn. Dodgers, 2–1
Jeff Tesreau	Sept. 6, 1912	N.Y. Giants at Phila. Phillies, 3–0
Paul Dean	Sept. 21, 1934	St.L. Cardinals vs. Bklyn. Dodgers, 3–0
Sam Jones	May 12, 1955	Chi. Cubs vs. Pitt. Pirates, 4–0
Don Wilson	June 18, 1967	Hous. Astros vs. Atl. Braves, 2–0
Burt Hooton	Apr. 16, 1972	Chi. Cubs vs. Phila. Phillies, 4–0
Jose Jimenez	June 25, 1999	St.L. Cardinals vs. Ariz. D'backs, 1–0
Bud Smith	Sept. 3, 2001	St.L. Cardinals at S.D. Padres, 4–0
Anibal Sanchez	Sept. 6, 2006	Fla. Marlins vs. Ariz. D'backs, 2–0
Chris Heston	June 9, 2015	S.F. Giants at N.Y. Mets, 6–0

Saves/Relief Pitchers

Saves by Decade

Pre-1900

16	Kid Nichols
15	Tony Mullane
14	Harry Wright
13	Al Spalding
12	Jack Manning
9	Brickyard Kennedy
9	Jack Taylor
8	Win Mercer
8	Cy Young
6	Frank Dwyer
6	George Hemming
6	Silver King
6	Adonis Terry
6	Kid Gleason

1900–09

22	Joe McGinnity
19	Mordecai Brown
19	Hooks Wiltse
16	Christy Mathewson
15	Ed Walsh
14	Jack Powell
11	Orval Overall
9	Tom Hughes
9	Cy Young
8	Frank Arellanes
8	Chief Bender
8	Cecil Ferguson
8	Sam Leever
8	Tully Sparks

1910–19

32	Slim Sallee
30	Mordecai Brown
29	Red Ames
26	Chief Bender
22	Eddie Plank
21	Jim Bagby
20	Walter Johnson
20	Ed Walsh
19	Larry Cheney
19	Eddie Cicotte
19	Doc Crandall
19	Hugh Bedient

1920–29

72	Firpo Marberry
30	Waite Hoyt
26	Hooks Dauss
25	Sarge Connally

1930–39

54	Johnny Murphy
49	Clint Brown
38	Jack Russell
35	Joe Heving

1940–49

63	Joe Page
53	Hugh Casey
53	Johnny Murphy
50	Al Benton

continued on next page

25 ..... Wilcy Moore
25 ..... Eddie Rommel
25 ..... Allen Russell
24 ..... Bill Sherdel
23 ..... Lefty Grove
23 ..... Sad Sam Jones
23 ..... Herb Pennock

33 ..... Dick Coffman
33 ..... Chief Hogsett
32 ..... Bob Smith
31 ..... Dizzy Dean
31 ..... Lefty Grove
30 ..... Carl Hubbell
30 ..... Syl Johnson
30 ..... Charlie Root

49 ..... Ace Adams
45 ..... Harry Gumbert
41 ..... Tom Ferrick
39 ..... George Caster
35 ..... Russ Christopher
33 ..... Ed Klieman
33 ..... Gordon Maltzberger

1950–59

98 ..... Ellis Kinder
80 ..... Clem Labine
67 ..... Jim Konstanty
58 ..... Ray Narleski
58 ..... Hoyt Wilhelm
57 ..... Marv Grissom
54 ..... Al Brazle
51 ..... Turk Lown
49 ..... Roy Face
45 ..... Tom Morgan
45 ..... Fritz Dorish

1960–69*

153 ..... Hoyt Wilhelm
142 ..... Roy Face
137 ..... Ron Perranoski
137 ..... Stu Miller
120 ..... Dick Radatz
113 ..... Lindy McDaniel
107 ..... Ted Abernathy
103 ..... Ron Kline
103 ..... John Wyatt
98 ..... Al Worthington

1970–79 ***

209 ..... Rollie Fingers
190 ..... Sparky Lyle
177 ..... Mike Marshall
140 ..... Dave Giusti
132 ..... Tug McGraw
122 ..... Dave LaRoche
115 ..... John Hiller
110 ..... Gene Garber
106 ..... Clay Carroll
105 ..... Bruce Sutter

1980–89

264 ..... Jeff Reardon
239 ..... Dan Quisenberry
234 ..... Lee Smith
206 ..... Goose Gossage
195 ..... Bruce Sutter
188 ..... Dave Righetti
176 ..... Dave Smith
161 ..... Steve Bedrosian
148 ..... John Franco
146 ..... Greg Minton

1990–99

295 ..... John Wetteland
293 ..... Dennis Eckersley
291 ..... Randy Myers
285 ..... Jeff Montgomery
282 ..... Rick Aguilera
268 ..... John Franco
260 ..... Rod Beck
244 ..... Lee Smith
234 ..... Roberto Hernandez
228 ..... Trevor Hoffman

2000–09

397 ..... Mariano Rivera
363 ..... Trevor Hoffman
284 ..... Jason Isringhausen
284 ..... Billy Wagner
250 ..... Francisco Cordero
246 ..... Joe Nathan
243 ..... Francisco Rodriguez
230 ..... Armando Benitez
219 ..... Troy Percival
195 ..... Brad Lidge
193 ..... Bob Wickman

2010–15

225 ..... Craig Kimbrel
198 ..... Jonathan Papelbon
186 ..... Huston Street
166 ..... Fernando Rodney
164 ..... Rafael Soriano
146 ..... Aroldis Chapman
145 ..... Greg Holland
143 ..... Francisco Rodriguez
142 ..... Kenley Jansen
140 ..... John Axford

*For games played before 1969, saves have been figured retroactively using the 1969 definition, which states that "a relief pitcher earned a save when he entered the game with his team in the lead and held the lead for the remainder of the game, provided that he was not credited with the victory."

**Before the 1974 season, the save rule was modified and simplified. Under this new rule, a relief pitcher earned a save under one of the following two conditions:

1. Pitcher had to enter the game with either the potential tying or winning run either on base or at the plate and preserve the lead.
2. Pitcher had to pitch at least three or more effective innings and preserve the lead.

***Beginning the 1975 season, the save rule was modified a final time, stating that a relief pitcher will be awarded a save when they met all of the three following conditions:

1. Pitcher must finish the game won by his club.
2. Pitcher is not the winning pitcher.
3. Pitcher qualifies under one of the following three conditions:
   a. Pitcher enters the game with a lead of no more than three runs and pitches for at least one inning.
   b. Pitcher enters the game, regardless of the score, with the potential tying run either on base, at bat, or on deck.
   c. Pitcher throws for at least three innings, regardless of the score.

Evolution of Saves Record

American League

1901	Bill Hoffer, Cle. Indians	3
1908	Ed Walsh, Chi. White Sox	6
1909	Frank Arellanes, Bost. Americans	8
1912	Ed Walsh, Chi. White Sox	10
1913	Chief Bender, Phila. A's	13
1924	Firpo Marberry, Wash. Senators	15
1926	Firpo Marberry, Wash. Senators	22
1949	Joe Page, N.Y. Yankees	27
1961	Luis Arroyo, N.Y. Yankees	29
1966	Jack Aker, K.C. A's	32
1970	Ron Perranoski, Min. Twins	34
1972	Sparky Lyle, N.Y. Yankees	35
1973	John Hiller, Det. Tigers	38
1983	Dan Quisenberry, K.C. Royals	45
1986	Dave Righetti, N.Y. Yankees	46
1990	Bobby Thigpen, Chi. White Sox	57
2008	Francisco Rodriguez, L.A. Angels	62

National League (Post-1899)

1900	Frank Kitson, Bklyn. Dodgers	4
1904	Joe McGinnity, N.Y. Giants	5
1905	Claude Elliott, Bost. Beaneaters	6
1906	Cecil Ferguson, N.Y. Giants	7
1911	Three Finger Brown, Chi. Cubs	13
1931	Jack Quinn, Phila. Phillies	15
1947	Hugh Casey, Bklyn. Dodgers	18
1950	Jim Konstanty, Phila. Phillies	22
1954	Jim Hughes, Bklyn. Dodgers	24
1960	Lindy McDaniel, St.L. Cardinals	26
1962	Roy Face, Pitt. Pirates	28
1965	Ted Abernathy, Chi. Cubs	31
1970	Wayne Granger, Cin. Reds	35
1972	Clay Carroll, Cin. Reds	37
1984	Bruce Sutter, St.L. Cardinals	45
1991	Lee Smith, St.L. Cardinals	47
1993	Randy Myers, Chi. Cubs	53
2002	John Smoltz, Atl. Braves	55

Pitchers with 100 Wins and 100 Saves, Career

	Wins	Saves
Dennis Eckersley (1975–98)	197	390
Roy Face (1953, 1955–69)	104	193
Rollie Fingers (1968–85)	114	341
Dave Giusti (1962, 1964–77)	100	145
Tom Gordon (1988–2009)	138	158
Goose Gossage (1972–94)	124	310
Ellis Kinder (1946–57)	102	102
Ron Kline (1952, 1955–70)	114	108
Firpo Marberry (1923–36)	148	101
Lindy McDaniel (1955–75)	141	172
Stu Miller (1952–54, 1956–68)	105	154

continued on next page

Ron Reed (1966–84)	146	103
John Smoltz (1998–2009)	213	154
Bob Stanley (1977–89)	115	132
Hoyt Wilhelm (1952–72)	143	227

Relief Pitchers with the Most Wins, Season

American League

John Hiller, Det. Tigers, 1974	17–14
Bill Campbell, Min. Twins, 1976	17–5
Tom Johnson, Min. Twins, 1977	16–7
Dick Radatz, Bost. Red Sox, 1964	16–9
Luis Arroyo, N.Y. Yankees, 1961	15–5
Dick Radatz, Bost. Red Sox, 1963	15–6
Eddie Fisher, Chi. White Sox, 1965	15–7

National League (Post-1900)

Roy Face, Pitt. Pirates, 1959	18–1
Jim Konstanty, Phila. Phillies, 1950	16–7
Ron Perranoski, L.A. Dodgers, 1963	16–3
Mace Brown, Pitt. Pirates, 1938	15–9*
Hoyt Wilhelm, N.Y. Giants, 1952	15–3
Mike Marshall, L.A. Dodgers, 1974	15–12
Dale Murray, Mont. Expos, 1975	15–8

*Started two games, no decisions

Most Games Won by Relief Pitcher, Career

Hoyt Wilhelm (1952–72)	124
Lindy McDaniel (1955–75)	119
Goose Gossage (1972–94)	115
Rollie Fingers (1968–85)	107
Sparky Lyle (1967–82)	99
Roy Face (1953–69)	96
Gene Garber (1969–87)	94
Kent Tekulve (1974–89)	94
Mike Marshall (1967–81)	92

Teams with Two Pitchers with 20 Saves, Season

1965	Chi. White Sox (AL)	Eddie Fisher	24	Hoyt Wilhelm	20
1983	S.F. Giants (NL)	Greg Minton	22	Gary Lavelle	20
1986	N.Y. Mets (NL)	Roger McDowell	22	Jesse Orosco	21

Pitchers Having 20-Win Seasons and 20-Save Seasons, Career

		Wins	Saves
Dennis Eckersley	Bost. Red Sox (AL), 1978	20	
	Oak. A's (AL), 1988		45
	Oak. A's (AL), 1989		33
	Oak. A's (AL), 1990		48
	Oak. A's (AL), 1991		43
	Oak. A's (AL), 1992		51
	Oak. A's (AL), 1993		36
	Oak. A's (AL), 1995		29
	St.L. Cardinals (NL), 1996		30
	St.L. Cardinals (NL), 1997		36
Mudcat Grant	Min. Twins (AL), 1965	21	
	Oak. A's (AL)–Pitt. Pirates (NL), 1970		24
Ellis Kinder	Bost. Red Sox (AL), 1949	23	
	Bost. Red Sox (AL), 1953		27
Johnny Sain	Bost. Braves (NL), 1946	20	
	Bost. Braves (NL), 1947	21	
	Bost. Braves (NL), 1948	24	

continued on next page

		Wins	Saves
	Bost. Braves (NL), 1950	20	
	N.Y. Yankees (AL), 1954		22
John Smoltz	Atl. Braves (NL), 1996	24	
	Atl. Braves (NL), 2002		55
	Atl. Braves (NL), 2003		45
	Atl. Braves (NL), 2004		45
Wilbur Wood	Chi. White Sox (AL), 1970		21
	Chi. White Sox (AL), 1971	22	
	Chi. White Sox (AL), 1972	24	
	Chi. White Sox (AL), 1973	24	
	Chi. White Sox (AL), 1974	20	

Pitchers with 15 Saves and 15 Wins in Relief, Same Season

American League

	Wins	Saves
Luis Arroyo, N.Y. Yankees, 1961	15	29
Dick Radatz, Bost. Red Sox, 1963	15	25
Dick Radatz, Bost. Red Sox, 1964	16	29
Eddie Fisher, Chi. White Sox, 1965	15	24
Bill Campbell, Min. Twins, 1976	17	20
Tom Johnson, Min. Twins, 1977	16	15

National League (Post-1900)

	Wins	Saves
Jim Konstanty, Phila. Phillies, 1950	16	22
Joe Black, Bklyn. Dodgers, 1952	15	15
Ron Perranoski, L.A. Dodgers, 1963	16	21
Mike Marshall, L.A. Dodgers, 1974	15	21

Pitching Miscellany

Best Winning Percentage by Decade (100 Decisions)

Pre-1900		1900–09		1910–19	
.701	Bill Hoffer	.713	Ed Reulbach	.682	Smoky Joe Wood
.690	Dave Foutz	.697	Sam Leever	.675	Grover C. Alexander
.688	Bob Caruthers	.689	Three Finger Brown	.663	Chief Bender
.665	Larry Corcoran	.678	Christy Mathewson	.659	Babe Ruth
.663	Kid Nichols	.636	Ed Walsh	.657	Eddie Plank
.650	Ted Lewis	.634	Hooks Wiltse	.656	Doc Crandall
.648	John Clarkson	.634	Jack Pfiester	.650	Walter Johnson
.640	Lady Baldwin	.634	Joe McGinnity	.643	Christy Mathewson
.639	Cy Young	.633	Jesse Tannehill	.621	Jack Coombs
.630	Nig Cuppy	.631	Deacon Phillippe	.615	Jeff Tesreau

1920–29		1930–39		1940–49	
.660	Ray Kremer	.724	Lefty Grove	.714	Spud Chandler
.638	Carl Mays	.706	Johnny Allen	.640	Tex Hughson
.627	Urban Shocker	.686	Firpo Marberry	.640	Harry Brecheen
.626	Freddie Fitzsimmons	.650	Lefty Gomez	.629	Howie Pollet
.626	Lefty Grove	.648	Dizzy Dean	.626	Mort Cooper

continued on next page

.620 ..... Dazzy Vance
.615 ..... Art Nehf
.612 ..... Waite Hoyt
.611 ..... Grover C. Alexander
.599 ..... Stan Coveleski

.644 ..... Carl Hubbell
.641 ..... Red Ruffing
.634 ..... Monte Pearson
.629 ..... Lon Warneke
.602 ..... Bill Lee

.626 ..... Bob Feller
.621 ..... Max Lanier
.619 ..... Schoolboy Rowe
.613 ..... Warren Spahn
.605 ..... Rip Sewell

1950–59

.708 ..... Whitey Ford
.669 ..... Allie Reynolds
.667 ..... Eddie Lopat
.663 ..... Sal Maglie
.643 ..... Vic Raschi
.633 ..... Don Newcombe
.618 ..... Bob Buhl
.615 ..... Bob Lemon
.612 ..... Early Wynn
.607 ..... Warren Spahn

1960–69

.695 ..... Sandy Koufax
.685 ..... Juan Marichal
.673 ..... Whitey Ford
.667 ..... Denny McLain
.626 ..... Jim Maloney
.621 ..... Dave McNally
.610 ..... Bob Gibson
.596 ..... Ray Culp
.593 ..... Bob Purkey
.582 ..... Dick Hall

1970–79

.686 ..... Don Gullett
.648 ..... John Candelaria
.647 ..... Pedro Borbon
.644 ..... Jim Palmer
.638 ..... Tom Seaver
.624 ..... Catfish Hunter
.613 ..... Tommy John
.612 ..... Gary Nolan
.610 ..... Clay Carroll
.607 ..... Luis Tiant

1980–89

.719 ..... Dwight Gooden
.679 ..... Roger Clemens
.639 ..... Ted Higuera
.613 ..... Ron Darling
.612 ..... John Tudor
.607 ..... Ron Guidry
.605 ..... Sid Fernandez
.605 ..... Orel Hershiser
.605 ..... Dennis Rasmussen
.602 ..... Jimmy Key

1990–99

.682 ..... Pedro Martinez
.673 ..... Mike Mussina
.667 ..... Randy Johnson
.667 ..... Greg Maddux
.653 ..... Tom Glavine
.642 ..... Kirk Rueter
.638 ..... Andy Pettitte
.631 ..... Roger Clemens
.626 ..... Jose Rijo
.624 ..... David Cone

2000–09

.691 ..... Pedro Martinez
.682 ..... Roger Clemens
.670 ..... Johan Santana
.668 ..... Roy Halladay
.662 ..... Roy Oswalt
.650 ..... Curt Schilling
.647 ..... Randy Johnson
.643 ..... Tim Hudson
.641 ..... Chris Carpenter
.634 ..... Cliff Lee

2010–15 (Min. 60 decisions)

.701 ..... Clayton Kershaw
.697 ..... Zack Greinke
.671 ..... Max Scherzer
.657 ..... David Price
.636 ..... Adam Wainwright
.630 ..... Justin Verlander
.628 ..... Johnny Cueto
.621 ..... C.J. Wilson
.619 ..... CC Sabathia
.617 ..... Jered Weaver

Walks Plus Hits Per Inning

Best WHIP by Decade (1000 Innings)

Pre-1900

1.043 ..... Monte Ward
1.067 ..... Charlie Sweeney
1.087 ..... Jim Devlin
1.090 ..... George Bradley
1.091 ..... Tommy Bond
1.105 ..... Larry Corcoran
1.108 ..... Ed Morris
1.111 ..... Will White
1.117 ..... Terry Larkin
1.117 ..... Charlie Ferguson

1900–09

0.963 ..... Addie Joss
0.967 ..... Ed Walsh
0.984 ..... Mordecai Brown
1.000 ..... Cy Young
1.035 ..... Christy Mathewson
1.048 ..... Ed Reulbach
1.079 ..... Chief Bender
1.085 ..... Frank Smith
1.089 ..... Doc White
1.089 ..... Barney Pelty

1910–19

0.953 ..... Walter Johnson
1.04 ..... Ed Walsh
1.052 ..... Grover C. Alexander
1.053 ..... Babe Adams
1.08 ..... Reb Russell
1.088 ..... Smoky Joe Wood
1.095 ..... Carl Mays
1.096 ..... Christy Mathewson
1.113 ..... Jeff Pfeffer
1.121 ..... Fred Toney

continued on next page

1920–29

1.191 ..... Grover C. Alexander
1.205 ..... Dazzy Vance
1.258 ..... Tommy Thomas
1.260 ..... Ray Kremer
1.264 ..... Dolf Luque
1.267 ..... Eppa Rixey
1.268 ..... Walter Johnson
1.275 ..... Urban Shocker
1.281 ..... Jesse Petty
1.283 ..... Carl Mays

1930–39

1.118 ..... Carl Hubbell
1.193 ..... Dizzy Dean
1.226 ..... Bill Swift
1.243 ..... Lefty Grove
1.257 ..... Syl Johnson
1.261 ..... Lon Warneke
1.268 ..... Red Lucas
1.277 ..... Charlie Root
1.28 ..... Ben Cantwell
1.29 ..... Curt Davis

1940–49

1.153 ..... Tiny Bonham
1.166 ..... Whit Wyatt
1.167 ..... Harry Brecheen
1.177 ..... Spud Chandler
1.185 ..... Mort Cooper
1.194 ..... Tex Hughson
1.232 ..... Curt Davis
1.236 ..... Paul Derringer
1.245 ..... Preacher Roe
1.246 ..... Dutch Leonard

1950–59

1.129 ..... Robin Roberts
1.18 ..... Warren Spahn
1.192 ..... Don Newcombe
1.214 ..... Harvey Haddix
1.224 ..... Warren Hacker
1.232 ..... Steve Gromek
1.237 ..... Billy Pierce
1.243 ..... Hoyt Wilhelm
1.244 ..... Dick Donovan
1.245 ..... Eddie Lopat

1960–69

0.993 ..... Hoyt Wilhelm
1.005 ..... Sandy Koufax
1.045 ..... Juan Marichal
1.085 ..... Ferguson Jenkins
1.094 ..... Denny McLain
1.118 ..... Don Drysdale
1.125 ..... Sonny Siebert
1.125 ..... Eddie Fisher
1.129 ..... Ralph Terry
1.142 ..... Jim Bunning

1970–79

1.073 ..... Tom Seaver
1.106 ..... Catfish Hunter
1.108 ..... Don Sutton
1.118 ..... Ferguson Jenkins
1.141 ..... Rollie Fingers
1.142 ..... Gaylord Perry
1.142 ..... Jim Palmer
1.144 ..... Frank Tanana
1.149 ..... Gary Nolan
1.160 ..... Andy Messersmith

1980–89

1.109 ..... Dwight Gooden
1.127 ..... Bret Saberhagen
1.136 ..... Roger Clemens
1.149 ..... Orel Hershiser
1.150 ..... Sid Fernandez
1.163 ..... Mario Soto
1.172 ..... Teddy Higuera
1.177 ..... Don Sutton
1.179 ..... Bryn Smith
1.179 ..... Dennis Eckersley

1990–99

1.055 ..... Greg Maddux
1.074 ..... Pedro Martinez
1.134 ..... Curt Schilling
1.154 ..... Bret Saberhagen
1.157 ..... Jose Rijo
1.174 ..... Mike Mussina
1.176 ..... Roger Clemens
1.180 ..... John Smoltz
1.193 ..... Dennis Martinez
1.197 ..... Randy Johnson

2000–09

1.036 ..... Pedro Martinez
1.113 ..... Johan Santana
1.114 ..... Randy Johnson
1.129 ..... Curt Schilling
1.151 ..... John Smoltz
1.171 ..... Roy Halladay
1.172 ..... Greg Maddux
1.178 ..... Dan Haren
1.182 ..... Jake Peavy
1.201 ..... Roger Clemens
1.201 ..... Ben Sheets

2010–15

0.970 ..... Clayton Kershaw
1.104 ..... Felix Hernandez
1.107 ..... Jered Weaver
1.111 ..... Madison Bumgarner
1.113 ..... David Price
1.115 ..... Johnny Cueto
1.121 ..... Zack Greinke
1.130 ..... Cole Hamels
1.141 ..... Jordan Zimmermann
1.146 ..... Max Scherzer

Most Seasons Leading League in Pitching Category

American League

	Seasons	
Games Pitched	6	Firpo Marberry, 1924–26, 1928–29, and 1932
Complete Games	6	Walter Johnson, 1910–11 and 1913–16
Innings Pitched	5	Walter Johnson, 1910 and 1913–16
	5	Bob Feller, 1939–41 and 1946–47
Games Won	6	Walter Johnson, 1913–16, 1918, and 1924
Games Lost	4	Bobo Newsom, 1934–35, 1941, and 1945
	4	Pedro Ramos, 1958–61
Won-Lost Percentage	5	Lefty Grove, 1929–31, 1933, and 1939
ERA	9	Lefty Grove, 1926, 1929–32, 1935–36, and 1938–39
Strikeouts	12	Walter Johnson, 1910, 1912–19, 1921, and 1923–24
Shutouts	7	Walter Johnson, 1911, 1913–15, 1918–19, and 1924

continued on next page

Saves	5	Firpo Marberry, 1924–26, 1929, and 1932
	5	Dan Quisenberry, 1980 and 1982–85

National League (Post-1900)

	Seasons	
Games Pitched	6	Joe McGinnity, 1900 and 1903–07
Complete Games	9	Warren Spahn, 1949, 1951, and 1957–63
Innings Pitched	7	Grover C. Alexander, 1911–12, 1914–17, and 1920
Games Won	8	Warren Spahn, 1949–50, 1953, and 1957–61
Games Lost	4	Phil Niekro, 1977–80
Won-Lost Percentage	4	Tom Seaver, 1969, 1975, 1979, and 1981
ERA	5	Christy Mathewson, 1905, 1908–09, 1911, and 1913
	5	Grover C. Alexander, 1915–17 and 1919–20
	5	Sandy Koufax, 1962–66
Strikeouts	7	Dazzy Vance, 1922–28
Shutouts	7	Grover C. Alexander, 1911, 1913, 1915–17, 1919, and 1921
Saves	5	Bruce Sutter, 1979–82 and 1984

Most Consecutive Seasons Leading League in Pitching Category

American League

	Seasons	
Winning Percentage	3	Lefty Grove, 1929–31
ERA	4	Lefty Grove, 1929–32
Shutouts	3	Walter Johnson, 1913–15
Strikeouts	8	Walter Johnson, 1912–19
Saves	4	Dan Quisenberry, 1982–85

National League (Post-1900)

	Seasons	
Winning Percentage	3	Ed Reulbach, 1906–08
ERA	5	Sandy Koufax, 1962–66
Shutouts	3	Grover C. Alexander, 1915–17
Strikeouts	7	Dazzy Vance, 1922–28
Saves	4	Three Finger Brown, 1908–11
	4	Bruce Sutter, 1979–82
	4	Craig Kimbrel, 2011–14

Most Consecutive Scoreless Innings Pitched

American League

Innings	
55⅔	Walter Johnson, 1913 Wash. Senators
53	Jack Coombs, 1910 Phila. A's
45	Doc White*, 1904 Chi. White Sox
45	Cy Young*, 1904 Bost. Red Sox
43⅔	Rube Waddell, 1905 Phila. A's
42	Rube Foster, 1914 Bost. Red Sox

*Left-handed.

National League

Innings	
59	Orel Hershiser, 1988 L.A. Dodgers
58⅔	Don Drysdale, 1968 L.A. Dodgers
47	Bob Gibson, 1968 St.L. Cardinals
45⅔	Zack Greinke, 2015 L.A. Dodgers
45⅓	Carl Hubbell*, 1933 N.Y. Giants
45	Sal Maglie, 1950 N.Y. Giants

Highest Career Pitching Totals by Pitchers Who Never Led League

American League		National League	
Games Pitched			
1115	Mariano Rivera	1119	John Franco
Complete Games			
395	Eddie Plank	290	Eppa Rixey

continued on next page

Innings Pitched

4269 ..... Eddie Plank	5282 ..... Don Sutton

Games Won

254 ..... Red Faber	324 ..... Don Sutton

Games Lost

279 ..... Walter Johnson	245 ..... Warren Spahn

Winning Percentage (Min. 100 Wins)

.630 ..... Allie Reynolds	.647 ..... Three Finger Brown

ERA

2.35 ..... Eddie Plank	2.23 ..... Orval Overall

Strikeouts

2416 ..... Luis Tiant	3574 ..... Don Sutton

Shutouts

47 ..... Rube Waddell	43 ..... Phil Niekro

Saves

377 ..... Joe Nathan	422 ..... Billy Wagner

Career Pitching Leaders Under Six Feet Tall

Games Pitched	1119	John Franco (5'10")
Games Won	361	Pud Galvin (5'8")
Games Won	361	Kid Nichols (5'10")
Games Lost	308	Pud Galvin (5'8")
Winning Percentage (Min. 150 Wins)	.690	Whitey Ford (5'10")
ERA (Min. 100 Wins)	2.03	Smoky Joe Wood (5'11")
Complete Games	639	Pud Galvin (5'8")
Innings Pitched	5941	Pud Galvin (5'8")
Games Started	681	Pud Galvin (5'8")
Strikeouts	3154	Pedro Martinez (5'11")
Shutouts	69	Eddie Plank (5'11½")
Walks	1570	Gus Weyhing (5'10")
Saves	424	John Franco (5'10")

Pitching's Triple Crown Winners (Led League in Wins, ERA, and Strikeouts, Same Season)

American League

	Wins	ERA	Strikeouts
Cy Young, Bost. Americans, 1901	33	1.62	158
Rube Waddell, Phila. A's, 1905	26	1.48	287
Walter Johnson, Wash. Senators, 1913	36	1.09	243
Walter Johnson, Wash. Senators, 1918	23	1.27	162
Walter Johnson, Wash. Senators, 1924	23	2.72	158
Lefty Grove, Phila. A's, 1930	28	2.54	209
Lefty Grove, Phila. A's, 1931	31	2.06	175
Lefty Gomez, N.Y. Yankees, 1934	26	2.33	158
Lefty Gomez, N.Y. Yankees, 1937	21	2.33	194
Bob Feller, Cle. Indians, 1940	27	2.61	261
Hal Newhouser, Det. Tigers, 1945	25	1.81	212

continued on next page

Roger Clemens, Tor. Blue Jays, 1997	21	2.05	292
Roger Clemens, Tor. Blue Jays, 1998	20	2.65	271
Pedro Martinez, Bost. Red Sox, 1999	23	2.07	313
Johan Santana, Min. Twins, 2006	19	2.77	245
Justin Verlander, Det. Tigers, 2011	24	2.40	250

National League (Post-1900)

	Wins	ERA	Strikeouts
Christy Mathewson, N.Y. Giants, 1905	31	1.27	206
Christy Mathewson, N.Y. Giants, 1908	37	1.43	259
Grover C. Alexander, Phila. Phillies, 1915	31	1.22	241
Grover C. Alexander, Phila. Phillies, 1916	33	1.55	167
Grover C. Alexander, Phila. Phillies, 1917	30	1.86	201
Hippo Vaughn, Chi. Cubs, 1918	22	1.74	148
Grover C. Alexander, Chi. Cubs, 1920	27	1.91	173
Dazzy Vance, Bklyn. Dodgers, 1924	28	2.16	262
Bucky Walters, Cin. Reds, 1939	27	2.29	137
Sandy Koufax, L.A. Dodgers, 1963	25	1.88	306
Sandy Koufax, L.A. Dodgers, 1965	26	2.04	382
Sandy Koufax, L.A. Dodgers, 1966	27	1.73	317
Steve Carlton, Phila. Phillies, 1972	27	1.97	310
Dwight Gooden, N.Y. Giants, 1985	24	1.53	268
Randy Johnson, Ariz. D'backs, 2002	24	2.32	334
Jake Peavy, S.D. Padres, 2007	19	2.54	240
Clayton Kershaw, L.A. Dodgers, 2011	21	2.28	248

Most Home Runs Given Up, Season

American League

50	Bert Blyleven, Min. Twins, 1986 (in 271 innings)
46	Bert Blyleven, Min. Twins, 1987 (in 267 innings)
44	Jamie Moyer, Sea. Mariners, 2004 (in 202 innings)
43	Pedro Ramos, Wash. Senators, 1957 (in 231 innings)
42	Denny McLain, Det. Tigers, 1966 (in 264 innings)
41	Rick Helling, Tex. Rangers, 1999 (in 219 innings)
40	Ralph Terry, N.Y. Yankees, 1962 (in 298 innings)
40	Orlando Pena, K.C. A's, 1964 (in 219 innings)
40	Ferguson Jenkins, Tex. Rangers, 1979 (in 259 innings)
40	Jack Morris, Det. Tigers, 1986 (in 267 innings)
40	Shawn Boskie, Cal. Angels, 1996 (in 189 innings)
40	Brad Radke, Min. Twins, 1996 (in 232 innings)
40	Ramon Ortiz, Ana. Angels, 2002 (in 217 innings)

National League (Post-1900)

48	Jose Lima, Hous. Astros, 2000 (in 196 innings)
46	Robin Roberts, Phila. Phillies, 1956 (in 297 innings)
46	Bronson Arroyo, Cin. Reds, 2011 (in 199 innings)
43	Eric Milton, Phila. Phillies, 2004 (in 201 innings)
41	Robin Roberts, Phila. Phillies, 1955 (in 305 innings)
41	Phil Niekro, Atl. Braves, 1979 (in 229 innings)
40	Robin Roberts, Phila. Phillies, 1957 (in 249 innings)
40	Phil Niekro, Atl. Braves, 1979 (in 342 innings)
40	Eric Milton, Cin. Reds, 2005 (in 186 innings)

Most Home Runs Given Up, Career

522 ..... Jamie Moyer (1986–91, 1993–2012)
505 ..... Robin Roberts (1948–66)
484 ..... Ferguson Jenkins (1965–83)
482 ..... Phil Niekro (1964–87)
472 ..... Don Sutton (1966–88)
448 ..... Frank Tanana (1973–93)
434 ..... Warren Spahn (1942, 1946–65)
430 ..... Bert Blyleven (1970–92)
418 ..... Tim Wakefield (1992–93, 1995–2011)
414 ..... Steve Carlton (1965–88)
411 ..... Randy Johnson (1988–2009)
407 ..... David Wells (1987–2007)
399 ..... Gaylord Perry (1962–83)

Pitchers Giving Up Most Grand Slams, Season

American League

4 ..... Ray Narleski, Det. Tigers, 1959
Mike Schooler, Sea. Mariners, 1992

National League

4 ..... Tug McGraw, Phila. Phillies, 1979
Chan Ho Park, L.A. Dodgers, 1999
Matt Clement, S.D. Padres, 2000

Pitchers with 2000 Innings Pitched, Allowing No Grand Slams

Old Hoss Radbourn (1880–91) 4535
Eddie Plank (1901–17) 4505
Jim McCormick (1878–87) 4275
Jim Palmer (1965–84) 3948
Herb Pennock (1912–17, 1919–34) 3558
Dazzy Vance (1915, 1918, 1922–35) 2967
Joaquin Andujar (1976–88) 2153
Gary Peters (1959–72) 2081

20-Game Winners Batting .300, Same Season

American League

	Wins	Batting Average
Clark Griffith, Chi. White Sox, 1901	24	.303
Cy Young, Bost. Americans, 1903	28	.321
Ed Killian, Det. Tigers, 1907	25	.320
Jack Coombs, Phila. A's, 1911	29	.319
Babe Ruth, Bost. Red Sox, 1917	24	.325
Carl Mays, N.Y. Yankees, 1921	27	.343
Joe Bush, N.Y. Yankees, 1922	26	.326
George Uhle, Cle. Indians, 1923	26	.361
Joe Shaute, Cle. Indians, 1924	20	.318
Walter Johnson, Wash. Senators, 1925	20	.433
Ted Lyons, Chi. White Sox, 1930	22	.311
Wes Ferrell, Cle. Indians, 1931	22	.319
Schoolboy Rowe, Det. Tigers, 1934	24	.303
Wes Ferrell, Bost. Red Sox, 1935	25	.347
Red Ruffing, N.Y. Yankees, 1939	21	.307
Ned Garver, St.L. Browns, 1951	20	.305
Catfish Hunter, Oak. A's, 1971	21	.350
Catfish Hunter, Oak. A's, 1973	21	1.000

National League (Post-1900)

	Wins	Batting Average
Brickyard Kennedy, Bklyn. Bridegrooms, 1900	20	.301
Jesse Tannehill, Pitt. Pirates, 1900	20	.336
Claude Hendrix, Pitt. Pirates, 1912	24	.322
Burleigh Grimes, Bklyn. Dodgers, 1920	23	.306
Wilbur Cooper, Pitt. Pirates, 1924	20	.346
Pete Donahue, Cin. Reds, 1926	20	.311
Burleigh Grimes, Pitt. Pirates, 1928	25	.321
Curt Davis, St.L. Cardinals, 1939	22	.381
Bucky Walters, Cin. Reds, 1939	27	.325
Johnny Sain, Bost. Braves, 1947	21	.346
Don Newcombe, Bklyn. Dodgers, 1955	20	.359
Warren Spahn, Milw. Braves, 1958	22	.333
Don Drysdale, L.A. Dodgers, 1965	23	.300
Bob Gibson, St.L. Cardinals, 1970	23	.303
Mike Hampton, Hous. Astros, 1999	22	.311

Pitchers with Two Seasons of 1.000 Batting Averages (Post-1900)

Bruce Chen ..... Balt. Orioles, 2006 .....1-for-1 (40 games)
K.C. Royals, 2009.....1-for-1 (17 games)
K.C. Royals, 2010.....1-for-1 (33 games)
Nick Altrock ..... Wash. Senators, 1924 .....1-for-1 (1 game)
Wash. Senators, 1929 .....1-for-1 (1 game)
Clark Griffith .... Wash. Senators, 1913 .....1-for-1 (1 game)
Wash. Senators, 1914 .....1-for-1 (1 game)
Scott Linebrink .... S.F. Giants–Hous. Astros.....
2000 1-for-1 (11 games)
S.D. Padres, 2006 .....1-for-1 (73 games)
John Morris ..... Sea. Pilots, 1969 .....1-for-1 (6 games)
S.F. Giants, 1974 .....1-for-1 (17 games)
Felix Rodriguez ..S.F. Giants, 2002 .....1-for-1 (78 games)
S.F. Giants, 2003 .....1-for-1 (81 games)
Al Schroll.....Bost. Red Sox, 1958 ....1-for-1 (5 games)
Chi. Cubs, 1960 .....1-for-1 (2 games)
Lefty Weinert.....Phila. Phillies, 1919 .....2-for-2 (1 game)
Phila. Phillies, 1921 .....1-for-1 (8 games)
Matt Wise .....Milw. Brewers, 2005..1-for-1 (49 games)
Milw. Brewers, 2007...1-for-1 (56 games)
Esteban Yan.....T.B. Devil Rays, 2000 ...1-for-1 (43 games)
St.L. Cardinals, 2003..1-for-1 (39 games)

Complete Games by Decade

Pre-1900

646.....Pud Galvin
554.....Tim Keefe
525.....Mickey Welch
525.....Bobby Mathews
488.....Old Hoss Radbourn
485.....John Clarkson
468.....Tony Mullane
466.....Jim McCormick
448.....Gus Weyhing
443.....Kid Nichols
418.....Cy Young

1900–09

337.....Cy Young
312.....Vic Willis
282.....Christy Mathewson
277.....Jack Powell
276.....Joe McGinnity
263.....Eddie Plank
258.....George Mullin
254.....Bill Dinneen
251.....Rube Waddell
246.....Bill Donovan

1910–19

327.....Walter Johnson
242.....Gover C. Alexander
193.....Eddie Cicotte
183.....Hippo Vaughn
172.....Claude Hendrix
167.....Dick Rudolph
163.....Slim Sallee
160.....Ray Caldwell
159.....Lefty Tyler
156.....Hooks Dauss

1920–29

234.....Burleigh Grimes
194.....Grover C. Alexander
185.....Eppa Rixey
182.....George Uhle
181.....Red Faber
181.....Herb Pennock
172.....Dazzy Vance
169.....Jesse Haines
168.....Dolf Luque
168.....Urban Shocker

1930–39

207.....Wes Ferrell
201.....Red Ruffing
197.....Lefty Grove
197.....Carl Hubbell
168.....Ted Lyons
163.....Paul Derringer
163.....Lefty Gomez
161.....Larry French
156.....Tommy Bridges
151.....Dizzy Dean

1940–49

181.....Hal Newhouser
155.....Bob Feller
153.....Bucky Walters
139.....Dutch Leonard
132.....Rip Sewell
132.....Dizzy Trout
130.....Claude Passeau
127.....Jim Tobin
120.....Mort Cooper
115.....Bobo Newsom

1950–59

237.....Robin Roberts
215.....Warren Spahn
162.....Billy Pierce
162.....Early Wynn
139.....Bob Lemon
125.....Ned Garver
116.....Don Newcombe
105.....Bob Rush
104.....Lew Burdette
103.....Mike Garcia

1960–69

197.....Juan Marichal
164.....Bob Gibson
135.....Don Drysdale
122.....Sandy Koufax
116.....Larry Jackson
108.....Jim Bunning
102.....Jim Kaat
95.....Warren Spahn
93.....Denny McLain
93.....Camilo Pascual

1970–79

197.....Gaylord Perry
184.....Ferguson Jenkins
175.....Jim Palmer
165.....Steve Carlton
164.....Nolan Ryan
160.....Phil Niekro
147.....Tom Seaver
145.....Bert Blyleven
140.....Catfish Hunter
133.....Mickey Lolich

1980–89

133.....Jack Morris
102.....Fernando Valenzuela
94.....Bert Blyleven
93.....Charlie Hough

1990–99

75.....Greg Maddux
65.....Randy Johnson
61.....Jack McDowell
58.....Kevin Brown

2000–09

47.....Roy Halladay
36.....Livan Hernandez
32.....Randy Johnson
28.....CC Sabathia

continued on next page

92 ..... Dave Stieb
70 ..... Mike Witt
70 ..... Mario Soto
64 ..... Bruce Hurst
62 ..... Mike Moore
62 ..... Scott McGregor

57 ..... Roger Clemens
57 ..... Curt Schilling
47 ..... Scott Erickson
46 ..... Chuck Finley
42 ..... John Smoltz
41 ..... Terry Mulholland
41 ..... Doug Drabek

26 ..... Curt Schilling
25 ..... Mark Mulder
24 ..... Mark Buehrle
23 ..... Bartolo Colon
23 ..... Sidney Ponson
23 ..... Javier Vazquez

2010–15

21 ..... Clayton Kershaw
18 ..... Felix Hernandez
18 ..... Adam Wainwright
18 ..... Roy Halladay
17 ..... James Shields
16 ..... Cliff Lee
15 ..... Justin Verlander
14 ..... R.A. Dickey
14 ..... David Price
12 ..... Johnny Cueto

Evolution of Complete Games Record

American League

1901 Joe McGinnity, Balt. Orioles 39
1902 Cy Young, Bost. Red Sox 41
1904 Jack Chesbro, N.Y. Yankees 48

National League (Pre-1900)

1876 Jim Devlin, Lou. Colonels 66
1879 Will White, Cin. Reds 75

National League (Post-1899)

1900 Pink Hawley, N.Y. Giants 34
1901 Noodles Hahn, Cin. Reds 41
1902 Vic Willis, Bost. Beaneaters 45

Most Games Started By a Pitcher, Career

Starts

815 ..... Cy Young (1890–1911)
773 ..... Nolan Ryan (1968–93)
756 ..... Don Sutton (1966–88)
740 ..... Greg Maddux (1986–2008)
716 ..... Phil Niekro (1964–87)
709 ..... Steve Carlton (1965–88)
707 ..... Roger Clemens (1984–2007)
700 ..... Tommy John (1963–74, 1976–89)
690 ..... Gaylord Perry (1962–83)
688 ..... Pud Galvin (1875, 1879–92)
685 ..... Bert Blyleven (1970–92)

Starts

682 ..... Tom Glavine (1987–2008)
666 ..... Walter Johnson (1907–27)
665 ..... Warren Spahn (1942, 1946–65)
647 ..... Tom Seaver (1967–86)
638 ..... Jamie Moyer (1986–91, 1993–2010, 2012)
625 ..... Jim Kaat (1959–83)
616 ..... Frank Tanana (1973–93)
612 ..... Early Wynn (1939, 1941–44, 1946–63)
609 ..... Robin Roberts (1948–66)
603 ..... Randy Johnson (1988–2009)
600 ..... Grover C. Alexander (1911–30)

Highest Percentage of Complete Games to Games Started

		Games Started	Complete Games
.898	Cy Young (1900–11*)	404	363
.825	George Mullin (1902–15)	428	353
.820	Vic Willis (1900–10*)	395	324
.797	Walter Johnson (1907–27)	666	531
.793	Jack Powell (1900–12*)	406	322

continued on next page

.788	Christy Mathewson (1900–16)	529	435
.775	Eddie Plank (1900–17*)	529	410
.736	Ted Lyons (1923–42, 1946)	484	356
.728	Grover C. Alexander (1911–30)	600	437
.652	Lefty Grove (1925–41)	457	298
.632	Burleigh Grimes (1916–34)	497	314
.623	Red Ruffing (1924–42, 1945–47)	538	335
.574	Warren Spahn (1942, 1946–65)	665	382

*Record only from 1900.

Pitchers Starting 20 Games in 20 Consecutive Seasons

	Seasons	Teams
Nolan Ryan, 1971–92	22	N.Y. Mets (NL), 1971; Cal. Angels (AL), 1972–79; Hous. Astros (NL), 1980–88; Tex. Rangers (AL), 1989–92
Don Sutton, 1966–87	22	L.A. Dodgers (NL), 1966–80, 1988; Hous. Astros (NL), 1980–82; Milw. Brewers (AL), 1982–85; Oak. A's (AL), 1985; Cal. Angels (AL), 1986–88
Greg Maddux, 1987–2008	22	Chi. Cubs (NL), 1987–92; Atl. Braves (NL), 1993–2003; Chi. Cubs (NL), 2004–06; L.A. Dodgers (NL), 2006; S.D. Padres (NL), 2007–08; L.A. Dodgers (NL), 2008
Phil Niekro, 1965–87	21	Atl. Braves (NL), 1967–83; N.Y. Yankees (AL), 1984–85; Cle. Indians (AL), 1986–87
Cy Young, 1891–1910	20	Cle. Spiders (NL), 1891–98; St.L. Cardinals (NL), 1899–1900; Bost. Americans (AL), 1901–08; Cle. Naps (AL), 1909–11; Bost. Rustlers (NL), 1911
Tom Seaver, 1967–86	20	N.Y. Mets (NL), 1967–77, 1983; Cin. Reds (NL), 1977–82; Chi. White Sox (AL), 1984–86; Bost. Red Sox (AL), 1986
Roger Clemens, 1986–2005	20	Bost. Red Sox (AL), 1986–96; Tor. Blue Jays (AL), 1997–98; N.Y. Yankees (AL), 1999–2003; Hous. Astros (NL), 2004–05
Tom Glavine, 1988–2007	20	Atl. Braves (NL), 1988–2002; N.Y. Mets (NL), 2003–07

Evolution of Record for Most Games Pitched in a Season

American League

1901	Joe McGinnity, Balt. Orioles	48
1904	Jack Chesbro, N.Y. Yankees	55
1907	Ed Walsh, Chi. White Sox	56
1908	Ed Walsh, Chi. White Sox	66
1953	Ellis Kinder, Bost. Red Sox	69
1960	Mike Fornieles, Bost. Red Sox	70
1963	Stu Miller, Balt. Orioles	71
1964	John Wyatt, K.C. A's	81
1965	Eddie Fisher, Chi. White Sox	82
1968	Wilbur Wood, Chi. White Sox	88
1979	Mike Marshall, Min. Twins	90

National League (Pre-1900)

1876	Jim Devlin, Lou. Colonels	68
1879	Will White, Cin. Reds	76

National League (Post-1899)

1900	Bill Carrick, N.Y. Giants	45
1902	Vic Willis, Bost. Beaneaters	51
1903	Joe McGinnity, N.Y. Giants	55
1908	Christy Mathewson, N.Y. Giants	56
1942	Ace Adams, N.Y. Giants	61
1943	Ace Adams, N.Y. Giants	70
1950	Jim Konstanty, Phila. Phillies	74
1965	Ted Abernathy, Chi. Cubs	84
1969	Wayne Granger, Cin. Reds	90
1973	Mike Marshall, Mont. Expos	92
1974	Mike Marshall, L.A. Dodgers	106

Evolution of Innings Pitched Record

American League

1901 Joe McGinnity, Balt. Orioles 382
1902 Cy Young, Bost. Americans 385
1904 Jack Chesbro, N.Y. Highlanders 455
1908 Ed Walsh, Chi. White Sox 464

National League (Pre-1900)

1876 Jim Devlin, Lou. Colonels 622
1879 Will White, Cin. Reds 680

National League (Post-1899)

1900 Joe McGinnity, Bklyn. Bridegrooms 343
1901 Noodles Hahn, Cin. Reds 375
1902 Vic Willis, Bost. Beaneaters 410
1903 Joe McGinnity, N.Y. Giants 434

Most Wild Pitches, Season (Since 1900)

American League

26 ..... Juan Guzman, 1993 Tor. Blue Jays
25 ..... A.J. Burnett, 2011 N.Y. Yankees
24 ..... Jack Morris, 1987 Det. Tigers
23 ..... Tim Leary, 1990 N.Y. Yankees

National League

30 ..... Red Ames, 1905 N.Y. Giants
27 ..... Tony Cloninger, 1966 Atl. Braves
26 ..... Larry Cheney, 1914 Chi. Cubs
23 ..... Christy Mathewson, 1901 N.Y. Giants
23 ..... Matt Clement, 2000 S.D. Padres

Last Legal Spitball Pitchers

American League

Doc Ayers ..... (1913–21)
Ray Caldwell ..... (1910–21)
Stan Coveleski ..... (1912–28)
Urban Faber ..... (1914–33)
Hub Leonard* ..... (1913–25)
Jack Quinn ..... (1909–33)
Allan Russell ..... (1915–25)
Urban Shocker ..... (1916–28)
Allan Sothoron ..... (1914–26)

*Left-hander.

National League

Bill Doak ..... (1912–29)
Phil Douglas ..... (1912–22)
Dana Fillingim ..... (1915–25)
Ray Fisher ..... (1910–20)
Marvin Goodwin ..... (1916–25)
Burleigh Grimes ..... (1916–34)
Claude Hendrix ..... (1911–20)
Clarence Mitchell* ..... (1911–32)
Dick Rudolph ..... (1910–27)

Left-Handed Pitchers Appearing in More Than 700 Games, Career

Jesse Orosco (1979, 1981–2003) 1252
Mike Stanton (1989–2007) 1178
John Franco (1984–2005) 1119
Dan Plesac (1986–2003) 1064
Eddie Guardado (1993–2009) 908
Arthur Rhodes (1991–2011) 900
Sparky Lyle (1967–82) 899
Jim Kaat (1959–83) 898
Paul Assenmacher (1986–99) 884
Mike Myers (1995–2007) 883
Alan Embree (1992–2009) 882
Billy Wagner (1995–2010) 853
Tug McGraw (1965–84) 824
Rick Honeycutt (1977–97) 797
Steve Kline (1997–2007) 796
Buddy Groom (1992–2005) 786
Jeremy Affeldt* (2002–) 774
Javier Lopez* (2003–) 771
Darren Oliver (1993–2004, 2006–13) 766
Darold Knowles (1965–80) 765
Mark Guthrie (1989–2003) 765
Kenny Rogers (1989–2008) 762
Tommy John (1963–74, 1976–89) 760
Warren Spahn (1942, 1946–65) 750
Tom Burgmeier (1968–84) 745
Gary Lavelle (1974–87) 745
Willie Hernandez (1977–89) 744
Steve Carlton (1965–88) 741
Ron Perranoski (1961–73) 737
Matt Thornton* (2004–) 730

*Still active.

continued on next page

Randy Myers (1985–98) 728
Jeff Fassero (1991–2006) 720
Dave Righetti (1979–95) 718
Ron Villone (1995–2009) 717

Pitchers Who Pitched for Both Yankees and Mets and Threw No-Hitters

No-Hitter

Dock Ellis (Yankees, 1976–77; Mets, 1979) ..... With Pitt. Pirates (vs. S.D. Padres), June 12, 1970
John Candelaria (Mets, 1987; Yankees, 1988–89) ..... With Pitt. Pirates (vs. L.A. Dodgers), Aug. 9, 1976
Scott Erickson (Mets 2004; Yankees 2006) ..... With Min. Twins (vs. Milw. Brewers), Apr. 27, 1994
Kenny Rogers (Yankees, 1996–97; Mets, 1999) ..... With Tex. Rangers (vs. Cal. Angels), July 28, 1994 (perfect game)
Dwight Gooden (Mets, 1984–94; Yankees, 1996–97) ..... With Yankees (vs. Sea. Mariners), May 14, 1996
Al Leiter (Yankees, 1987–89; Mets, 1998–2004) ..... With Fla. Marlins (vs. Colo. Rockies), May 11, 1996
David Cone (Mets, 1987–92; Yankees, 1995–99) ..... With Yankees (vs. Mont. Expos), July 18, 1999 (perfect game)

Pitchers Who Have Stolen Home

American League

Frank Owen, Chi. White Sox (vs. Wash. Senators), Aug. 2, 1904
Bill Donovan, Det. Tigers (vs. Cle. Indians), May 7, 1906
Frank Owen, Chi. White Sox (vs. St.L. Browns), Apr. 27, 1908
Ed Walsh, Chi. White Sox (vs. N.Y. Yankees), June 13, 1908
Ed Walsh, Chi. White Sox (vs. St.L. Browns), June 2, 1909
Eddie Plank, Phila. A's (vs. Chi. White Sox), Aug. 30, 1909
Jack Warhop, N.Y. Yankees (vs. Chi. White Sox), Aug. 27, 1910
Jack Warhop, N.Y. Yankees (vs. St.L. Browns), July 12, 1912
Red Faber, Chi. White Sox (vs. Phila. A's), July 14, 1915
Reb Russell, Chi. White Sox (vs. Bost. Red Sox), Aug. 7, 1916
Babe Ruth, Bost. Red Sox (vs. St.L. Browns), Aug. 24, 1918
Dickie Kerr, Chi. White Sox (vs. N.Y. Yankees), July 8, 1921
Red Faber, Chi. White Sox (vs. St.L. Browns), Apr. 23, 1923
George Mogridge, Wash. Senators (vs. Chi. White Sox), Aug. 15, 1923
Joe Haynes, Chi. White Sox (vs. St.L. Browns), Sept. 17, 1944
Fred Hutchinson, Det. Tigers (vs. St.L. Browns), Aug. 29, 1947
Harry Dorish, St.L. Browns (vs. Wash. Senators), June 2, 1950

National League (Post-1900)

John Menafee, Chi. Cubs (vs. Bklyn. Dodgers), July 15, 1902
Joe McGinnity, N.Y. Giants (vs. Bklyn. Dodgers), Aug. 8, 1903
Joe McGinnity, N.Y. Giants (vs. Bost. Beaneaters), Apr. 29, 1904
Christy Mathewson, N.Y. Giants (vs. Bost. Rustlers), Sept. 12, 1911
Leon Ames, N.Y. Giants (vs. Bklyn. Dodgers), May 22, 1912
Christy Mathewson, N.Y. Giants (vs. Bost. Braves), June 28, 1912
Slim Sallee, N.Y. Giants (vs. St.L. Cardinals), July 22, 1913
Sherry Smith, Bklyn. Dodgers (vs. N.Y. Giants), Apr. 16, 1916
Tom Seaton, Chi. Cubs (vs. Cin. Reds), June 23, 1916
Bob Steele, N.Y. Giants (vs. St.L. Cardinals), July 26, 1918
Hippo Vaughn, Chi. Cubs (vs. N.Y. Giants), Aug. 9, 1919
Dutch Reuther, Cin. Reds (vs. Chi. Cubs), Sept. 3, 1919
Jesse Barnes, N.Y. Giants (vs. St.L. Cardinals), July 27, 1920
Dutch Reuther, Bklyn. Dodgers (vs. N.Y. Giants), May 4, 1921
Johnny Vander Meer, Cin. Reds (vs. N.Y. Giants), Sept. 23, 1943
Bucky Walters, Cin. Reds (vs. Pitt. Pirates), Apr. 20, 1946
Don Newcombe, Bklyn. Dodgers (vs. Pitt. Pirates), May 26, 1955
Curt Simmons, St.L. Cardinals (vs. Phila. Phillies), Sept. 1, 1963
Pascual Perez, Atl. Braves (vs. S.F. Giants). Sept. 7, 1984
Rick Sutcliffe, Chi. Cubs (vs. Phila. Phillies), July 29, 1988
Kevin Ritz, Colo. Rockies (vs. S.D. Padres), June 5, 1997
Darren Dreifort, L.A. Dodgers (vs. Tex. Rangers), June 12, 2001

3

HALL OF FAME

First Players Elected to Hall of Fame from Each Position

First Base	Cap Anson, 1939
	George Sisler, 1939
Second Base	Nap Lajoie, 1937
Third Base	Jimmy Collins, 1945
Shortstop	Honus Wagner, 1936
Left Field	Fred Clarke, 1945
Center Field	Ty Cobb, 1936
Right Field	Babe Ruth, 1936
Catcher	Roger Bresnahan, 1945
	King Kelly, 1945
Right-Handed Pitcher	Walter Johnson, 1936
	Christy Mathewson, 1936
Left-Handed Pitcher	Eddie Plank, 1946
	Rube Waddell, 1946
Relief Pitcher	Hoyt Wilhelm, 1985
Designated Hitter	Paul Molitor, 2004

Highest Lifetime Batting Average for Hall of Fame Pitchers

	At Bats	Hits	Average
Red Ruffing (1924–42, 1945–47)	1937	521	.269
Burleigh Grimes (1916–34)	1535	380	.248
Amos Rusie (1889–98, 1901)	1730	428	.247
Walter Johnson (1907–27)	2324	547	.235
Old Hoss Radbourn (1880–91)	2487	585	.235
Ted Lyons (1923–42, 1946)	1563	364	.233
Bob Lemon (1941–42, 1946–58)	1183	274	.232
Catfish Hunter (1965–79)	658	149	.226
Kid Nichols (1890–1901, 1904–06)	2086	471	.226
Dizzy Dean (1930, 1932–41, 1947)	717	161	.225

Hall of Famers with Lifetime Batting Averages Below .265 (Excluding Pitchers)

Joe Tinker, shortstop (1902–16)	.262	Elected 1946
Luis Aparicio, shortstop (1956–73)	.262	Elected 1984
Reggie Jackson, outfield (1967–87)	.262	Elected 1993
Ozzie Smith, shortstop (1978–96)	.262	Elected 2002
Gary Carter, catcher (1974–92)	.262	Elected 2003
Bill Mazeroski, second base (1956–72)	.260	Elected 2001

continued on next page

Rabbit Maranville, shortstop and second base (1912–35)	.258	Elected 1954
Harmon Killebrew, first base and third base (1954–75)	.256	Elected 1984
Ray Schalk, catcher (1912–29)	.253	Elected 1955

Hall of Famers with Lowest Marks in Offensive Categories*

Games	Ross Youngs (1917–26)	1211
At Bats	Roy Campanella (1948–57)	4205
Hits	Roy Campanella (1948–57)	1161
Batting Average	Ray Schalk (1912–29)	.253
Doubles	Roy Campanella (1948–57)	178
Triples	Roy Campanella (1948–57)	18
Home Runs	Ray Schalk (1912–29) and Johnny Evers (1902–17, 1922, 1929)	12
Runs Scored	Ray Schalk (1912–29)	.579
Runs Batted In	Johnny Evers (1902–17, 1922, 1929)	.538
Stolen Bases	Ernie Lombardi (1931–47)	8

* Position players with at least 10 years.

Teams Fielding Most Future Hall of Fame Players

8	N.Y. Giants (NL), 1923	Dave Bancroft (shortstop), Frankie Frisch (second base), Travis Jackson (infield), George Kelly (first base), Casey Stengel (outfield), Bill Terry (first base), Hack Wilson (outfield), and Ross Youngs (outfield)
8	N.Y. Yankees (AL), 1930	Earle Combs (outfield), Bill Dickey (catcher), Lou Gehrig (first base), Lefty Gomez (pitcher), Waite Hoyt (pitcher), Herb Pennock (pitcher), Red Ruffing (pitcher), and Babe Ruth (outfield)
8	N.Y. Yankees (AL), 1931	Earle Combs (outfield), Bill Dickey (catcher), Lou Gehrig (first base), Lefty Gomez (pitcher), Herb Pennock (pitcher), Red Ruffing (pitcher), Babe Ruth (outfield), and Joe Sewell (third base)
8	N.Y. Yankees (AL), 1933	Earle Combs (outfield), Bill Dickey (catcher), Lou Gehrig (first base), Lefty Gomez (pitcher), Herb Pennock (pitcher), Red Ruffing (pitcher), Babe Ruth (outfield), and Joe Sewell (third base)

Infields Fielding Four Future Hall of Famers

N.Y. Giants (NL), 1925
First Base: Bill Terry
Second Base: George Kelly
Third Base: Fred Lindstrom
Shortstop: Travis Jackson

N.Y. Giants (NL), 1926
First Base: George Kelly
Second Base: Frankie Frisch
Third Base: Fred Lindstrom
Shortstop: Travis Jackson

N.Y. Giants (NL), 1927
First Base: Bill Terry
Second Base: Rogers Hornsby
Third Base: Fred Lindstrom
Shortstop: Travis Jackson

Hall of Fame Pitchers Who Batted Right and Threw Left

Carl Hubbell (1928–43)
Randy Johnson (1988–2009)
Eppa Rixey (1912–33)
Rube Waddell (1897, 1899–1910)

Switch-Hitting Pitchers in Hall of Fame

Three Finger Brown (1903–16)
Red Faber (1914–24, 1926–33)*
Herb Pennock (1912–17, 1919–34)
Ted Lyons (1923–42, 1946)
Rube Marquard (1908–24)**
Kid Nichols (1890–1901, 1904–06)
Robin Roberts (1948–66)
Early Wynn (1946–63)***

* Batted right-handed in 1925.
** Batted left-handed in 1925.
*** Batted right-handed 1939–44.

Hall of Fame Pitchers Who Played Most Games at Other Positions

	Games
John Clarkson (outfield: 27; third base: 4; first base: 2)	33
Bob Lemon (outfield: 14; third base: 2)	16
Walter Johnson (outfield)	15

Hall of Fame Position Players Who Also Pitched

	Appearances	
Cap Anson	3	1883 (2) and 1884 (1)
Jake Beckley	1	1902
Wade Boggs	2	1997 (1) and 1999 (1)
Roger Bresnahan	9	1897 (6), 1901 (2), and 1901 (1)
Dan Brouthers	4	1897 (3) and 1883 (1)
Jesse Burkett	23	1890 (21), 1894 (1), and 1902 (1)
Ty Cobb	3	1918 (2) and 1925 (1)
George Davis	3	1891
Buck Ewing	9	1882 (1), 1884 (1), 1885 (1), 1888 (2), 1889 (3), and 1890 (1)
Jimmie Foxx	10	1939 (1) and 1945 (9)
Harry Hooper	1	1913
George Kelly	1	1917
King Kelly	12	1880 (1), 1883 (1), 1884 (2), 1888 (3), 1890 (1), 1891 (3), and 1892 (1)
Tommy McCarthy	13	1884 (7), 1886 (1), 1888 (2), 1889 (1), 1891 (1), and 1894 (1)
Stan Musial	1	1952
Jim O'Rourke	6	1883 (2) and 1884 (4)
Sam Rice	9	1915 (4) and 1916 (5)
Babe Ruth	163	1914 (4), 1915 (32), 1916 (44), 1917 (41), and 1918 (20), 1919 (17), 1920 (1), 1921 (2), 1930 (1), and 1933 (1)
George Sisler	23	1915 (15), 1916 (3), and 1918 (2)
Tris Speaker	1	1914 (1)
Honus Wagner	2	1900 (1) and 1902 (1)
Bobby Wallace	57	1894 (4), 1895 (30), 1896 (22), and 1902 (1)
Ted Williams	1	1940

Hall of Fame Pitchers with Losing Records

	Wins-Losses
Rollie Fingers (1968–82, 1984–85)	114–118
Bruce Sutter (1976–86, 1988)	68–71
Satchel Paige (1948–49, 1951–53, 1965)	28–31

Leading Career Pitching Marks by Those Not In Hall of Fame

Most Games Pitched	Jesse Orosco (1979–2003)	1252
Most Games Started	Roger Clemens (1984–2007)	707
Most Complete Games	Tony Mullane (1881–94)	468
Most Innings Pitched	Roger Clemens (1984–2007)	4917
Most Walks Allowed	Bobo Newsom (1929–30, 1932, 1934–48, 1952–53)	1732
Most Strikeouts	Roger Clemens (1984–2007)	4672
Most Shutouts	Luis Tiant (1964–82)	49
Most Games Won	Roger Clemens (1984–2007)	354
Most Games Lost	Jack Powell (1897–1912)	254
Most Saves	Mariano Rivera* (1995–2013)	652
Lowest ERA	Smoky Joe Wood (1908–20)	2.03
Winning Percentage	Spud Chandler (1937–47)	.717

* Will be eligible for Hall of Fame in 2019.

Leading Career Batting Marks by Players Not In Hall of Fame

Most Games Played	Pete Rose (1963–86)	3562
Most At Bats	Pete Rose (1963–86)	14,053
Most Base Hits	Pete Rose (1963–86)	4256
Most Singles	Pete Rose (1963–86)	2264
Most Doubles	Barry Bonds (1986–2007)	746
Most Triples	Ed Konetchy (1907–21)	182

continued on next page

Most Home Runs	Barry Bonds (1986–2007)	762
Most Runs Scored	Barry Bonds (1986–2007)	2227
Most RBIs	Barry Bonds (1986–2007)	1996
Most Walks	Barry Bonds (1986–2007)	2558
Most Strikeouts	Jim Thome* (1991–2012)	2548
Most Stolen Bases	Tim Raines (1979–2002)	808
Highest Lifetime Batting Average	Joe Jackson (1908–20)	.356
Highest Lifetime Slugging Average	Barry Bonds (1986–2007	607
Highest Lifetime On-Base Percentage	John McGraw** (1891–1906)	.466
Highest Lifetime On-Base Plus Slugging	Barry Bonds (1986–2007)	1.051

* Will be eligible for Hall of Fame in 2018.
** Elected to Hall of Fame in 1937 as a manager.

Most Career Hits by Players Not in Hall of Fame

4256	Pete Rose (1963–86)
3465	Derek Jeter*** (1995–2014)
3020	Rafael Palmeiro (1986–2005)
2935	Barry Bonds (1986–2007)
2877	Omar Vizquel** (1989–2012)
2866	Harold Baines (1980–2001)
2844	Ivan Rodriguez* (1991–2011)
2769	Johnny Damon*** (1995–2012)
2757	Vada Pinson (1958–75)
2743	Al Oliver (1968–85)
2726	Chipper Jones** (1993–2012)
2716	Rusty Staub (1963–85)
2715	Bill Buckner (1969–90)
2712	Dave Parker (1973–91)
2705	Doc Cramer (1929–48)
2689	Gary Sheffield (1988–2009)
2651	Lave Cross (1887–1907)
2605	Tim Raines (1979–2002)
2599	Steve Garvey (1969–87)
2591	Luis Gonzalez (1990–2008)
2590	Vladimir Guerrero* (1996–2011)
2586	Julio Franco (1982–94, 1996–97, 1999, 2001–07)
2574	Manny Ramirez* (1993–2011)
2561	Willie Davis (1960–79)

* Will be eligible for Hall of Fame in 2017.
** Will be eligible for Hall of Fame in 2018.
*** Will be eligible for Hall of Fame in 2020.

Most Career Wins by Pitchers Not In Hall of Fame

354	Roger Clemens (1984–2007)
288	Tommy John (1963–89)
284	Tony Mullane (1881–94)
283	Jim Kaat (1959–83)
270	Mike Mussina (1991–2008)
269	Jamie Moyer* (1986–2012)
264	Gus Weyhing (1887–1901)
256	Andy Pettitte** (1995–2013)
254	Jack Morris (1977–94)
247	Jack Quinn (1909–33)

* Will be eligible for Hall of Fame in 2018.
** Will be eligible for Hall of Fame in 2019.

Most Career Home Runs by Players Not In Hall of Fame

762	Barry Bonds (1986–2007)
612	Jim Thome** (1991–2012)
609	Sammy Sosa (1989–2007)
583	Mark McGwire (1986–2001)
569	Rafael Palmeiro (1986–2005)
555	Manny Ramirez* (1993–2011)
509	Gary Sheffield (1988–2009)
493	Fred McGriff (1986–2004)
473	Carlos Delgado (1993–2009)
468	Chipper Jones** (1993–2012)
462	Jose Canseco (1986–2001)
462	Adam Dunn*** (2001–14)
449	Jeff Bagwell (1991–2005)
449	Vladimir Guerrero** (1996–2011)
442	Dave Kingman (1971–86)
440	Jason Giambi*** (1995–2014)
439	Paul Konerko*** (1997–2014)
434	Juan Gonzalez (1989–2005)
434	Andruw Jones** (1996–2012)
414	Darrell Evans (1969–89)
412	Alfonso Soriano*** (1999–2014)

* Will be eligible for Hall of Fame in 2017.
**Will be eligible for Hall of Fame in 2018.
***Will be eligible for Hall of Fame in 2020.

Hall of Fame Inductees Receiving 90 Percent of Vote

Ken Griffey Jr., 2016 (440 ballots cast)	99.3
Tom Seaver, 1992 (425 ballots cast)	98.8
Nolan Ryan, 1999 (491 ballots cast)	98.8
Cal Ripken Jr., 2007 (532 ballots cast)	98.5

continued on next page

Ty Cobb, 1936 (226 ballots cast) 98.2
Hank Aaron, 1982 (415 ballots cast) 97.8
Tony Gwynn, 2007 (532 ballots cast) 97.6
Randy Johnson, 2015 (549 ballots cast) 97.3
Greg Maddux, 2014 (571 ballots cast) 97.2
Johnny Bench, 1989 (431 ballots cast) 96.4
Babe Ruth, 1936 (226 ballots cast) 95.1
Honus Wagner, 1936 (226 ballots cast) 95.1
Rickey Henderson, 2009 (539 ballots cast) 94.8
Carl Yastrzemski, 1989 (423 ballots cast) 94.6
Willie Mays, 1979 (432 ballots cast) 94.6
Bob Feller, 1962 (160 ballots cast) 93.8
Reggie Jackson, 1993 (396 ballots cast) 93.6
Ted Williams, 1966 (302 ballots cast) 93.4
Stan Musial, 1969 (340 ballots cast) 93.2
Roberto Clemente, 1973 (424 ballots cast) 92.7
Jim Palmer, 1990 (444 ballots cast) 92.5
Brooks Robinson, 1983 (374 ballots cast) 92.0
Tom Glavine, 2014 (571 ballots cast) 91.9
Wade Boggs, 2005 (516 ballots cast) 91.9
Pedro Martinez, 2015 (549 ballots cast) 91.1
Christy Mathewson, 1936 (226 ballots cast) 90.7
Rod Carew, 1991 (401 ballots cast) 90.5
Roberto Alomar, 2011 (523 ballots cast) 90.0

Won-Lost Percentage of Hall of Famers Elected as Players Who Managed in Majors

		Teams Managed	Career Wins-Losses
.593	Frank Chance	Chi. Cubs (NL), 1905–12	932–640
		N.Y. Yankees (AL), 1913–14	
		Bost. Red Sox (AL), 1923	
.582	Mickey Cochrane	Det. Tigers (AL), 1934–38	413–297
.576	Fred Clarke	Lou. Colonels (NL), 1897–99	1602–1179
		Pitt. Pirates (NL), 1900–15	
.575	Cap Anson	Chi. White Stockings/Colts (NL), 1879–97	1297–957
		N.Y. Giants (NL), 1898	
.562	Monte Ward	N.Y. Gothams (NL), 1884	394–307
		Bklyn. Wonders (PL), 1890	
		Bklyn. Bridegrooms (NL), 1891–92	
		N.Y. Giants (NL), 1893–94	
.555	Bill Terry	N.Y. Giants (NL), 1932–41	823–661
.553	Buck Ewing	N.Y. Giants (PL), 1890	489–395
		Cin. Reds (NL), 1895–99	
		N.Y. Giants (NL), 1900	
.551	Walter Johnson	Wash. Senators (AL), 1929–32	530–432
		Cle. Indians (AL), 1933–35	
.546	Nap Lajoie	Cle. Naps (AL), 1905–09	397–330
.544	Jimmy Collins	Bost. Americans (AL), 1901–06	464–389
.543	Bill Dickey	N.Y. Yankees (AL), 1946	57–48
.542	Tris Speaker	Cle. Indians (AL), 1919–26	616–520
.541	King Kelly	Bost. Reds (PL), 1890	124–105
		Cin. Reds–Milw. Brewers (AA), 1891	
.540	Joe Cronin	Wash. Senators (AL), 1933–34	1236–1055
		Bost. Red Sox (AL), 1935–47	
.538	Hughie Jennings	Det. Tigers (AL), 1907–20	1131–972
.536	Gabby Hartnett	Chi. Cubs (NL), 1938–40	203–176
.530	Pie Traynor	Pitt. Pirates (NL), 1934–39	457–406
.522	Yogi Berra	N.Y. Yankees (AL), 1964	484–444
		N.Y. Mets (NL), 1972–75	
		N.Y. Yankees (AL), 1984–85	
.521	Eddie Collins	Chi. White Sox (AL), 1925–26	160–147
.521	Red Schoendienst	St.L. Cardinals (NL), 1965–76 and 1980	1028–944
.519	Ty Cobb	Det. Tigers (AL), 1921–26	479–444
.519	Bob Lemon	K.C. Royals (AL), 1970–72	432–401
		Chi. White Sox (AL), 1977–78	
		N.Y. Yankees (AL), 1978–79 and 1981–82	

continued on next page

.513	Frankie Frisch	St.L. Cardinals (NL), 1933–38	1137–1078
		Pitt. Pirates (NL), 1940–46	
		Chi. Cubs (NL), 1949–51	
.500	Deacon White	Cin. Reds (NL), 1879	9–9
.512	Joe Kelley	Cin. Reds (NL), 1902–05	337–321
		Bost. Rustlers (NL), 1908	
.498	Joe Gordon	Cle. Indians (AL), 1958–60	305–308
		Det.Tigers (AL), 1960	
		K.C. A's (AL), 1961	
		K.C. Royals (AL), 1969	
.497	Joe Tinker	Cin. Reds (NL), 1913	304–308
		Chi. Whales (FL), 1914–15	
		Chi. Cubs (NL), 1916	
.488	Jim O'Rourke	Buff. Bisons (NL), 1881–84	246–258
		Wash. Senators (NL), 1893	
.487	Lou Boudreau	Cle. Indians (AL), 1942–50	1162–1224
		Bost. Red Sox (AL), 1952–54	
		K.C. A's (AL), 1955–57	
		Chi. Cubs (NL), 1960	
.485	Johnny Evers	Chi. Cubs (NL), 1913 and 1921	196–208
		Chi. White Sox (AL), 1924	
.482	Christy Mathewson	Cin. Reds (NL), 1916–18	164–176
.481	Eddie Mathews	Atl. Braves (NL), 1972–74	149–161
.476	Max Carey	Bklyn. Dodgers (NL), 1932–33	146–161
.476	Frank Robinson	Cle. Indians (AL), 1975–77	913–1004
		S.F. Giants (NL), 1981–84	
		Balt. Orioles (AL), 1988–91	
		Mont. Expos (NL), 2002–04	
.475	George Sisler	St.L. Browns (AL), 1924–26	218–241
.467	Mel Ott	N.Y. Giants (NL), 1942–48	464–530
.460	Rogers Hornsby	St.L. Cardinals (NL), 1925–26	680–798
		Bost. Braves (NL), 1928	
		Chi. Cubs (NL), 1930–32	
		St.L. Browns (AL), 1933–37 and 1952	
		Cin. Reds (NL), 1952–53	
.444	Hugh Duffy	Milw. Brewers (AL), 1901	535–671
		Phila. Phillies (NL), 1904–06	
		Chi. White Sox (AL), 1910–11	
		Bost. Red Sox (AL), 1921–22	
.442	Three Finger Brown	St.L. Terriers (FL), 1914	50–63
.434	Rabbit Maranville	Chi. Cubs (NL), 1925	23–30
.432	Roger Bresnahan	St.L. Cardinals (NL), 1909–12	328–432
		Chi. Cubs (NL), 1915	
.432	Burleigh Grimes	Bklyn. Dodgers (NL), 1937–38	130–171
.430	Ted Lyons	Chi. White Sox (AL), 1946–48	185–245
.429	Cy Young	Bost. Americans (AL), 1907	3–4
.429	Ted Williams	Wash. Senators II (AL), 1969–71	273–364
		Tex. Rangers (AL), 1972	
.425	Larry Doby	Chi. White Sox (AL), 1978	37–50
.408	Billy Herman	Pitt. Pirates (NL), 1947	189–274
		Bost. Red Sox (AL), 1964–66	

continued on next page

.407	Dave Bancroft	Bost. Braves (NL), 1924–27	249–363
.389	Bid McPhee	Cin. Reds (NL), 1901–02	79–124
.287	Bobby Wallace	St.L. Browns (AL), 1911–12 Cin. Reds (NL), 1937	62–154
.267	Pud Galvin	Buff. Bisons (NL), 1885	8–22
.266	Jim Bottomley	St.L. Browns (AL), 1937	21–58
.250	Luke Appling	K.C. A's (AL), 1967	10–30
.200	Honus Wagner	Pitt. Pirates (NL), 1917	1–4

Hall of Famers Making Last Out in World Series

1903	Honus Wagner (Pitt. Pirates, NL)	strikeout
1926	Babe Ruth (N.Y. Yankees, AL)	caught stealing
1938	Billy Herman (Chi. Cubs, NL)	ground out
1940	Earl Averill (Det. Tigers, AL)	ground out
1952	Pee Wee Reese (Bklyn. Dodgers, NL)	fly out
1958	Red Schoendienst (Milw. Brewers, NL)	fly out
1959	Luis Aparicio (Chi. White Sox, AL)	line out
1962	Willie McCovey (S.F. Giants, NL)	line out
1975	Carl Yazstremski (Bost. Red Sox, AL)	fly out
1984	Tony Gwynn (S.D. Padres, NL)	fly out
2000	Mike Piazza (N.Y. Mets, NL)	fly out

Hall of Famers Who Played for the Harlem Globetrotters

Ernie Banks
Lou Brock
Bob Gibson
Ferguson Jenkins
Satchel Paige

Hall of Famers Who Died on Their Birthday

Stanley "Bucky" Harris, born Nov. 8, 1896, and died Nov. 8, 1977
Charles "Gabby" Hartnett, born Dec. 20, 1900, and died Dec. 20, 1972
Joe Tinker, born July 27, 1880, and died July 27, 1948

4

AWARDS

Most Valuable Player

Unanimous Choice for MVP

American League

Ty Cobb, outfield, Det. Tigers, 1911
Babe Ruth, outfield, N.Y. Yankees, 1923
Hank Greenberg, first base, Det. Tigers, 1935
Al Rosen, third base, Cle. Indians, 1953
Mickey Mantle, outfield, N.Y. Yankees, 1956
Frank Robinson, outfield, Balt. Orioles, 1966
Denny McLain, pitcher, Det. Tigers, 1968
Reggie Jackson, outfield, Oak. A's, 1973
Jose Canseco, outfield, Oak. A's, 1988
Frank Thomas, first base, Chi. White Sox, 1993
Ken Griffey Jr., outfield, Sea. Mariners, 1997
Mike Trout, outfield, L.A. Angels, 2014

National League

Carl Hubbell, pitcher, N.Y. Giants, 1936
Orlando Cepeda, first base, St.L. Cardinals, 1967
Mike Schmidt, third base, Phila. Phillies, 1980
Jeff Bagwell, first base, Hous. Astros, 1994
Ken Caminiti, third base, S.D. Padres, 1996
Barry Bonds, outfield, S.F. Giants, 2002
Albert Pujols, first base, St.L. Cardinals, 2009
Bryce Harper, outfield, Wash. Nationals, 2015

Closest Winning Margins in MVP Voting

American League

Margin	Season	MVP	Votes	Runner-Up	Votes
+1	1947	Joe DiMaggio, N.Y. Yankees	202	Ted Williams, Bost. Red Sox	201
+2	1928	Mickey Cochrane, Phila. A's	53	Heinie Manush, St.L. Browns	51
+2	1934	Mickey Cochrane, Det. Tigers	67	Charlie Gehringer, Det. Tigers	65
+3	1960	Roger Maris, N.Y. Yankees	225	Mickey Mantle, N.Y. Yankees	222
+3	1996	Juan Gonzalez, Tex. Rangers	290	Alex Rodriguez, Sea. Mariners	287
+4	1925	Roger Peckinpaugh, Wash. Senators	45	Al Simmons, Phila. A's	41
+4	1937	Charlie Gehringer, Det. Tigers	78	Joe DiMaggio, N.Y. Yankees	74
+4	1944	Hal Newhouser, Det. Tigers	236	Dizzy Trout, Det. Tigers	232
+4	1961	Roger Maris, N.Y. Yankees	202	Mickey Mantle, N.Y. Yankees	198

National League

Margin	Season	MVP	Votes	Runner-Up	Votes
0 (Tie)	1979	Keith Hernandez, St.L. Cardinals	216	Willie Stargell, Pitt. Pirates	216
+1	1944	Marty Marion, St.L. Cardinals	190	Bill Nicholson, Chi. Cubs	189
+2	1937	Joe Medwick, St.L. Cardinals	70	Gabby Hartnett, Chi. Cubs	68
+4	1911	Frank Schulte, Chi. Cubs	29	Christy Mathewson, N.Y. Giants	25
+5	1912	Larry Doyle, N.Y. Giants	48	Honus Wagner, Pitt. Pirates	43
+5	1955	Roy Campanella, Bklyn. Dodgers	226	Duke Snider, Bklyn. Dodgers	221

Widest Winning Margins in MVP Voting

American League

Margin	Season	MVP	Votes	Runner-Up	Votes
+191	2014	Mike Trout, L.A. Angels	420	Victor Martinez, Det. Tigers	229
+183	1993	Frank Thomas, Chi. White Sox	392	Paul Molitor, Tor. Blue Jays	209
+169	1953	Al Rosen, Cle. Indians	336	Yogi Berra, N.Y. Yankees	167
+169	1975	Fred Lynn, Bost. Red Sox	326	John Mayberry, K.C. Royals	157
+164	1973	Reggie Jackson, Oak. A's	336	Jim Palmer, Balt. Orioles	172
+157	1972	Dick Allen, Chi. White Sox	321	Joe Rudi, Oak. A's	164
+157	1982	Robin Yount, Milw. Brewers	385	Eddie Murray, Balt. Orioles	228
+150	1956	Mickey Mantle, N.Y. Yankees	336	Yogi Berra, N.Y. Yankees	186
+150	1988	Jose Canseco, Oak. A's	392	Mike Greenwell, Bost. Red Sox	242

National League

Margin	Season	MVP	Votes	Runner-Up	Votes
+215	2009	Albert Pujols, St.L. Cardinals	448	Hanley Ramirez, Fla. Marlins	233
+191	1994	Jeff Bagwell, Hous. Astros	392	Matt Williams, S.F. Giants	201
+186	2015	Bryce Harper, Wash. Nationals	420	Paul Goldscmidt, Ariz. D'backs	234
+172	2002	Barry Bonds, S.F. Giants	448	Albert Pujols, St.L. Cardinals	276
+167	2013	Andrew McCutchen, Pitt. Pirates	409	Paul Goldschmidt, Ariz. D'backs	242
+166	1998	Sammy Sosa, Chi. Cubs	438	Mark McGwire, St.L. Cardinals	272
+164	2010	Joey Votto, Cin. Reds	443	Albert Pujols, St.L. Cardinals	279
+160	2001	Barry Bonds, S.F. Giants	438	Sammy Sosa, Chi. Cubs	278
+156	1999	Chipper Jones, Atl. Braves	432	Jeff Bagwell, Hous. Astros	276
+155	1996	Ken Caminiti, S.D. Padres	392	Mike Piazza, L.A. Dodgers	237

Won MVP Award in Consecutive Years, by Position

First Base	Jimmie Foxx, Phila. A's (AL), 1932–33
	Frank Thomas, Chi. White Sox (AL), 1993–94
	Albert Pujols, St.L. Cardinals (NL), 2008–09
Second Base	Joe Morgan, Cin. Reds (NL), 1975–76
Third Base	Mike Schmidt, Phila. Phillies (NL), 1980–81
Shortstop	Ernie Banks, Chi. Cubs (NL), 1959–60
Outfield	Mickey Mantle, N.Y. Yankees (AL), 1956–57
	Roger Maris, N.Y. Yankees (AL), 1960–61
	Dale Murphy, Atl. Braves (NL), 1982–83
	Barry Bonds, Pitt. Pirates (NL), 1992, and S.F. Giants (NL), 1993
	Barry Bonds, S.F. Giants (NL), 2001–04
Catcher	Yogi Berra, N.Y. Yankees (AL), 1954–55
Pitcher	Hal Newhouser, Det. Tigers (AL), 1944–45

Teammates Finishing One-Two in MVP Balloting

American League

Season	Team	Leader	Position	Runner-Up	Position
1934	Det. Tigers	Mickey Cochrane	Catcher	Charlie Gehringer	Second base
1944	Det. Tigers	Hal Newhouser	Pitcher	Dizzy Trout	Pitcher
1945	Det. Tigers	Hal Newhouser	Pitcher	Eddie Mayo	Second base
1956	N.Y. Yankees	Mickey Mantle	Outfield	Yogi Berra	Catcher
1959	Chi. White Sox*	Nellie Fox	Second base	Luis Aparicio	Shortstop
1960	N.Y. Yankees	Roger Maris	Outfield	Mickey Mantle	Outfield
1961	N.Y. Yankees	Roger Maris	Outfield	Mickey Mantle	Outfield
1962	N.Y. Yankees	Mickey Mantle	Outfield	Bobby Richardson	Second base

continued on next page

1965	Min. Twins	Zoilo Versalles	Shortstop	Tony Oliva	Outfield
1966	Balt. Orioles*	Frank Robinson	Outfield	Brooks Robinson	Third base
1968	Det. Tigers	Denny McLain	Pitcher	Bill Freehan	Catcher
1971	Oak. A's	Vida Blue	Pitcher	Sal Bando	Third base
1983	Balt. Orioles	Cal Ripken Jr.	Shortstop	Eddie Murray	First base

National League

Season	Team	Leader	Position	Runner-Up	Position
1914	Bost. Braves*	Johnny Evers	Second base	Rabbit Maranville	Shortstop
1941	Bklyn. Dodgers*	Dolph Camilli	First base	Pete Reiser	Outfield
1942	St.L. Cardinals	Mort Cooper	Pitcher	Enos Slaughter	Outfield
1943	St.L. Cardinals	Stan Musial	Outfield	Mort Cooper	Pitcher
1955	Bklyn. Dodgers	Roy Campanella	Catcher	Duke Snider	Outfield
1956	Bklyn. Dodgers	Don Newcombe	Pitcher	Sal Maglie	Pitcher
1960	Pitt. Pirates	Dick Great	Shortstop	Don Hoak	Third base
1967	St.L. Cardinals	Orlando Cepeda	First base	Tim McCarver	Catcher
1976	Cin. Reds	Joe Morgan	Second base	George Foster	Outfield
1989	S.F. Giants	Kevin Mitchell	Outfield	Will Clark	First base
1990	Pitt. Pirates	Barry Bonds	Outfield	Bobby Bonilla	Outfield
2000	S.F. Giants	Jeff Kent	Second base	Barry Bonds	Outfield

*Teammates finished one-two-three in voting (AL 1959: Early Wynn, pitcher; AL 1966: Boog Powell, first base; NL 1914: Bill James, pitcher; and NL 1941: Whit Wyatt, pitcher).

Triple Crown Winners *Not* Winning MVP

American League

Season	Triple Crown Winner	MVP Winner
1934	Lou Gehrig, N.Y. Yankees	Mickey Cochrane, Det. Tigers
1942	Ted Williams, Bost. Red Sox	Joe Gordon, N.Y. Yankees
1947	Ted Williams, Bost. Red Sox	Joe DiMaggio, N.Y. Yankees

National League

Season	Triple Crown Winner	MVP Winner
1912	Heinie Zimmerman, Chi. Cubs	Larry Doyle, N.Y. Giants
1933	Chuck Klein, Phila. Phillies	Carl Hubbell, N.Y. Giants

MVPs on Nonwinning Teams

American League

Team	Wins–Losses
Robin Yount, Milw. Brewers, 1989	81–81
Alex Rodriguez, Tex. Rangers, 2003	71–91

National League

Team	Wins–Losses
Hank Sauer, Chi. Cubs, 1952	77–77
Ernie Banks, Chi. Cubs, 1958	72–82
Ernie Banks, Chi. Cubs, 1959	74–80
Andre Dawson, Chi. Cubs, 1987	76–85

MVPs *Not* Batting .300, Hitting 30 Home Runs, or Driving in 100 Runs (Not Including Pitchers)

American League

	Batting Average	Home Runs	RBIs
Roger Peckinpaugh, Wash. Senators, 1925	.294	4	64
Mickey Cochrane, Phila. A's, 1928	.293	10	57
Yogi Berra, N.Y. Yankees, 1951	.294	27	88
Elston Howard, N.Y. Yankees, 1963	.287	28	85
Zoilo Versalles, Min. Twins, 1965	.273	19	77

continued on next page

National League

	Batting Average	Home Runs	RBIs
Johnny Evers, Bost. Braves, 1914	.279	1	40
Bob O'Farrell, St.L Cardinals, 1926	.293	7	68
Marty Marion, St.L. Cardinals, 1944	.267	6	63
Maury Wills, L.A. Dodgers, 1962	.299	6	48
Kirk Gibson, L.A. Dodgers, 1988	.273	25	76

Pitchers Winning MVP Award

American League

Walter Johnson, Wash. Senators, 1912*
Walter Johnson, Wash. Senators, 1924**
Lefty Grove, Phila. A's, 1931
Spud Chandler, N.Y. Yankees, 1943
Hal Newhouser, Det. Tigers, 1944
Hal Newhouser, Det. Tigers, 1945
Bobby Shantz, Phila. A's, 1952
Denny McLain, Det. Tigers, 1968
Vida Blue, Oak. A's, 1971
Rollie Fingers, Milw. Brewers, 1981
Willie Hernandez, Det. Tigers, 1984
Roger Clemens, Bost. Red Sox, 1986
Dennis Eckersley, Oak. A's, 1992
Justin Verlander, Det. Tigers, 2011

*Chalmers Award.
**League Award.

National League

Dazzy Vance, Bklyn. Dodgers, 1924*
Carl Hubbell, N.Y. Giants, 1933
Dizzy Dean, St.L. Cardinals, 1934
Carl Hubbell, N.Y. Giants, 1936
Bucky Walters, Cin. Reds, 1939
Mort Cooper, St.L. Cardinals, 1942
Jim Konstanty, Phila. Phillies, 1950
Don Newcombe, Bklyn. Dodgers, 1956
Sandy Koufax, L.A. Dodgers, 1963
Bob Gibson, St.L. Cardinals, 1968
Clayton Kershaw, L.A. Dodgers, 2014

Players Winning MVP Award First Season in League

American League

Frank Robinson, Balt. Orioles, 1966
Dick Allen, Chi. White Sox, 1972
Fred Lynn, Bost. Red Sox, 1975
Willie Hernandez, Det. Tigers, 1984
Ichiro Suzuki, Sea. Mariners, 2001
Vladimir Guerrero, Ana. Angels, 2004

National League

Kirk Gibson, L.A. Dodgers, 1988

MVPs Receiving Fewer First-Place Votes Than Runner-Up

American League

1944 Hal Newhouser (Det. Tigers, pitcher) winner over Dizzy Trout (Det. Tigers, pitcher), 236–232
1960 Roger Maris (N.Y. Yankees, outfield) winner over Mickey Mantle (N.Y. Yankees, outfield), 225–222
1991 Ivan Rodriguez (Tex. Rangers, catcher) winner over Pedro Martinez (Bost. Red Sox, pitcher), 252–239

National League

1966 Roberto Clemente (Pitt. Pirates, outfield) winner over Sandy Koufax (L.A. Dodgers, pitcher), 218–205

Teams with Most Consecutive MVP Awards

5	S.F. Giants (NL), 2000–04	Jeff Kent, second base, 2000
		Barry Bonds, outfield, 2001–04
4	N.Y. Yankees (AL), 1954–57	Yogi Berra, catcher, 1954 and 1955
		Mickey Mantle, outfield, 1956 and 1957
4	N.Y. Yankees (AL), 1960–63	Roger Maris, outfield, 1960 and 1961
		Mickey Mantle, outfield, 1962
		Elston Howard, catcher, 1963

Players Winning MVP Award with Two Different Teams

		MVP Seasons
Barry Bonds	Pitt. Pirates (NL)	1990 and 1992
	S.F. Giants (NL)	1993 and 2001–04
Mickey Cochrane	Phila. A's (AL)	1928
	Det. Tigers (AL)	1934
Jimmie Foxx	Phila. A's (AL)	1932–33
	Bost. Red Sox (AL)	1938
Rogers Hornsby	St.L. Cardinals (NL)	1925
	Chi. Cubs (NL)	1929
Frank Robinson	Cin. Reds (NL)	1961
	Balt. Orioles (AL)	1966
Alex Rodriguez	Tex. Rangers (AL)	2003
	N.Y. Yankees (AL)	2005 and 2007

MVPs with Fewest Hits

119 ..... Willie Stargell, 1979, National League
124 ..... Roger Peckinpaugh, 1925, American League
133 ..... Barry Bonds, 2003, National League
135 ..... Marty Marion, 1944, National League
135 ..... Barry Bonds, 2004, National League

Switch-Hitting MVPs

American League

Mickey Mantle, N.Y. Yankees, 1956
Mickey Mantle, N.Y. Yankees, 1957
Mickey Mantle, N.Y. Yankees, 1962
Vida Blue, Oak. A's, 1971

National League

Frankie Frisch, St.L. Cardinals, 1931
Maury Wills, L.A. Dodgers, 1962
Pete Rose, Cin. Reds, 1973
Willie McGee, St.L. Cardinals, 1985
Terry Pendleton, Atl. Braves, 1991
Ken Caminiti, S.D. Padres, 1996
Chipper Jones, Atl. Braves, 1999
Jimmy Rollins, Phila. Phillies, 2007

Cy Young Award

Pitchers Winning 25 Games, Not Winning Cy Young Award

American League

		Wins–Losses	Cy Young Award Winner	Wins–Losses
1966	Jim Kaat, Min. Twins	25–13	Sandy Koufax, L.A. Dodgers (NL)	27–9*
1971	Mickey Lolich, Det. Tigers	25–14	Vida Blue, Oak. A's	24–8
1974	Ferguson Jenkins, Tex. Rangers	25–12	Catfish Hunter, Oak. A's	25–12

National League

		Wins–Losses	Cy Young Award Winner	Wins–Losses
1963	Juan Marichal, S.F. Giants	25–8	Sandy Koufax, L.A. Dodgers	25–5*
1966	Juan Marichal, S.F. Giants	25–6	Sandy Koufax, L.A. Dodgers	27–9*
1968	Juan Marichal, S.F. Giants	26–9	Bob Gibson, St.L. Cardinals	22–9

*One winner, both leagues, 1956–67.

Pitchers Winning 20 Games Only Once and Cy Young Award Same Season

American League

	Wins
Jim Lonborg, Bost. Red Sox, 1967	22
Mike Flanagan, Balt. Orioles, 1979	23
Steve Stone, Balt. Orioles, 1980	25
Bob Welch, Oak. A's, 1990	27
Pat Hentgen, Tor. Blue Jays, 1996	20
Barry Zito, Oak. A's, 2002	23
Johan Santana, Min. Twins, 2004	20
Cliff Lee, Cle. Indians, 2008	22
Justin Verlander*, Det. Tigers, 2011	24
David Price*, T.B. Rays, 2012	20
Max Scherzer*, Det. Tigers, 2013	21

*Still active.

National League

	Wins
Vern Law, Pitt. Pirates, 1960	20
Mike McCormick, S.F. Giants, 1967	22
Doug Drabek, Pitt. Pirates, 1990	22
John Smoltz, Atl. Braves, 1996	24
Chris Carpenter, St.L. Cardinals, 2005	21
R.A. Dickey*, N.Y. Mets, 2012	20

Cy Young Winners *Not* in Top 10 in League in ERA, Season

American League

	ERA	Place in League
Jim Lonborg, Bost. Red Sox, 1967	3.16	18th
LaMarr Hoyt, Chi. White Sox, 1983	3.66	17th

National League

	ERA	Place in League
Mike McCormick, S.F. Giants, 1967	2.85	16th

Relief Pitchers Winning Cy Young Award

American League

Sparky Lyle, N.Y. Yankees, 1977
Rollie Fingers, Milw. Brewers, 1981
Willie Hernandez, Det. Tigers, 1984
Dennis Eckersley, Oak. A's, 1992

National League

Mike Marshall, L.A. Dodgers, 1974
Bruce Sutter, Chi. Cubs, 1979
Steve Bedrosian, Phila. Phillies, 1987
Mark Davis, S.D. Padres, 1989
Eric Gagne, L.A. Dodgers, 2003

Cy Young Winners Increasing Their Number of Victories the Following Season

American League

	Award-Winning Season	Following Season
Mike Cuellar, Balt. Orioles, 1969	23–11	24–8
David Cone, K.C. Royals, 1994	16–5	18–8
Felix Hernandez, Sea. Mariners, 2010	13–12	14–14

National League

	Award-Winning Season	Following Season
Warren Spahn, Milw. Braves, 1957	21–11	22–11
Sandy Koufax, L.A. Dodgers, 1965	26–8	27–9
Steve Bedrosian, Phila. Phillies, 1987	5–3	6–6
Greg Maddux, Atl. Braves, 1994	16–6	19–2
Pedro Martinez, Mont. Expos, 1997	17–8	19–7
Randy Johnson, Ariz. D'backs, 1999	17–9	19–7
Randy Johnson, Ariz. D'backs, 2000	19–7	21–6
Randy Johnson, Ariz. D'backs, 2001	21–6	24–5
Eric Gagne, L.A. Dodgers, 2003	2–3	7–3
Brandon Webb, Ariz. D'backs, 2007	16–8	18–10
Tim Lincecum, S.F. Giants, 2009	15–7	16–10
Clayton Kershaw, L.A. Dodgers, 2013	16–9	21–3

Won Both Cy Young and MVP Same Season

American League

1968 ..... Denny McLain, Det. Tigers
1971 ..... Vida Blue, Oak. A's
1981 ..... Rollie Fingers, Milw. Brewers
1984 ..... Willie Hernandez, Det. Tigers
1986 ..... Roger Clemens, Bost. Red Sox
1992 ..... Dennis Eckersley, Oak. A's
2011 ..... Justin Verlander, Det. Tigers

National League

1956 ..... Don Newcombe, Bklyn. Dodgers
1963 ..... Sandy Koufax, L.A. Dodgers
1968 ..... Bob Gibson, St.L. Cardinals

Cy Young Winners with Higher Batting Averages Than That Year's Home Run Leader

American League

Cy Young Winner	Home Run Leader
1959 ..... Early Wynn, Chi. White Sox, .244	Harmon Killebrew, Min. Twins, .242 (Tie)

National League (Post-1900)

Cy Young Winner	Home Run Leader
1970 ..... Bob Gibson, St.L. Cardinals, .303	Johnny Bench, Cin. Reds, .293
1982 ..... Steve Carlton, Phila. Phillies, .218	Dave Kingman, N.Y. Mets, .204

Rookie of the Year

Rookie of the Year Winners on Team Other Than the One First Played On

	Team First Played On
Tommie Agee, Chi. White Sox (AL), 1966	First came up for 5 games with Cle. Indians (AL), 1962
Jason Bay, Pitt. Pirates (NL), 2004	First came up for 3 games with S.D. Padres (NL), 2003
Alfredo Griffin, Tor. Blue Jays (AL), 1979 (cowinner)	First came up for 12 games with Cle. Indians (AL), 1976
Lou Piniella, K.C. Royals (AL), 1969	First came up for 4 games with Balt. Orioles (AL), 1964
Hanley Ramirez, Fla. Marlins (NL), 2006	First came up for 4 games with Bost. Red Sox (AL), 2005

Relief Pitchers Winning Rookie of the Year

American League

Kazuhiro Sasaki, Sea. Mariners, 2000
Huston Street, Oak. A's, 2005
Andrew Bailey, Oak. A's, 2009
Neftali Feliz, Tex. Rangers, 2010

National League

Joe Black, Bklyn. Dodgers, 1952
Butch Metzger, S.D. Padres, 1976 (Tie)
Steve Howe, L.A. Dodgers, 1980
Todd Worrell, St.L. Cardinals, 1986
Scott Williamson, Cin. Reds, 1999
Craig Kimbrel, Atl. Braves, 2011

Rookie of the Year on Pennant-Winning Teams

American League

Gil McDougald, second base and third base, N.Y. Yankees, 1951
Tony Kubek, outfield and shortstop, N.Y. Yankees, 1957
Tom Tresh, shortstop, N.Y. Yankees, 1962
Fred Lynn, outfield, Bost. Red Sox, 1975
Dave Righetti, pitcher, N.Y. Yankees, 1981
Walt Weiss, shortstop, Oak. A's, 1988
Chuck Knoblauch, second base, Min. Twins, 1991
Derek Jeter, shortstop, N.Y. Yankees, 1996
Dustin Pedroia, shortstop, Bost. Red Sox, 2007
Evan Longoria, third base, T.B. Rays, 2008
Neftali Feliz, pitcher, Tex. Rangers, 2010

National League

Jackie Robinson, first base, Bklyn. Dodgers, 1947
Alvin Dark, shortstop, Bost. Braves, 1948
Don Newcombe, pitcher, Bklyn. Dodgers, 1949
Willie Mays, outfield, N.Y. Giants, 1951
Joe Black, pitcher, Bklyn. Dodgers, 1952
Junior Gilliam, second base, Bklyn. Dodgers, 1953
Jim Lefebvre, second base, L.A. Dodgers, 1965
Pat Zachry, pitcher, Cin. Reds, 1976
Fernando Valenzuela, pitcher, L.A. Dodgers, 1981
Vince Coleman, outfield, St.L. Cardinals, 1985
Buster Posey, catcher, S.F. Giants, 2010

Rookies of the Year Elected to Hall of Fame

	Rookie of the Year	HOF
1947	Jackie Robinson	1962
1951	Willie Mays	1979
1956	Frank Robinson	1982
1956	Luis Aparicio	1984
1958	Orlando Cepada	1999
1959	Willie McCovey	1986
1961	Billy Williams	1978
1967	Tom Seaver	1992
1967	Rod Carew	2003
1968	Johnny Bench	1989
1972	Carlton Fisk	2000
1977	Eddie Murray	2003
1977	Andre Dawson	2010
1982	Cal Ripken Jr.	2007
1989	Ken Griffey Jr.	2016
1993	Mike Piazza	2016

Gold Gloves

Most Gold Gloves, by Position

American League

First Base	9	Don Mattingly (1985–89, 1991–94)
Second Base	10	Roberto Alomar (1991–96, 1998–2001)
Third Base	16	Brooks Robinson (1960–75)
Shortstop	9	Luis Aparicio (1958–62, 1964, 1966, 1968, 1970)
	9	Omar Vizquel (1993–2001)
Outfield	10	Al Kaline (1957–59, 1961–67)
	10	Ken Griffey Jr. (1990–99)
	10	Ichiro Suzuki* (2001–10)
Catcher	13	Ivan Rodriguez (1992–2001, 2004, 2006–07)
Pitcher	14	Jim Kaat (1962–75)

*Still active.

National League

First Base	11	Keith Hernandez (1978–88)
Second Base	9	Ryne Sandberg (1983–91)
Third Base	10	Mike Schmidt (1976–84, 1986)
Shortstop	13	Ozzie Smith (1980–92)
Outfield	12	Roberto Clemente (1961–72)
	12	Willie Mays (1957–68)
Catcher	10	Johnny Bench (1968–77)
Pitcher	18	Greg Maddux (1990–2002, 2004–08)

5

MANAGERS

Winningest Managers by First Letter of Last Name

			Percentage
A	Sparky Anderson (1970–95)	2194–1834	.545
B	Bruce Bochy* (1995–)	1702–1682	.503
C	Bobby Cox (1978–2010)	2504–2001	.521
D	Leo Durocher (1939–46, 1948–55, 1966–73)	2008–1709	.540
E	Buck Ewing (1890, 1895–1900)	489–395	.553
F	Terry Francona* (1997–2000, 2004–11, 2013–)	1287–1142	.530
G	Clark Griffith (1901–20)	1491–1367	.522
H	Bucky Harris (1924–43, 1947–48, 1950–56)	2158–2219	.493
I	Arthur Irwin (1889, 1891–92, 1894–96, 1898–99)	416–427	.493
J	Davey Johnson (1984–90, 1993–97, 1999–2000, 2011–2013)	1372–1071	.562
K	Tom Kelly (1986–2000)	1140–1244	.478
L	Tony La Russa (1979–2011)	2728–2365	.536
M	Connie Mack (1894–96, 1901–50)	3731–3948	.486
N	Jerry Narron (2001–07)	291–341	.460
O	Steve O'Neill (1935–37, 1943–48, 1950–54)	1040–821	.559
P	Lou Piniella (1986–88, 1990–2010)	1835–1713	.517
Q	Frank Quilici (1972–75)	280–267	.494
R	Wilbert Robinson (1902, 1914–31)	1399–1398	.503
S	Casey Stengel (1934–36, 1938–43, 1949–60, 1962–65)	1905–1842	.508
T	Joe Torre (1977–84, 1990–2010)	2326–1997	.540
U	Bob Unglaub (1907)	9–20	.310
V	Bobby Valentine (1985–92, 1996–2002, 2012)	1186–1165	.504
W	Dick Williams (1967–69, 1971–88)	1571–1451	.520
X	[No manager]		
Y	Ned Yost* (2003–08, 2010–)	925–971	.488
Z	Don Zimmer (1972–73, 1976–82, 1988–91, 1999)	885–858	.508

*Still active.

Winningest Managers by Zodiac Sign

Aquarius (Jan. 20–Feb. 18)	Davey Johnson	1372
Pisces (Feb. 19–Mar. 20)	Sparky Anderson	2194
Aries (Mar. 21–Apr. 19)	John McGraw	2763
Taurus (Apr. 20–May 20)	Joe McCarthy	2125
Gemini (May 21–June 21)	Bobby Cox	2504
Cancer (June 22–July 22)	Joe Torre	2326
Leo (July 23–Aug. 22)	Leo Durocher	2008

continued on next page

Virgo (Aug. 23–Sept. 22)	Lou Piniella	1835
Libra (Sept. 23–Oct. 23)	Tony La Russa	2728
Scorpio (Oct. 24–Nov. 21)	Bucky Harris	2158
Sagittarius (Nov. 22–Dec. 21)	Walter Alston	2040
Capricorn (Dec. 22–Jan. 19)	Connie Mack	3637

Managers During Most Presidential Administrations

10	Connie Mack	Cleveland, McKinley, T. Roosevelt, Taft, Wilson, Harding, Hoover, F. Roosevelt, Truman
7	Gene Mauch	Eisenhower, Kennedy, L. Johnson, Nixon, Ford, Carter, Reagan
7	John McGraw	McKinley, T. Roosevelt, Taft, Wilson, Harding, Coolidge, Hoover
7	Harry Wright	Grant, Hayes, Garfield, Arthur, Cleveland, B. Harrison, Cleveland
6	Bobby Cox	Carter, Reagan, G. Bush, Clinton, G. Bush, G.W. Bush, Obama
6	Ralph Houk	Kennedy, L. Johnson, Nixon, Ford, Carter, Reagan
6	Tony La Russa	Carter, Reagan, G. Bush, Clinton, G.W. Bush, Obama
6	Bill McKechnie	Wilson, Harding, Coolidge, Hoover, F. Roosevelt, Truman
6	John McNamara	Nixon, Ford, Carter, Reagan, G. Bush, Clinton
6	Joe Torre	Carter, Reagan, G. Bush, Clinton, G.W. Bush, Obama

Managers Winning 1000 Games with One Franchise

Connie Mack, Phila. A's (AL), 1901–50	3637
John McGraw, N.Y. Giants (NL), 1902–32	2658
Bobby Cox, Atl. Braves (NL), 1978–81 and 1990–2010	2149
Walter Alston, Bklyn.–L.A. Dodgers (NL), 1954–76	2040
Tommy Lasorda, L.A. Dodgers (NL), 1976–96	1599
Earl Weaver, Balt. Orioles (AL), 1968–82 and 1985–86	1480
Joe McCarthy, N.Y. Yankees (AL), 1931–46	1460
Fred Clarke, Pitt. Pirates (NL), 1900–1915	1422
Mike Scioscia*, Ana.–L.A. Angels (AL), 2000–	1416
Tony La Russa, St.L. Cardinals (NL) 1996–2011	1408
Wilbert Robinson, Bklyn. Robins (NL), 1914–31	1375
Bucky Harris, Wash. Senators (AL), 1924–28, 1935–42, and 1950–54	1336
Sparky Anderson, Det. Tigers (AL) 1979–95	1331
Cap Anson, Chi. Colts–Cubs (NL), 1879–97	1288
Joe Torre, N.Y. Yankees (AL), 1996–2007	1173
Casey Stengel, N.Y. Yankees (AL), 1949–60	1149
Tom Kelly, Min. Twins (AL), 1986–2001	1140
Hughie Jennings, Det. Tigers (AL), 1907–20	1131
Danny Murtaugh, Pitt. Pirates (NL), 1957–64, 1967, 1970–71, and 1973–76	1115
Joe Cronin, Bost. Red Sox (AL), 1935–47	1071
Ron Gardenhire, Min. Twins (AL), 2002–14	1068
Miller Huggins, N.Y. Yankees (AL), 1918–29	1067
Red Schoendienst, St.L. Cardinals (NL), 1965–76 and 1980	1028
Frank Selee, Bost. Beaneaters (NL), 1890–1901	1004

*Still active.

Managers with Over 1000 Career Wins and sub-.500 Winning Percentage

	Record	Percentage	
Frank Robinson	1065–1176	.475	Cle. Indians (AL), 1975–77
			S.F. Giants (NL), 1981–84
			Balt. Orioles (AL), 1988–91
			Mont. Expos (NL), 2002–04
			Wash. Nationals (NL), 2005–06
Jimmy Dykes	1406–1541	.477	Chi. White Sox (AL), 1934–46
			Phila. A's (AL), 1951–53
			Balt. Orioles (AL), 1954
			Cin. Reds (NL), 1958
			Det. Tigers (AL), 1959–60
			Cle. Indians (AL), 1960–61
Tom Kelly	1140–1244	.478	Min. Twins (AL), 1986–2001
Gene Mauch	1902–2037	.483	Phila. Phillies (NL), 1960–68
			Mont. Expos (NL), 1969–75
			Min. Twins (AL), 1976–80
			Cal. Angels (AL), 1981–87
Jim Fregosi	1028–1094	.484	Cal. Angels (AL), 1978–81
			Chi. White Sox (AL), 1986–88
			Phila. Phillies (NL), 1991–96
			Tor. Blue Jays (NL), 1999–2000
Bill Rigney	1239–1321	.484	N.Y. Giants (NL), 1956–57
			S.F. Giants (NL), 1958–60
			L.A. Angels (AL), 1961–64
			Cal. Angels (AL), 1965–69
			Min. Twins (AL), 1970–72
John McNamara	1160–1233	.485	Oak A's (AL), 1969–70
			S.D. Padres (NL), 1974–77
			Cin. Reds (NL), 1979–82
			Cal. Angels (AL), 1983–84, 1996
			Bost. Red Sox (AL), 1985–88
			Cle. Indians (AL), 1900–91
Connie Mack	3731–3948	.486	Pitt. Pirates (NL), 1894–96
			Phila. A's (AL), 1901–50
Lou Boudreau	1162–1224	.487	Cle. Indians (AL), 1942–50
			Bost. Red Sox (AL), 1942–50
			K.C. A's (AL), 1955–57
			Chi. Cubs (NL), 1960
Bucky Harris	2158–2218	.493	Wash. Senators (AL), 1924–28, 1935–42, 1950–54
			Det. Tigers (AL), 1929–33, 1955–56
			Bost. Red Sox (AL), 1934
			Phila. Phillies (NL), 1943
			N.Y. Yankees (AL), 1947–48
Chuck Tanner	1352–1381	.495	Chi. White Sox (AL), 1970–75
			Oak. A's (AL), 1976
			Pitt. Pirates (NL), 1977–85
			Atl. Braves (NL), 1986–88
Art Howe	1129–1137	.498	Hous. Astros (NL), 1989–93
			Oak. A's (AL), 1996–2002
			N.Y. Mets (NL), 2003–04

Managers with Most Career Victories for Each Franchise

American League

Balt. Orioles	Earl Weaver, 1968–82 and 1985–86	1480–1060	.583
Bost. Red Sox	Joe Cronin, 1935–47	1071–916	.539
Chi. White Sox	Jimmy Dykes, 1934–46	899–938	.489
Cle. Indians	Lou Boudreau, 1942–50	728–649	.529
Det. Tigers	Sparky Anderson, 1979–95	1331–972	.516
Hous. Astros*	Bill Virdon, 1975–82	544–522	.510
K.C. A's	Harry Craft, 1957–59	162–196	.452
K.C. Royals	Ned Yost**, 2010–	468–469	.499
Ana.–L.A. Angels	Mike Scioscia**, 2000–	1416–1176	.546
Min. Twins	Tom Kelly, 1986–2001	1140–1244	.478
N.Y. Yankees	Joe McCarthy, 1931–46	1460–867	.627
Oak. A's	Tony La Russa, 1986–95	798–673	.542
Phila. A's	Connie Mack, 1901–50	3627–3891	.482
Sea. Mariners	Lou Piniella, 1993–2002	840–711	.542
Sea. Pilots	Joe Schultz, 1969	64–98	.395
St.L. Browns	Jimmy McAleer, 1902–09	551–632	.466
T.B. Rays	Joe Maddon, 2006–14	754–705	.517
Tex. Rangers	Ron Washington, 2007–14	664–611	.521
Tor. Blue Jays	Cito Gaston, 1989–97 and 2008–10	894–837	.516
Wash. Senators	Bucky Harris, 1924–28, 1935–42, and 1950–54	1336–1416	.485
Wash. Senators II	Gil Hodges, 1963–67	321–445	.419

National League (Post-1900)

Ariz. D'backs	Kirk Gibson, 2010–14	353–375	.485
Atl. Braves	Bobby Cox, 1978–81 and 1990–2010	2149–1709	.557
Bost. Braves	George Stallings, 1913–20	579–597	.492
Bklyn. Dodgers	Wilbert Robinson, 1914–31	1375–1341	.504
Chi. Cubs	Charlie Grimm, 1932–38, 1944–49, and 1960	946–784	.547
Cin. Reds	Sparky Anderson, 1970–78	863–586	.596
Colo. Rockies	Clint Hurdle, 2002–09	534–625	.461
Mia. Marlins	Jack McKeon, 2003–05 and 2011	281–257	.522
L.A. Dodgers	Walter Alston, 1958–76	1673–1355	.552
Milw. Braves	Fred Haney, 1956–59	341–231	.596
Milw. Brewers	George Bamberger***, 1978–80 and 1985–86	377–351	.518
Mont. Expos	Gene Mauch, 1969–75	499–627	.443
N.Y. Giants	John McGraw, 1902–32	2658–1823	.593
N.Y. Mets	Davey Johnson, 1984–90	595–417	.588
Phila. Phillies	Charlie Manuel, 2005–13	780–636	.551
Pitt. Pirates	Fred Clarke, 1900–15	1422–969	.595
St.L. Cardinals	Tony La Russa, 1996–2011	1408–1182	.544
S.D. Padres	Bruce Bochy, 1995–2006	951–975	.494
S.F. Giants	Dusty Baker, 1993–2002	840–715	.540
Wash. Nationals	Davey Johnson, 2011–13	224–183	.550

*Played in NL from 1962–2012.

**Still active with team.

***Played in AL from 1970–97.

Best Winning Percentage as Manager with One Team (Post-1900; Min. 150 Games)

Percentage		Wins–Losses
.664	Frank Chance, Chi. Cubs (NL), 1905–12	768–389
.642	Chuck Dressen, Bklyn. Dodgers (NL), 1951–53	298–166
.642	Billy Southworth, St.L. Cardinals (NL), 1939–45	620–346
.632	Dick Howser, N.Y. Yankees (AL), 1978 and 1980	103–60
.627	Joe McCarthy, N.Y. Yankees (AL), 1931–46	1460–867
.623	Casey Stengel, N.Y. Yankees (AL), 1949–60	1149–696
.621	Jake Stahl, Bost. Red Sox (AL), 1912–13	144–88
.620	Bucky Harris, N.Y. Yankees (AL), 1947–48	191–117
.617	Al Lopez, Cle. Indians (AL), 1951–56	570–354
.606	Joe McCarthy, Bost. Red Sox (AL), 1948–50	223–145
.605	Joe Torre, N.Y. Yankess (AL), 1996–2007	1173–767

Managers with 500 Wins in Each League

2728 Tony La Russa (1408 NL, 1320 AL)
2326 Joe Torre (1173 AL, 1153 NL)
2194 Sparky Anderson (1331 NL, 863 AL)
1905 Casey Stengel (1149 AL, 756 NL)
1902 Gene Mauch (1145 NL, 757 AL)
1835 Lou Piniella (1264 AL, 571 NL)
1769 Jim Leyland (700 AL, 1069 NL)
1186 Dick Williams (650 AL, 536 NL)
1168 John McNamara (665 AL, 503 NL)

Played in 2000 Games, Managed in 2000 Games

	Games Played	Games Managed
Cap Anson	2276 (1876–97)	2296 (1879–98)
Charlie Grimm	2164 (1916, 1918–36)	2370 (1932–38, 1944–49, 1952–56, 1960)
Dusty Baker*	2039 (1968–86)	3176 (1993–2006, 2008–13)
Felipe Alou	2082 (1958–74)	2055 (1992–2001, 2003–06)
Frankie Frisch	2311 (1919–37)	2245 (1933–38, 1940–46, 1949–51)
Frank Robinson	2808 (1956–76)	2241 (1975–77, 1981–84, 1988–91, 2002–06)
Fred Clarke	2245 (1894–1915)	2822 (1897–1915)
Jimmy Dykes	2282 (1918–39)	2960 (1934–46, 1951–54, 1958–61)
Joe Cronin	2124 (1926–45)	2315 (1933–47)
Joe Torre	2209 (1960–77)	4329 (1977–84, 1990–2010)

*Hired as manager of Wash. Nationals for 2016 season.

Managers Managing 100-Loss Teams After 1000th Career Victory

Lou Boudreau, K.C. A's (AL), 1956
Leo Durocher, Chi. Cubs (NL), 1966
Jimmy Dykes, Balt. Orioles (AL), 1954
Ned Hanlon, Bklyn. Dodgers (NL), 1905
Ralph Houk, Det. Tigers (AL), 1975
Connie Mack, Phila. A's (AL), 1915–16, 1919–20, 1943, and 1946
Bill McKechnie, Bost. Braves (NL), 1935
Casey Stengel, N.Y. Mets (NL), 1962–64
Chuck Tanner, Pitt. Pirates (NL), 1985

Managers with Both 100-Win and 100-Loss Seasons

	100 Wins	100 Losses
Sparky Anderson	Cin. Reds (NL) 1970, 1975, 1976	Det. Tigers (AL), 1989
Chuck Dressen	Bklyn. Dodgers (NL) 1953	Wash. Senators (AL) 1955
Leo Durocher	Bklyn. Dodgers (NL) 1941, 1942	Chi. Cubs (NL) 1966
Ralph Houk	N.Y. Yankees (AL), 1961, 1963	Det. Tigers (AL) 1975
Connie Mack	Phila. A's (AL), 1910, 1911, 1929, 1930, 1931	Phila. A's (AL), 1915, 1916, 1919, 1920, 1921, 1936, 1940, 1943, 1946, 1950

continued on next page

Bill McKechnie.....Cin. Reds (NL), 1940 ..... Bost. Braves (NL), 1935
Casey Stengel.....N.Y. Yankees (AL), 1954 ..... N.Y. Mets (NL), 1962, 1963, 1964

Former Pitchers Winning Pennants as Managers (Post-1900)

Eddie Dyer, St.L. Cardinals (NL), 1946
Dallas Green, Phila. Phillies (NL), 1980
Clark Griffith, Chi. White Sox (AL), 1901
Roger Craig, S.F. Giants (NL), 1989
John Farrell, Bost. Red Sox (AL), 2013
Fred Hutchinson, Cin. Reds (NL), 1961
Tommy Lasorda, L.A. Dodgers (NL), 1977–78, 1981, and 1988
Bob Lemon, N.Y. Yankees (AL), 1978 and 1981
Kid Gleason, Chi. White Sox (AL), 1919

Managers Taking Over World Series Teams in Midseason

American League

Season	Manager	Wins–Losses	Former Manager
1978	Bob Lemon, N.Y. Yankees*	48–20	Billy Martin (52–42), Dick Howser (0–1)
1981	Bob Lemon, N.Y. Yankees	13–15	Gene Michael (46–33)
1982	Harvey Kuenn, Milw. Brewers	72–49	Buck Rodgers (23–24)

National League

Season	Manager	Wins–Losses	Former Manager
1932	Charlie Grimm, Chi. Cubs	37–20	Rogers Hornsby (53–44)
1938	Gabby Hartnett, Chi. Cubs	44–27	Charlie Grimm (45–36)
1947	Burt Shotton, Bklyn. Dodgers	93–60	Clyde Sukeforth (1–0)
1983	Paul Owens, Phila. Phillies	47–30	Pat Corrales (43–42)
2003	Jack McKeon, Fla. Marlins*	75–49	Jeff Torborg (17–22)

*World Series winner.

Managers Replaced While Team Was in First Place

Season	Team	Former Manager	Wins–Losses	New Manager	Wins–Losses
1947	Bklyn. Dodgers (NL)	Clyde Sukeforth	1–0	Burt Shotton	93–60
1983	Phila. Phillies (NL)	Pat Corrales	43–42	Paul Owens	47–30

Managers Winning Pennant in First Year as Manager of Team

American League

Clark Griffith, Chi. White Sox, 1901
Hughie Jennings, Det. Tigers, 1907
Kid Gleason, Chi. White Sox, 1919
Tris Speaker*, Cle. Indians, 1920
Bucky Harris, Wash. Senators, 1924
Joe Cronin, Wash. Senators, 1933
Mickey Cochrane, Det. Tigers, 1934
Ralph Houk, N.Y. Yankees, 1961
Yogi Berra, N.Y. Yankees, 1964
Dick Williams, Bost. Red Sox, 1967
Bob Lemon**, N.Y. Yankees, 1978
Earl Weaver*, Balt. Orioles, 1979
Jim Frey, K.C. Royals, 1980
Joe Torre, N.Y. Yankees, 1996
Terry Francona, Bost. Red Sox, 2004
John Farrell, Bost. Red Sox, 2013
Jim Leyland, Det. Tigers, 2006

*First full season as manager.
**Took over in mid-season.

National League

Frank Chance*, Chi. Cubs, 1906
Pat Moran, Phila. Phillies, 1915
Pat Moran, Cin. Reds, 1919
Charlie Grimm**, Chi. Cubs, 1932
Gabby Hartnett**, Chi. Cubs, 1938
Eddie Dyer, St.L. Cardinals, 1946
Burt Shotton, Bklyn. Dodgers, 1947
Tommy Lasorda*, L.A. Dodgers, 1977
Jim Leyland, Fla. Marlins, 1997
Bob Brenly*, Ariz. D'backs, 2001
Jack McKeon**, Fla. Marlins, 2003

Managers Undefeated in World Series Play

George Stallings, Bost. Braves (NL), 1914 ..... 4–0 over Phila. A's (AL)
Hank Bauer, Balt. Orioles (AL), 1966 ..... 4–0 over L.A. Dodgers (NL)
Lou Piniella, Cin. Reds (NL), 1990 ..... 4–0 over Oak. A's (AL)
Terry Francona, Bost. Red Sox (AL), 2004 ..... 4–0 over St.L. Cardinals (NL),
2007 ..... 4–0 over Colo. Rockies (NL)
Ozzie Guillen, Chi. White Sox (AL), 2005 ..... 4–0 over Hous. Astros (NL)

Managers with Fewest Career Wins to Win World Series

	Wins
Bob Brenly, Ariz. D'backs (NL), 2001	92
Tom Kelly, Min. Twins (AL), 1987	97
Eddie Dyer, St.L. Cardinals (NL), 1946	98
Dallas Green, Phila. Phillies (NL), 1980	110
Ed Barrow, Bost. Red Sox (AL), 1918	172
Ozzie Guillen, Chi. White Sox (AL), 2005	182
Mickey Cochrane, Det. Tigers (AL), 1935	194
Gabby Street, St.L. Cardinals (NL), 1931	194
Jake Stahl, Bost. Red Sox (AL), 1912	224
Bill Carrigan, Bost. Red Sox (AL), 1915	232
Jimmy Collins, Bost. Red Sox (AL), 1903	247
John Farrell, Bost. Red Sox (AL), 2013	251
Mike Scioscia, Ana. Angels (AL), 2002	256
Joe Girardi, N.Y. Yankees (AL), 2009	270
Pants Rowland, Chi. White Sox (AL), 1917	281
Davey Johnson, N.Y. Mets (NL), 1986	296
Lou Piniella, Cin. Reds (NL), 1990	315
Johnny Keane, St.L. Cardinals (NL), 1964	317
Joe Altobelli, Balt. Orioles (AL), 1983	323
Cito Gaston, Tor. Blue Jays, 1992	331
Bill Carrigan, Bost. Red Sox (AL), 1916	323
Bob Lemon, N.Y. Yankees (AL), 1978	379

Managers with Most Career Wins *Never* to Manage a World Series Team (Post-1903)

	Wins	Seasons
Gene Mauch	1901	26 (1960–82, 1985–87)
Jimmy Dykes	1407	21 (1934–46, 1951–54, 1958–61)
Buck Showalter*	1340	13 (1992–95, 1998–2000, 2003–06, 2010–)
Bill Rigney	1239	18 (1956–72, 1976)
Art Howe	1129	14 (1989–93, 1996–2004)
Ron Gardenhire	1068	10 (2002–14)
Frank Robinson	1065	14 (1975–77, 1981–84, 1988–91, 2002–06)
Felipe Alou	1033	14 (1992–2001, 2003–06)
Bill Virdon	995	13 (1972–84)
Paul Richards	923	12 (1951–61, 1976)
Jimy Williams	910	12 (1986–89, 1997–2004)
Don Zimmer	906	14 (1972–73, 1976–82, 1988–91, 1999)
Jim Tracy	856	10 (2001–07, 2009–12)
Johnny Oates	797	11 (1991–2001)
Buck Rodgers	784	13 (1980–82, 1985–94)

*Still active.

Pennant-Winning Managers with Fewest Career Wins (Since 1900)

44...Gabby Hartnett, 1938 Chi. Cubs (NL)
73...Harvey Kuenn, 1982 Milw. Brewers (AL)
80...Paul Owens, 1983 Phila. Phillies (NL)
88...Kid Gleason, 1919 Chi. White Sox (AL)
92...Bucky Harris, 1924 Wash. Senators (AL)*
92...Bob Brenly, 2001 Ariz. D'backs (NL)*
93...Gabby Street, 1930 St.L. Cardinals (NL)
97...Jim Frey, 1980 K.C. Royals (AL)
98...Eddie Dyer, 1946 St.L. Cardinals (NL)*
99...Joe Cronin, 1933 Wash. Senators (AL)
99 ..... Yogi Berra, 1964 N.Y. Yankees (AL)
101 ..... Mickey Cochrane, 1934 Det. Tigers (AL)
109 ..... Ralph Houk, 1961 N.Y. Yankees (AL)*
110 ..... Dallas Green, 1980 Phila. Phillies (NL)*
172 ..... Ed Barow, 1918 Bost. Red Sox (AL)*
182 ..... Ozzie Guillen, 2005 Chi. White Sox (AL)*
188 ..... Bucky Harris, 1925 Wash. Senators (AL)
194 ..... Gabby Street, 1931 St.L. Cardinals (NL)*
194 ..... Mickey Cochrane, 1935 Det. Tigers (AL)*
205 ..... Ralph Houk, 1962 N.Y. Yankees (AL)

*Won World Series.

Most Times Managing the Same Club

5	Billy Martin, N.Y. Yankees, 1975–78, 1979, 1983, 1985, and 1988
4	Danny Murtaugh, Pitt. Pirates, 1957–64, 1967, 1970–71, and 1973–76
3	Bucky Harris, Wash. Senators, 1924–28, 1935–42, and 1950–54
3	Charlie Grimm, Chi. Cubs, 1932–38, 1944–49, and 1960

Managers with Best Winning Percentage for First Five Full Years of Managing

	Wins–Losses	Percentage
Frank Chance, Chi. Cubs (NL), 1906–10	530–235	.693
Al Lopez, Cle. Indians (AL), 1951–55	482–288	.626
Earl Weaver, Balt. Orioles (AL), 1969–73	495–303	.620
John McGraw, Balt. Orioles (NL), 1899; Balt. Orioles (AL), 1901; and N.Y. Giants (NL), 1903–05	449–277	.618
Davey Johnson, N.Y. Mets (NL), 1984–88	488–320	.604
Hughie Jennings, Det. Tigers (AL), 1907–11	455–308	.596
Leo Durocher, Bklyn. Dodgers (NL), 1939–43	457–310	.596
Sparky Anderson, Cin. Reds (NL), 1970–74	473–329	.590
Fielder Jones, Chi. White Sox (AL), 1904–07; and St.L. Terriers (FL), 1915	447–313	.588
Joe McCarthy, Chi. Cubs (NL), 1926–29; and N.Y. Yankees (AL), 1931	450–316	.587
Pat Moran, Phila. Phillies (NL), 1915–18; and Cin. Reds (NL), 1919	419–301	.582

Managers Never Experiencing a Losing Season (Post-1900; Min. Two Full Seasons)

	Winning Seasons	Wins–Losses	Percentage
Joe McCarthy (1926–46, 1948–50)	24	2136–1335	.614
Steve O'Neill (1935–37, 1943–48, 1950–54)	14	1039–819	.559
Don Mattingly* (2011–)	5	446–363	.551
Eddie Dyer (1946–50)	5	446–325	.578
Eddie Kasko (1970–73)	4	345–295	.539
Joe Morgan (1989–91)	4	255–231	.525
Mike Matheny* (2012–)	4	375–273	.579
Ossie Vitt (1938–40)	3	262–198	.570
Harvey Kuenn (1975, 1982–83)	3	160–118	.576
Eddie Collins (1925–26)	2	160–147	.521
Matt Williams (2014–15)	2	179–145	552
Dick Sisler (1964–65)	2	121–94	.563

*Still active.

Career One-Game Managers

American League		National League	
Bibb Falk, Cle. Indians, 1933	1–0	Vern Benson, Atl. Braves, 1977	1–0
Marty Martinez, Sea. Mariners, 1986	0–1	Bill Burwell, Pitt. Pirates, 1947	1–0
Bob Schaefer, K.C. Royals, 1991	1–0	Andy Cohen, Phila. Phillies, 1960	1–0
Jo-Jo White, Cle. Indians, 1960	1–0	Bill Holbert, Syr. Stars, 1879	0–1
Del Wilber, Tex. Rangers, 1973	1–0	Brandon Hyde, Fla. Marlins, 2011	0–1
Rudy York, Bost. Red Sox, 1959	0–1	Roy Johnson, Chi. Cubs, 1944	1–0
Eddie Yost, Wash. Senators II, 1963	0–1	Ted Turner, Atl. Braves, 1977	0–1

Managers Managing in Civilian Clothes

Bill Armour, Cle. Indians (AL), 1902–04; and Det. Tigers (AL), 1905–06

Judge Emil Fuchs, Bost. Braves (NL), 1929

Connie Mack, Pitt. Pirates (NL), 1894–96; and Phila. A's (AL), 1901–50

John McGraw, N.Y. Giants (NL), 1930–32

Burt Shotton, Phila. Phillies (NL), 1928–33; Cin. Reds (NL), 1934; and Bklyn. Dodgers (NL), 1947–48 and 1949–50

George Stallings, Phila. Phillies (NL), 1897–99; Det. Tigers (AL), 1901; N.Y. Yankees (AL), 1909–10; and Bost. Braves (NL), 1913–20

Managers Who Were Lawyers

Bill Armour, Cle. Indians (AL), 1902–04; Det. Tigers (AL), 1905–06

Judge Emil Fuchs, Bost. Braves (NL), 1929

Miller Huggins, St.L. Cardinals (NL), 1913–17; and N.Y. Yankees (AL), 1918–29

Hughie Jennings, Det. Tigers (AL), 1907–20

Tony La Russa, Chi. White Sox (AL), 1979–86; Oak. A's (AL), 1986–88; and St.L. Cardinals (NL), 1996–2011

Branch Rickey, St.L. Browns (AL), 1913–15; and St.L. Cardinals (NL), 1919–25

Muddy Ruel, St.L. Browns (AL), 1947

Monte Ward, N.Y. Gothams (NL), 1884; Bklyn. Wonders (PL), 1890; Bklyn. Bridegrooms (NL), 1891–92; and N.Y. Giants (NL), 1893–94

Pennant-Winning Managers Who Won Batting Titles

Manager of Pennant Winner	Batting Champion
Lou Boudreau.....Cle. Indians (AL), 1948	Cle. Indians (AL), 1944 (.327)
Rogers Hornsby.....St.L. Cardinals (NL), 1926	St.L. Cardinals (NL), 1920 (.370), 1921 (.397), 1922 (.401), 1923 (.384), 1924 (.424), 1925 (.403)
	Bost. Braves (NL), 1928 (.387)
Harvey Kuenn.....Milw. Brewers (AL), 1982	Det. Tigers (AL), 1959 (.353)
Tris Speaker.....Cle. Indians (AL), 1920	Cle. Indians (AL), 1916 (.386)
Bill Terry.....N.Y. Giants (NL), 1933, 1936–37	N.Y. Giants (NL), 1930 (.401)
Joe Torre.....N.Y. Yankees (AL), 1996, 1998–2001, 2003	St.L. Cardinals (NL), 1971 (.363)

Managers with Same Initials as Team They Managed

Billy Barnie, Bklyn. Bridegrooms (1897–98)

Harry Craft, Hous. Colt .45s (1962)

Bill Dahlen, Bklyn. Dodgers (1910–13)

Dick Tracewski, Det. Tigers (1979)

Playing Managers After 1950

American League

Lou Boudreau (shortstop), Cle. Indians, 1950 (81 games)

Lou Boudreau (shortstop), Bost. Red Sox, 1952 (4 games)

Fred Hutchinson (pitcher), Det. Tigers, 1952–53 (12 games in 1952; 3 games in 1953)

Marty Marion (shortstop, third base), St.L. Browns, 1952–53 (67 games in 1952; 3 games in 1953)

Eddie Joost (infield), Phila. A's, 1954 (19 games)

Hank Bauer (outfield), K.C. A's, 1961 (43 games)

continued on next page

Frank Robinson (designated hitter), Cle. Indians, 1976 (36 games)
Don Kessinger (shortstop), Chi. White Sox, 1979 (56 games)

National League

Tommy Holmes (outfield), Bost. Braves, 1951 (27 games)
Phil Cavaretta (first base), Chi. Cubs, 1951–53 (89 games in 1951; 41 games in 1952; 27 games in 1953)
Eddie Stanky (second base), St.L. Cardinals, 1952–53 (53 games in 1952; 17 games in 1953)
Harry Walker (outfield), St.L. Cardinals, 1955 (11 games)
Solly Hemus (infield), St.L. Cardinals, 1959 (24 games)
El Tappe (catcher), Chi. Cubs, 1962 (26 games)
Joe Torre (first base, pinch hitter), N.Y. Mets, 1977 (26 games)
Pete Rose (first base), Cin. Reds, 1984–86 (26 games in 1984; 119 games in 1985; 72 games in 1986)

1000 Wins as Manager and 2000 Hits as Player

Felipe Alou ..... Manager (1992–2006) 1033 wins
Player (1958–74) 2101 hits
Cap Anson ..... Manager (1875, 1879–98) 2196 wins
Player (1871–97) 3012 hits
Fred Clarke ..... Manager (1897–15) 1602 wins
Player (1894–1915) 2678 hits
Joe Cronin ..... Manager (1933–47) 1236 wins
Player (1926–45) 2285 hits
Jimmy Dykes ..... Manager (1934–46, 1951–54, 1958–61) 1406 wins
Player (1918–38) 2256 hits
Frankie Frisch ..... Manager (1933–38, 1940–46, 1949–51) 1138 wins
Player (1919–37) 2880 hits
Charlie Grimm ..... Manager (1932–38, 1944–49, 1952–56, 1960) 1287 wins
Player (1916, 1918–36) 2299 hits
Frank Robinson ..... Manager (1975–77, 1981–84, 1988–91, 2002–06) 1065 wins
Player (1957–76) 2943 hits
Red Schoendienst ..... Manager (1965–76, 1980, 1990) 1041 wins
Player (1945–63) 2449 hits
Joe Torre ..... Manager (1977–84, 1990–2010) 2326 wins
Player (1960–77) 2342 hits

6

FIELDING

Most Games Played by Position, Career

First Base	2413	Eddie Murray (1977–97)
Second Base	2650	Eddie Collins (1906, 1908–28)
Third Base	2870	Brooks Robinson (1955–77)
Shortstop	2709	Omar Vizquel (1989–2012)
Left Field	2715	Barry Bonds (1986–2007)
Centerfield	2832	Willie Mays (1951–52, 1954–73)
Right Field	2307	Roberto Clemente (1955–72)
Catcher	2427	Ivan Rodriguez (1991–2011)
Pitcher	1252	Jesse Orosco (1979, 1981–2004)
Designated Hitter	1887	David Ortiz (1997–)

Most Consecutive Games Played at Each Position

American League

First Base	885	Lou Gehrig, N.Y. Yankees, 1925–30
Second Base	798	Nellie Fox, Chi. White Sox, 1955–60
Third Base	576	Eddie Yost, Wash. Senators, 1951–55
Shortstop	2216	Cal Ripken Jr., Balt. Orioles, 1983–95
Outfield	511	Clyde Milan, Wash. Senators, 1910–13
Catcher	312	Frankie Hayes, St.L. Browns–Phila. A's–Cle. Indians, 1943–46
Pitcher	13	Dale Mohoric, Tex. Rangers, 1986

National League

First Base	652	Frank McCormick, Cin. Reds, 1938–42
Second Base	443	Dave Cash, Pitt. Pirates–Phila. Phillies, 1973–76
Third Base	364	Ron Santo, Chi. Cubs, 1964–66
Shortstop	584	Roy McMillan, Cin. Reds, 1951–55
Outfield	897	Billy Williams, Chi. Cubs, 1963–69
Catcher	217	Ray Mueller, Cin. Reds, 1943–44
Pitcher	13	Mike Marshall, L.A. Dodgers, 1974

Players Who Played 1000 Games at Two Positions, Career

Ernie Banks	1125 at shortstop, 1259 at first base
Rod Carew	1130 at second base, 1184 at first base
Ron Fairly	1218 at first base, 1037 in the outfield
Stan Musial	1890 in the outfield, 1016 at first base
Alex Rodriguez	1272 at shortstop, 1193 at third base
Robin Yount	1479 at shortstop, 1150 in center field
Babe Ruth	1054 in left field, 1133 in right field

Unassisted Triple Plays

Neal Ball, shortstop, Cle. Indians (vs. Bost. Red Sox) (AL), July 19, 1909, 2nd inning; Batter: Amby McConnell
Ball spears McConnell's line drive, comes down on second to double up Heinie Wagner, and tags out Jake Stahl, coming from first.

Bill Wambsganss, second base, Cle. Indians (vs. Bklyn. Dodgers) (AL), Oct. 10, 1920*, 5th inning; Batter: Clarence Mitchell
"Wamby" catches Mitchell's liner, steps on second to retire Pete Kilduff, and wheels around to tag Otto Miller, coming down from first.

George H. Burns, first base, Bost. Red Sox (vs. Cle. Indians) (AL), Sept. 14, 1923, 2nd inning; Batter: Frank Brower
Burns takes Brower's line drive, reaches out and tags Walter Lutzke, who was on first base, and then rushes down to second to tag the base before base runner Joe Stephenson can return.

Ernie Padgett, shortstop, Bost. Braves (vs. Phila. Phillies) (NL), Oct. 6, 1923, 4th inning; Batter: Walter Holke
Padgett takes Holke's line drive, tags second to retire Cotton Tierney, and then tags out Cliff Lee, coming into second.

Glenn Wright, shortstop, Pitt. Pirates (vs. St.L. Cardinals) (NL), May 7, 1925, 9th inning; Batter: Jim Bottomley
Wright snares Bottomley's liner, touches second to retire Jimmy Cooney, and then tags out Rogers Hornsby, on his way into second.

Jimmy Cooney, shortstop, Chi. Cubs (vs. Pitt. Pirates) (NL), May 30, 1927, 4th inning; Batter: Paul Waner
Cooney grabs Waner's line drive, doubles Lloyd Waner off second, and then tags out Clyde Barnhart, coming down from first.

Johnny Neun, first base, Det. Tigers (vs. Cle. Indians) (AL), May 31, 1927, 9th inning; Batter: Homer Summa
Neun snares Summa's liner, tags first to double up Charlie Jamieson, and then races down toward second to tag out base runner Glenn Myatt before he can return to second, ending the game.

Ron Hansen, shortstop, Wash. Senators II (vs. Cle. Indians) (AL), July 29, 1968, 1st inning; Batter: Joe Azcue
Hansen grabs Azcue's liner, steps on second to double up Dave Nelson, and then tags out Russ Snyder, barreling down from first.

Mickey Morandini, second base, Phila. Phillies (vs. Pitt. Pirates) (NL), Sept. 20, 1992, 6th inning; Batter: Jeff King
Morandini makes a diving catch of King's line drive, runs to second to double off Andy Van Slyke, and then tags out Barry Bonds running down from first.

John Valentin, shortstop, Bost. Red Sox (vs. Sea. Mariners) (AL), July 8, 1994, 6th inning; Batter: Marc Newfield
Valentin catches Newfield's line drive, steps on second to double up Mike Blowers, and then tags out Kevin Mitchell coming down from first.

Randy Velarde, second base, Oak. A's (vs. N.Y. Yankees) (AL), May 29, 2000, 6th inning; Batter: Shane Spencer
Velarde catches Spencer's liner, tags Jorge Posada running from first to second, and then runs over to step on second to retire Tino Martinez.

Rafael Furcal, shortstop, Atl. Braves (vs. St.L. Cardinals) (NL), Aug. 10, 2003, 6th inning; Batter: Woody Williams
Furcal grabs Williams's liner, steps on second to retire Mike Matheny, and then tags Orlando Palmeiro coming down the line from first.

Troy Tulowitzki, shortstop, Colo. Rockies (vs. Atl. Braves) (NL), Apr. 29, 2007, 7th inning; Batter: Chipper Jones
Jones hits a line drive to Tulowitzki, who then steps on second to double up Kelly Johnson and tags Edgar Renteria between first and second base.

Asdrubal Cabrera, second base, Cle. Indians (vs. Tor. Blue Jays) (AL), May 12, 2008, 5th inning; Batter: Lyle Overbay
Overbay hits a line drive that is caught by a diving Cabrera, who steps on second to double up Kevin Mench and then tags out Marco Scutaro.

Eric Bruntlett, second base, Phila. Phillies (vs. N.Y. Mets) (NL), Aug. 23, 2009, 9th inning; Batter: Jeff Francoeur
Francoeur hits a line drive to Bruntlett, who steps on second to double up Luis Castillo and then tags Daniel Murphy between first and second, ending the game.

*World Series game.

Most No-Hitters Caught

	Catcher	Pitcher
4	Jason Varitek, Bost. Red Sox (AL)	Hideo Nomo, Apr. 4, 2001, vs. Balt. Orioles, 3–0
		Derek Lowe, Apr. 27, 2002, vs. T.B. Devil Rays, 10–0
		Clay Buchholz, Sept. 1, 2007, vs. Balt. Orioles, 10–0
		Jon Lester, May 19, 2008, vs. K.C. Royals, 7–0

continued on next page

4	Carlos Ruiz, Phila. Phillies (NL)	Roy Halladay, May 29, 2010, vs. Fla. Marlins, 1–0 (perfect game)
		Roy Halladay, Oct. 6, 2010, vs. Cin. Reds, 4–0 (Division Series)
		Cole Hamels, Jake Diekman, Ken Giles, Jonathan Papelbon, Sept. 1, 2014, vs. Atl. Braves 7–0
		Cole Hamels, July 25, 2015, vs. Chi. Cubs, 5–0
3	Lou Criger, Bost. Red Sox (AL)	Cy Young, May 5, 1904, vs. Phila. A's, 3–0 (perfect game)
		Bill Dinneen, Sept. 27, 1905, vs. Chi. White Sox, 2–0
		Cy Young, June 30, 1908, vs. N.Y. Highlanders, 8–0
3	Bill Carrigan, Bost. Red Sox (AL)	Smoky Joe Wood, July 29, 1911, vs. St.L. Browns, 5–0
		Rube Foster, June 16, 1916, vs. N.Y. Yankees, 2–0
		Dutch Leonard, Aug. 30, 1916, vs. St.L. Browns, 4–0
3	Ray Schalk, Chi. White Sox (AL)	Joe Benz, May 31, 1914, vs. Cle. Indians, 6–1
		Jim Scott, May 14, 1914, vs. Wash. Senators, 0–1*
		Eddie Cicotte, Apr. 14, 1917, vs. St.L. Browns, 11–0
		Charlie Robertson, Apr. 30, 1922, vs. Det. Tigers, 2–0 (perfect game)
3	Val Picinich, Phila. A's (AL)	Joe Bush, Aug. 26, 1916, vs. Cle. Indians, 5–0
	Wash. Senators (AL)	Walter Johnson, July 1, 1920, vs. Bost. Red Sox, 1–0
	Bost. Red Sox (AL)	Howard Ehmke, Sept. 7, 1923, vs. Phila. A's, 4–0
3	Luke Sewell, Cle. Indians (AL)	Wes Ferrell, Apr. 29, 1931, vs. St.L. Browns, 9–0
	Chi. White Sox (AL)	Vern Kennedy, Aug. 31, 1935, vs. Cle. Indians, 5–0
		Bill Dietrich, June 1, 1937, vs. St.L. Browns, 8–0
3	Jim Hegan, Cle. Indians (AL)	Don Black, July 10, 1947, vs. Phila. A's, 3–0
		Bob Lemon, June 30, 1948, vs. Det. Tigers, 2–0
		Bob Feller, July 1, 1951, vs. Det. Tigers, 2–1
3	Yogi Berra, N.Y. Yankees (AL)	Allie Reynolds, July 12, 1951, vs. Cle. Indians, 1–0
		Allie Reynolds, Sept. 28, 1951, vs. Bost. Red Sox, 8–0
		Don Larsen, Oct. 8, 1956, vs. Bklyn. Dodgers, 2–0 (World Series, perfect game)
3	Roy Campanella, Bklyn. Dodgers (NL)	Carl Erskine, June 19, 1952, vs. Chi. Cubs, 5–0
		Carl Erskine, May 12, 1956, vs. N.Y. Giants, 3–0
		Sal Maglie, Sept. 25, 1956, vs. Phila. Phillies, 5–0
3	Del Crandall, Milw. Braves (NL)	Jim Wilson, June 12, 1954, vs. Phila. Phillies, 2–0
		Lew Burdette, Aug. 18, 1960, vs. Phila. Phillies, 1–0
		Warren Spahn, Sept. 16, 1960, vs. Phila. Phillies, 4–0
3	Jeff Torborg, L.A. Dodgers (NL)	Sandy Koufax, Sept. 9, 1965, vs. Chi. Cubs, 1–0 (perfect game)
		Bill Singer, July 20, 1970, vs. Phila. Phillies, 5–0
	Cal. Angels (AL)	Nolan Ryan, May 15, 1973, vs. K.C. Royals, 3–0
3	Alan Ashby, Hous. Astros (NL)	Ken Forsch, Apr. 7, 1979, vs. Atl. Braves, 6–0
		Nolan Ryan, Sept. 26, 1981, vs. L.A. Dodgers, 5–0
		Mike Scott, Sept. 25, 1986, vs. S.F. Giants, 2–0
3	Charles Johnson, Fla. Marlins (NL)	Al Leiter, May 11, 1996, vs. Colo. Rockies, 11–0
		Kevin Brown, June 10, 1997, vs. S.F. Giants, 9–0
		A.J. Burnett, May 12, 2001, vs. S.D. Padres, 3–0
3	Buster Posey, S.F. Giants (NL)	Matt Cain, June 13, 2012, vs. Hous. Astros, 10–0 (perfect game)
		Tim Lincecum, July 13, 2013, vs. S.D. Padres, 9–0
		Chris Heston, June 9, 2015, vs. N.Y. Mets, 5–0
3	Wilson Ramos, Wash. Nationals (NL)	Jordan Zimmermann, Sept. 28, 2014, vs. Mia. Marlins, 1–0
		Max Scherzer, June 20, 2015, vs. Pitt. Pirates, 6–0
		Max Scherzer, Oct. 3, 2015, vs. N.Y. Mets, 2–0

Games Caught by Left-Handed Catchers

1073 ..... Jack Clements, 1884–1900
272 ..... Sam Trott, 1880–85 and 1887–88
202 ..... Pop Tate, 1885–90
186 ..... Sy Sutcliffe, 1885, 1888–91
125 ..... Bill Harbridge, 1876–78, 1880–83
99 ..... Mike Hines, 1883–85, 1888
75 ..... John Humphries, 1883–84
71 ..... Fred Tenney, 1894–96, 1898, 1901
62 ..... Phil Baker, 1883–84, 1886
52 ..... Art Twineham, 1893–94
45 ..... Jiggs Donahue, 1900–02
35 ..... Dave Oldfield, 1883, 1885–86
34 ..... Charlie Householder, 1882, 1884
21 ..... Fergy Malone, 1876, 1884
16 ..... Jack McMahon, 1892–93
12 ..... Charlie Krehmeyer, 1884–85
7 ..... Joe Wall, 1901–02
5 ..... Elmer Foster, 1884
3 ..... Homer Hillebrand, 1905
3 ..... Benny Distefano, 1989
2 ..... Jim Egan, 1882
2 ..... Dale Long, 1958
2 ..... Mike Squires, 1980
1 ..... John Mullen, 1876
1 ..... Billy Redmond, 1878
1 ..... Charlie Eden, 1879
1 ..... Martin Powell, 1881
1 ..... John Cassidy, 1887
1 ..... Lefty Marr, 1889
1 ..... Chris Short, 1961

Players Pitching and Catching, Same Game

American League

Bert Campaneris, K.C. A's ..... Sept. 8, 1965
Cesar Tovar, Min. Twins ..... Sept. 22, 1968
Jeff Newman, Oak. A's ..... Sept. 14, 1977
Rick Cerone, N.Y. Yankees ..... July 19 and Aug. 9, 1987
Scott Sheldon, Tex. Rangers ..... Sept. 6, 2000
Shane Halter, Det. Tigers ..... Oct. 1, 2000

National League (Post-1900)

Roger Bresnahan, St.L. Cardinals ..... Aug. 3, 1910

7

RELATIVES

Father-Son Combinations with 250 Home Runs, Career

Total	Father	Home Runs	Son	Home Runs
1094	Bobby Bonds (1968–81)	332	Barry Bonds (1986–2007)	762
782	Ken Griffey Sr. (1973–91)	152	Ken Griffey Jr. (1989–2010)	630
630	Cecil Fielder (1985–88, 1990–98)	319	Prince Fielder (2005–)	311
538	Felipe Alou (1958–74)	206	Moises Alou (1990,1992–98, 2000–08)	332
458	Tony Perez (1964–86)	374	Eduardo Perez (1993–2000, 2002–06)	74
407	Gus Bell (1950–64)	206	Buddy Bell (1972–88)	201
407	Yogi Berra (1946–65)	358	Dale Berra (1977–87)	49
369	Jose Cruz (1970–88)	165	Jose Cruz Jr. (1997–2008)	204
357	Bob Boone (1972–89)	105	Bret Boone (1992–2005)	252
342	Gary Matthews Sr. (1972–1987)	234	Gary Matthews Jr. (1999–2010)	108
324	Buddy Bell (1972–88)	201	David Bell (1995–2006)	123
311	John Mayberry (1968–82)	191	John Mayberry Jr. (2009–)	56
294	Hal McRae (1968, 1970–87)	82	Brian McRae (1990–99)	103
284	Randy Hundley (1964–77)	238	Todd Hundley (1990–2003)	202
282	Earl Averill Sr. (1929–41)	255	Earl Averill Jr. (1956–63)	44
264	Jose Tartabull (1962–70)	2	Danny Tartabull (1984–97)	262
257	Jesse Barfield (1981–92)	241	Josh Barfield (2006–09)	16
257	Dolph Camilli (1933–45)	239	Doug Camilli (1960–69)	18
256	Ray Boone (1948–60)	151	Bob Boone (1972–89)	105
252	Jeff Burroughs (1970–85)	240	Sean Burroughs (2002–06, 2011–12)	12

Brother Batteries*

Jim and Ed Bailey ..... Cin. Reds (NL), 1959
Dick and Bill Conway ..... Balt. Orioles (AA), 1886
Mort and Walker Cooper ..... St.L. Cardinals (NL), 1940–45; and N.Y. Giants (NL), 1947
Ed and Bill Dugan ..... Rich. Virginians (AA), 1884
John and Buck Ewing ..... N.Y. Giants (NL), 1890–91
Wes and Rick Ferrell ..... Bost. Red Sox (AL), 1934–37; and Wash. Senators (AL), 1937–38
Milt and Alex Gaston ..... Bost. Red Sox (AL), 1929
Mike and John O'Neill ..... St.L. Cardinals (NL), 1902–03
Elmer and Johnny Riddle ..... Cin. Reds (NL), 1941 and 1944–45; and Pitt. Pirates (NL), 1948
Bobby and Billy Shantz ..... Phila. A's (AL), 1954; K.C. A's (AL), 1955; and N.Y. Yankees (AL), 1960
Larry and Norm Sherry ..... L.A. Dodgers (NL), 1960–62
Tom and Homer Thompson ..... N.Y. Yankees (AL), 1912
Lefty and Fred Tyler ..... Bost. Braves (NL), 1914
Will and Deacon White ..... Bost. Red Caps (NL), 1877; and Cin. Reds (NL) 1878–79
Pete and Fred Wood ..... Buff. Bisons (NL), 1885

*Pitcher listed first; catcher second.

Twins Who Played Major League Baseball

Canseco ..... Jose, outfield (1985–2001)
Ozzie, outfield (1990, 1992–93)
Cliburn ..... Stan, catcher (1980)
Stu, pitcher (1984–85)
Edwards ..... Marshall, outfield (1981–83)
Mike, second base (1977–80)
Grimes ..... Ray, first base (1920–26)
Roy, second base (1920)
Hunter ..... Bill, outfield (1912)
George, outfield and pitcher (1909–10)
Minor ..... Ryan, first base (1998–2001)
Damon, first base (2000–04)
Jonnard ..... Bubber, catcher (1920, 1922, 1926–27, 1929, 1935)
Claude, pitcher (1921–24, 1926, 1929)
O'Brien..... Eddie, shortstop, outfield, and pitcher (1953, 1955–58)
Johnny, infield and pitcher (1953, 1955–59)
Reccius ..... John, outfield and pitcher (1882–88, 1890)
Phil, infield, outfield, and pitcher (1882–83)
Shannon ..... Joe, outfield and second base (1915)
Red, shortstop (1915, 1917–21, 1926)

Hall of Famers Whose Sons Played in Majors

Father	Sons
Earl Averill Sr. (1929–41)	Earl Averill Jr. (1956, 1958–63)
Yogi Berra (1946–63, 1965)	Dale Berra (1977–87)
Eddie Collins Sr. (1906–30)	Eddie Collins Jr. (1939, 1941–42)
Freddie Lindstrom (1924–36)	Charlie Lindstrom (1958)
Connie Mack (1886–96)	Earle Mack (1910–11, 1914)
Jim O'Rourke (1876–93, 1904)	Queenie O'Rourke (1908)
Tony Perez (1964–86)	Eduardo Perez (1993–2000, 2002–06)
George Sisler (1915–22, 1924–30)	Dick Sisler (1946–53)
	Dave Sisler (1956–62)
Ed Walsh Sr. (1904–17)	Ed Walsh Jr. (1928–30)
Tony Gwynn Sr. (1982–2001)	Tony Gwynn Jr. (2006–12, 2014)

Players with Two Sons Who Played in Majors

Father	Sons
Sandy Alomar (1964–78)	Sandy Alomar Jr. (1988–2007)
	Roberto Alomar (1988–2004)
Buddy Bell (1972–89)	David Bell (1995–2006)
	Mike Bell (2000)
Bob Boone (1972–90)	Aaron Boone (1997–2009)
	Bret Boone (1992–2005)
Jimmy Cooney (1890–92)	Jimmy Cooney (1917, 1919, 1924–28)
	Johnny Cooney (1921–44)
Dave Duncan (1964–76)	Chris Duncan (2005–09)
	Shelley Duncan (2007–13)
Larry Gilbert (1914–15)	Charlie Gilbert (1940–43, 1946–47)
	Tookie Gilbert (1950, 1953)
Jerry Hairston (1973–88)	Jerry Hairston Jr. (1998–2013)
	Scott Hairston (2004–14)
Sam Hairston (1951)	Jerry Hairston (1973–88)
	John Hairston (1969)
Dave LaRoche (1970–83)	Adam LaRoche* (2004–)

continued on next page

	Andy LaRoche (2007–11, 2013)
Manny Mota (1962–82)	Andy Mota (1991)
	Jose Mota (1991–95)
Kevin Romine (1985–91)	Andrew Romine* (2010–)
	Austin Romine* (2011, 2013–)
George Sisler (1915–22, 1924–30)	Dave Sisler (1956–62)
	Dick Sisler (1946–53)
Mel Stottlemyre (1964–74)	Mel Stottlemyre Jr. (1990)
	Todd Stottlemyre (1988–2002)
Dixie Walker (1909–12)	Dixie Walker (1931, 1933–49)
	Harry Walker (1940–43, 1946–55)

*Still active.

Brother Double-Play Combinations

Garvin Hamner, second base, and Granny Hamner, shortstop, Phila. Phillies (NL), 1945
Eddie O'Brien, shortstop, and Johnny O'Brien, second base, Pitt. Pirates (NL), 1953, 1955–56
Billy Ripken, second base, and Cal Ripken Jr., shortstop, Balt. Orioles (AL), 1987–92

Most Home Runs, Brothers

Total	Brothers	Home Runs
768	Hank Aaron (1954–76)	755
	Tommie Aaron (1962–63, 1965, 1968–71)	13
573	Joe DiMaggio (1936–42, 1946–51)	361
	Vince DiMaggio (1937–46)	125
	Dom DiMaggio (1940–42, 1946–53)	87
508	Eddie Murray (1977–97)	504
	Rich Murray (1980,1983)	4
492	Jason Giambi (1995–2014)	440
	Jeremy Giambi (1998–2003)	52
462	Jose Canseco (1985–2001)	462
	Ozzie Canseco (1990, 1992–93)	0
451	Cal Ripken Jr. (1981–2001)	431
	Billy Ripken (1987–98)	20
444	Ken Boyer (1955–69)	282
	Clete Boyer (1955–71)	162
444	Lee May (1965–82)	354
	Carlos May (1968–77)	90
406	Graig Nettles (1967–88)	390
	Jim Nettles (1970–72, 1974, 1979, 1981)	16
378	Bret Boone (1992–2005)	252
	Aaron Boone (1997–2009)	126
363	Brian Giles (1995–2009)	287
	Marcus Giles (2001–07)	76
356	J.D. Drew (1998–2011)	242
	Stephen Drew* (2006–)	114
358	Dick Allen (1963–77)	351
	Hank Allen (1966–70, 1972–73)	6
	Ron Allen (1972)	1
346	Bob Johnson (1933–45)	288
	Roy Johnson (1929–38)	58
334	Justin Upton* (2007–)	190
	Melvin Upton* (2004, 2006–)	144

*Still active

Pitching Brothers Each Winning 20 Games in Same Season

1970 Gaylord Perry, S.F. Giants (NL) 23–13
Jim Perry, Min. Twins (AL) 24–12

1979 Joe Niekro, Hous. Astros (NL) 21–11
Phil Niekro, Atl. Braves (NL) 21–20

Hall of Famers' Brothers Who Played 10 or More Seasons in Majors (Post-1900)

Hall of Famer	Brother
Roberto Alomar (1988–2004)	Sandy Alomar Jr. (1988–2007)
George Brett (1973–93)	Ken Brett (1967, 1969–81)
Ed Delahanty (1888–1903)	Jim Delahanty (1901–02, 1904–12, 1914–15)
Joe DiMaggio (1936–42, 1946–51)	Dom DiMaggio (1940–42, 1946–53)
Joe DiMaggio (1936–42, 1946–51)	Vince DiMaggio (1937–46)
Rick Ferrell (1929–45, 1947)	Wes Ferrell (1927–41)
Tony Gwynn (1982–2001)	Chris Gwynn (1987–96)
Greg Maddux (1986–2008)	Mike Maddux (1986–2000)
Pedro Martinez (1992–2009)	Ramon Martinez (1998–2001)
Phil Niekro (1964–87)	Joe Niekro (1967–88)
Gaylord Perry (1962–83)	Jim Perry (1959–75)
Cal Ripken Jr. (1981–2001)	Billy Ripken (1987–1998)
Joe Sewell (1920–33)	Luke Sewell (1921–39, 1942)
Lloyd Waner (1927–42, 1944–45)	Paul Waner (1926–45)
Paul Waner (1926–45)	Lloyd Waner (1927–42, 1944–45)

Father-Son Tandems Who Both Played for Same Manager

		Manager
Brucker	Earle Sr., Phila. A's (AL), 1937–40 and 1943	Connie Mack
	Earle Jr., Phila. A's (AL), 1948	
Collins	Eddie Sr., Phila. A's (AL), 1906–14	Connie Mack
	Eddie Jr., Phila. A's (AL), 1939 and 1941–42	
Hairston	Sam, Chi. White Sox (AL), 1951	Paul Richards
	Jerry, Chi. White Sox (AL), 1976	
Griffey	Ken Sr., Sea. Mariners (AL), 1990–91	Jim Lefebvre
	Ken Jr., Sea. Mariners (AL), 1989–91	
Raines	Tim Sr., Balt. Orioles (AL), 2001	Mike Hargrove
	Tim Jr., Balt. Orioles (AL), 2001	

Sons Who Played for Their Fathers

Son	Father-Manager
Moises Alou, Mont. Expos (NL), 1992–96; S.F. Giants (NL), 2005	Felipe Alou
Dale Berra, N.Y. Yankees (AL), 1985	Yogi Berra
Aaron Boone, Cin. Reds (NL), 2001–03	Bob Boone
Earle Mack, Phila. A's (AL), 1910–11 and 1914	Connie Mack
Brian McRae, K.C. Royals (AL), 1991–94	Hal McRae
Billy Ripken, Balt. Orioles (AL), 1987–88	Cal Ripken Sr.
Cal Ripken Jr., Balt. Orioles (AL), 1985 and 1987–88	Cal Ripken Sr.

Best Won-Lost Percentage for Pitching Brothers

Percentage	Brothers	Wins–Losses	Total
1.000	George Kelly (1917)	1–0	1–0
	Ren Kelly (1923)	0–0	
.800	Hick Hovlik (1918–19)	2–1	4–1
	Joe Hovlik (1909–11)	2–0	

continued on next page

.664	Christy Mathewson (1900–16)	373–188	373–189
	Henry Mathewson (1906–07)	0–1	
.660	Larry Corcoran (1880–87)	177–90	177–91
	Mike Corcoran (1884)	0–1	
.653	Pedro Martinez (1992–2009)	219–100	354–188
	Ramon Martinez (1988–2001)	135–88	
.639	Jim Hughes (1898–99, 1901–02)	83–41	122–69
	Mickey Hughes (1888–90)	39–28	
.631	Dizzy Dean (1930, 1932–41, 1947)	150–83	200–117
	Paul Dean (1934–41, 1943)	50–34	
.623	Dad Clarkson (1891–96)	39–39	385–233
	John Clarkson (1882, 1884–94)	328–178	
	Walter Clarkson (1904–08)	18–16	
.616	George Radbourn (1883)	1–2	309–193
	Old Hoss Radbourn (1880–91)	301–191	
.600	Harry Coveleski (1907–10, 1014–18)	81–55	296–197
	Stan Coveleski (1912, 1916–28)	215–142	
.599	Greg Maddux (1986–2008)	355–227	394–264
	Mike Maddux (1986–2000)	39–37	
.591	Dave Gregg (1913)	0–0	91–63
	Vean Gregg (1911–16, 1918, 1925)	91–63	
.588	Cy Ferry (1904–05)	0–1	10–7
	Jack Ferry (1910–13)	10–6	
.583	Hooks Wiltse (1904–15)	139–90	169–121
	Snake Wiltse (1901–03)	30–31	
.580	Ed Pipgras (1932)	0–1	102–74
	George Pipgras (1923–24, 1927–35)	102–73	
.580	Deacon White (1876, 1890)	0–0	229–166
	Will White (1877–86)	229–166	
.576	Gene Ford (1905)	0–1	98–72
	Russ Ford (1909–15)	98–71	
.565	Erskine Mayer (1912–19)	91–70	91–70
	Sam Mayer (1915)	0–0	
.563	Johnny Morrison (1920–27, 1929–30)	103–80	103–80
	Phil Morrison (1921)	0–0	
.558	Harry Camnitz (1909, 1911)	1–0	134–106
	Howie Camnitz (1904, 1906–15)	133–106	
.556	Charlie Getting (1896–99)	15–12	15–12
	Tom Gettinger (1895)	0–0	
.556	Chet Johnson (1946)	0–0	40–32
	Earl Johnson (1940–41, 1946–51)	40–32	
.554	Big Jeff Pfeffer (1905–08, 1910–11)	31–40	189–152
	Jeff Pfeffer (1911, 1913–24)	158–112	
.547	Jeff Weaver (1999–2007, 2009–10)	104–119	242–200
	Jered Weaver (2006–)	138–81	
.546	Gaylord Perry (1962–83)	314–265	529–439
	Jim Perry (1959–75)	215–174	
.544	Lindy McDaniel (1955–75)	141–119	148–124
	Von McDaniel (1957–58)	7–5	
.542	Ad Gumbert (1888–96)	122–101	129–109
	Billy Gumbert (1890, 1892–93)	7–8	
.538	Denny O'Toole (1969–73)	0–0	98–84
	Jim O'Toole (1958–67)	98–84	

continued on next page

.536	Lou Galvin (1884)	0–2	361–312	
	Pud Galvin (1879–92)	361–310		
.535	Enrique Romo (1977–82)	44–33	76–66	
	Vicente Romo (1968–74, 1982)	32–33		
.531	Bob Forsch (1974–89)	168–136	282–249	
	Ken Forsch (1970–84, 1986)	114–113		
.531	Gus Weyhing (1887–96, 1898–1901)	264–232	267–236	
	John Weyhing (1888–89)	3–4		
.530	Joe Niekro (1967–88)	221–204	539–478	
	Phil Niekro (1964–87)	318–274		
.526	Paul Reuschel (1975–79)	16–16	230–207	
	Rick Reuschel (1972–81, 1983–91)	214–191		
.525	Livan Hernandez (1996–2012)	178–177	268–242	
	Orlando Hernandez (1998–2007)	90–65		
.524	Andy Benes (1989–2002)	155–139	184–167	
	Alan Benes (1995–97, 1999–2003)	29–28		
.522	Al Lary (1954–55)	0–1	128–117	
	Frank Lary (1954–65)	128–116		
.514	Art Fowler (1954–57, 1959, 1961–64)	54–51	55–52	
	Jesse Fowler (1924)	1–1		
.509	Matt Kilroy (1886–94, 1898)	142–134	142–137	
	Mike Kilroy (1888, 1890)	0–3		
.507	Jesse Barnes (1915–27)	153–149	214–208	
	Virgil Barnes (1919–20, 1922–28)	61–59		
.507	Brownie Foreman (1895–96)	11–13	109–106	
	Frank Foreman (1884–85, 1889–93, 1895–96, 1901–02)	98–93		
.506	Camilo Pascual (1954–71)	174–170	175–171	
	Carlos Pascual (1950)	1–1		
.500	Chi Chi Olivo (1961, 1964–66)	7–6	12–12	
	Diomedes Olivo (1960, 1962–63)	5–6		

Most Total Combined Career Wins for Pitching Brothers

Total	Brothers	Wins
539	Phil Niekro (1964–87)	318
	Joe Niekro (1967–88)	221
529	Gaylord Perry (1962–83)	314
	Jim Perry (1959–75)	215
394	Greg Maddux (1986–2008)	355
	Mike Maddux (1986–2000)	39
385	John Clarkson (1882–94)	328
	Dad Clarkson (1891–96)	39
	Walter Clarkson (1904–08)	18
373	Christy Mathewson (1900–16)	373
	Henry Mathewson (1906–07)	0
361	Pud Galvin (1879–92)	361
	Lou Galvin (1884)	0
354	Pedro Martinez (1992–2009)	219
	Ramon Martinez (1988–2001)	135
296	Stan Coveleski (1912, 1916–28)	215
	Harry Coveleski (1907–10, 1914–18)	81
268	Livan Hernandez (1996–2012)	178
	Orlando Hernandez (1998–2007)	90
282	Bob Forsch (1974–89)	168
	Ken Forsch (1970–84, 1986)	114
242	Jered Weaver (2006–)	138
	Jeff Weaver (1999–2007, 2009–10)	104

continued on next page

230	Rick Reuschel (1972–89)	214
	Paul Reuschel (1975–79)	16
214	Jesse Barnes (1905–27)	153
	Virgil Barnes (1919–20, 1922–28)	61
200	Dizzy Dean (1930, 1932–41, 1947)	150
	Paul Dean (1934–41, 1947)	50

Pitching Brothers Facing Each Other, Regular Season

Frank Foreman, Cin. Reds (NL), vs. Brownie Foreman, Pitt. Pirates (NL), 1896*

Stan Coveleski, Cle. Indians (AL), vs. Harry Coveleski Det. Tigers (AL), 1916*

Virgil Barnes, N.Y. Giants (NL), vs. Jesse Barnes, Bost. Braves (NL), 1923

Virgil Barnes, N.Y. Giants (NL), vs. Jesse Barnes, Bklyn. Dodgers (NL), 1927

Phil Niekro, Atl. Braves (NL), vs. Joe Niekro, Chi. Cubs (NL), 1968

*Same game but not at same time.

**Interleague play.

Gaylord Perry, Cle. Indians (AL), vs. Jim Perry, Det. Tigers (AL), 1973

Bob Forsch, St.L. Cardinals (NL), vs. Ken Forsch, Hous. Astros (NL), 1974

Tom Underwood, Tor. Blue Jays (AL), vs. Pat Underwood, Det. Tigers (AL), 1979

Greg Maddux, Chi. Cubs (NL), vs. Mike Maddux, Phila. Phillies (NL), 1986

Greg Maddux, Chi. Cubs (NL), vs. Mike Maddux, Phila. Phillies (NL), 1988

Jeff Weaver, L.A. Dodgers (NL), vs. Jered Weaver, L.A. Angels (AL), 2009**

Jeff Weaver, L.A. Dodgers (NL), vs. Jered Weaver, L.A. Angels (AL), 2010**

Most Career Victories by Father-Son Combination (Post-1900)

Total	Father	Wins	Son	Wins
302	Mel Stottlemyre (1964–74)	164	Todd Stottlemyre (1988–2002)	138
258	Dizzy Trout (1939–52, 1957)	170	Steve Trout (1978–89)	88
224	Jim Bagby Sr. (1912, 1916–23)	127	Jim Bagby Jr. (1938–47)	97
206	Ed Walsh Sr. (1904–17)	195	Ed Walsh Jr. (1928–30, 1932)	11
194	Joe Coleman Sr. (1942, 1946–51, 1953–55)	52	Joe Coleman Jr. (1965–79)	142
171	Floyd Bannister (1977–89, 1991–92)	134	Brian Bannister (2006–10)	37
168	Clyde Wright (1966–75)	100	Jaret Wright (1997–2007)	68
163	Doug Drabek (1986–98)	155	Kyle Drabek (2010–)	8
157	Thornton Lee (1933–48)	117	Don Lee (1957–58, 1960–66)	40
150	Joe Coleman (1965–79)	142	Casey Coleman (2010–12, 2014)	8
124	Ross Grimsley Sr. (1951)	0	Ross Grimsley Jr. (1971–80, 1982)	124
123	Julio Navarro (1962–70)	7	Jaime Navarro (1989–2000)	116
117	Smoky Joe Wood (1908–15, 1917, 1919–20)	117	Joe Wood Jr. (1944)	0
116	Dick Ellsworth (1958, 1960–71)	115	Steve Ellsworth (1988)	1
73	Lew Krausse Sr. (1931–32)	5	Lew Krausse Jr. (1961, 1964–74)	68
7	Steve Bedrosian (1981–91, 1993–95)	76	Cam Bedrosian (2015)	1
61	Bruce Ruffin (1986–97)	60	Chance Ruffin (2011, 2013)	1
72	Herman Pillette (1917, 1922–24)	34	Duane Pillette (1949–56)	38
58	Jeff Russell (1983–96)	56	James Russell (2010–)	2
47	Mel Queen Sr. (1942, 1944, 1946–48, 1950–52)	27	Mel Queen Jr. (1964–72)	20

Brothers Who Played Together on Three Major League Teams

Sandy Jr. and Roberto Alomar ..... S.D. Padres (NL), 1988–89
Cle. Indians (AL), 1999–2000
Chi. White Sox (AL), 2003–04

Arthur and John Irwin ..... Worc. Brown Stockings (NL), 1882
Wash. Statesmen (NL), 1889
Bost. Reds (AA), 1891

Paul and Lloyd Waner ..... Pitt. Pirates (NL), 1927–40
Bost. Braves (NL), 1941
Bklyn. Dodgers (NL), 1944

8

WORLD SERIES

Teams Never to Trail in a World Series

1963 ..... L.A. Dodgers (NL) vs. N.Y. Yankees (AL)
1966 ..... Balt. Orioles (AL) vs. L.A. Dodgers (NL)
1989 ..... Oak. A's (AL) vs. S.F. Giants (NL)
2004 ..... Bost. Red Sox (AL) vs. St.L. Cardinals (NL)

Highest Batting Average for a World Series Team

American League

Batting Average	
.338	N.Y. Yankees, 1960*
.333	Bost. Red Sox, 2007
.316	Phila. A's, 1910
.313	N.Y. Yankees, 1932
.311	Tor. Blue Jays, 1993
.310	Ana. Angels, 2002
.309	N.Y. Yankees, 1998
.302	N.Y. Yankees, 1936
.309	Oak. A's, 1989

*Lost World Series.

National League

Batting Average	
.323	Pitt. Pirates, 1979
.317	Cin. Reds, 1990
.309	N.Y. Giants, 1922
.300	Bklyn. Dodgers, 1953

Lowest Batting Average for a World Series Team

American League

Batting Average	
.146	Balt. Orioles, 1969
.149	Det. Tigers, 2006
.161	Phila. A's, 1905
.172	Phila. A's, 1914
.177	Oak. A's, 1988
.179	Cle. Indians, 1995
.183	St.L. Browns, 1944
.183	N.Y. Yankees, 2001
.186	Bost. Red Sox, 1918*
.190	Cle. Indians, 1954
.190	Tex. Rangers, 2010
.197	Phila. A's, 1930*
.198	Chi. White Sox, 1906*
.199	Cle. Indians, 1948*
.199	N.Y. Yankees, 1962*

*Won World Series.

National League

Batting Average	
.142	L.A. Dodgers, 1966
.175	N.Y. Giants, 1911
.182	Phila. Phillies, 1915
.182	Bklyn. Dodgers, 1941
.185	St.L. Cardinals, 1985
.190	St.L. Cardinals, 2004
.193	N.Y. Mets, 2015
.195	Bklyn. Dodgers, 1956
.195	Phila. Phillies, 1983
.196	Chi. Cubs, 1906

Most Regular Season Losses, Reaching World Series

American League

Losses	
77	1987 Min. Twins* (Record: 85–77)
75	1997 Cle. Indians (Record: 86–75)
74	2000 N.Y. Yankees* (Record: 87–74)
74	2012 Det. Tigers (Record:88–74)
73	2014 K.C. Royals (Record: 89–73)
72	1974 Oak. A's* (Record: 90–72)
72	2010 Tex. Rangers (Record: 90–72)
71	1985 K.C. Royals* (Record: 91–71)
70	1967 Bost. Red Sox (Record: 92–70)
70	1996 N.Y. Yankees* (Record: 92–70)
68	1973 Oak. A's* (Record: 94–68)
67	1982 Milw. Brewers (Record: 95–67)
67	1991 Min. Twins* (Record: 95–67)
67	1993 Tor. Blue Jays* (Record: 95–67)

National League

Losses	
79	1973 N.Y. Mets (Record: 82–79)
78	2006 St.L. Cardinals* (Record: 83–78)
74	2014 S.F. Giants* (Record: 88–74)
73	2005 Hous. Astros (Record: 89–73)
73	2007 Colo. Rockies (Record: 90–73)
72	1983 Phila. Phillies* (Record: 90–72)
72	2011 St.L. Cardinals* (Record: 90–72)
71	1980 Phila. Phillies* (Record: 91–71)
71	1990 Cin. Reds* (Record: 91–71)
71	2003 Fla. Marlins* (Record: 91–71)
70	1982 St.L. Cardinals* (Record: 92–70)
70	1984 S.D. Padres (Record: 92–70)
70	1989 S.F. Giants (Record: 92–70)
70	1997 Fla. Marlins* (Record: 92–70)
70	2001 Ariz. D'backs* (Record: 92–70)
70	2008 Phila. Phillies* (Record 92–70)
70	2010 S.F. Giants* (Record: 92–70)
69	1964 St.L. Cardinals (Record: 93–69)
69	2009 Phila. Phillies (Record: 93–69)
68	1959 L.A. Dodgers* (Record: 88–68)
68	1991 Atl. Braves (Record: 94–68)
68	2000 N.Y. Mets (Record: 94–68)
68	2012 S.F. Giants* (Record: 94–68)
67	1966 L.A. Dodgers (Record: 95–67)
67	1978 L.A. Dodgers (Record: 95–67)
67	1987 St.L. Cardinals (Record: 95–67)
67	1988 L.A. Dodgers* (Record: 95–67)

*Won World Series

Teams Winning World Series a Year After Finishing with a Losing Record

Team	WS-Winning Season	Losing Season
Bost. Braves (NL)	1914 (94–59)	1913 (69–82)
Wash. Senators (AL)	1924 (92–62)	1923 (75–78)
N.Y. Giants (NL)	1954 (97–57)	1953 (70–84)
L.A. Dodgers (NL)	1959 (88–68)	1958 (71–83)
L.A. Dodgers (NL)	1965 (97–65)	1964 (80–82)
N.Y. Mets (NL)	1969 (100–62)	1968 (73–89)
Min. Twins (AL)	1987 (85–77)	1986 (71–91)
L.A. Dodgers (NL)	1988 (94–67)	1987 (73–89)
Cin. Reds (NL)	1990 (91–71)	1989 (75–87)
Min. Twins (AL)	1991 (95–67)	1990 (74–88)*
Ana. Angels (AL)	2002 (99–63)	2001 (75–87)
Fla. Marlins (NL)	2003 (91–71)	2002 (79–83)
Bost. Red Sox (AL)	2013 (97–65)	2012 (69–93)*
S.F. Giants (NL)	2014 (88–74)	2013 (76–86)

*Finished in last place.

Players Hitting .500 in World Series (Min. 10 At Bats)

Billy Hatcher, Cin. Reds (NL), 1990	9-for-12	.750
David Ortiz, Bost. Red Sox (AL), 2013	11-for-16	.688
Babe Ruth, N.Y. Yankees (AL), 1928	10-for-16	.625
Hideki Matsui, N.Y. Yankees (AL), 2009	8-for-13	.615
Ricky Ledee, N.Y. Yankees (AL), 1998	6-for-10	.600

continued on next page

Chris Sabo, Cin. Reds (NL), 1990	9-for-16	.563
Hank Gowdy, Bost. Braves (NL), 1914	6-for-11	.545
Lou Gehrig, N.Y. Yankees (AL), 1928	6-for-11	.545
Bret Boone*, Atl. Braves (NL), 1999	7-for-13	.538
Johnny Bench, Cin. Reds (NL), 1976	8-for-15	.533
Lou Gehrig, N.Y. Yankees (AL), 1932	9-for-17	.529
Thurman Munson*, N.Y. Yankees (AL), 1976	9-for-17	.529
Dane Iorg, St.L. Cardinals (NL), 1982	9-for-17	.529
Larry McLean, N.Y. Giants (NL), 1913	6-for-12	.500
Dave Robertson, N.Y. Giants (NL), 1917	11-for-22	.500
Mark Koenig, N.Y. Yankees (AL), 1927	9-for-18	.500
Pepper Martin, St.L. Cardinals (NL), 1931	12-for-24	.500
Joe Gordon, N.Y. Yankees (AL), 1941	7-for-14	.500
Billy Martin, N.Y. Yankees (AL), 1953	12-for-24	.500
Vic Wertz*, Cle. Indians (AL), 1954	8-for-16	.500
Phil Garner, Pitt. Pirates (NL), 1979	12-for-24	.500
Paul Molitor, Tor. Blue Jays (AL), 1993	12-for-24	.500
Tony Gwynn*, S.D. Padres (NL), 1998	8-for-16	.500
Pablo Sandoval, S.F. Giants (NL), 2012	8-for-16	.500

*Member of losing team.

0-for-the Series (10 or More At Bats)

Dal Maxvill, St.L. Cardinals (NL), 1968	0-for-22
Jimmy Sheckard, Chi. Cubs (NL), 1906	0-for-21
Billy Sullivan, Chi. White Sox (AL), 1906	0-for-21
Red Murray, N.Y. Giants (NL), 1911	0-for-21
Gil Hodges, Bklyn. Dodgers (NL), 1952	0-for-21
Lonny Frey, Cin. Reds (NL), 1939	0-for-17
Flea Clifton, Det. Tigers (AL), 1935	0-for-16
Mike Epstein, Oak. A's (AL), 1972	0-for-16
Rafael Belliard, Atl. Braves (NL), 1995	0-for-16
Bill Dahlen, N.Y. Giants (NL), 1905	0-for-15
Wally Berger, Cin. Reds (NL), 1939	0-for-15
Scott Rolen, St.L. Cardinals (NL), 2004	0-for-15
Hal Wagner, Bost. Red Sox (AL), 1946	0-for-13
Dick Green, Oak. A's (AL), 1974	0-for-13
Pat Burrell, S.F. Giants (NL), 2010	0-for-13
Carl Reynolds, Chi. Cubs (NL), 1938	0-for-12
Joe Collins, N.Y. Yankees (AL), 1952	0-for-12
Barbaro Garbey, Det. Tigers (AL), 1984	0-for-12
Birdie Tebbetts, Det. Tigers (AL), 1940	0-for-11
Davey Williams, N.Y. Giants (NL), 1954	0-for-11
Jim Rivera, Chi. White Sox (AL), 1959	0-for-11
Roy Howell, Milw. Brewers (AL), 1982	0-for-11
Hippo Vaughn, Chi. Cubs (NL), 1918	0-for-10
Lefty Grove, Phila. A's (AL), 1931	0-for-10
Felix Mantilla, Milw. Braves (NL), 1957	0-for-10
Jim Leyritz, S.D. Padres (NL), 1998	0-for-10
Pete Kozma, St.L. Cardinals (NL), 2013	0-for-10

Players on World Series–Winning Teams in Both Leagues

American League	National League
Rick Aguilera ... Min. Twins, 1991	N.Y. Mets, 1986
Doug Bair ... Det. Tigers, 1984	St.L. Cardinals, 1982
Josh Beckett ... Bost. Red Sox, 2007	Fla. Marlins, 2003
Joe Blanton ... K.C. Royals, 2015	Phila. Phillies, 2008
Bert Blyleven ... Min. Twins, 1987	Pitt. Pirates, 1979
A.J. Burnett ... N.Y. Yankees, 2009	Fla. Marlins, 2003*
Terry Crowley ... Balt. Orioles, 1970	Cin. Reds, 1975
Mike Cuellar ... Balt. Orioles, 1970	St.L. Cardinals, 1964*
Vic Davalillo ... Oak. A's, 1973	Pitt. Pirates, 1971
Murry Dickson ... N.Y. Yankees, 1958	St.L. Cardinals, 1942 and 1946
Mariano Duncan ... N.Y. Yankees, 1996	Cin. Reds, 1990
Leo Durocher ... N.Y. Yankees, 1928	St.L. Cardinals, 1934
David Eckstein ... Ana. Angels, 2002	St.L. Cardinals, 2006
Lonny Frey ... N.Y. Yankees, 1947	Cin. Reds, 1940
Billy Gardner ... N.Y. Yankees, 1961	N.Y. Giants, 1954*
Kirk Gibson ... Det. Tigers, 1984	L.A. Dodgers, 1988
Dwight Gooden ... N.Y. Yankees, 1996*	N.Y. Mets, 1986
Alfredo Griffin ... Tor. Blue Jays, 1992–93	L.A. Dodgers, 1988
Don Gullett ... N.Y. Yankees, 1977	Cin. Reds, 1975–76

continued on next page

Mule Haas	Phila. A's, 1929–30	Pitt. Pirates, 1925*
Johnny Hopp	N.Y. Yankees, 1950–51	St.L. Cardinals, 1942 and 1944
Dane Iorg	K.C. Royals, 1985	St.L. Cardinals, 1982
Danny Jackson	K.C. Royals, 1985	Cin. Reds, 1990
Howard Johnson	Det. Tigers, 1984	N.Y. Mets, 1986
Jay Johnstone	N.Y. Yankees, 1978	L.A. Dodgers, 1981
David Justice	N.Y. Yankees, 2000	Atl. Braves, 1995
Byung-Hyun Kim	Bost. Red Sox, 2004*	Ariz. D'backs, 2001
Al Leiter	Tor. Blue Jays, 1993	Fla. Marlins, 1997
Javier Lopez	Bost. Red Sox, 2007	S.F. Giants, 2010, 2012* and 2014
Mike Lowell	Bost. Red Sox, 2007	Fla. Marlins, 2003
Ryan Madsen	K.C. Royals, 2015	Phila. Phillies, 2008
Roger Maris	N.Y. Yankees, 1960–61	St.L. Cardinals, 1967
Eddie Mathews	Det. Tigers, 1968	Milw. Braves, 1957
Dal Maxvill	Oak. A's, 1972* and 1974	St.L. Cardinals, 1964 and 1967
Stuffy McInnis	Phila. A's, 1911 and 1913, and Bost. Red Sox, 1918	Pitt. Pirates, 1925
Don McMahon	Det. Tigers, 1968	Milw. Braves, 1957
Paul O'Neill	N.Y. Yankees, 1996 and 1998–2000	Cin. Reds, 1990
Dave Parker	Pitt. Pirates, 1979	Oak. A's, 1989
Paul Richards	Det. Tigers, 1945	N.Y. Giants, 1933*
Dutch Ruether	N.Y. Yankees, 1927*	Cin. Reds, 1919
Rosy Ryan	N.Y. Yankees, 1928*	N.Y. Giants, 1921* and 1923
Curt Schilling	Bost. Red Sox, 2004 and 2007	Ariz. D'backs, 2001
John Shelby	Balt. Orioles, 1983	L.A. Dodgers, 1988
Bill Skowron	N.Y. Yankees, 1956, 1958, and 1961–62	L.A. Dodgers, 1963
Enos Slaughter	N.Y. Yankees, 1956 and 1958	St.L. Cardinals, 1942 and 1944
Lonnie Smith	K.C. Royals, 1985	Phila. Phillies, 1980, and St.L. Cardinals, 1982
Scott Spiezio	Ana. Angels, 2002	St.L. Cardinals, 2006
Dave Stewart	Oak. A's, 1989	L.A. Dodgers, 1981
Darryl Strawberry	N.Y. Yankees, 1996 and 1999*	N.Y. Mets, 1986
Gene Tenace	Oak. A's, 1972–74	St.L. Cardinals, 1982
Dick Tracewski	Det. Tigers, 1968	L.A. Dodgers, 1963 and 1965
Juan Uribe	Chi. White Sox, 2005	S.F. Giants, 2010
Bob Welch	Oak. A's, 1989	L.A. Dodgers, 1981
Devon White	Tor. Blue Jays, 1992–93	Fla. Marlins, 1997

*Did not play.

Pitchers in World Series with Highest Slugging Percentage

Slugging %	Pitcher	Games	At Bats	Hits	Doubles	Triples	Home Runs	Batting Avg.
1.667	Orel Hershiser	2	3	3	2	0	0	1.000
.833	Ken Holtzman	8	12	4	3	0	1	.333
.800	Joe Blanton	2	7	1	0	0	1	.200
.818	Dutch Ruether	7	11	4	1	2	0	.364
.777	Pop Haines	6	9	4	0	0	2	.444
.750	Jack Bentley	10	12	5	1	0	1	.417
.667	Mike Moore	2	3	1	1	0	0	.333
.500	Dave McNally	9	16	2	0	0	2	.125
.467	Dizzy Dean	6	15	5	2	0	0	.333
.375	Jack Coombs	6	24	8	1	0	0	.333
.375	Johnny Podres	7	16	5	1	0	0	.313
.357	Bob Gibson	9	28	4	0	0	2	.143
.346	Allie Reynolds	15	26	8	1	0	0	.308
.316	Burleigh Grimes	9	19	6	0	0	0	.316

World Series–Ending Hits

1912..... Bost. Red Sox (AL) Larry Gardner hits a deep sacrifice drive to N.Y. Giant (NL) right fielder Josh Devore to score Boston second baseman Steve Yerkes with the winning run in the eighth game of the Series (one had ended in a tie) as Boston scored two in the bottom of the 10th inning for a comeback 3–2 win to win Series 4 games to 3.

1924..... Earl McNeeley's single over Freddie Lindstrom's head in the 12th inning of Game 7 drives in Muddy Ruel with the winning run as the Wash. Senators (AL) beat the N.Y. Giants (NL), 4 games to 3.

1929..... Bing Miller's double in the 9th inning of Game 5 drives in Al Simmons with the winning run as the Phila. A's (AL) beat the Chi. Cubs (NL), 4 games to 1.

1935..... Goose Goslin's single in the ninth inning drives in Charlie Gehringer with the winning run as the Det. Tigers (AL) beat the Chi. Cubs (NL), 4 games to 2.

1953..... Billy Martin's 12th hit of the Series, a single, drives in Hank Bauer with the winning run as the N.Y. Yankees (AL) beat the Bklyn. Dodgers (NL), 4 games to 2.

1960..... Bill Mazeroski's lead-off home run in the bottom of the 9th inning of Game 7 wins the Series for the Pittsburgh Pirates (NL) over the N.Y. Yankees (AL), 4 games to 3.

1993..... Joe Carter's bottom-of-the-ninth home run off pitcher Mitch Williams with Rickey Henderson and Paul Molitor aboard gives the Tor. Blue Jays (AL) an 8–6 victory over the Phila. Phillies (NL) (and their second straight World Championship), 4 games to 2.

1997..... Edgar Renteria's ground-ball single up the middle scored Craig Counsell as the Fla. Marlins (NL) rallied with two in the 9th inning against the Cle. Indians (AL) to win Game 7, 3–2.

2001..... Luis Gonzalez's bloop single over a drawn-in N.Y. Yankees (AL) infield in the bottom of the 9th inning of Game 7 wins the Series for the Ariz. D'backs (NL), 4 games to 3.

Pitchers in World Series with 300 Career Wins

	Wins
Cy Young, Bost. Red Sox (AL), 1903	379
Christy Mathewson, N.Y. Giants (NL), 1912	312
Christy Mathewson, N.Y. Giants (NL), 1913	337
Walter Johnson, Wash. Senators (AL), 1924	377
Walter Johnson, Wash. Senators (AL), 1925	397
Grover C. Alexander, St.L. Cardinals (NL), 1926	327
Grover C. Alexander, St.L. Cardinals (NL), 1928	364
Steve Carlton, Phila. Phillies (NL), 1983	300
Roger Clemens, N.Y. Yankees (AL), 2003	310
Hous. Astros (NL), 2005	341

Players on World Series Teams in Three Decades

Yogi Berra	N.Y. Yankees (AL)	1947 and 1949
	N.Y. Yankees (AL)	1950–53 and 1955–58
	N.Y. Yankees (AL)	1960–61 and 1963
Roger Clemens	Bost. Red Sox (AL)	1986
	N.Y. Yankees (AL)	1999
	N.Y. Yankees (AL)	2000–01, 2003
	Hous. Astros (NL)	2005
Bill Dickey	N.Y. Yankees (AL)	1928*
	N.Y. Yankees (AL)	1932 and 1936–39
	N.Y. Yankees (AL)	1941–43
Joe DiMaggio	N.Y. Yankees (AL)	1936–39
	N.Y. Yankees (AL)	1941–42, 1947, and 1949
	N.Y. Yankees (AL)	1950–51
Leo Durocher	N.Y. Yankees (AL)	1928
	St.L. Cardinals (NL)	1934
	Bklyn. Dodgers (NL)	1941*
Willie Mays	N.Y. Giants (NL)	1951 and 1954
	S.F. Giants (NL)	1962
	N.Y. Mets (NL)	1973
Tug McGraw	N.Y. Mets (NL)	1969*
	N.Y. Mets (NL)	1973
	Phila. Phillies (NL)	1980
Jim Palmer	Balt. Orioles (AL)	1966 and 1969
	Balt. Orioles (AL)	1970–71 and 1979
	Balt. Orioles (AL)	1983

continued on next page

Herb Pennock	Phila. A's (AL)	1913* and 1914
	N.Y. Yankees (AL)	1923 and 1926–28*
	N.Y. Yankees (AL)	1932
Billy Pierce	Det. Tigers (AL)	1945*
	Chi. White Sox (AL)	1959
	S.F. Giants (NL)	1962
Babe Ruth	Bost. Red Sox (AL)	1915–16 and 1918
	N.Y. Yankees (AL)	1921–23 and 1926–28
	N.Y. Yankees (AL)	1932
Wally Schang	Phila. A's (AL); and Bost. Red Sox (AL)	1913–14 and 1918
	N.Y. Yankees (AL)	1921–23
	Phila. A's (AL)	1930*
Bob Welch	L.A. Dodgers (NL)	1978
	L.A. Dodgers (NL)	1981
	Oak. A's (AL)	1990
Matt Williams	S.F. Giants (NL)	1989
	Cle. Indians (AL)	1997
	Ariz. D'backs (NL)	2001
Jimmy Wilson	St.L. Cardinals (NL)	1928
	St.L. Cardinals (NL)	1930–31
	Cin. Reds (NL)	1940

*Did not play.

Players with World Series Home Runs in Three Decades

Yogi Berra	N.Y. Yankees (AL)	1947
	N.Y. Yankees (AL)	1950, 1952–53, and 1955–57
	N.Y. Yankees (AL)	1960–61
Joe DiMaggio	N.Y. Yankees (AL)	1937–39
	N.Y. Yankees (AL)	1947 and 1949
	N.Y. Yankees (AL)	1950–51
Matt Williams	S.F. Giants (NL)	1989
	Cle. Indians (AL)	1997
	Ariz. D'backs (NL)	2001
Eddie Murray	Balt. Orioles (AL)	1979
	Balt. Orioles (AL)	1983
	Cle. Indians (AL)	1995

Player-Managers on World Series-Winning Teams

Jimmy Collins	Bost. Red Sox (AL), 1903
John McGraw	N.Y. Giants (NL), 1905
Fielder Jones	Chi. White Sox (AL), 1906
Frank Chance	Chi. Cubs (NL), 1907, 1908
Fred Clarke	Pitt. Pirates (NL), 1909
Jake Stahl	Bost. Red Sox (AL), 1912
John Carrigan	Bost. Red Sox (AL), 1915, 1916
Tris Speaker	Cle. Indians (AL), 1920
Bucky Harris	Wash. Senators (AL), 1924
Rogers Hornsby	St.L. Cardinals (NL), 1926
Gabby Street	St.L. Cardinals (NL), 1931
Bill Terry	N.Y. Giants (NL), 1933
Frankie Frisch	St.L. Cardinals (NL), 1934
Mickey Cochrane	Det. Tigers (NL), 1935
Lou Boudreau	Cle. Indians (AL), 1948

World Series-Winning Managers Who Never Played in Majors

Ed Barrow	Bost. Red Sox (AL)	1918
Johnny Keane	St.L. Cardinals (NL)	1964
Jim Leyland	Fla. Marlins (NL)	1997
Joe McCarthy	N.Y. Yankees (AL)	1932, 1936, 1937, 1938, 1939, 1941, and 1943
Jack McKeon	Fla. Marlins (NL)	2003
Pants Rowland	Chi. White Sox (AL)	1917
Earl Weaver	Balt. Orioles (AL)	1966 and 1970

Leaders in Offensive Categories, Never Appearing in World Series (Post-1903)

Games	Rafael Palmeiro	2831
Base Hits	Rod Carew	3053
Runs	Rafael Palmeiro	1663
Singles	Rod Carew	2404
Doubles	Rafael Palmeiro	585
Triples	George Sisler	164
Home Runs	Ken Griffey Jr.	630
Grand Slams	Carlos Lee	17
Pinch-Hit Home Runs	Dave Hansen	15
Total Bases	Rafael Palmeiro	5388
Extra-Base Hits	Rafael Palmeiro	1192
	Ken Griffery Jr.	1192
RBIs	Ken Griffey Jr.	1836
Walks	Frank Thomas	1667
Strikeouts	Adam Dunn	2379
Slugging Average (Min. 4000 Total Bases)	Frank Thomas	.555
Batting Average (Min. 10 Seasons)	Lefty O'Doul	.349
.300 Seasons	Luke Appling	13
Stolen Bases	Ichiro Suzuki*	498

*Still active.

Most Seasons, Never Appearing in World Series (Post-1903)

24 .....Phil Niekro, pitcher (1964–87)
23 ..... Julio Franco, first base (1982–94, 1996–97,1999, 2001–07)
22 ..... Harold Baines, outfield and designated hitter (1980–2001)
22 ..... Gaylord Perry, pitcher (1962–83)
21 ..... Tom Gordon, pitcher (1988–1999, 2001–09)
22 ..... Ken Griffey Jr., outfield (1989–2010)
21 ..... Ted Lyons, pitcher (1923–42, 1946)
21 ..... Lindy McDaniel, pitcher (1955–75)
21 ..... Danny Darwin, pitcher (1978–98)
21 ..... Frank Tanana, pitcher (1973–93)
20 ..... Johnny Cooney, outfield (1921–30, 1935–44)
20 ..... Mel Harder, pitcher (1928–47)
20 ..... Luke Appling, shortstop (1930–43, 1945–50)
20 ..... Dutch Leonard, pitcher (1933–36, 1938–53)
20.....Mickey Vernon, first base (1939–43, 1946–60)
20.....Elmer Valo, outfield (1940–43, 1946–61)
20.....Brian Downing, outfielder (1973–92)
20.....Rafael Palmeiro, first base (1986–2005)
19.....Cy Williams, outfield (1912–30)
19.....Rube Bressler, outfield and pitcher (1914–32)
19.....Al Lopez, catcher (1928, 1930–47)
19.....Ernie Banks, shortstop and first base (1953–71)
19.....Tony Taylor, second base (1958–76)
19.....Ferguson Jenkins, pitcher (1965–83)
19.....Rod Carew, infield (1967–85)
19.....Gene Garber, pitcher (1969–70, 1972–88)
19.....Jose Cruz, outfield (1970–88)
19.....Torii Hunter, outfield (1997–2015)
19.....Mark McLemore, infield and outfield (1986–2004)
19.....Chris Speier, infield (1971–89)
19.....Andres Galarraga, first base (1985–2004)
19.....B.J. Surhoff, infield (1987–2005)
19.....Frank Thomas, first base (1990–2008)

Playing Most Games, Never Appearing in World Series (Post-1903)

Rafael Palmeiro (1986–2005)..... 2831
Ken Griffey Jr. (1989–2010) 2671
Andre Dawson (1976–86)..... 2627
Ernie Banks (1953–71) 2528
Julio Franco (1982–94, 1996–97, 1999, 2001–07).. 2527
Billy Williams (1959–76) 2488
Rod Carew (1967–85) 2469
Bobby Abreu (1996–2012, 2014)..... 2425
Luke Appling (1930–43, 1945–50)..... 2422
Mickey Vernon (1939–43, 1946–60)..... 2409
Buddy Bell (1972–89) 2405

Players with the Most Home Runs, Never Appearing in World Series

Ken Griffey Jr. (1989–2010) 630
Sammy Sosa (1989–2005, 2007)..... 609
Rafael Palmeiro (1986–2005)..... 569
Frank Thomas (1990–2008) 521
Ernie Banks (1953–71) 512
Carlos Delgado (1993–2009)..... 473
Adam Dunn (2001–2014) 462
Dave Kingman (1971–86)..... 442
Andre Dawson (1976–96)..... 438
Juan Gonzalez (1990–2005)..... 434

continued on next page

Billy Williams (1959–76)	426
Andres Galarraga (1985–2004)	399
Dale Murphy (1976–93)	398
Aramis Ramirez (1998–2015)	386
Harold Baines (1980–2000)	384
Rocky Colavito (1955–68)	374
Ralph Kiner (1946–55)	369
Ellis Burks (1987–2004)	352
Dick Allen (1963–77)	351
Ron Santo (1960–74)	342
Bobby Bonds (1968–81)	332

Players with Highest Lifetime Batting Average, Never Appearing in World Series (Post-1903; Min. 10 Seasons)

Harry Heilmann (1914, 1916–30, 1932)	.342
George Sisler (1915–22, 1924–30)	.340
Nap Lajoie (1903–16)	.328
Rod Carew (1967–85)	.328
Fats Fothergill (1922–33)	.325
Babe Herman (1926–37, 1945)	.324
Ken Williams (1915–29)	.319
Bibb Falk (1920–31)	.314
Ichiro Suzuki* (2001–)	.314
Cecil Travis (1933–41, 1945–47)	.314
Jack Fournier (1912–18, 1920–27)	.313
Joe Mauer* (2004–)	.313
Edgar Martinez (1987–2004)	.312
Nomar Garciaparra (1996–2009)	.313
Baby Doll Jacobson (1915, 1917, 1919–27)	.311
Rip Radcliff (1934–43)	.311

*Still active.

Players with Most Hits, Never Appearing in World Series (Post-1903)

Rod Carew (1967–85)	3053
Rafael Palmeiro (1986–2005)	3020
Ichiro Suzuki* (2001–)	2935
Harold Baihes (1980–2001)	2866
George Sisler (1915–22, 1924–30)	2812
Ken Griffey Jr. (1989–2010)	2781
Andre Dawson (1976–96)	2774
Luke Appling (1930–43, 1945–50)	2749
Al Oliver (1968–85)	2743
Billy Williams (1959–76)	2711
Harry Heilmann (1914, 1916–30, 1932)	2660
Julio Franco (1982–94, 1996–97, 1999, 2001–07)	2586
Ernie Banks (1953–71)	2583
Buddy Bell (1972–89)	2514
Mickey Vernon (1939–43, 1946–60)	2495
Bobby Abreu (1996–2012, 2014)	2470
Frank Thomas (1990–2008)	2468
Torii Hunter (1997–2015))	2452
Sammy Sosa (1989–2007)	2408
Miguel Tejada (1997–2011, 2013)	2407
Ryne Sandberg (1981–97)	2386
Brett Butler (1981–97)	2375
Joe Torre (1960–77)	2342
Andres Galarraga (1985–2004)	2333

*Still active.

Leaders in Pitching Categories, Never Pitching in World Series (Post-1903)

Victories	Phil Niekro (1964–87)	318
Games Pitched	Dan Plesac (1986–2003)	1064
Games Started	Phil Niekro (1964–87)	716
Complete Games	Ted Lyons (1923–42, 1946)	356
Innings Pitched	Phil Niekro (1964–87)	5404
ERA (Min. 2000 Innings)	Addie Joss (1903–10)	1.89
Hits Allowed	Phil Niekro (1964–87)	5044
Runs Allowed	Phil Niekro (1964–87)	2337
Losses	Phil Niekro (1964–87)	274
Grand Slams Allowed	Ned Garver (1948–61)	9
	Milt Pappas (1957–73)	9
	Tom Gordon (1988–99, 2001–09)	9
	Lee Smith (1980–97)	9

continued on next page

20-Win Seasons	Ferguson Jenkins (1965–83)	7
Saves	Lee Smith (1980–97)	478
Shutouts	Gaylord Perry (1962–83)	53
Walks	Phil Niekro (1964–87)	1809
Strikeouts	Gaylord Perry (1962–83)	3534

Pitchers with Most Wins, Never Appearing in World Series (Post-1903)

Phil Niekro (1964–87)	318
Gaylord Perry (1961–83)	314
Ferguson Jenkins (1965–83)	284
Ted Lyons (1923–42, 1946)	260
Frank Tanana (1973–93)	240
Jim Bunning (1955–71)	224
Mel Harder (1928–47)	223
Hooks Dauss (1912–26)	223
Joe Niekro (1967–88)	221
Jerry Reuss (1969–90)	220
Wilbur Cooper (1912–26)	216
Jim Perry (1959–75)	215
Milt Pappas (1957–73)	209
George Uhle (1919–34, 1936)	200
Chuck Finley (1986–2003)	200

Pitchers with World Series Wins in Both Leagues

Hank Borowy	N.Y. Yankees (AL), 1943; Chi. Cubs (NL), 1945
Jack Coombs	Phila. A's (AL), 1910, 1911; Bklyn. Robins (NL), 1916
Don Larsen	N.Y. Yankees (AL), 1956, 1957, 1958; S.F. Giants (NL), 1962
Johnny Sain	Bost. Braves (NL), 1948; N.Y. Yankees (AL), 1953
Curt Schilling	Phila. Phillies (NL), 1993; Ariz. D'backs (NL), 2001; Bost. Red Sox (AL), 2004
Josh Beckett	Fla. Marlins (NL), 2003; Bost. Red Sox (AL), 2007

Pitchers with World Series Losses in Both Leagues

Al Downing	N.Y. Yankees (AL), 1963, 1964; L.A. Dodgers (NL), 1974
Dock Ellis	Pitt. Pirates (NL), 1971; N.Y. Yankees (AL), 1976
Don Gullett	Cin. Reds (NL), 1975; N.Y. Yankees (AL), 1976–77
Pat Malone	Chi. Cubs (NL), 1929; N.Y. Yankees (AL), 1936
Johnny Sain	Bost. Braves (NL), 1948; N.Y. Yankees (AL), 1952

Players Whose Home Run Won World Series Game 1–0

Casey Stengel, N.Y. Giants (NL), 1923, Game 3, 7th inning, off Sam Jones, N.Y. Yankees (AL)
Tommy Henrich, N.Y. Yankees (AL), 1949, Game 1, 9th inning, off Don Newcombe, Bklyn. Dodgers (NL)
Paul Blair, Balt. Orioles (AL), 1966, Game 3, 5th inning, off Claude Osteen, L.A. Dodgers (NL)
Frank Robinson, Balt. Orioles (AL), 1966, Game 4 (final game), 4th inning, off Don Drysdale, L.A. Dodgers (NL)
David Justice, Atl. Braves (NL), 1995, Game 6 (final game), 6th inning, off Jim Poole, Cle. Indians (AL)

Brothers Who Were World Series Teammates

Felipe Alou, outfield, and Matty Alou, outfield, S.F. Giants (NL), 1962
Jesse Barnes, pitcher, and Virgil Barnes, pitcher, N.Y. Giants (NL), 1922
George Brett, third base, and Ken Brett, pitcher, K.C. Royals (AL), 1980
Mort Cooper, pitcher, and Walker Cooper, catcher, St.L. Cardinals (NL), 1942–44
Dizzy Dean, pitcher, and Paul Dean, pitcher, St.L. Cardinals (NL), 1934
Lloyd Waner, outfield, and Paul Waner, outfield, Pitt. Pirates (NL), 1927

Brothers Facing Each Other in World Series

Clete Boyer, third base, N.Y. Yankees (AL), and Ken Boyer, third base, St.L. Cardinals (NL), 1964
Doc Johnston, first base, Cle. Indians (AL), and Jimmy Johnston, third base, Bklyn. Dodgers (NL), 1920
Bob Meusel, outfield, N.Y. Yankees (AL), and Irish Meusel, outfield, N.Y. Giants (NL), 1921–23

Fathers and Sons in World Series Competition

Father	Son
Felipe Alou, outfielder, S.F. Giants (NL), 1962	Moises Alou, outfielder, Fla. Marlins (NL), 1997
Jim Bagby Sr., pitcher, Cle. Indians (AL), 1920	Jim Bagby Jr., pitcher, Bost. Red Sox (AL), 1946
Pedro Borbon, pitcher, Cin. Reds (NL), 1972, 1975–76	Pedro Borbon Jr., pithcer, Atl. Braves (NL), 1995
Ray Boone, pinch hitter, Cle. Indians (AL), 1948	Bob Boone, catcher, Phila. Phillies (NL), 1980
Bob Boone, catcher, Phila. Phillies (NL), 1980	Aaron Boone, third base, N.Y. Yankees (AL), 2003
Cecil Fielder, first base and designated hitter, N.Y. Yankees (AL), 1996	Prince Fielder, first base, Det. Tigers (AL), 2012
Dave Duncan, Catcher, Oak. A's (AL), 1972	Chris Duncan, outfielder, St.L. Cardinals (NL), 2006
Jim Hegan, catcher, Cle. Indians (AL), 1948 and 1954	Mike Hegan, pinch hitter and first base, N.Y. Yankees (AL), 1964, and Oak. A's (AL), 1972
Julian Javier, second base and pinch hitter, St.L. Cardinals (NL), 1964, 1967–68, Cin,. Reds (NL), 1972	Stan Javier, outfielder and pinch runner, Oak. A's (1988–89)
Ernie Johnson, shortstop, N.Y. Yankees (AL), 1923	Don Johnson, second base, Chi. Cubs (NL), 1945
Bob Kennedy, outfield, Cle. Indians (AL), 1948	Terry Kennedy, catcher, S.D. Padres (NL), 1984
Mel Stottlemyre, pitcher, N.Y. Yankees (AL), 1964	Todd Stottlemyre, pithcer, Tor. Blue Jays (AL), 1992–93
Ed Spiezio, infielder, St.L. Cardinals, 1967–68	Scott Spiezio, infielder, Ana. Angels (AL) 2002, St.L. Cardinals (NL), 2006
Billy Sullivan Sr., catcher, Chi. White Sox (AL), 1906	Billy Sullivan Jr., catcher, Det. Tigers (AL), 1940

Batting Average of .400 Hitters in World Series Play

.345... Joe Jackson, 1919 World Series, Chi. White Sox ..... .408 in 1910
.295... Bill Terry, 1924, 1933, and 1934 World Series, N.Y. Giants ..... .401 in 1930
.262... Ty Cobb, 1907, 1908 and 1909 World Series, Det. Tigers ..... .420 in 1911, .410 in 1912, .401 in 1922
.245... Rogers Hornsby, 1926 World Series, St.L. Cardinals, 1929 World Series Chi. Cubs ..... .401 in 1922, .424 in 1924, .403 in 1925
.200... Ted Williams, 1946 World Series, Bost. Red Sox ..... .406 in 1941

Batting Averages of .400 in World Series Play

Career Leaders

	BA	PA
Phil Garner	.500	28
Amos Otis	.478	26
Barry Bonds	.471	30
David Ortiz	.455	59
Max Carey	.458	31
Bobby Brown	.439	46
Jake Powell	.435	27
Pablo Sandoval	.426	50
Marty Barrett	.433	35
Paul Molitor	.418	61
Pepper Martin	.418	60

Single-Season Leaders

	BA	PA	Series/Year
Billy Hatcher	.750	15	1990 World Series
David Ortiz	.688	25	2013 World Series
Babe Ruth	.625	17	1928 World Series
Hideki Matsui	.615	14	2009 World Series
Ricky Ledee	.600	13	1998 World Series
Danny Bautista	.583	13	2001 World Series
Ivey Wingo	.571	11	1919 World Series
Chris Sabo	.562	18	1990 World Series
Lou Gehrig	.545	17	1928 World Series
Hank Gowdy	.545	16	1914 World Series

Players Hitting World Series Home Runs in Each League

American League	National League
Miguel Cabrera ..... Det. Tigers, 2012	Fla. Marlins, 2003
Kirk Gibson ..... Det. Tigers, 1984	L.A. Dodgers, 1988
Roger Maris ..... N.Y. Yankees, 1960–62 and 1964	St.L. Cardinals, 1967
Frank Robinson ..... Balt. Orioles, 1966 and 1969–71	Cin. Reds, 1961
Bill Skowron ..... N.Y. Yankees, 1955–56, 1958, and 1960–61	L.A. Dodgers, 1963
Enos Slaughter ..... N.Y. Yankees, 1956	St.L. Cardinals, 1942 and 1946
Matt Williams ..... Cle. Indians, 1997	S.F. Giants, 1989, and Ariz. D'backs, 2001
Reggie Smith ..... Bost. Red Sox, 1967	St.L. Cardinals, 1977–78

World Series Inside-The-Park Home Runs

	HRs		Player's Team	Opponent's Team
1903	1	Jimmy Sebrig	Pitt. Pirates	Bost. Americans
1903	1	Patsy Dougherty	Bost. Americans	Pitt. Pirates
1915	1	Duffy Lewis	Bost. Red Sox	Phila. Phillies
1916	1	Hy Myers	Bklyn. Robins	Bost. Red Sox
1916	1	Larry Gardner	Bost. Red Sox	Bklyn. Robins
1923	1	Casey Stengel	N.Y. Giants	N.Y. Yankees
1926	1	Tommy Thevenow	St.L. Cardinals	N.Y. Yankees
1928	1	Lou Gehrig	N.Y. Yankees	St.L. Cardinals
1929	2	Mule Haas	Phila. A's	Chi. Cubs
2015	1	Alcides Escobar	K.C. Royals	N.Y. Mets

World Series Teams Using Six Different Starting Pitchers

Bklyn. Dodgers (NL), 1947	Game 1	Ralph Branca (lost)
	Games 2 and 6	Vic Lombardi (lost and won)
	Game 3	Joe Hatten (won)
	Game 4	Harry Taylor (won)
	Game 5	Rex Barney (lost)
	Game 7	Hal Gregg (lost)
Bklyn. Dodgers (NL), 1955	Game 1	Don Newcombe (lost)
	Game 2	Billy Loes (lost)
	Games 3 and 7	Johnny Podres (won and won)
	Game 4	Carl Erskine (won)
	Game 5	Roger Craig (won)
	Game 6	Karl Spooner (lost)
Pitt. Pirates (NL), 1971	Game 1	Dock Ellis (lost)
	Game 2	Bob Johnson (lost)
	Games 3 and 7	Steve Blass (won and won)
	Game 4	Luke Walker (won)
	Game 5	Nelson Briles (won)
	Game 6	Bob Moose (lost)

Rookies Starting Seventh Game of World Series

Babe Adams, Pitt. Pirates (NL) (vs. Det. Tigers, AL), 1909	Pitched complete game and wins 8–0
Hugh Bedient, Bost. Red Sox (AL) (vs. N.Y. Giants, NL), 1912	Pitched 7 innings, no decision* (Bost. wins 3–2)
Spec Shea, N.Y. Yankees (AL) (vs. Bklyn. Dodgers, NL), 1947	Pitched 1⅓ innings, no decision (N.Y. wins 5–2)
Joe Black, Bklyn. Dodgers (NL) (vs. N.Y. Yankees, AL), 1952	Pitched 5⅓ innings and loses 4–2
Mel Stottlemyre, N.Y. Yankees (AL) (vs. St.L. Cardinals, NL), 1964	Pitched 4 innings and loses 7–5
Joe Magrane, St.L. Cardinals (NL) (vs. Min. Twins, AL), 1987	Pitched 4⅓ innings, no decision (Min. wins 4–2)
John Lackey, Ana. Angels (AL) (vs. S.F. Giants, NL), 2002	Pitched 5 innings and wins 4–1

*Started last game of eight-game Series.

Players Playing Four Different Positions in World Series Competition, Career

Elston Howard	Left field, right field, first base, catcher
Tony Kubek	Left field, third base, center field, shortstop
Jackie Robinson	First base, second base, left field, third base
Pete Rose	Right field, left field, third base, first base
Babe Ruth	Pitcher, left field, right field, first base

Players Stealing Home in World Series Game

Bill Dahlen, N.Y. Giants (NL) (vs. Phila. A's, AL), 1905, Game 3, 5th inning*

George Davis, Chi. White Sox (AL) (vs. Chi. Cubs, NL), 1906, Game 5, 3rd inning*

Jimmy Slagle, Chi. Cubs (NL) (vs. Det. Tigers, AL), 1907, Game 4, 7th inning*

Ty Cobb, Det. Tigers (AL) (vs. Pitt. Pirates, NL), 1909, Game 2, 3rd inning

Buck Herzog, N.Y. Giants (NL) (vs. Bost. Red Sox, AL), 1912, Game 6, 1st inning

Butch Schmidt, Bost. Braves (NL) (vs. Phila. A's, AL), 1914, Game 1, 8th inning*

Mike McNally, N.Y. Yankees (AL) (vs. N.Y. Giants, NL), 1921, Game 1, 5th inning

Bob Meusel, N.Y. Yankees (AL) (vs. N.Y. Giants, NL), 1921, Game 2, 8th inning

Bob Meusel, N.Y. Yankees (AL) (vs. St.L. Cardinals, NL), 1928, Game 3, 6th inning*

Hank Greenberg, Det. Tigers (AL) (vs. St.L. Cardinals, NL), 1934, Game 4, 8th inning*

Monte Irvin, N.Y. Giants (NL) (vs. N.Y. Yankees, AL),1951, Game 1, 1st inning

Jackie Robinson, Bklyn. Dodgers (NL) (vs. N.Y. Yankees, AL), 1955, Game 1, 8th inning

Tim McCarver, St.L. Cardinals (NL) (vs. N.Y. Yankees, AL), 1964, Game 7, 4th inning*

Brad Fullmer, Ana. Angels (AL) (vs. S.F. Giants, NL), 2002, Game 2 1st inning

*Front end of double steal.

Pitchers Hitting Home Runs in World Series Play

Jim Bagby Sr., Cle. Indians (AL) (vs. Bklyn. Dodgers, NL), 1920, Game 5

Rosy Ryan, N.Y. Giants (NL) (vs. Wash. Senators, AL), 1924, Game 3

Jack Bentley, N.Y. Giants (NL) (vs. Wash. Senators, AL), 1924, Game 5

Jesse Haines, St.L. Cardinals (NL) (vs. N.Y. Yankees, AL), 1926, Game 3

Bucky Walters, Cin. Reds (NL) (vs. Det. Tigers, AL), 1940, Game 6

Lew Burdette, Milw. Braves (NL) (vs. N.Y. Yankees, AL), 1958, Game 2

Mudcat Grant, Min. Twins (AL) (vs. L.A. Dodgers, NL), 1965, Game 6

Jose Santiago, Bost. Red Sox (AL) (vs. St.L. Cardinals, NL), 1967, Game 1*

Bob Gibson, St.L. Cardinals (NL) (vs. Bost. Red Sox, AL), 1967, Game 4

Mickey Lolich, Det. Tigers (AL) (vs. St.L. Cardinals, NL), 1968, Game 2

Dave McNally, Balt. Orioles (AL) (vs. N.Y. Mets, NL), 1969, Game 5*

Dave McNally**, Balt. Orioles (AL) (vs. Cin. Reds, NL), 1970, Game 3

Joe Blanton, Phila. Phillies (NL) (vs. T.B. Rays, AL), 2008, Game 4

Ken Holtzman, Oak. A's (AL) (vs. L.A. Dodgers, NL), 1974, Game 4

*Hit home run in losing effort.
**Hit grand slam home run.

Cy Young Winners Facing Each Other in World Series Games

Denny McLain, Det. Tigers (AL), vs. Bob Gibson, St.L. Cardinals (NL), 1968, Games 1 and 4

Mike Cuellar, Balt. Orioles (AL), vs. Tom Seaver, N.Y. Mets (NL), 1969, Games 1 and 4

Catfish Hunter, Oak. A's (AL), vs. Mike Marshall, L.A. Dodgers (NL), 1974, Games 1 and 3

World Series in Which Neither Team Had a 20-Game Winner

Bost. Red Sox (AL) vs. Cin. Reds (NL), 1975

N.Y. Yankees (AL) vs. Cin. Reds (NL), 1976

N.Y. Yankees (AL) vs. L.A. Dodgers (NL), 1981

Milw. Brewers (AL) vs. St.L. Cardinals (NL), 1982

Balt. Orioles (AL) vs. Phila. Phillies (NL), 1983

Det. Tigers (AL) vs. S.D. Padres (NL), 1984

Min. Twins (AL) vs. St.L. Cardinals (NL), 1987

Tor. Blue Jays (AL) vs. Phila. Phillies (NL), 1993

Cle. Indians (AL) vs. Atl. Braves (NL), 1995

Cle. Indians (AL) vs. Fla. Marlins (NL), 1997

N.Y. Yankees (AL) vs. N.Y. Mets (NL), 2000

Ana. Angels (AL) vs. S.F. Giants (NL), 2002

Continued on next page

Det. Tigers (AL) vs. St.L. Cardinals (NL), 2006
Bost. Red Sox (AL) vs. Colo. Rockies (NL), 2007
T.B. Rays (AL) vs. Phila. Phillies (NL), 2008
N.Y. Yankees (AL) vs. Phila. Phillies (NL), 2009
Tex. Rangers (AL) vs. S.F. Giants (NL), 2010
Tex. Rangers (AL)) vs. St.L. Cardinals (NL), 2011
Det. Tigers (AL) vs. S.F. Giants (NL), 2012
Bost. Red Sox (AL) vs. St.L. Cardinals (NL), 2013
K.C. Royals (AL) vs. S.F. Giants (NL), 2014
K.C. Royals (AL) vs. N.Y. Mets (NL), 2015

Pitchers with Lowest ERA in Total World Series Play (Min. 25 Innings)

Career Leaders

	ERA	IP
Madison Bumgarner	0.25	36
Jack Billingham	0.36	25⅓
Harry Brecheen	0.83	32⅔
Claude Osteen	0.86	21
Babe Ruth	0.87	31
Sherry Smith	0.89	30⅓
Sandy Koufax	0.95	57
Christy Mathewson	0.97	101⅔
Mariano Rivera	0.99	36⅓
Hippo Vaughn	1.00	27

Single-Season Leaders

	ERA	IP	Series/Year
Waite Hoyt	0.00	27	1921 World Series
Christy Mathewson	0.00	27	1905 World Series
Carl Hubbell	0.00	20	1933 World Series
Whitey Ford	0.00	18	1960 World Series
Joe McGinnity	0.00	17	1905 World Series
Duster Mails	0.00	15⅔	1920 World Series
Rube Benton	0.00	14	1917 World Series
Whitey Ford	0.00	14	1961 World Series
Jack Billingham	0.00	13⅔	1972 World Series
Joe Dobson	0.00	12⅔	1946 World Series
Allie Reynolds	0.00	12⅓	1949 World Series
Clem Labine	0.00	12	1956 World Series
Mordecai Brown	0.00	11	1908 World Series
Bill James	0.00	11	1914 World Series
Jack Kramer	0.00	11	1944 World Series
Gene Bearden	0.00	10⅔	1948 World Series
Don Larsen	0.00	10⅔	1956 World Series

World Series Grand Slams

Elmer Smith, Cle. Indians (AL), 1920, Game 5, 1st inning, off Burleigh Grimes, Bklyn. Dodgers (NL)

Tony Lazzeri, N.Y. Yankees (AL), 1936, Game 2, 3rd inning, off Dick Coffman, N.Y. Giants (NL)

Gil McDougald, N.Y. Yankees (AL), 1951, Game 5, 3rd inning, off Larry Jansen, N.Y. Giants (NL)

Mickey Mantle, N.Y. Yankees (AL), 1953, Game 5, 3rd inning, off Russ Meyer, Bklyn. Dodgers (NL)

Yogi Berra, N.Y. Yankees (AL), 1956, Game 2, 2nd inning, off Don Newcombe, Bklyn. Dodgers (NL)

Bill Skowron, N.Y. Yankees (AL), 1956, Game 7, 7th inning, off Roger Craig, Bklyn. Dodgers (NL)

Bobby Richardson, N.Y. Yankees (AL), 1960, Game 3, 1st inning, off Clem Labine, Pitt. Pirates (NL)

Chuck Hiller, S.F. Giants (NL), 1962, Game 4, 7th inning, off Marshall Bridges, N.Y. Yankees (AL)

Ken Boyer, St.L. Cardinals (NL), 1964, Game 4, 6th inning, off Al Downing, N.Y. Yankees (AL)

Joe Pepitone, N.Y. Yankees (AL), 1964, Game 6, 8th inning, off Gordie Richardson, St.L. Cardinals (NL)

Jim Northrup, Det. Tigers (AL), 1968, Game 6, 3rd inning, off Larry Jaster, St.L. Cardinals (NL)

Dave McNally, Balt. Orioles (AL), 1970, Game 3, 6th inning, off Wayne Granger, Cin. Reds (NL)

Dan Gladden, Min. Twins (AL), 1987, Game 1, 4th inning, off Bob Forsch, St.L. Cardinals (NL)

Kent Hrbek, Min. Twins (AL), 1987, Game 6, 6th inning, off Ken Dayley, St.L. Cardinals (NL)

Jose Canseco, Oak. A's (AL), 1988, Game 1, 2nd inning, off Tim Belcher, L.A. Dodgers (NL)

Lonnie Smith, Atl. Braves (NL), 1992, Game 5, 5th inning, off Jack Morris, Tor. Blue Jays (AL)

Tino Martinez, N.Y. Yankees (AL), 1998, Game 1, 7th inning, off Mark Langston, S.D. Padres (NL)

Paul Konerko, Chi. White Sox (AL), 2005, Game 2, 7th inning, off Chad Qualls, Hous. Astros (NL)

Players on Three Different World Series Clubs

Don Baylor ..... Bost. Red Sox (AL), 1986
Min. Twins (AL), 1987
Oak. A's (AL), 1988

Joe Bush ..... Phila. A's (AL), 1913–14
Bost. Red Sox (AL), 1918
N.Y. Yankees (AL), 1922–23

Bobby Byrne ..... Pitt. Pirates (NL), 1909
Phila. Phillies (NL), 1915
Chi. White Sox (AL), 1917*

Roger Clemens ..... Bost. Red Sox (AL), 1986
N.Y. Yankees (AL), 1999–2001, 2003
Hous. Astros (NL), 2005

Vic Davalillo ..... Pitt. Pirates (NL), 1971
Oak. A's (AL), 1973
L.A. Dodgers (NL), 1977–78

Paul Derringer ..... St.L. Cardinals (NL), 1931
Cin. Reds (NL), 1939–40
Chi. Cubs (NL), 1945

Leo Durocher ..... N.Y. Yankees (AL), 1928
St.L. Cardinals (NL), 1934
Bklyn. Dodgers (NL), 1941*

Mike Gonzalez ..... N.Y. Giants (NL), 1921*
Chi. Cubs (NL), 1929
St.L. Cardinals (NL), 1931*

Burleigh Grimes ..... Bklyn. Dodgers (NL), 1920
St.L. Cardinals (NL), 1930–31
Chi. Cubs (NL), 1932

Heinie Groh ..... N.Y. Giants (NL), 1912* and 1922–24
Cin. Reds (NL), 1919
Pitt. Pirates (NL), 1927

Pinky Higgins ..... Phila. A's (AL), 1930*
Det. Tigers (AL), 1940
Bost. Red Sox (AL), 1946

Grant Jackson ..... Balt. Orioles (AL), 1971
N.Y. Yankees (AL), 1976
Pitt. Pirates (NL), 1979

Mark Koenig ..... N.Y. Yankees (AL), 1926–28
Chi. Cubs (NL), 1932
N.Y. Giants (NL), 1936

Mike McCormick ..... Cin. Reds (NL), 1940
Bost. Braves (NL), 1948
Bklyn. Dodgers (NL), 1949

Stuffy McInnis . Phila. A's (AL), 1910*, 1911, and 1913–14
Bost. Red Sox (AL), 1918
Pitt. Pirates (NL), 1925

Fred Merkle ..... N.Y. Giants (NL), 1911–13
Bklyn. Dodgers (NL), 1916
Chi. Cubs (NL), 1918
N.Y. Yankees (AL), 1926*

Jack Morris ..... Det. Tigers (AL), 1984
Min. Twins (AL), 1991
Tor. Blue Jays (AL), 1992 and 1993*

Andy Pafko ..... Chi. Cubs (NL), 1945
Bklyn. Dodgers (NL), 1952
Milw. Braves (NL), 1957–58

Billy Pierce ..... Det. Tigers (AL), 1945*
Chi. White Sox (AL), 1959
S.F. Giants (NL), 1962

Edgar Renteria ..... Flo. Marins (NL) 1997
St.L. Cardinals (NL), 2004
S.F. Giants (NL), 2010

Dutch Ruether ..... Cin. Reds (NL), 1919
Wash. Senators (AL), 1925
N.Y. Yankees (AL), 1926 and 1927*

Wally Schang ..... Phila. A's (AL), 1913–14 and 1930*
Bost. Red Sox (AL), 1918
N.Y. Yankees (AL), 1921–22

Everett Scott ..... Bost. Red Sox (AL), 1915–16 and 1918
N.Y. Yankees (AL), 1922–23
Wash. Senators (AL), 1925*

Earl Smith ..... N.Y. Giants (NL), 1921–22
Pitt. Pirates (NL), 1925 and 1927
St.L. Cardinals (NL), 1928

Lonnie Smith ..... Phila. Phillies (NL), 1980
St.L. Cardinals (NL), 1982
K.C. Royals (AL), 1985

Tuck Stainback ..... Chi. Cubs (NL), 1935*
Det. Tigers (AL), 1940*
N.Y. Yankees (AL), 1942–43

Matt Williams ..... S.F. Giants (NL), 1989
Cle. Indians (AL), 1997
Ariz. D'backs (NL), 2001

Eddie Stanky ..... Bklyn. Dodgers (NL), 1947
Bost. Braves (NL), 1948
N.Y. Giants (NL), 1951

*Did not play in Series.

Players Playing for Two Different World Series Champions in Successive Years

Allie Clark, outfield ..... 1947 N.Y. Yankees; 1948 Cle. Indians
Clem Labine, pitcher ..... 1959 L.A. Dodgers; 1960 Pitt. Pirates
Moose Skowron, first base ..... 1962 N.Y. Yankees; 1963 L.A. Dodgers
Don Gullett, pitcher ..... 1976 Cin. Reds; 1977 N.Y. Yankees
Jack Morris, pitcher ..... 1991 Min. Twins; 1992 Tor. Blue Jays

Players with Same Lifetime Batting Average as Their World Series Overall Average

	Lifetime/World Series Batting Average	World Series Appearance(s)
Duffy Lewis (1910–17, 1919–21)	.284	1912 and 1915–16
Phil Linz (1962–68)	.235	1963–64
Danny Murphy (1900–15)	.288	1905 and 1910–11
Paul Waner (1926–45)	.333	1927

Batting Champions Facing Each Other in World Series

Ty Cobb (.377), Det. Tigers (AL), and Honus Wagner (.339), Pitt. Pirates (NL), 1909
Al Simmons (.390), Phila. A's (AL), and Chick Hafey (.349), St.L. Cardinals (NL), 1931
Bobby Avila (.341), Cle. Indians (AL), and Willie Mays (.345), N.Y. Giants (NL), 1954
Miguel Cabrera (.330), Det. Tigers (AL), and Buster Posey (.336), S.F. Giants (NL), 2012

Home Run Champions Facing Each Other in World Series

Babe Ruth (59), N.Y. Yankees (AL), and George Kelly (23), N.Y. Giants (NL), 1921
Babe Ruth (54), N.Y. Yankees (AL), and Jim Bottomley (31), St.L. Cardinals (NL), 1928
Lou Gehrig (49), N.Y. Yankees (AL), and Mel Ott (33), N.Y. Giants (NL), 1936
Joe DiMaggio (46), N.Y. Yankees (AL), and Mel Ott (31), N.Y. Giants (NL), 1937
Mickey Mantle (52), N.Y. Yankees (AL), and Duke Snider (43), Bklyn. Dodgers (NL), 1956

Players Hitting Home Run in First World Series At Bat

Joe Harris, Wash. Senators (AL), 1925
George Watkins, St.L. Cardinals (NL), 1930
Mel Ott, N.Y. Giants (NL), 1933
George Selkirk, N.Y. Yankees (AL), 1936
Dusty Rhodes, N.Y. Giants (NL), 1954
Elston Howard, N.Y. Yankees (AL), 1955
Roger Maris, N.Y. Yankees (AL), 1960
Don Mincher, Min. Twins (AL), 1965
Brooks Robinson, Balt. Orioles (AL), 1966
Jose Santiago, Bost. Red Sox (AL), 1967
Mickey Lolich, Det. Tigers (AL), 1968
Don Buford, Balt. Orioles (AL), 1969
Gene Tenace*, Oak. A's (AL), 1972
Jim Mason, N.Y. Yankees (AL), 1976
Doug DeCinces, Balt. Orioles (AL), 1979
Amos Otis, K.C. Royals (AL), 1980
Bob Watson, N.Y. Yankees (AL), 1981
Jim Dwyer, Balt. Orioles (AL), 1983
Jose Canseco, Oak. A's (AL), 1988
Mickey Hatcher, L.A. Dodgers (NL), 1988
Bill Bathe, S.F. Giants (NL), 1989
Eric Davis, Cin. Reds (NL), 1990
Ed Sprague Jr., Tor. Blue Jays (AL), 1992
Fred McGriff, Atl. Braves (NL), 1995
Andruw Jones, Atl. Braves (NL), 1996
Troy Glaus. Ana. Angels (AL), 2002
Barry Bonds, S.F. Giants (NL), 2002
David Ortiz, Bost. Red Sox (AL), 2004
Mike Lamb, Hous. Astros (NL), 2005
Geoff Blum, Chi. White Sox (AL), 2005
Bobby Kielty, Bost. Red Sox (AL), 2007
Dustin Pedroia, Bost. Red Sox (AL), 2007
Chase Utley, Phila. Phillies (NL), 2008
Alcides Escobar**, K.C. Royals (AL), 2015

*Hit home runs in first two times at bat in World Series.
**Inside-the-park home run.

World Series Pitchers with Most Losses, Season

American League

George Mullin, Det. Tigers, 1907 20
Ken Holtzman, Oak. A's, 1974 17
Dennis Martinez, Balt. Orioles, 1979 16
Dennis Martinez, Balt. Orioles, 1983 16
Joe Bush, Bost. Red Sox, 1918 15
Joe Bush, N.Y. Yankees, 1923 15
Tom Zachary, Wash. Senators, 1925 15
General Crowder, Wash. Senators, 1933 15
Dizzy Trout, Det. Tigers, 1945 15
Bob Feller, Cle. Indians, 1948 15
Billy Pierce, Chi. White Sox, 1959 15
Ralph Terry, N.Y. Yankees, 1963 15
Vida Blue, Oak. A's, 1974 15
Catfish Hunter, N.Y. Yankees, 1976 15
Bud Black, K.C. Royals, 1985 15
Mike Moore, Oak. A's, 1990 15

National League

Larry French, Chi. Cubs, 1938 19
Pat Malone, Chi. Cubs, 1932 17
Don Drysdale, L.A. Dodgers, 1963 17
Don Drysdale, L.A. Dodgers, 1966 16
Jon Matlack, N.Y. Mets, 1973 16
Steve Carlton, Phila. Phillies, 1983 16
Livan Hernandez, S.F. Giants, 2002 16
Jason Marquis, St.L. Cardinals, 2006 16
Joe McGinnity, N.Y. Giants, 1905 15
Erskine Mayer, Phila. Phillies, 1915 15
Harry Brecheen, St.L. Cardinals, 1946 15
Johnny Sain, Bost. Braves, 1948 15
Claude Osteen, L.A. Dodgers, 1965 15
Jerry Koosman, N.Y. Mets, 1973 15
Tim Lincecum, S.F. Giants, 2012 15

Teams Winning a World Series in First Year in New Ballpark

Team	Ballpark	Opponent	Series
Pitt. Pirates (NL)	Forbes Field, 1909	Det Tigers (AL)	4 games to 3
Bost. Red Sox (AL)	Fenway Park, 1912	N.Y. Giants (NL)	4 games to 3
N.Y. Yankees (AL)	Yankee Stadium I, 1923	N.Y. Giants (NL)	4 games to 2
St.L. Cardinals (NL)	Busch Stadium III, 2006	Det. Tigers (AL)	4 games to 2
N.Y. Yankees (AL)	Yankee Stadium II, 2009	Phila. Phillies (NL)	4 games to 2

Pitchers on World Series Winning Teams, Both Winning 20 Games and *All* of Their Team's Series Victories

American League

1903 Cy Young (28 season wins, 2 Series wins) and Bill Dinneen (21 season wins, 3 Series wins), Bost. Americans
1910 Jack Coombs (31 season wins, 3 Series wins) and Chief Bender (23 season wins, 1 Series win), Phila. A's
1912 Smoky Joe Wood (34 season wins, 3 Series wins) and Hugh Bedient (20 season wins, 1 Series win), Bost. Red Sox
1930 Lefty Grove (28 season wins, 2 Series wins) and George Earnshaw (22 season wins, 2 Series wins), Phila. A's

National League

1905 Christy Mathewson (31 season wins, 3 Series wins) and Joe McGinnity (21 season wins, 1 Series win), N.Y. Giants
1914 Bill James (26 season wins, 2 Series wins) and Dick Rudolph (26 season wins, 2 Series wins), Bost. Braves
1940 Bucky Walters (22 season wins, 2 Series wins) and Paul Derringer (20 season wins, 2 Series wins), Cin. Reds
2001 Curt Schilling (22 season wins, 1 Series win) and Randy Johnson (21 season wins, 3 Series wins), Ariz. D'backs

Teams' Overall Won-Lost Percentage in World Series Games Played

American League

	Games Won–Lost	Percentage
Tor. Blue Jays (2 appearances, 2–0)	8–4	.667
N.Y. Yankees (40 appearances, 27–13)	1131–85–1	..606
Bost. Red Sox (12 appearances, 8–4)	41–28–1	.594
Balt. Orioles (6 appearances, 3–3)	19–14	.576
Ana. Angels (1 appearance, 1–0)	4–3	.571
Chi. White Sox (5 appearances, 3–2)	17–13	.567

continued on next page

Phila. A's (8 appearances, 5–3)	24–19	.558
Oak. A's (6 appearances, 4–2)	17–15	.531
Min. Twins (3 appearances, 2–1)	11–10	.524
K.C. Royals (4 appearances, 2–2)	13–12	.520
Cle. Indians (5 appearances, 2–3)	14–16	.467
Det. Tigers (11 appearances, 4–7)	27–37–1	.450
Milw. Brewers* (1 appearance, 0–1)	3–4	.429
Wash. Senators (3 appearances, 1–2)	8–11	.421
St.L. Browns (1 appearance, 0–1)	2–4	.333
Tex. Rangers (2 appearances, 0–2)	4–8	.333
T.B. Rays (1 appearance, 0–1)	1–4	.200

National League

	Games Won–Lost	Percentage
Fla.–Mia. Marlins (2 appearances, 2–0)	8–5	.615
Bost. Braves (2 appearances, 1–1)	6–4	.600
Ariz. D'backs (1 appearance, 1–0)	4–3	.571
S.F. Giants (6 appearances, 3–3)	18–16	.529
Cin. Reds (9 appearances, 5–4)	26–25	.510
L.A. Dodgers (9 appearances, 5–4)	25–24	.510
Milw. Braves (2 appearances, 1–1)	7–7	.500
St.L. Cardinals (19 appearances, 11–8)	58–60	.492
N.Y. Giants (14 appearances, 5–9)	39–41–2	.488
Pitt. Pirates (7 appearances, 5–2)	23–24	.489
N.Y. Mets (5 appearances, 2–3)	13–16	.448
Atl. Braves (5 appearances, 1–4)	11–18	.379
Phila. Phillies (7 appearances, 2–5)	14–23	.378
Chi. Cubs (10 appearances, 2–8)	19–33–1	.365
Bklyn. Dodgers (9 appearances, 1–8)	20–36	.357
S.D. Padres (2 appearances, 0–2)	1–8	.111
Colo. Rockies (1 appearance, 0–1)	0–4	.000
Hous. Astros** (1 appearance, 0–1)	0–4	.000

* Were in American League from 1970–97.

** Were in National League from 1962–2012.

Oldest Players to Appear in World Series

47 years, 3 months	Jack Quinn, Phila. A's, 1929, pitcher
46 years, 10 months	Jamie Moyer, Phila. Phillies, 2009, pitcher
46 years, 3 months	Jack Quinn, Phila. A's, 1930, pitcher
45 years, 10 months	Jamie Moyer, Phila. Phillies, 2008, pitcher
42 years, 5 months	Bartolo Colon, N.Y. Mets, 2015, pitcher
42 years, 3 months	Satchel Paige, Cle. Indians, 1948, pitcher
42 years, 1 month	Chuck Hostetler, Det. Tigers, 1945, pinch hitter
42 years, 0 months	Arthur Rhodes, St.L. Cardinals, 2011, pitcher
41 years, 9 months	Grover C. Alexander, St.L. Cardinals, 1928, pitcher
41 years, 0 months	Darren Oliver, Tex. Rangers, 2011, pitcher
40 years, 5 months	Rick Reuschel, S.F. Giants, 1989, pitcher
40 years, 3 months	Freddie Fitzsimmons, Bklyn. Dodgers, 1941, pitcher
40 years, 3 months	Bobo Newsom, N.Y. Yankees, 1947, pitcher
40 years, 0 months	Darren Oliver, Tex. Rangers, 2010, pitcher

Players with 3000 Hits Playing in World Series

	Number of Hits at Time
Willie Mays (1973 N.Y. Mets)	3283
Pete Rose (1980 Phila. Phillies)	3557
Pete Rose (1983 Phila. Phillies)	3990
Eddie Murray (1995 Cle. Indians)	3071

9

ALL-STAR GAME

Players Who Made All-Star Roster After Starting Season in Minors

Don Newcombe, Bklyn. Dodgers (NL), 1949 ..... Started season with Montreal (IL)
Don Schwall, Bost. Red Sox (AL), 1961 ..... Started season with Seattle (PCL)
Alvin Davis, Sea. Mariners (AL), 1984 ..... Started season with Salt Lake City (PCL)
Evan Longoria, T.B. Rays (AL), 2008 ..... Started season with Durham (IL)
Mike Trout, L.A. Angels (AL), 2012 ..... Started season with Salt Lake (PCL)
Kris Bryant, Chi. Cubs (NL), 2015 ..... Started season with Iowa (PCL)

Pitchers Winning All-Star Game and World Series Game, Same Season

Lefty Gomez, N.Y. Yankees (AL), 1937
Paul Derringer, Cin. Reds (NL), 1940
Spec Shea, N.Y. Yankees (AL), 1947
Vern Law, Pitt. Pirates (NL), 1960
Sandy Koufax, L.A. Dodgers (NL), 1965
Don Sutton, L.A. Dodgers (NL), 1977
John Smoltz, Atl. Braves (NL), 1996
Josh Beckett, Bost. Red Sox (AL), 2007

Pitchers Who Pitched More Than Three Innings in One All-Star Game

Lefty Gomez (AL), 1935 6
Mel Harder (AL), 1934 5
Al Benton (AL), 1942 5
Larry Jansen (NL), 1950 5
Catfish Hunter (AL), 1967 5
Lon Warneke (NL), 1933 4
Hal Schumacher (NL), 1935 4
Spud Chandler (AL), 1942 4
Johnny Antonelli (NL), 1956 4
Lew Burdette (NL), 1957 4
Bob Feller (AL), 1939 ..... 3⅔
Frank Sullivan (AL), 1955 ..... 3⅓
Joe Nuxhall (NL), 1955 ..... 3⅓
Ray Narleski (AL), 1958 ..... 3⅓

All-Star Game Managers Who Never Managed in World Series

Paul Richards, Balt. Orioles (AL), 1961 ..... Replaced Casey Stengel, N.Y. Yankees
Gene Mauch, Phila. Phillies (NL), 1965 ..... Replaced Johnny Keane, St.L. Cardinals

Brothers Selected to Play in All-Star Game, Same Season

Sandy Alomar Jr., Cle. Indians (AL), and Roberto Alomar, S.D. Padres (NL) and Balt. Orioles (AI), 1990, 1996–98
Felipe Alou, Atl. Braves (NL), and Matty Alou, Pitt. Pirates (NL), 1968
Aaron Boone, Cin. Reds (NL), and Bret Boone, Sea. Mariners (AL), 2003
Mort Cooper, St.L. Cardinals (NL), and Walker Cooper, St.L. Cardinals (NL), 1942–43
Joe DiMaggio, N.Y. Yankees (AL), and Dom DiMaggio, Bost. Red Sox (AL), 1941–42, 1946, and 1949–51
Carlos May, Chi. White Sox (AL), and Lee May, Cin. Reds (NL), 1969 and 1971
Gaylord Perry, S.F. Giants (NL), and Jim Perry, Min. Twins (AL), 1970
Dixie Walker, Bklyn. Dodgers (NL), and Harry Walker, St.L. Cardinals and Phila. Phillies (NL), 1943 and 1947

Players Hitting Home Runs in All-Star Game and World Series, Same Season

Joe Medwick, St.L. Cardinals (NL), 1934
Lou Gehrig, N.Y. Yankees (AL), 1936
Lou Gehrig, N.Y. Yankees (AL), 1937
Joe DiMaggio, N.Y. Yankees (AL), 1939

continued on next page

Jackie Robinson, Bklyn. Dodgers (NL), 1952
Mickey Mantle, N.Y. Yankees (AL), 1955
Mickey Mantle, N.Y. Yankees (AL), 1956
David Ortiz, Bost. Red Sox (AL), 2004
Ken Boyer, St.L. Cardinals (NL), 1964
Harmon Killebrew, Min. Twins (AL), 1965
Roberto Clemente, Pitt. Pirates (NL), 1971
Frank Robinson, Balt. Orioles (AL), 1971
Steve Garvey, L.A. Dodgers (NL), 1977
Sandy Alomar, Cle. Indians (AL), 1997
Barry Bonds, S.F. Giants (NL), 2002
Manny Ramirez, Bost. Red Sox (AL), 2004

Fathers and Sons, Both of Whom Played in All-Star Games

Father	Son
Sandy Alomar Sr., Cal. Angels (AL), 1970	Roberto Alomar, S.D. Padres (NL), 1990; Tor. Blue Jays (AL), 1991–95; Balt. Orioles (AL), 1996–98; Cle. Indians (AL), 1999–2001
	Sandy Alomar Jr., Cle. Indians (AL), 1990–92, 1996–98
Felipe Alou, S.F. Giants (NL), 1962; Atl. Braves (NL), 1966 and 1968	Moises Alou, Mont. Expos (NL), 1994; Fla. Marlins (NL), 1997; Hous. Astros (NL), 1998 and 2001
Gus Bell, Cin. Reds (NL), 1953–54, 1956–57	Buddy Bell, Cle. Indians (AL), 1973; Tex. Rangers (AL), 1980–82 and 1984
Bobby Bonds, S.F. Giants (NL), 1971 and 1973; N.Y. Yankees (AL), 1975	Barry Bonds, Pitt. Pirates (NL), 1990 and 1992; S.F. Giants (NL), 1993–98, 2000–04
Bob Boone, Phila. Phillies (NL), 1976 and 1978–79; Cal. Angels (AL), 1983	Aaron Boone, Cin. Reds (NL), 2003
	Bret Boone, Cin. Reds (NL), 1998; Sea. Mariners (AL), 2001 and 2003
Ray Boone, Det. Tigers (AL), 1954 and 1956	Bob Boone, Phila. Phillies (NL), 1976 and 1978–79; Cal. Angels (AL), 1983
Tom Gordon, Bost. Red Sox (AL), 1998; N.Y. Yankees (AL), 2004; Phila. Phillies (NL), 2008	Dee Gordon, L.A. Dodgers (NL), 2014; Mia. Marlins (NL), 2015
Cecil Fielder, Det. Tigers (AL), 1990–91 and 1993	Prince Fielder, Milw. Brewers (NL), 2007, 2008 and 2011; Det. Tigers, 2012–13; Tex. Rangers (AL), 2015
Ken Griffey Sr., Cin. Reds (NL), 1976–77, 1980	Ken Griffey Jr., Sea. Mariners (AL), 1990–99; Cin. Reds (NL), 2000
Jim Hegan, Cle. Indians (AL), 1947, 1949–52	Mike Hegan, Sea. Pilots (AL), 1969
Randy Hundley, Chi. Cubs (NL), 1969	Todd Hundley, N.Y. Mets (NL), 1996–97
Vern Law, Pitt. Pirates (NL), 1960	Vance Law, Chi. Cubs (NL), 1988
Gary Matthews Sr., Atl. Braves (NL), 1979	Gary Matthews Jr., Tex. Rangers (AL), 2006
Steve Swisher, Chi. Cubs (NL), 1976	Nick Swisher, N.Y. Yankees (AL), 2010

Pitchers with No Victories, Named to All-Star Team

Dave LaRoche, Cle. Indians (AL), 1976
Tom Henke, Tor. Blue Jays (AL), 1987

Oldest Players Named to All-Star Team

Satchel Paige, pitcher, Cle. Indians (AL), 1952 ..... 46 years, 1 day
Mariano Rivera, pitcher, N.Y. Yankees (AL), 2013 ..... 43 years, 233 days
Roger Clemens, pitcher, Hous. Astros (NL), 2004 ..... 41 years, 344 days
Mariano Rivera, pitcher, N.Y. Yankees (NL), 2011 ..... 41 years, 225 days
Arthur Rhodes, pitcher, Cin. Reds (NL), 2010, ... 40 years, 263 days
Jamie Moyer, pitcher, Sea. Mariners (AL), 2003 ..... 40 years, 239 days
Mariano Rivera, pitcher, N.Y. Yankees (AL), 2010 ..... 40 years, 226 days
Connie Marrero, pitcher, Wash. Senators (AL), 1951 ..... 40 years, 70 days

10

TEAMS

Teams' Won-Lost Percentage by Decade

1901–09

American League

	Wins	Losses	%
Phila. A's	734	568	.564
Chi. White Sox	744	575	.564
Cle. Indians	609	632	.525
Bost. Red Sox	691	634	.522
Det. Tigers	683	632	.519
Balt. Orioles–N.Y. Yankees*	638	671	.487
Milw. Brewers–St.L. Browns**	599	721	.454
Wash. Senators	480	834	.365

*Baltimore franchise moved to New York in 1903.

**Milwaukee moved to St. Louis in 1902.

National League

	Wins	Losses	%
Pitt. Pirates	859	478	.642
Chi. Cubs	814	517	.612
N.Y. Giants	763	567	.574
Cin. Reds	642	691	.482
Phila. Phillies	634	689	.479
Bklyn. Dodgers	567	755	.429
Bost. Beaneaters–Doves	521	805	.393
St.L. Cardinals	515	813	.388

1910–19

American League

	Wins	Losses	%
Bost. Red Sox	857	624	.579
Chi. White Sox	796	692	.535
Det. Tigers	790	704	.529
Wash. Senators	755	737	.506
Cle. Indians	742	749	.498
Phila. A's	710	774	.478
N.Y. Yankees	701	780	.473
St.L. Browns	597	892	.401

National League

	Wins	Losses	%
N.Y. Giants	889	597	.598
Chi. Cubs	826	668	.553
Phila. Phillies	762	717	.515
Pitt. Pirates	736	751	.495
Cin. Reds	717	779	.479
Bklyn. Dodgers	696	787	.469
Bost. Braves	666	815	.450
St.L. Cardinals	652	830	.440

continued on next page

1920–29

American League

	Wins	Losses	%
N.Y. Yankees	933	602	.608
Wash. Senators	791	735	.518
Cle. Indians	786	749	.512
Phila. A's	770	754	.505
St.L. Browns	762	769	.496
Det. Tigers	760	778	.494
Chi. White Sox	731	804	.476
Bost. Red Sox	595	938	.388

National League

	Wins	Losses	%
N.Y. Giants	890	639	.582
Pitt. Pirates	887	656	.572
St.L. Cardinals	822	712	.536
Chi. Cubs	807	728	.526
Cin. Reds	798	736	.520
Bklyn. Dodgers	765	768	.499
Bost. Braves	603	928	.394
Phila. Phillies	566	962	.370

1930–39

American League

	Wins	Losses	%
N.Y. Yankees	970	554	.636
Cle. Indians	824	708	.538
Det. Tigers	818	716	.533
Wash. Senators	806	722	.527
Phila. A's	723	795	.476
Bost. Red Sox	705	815	.464
Chi. White Sox	678	841	.446
St.L. Browns	578	951	.378

National League

	Wins	Losses	%
Chi. Cubs	889	646	.579
N.Y. Giants	868	657	.569
St.L. Cardinals	869	665	.566
Pitt. Pirates	812	718	.531
Bklyn. Dodgers	724	793	.477
Bost. Braves	700	829	.458
Cin. Reds	664	866	.434
Phila. Phillies	581	943	.381

1940–49

American League

	Wins	Losses	%
N.Y. Yankees	929	609	.604
Bost. Red Sox	754	683	.556
Det. Tigers	834	705	.542
Cle. Indians	800	731	.523
Chi. White Sox	707	820	.463
St.L. Browns	698	833	.456
Wash. Senators	677	858	.441
Phila. A's	638	898	.415

National League

	Wins	Losses	%
St.L. Cardinals	960	580	.623
Bklyn. Dodgers	894	646	.581
Cin. Reds	767	769	.499
Pitt. Pirates	756	776	.493
Chi. Cubs	736	802	.479
N.Y. Giants	724	808	.473
Bost. Braves	719	808	.470
Phila. Phillies	584	951	.380

1950–59

American League

	Wins	Losses	%
N.Y. Yankees	955	582	.621
Cle. Indians	904	634	.588
Chi. White Sox	847	693	.550
Bost. Red Sox	814	725	.529
Det. Tigers	738	802	.479
Wash. Senators	640	898	.416
St.L. Browns–Balt. Orioles*	632	905	.412
Phila.–K.C. A's	624	915	.405

*St. Louis franchise moved to Baltimore in 1954.

**Philadelphia franchise moved to Kansas City in 1955.

National League

	Wins	Losses	%
Bklyn.–L.A. Dodgers*	913	630	.592
Bost.–Milw. Braves**	854	687	.554
N.Y.–S.F. Giants***	822	721	.531
St.L. Cardinals	776	763	.504
Phila. Phillies	767	773	.498
Cin. Reds	741	798	.481
Chi. Cubs	672	866	.437
Pitt. Pirates	616	923	.400

*Brooklyn franchise moved to Los Angeles in 1958.

**Boston franchise moved to Milwaukee in 1953.

***New York franchise moved to San Francisco in 1958.

continued on next page

1960–69

American League

	Wins	Losses	%
Balt. Orioles	911	698	.566
N.Y. Yankees	887	720	.552
Det. Tigers	882	729	.547
Min. Twins*	852	747	.536
Chi. White Sox	783	760	.529
Cle. Indians	764	826	.487
Bost. Red Sox	685	845	.475
L.A.–Cal. Angels**	685	770	.471
K.C.–Oak. A's***	686	922	.427
K.C. Royals***	69	93	.426
Wash. Senators*	607	844	.418
Sea. Pilots–Milw. Brewers****	64	98	.395

*Original Washington Senators franchise moved to Minnesota in 1961.

**New team awarded Washington by League in expansion in 1961 along with Los Angeles in 1961.

***Kansas City franchise moved to Oakland in 1968.

****Kansas City and Seattle (now Milwaukee) entered the league in 1961 as expansion teams.

National League

	Wins	Losses	%
N.Y. Giants	902	704	.562
St.L. Cardinals	884	718	.552
L.A. Dodgers	878	729	.546
Cin. Reds	860	742	.537
Milw.–Atl. Braves*	851	753	.531
Pitt. Pirates	848	755	.529
Phila. Phillies	759	843	.474
Chi. Cubs	735	868	.459
Hous. Astros*	555	739	.429
N.Y. Mets**	494	799	.382
Mont. Expos***	52	110	.321
S.D. Padres***	52	110	.321

*Milwaukee franchise moved to Atlanta in 1966.

**Houston and New York joined League as expansion teams in 1962.

***San Diego and Montreal joined League as expansion teams in 1969.

1970–79

American League

	Wins	Losses	%
Balt. Orioles	944	656	.590
Bost. Red Sox	895	714	.556
N.Y. Yankees	892	715	.555
K.C. Royals	851	760	.528
Oak. A's	838	772	.520
Min. Twins	812	794	.506
Det. Tigers	789	820	.490
Cal. Angels	781	831	.484
Chi. White Sox	752	853	.469
Wash. Senators–Tex. Rangers	747	860	.465
Cle. Indians	737	866	.460
Milw. Brewers	838	873	.458
Sea. Mariners**	187	297	.386
Tor. Blue Jays**	166	318	.343

*The second edition of the Washington Senators moved to Texas in 1972.

**The Seattle Mariners and Toronto Blue Jays entered the League as expansion teams in 1977.

National League

	Wins	Losses	%
Cin. Reds	953	657	.592
Pitt. Pirates	916	695	.569
L.A. Dodgers	910	701	.565
Phila. Phillies	812	801	.503
St.L. Cardinals	800	813	.496
S.F. Giants	794	818	.493
Hous. Astros	793	817	.493
Chi. Cubs	785	827	.487
N.Y. Mets	763	850	.473
Mont. Expos	748	862	.465
Atl. Braves	725	883	.451
S.D. Padres	667	942	.415

continued on next page

1980–89

American League

	Wins	Losses	%
N.Y. Yankees	854	708	.547
Det. Tigers	839	727	.536
K.C. Royals	826	734	.529
Bost. Red Sox	821	742	.525
Tor. Blue Jays	817	746	.523
Milw. Brewers	804	760	.514
Balt. Orioles	800	761	.512
Oak. A's	803	764	.512
Cal. Angels	783	783	.500
Chi. White Sox	758	802	.486
Min. Twins	733	833	.468
Tex. Rangers	720	839	.462
Cle. Indians	710	849	.455
Sea. Mariners	673	893	.430

National League

	Wins	Losses	%
St.L. Cardinals	825	734	.529
L.A. Dodgers	825	741	.527
N.Y. Mets	816	743	.523
Hous. Astros	819	750	.522
Mont. Expos	811	752	.519
Phila. Phillies	783	780	.501
Cin. Reds	781	783	.499
S.F. Giants	773	795	.493
S.D. Padres	762	805	.486
Chi. Cubs	735	821	.472
Pitt. Pirates	732	825	.470
Atl. Braves	712	845	.457

1990–99

American League

	Wins	Losses	%
N.Y. Yankees	851	702	.548
Cle. Indians	823	728	.531
Chi. White Sox	816	735	.526
Bost. Red Sox	814	741	.523
Tex. Rangers	807	747	.519
Tor. Blue Jays	801	754	.515
Balt. Orioles	794	757	.512
Oak. A's	773	781	.497
Sea. Mariners	764	787	.493
Milw. Brewers*	594	636	.483
Ana. Angels	738	817	.475
K.C. Royals	725	825	.468
Min. Twins	718	833	.463
Det. Tigers	702	852	.452
T.B. Devil Rays**	132	192	.407

*Milwaukee Brewers switched to National League in 1998.

**Tampa Bay entered League as an expansion team in 1998.

National League

	Wins	Losses	%
Atl. Braves	925	629	.595
Hous. Astros	813	742	.523
Cin. Reds	809	746	.520
L.A. Dodgers	797	757	.513
Ariz. D'backs*	165	159	.509
S.F. Giants	790	766	.508
Mont. Expos	776	777	.499
Pitt. Pirates	774	779	.498
N.Y. Mets	767	786	.494
St.L. Cardinals	758	794	.488
S.D. Padres	758	799	.486
Colo. Rockies*	512	559	.478
Chi. Cubs	739	813	.476
Phila. Phillies	732	823	.471
Milw. Brewers	148	175	.458
Fla. Marlins**	472	596	.442

*Arizona entered League as an expansion team in 1998.

**Colorodo and Florida entered League as expansion teams in 1993.

2000–09

American League

	Wins	Losses	%
N.Y. Yankees	965	651	.597
Bost. Red Sox	920	699	.568
L..A. Angels	900	720	.556
Oak. A's	890	728	.550
Min. Twins	863	758	.532
Chi. White Sox	857	764	.529
Sea. Mariners	837	783	.517
Cle. Indians	816	804	.504
Tor. Blue Jays	805	814	.497
Tex. Rangers	776	844	.479
Det. Tigers	.729	891	.450
Balt. Orioles	698	920	.431
T.B. Rays	694	923	.429
K.C. Royals	672	948	.415

National League

	Wins	Losses	%
St.L. Cardinals	913	706	.564
Atl. Braves	.892	726	.551
L.A. Dodgers	862	758	.532
S.F. Giants	855	762	.529
Phila. Phillies	850	769	.525
Hous. Astros	832	787	.514
N.Y. Mets	815	803	.504
Fla. Marlins	811	807	.501
Chi. Cubs	807	811	.499
Ariz. D'backs	805	815	.497
Colo. Rockies	769	852	.474
S.D. Padres	769	852	.474
Cin. Reds	751	869	.464
Milw. Brewers	741	878	.458
Mont. Expos–Wash. Nationals*	711	908	.439
Pitt. Pirates	681	936	421

*Montreal franchise moved to Washington in 2005.

continued on next page

2010–15

American League

	Wins	Losses	%
N.Y. Yankees	543	429	.559
T.B. Rays	526	447	.541
Tex. Rangers	525	448	.540
Det. Tigers	521	450	.537
L.A. Angels	516	456	.531
Oak. A's	501	471	.515
Bost. Red Sox	494	478	.508
Balt. Orioles	490	482	.504
Tor. Blue Jays	489	483	.503
K.C. Royals	480	492	.494
Cle. Indians	475	496	.489
Chi. White Sox	464	508	.470
Min. Twins	442	530	.455
Sea. Mariners	437	535	.450
Hous. Astros	394	578	.405

*Houston Astros switched to American League in 2013.

National League

	Wins	Losses	%
St.L. Cardinals	551	421	.567
L.A. Dodgers	526	445	.541
S.F. Giants	520	452	.535
Atl. Braves	516	456	.531
Wash. Nationals	512	459	.527
Cin. Reds	497	475	.511
Phila. Phillies	489	483	.503
Pitt. Pirates	488	484	.502
Milw. Brewers	480	492	.494
N.Y. Mets	473	499	.487
Ariz. D'backs	464	508	.477
S.D. Padres	464	508	.470
Chi. Cubs	443	529	.456
Fla.–Mia. Marlins	431	541	.443
Colo. Rockies	.428	544	.440

Clubs Winning 100 Games, Not Winning Pennant

American League

Wins

116 ..... Sea. Mariners, 2001 (116–46, .716)
(Lost League Championship Series to N.Y. Yankees)

103 ..... N.Y. Yankees, 1954 (103–51, .667)
(Finished second to Cle. Indians by 8 games)

103 ..... N.Y. Yankees, 1980 (103–59, .636)
(Lost League Championship Series to K.C. Royals)

103 ..... N.Y. Yankees, 2002 (103–58, .640)
(Lost Division Series to Ana. Angels)

103 ..... Oak. A's, 2002 (103–59, .636)
(Lost Division Series to Min. Twins)

102 ..... K.C. Royals, 1977 (102–60, .630)
(Lost League Championship Series to N.Y. Yankees)

102 ..... Oak. A's, 2001 (102–60, .630)
(Lost Division Series to N.Y. Yankees)

101 ..... Det. Tigers, 1961 (101–61, .623)
(Finished second to N.Y. Yankees by 8 games)

101 ..... Oak. A's, 1971 (101–60, .627)
(Lost League Championship Series to Balt. Orioles)

101 ..... N.Y. Yankees, 2004 (101–61, .623)
(Lost League Championship Series to Bost. Red Sox)

100 ..... Det. Tigers, 1915 (100–54, .649)
(Finished second to Bost. Red Sox by 2.5 games)

100 ..... Balt. Orioles, 1980 (100–62, .617)
(Finished second in AL East to N.Y. Yankees by 3 games)

100 ..... L.A. Angels, 2008 (100–62, .617)
(Lost Division Series to Bost. Red Sox)

National League

Wins

106 ..... Atl. Braves, 1998 (106–56, .654)
(Lost League Championship Series to S.D. Padres)

104 ..... Chi. Cubs, 1909 (104–49, .680)
(Finished second to Pitt. Pirates by 6.5 games)

104 ..... Bklyn. Dodgers, 1942 (104–50, .675)
(Finished second to St.L. Cardinals by 2 games)

104 ..... Atl. Braves, 1993 (104–58, .642)
(Lost League Championship Series to Phila. Phillies)

103 ..... S.F. Giants, 1993 (103–59, .636)
(Finished second to Atl. Braves in NL West by 1 game)

102 ..... L.A. Dodgers, 1962 (102–63, .618)
(Lost Pennant Playoff to S.F. Giants)

102 ..... Hous. Astros, 1998 (102–60, .630)
(Lost Division Series to S.D. Padres)

102 ..... Phila. Phillies, 2011 (102–60, .630)
(Lost Division Series to St.L. Cardinals)

101 ..... Phila. Phillies, 1976 (101–61, .623)
(Lost League Championship Series to Cin. Reds)

101 ..... Phila. Phillies, 1977 (101–61, .623)
(Lost League Championship Series to L.A. Dodgers)

101 ..... Atl. Braves, 2002 (101–59, .631)
(Lost Division Series to S.F. Giants)

101 ..... Atl. Braves, 2003 (101–61, .623)
(Lost Division Series to Chi. Cubs)

100 ..... N.Y. Mets, 1988 (100–60, .625)
(Lost League Championship Series to L.A. Dodgers)

100 ..... Ariz. D'backs, 1999 (100–62, .617)
(Lost Division Series to St.L. Cardinals)

100 ..... S.F. Giants, 2003 (100–62, .617)
(Lost Division Series to Chi. Cubs)

100 ..... St.L. Cardinals, 2005 (100–62, .617)
(Lost Division Series to Hous. Astros)

100 ..... St.L. Cardinals, 2015 (100–62, .617)
(Lost Division Series to Chi. Cubs)

Pennant Winners One Year, Losing Record Next (Post-1900)

American League

Won Pennant		Losing Record	%
1914	Phila. A's	1915: 43–109	.283
1917	Chi. White Sox	1918: 57–67	.460
1918	Bost. Red Sox*	1919: 66–71	.482
1933	Wash. Senators	1934: 66–86	.434
1964	N.Y. Yankees	1965: 77–85	.475
1966	Balt. Orioles*	1967: 76–85	.472
1980	K.C. Royals	1981: 50–53	.485
1981	N.Y. Yankees	1982: 79–83	.488
1985	K.C. Royals*	1986: 76–86	.469
1986	Bost. Red Sox	1987: 78–84	.481
1993	Tor. Blue Jays*	1994: 55–60	.478
2002	Ana. Angels*	2003: 77–85	.475
2013	Bost. Red Sox*	2014: 71–91	.438

National League

Won Pennant		Losing Record	%
1916	Bklyn. Dodgers	1917: 70–81	.464
1931	St.L. Cardinals*	1932: 72–82	.468
1948	Bost. Braves	1949: 75–79	.487
1950	Phila. Phillies	1951: 73–81	.474
1960	Pitt. Pirates*	1961: 75–79	.487
1963	L.A. Dodgers*	1964: 80–82	.494
1964	St.L. Cardinals*	1965: 80–81	.497
1966	L.A. Dodgers	1967: 73–89	.451
1970	Cin. Reds	1971: 79–83	.488
1973	N.Y. Mets	1974: 71–91	.438
1978	L.A. Dodgers	1979: 79–83	.488
1982	St.L. Cardinals*	1983: 79–83	.488
1985	St.L. Cardinals	1986: 79–83	.488
1987	St.L. Cardinals	1988: 76–86	.469
1990	Cin. Reds	1991: 74–88	.457
1993	Phila. Phillies	1994: 54–61	.470
1997	Fla. Marlins*	1998: 54–108	.333
1998	S.D. Padres	1999: 74–88	.457
2006	St.L. Cardinals*	2007: 78–84	.481
2007	Colo. Rockies	2008: 74–88	.457
2012	S.F. Giants*	2013: 76–86	.469

*World Series winner.

Pennant-Winning Season After Losing Record Year Before

American League

Won Pennant		Losing Record	%
1907	Det. Tigers	1906: 71–78	.477
1919	Chi. White Sox	1918: 57–67	.460
1924	Wash. Senators*	1923: 75–78	.490
1926	N.Y. Yankees	1925: 69–85	.448
1934	Det. Tigers	1933: 75–79	.487
1944	St.L. Browns	1943: 72–80	.474
1946	Bost. Red Sox	1945: 71–83	.461
1965	Min. Twins	1964: 79–83	.488
1967	Bost. Red Sox	1966: 72–90	.444
1987	Min. Twins*	1986: 71–91	.438
1991	Min. Twins*	1990: 74–88	.457
2002	Ana. Angels*	2001: 75–87	.463
2008	T.B. Rays	2007: 66–96	.407

continued on next page

National League

Won Pennant		Losing Record	%
1914	Bost. Braves*	1913: 69–82	.457
1915	Phila. Phillies	1914: 74–80	.481
1918	Chi. Cubs	1917: 74–80	.481
1920	Bkly. Dodgers	1919: 69–71	.493
1933	N.Y. Giants*	1932: 72–82	.468
1945	Chi. Cubs	1944: 75–79	.487
1954	N.Y. Giants*	1953: 70–84	.455
1959	L.A. Dodgers*	1958: 71–83	.461
1961	Cin. Reds	1960: 67–87	.435
1965	L.A. Dodgers*	1964: 80–82	.494
1969	N.Y. Mets*	1968: 73–89	.451
1972	Cin. Reds	1971: 77–83	.488
1987	St.L. Cardinals	1986: 76–82	.491
1988	L.A. Dodgers*	1987: 73–89	.451
1990	Cin. Reds*	1989: 75–87	.463
1991	Atl. Braves	1990: 65–97	.401
1993	Phila. Phillies	1992: 70–92	.432
1997	Fla. Marlins*	1996: 80–82	.494
1998	S.D. Padres	1997: 76–86	.469
2003	Fla. Marlins*	2002: 79–83	.488
2007	Colo. Rockies	2006: 76–86	.469

*World Series winner.

Teams Winning 100 Games in a Season, Three Years in a Row

American League

1929–31 Phila. A's	1929: 104 wins
	1930: 102 wins
	1931: 107 wins
1969–71 Balt. Orioles	1969: 109 wins
	1970: 108 wins
	1971: 101 wins
2002–04 N.Y. Yankees	2002: 103 wins
	2003: 101 wins
	2004: 101 wins

National League

1942–44 St.L. Cardinals	1942: 106 wins
	1943: 106 wins
	1944: 105 wins
1997–99 Atl. Braves	1997: 101 wins
	1998: 106 wins
	1999: 103 wins

Largest Increase in Games Won by Team Next Season

American League

Wins

+34 ....Cle. Indians, 1995 (100 wins vs. 66 wins in 1994)*
+33 . Bost. Red Sox, 1946 (104 wins vs. 71 wins in 1945)
+33 ..... Balt. Orioles, 1989 (87 wins vs. 54 wins in 1988)
+32 ... Bost. Red Sox, 1995 (86 wins vs. 54 wins in 1994)*
+31 ..... Cal. Angels, 1995 (78 wins vs. 47 wins in 1994)*
+31 .Chi. White Sox, 1919 (88 wins vs. 57 wins in 1918)*
+31 ..... T.B. Rays, 2008 (97 wins vs. 66 wins in 2007)
+30 ..... Det. Tigers, 1961 (101 wins vs. 71 wins in 1960)
+30 ... Bost. Red Sox, 1967 (92 wins vs. 72 wins in 1966)
+30 ...Sea. Mariners, 1995 (79 wins vs. 49 wins in 1994)*
+29 ..... Det. Tigers, 2004 (72 wins vs. 43 wins in 2003)
+28 ..... Bost. Red Sox, 2013 (97 wins vs. 69 wins in 2012)

*1994 was a strike-shortened season; 1918 was shortened by WWI.

National League (Post-1900)

Wins

+36 ..... N.Y. Giants, 1903 (84 wins vs. 48 wins in 1902)
+35 .. Ariz. D'backs, 1999 (100 wins vs. 65 wins in 1998)
+34 ..... Phila. Phillies, 1962 (81 wins vs. 47 wins in 1961)
+33 ..... Bost. Braves, 1936 (71 wins vs. 38 wins in 1935)
+32 ...St.L. Cardinals, 1904 (75 wins vs. 43 wins in 1903)
+31 .....Phila. Phillies, 1905 (83 wins vs. 52 wins in 1904)
+31 .....S.F. Giants, 1993 (103 wins vs. 72 wins in 1992)
+30 ...St.L. Cardinals, 1914 (81 wins vs. 51 wins in 1913)

Largest Decrease in Games Won Next Season

American League

Wins

-56 ..... Phila. A's, 1915 (43 wins vs. 99 wins in 1914)
-47 ..... K.C. Royals, 1981 (50 wins vs. 97 wins in 1980)*
-44 ..... N.Y. Yankees, 1981 (59 wins vs. 103 wins in 1980)*
-43 ..... Chi. White Sox, 1918 (57 wins vs. 100 wins in 1917)
-41 .. Balt. Orioles, 1981 (59 wins vs. 100 wins in 1980)*
-40 .. Tor. Blue Jays, 1994 (55 wins vs. 95 wins in 1993)*
-36 ..... Min. Twins, 1981 (41 wins vs. 77 wins in 1980)*
-35 ..... Cle. Naps, 1914 (51 wins vs. 86 wins in 1913)
-34 ... Tex. Rangers, 1994 (52 wins vs. 86 wins in 1993)*
-34 .... Chi. White Sox, 1921 (62 wins vs. 96 wins in 1920)
-33 .... Wash. Senators, 1934 (66 wins vs. 99 wins in 1933)
-33 .. Sea. Mariners, 1994 (49 wins vs. 82 wins in 1993)*
-32 ..... Det. Tigers, 1994 (53 wins vs. 85 wins in 1993)*

*1981 and 1994 were strike-shortened seasons; 1918 was shortened by WWI.

National League

Wins

-48 ... S.F. Giants, 1994 (55 wins vs. 103 wins in 1993)*
-43 .. Phila. Phillies, 1994 (54 wins vs. 97 wins in 1993)*
-40 .... Bost. Braves, 1935 (38 wins vs. 78 wins in 1934)
-38 .... Fla. Marlins, 1998 (54 wins vs. 92 wins in 1997)
-37 ..... Pitt. Pirates, 1981 (46 wins vs. 83 wins in 1980)*
-36 ... Atl. Braves, 1994 (68 wins vs. 104 wins in 1993)*
-35 ..... Chi. Cubs, 1994 (49 wins vs. 84 wins in 1993)*
-34 .... St.L. Cardinals, 1994 (53 wins vs. 87 wins in 1993)*
-33 .. Ariz. D'backs, 2004 (51 wins vs. 84 wins in 2003)
-32 .. Phila. Phillies, 1918 (55 wins vs. 87 wins in 1917)
-32 ... Hous. Astros, 1981 (61 wins vs. 93 wins in 1980)*
-32 .. Phila. Phillies, 1981 (59 wins vs. 91 wins in 1980)*
-32 .... S.D. Padres, 1981 (41 wins vs. 73 wins in 1980)*

Teams with Worst Won-Lost Percentage

American League

	Wins–Losses	Percentage
Phila. A's, 1916	36–117	.235
Wash. Senators, 1904	38–113	.252
Phila. A's, 1919	36–104	.257
Det. Tigers, 2003	43–119	.265
Wash. Senators, 1909	42–110	.276
Bost. Red Sox, 1932	43–111	.279
St.L. Browns, 1939	43–111	.279
Phila. A's, 1915	43–109	.283
St.L. Browns, 1911	45–107	.296
St.L. Browns, 1937	46–108	.299

National League (Post-1900)

	Wins–Losses	Percentage
Bost. Braves, 1935	38–115	.248
N.Y. Mets, 1962	40–120	.250
Pitt. Pirates, 1952	42–112	.273
Phila. Phillies, 1942	42–109	.278
Phila. Phillies, 1941	43–111	.279
Phila. Phillies, 1928	43–109	.283
Bost. Rustlers, 1911	44–107	.291
Bost. Rustlers, 1909	45–108	.294
Phila. Phillies, 1939	45–106	.298
Phila. Phillies, 1945	46–108	.299
Phila. Phillies, 1938	45–105	.300

Teams Hitting .300

American League

St.L. Browns, 1920	.308
Cle. Indians, 1920	.303
Det. Tigers, 1921	.316
Cle. Indians, 1921	.308
St.L. Browns, 1921	.304
N.Y. Yankees, 1921	.300
St.L. Browns, 1922	.313
Det. Tigers, 1922	.305
Cle. Indians, 1923	.301
Det. Tigers, 1923	.300
Phila. A's, 1925	.307
Wash. Senators, 1925	.303
Det. Tigers, 1925	.302
N.Y. Yankees, 1927	.307
Phila. A's, 1927	.303
N.Y. Yankees, 1930	.309
Cle. Indians, 1930	.304
Wash. Senators, 1930	.302
Det. Tigers, 1934	.300
Cle. Indians, 1936	.304
Det. Tigers, 1936	.300
N.Y. Yankees, 1936	.300
Bost. Red Sox, 1950	.302

National League (Post-1900)

St.L. Cardinals, 1921	.308
Pitt. Pirates, 1922	.308
N.Y. Giants, 1922	.305
St.L. Cardinals, 1922	.301
N.Y. Giants, 1924	.300
Pitt. Pirates, 1925	.307
Pitt. Pirates, 1927	.305
Pitt. Pirates, 1928	.309
Phila. Phillies, 1929	.309
Chi. Cubs, 1929	.303
Pitt. Pirates, 1929	.303
N.Y. Giants, 1930	.319
Phila. Phillies, 1930	.315
St.L. Cardinals, 1930	.314
Chi. Cubs, 1930	.309
Bklyn. Dodgers, 1930	.304
Pitt. Pirates, 1930	.303

Teams with Three 20-Game Winners

American League

Bost. Americans, 1903	Cy Young (28), Bill Dinneen (21), Long Tom Hughes (20)
Bost. Americans, 1904	Cy Young (27), Bill Dinneen (23), Jesse Tannehill (21)
Cle. Indians, 1906	Otto Hess (22), Addie Joss (21), Bob Rhoads (21)
Chi. White Sox, 1907	Doc White (27), Ed Walsh (25), Frank Smith (23)
Det. Tigers, 1907	Bill Donovan (25), Ed Killian (25), George Mullin (20)
Chi. White Sox, 1920*	Red Faber (23), Lefty Williams (22), Eddie Cicotte (21), Dickie Kerr (21)
Cle. Indians, 1920	Jim Bagby Sr. (31), Stan Coveleski (24), Ray Caldwell (20)
Phila. A's, 1931	Lefty Grove (31), George Earnshaw (21), Rube Walberg (20)
Cle. Indians, 1951	Bob Feller (22), Mike Garcia (20), Early Wynn (20)
Cle. Indians, 1952	Early Wynn (23), Mike Garcia (22), Bob Lemon (22)
Cle. Indians, 1956	Bob Lemon (20), Herb Score (20), Early Wynn (20)
Balt. Orioles, 1970	Mike Cuellar (24), Dave McNally (24), Jim Palmer (20)
Balt. Orioles, 1971*	Dave McNally (21), Mike Cuellar (20), Pat Dobson (20), Jim Palmer (20)
Oak. A's, 1973	Ken Holtzman (21), Catfish Hunter (21), Vida Blue (20)

continued on next page

National League

Pitt. Pirates, 1902	Jack Chesbro (28), Deacon Phillippe (20), Jesse Tannehill (20)
Chi. Cubs, 1903	Jack Taylor (21), Jake Weimer (21), Bob Wicker (20)**
N.Y. Giants, 1904	Joe McGinnity (35), Christy Mathewson (33), Dummy Taylor (21)
N.Y. Giants, 1905	Christy Mathewson (31), Red Ames (22), Joe McGinnity (21)
Chi. Cubs, 1906	Three Finger Brown (26), Ed Reulbach (20), Jack Taylor (20)***
N.Y. Giants, 1913	Christy Mathewson (25), Rube Marquard (23), Jeff Tesreau (22)
N.Y. Giants, 1920	Art Nehf (21), Fred Toney (21), Jesse Barnes (20)
Cin. Reds, 1923	Dolf Luque (27), Pete Donohue (21), Eppa Rixey (20)

*Four 20-game winners on staff.
**Wicker started 1903 season with St.L. Cardinals (1 game, 0–0).
***Taylor started 1906 season with St.L. Cardinals (17 games, 8–9).

Teams with 30-Game Winners, Not Winning Pennant

American League

Team	Pitcher	Finish
Bost. Americans, 1901	Cy Young (33)	2nd, 4 games behind Chi. White Sox
Bost. Americans, 1902	Cy Young (32)	3rd, 6.5 games behind Phila. A's
N.Y. Highlanders, 1904	Jack Chesbro (41)	2nd, 1.5 games behind Bost. Red Sox
Chi. White Sox, 1908	Ed Walsh (40)	3rd, 1.5 games behind Det. Tigers
Wash. Senators, 1912	Walter Johnson (32)	2nd, 14 games behind Bost. Red Sox
Wash. Senators, 1913	Walter Johnson (36)	2nd, 6.5 games behind Phila. A's

National League

Team	Pitcher	Finish
N.Y. Giants, 1903	Joe McGinnity (31), Christy Mathewson (30)	2nd, 6.5 games behind Pitt. Pirates
N.Y. Giants, 1908	Christy Mathewson (37)	2nd, 1 game behind Chi. Cubs
Phila. Phillies, 1916	Grover C. Alexander (33)	2nd, 2.5 games behind Bklyn. Dodgers
Phila. Phillies, 1917	Grover C. Alexander (30)	2nd, 10 games behind N.Y. Giants

Teams Leading or Tied for First Place Entire Season

American League

1927	N.Y. Yankees (Record: 110–44)
1984	Det. Tigers (Record: 104–58)
1997	Balt. Orioles (Record: 98–64)
1998	Cle. Indians (Record: 89–73)
2001	Sea. Mariners (Record: 116–46)
2005	Chi. White Sox (Record: 99–63)

National League

1923	N.Y. Giants (Record: 95–58)
1955	Bklyn. Dodgers (Record: 98–55)
1990	Cin. Reds (Record: 91–71)
2003	S.F. Giants (Record: 100–61)

Teams Scoring in Every Inning

American League

Bost. Red Sox vs. Cle. Indians, Sept. 16, 1903	Cle. Indians	0 4 3 0 0 0 0 0 0 – 7
	Bost. Red Sox	2 2 3 1 1 3 1 1 X – 14
Cle. Indians vs. Bost. Red Sox, July 7, 1923 (First Game)	Bost. Red Sox	0 0 0 2 0 0 0 0 1 – 3
	Cle. Indians	3 2 3 1 2(13)1 2 X – 27
N.Y. Yankees vs. St.L. Browns, July 26, 1939	St.L. Browns	0 0 0 0 0 0 0 1 0 – 1
	N.Y. Yankees	2 1 1 4 1 3 1 1 X – 14
Chi. White Sox vs. Bost. Red Sox, May 11, 1949	Bost. Red Sox	0 0 0 5 0 1 0 2 0 – 8
	Chi. White Sox	1 1 2 1 2 1 1 3 X – 12

continued on next page

K.C. Royals vs. Oak. A's, Sept. 14, 1998	Oak. A's	1 0 0 0 5 0 0 0 0–6
	K.C. Royals	1 1 3 1 1 3 2 4 X–16
N.Y. Yankees vs. Tor. Blue Jays, Apr. 29, 2006	Tor. Blue Jays	2 0 3 0 1 0 0 0 0–6
	N.Y. Yankees	4 1 2 2 3 1 3 1 X–17
Det. Tigers vs. Colo. Rockies (NL), Aug. 3, 2014	Colo. Rockies	0 2 0 0 0 0 0 0 3–5
	Det. Tigers	1 1 1 2 3 1 1 1 X–11

National League (Post-1900)

N.Y. Giants vs. Phila. Phillies, June 1, 1923	N.Y. Giants	4 2 1 1 5 5 1 2 1–22
	Phila. Phillies	1 4 0 1 1 0 0 1 0–8
St.L. Cardinals vs. Chi. Cubs, Sept. 13, 1964	St.L. Cardinals	2 1 2 2 2 1 3 1 1–15
	Chi. Cubs	1 0 0 0 0 1 0 0 0–2
Chi. Cubs vs. Hous. Astros, Sept. 1, 1978	Hous. Astros	0 6 0 3 0 0 1 1 0–11
	Chi. Cubs	5 1 1 1 1 2 1 2 X–14
Colo. Rockies vs. Chi. Cubs, May 5, 1999	Colo. Rockies	1 1 1 1 2 1 2 2 2–13
	Chi. Cubs	0 2 3 0 0 0 0 1 0–6
Colo. Rockies vs. S.D. Padres, Sept. 24, 2001	S.D. Padres	1 0 1 2 0 4 0 2 1–11
	Colo. Rockies	1 2 2 1 2 5 1 1 X–15

Most Lopsided Shutouts

American League

22–0 ..... Cle. Indians over N.Y. Yankees, Aug. 31, 2004
21–0 ..... Det. Tigers over Cle. Blues, Sept. 15, 1901
21–0 ..... N.Y. Yankees over Phila. A's, Aug. 13, 1939

National League

22–0 ..... Pitt. Pirates over Chi. Cubs, Sept. 16, 1975
20–0 ..... Milw. Brewers over Pitt. Pirates, Apr. 22, 2010

11

MISCELLANY

Players with Both Little League and Major League World Series Teams

Boog Powell	1954 (Lakeland, Florida)	1966 World Series
Jim Barbieri	1954 (Schenectady, New York)	1966 World Series
Rick Wise	1958 (Portland, Oregon)	1988 World Series, 1975 World Series
Carney Lansford	1969 (Santa Clara, California)	1990 World Series
Ed Vosberg	1973 (Tucson, Arizona)	1997 World Series
Charlie Hayes	1977 (Hattiesburg, Mississippi)	1996 World Series
Dwight Gooden	1979 (Tampa, Florida) 1980 (Tampa, Florida)	1986 World Series
Gary Sheffield	1980 (Tampa, Florida)	1997 World Series
Derek Bell	1981 (Tampa, Florida)	1992 World Series
Jason Varitek	1984 (Altamonte Springs, Florida)	2004 World Series, 2007 World Series
Jason Marquis	1991 (Staten Island, New York)	2004 World Series
Yusmeiro Petit	1994 (Maracaibo, Venezuela)	2014 World Series
Lance Lynn	1999 (Brownsburg, Indiana)	2011 World Series, 2013 World Series
Michael Conforto	2004 (Redmond, Washington)	2015 World Series

Olympians (in Sports Other Than Baseball) Who Played Major League Baseball

Ed "Cotton" Minahan, pitcher, Cin. Reds (NL), 1907	Track and field, Paris, 1900
Al Spalding, pitcher, Chi. Cubs (NL), 1876–78	Shooting, Paris, 1900
Jim Thorpe, outfield, N.Y. Giants (NL), 1913–15 and 1917–18; Cin. Reds (NL), 1917; Bost. Braves (NL), 1919	Decathlon, Stockholm, 1912

Babe Ruth's Yearly Salary

Bost. Red Sox (AL), 1914	$1,900
Bost. Red Sox (AL), 1915	$3,500
Bost. Red Sox (AL), 1916	$3,500
Bost. Red Sox (AL), 1917	$5,000
Bost. Red Sox (AL), 1918	$7,000
Bost. Red Sox (AL), 1919	$10,000
N.Y. Yankees (AL), 1920	$20,000
N.Y. Yankees (AL), 1921	$30,000
N.Y. Yankees (AL), 1922	$52,000
N.Y. Yankees (AL), 1923	$52,000
N.Y. Yankees (AL), 1924	$52,000
N.Y. Yankees (AL), 1925	$52,000
N.Y. Yankees (AL), 1926	$52,000
N.Y. Yankees (AL), 1927	$70,000
N.Y. Yankees (AL), 1928	$70,000
N.Y. Yankees (AL), 1929	$70,000
N.Y. Yankees (AL), 1930	$80,000
N.Y. Yankees (AL), 1931	$80,000
N.Y. Yankees (AL), 1932	$75,000
N.Y. Yankees (AL), 1933	$52,000
N.Y. Yankees (AL), 1934	$37,500
Bost. Braves (NL), 1935	$25,000
22 Seasons Total	**$900,400**

Players Leading N.Y. Yankees in Home Runs One Season, Playing Elsewhere Next Season

Danny Hoffman, 1907	4	Traded to St.L. Browns (AL) with Jimmy Williams and Hobe Ferris for Fred Glade and Charlie Hemphill
Guy Zinn, 1912	6	Sold to Bost. Braves (NL) for cash
Joe Pepitone, 1969	27	Traded to Hous. Astros (NL) for Curt Blefary
Bobby Bonds, 1975	32	Traded to Cal. Angels (AL) for Mickey Rivers and Ed Figueroa
Jack Clark, 1988	27	Traded to S.D. Padres (NL) for Jimmy Jones, Lance McCullers, and Stan Jefferson
Tino Martinez, 2001	34	Filed for free agency, signed with St.L. Cardinals (NL)
Robinson Cano, 2013	27	Filed for free agency, signed with Sea. Mariners (AL)

Billy Martin's Fights

May 1952	vs. Jimmy Piersall, Bost. Red Sox (AL)
July 14, 1952	vs. Clint Courtney, St.L. Browns (AL)
Apr. 30, 1953	vs. Clint Courtney, St.L. Browns (AL)
July 1953	vs. Matt Batts, Det. Tigers (AL)
May 16, 1957	with Hank Bauer, Whitey Ford, Yogi Berra, Mickey Mantle, and Johnny Kucks vs. patron at Copacabana nightclub, New York City
Aug. 4, 1960	vs. Jim Brewer, Chi. Cubs (NL)
July 12, 1966	vs. Howard Fox, traveling secretary, Min. Twins (AL)
Aug. 6, 1969	vs. Jim Boswell, Min. Twins (AL)
Apr. 20, 1972	vs. Det. Tigers (AL) fan
Mar. 8, 1973	vs. Lakeland, Florida, policeman
May 30, 1974	vs. Cle. Indians (AL) team
Sept. 26, 1974	vs. Burt Hawkins, traveling secretary, Tex. Rangers (AL)
June 18, 1977	vs. Reggie Jackson, N.Y. Yankees (AL)
Nov. 10, 1978	vs. Ray Hagar, sportswriter, in Reno, Nevada
Oct. 25, 1979	vs. Joseph Cooper, marshmallow salesman, Minneapolis, Minnesota
May 25, 1983	vs. Robin Wayne Olson, nightclub patron, in Anaheim, California
Sept. 20, 1985	vs. patron at Cross Keys Inn, Baltimore, Maryland
Sept. 21, 1985	vs. Ed Whitson, N.Y. Yankees (AL), in Cross Keys Inn, Baltimore, Maryland
May 6, 1988	vs. unidentified assailant(s) in bathroom, Lace Nightclub, Arlington, Texas

Four-Decade Players

1870s–1900s

Dan Brouthers, first base (1879–96, 1904)

Jim O'Rourke, outfield (1876–93, 1904)

1880s–1910s

Kid Gleason, pitcher and second base (1888–1908, 1912)

Deacon McGuire, catcher (1884–88, 1890–1908, 1910, 1912)

Jack O'Connor, catcher (1887–1904, 1906–07, 1910)

John Ryan, catcher (1889–91, 1894–96, 1898–1903, 1912–13)

1890s–1920s

Nick Altrock, pitcher (1898, 1902–09, 1912–15, 1918–19, 1924, 1929, 1931, 1933)*

1900s–30s

Eddie Collins, second base (1906–30)

Jack Quinn, pitcher (1909–15, 1918–33)

1910s–40s

[No player]

1920s–50s

Bobo Newsom, pitcher (1929–30, 1932, 1934–48, 1952–53)

continued on next page

1930s–60s

Elmer Valo, outfield (1939–43, 1946–61)**
Mickey Vernon, first base (1939–43, 1946–60)
Ted Williams, outfield (1939–42, 1946–60)
Early Wynn, pitcher (1939, 1941–44, 1946–63)

1940s–70s

Minnie Minoso, outfield (1949, 1951–64, 1976, 1980)*

1950s–80s

Jim Kaat, pitcher (1959–83)
Tim McCarver, catcher (1959–61, 1963–80)
Willie McCovey, first base (1959–80)

1960s–90s

Bill Buckner, outfield and first base (1969–90)
Rick Dempsey, catcher (1969–92)
Carlton Fisk, catcher (1969, 1971–90)
Jerry Reuss, pitcher (1969–90)
Nolan Ryan, pitcher (1966, 1968–93)

1970s–2000s

Rickey Henderson, outfield (1979–2003)
Mike Morgan, pitcher (1979, 1982–83, 1985–2002)
Jesse Orosco, pitcher (1979, 1981–2003)
Tim Raines, outfield (1979–99, 2001–02)

1980s–2010s

Ken Griffey Jr., outfield (1989–2010)
Jamie Moyer, pitcher (1986–91, 1993–2010, 2012)
Omar Vizquel, shortstop (1989–12)

*Played five decades.

**Played in last game of 1939 season for Phila. A's (AL) but manager Connie Mack kept his name off the official line-up card.

First Players Chosen in Draft by Expansion Teams

American League		National League	
K.C. Royals	Roger Nelson, pitcher	Ariz. D'backs	Brian Anderson, pitcher
L.A. Angels	Eli Grba, pitcher	Colo. Rockies	David Nied, pitcher
Sea. Pilots	Marv Staehle, second base	Fla. Marlins	Nigel Wilson, outfield
Sea. Mariners	Dave Johnson, second base	Hous. Colt .45s	Ed Bressoud, shortstop
T.B. Devil Rays	Tony Saunders, pitcher	Mont. Expos	Manny Mota, outfield
Tor. Blue Jays	Phil Roof, catcher	N.Y. Mets	Hobie Landrith, catcher
Wash. Senators II	John Gabler, pitcher	S.D. Padres	Ollie Brown, outfield

Last Active Player Once Playing for . . .

Bklyn. Dodgers (NL) ..... Bob Aspromonte (played for Bklyn. Dodgers in 1956; active until 1971)
N.Y. Giants (NL) ..... Willie Mays (played for N.Y. Giants in 1957; active until 1973)
Bost. Braves (NL) ..... Eddie Mathews (played for Bost. Braves in 1952; active until 1968)
Phila. A's (AL) ..... Vic Power (played for Phila. A's in 1954; active until 1965)
St.L. Browns (AL) ..... Don Larsen (played for St.L. Browns in 1953; active until 1967)
Milw. Braves (NL) ..... Phil Niekro (played for Milw. Braves in 1965; active until 1987)
K.C. A's (AL) ..... Reggie Jackson (played for K.C. A's in 1967; active until 1987)
Hous. Colt .45s (NL) ..... Rusty Staub (played for Hous. Astros in 1964; active until 1985)
L.A. Angels (AL) ..... Jim Fregosi (played for L.A. Angels in 1964; active until 1978)
Sea. Pilots (AL) ..... Fred Stanley (played for Sea. Pilots in 1969; active until 1982)
Wash. Senators (AL) ..... Jim Kaat (played for Wash. Senators in 1960; active until 1983)
Wash. Senators II (AL) ..... Toby Harrah (played for Wash. Senators II in 1971; active until 1986)

Last Players Born in Nineteenth Century to Play in Majors

American League

Fred Johnson, pitcher (b. Mar. 5, 1894) ..... Played in 1939 with St.L. Browns
Jimmy Dykes, third base (b. Nov. 10, 1896) ..... Played in 1939 with Chi. White Sox

National League

Hod Lisenbee, pitcher (b. Sept. 23, 1898) ..... Played in 1945 with Cin. Reds
Charlie Root, pitcher (b. Mar. 17, 1899) ..... Played in 1941 with Chi. Cubs

First Players Born in Twentieth Century to Play in Majors

American League

Ed Corey, pitcher (b. July 13, 1900) ..... Played in 1918 with Chi. White Sox

National League

John Cavanaugh, third base (b. June 5, 1900) ..... Played in 1919 with Phila. Phillies

Second African American to Play for Each of 16 Original Major League Teams

American League

	Second African American	First African American
Bost. Red Sox	Earl Wilson, pitcher, 1959	Pumpsie Green, infield, 1959
Chi. White Sox	Sammy Hairston, catcher, 1951	Minnie Minoso, outfield, 1951
Cle. Indians	Satchel Paige, pitcher, 1948	Larry Doby, outfield, 1947
Det. Tigers	Larry Doby, outfield, 1959	Ozzie Virgil, third base, 1958
N.Y. Yankees	Harry "Suitcase" Simpson, outfield, 1957	Elston Howard, catcher, 1955
Phila. A's	Vic Power, outfield and first base, 1954	Bob Trice, pitcher, 1953
St.L. Browns	Willard Brown, outfield, 1947	Hank Thompson, second base, 1947
Wash. Senators	Joe Black, pitcher, 1957	Carlos Paula, outfield, 1954

National League

	Second African American	First African American
Bost. Braves	Luis Marquez, outfield, 1951	Sam Jethroe, outfield, 1950
Bklyn. Dodgers	Dan Bankhead, pitcher, 1947	Jackie Robinson, first base, 1947
Chi. Cubs	Gene Baker, second base, 1953	Ernie Banks, shortstop, 1953
Cin. Reds	Chuck Harmon, infield, 1954	Nino Escalera, outfield, 1954
N.Y. Giants	Monte Irvin, outfield, 1949	Hank Thompson, second base, 1949
Phila. Phillies	Chuck Harmon, infield, 1957	John Kennedy, third base, 1957
Pitt. Pirates	Sam Jethroe, outfield, 1954	Curt Roberts, second base, 1954
St.L. Cardinals	Brooks Lawrence, pitcher, 1954	Tom Alston, first base, 1954

Players and Mangers Having Same Number Retired on Two Different Clubs

Hank Aaron	Atl. Braves (NL) and Milw. Brewers (AL)	44
Rod Carew	Cal. Angels (AL) and Min. Twins (AL)	29
Rollie Fingers	Milw. Brewers (NL) and Oak. A's (AL)	34
Greg Maddux	Atl. Braves (NL) and Chi. Cubs (NL)	31
Frank Robinson	Balt. Orioles (AL) and Cin. Reds (NL)	20
Nolan Ryan	Hous. Astros (AL) and Tex. Rangers (AL)	34
Casey Stengel	N.Y. Mets (NL) and N.Y. Yankees (AL)	37

Major Leaguers Who Played Pro Football in Same Year(s)

	Baseball Team	Year(s)	Football Team
Red Badgro, outfield	St.L. Browns (AL)	1929–30	N.Y. Giants
Charlie Berry, catcher	Phila. A's (AL)	1925	Pottsville (PA) Maroons
Joe Berry, second base	N.Y. Giants (NL)	1921	Rochester (NY) Jeffs
Garland Buckeye, pitcher	Cle. Indians (AL)	1926	Chi. Bulls
Bruce Caldwell, outfield	Cle. Indians (AL)	1928	N.Y. Giants
Chuck Corgan, infield	Bklyn. Dodgers (NL)	1925	K.C. Cowboys
	Bklyn. Dodgers (NL)	1927	N.Y. Giants
Steve Filipowicz, outfield	N.Y. Giants (NL)	1945	N.Y. Giants
	Cin. Reds (NL)	1946	N.Y. Giants
Walter French, outfield	Phila. A's (AL)	1925	Pottsville (PA) Maroons
George Halas, outfield	N.Y. Yankees (AL)	1919	Decatur (IL) Staleys
Bo Jackson, outfield	K.C. Royals (AL)	1987–90	L.A. Raiders
Vic Janowicz, catcher	Pitt. Pirates (NL)	1954	Wash. Redskins
Bert Kuczynski, pitcher	Phila. A's (AL)	1943	Det. Lions
Pete Layden, outfield	St.L. Browns (AL)	1948	N.Y. Yankees
Christy Mathewson, pitcher	N.Y. Giants (NL)	1902	Pitt. Pros
John Mohardt, second base	Det. Tigers (AL)	1922	Chi. Cardinals
Ernie Nevers, pitcher	St.L. Browns (AL)	1926–27	Duluth Eskimos
Ace Parker, shortstop	Phila. A's (AL)	1937–38	Bklyn. Dodgers
Al Pierotti, pitcher	Bost. Braves (NL)	1920	Cle. Tigers
	Bost. Braves (NL)	1921	N.Y. Giants
Pid Purdy, outfield	Cin. Reds (NL), Chi. White Sox (AL)	1926–27	G.B. Packers
Dick Reichle, outfield	Bost. Red Sox (AL)	1923	Milw. Badgers
Deion Sanders, outfield	N.Y. Yankees (AL)	1989–90	Atl. Falcons
	Atl. Braves (NL)	1991–94	Atl. Falcons (until 1993)
	Cin. Reds (NL)	1994–95, 1997	S.F. 49ers (1994)
	S.F. Giants (NL)	1995	Dal. Cowboys
John Scalzi, outfield	Bost. Braves (NL)	1931	Bklyn. Dodgers
Red Smith, catcher	N.Y. Giants (NL)	1927	G.B. Packers
Jim Thorpe, outfield	N.Y. Giants (NL)	1915, 1917	Canton Bulldogs
	Cin. Reds (NL)	1917	Canton Bulldogs
	Bost. Braves (NL)	1919	Canton Bulldogs
Ernie Vick, catcher	St.L. Cardinals (NL)	1925	Det. Panthers
Rube Waddell, pitcher	Phila. A's (AL)	1902	Pitt. Pros
Tom Whelan, first base	Bost. Braves (NL)	1920	Canton Bulldogs

Performances by Oldest Players

Pitched	Satchel Paige, K.C. A's (AL), Sept. 25, 1965	59 years, 2 months
Batted (0-for-1)	Satchel Paige, K.C. A's (AL), Sept. 25, 1965	59 years, 2 months
Caught	Jim O'Rourke, N.Y. Giants (NL), Sept. 20, 1904	52 years, 1 month
At Bat	Nick Altrock, Wash. Senators (AL), Sept. 30, 1933	57 years, 0 months
Base Hit	Minnie Minoso, Chi. White Sox (AL), Sept. 12, 1976	53 years, 9 months
Double	Julio Franco, Atl. Braves (NL), July 27, 2007	48 years, 11 months
Triple	Nick Altrock, Wash. Senators (AL), Sept. 30, 1924	48 years, 0 months
Home Run	Julio Franco, N.Y. Mets (NL), May 4, 2007	48 years, 9 months
Grand Slam Home Run	Julio Franco, Atl. Braves (NL), June 3, 2004	45 years, 10 months
Run Scored	Charlie O'Leary, St.L. Browns (AL), Sept. 30, 1934	52 years, 11 months
RBI	Julio Franco, Atl. Braves (NL), Sept. 27, 2007	49 years, 1 months
Stolen Base	Arlie Latham, N.Y. Giants (NL), Aug. 18, 1909	50 years, 5 months

continued on next page

100 Games, Season	Cap Anson, Chi. Colts (NL), 1897	45 years, 0 months
Game Won, Relief	Jack Quinn, Bklyn. Dodgers (NL), Aug. 14, 1932	48 years, 1 month
Game Lost, Relief	Hoyt Wilhelm, L.A. Dodgers (NL), June 24, 1972	48 years, 11 months
Complete Game	Phil Niekro, N.Y. Yankees (AL), Oct. 6, 1985	46 years, 6 months
Shutout	Phil Niekro, N.Y. Yankees (AL), Oct. 6, 1985	46 years, 6 months
No-Hitter	Cy Young, Bost. Red Sox (AL), June 30, 1908	41 years, 3 months
Perfect Game	Randy Johnson, Ariz. D'backs (NL), May 18, 2004	39 years, 8 months

Oldest Players, by Position

First Base	Julio Franco, Atl. Braves (NL), 2007	48
Second Base	Arlie Latham, N.Y. Giants (NL), 1909	49
Third Base	Jimmy Austin, St.L. Browns (AL), 1929	49
Shortstop	Bobby Wallace, St.L. Cardinals (NL), 1918	44
Outfield	Sam Thompson, Det. Tigers (AL), 1906	46
Catcher	Jim O'Rourke, N.Y. Giants (NL), 1904	52
Pitcher	Satchel Paige, K.C. A's (AL), 1965	59
Designated Hitter	Minnie Minoso, Chi. White Sox (AL), 1976	53
Pinch Hitter	Nick Altrock, Wash. Senators (AL), 1933	57

Youngest Players to Play in Majors

Fred Chapman, pitcher, Phila. A's (AA), July 22, 1887	14 years, 8 months
Joe Nuxhall, pitcher, Cin. Reds (NL), June 10, 1944	15 years, 10 months
Willie McGill, pitcher, Cle. (P), May 8, 1890	16 years, 6 months
Joe Stanley, outfield, Balt. (U), Sept. 11, 1897	16 years, 6 months
Carl Scheib, pitcher, Phila. A's (AL), Sept. 6, 1943	16 years, 8 months
Tommy Brown, shortstop, Bklyn. Dodgers (NL) Aug. 3, 1944	16 years, 8 months
Milton Scott, first base, Chi. Cubs (NL), Sept. 30, 1882	16 years, 9 months
Putsy Caballero, third base, Phila. Phillies (NL), Sept. 14, 1944	16 years, 10 months
Jim Derrington, pitcher, Chi. White Sox (AL), Sept. 30, 1956	16 years, 10 months
Rogers McKee, pitcher, Phila. Phillies (NL), Aug. 18, 1943	16 years, 11 months
Alex George, shortstop, K.C. A's (AL), Sept. 16, 1955	16 years, 11 months
Merito Acosta, outfield, Wash. Senators (AL), June 5, 1913	17 years, 0 months

Youngest Players, by Position

First Base	Milton Scott, Chi. Cubs (NL), 1882	16
Second Base	Ted Sepkowski, Cle. Indians (AL), 1942	18
Third Base	Putsy Caballero, Phila. Phillies (NL), 1944	16
Shortstop	Tommy Brown, Bklyn. Dodgers (NL), 1944	16
Outfield	Merito Acosta, Wash. Senators (AL), 1913	17
	Mel Ott, N.Y. Giants (NL), 1926	17
	Willie Crawford, L.A. Dodgers (NL), 1964	17
Catcher	Jimmie Foxx, Phila. A's (AL), 1925	17
Right-Handed Pitcher	Fred Chapman, Phila. A's (AA), 1887	14
Left-Handed Pitcher	Joe Nuxhall, Cin. Reds (NL), 1944	15

Players Who Played During Most Presidential Administrations

Cap Anson (1876–97)	8	Ulysses S. Grant (1876–77)
		Rutherford B. Hayes (1887–81)
		James A. Garfield (1881)
		Chester A. Arthur (1881–85)
		Grover Cleveland (1885–89)
		Benjamin Harrison (1889–93)
		Grover Cleveland (1893–97)
		William McKinley (1897)
Jim O'Rourke (1876–93, 1904)	8	Ulysses S. Grant (1876–77)
		Rutherford B. Hayes (1877–81)
		James A. Garfield (1881)
		Chester A. Arthur (1881–85)
		Grover Cleveland (1885–89)
		Benjamin Harrison (1889–93)
		Grover Cleveland (1893–97)
		Theodore Roosevelt (1904)
Nick Altrock (1898, 1902–09, 1912–15, 1918–19, 1924, 1929, 1931, 1933)	7	William McKinley (1898)
		Theodore Roosevelt (1902–09)
		William Howard Taft (1909–13)
		Woodrow Wilson (1913–19)
		Calvin Coolidge (1924)
		Herbert Hoover (1929, 1931)
		Franklin D. Roosevelt (1933)
Jim Kaat (1959–83)	7	Dwight D. Eisenhower (1959–61)
		John F. Kennedy (1961–63)
		Lyndon B. Johnson (1963–69)
		Richard M. Nixon (1969–75)
		Gerald Ford (1975–77)
		Jimmy Carter (1977–81)
		Ronald Reagan (1981–83)

Players Playing Most Seasons with One Address (One Club, One City in Majors)

23	Brooks Robinson, Balt. Orioles (AL), 1955–77
23	Carl Yastrzemski, Bost. Red Sox (AL), 1961–83
22	Cap Anson, Chi. Cubs (Colts) (NL), 1876–97
22	Al Kaline, Det. Tigers (AL), 1953–74
22	Stan Musial, St.L. Cardinals (NL), 1941–44 and 1946–63
22	Mel Ott, N.Y. Giants (NL), 1926–47
21	George Brett, K.C. Royals (AL), 1973–93
21	Walter Johnson, Wash. Senators (AL), 1907–27
21	Ted Lyons, Chi. White Sox (AL), 1923–42 and 1946
21	Cal Ripken Jr., Balt. Orioles (AL), 1981–2001
21	Willie Stargell, Pitt. Pirates (NL), 1962–82
20	Luke Appling, Chi. White Sox (AL), 1930–43 and 1945–50
20	Red Faber, Chi. White Sox (AL), 1914–33
20	Tony Gwynn, S.D. Padres (NL), 1982–2001
20	Mel Harder, Cle. Indians (AL), 1928–47
20	Alan Trammell, Det. Tigers (AL), 1977–96
20	Robin Yount, Milw. Brewers (AL), 1974–93
20	Derek Jeter, N.Y. Yankees (AL), 1995–2014

Players Who Played 2500 Games in One Uniform (Post-1900)

3308 ..... Carl Yastrzemski, Bost. Red Sox (AL), 1961–83
3026 ..... Stan Musial, St.L. Cardinals (NL), 1941–44 and 1946–63
3001 ..... Cal Ripken Jr., Balt. Orioles (AL), 1981–2001
2896 ..... Brooks Robinson, Balt. Orioles (AL), 1955–77
2856 ..... Robin Yount, Milw. Brewers (AL), 1974–93
2850 ..... Craig Biggio, Hous. Astros (NL), 1988–2007
2834 ..... Al Kaline, Det. Tigers (AL), 1953–74
2747 ..... Derek Jeter, N.Y. Yankees, (AL), 1995–2004
2732 ..... Mel Ott, N.Y. Giants (NL), 1926–47
2707 ..... George Brett, K.C. Royals (AL), 1973–93
2528 ..... Ernie Banks, Chi. Cubs (NL), 1953–71

Players Playing Most Seasons in City of Birth

22 ..... Phil Cavarretta, Chi. Cubs (NL), 1934–53, and Chi. White Sox (AL), 1954–55
19 ..... Pete Rose, Cin. Reds (NL), 1963–78 and 1984–86
19 ..... Barry Larkin, Cin. Reds (NL), 1986–2004
18 ..... Ed Kranepool, N.Y. Mets (NL), 1962–79
17 ..... Lou Gehrig, N.Y. Yankees (AL), 1923–39
16 ..... Harry Davis, Phila. A's (AL), 1901–11 and 1913–17
16 ..... Whitey Ford, N.Y. Yankees (AL), 1950 and 1953–67

Players with Same Surname as Town of Birth

Loren Bader, pitcher (1912, 1917–18), born in Bader, Illinois
Verne Clemons, catcher (1916, 1919–24), born in Clemons, Iowa
Estel Crabtree, outfield (1929, 1931–33, 1941–44), born in Crabtree, Ohio
Charlie Gassaway, pitcher, (1944–46), born in Gassaway, Tennessee
Elmer "Slim" Love, pitcher, (1913, 1916–20), born in Love, Missouri
Jack Ogden, pitcher, (1918, 1928–29, 1931–32), born in Ogden, Pennsylvania
Curly Ogden, pitcher, (1922–26), born in Ogden, Pennsylvania
Steve Phoenix, pitcher (1984–95), born in Phoenix, Arizona
Happy Townsend, pitcher (1901–06), born in Townsend, Delaware
George Turbeville, pitcher (1935–37), born in Turbeville, South Carolina

Players with Longest Given Names

Alan Mitchell Edward George Patrick Henry Gallagher ("Al"), third base (1970–73) ..... 45 characters
Christian Frederick Albert John Henry David Betzel ("Bruno"), infield (1914–18) ..... 44 characters
Calvin Coolidge Julius Caesar Tuskahoma McLish ("Cal"), pitcher, (1944, 1946–49, 1951, 1956–64) ..... 41 characters

Players with Palindromic Surnames*

Truck Hannah, catcher (1918–20)
Toby Harrah, infield (1969, 1971–86)
Eddie Kazak, shortstop (1948–52)
Dick Nen, first base (1963, 1965–68, 1970)
Robb Nen, pitcher (1993–2002)
Dave Otto, pitcher (1987–94)
Johnny Reder, first base (1932)
Mark Salas, catcher (1984–91)
Juan Salas, pitcher (2006–08)
Marino Salas, pitcher (2008)
Fernando Salas, pitcher (2010–)
Dean Anna, pitcher (2014–)

*Last name spelled the same forward and backward.

Most Common Last Names in Baseball History

Smith	149	Miller	87
Johnson	109	Williams	75
Jones	97	Wilson	73
Brown	87	Davis	68

Number of Major League Players by First Letter of Last Name*

A	551	N	322
B	1776	O	343
C	1453	P	885
D	909	Q	47
E	341	R	1017
F	661	S	1809
G	1002	T	607
H	1348	U	56
I	57	V	248
J	482	W	1037
K	683	X	0
L	853	Y	108
M	1931	Z	88

*From 1871 through 2015.

Third Basemen on Tinker-to-Evers-to-Chance Chicago Cubs Teams*

Doc Casey	1903–05	388 games
Harry Steinfeldt	1906–10	729 games
Heinie Zimmerman	1908, 1910	23 games
Solly Hoffman	1905–08	20 games
Otto Williams	1903–04	7 games
John Kane	1909–10	7 games
Tommy Raub	1903	4 games
George Moriarty	1903–04	3 games
Bobby Lowe	1903	1 game
Broadway Aleck Smith	1904	1 game

*Famed Hall of Fame double-play combination for the Chi. Cubs, 1903–10.

First Designated Hitter for Each Major League Team

American League

Balt. Orioles	Terry Crowley (vs. Milw. Brewers), Apr. 6, 1973	2-for-4
Bost. Red Sox	Orlando Cepeda (vs. N.Y. Yankees), Apr. 6, 1973	0-for-6
Cal. Angels	Tom McCraw (vs. K.C. Royals), Apr. 6, 1973	1-for-4
Chi. White Sox	Mike Andrews (vs. Tex. Rangers), Apr. 7, 1973	1-for-3
Cle. Indians	John Ellis (vs. Det. Tigers), Apr. 7, 1973	0-for-4
Det. Tigers	Gates Brown (vs. Cle. Indians), Apr. 7, 1973	0-for-4
K.C. Royals	Ed Kirkpatrick (vs. Cal. Angels), Apr. 6, 1973	0-for-3

continued on next page

Milw. Brewers	Ollie Brown (vs. Balt. Orioles), Apr. 6, 1973	0-for-3
Min. Twins	Tony Oliva (vs. Oak. A's), Apr. 6, 1973	2-for-4
N.Y. Yankees	Ron Blomberg* (vs. Bost. Red Sox), Apr. 6, 1973	1-for-3
Oak. A's	Bill North (vs. Min. Twins), Apr. 6, 1973	2-for-5
Sea. Mariners	Dave Collins (vs. Cal. Angels), Apr. 6, 1977	0-for-4
T.B. Devil Rays	Paul Sorrento (vs. Det. Tigers), Mar. 31, 1998	1-for-5
Tex. Rangers	Rico Carty (vs. Chi. White Sox), Apr. 7, 1973	1-for-4
Tor. Blue Jays	Otto Velez (vs. Chi. White Sox), Apr. 7, 1977	2-for-4

National League

Ariz. D'backs	Kelly Stinnett (vs. Oak. A's, AL), June 5, 1998	1-for-3
Atl. Braves	Keith Lockhart (vs. Tor. Blue Jays, AL), June 16, 1997	0-for-4
Chi. Cubs	Dave Clark (vs. Chi. White Sox, AL), June 16, 1997	1-for-4
Cin. Reds	Eddie Taubensee (vs. Cle. Indians, AL), June 16, 1997	0-for-3
Colo. Rockies	Dante Bichette (vs. Sea. Mariners, AL), June 12, 1997	3-for-5
Fla. Marlins	Jim Eisenreich (vs. Det. Tigers, AL), June 16, 1997	1-for-5
Hous. Astros	Sean Berry (vs. K.C. Royals, AL), June 16, 1997	1-for-4
L.A. Dodgers	Mike Piazza (vs. Oak. A's, AL), June 12, 1997	3-for-4
Mont. Expos	Jose Vidro (vs. Balt. Orioles, AL), June 16, 1997	0-for-4
N.Y. Mets	Butch Huskey (vs. N.Y. Yankees, AL), June 16, 1997	2-for-4
Phila. Phillies	Darren Daulton (vs. Bost. Red Sox, AL), June 16, 1997	1-for-5
Pitt. Pirates	Mark Smith (vs. Min. Twins, AL), June 16, 1997	1-for-4
St.L. Cardinals	Dmitri Young (vs. Milw. Brewers, AL), June 16, 1997	1-for-4
S.D. Padres	Rickey Henderson (vs. Ana. Angels, AL), June 12, 1997	2-for-5
S.F. Giants	Glenallen Hill** (vs. Tex. Rangers, AL), June 12, 1997	0-for-3

*First AL designated hitter.

**First NL designated hitter.

Players Killed as Direct Result of Injuries Sustained in Major League Games

Maurice "Doc" Powers, catcher, Phila. A's (AL) ..... Died Apr. 26, 1909, after three operations for "intestinal problems" after running into railing on Apr. 12, 1909, at Shibe Park inaugural game.

Ray Chapman, shortstop, Cle. Indians (AL) ..... Died Aug. 17, 1920, after being hit by pitch thrown by N.Y. Yankees pitcher Carl Mays at the Polo Grounds on Aug. 16, 1920.

Players Who Played for Three New York Teams

Dan Brouthers ..... Troy Trojans (NL), 1879–80
Buff. Bisons (NL), 1881–85
N.Y. Giants (NL), 1904

Jack Doyle ..... N.Y. Giants (NL), 1893–95, 1898–1900, and 1902
Bklyn. Dodgers (NL), 1903–04
N.Y. Yankees (AL), 1905

Dude Esterbrook ..... Buff. Bisons (NL), 1880
N.Y. Metropolitans (AA), 1883–84 and 1887
N.Y. Gothams/Giants (NL), 1885–86 and 1890
Bklyn. Dodgers (NL), 1891

Burleigh Grimes ..... Bklyn. Dodgers (NL), 1918–26
N.Y. Giants (NL), 1927
N.Y. Yankees (AL), 1934

Benny Kauff ..... N.Y. Yankees (AL), 1912
Bklyn. Tip-Tops (FL), 1915
N.Y. Giants (NL), 1916–20

continued on next page

Willie Keeler ..... N.Y. Giants (NL), 1892–93 and 1910
Bklyn. Dodgers (NL), 1893 and 1899–1902
N.Y. Yankees (AL), 1903–09
Tony Lazzeri ..... N.Y. Yankees (AL), 1926–37
Bklyn. Dodgers (NL), 1939
N.Y. Giants (NL), 1939
Sal Maglie ..... N.Y. Giants (NL), 1945 and 1950–55
Bklyn. Dodgers (NL), 1956–57
N.Y. Yankees (AL), 1957–58
Fred Merkle ..... N.Y. Giants (NL), 1907–16
Bklyn. Dodgers (NL), 1916–17
N.Y. Yankees (AL), 1925–26
Jack Nelson ..... Troy Trojans (NL), 1879
N.Y. Metropolitans (AA), 1883–87
N.Y. Giants (NL), 1887
Bklyn. Bridegrooms (AA), 1890
Lefty O'Doul ..... N.Y. Yankees (AL), 1919–20 and 1922
N.Y. Giants (NL), 1928 and 1933–34
Bklyn. Dodgers (NL), 1931–33
Dave Orr ..... N.Y. Gothams (NL), 1883
N.Y. Metropolitans (AA), 1884–87
Bklyn. Bridegrooms (AA), 1888
Bklyn. Wonders (PL), 1890
Jack Taylor ..... Bklyn. Dodgers (NL), 1920–25 and 1935
N.Y. Giants (NL), 1927
N.Y. Yankees (AL), 1934
Monte Ward ..... N.Y. Gothams/Giants (NL), 1883–89 and 1893–94
Bklyn. Wonders (PL), 1890
Bklyn. Bridegrooms (NL), 1891–92

Players Who Played for Both Original and Expansion Washington Senators

Rudy Hernandez, pitcher ..... Original Senators, 1960 ..... Expansion Senators, 1961
Hector Maestri, pitcher ..... Original Senators, 1960 ..... Expansion Senators, 1961
Pedro Pamos, pitcher ..... Original Senators, 1955–60 ..... Expansion Senators, 1970
Camilo Pascual, pitcher ..... Original Senators, 1954–60 ..... Expansion Senators, 1967–69
Zoilo Versalles, shortstop ..... Original Senators, 1959–60 ..... Expansion Senators, 1969

Players Who Played for Both Kansas City Athletics and Kansas City Royals

Moe Drabowsky, pitcher ..... K.C. A's, 1963–65 ..... K.C. Royals, 1969–70
Aurelio Monteagudo, pitcher ..... K.C. A's, 1963–66 ..... K.C. Royals, 1970
Ken Sanders, pitcher ..... K.C. A's, 1964, 1966 ..... K.C. Royals, 1976
Dave Wickersham, pitcher ..... K.C. A's, 1960–63 ..... K.C. Royals, 1969

Players Who Played for Both Milwaukee Braves and Milwaukee Brewers

Hank Aaron, outfielder and DH ..... Milw. Braves, 1954–65 ..... Milw. Brewers, 1975–76
Felipe Alou, outfielder ..... Milw. Braves, 1964–65 ..... Milw. Brewers, 1974
Phil Roof, catcher ..... Milw. Braves, 1961 and 1964 ..... Milw. Brewers, 1970–71

Pitchers Who Gave Up Most Hits to Pete Rose

Phil Niekro 64
Don Sutton 60
Juan Marichal 42
Gaylord Perry 42

continued on next page

Joe Niekro 39
Claude Osteen 38
Ron Reed 38
Bob Gibson 36
Ferguson Jenkins 36

Pitchers Who Gave Up Home Runs to Both Mark McGwire and Barry Bonds in Their Record-Breaking Seasons (1998 and 2001)

Scott Elarton ..... Pitching for Hous. Astros (NL), gave up #40 to McGwire
Pitching for Colo. Rockies (NL), gave up #61 and #62 to Bonds
Bobby Jones ..... Pitching for N.Y. Mets (NL), gave up #47 to McGwire
Pitching for S.D. Padres (NL), gave up #30 to Bonds
John Thomson ..... Pitching for Colo. Rockies (NL), gave up #25 and #44 to McGwire
Pitching for Colo. Rockies (NL), gave up #25 and #57 to Bonds
Steve Trachsel ..... Pitching for Chi. Cubs (NL), gave up #62 to McGwire
Pitching for N.Y. Mets (NL), gave up #15 to Bonds

Major League Shortstops from San Pedro de Macoris, Dominican Republic

Manny Alexander (1992–2006)
Juan Bell (1989–95)
Robinson Cano (2005–)
Juan Castillo (1986–89)
Pedro Ciriaco (2010–)
Mariano Duncan (1985–97)
Tony Fernandez (1983–2001)
Pepe Frias (1973–81)
Hector Gomez (2011, 2014–)
Pedro Gonzalez (1963–97)
Luis Garcia (1999)
Jerry Gil (2004–07)
Diory Hernandez (2009–)
Elian Herrera (2012–)
Julian Javier (1960–72)
Manuel Lee (1985–95)
Norberto Martin (1993–98)
Yamaico Navarro (2010–13)
Nelson Norman (1978–82, 1987)
Jose Offerman (1990–2005)
Elvis Pena (2000–01)
Santiago Perez (2000–01)
Jorge Polanco (2014–)
Rafael Ramirez (1980–92)
Rafael Robles (1969–72)
Eddie Rogers (2002–06)
Amado Samuel (1962–64)
Andres Santana (1990)
Alfonso Soriano (1999–2014)
Juan Sosa (1999–2001)
Fernando Tatis (1997–03, 2006, 2008–2010)
Jordany Valdespin (2012–)

Players Born on Leap Year Day (February 29)

	Year of Birth
Ed Appleton, pitcher (1913, 1916)	1892
Sadie Houck, shortstop (1879–81, 1883–87)	1856
Al Autry, pitcher (1976)	1952
Jerry Fry, catcher (1978)	1956
Bill Long, pitcher (1985, 1987–91)	1960
Terrence Long, outfield (1999–2006)	1976
Al Rosen, third base (1947–56)	1924
Pepper Martin, outfield (1928, 1930–40, 1944)	1904
Ralph Miller, infield (1920–21, 1924)	1896
Steve Mingori, pitcher (1970–79)	1944
Roy Parker, pitcher (1919)	1896
Dickey Pearce, shortstop (1871–77)	1836

Players Who Played on Four of California's Five Major League Teams

Mike Aldrete ..... S.F. Giants, 1986–88; S.D. Padres, 1991; Oak. A's, 1993–95; and Cal. Angels, 1995–96
John D'Acquisto ..... S.F. Giants, 1973–76; S.D. Padres, 1977–80; Cal. Angels, 1981; and Oak. A's, 1982
Steve Finley ..... S.D. Padres ,1995–98; L.A. Dodgers, 2004; L.A. Angels , 2005, and S.F. Giants, 2006
Rickey Henderson ..... Oak. A's, 1979–84, 1989–93, 1994–95, and 1998; S.D. Padres, 1996–97; Ana. Angels, 1997; and L.A. Dodgers, 2003
Stan Javier ..... Oak. A's, 1986–90 and 1994–95; L.A. Dodgers, 1990–92; Cal. Angels, 1993; and S.F. Giants, 1996–99
Jay Johnstone ..... Cal. Angels, 1966–70; Oak. A's, 1973; S.D. Padres, 1979; and L.A. Dodgers, 1980–82 and 1985
Dave Kingman ..... S.F. Giants, 1971–74; S.D. Padres, 1977; Cal. Angels, 1977; and Oak. A's, 1984–86
Elias Sosa ..... S.F. Giants, 1972–74; L.A. Dodgers, 1976–77; Oak. A's, 1978; and S.D. Padres, 1983
Derrel Thomas .... S.D. Padres, 1972–74 and 1978; S.F. Giants, 1975–77; L.A. Dodgers, 1979–83; and Cal. Angels, 1984
Brett Tomko ..... S.D. Padres, 2002, 2007–08; S.F. Giants, 2004–05; L.A. Dodgers, 2006–07; and Oak. A's, 2009

Tallest Players in Major League History

6'11" ..... Jon Rauch, pitcher (2002, 2004–13)
6'10" ..... Andrew Brackman, pitcher (2011)
Eric Hillman, pitcher (1992–94)
Randy Johnson, pitcher (1988–2009)
Andy Sisco, pitcher (2005–07)
Chris Young*, pitcher (2004–)
6'9" ..... Terry Bross, pitcher (1991, 1993)
Johnny Gee, pitcher (1939, 1941, 1943–46)
Mark Hendrickson*, pitcher (2002–)
John Holdzkom, pitcher (2014)
Alex Meyer*, pitcher (2015–)
Kam Mickolio pitcher (2008–11)
Jeff Niemann pitcher (2008–12)
6'8" ..... Mark Acre, pitcher (1994–97)
Dellin Betances*, pitcher (2011–)
Darren Clarke, pitcher (2007)
Tony Clark, first baseman (1995–2009)
Gene Conley, pitcher (1952, 1954–63)
Steve Ellsworth, pitcher (1988)
Doug Fister*, pitcher (2009–)
Nate Freiman, first baseman (2013–14)
Lee Guetterman, pitcher (1984, 1986–93, 1995–96)
Jason Hirsh, pitcher (2006–08)
Graeme Lloyd, pitcher (1993–2003)
Kameron Loe*, pitcher (2004–08, 2010–13)
Chris Martin*, pitcher (2014–)
Nate Minchey, pitcher (1993–97)
Mike Naymick, pitcher (1939–40, 1943–44)
Jeff Nelson, pitcher (1992–2006)
Logan Ondrusek pitcher (2010–14)
J.R. Richard, pitcher (1971–80)
Adam Russell pitcher (2008–11)
Michael Schwimer pitcher (2011–12)
Mike Smithson, pitcher (1982–89)
Kyle Snyder, pitcher (2003–2008)
Phil Stockman, pitcher (2006–2008)
Billy Taylor, pitcher (1994, 1996–98)
Joe Vitko, pitcher (1992)
Chris Volstad*, pitcher (2008–13, 2015)
Sean West, pitcher (2009–10)
Stefan Wever, pitcher (1982)

*Still active.

Shortest Players in Major League History

3'7" ..... Eddie Gaedel, pinch hitter (1951)
5'3" ..... Jess Cortazzo, pinch hitter (1923)
Yo-Yo Davalillo, shortstop (1953)
Bob Emmerich, outfield (1923)
Bill Finley, outfield/catcher (1886)
Stubby Magner, infield (1911)
Mike McCormick, third base (1904)
Tom Morrison, infield (1895–96)
Yale Murphy, shortstop/outfield (1894–95, 1897)
Dickey Pearce, shortstop (1871–77)
Frank Shannon, infield (1892, 1896)
Cub Stricker, second base (1882–85, 1887–93)

Teammates the Longest

19 years	Derek Jeter (shortstop) and Mariano Rivera (pitcher), N.Y. Yankees, 1995–2013
18 years	Joe Judge (first base) and Sam Rice (outfield), Wash. Senators, 1915–32
18 years	Alan Trammell (shortstop) and Lou Whitaker (second base), Det. Tigers, 1977–95
17 years	Derek Jeter (shortstop) and Jorge Posada (catcher), N.Y. Yankees, 1995–2011
17 years	Jorge Posada (catcher) and Mariano Rivera (pitcher), N.Y. Yankees, 1995–2011
15 years	Derek Jeter (shortstop) and Andy Pettitte (pitcher), N.Y. Yankees, 1995–2003, 2007–10, 2012–13
15 years	Andy Pettitte (pitcher) and Mariano Rivera (pitcher), N.Y. Yankees, 1995–2003, 2007–10, 2012–13
15 years	Jeff Bagwell (first base) and Craig Biggio (second base/outfield), Hous. Astros, 1991–2005
14 years	Duke Snider (outfield) and Carl Furillo (outfield), Bklyn./L.A. Dodgers, 1947–60
13 years	Joe Judge (first base) and Walter Johnson (pitcher), Wash. Senators, 1915–27
13 years	Andy Pettitte (pitcher) and Jorge Posada (catcher), N.Y. Yankees, 1995–2003, 2007–10

Teammates with 300 Wins and 500 Home Runs

Lefty Grove (pitcher) and Jimmie Foxx (batter) ..... 1941 Bost. Red Sox (AL)
Warren Spahn (pitcher) and Willie Mays (batter) ..... 1965 S.F. Giants (NL)
Don Sutton (pitcher) and Reggie Jackson (batter) ..... 1985 Cal. Angels (AL)
Greg Maddux (pitcher) and Sammy Sosa (batter) ..... 2004 Chi. Cubs (NL)

New Baseball Stadiums Built Since 2005

Team	Stadium	Opened	Capacity	Surface	Approximate Cost (in millions)	Center Field Distance
Mia. Marlins	Marlins Park	2012	37,422	Grass	$515	415′ (126 m)
Min. Twins	Target Field	2010	40,000	Grass	$522	404′ (124 m)
N.Y. Mets	Citi Field	2009	41,800	Grass	$850	408′ (124 m)
N.Y. Yankees	Yankee Stadium	2009	52,325	Grass	$1300	408′ (124.3 m)
Wash. Nationals	Nationals Park	2008	41,888	Grass	$611	402′ (122.5 m)
St.L. Cardinals	Busch Stadium	2006	46,861	Grass	$346	400′ (122 m)

Players Traded for Themselves

Harry Chiti (Apr. 26, 1962 and June 15, 1962)
Archie Corbin (Nov. 20, 1992 and Feb. 5, 1993)
Clint Courtney (Jan. 24, 1961 and Mar. 14, 1961)
Brad Gulden (Nov. 18, 1980 and May 18, 1981)
John MacDonald (July 22, 2005 and Nov. 10, 2005)
Dickie Noles (Sept. 22, 1987 and Oct. 23, 1987)
Mark Ross (Dec. 9, 1985 and Mar. 31, 1986)

Players Wearing Numbers "0" and "00"

"0"

Oscar Gamble, Chi. White Sox
Terrance Gore, K.C. Royals
L.J. Hoes, Hous. Astros
Candy Maldonado, Tor. Blue Jays
Terry McDaniel, N.Y. Mets
Oddibe McDowell, Tex. Ranger
Al Oliver, L.A. Dodgers, S.F. Giants, Mont. Expos, Phila. Phillies, Tex. Rangers, Tor. Blue Jays
Junior Ortiz, Cle. Indians, Tex. Rangers
Adam Ottavino, Colo. Rockies
Rey Ordonez, N.Y. Mets
Omar Quintanilla, N.Y. Mets
Kerry Robinson, St.L. Cardinals
Mark Ryal, Chi. White Sox
George Scott, K.C. Royals
Franklin Stubbs, Milw. Brewers
U.L. Washington, Pitt. Pirates

"00"

Don Baylor, Oak. A's
Brennen Boesch, L.A. Angels
Bobby Bonds, St.L. Cardinals
Jose Canseco, Tor. Blue Jays
Jack Clark, S.D. Padres
Tony Clark, N.Y. Mets
Paul Dade, Cle. Indians
Curtis Goodwin, Cin. Reds
Jerry Hairston, Chi. White Sox
Cliff Johnson, Tor. Blue Jays
Jeff Leonard, Milw. Brewers, S.F. Giants, Sea. Mariners
Curt Leskanic, Milw. Brewers
John Maybery, Hous. Astros
Eddie Milner, Cin. Reds
Bobo Newsom, Wash. Senators
Omar Olivares, St.L. Cardinals, Phila. Phillies
Joe Page, Pitt. Pirates
Kerry Robinson, Cin. Reds
Brandon Watson, Cin. Reds, Wash. Nationals
Rick White, Cle. Indians, Pit. Pirates, Cin. Reds, Phila. Phillies
Brian Wilson, L.A. Dodgers

PART 2
Team-by-Team Histories

AMERICAN LEAGUE

Baltimore Orioles

Dates of Operation: 1954–present (62 years)
Overall Record: 5041 wins, 4791 losses (.512)
Stadiums: Memorial Stadium, 1954–91; Oriole Park at Camden Yards, 1992–present (capacity: 45,971)

Year-by-Year Finishes

Year	Finish	Wins	Losses	Percentage	Games Behind	Manager	Attendance
1954	7th	54	100	.351	57.0	Jimmy Dykes	1,060,910
1955	7th	57	97	.370	39.0	Paul Richards	852,039
1956	6th	69	85	.448	28.0	Paul Richards	901,201
1957	5th	76	76	.500	21.0	Paul Richards	1,029,581
1958	6th	74	79	.484	17.5	Paul Richards	829,991
1959	6th	74	80	.481	20.0	Paul Richards	891,926
1960	2nd	89	65	.578	8.0	Paul Richards	1,187,849
1961	3rd	95	67	.586	14.0	Paul Richards, Luman Harris	951,089
1962	7th	77	85	.475	19.0	Billy Hitchcock	790,254
1963	4th	86	76	.531	18.5	Billy Hitchcock	774,343
1964	3rd	97	65	.599	2.0	Hank Bauer	1,116,215
1965	3rd	94	68	.580	8.0	Hank Bauer	781,649
1966	1st	97	63	.606	+9.0	Hank Bauer	1,203,366
1967	6th (Tie)	76	85	.472	15.5	Hank Bauer	955,053
1968	2nd	91	71	.562	12.0	Hank Bauer, Earl Weaver	943,977
					East Division		
1969	1st	109	53	.673	+19.0	Earl Weaver	1,058,168
1970	1st	108	54	.667	+15.0	Earl Weaver	1,057,069
1971	1st	101	57	.639	+12.0	Earl Weaver	1,023,037
1972	3rd	80	74	.519	5.0	Earl Weaver	899,950
1973	1st	97	65	.599	+8.0	Earl Weaver	958,667
1974	1st	91	71	.562	+2.0	Earl Weaver	962,572
1975	2nd	90	69	.566	4.5	Earl Weaver	1,002,157
1976	2nd	88	74	.543	10.5	Earl Weaver	1,058,609
1977	2nd (Tie)	97	64	.602	2.5	Earl Weaver	1,195,769
1978	4th	90	71	.559	9.0	Earl Weaver	1,051,724
1979	1st	102	57	.642	+8.0	Earl Weaver	1,681,009
1980	2nd	100	62	.617	3.0	Earl Weaver	1,797,438
1981*	2nd/4th	59	46	.562	2.0/2.0	Earl Weaver	1,024,652
1982	2nd	94	68	.580	1.0	Earl Weaver	1,613,031
1983	1st	98	64	.605	+6.0	Joe Altobelli	2,042,071
1984	5th	85	77	.525	19.0	Joe Altobelli	2,045,784

1985	4th	83	78	.516	16.0	Joe Altobelli, Earl Weaver	2,132,387
1986	7th	73	89	.451	22.5	Earl Weaver	1,973,176
1987	6th	67	95	.414	31.0	Cal Ripken Sr.	1,835,692
1988	7th	54	107	.335	34.5	Cal Ripken Sr., Frank Robinson	1,660,738
1989	2nd	87	75	.537	2.0	Frank Robinson	2,535,208
1990	5th	76	85	.472	11.5	Frank Robinson	2,415,189
1991	6th	67	95	.414	24.0	Frank Robinson, Johnny Oates	2,552,753
1992	3rd	89	73	.549	7.0	Johnny Oates	3,567,819
1993	3rd (Tie)	85	77	.525	10.0	Johnny Oates	3,644,965
1994	2nd	63	49	.563	6.5	Johnny Oates	2,535,359
1995	3rd	71	73	.493	15.0	Phil Regan	3,098,475
1996	2nd	88	74	.543	4.0	Davey Johnson	3,646,950
1997	1st	98	64	.605	+2.0	Davey Johnson	3,711,132
1998	4th	79	83	.488	35.0	Ray Miller	3,685,194
1999	4th	78	84	.481	20.0	Ray Miller	3,433,150
2000	4th	74	88	.457	13.5	Mike Hargrove	3,295,128
2001	4th	63	98	.391	32.5	Mike Hargrove	3,094,841
2002	4th	67	95	.414	36.5	Mike Hargrove	2,682,917
2003	4th	71	91	.438	30.0	Mike Hargrove	2,454,523
2004	3rd	78	84	.481	23.0	Lee Mazzilli	2,747,573
2005	4th	74	88	.457	21.0	Lee Mazzilli, Sam Perlozzo	2,624,740
2006	4th	70	92	.432	27.0	Sam Perlozzo	2,153,139
2007	4th	69	93	.426	27.0	Sam Perlozzo, Dave Trembley	2,164,822
2008	5th	68	93	.422	28.5	Dave Trembley	1,950,075
2009	5th	64	98	.395	39.0	Dave Trembley	1,907,163
2010	5th	66	96	.407	30.0	Dave Trembley, Juan Samuel, Buck Showalter	1,733,019
2011	5th	69	93	.425	28.0	Buck Showalter	1,755,461
2012	2nd	93	69	.574	2.0	Buck Showalter	2,102,240
2013	3rd	85	77	.525	12.0	Buck Showalter	2,357,561
2014	1st	96	66	.593	+12.0	Buck Showalter	2,464,473
2015	3rd	81	81	.500	12.0	Buck Showalter	2,281,202

*Split season.

Awards

Most Valuable Player

Brooks Robinson, third base, 1964
Frank Robinson, outfield, 1966
Boog Powell, first base, 1970
Cal Ripken Jr., shortstop, 1983
Cal Ripken Jr., shortstop, 1991

Rookie of the Year

Ron Hansen, shortstop, 1960
Curt Blefary, outfield, 1965
Al Bumbry, outfield, 1973
Eddie Murray, first base, 1977
Cal Ripken Jr., shortstop and third base, 1982
Gregg Olson, pitcher, 1989

Cy Young

Mike Cuellar (co-winner), 1969
Jim Palmer, 1973
Jim Palmer, 1975
Jim Palmer, 1976
Mike Flanagan, 1979
Steve Stone, 1980

Hall of Famers Who Played for the Orioles

Luis Aparicio, shortstop, 1963–67
Reggie Jackson, outfield, 1976
George Kell, third base, 1956–57
Eddie Murray, first base and designated hitter, 1977–88 and 1996
Jim Palmer, pitcher, 1965–84
Cal Ripken Jr., shortstop and third base, 1981–2001
Robin Roberts, pitcher, 1962–65
Brooks Robinson, third base, 1955–77
Frank Robinson, outfield, 1966–71
Hoyt Wilhelm, pitcher, 1958–62

Retired Numbers

4 ..... Earl Weaver
5 ..... Brooks Robinson
8 ..... Cal Ripken Jr.
20 ..... Frank Robinson
22 ..... Jim Palmer
33 ..... Eddie Murray

League Leaders, Batting

Batting Average, Season

Frank Robinson, 1966 ..... .316

Home Runs, Season

Frank Robinson, 1966 49
Eddie Murray, 1981 ..... 22 (Tie)
Chris Davis, 2013 53
Nelson Cruz, 2014 40
Chris Davis, 2015 47

RBIs, Season

Brooks Robinson, 1964 118
Frank Robinson, 1966 122
Lee May, 1976 109
Eddie Murray, 1981 78
Miguel Tejada, 2004 150
Chris Davis, 2013 138

Stolen Bases, Season
Luis Aparicio, 1963 40
Luis Aparicio, 1964 57
Brady Anderson, 1992 53
Brian Roberts, 2008 50

Total Bases, Season
Frank Robinson, 1966 367
Cal Ripken Jr., 1991 368
Chris Davis, 2013 370

Most Hits, Season
Cal Ripken Jr., 1983 211

Most Runs, Season
Frank Robinson, 1966 122
Don Buford, 1971 99
Cal Ripken Jr., 1983 121

Batting Feats

Triple Crown Winners
Frank Robinson, 1966 (.316 BA, 49 HRs, 122 RBIs)

Hitting for the Cycle
Brooks Robinson, July 15, 1960
Cal Ripken Jr., May 6, 1984
Aubrey Huff, June 29, 2007
Felix Pie, Aug. 14, 2009

Six Hits in a Game
Cal Ripken Jr., June 13, 1999

40 or More Home Runs, Season
53 ..... Chris Davis, 2013
50 ..... Brady Anderson, 1996
49 ..... Frank Robinson, 1966
47 ..... Chris Davis, 2015
46 ..... Jim Gentile, 1961
43 ..... Rafael Palmeiro, 1998
40 ..... Nelson Cruz, 2014

League Leaders, Pitching

Most Wins, Season
Chuck Estrada, 1960 ..... 18 (Tie)
Mike Cuellar, 1970 ..... 24 (Tie)
Dave McNally, 1970 ..... 24 (Tie)
Jim Palmer, 1975 ..... 23 (Tie)
Jim Palmer, 1976 22
Jim Palmer, 1977 ..... 20 (Tie)
Mike Flanagan, 1979 23
Steve Stone, 1980 25
Dennis Martinez, 1981 ..... 14 (Tie)
Mike Boddicker, 1984 20
Mike Mussina, 1995 19

Most Strikeouts, Season
Bob Turley, 1954 185

Lowest ERA, Season
Hoyt Wilhelm, 1959 ..... 2.19
Jim Palmer, 1973 ..... 2.40
Jim Palmer, 1975 ..... 2.09
Mike Boddicker, 1984 ..... 2.79

Most Saves, Season
Lee Smith, 1994 33
Randy Myers, 1997 45
Jim Johnson, 2012 51
Jim Johnson, 2013 50

Best Won–Lost Percentage, Season
Wally Bunker, 1964 .. 19–5 ..... .792
Jim Palmer, 1969 ..... 16–4 ..... .800
Mike Cuellar, 1970 ... 24–8 ..... .750
Dave McNally, 1971 . 21–5 ..... .808
Mike Cuellar, 1974 . 22–10 ..... .688
Mike Torrez, 1975 .... 20–9 ..... .690
Steve Stone, 1980 ..... 25–7 ..... .781
Mike Mussina, 1992 . 18–5 ..... .783

Pitching Feats

20 Wins, Season
Steve Barber, 1963 20–13
Dave McNally, 1968 22–10
Mike Cuellar, 1969 23–11
Dave McNally, 1969 20–7
Mike Cuellar, 1970 24–8
Dave McNally, 1970 24–9
Jim Palmer, 1970 20–10
Dave McNally, 1971 21–5
Pat Dobson, 1971 20–8
Mike Cuellar, 1971 20–9
Jim Palmer, 1971 20–9
Jim Palmer, 1972 21–10
Jim Palmer, 1973 22–9
Mike Cuellar, 1974 22–10
Jim Palmer, 1975 23–11
Mike Torrez, 1975 20–9
Jim Palmer, 1976 22–13
Wayne Garland, 1976 20–7
Jim Palmer, 1977 20–11
Jim Palmer, 1978 21–12
Mike Flanagan, 1979 23–9
Steve Stone, 1980 25–7
Scott McGregor, 1980 20–8
Mike Boddicker, 1984 20–11

No-Hitters
Hoyt Wilhelm (vs. N.Y. Yankees), Sept. 2, 1958 (final: 1–0)
Steve Barber and Stu Miller (vs. Det. Tigers), Apr. 30, 1967 (final: 1–2)
Tom Phoebus (vs. Bost. Red Sox), Apr. 27, 1968 (final: 6–0)
Jim Palmer (vs. Oak. A's), Aug. 13, 1969 (final: 8–0)
Bob Milacki, Mike Flanagan, Mark Williamson, and Gregg Olson (vs. Oak. A's), July 13, 1991 (final: 2–0)

No-Hitters Pitched Against
Bo Belinsky, L.A. Angels, May 5, 1962 (final: 2–0)
Nolan Ryan, Cal. Angels, June 1, 1975 (final: 1–0)
Juan Nieves, Milw. Brewers (AL), Apr. 15, 1987 (final: 7–0)
Wilson Alvarez, Chi. White Sox, Aug. 11, 1991 (final: 7–0)
Hideo Nomo, Bost. Red Sox, Apr. 4, 2001 (final: 3–0)
Clay Buchholz, Bost. Red Sox, Sept. 1, 2007 (final: 10–0)
Hisashi Iwakuma, Sea. Mariners, Aug. 12, 2015 (final: 3–0)

Postseason Play

1966 World Series vs. L.A. Dodgers (NL), won 4 games to 0
1969 League Championship Series vs. Min. Twins, won 3 games to 0
World Series vs. N.Y. Mets (NL), lost 4 games to 1
1970 League Championship Series vs. Min. Twins, won 3 games to 0
World Series vs. Cin. Reds (NL), won 4 games to 1
1971 League Championship Series vs. Oak. A's, won 3 games to 0
World Series vs. Pitt. Pirates (NL), lost 4 games to 3

1973 League Championship Series vs. Oak. A's, lost 3 games to 2

1974 League Championship Series vs. Oak. A's, lost 3 games to 1

1979 League Championship Series vs. Cal. Angels, won 3 games to 1
World Series vs. Pitt. Pirates (NL), lost 4 games to 3

1983 League Championship Series vs. Chi. White Sox, won 3 games to 1
World Series vs. Phila. Phillies (NL), won 4 games to 1

1996 Division Series vs. Cle. Indians, won 3 games to 1
League Championship Series vs. N.Y. Yankees, lost 4 games to 1

1997 Division Series vs. Sea. Mariners, won 3 games to 1
League Championship Series vs. Cle. Indians, lost 4 games to 2

2012 AL Wild Card Playoff Game vs. Tex. Rangers, won
Division Series vs. N.Y. Yankees, lost 3 games to 2

2014 Division Series vs. Det. Tigers, won 3 games to 0
League Championship Series vs. K.C. Royals, lost 4 games to 0

Boston Red Sox

Dates of Operation: 1901–present (115 years)
Overall Record: 9224 wins, 8638 losses (.516)
Stadiums: Huntington Avenue Baseball Grounds, 1901–11; Braves Field, 1915–16 World Series and 1929–32 (Sundays only); Fenway Park, 1912–present (capacity: 37,673)
Other Names: Americans, Puritans, Pilgrims, Plymouth Rocks, Somersets

Year-by-Year Finishes

Year	Finish	Wins	Losses	Percentage	Games Behind	Manager	Attendance
1901	2nd	79	57	.581	4.0	Jimmy Collins	289,448
1902	3rd	77	60	.562	6.5	Jimmy Collins	348,567
1903	1st	91	47	.659	+14.5	Jimmy Collins	379,338
1904	1st	95	59	.617	+1.5	Jimmy Collins	623,295
1905	4th	78	74	.513	16.0	Jimmy Collins	468,828
1906	8th	49	105	.318	45.5	Jimmy Collins, Chick Stahl	410,209
1907	7th	59	90	.396	32.5	George Huff, Bob Unglaub, Deacon McGuire	436,777
1908	5th	75	79	.487	15.5	Deacon McGuire, Fred Lake	473,048
1909	3rd	88	63	.583	9.5	Fred Lake	668,965
1910	4th	81	72	.529	22.5	Patsy Donovan	584,619
1911	5th	78	75	.510	24.0	Patsy Donovan	503,961
1912	1st	105	47	.691	+14.0	Jake Stahl	597,096
1913	4th	79	71	.527	15.5	Jake Stahl, Bill Carrigan	437,194
1914	2nd	91	62	.595	8.5	Bill Carrigan	481,359
1915	1st	101	50	.669	+2.5	Bill Carrigan	539,885
1916	1st	91	63	.591	+2.0	Bill Carrigan	496,397
1917	2nd	90	62	.592	9.0	Jack Barry	387,856
1918	1st	75	51	.595	+2.5	Ed Barrow	249,513
1919	6th	66	71	.482	20.5	Ed Barrow	417,291
1920	5th	72	81	.471	25.5	Ed Barrow	402,445
1921	5th	75	79	.487	23.5	Hugh Duffy	279,273
1922	8th	61	93	.396	33.0	Hugh Duffy	259,184
1923	8th	61	91	.401	37.0	Frank Chance	229,668
1924	7th	67	87	.435	25.0	Lee Fohl	448,556
1925	8th	47	105	.309	49.5	Lee Fohl	267,782
1926	8th	46	107	.301	44.5	Lee Fohl	285,155
1927	8th	51	103	.331	59.0	Bill Carrigan	305,275
1928	8th	57	96	.373	43.5	Bill Carrigan	396,920
1929	8th	58	96	.377	48.0	Bill Carrigan	394,620
1930	8th	52	102	.338	50.0	Heinie Wagner	444,045
1931	6th	62	90	.408	45.0	Shano Collins	350,975
1932	8th	43	111	.279	64.0	Shano Collins, Marty McManus	182,150
1933	7th	63	86	.423	34.5	Marty McManus	268,715
1934	4th	76	76	.500	24.0	Bucky Harris	610,640
1935	4th	78	75	.510	16.0	Joe Cronin	558,568
1936	6th	74	80	.481	28.5	Joe Cronin	626,895
1937	5th	80	72	.526	21.0	Joe Cronin	559,659
1938	2nd	88	61	.591	9.5	Joe Cronin	646,459
1939	2nd	89	62	.589	17.0	Joe Cronin	573,070

1940	4th (Tie)	82	72	.532	8.0	Joe Cronin	716,234
1941	2nd	84	70	.545	17.0	Joe Cronin	718,497
1942	2nd	93	59	.612	9.0	Joe Cronin	730,340
1943	7th	68	84	.447	29.0	Joe Cronin	358,275
1944	4th	77	77	.500	12.0	Joe Cronin	506,975
1945	7th	71	83	.461	17.5	Joe Cronin	603,794
1946	1st	104	50	.675	+12.0	Joe Cronin	1,416,944
1947	3rd	83	71	.539	14.0	Joe Cronin	1,427,315
1948	2nd	96	59	.619	1.0	Joe McCarthy	1,558,798
1949	2nd	96	58	.623	1.0	Joe McCarthy	1,596,650
1950	3rd	94	60	.610	4.0	Joe McCarthy, Steve O'Neill	1,344,080
1951	3rd	87	67	.565	11.0	Steve O'Neill	1,312,282
1952	6th	76	78	.494	19.0	Lou Boudreau	1,115,750
1953	4th	84	69	.549	16.0	Lou Boudreau	1,026,133
1954	4th	69	85	.448	42.0	Lou Boudreau	931,127
1955	4th	84	70	.545	12.0	Pinky Higgins	1,203,200
1956	4th	84	70	.545	13.0	Pinky Higgins	1,137,158
1957	3rd	82	72	.532	16.0	Pinky Higgins	1,181,087
1958	3rd	79	75	.513	13.0	Pinky Higgins	1,077,047
1959	5th	75	79	.487	19.0	Pinky Higgins, Billy Jurges	984,102
1960	7th	65	89	.422	32.0	Billy Jurges, Pinky Higgins	1,129,866
1961	6th	76	86	.469	33.0	Pinky Higgins	850,589
1962	8th	76	84	.475	19.0	Pinky Higgins	733,080
1963	7th	76	85	.472	28.0	Johnny Pesky	942,642
1964	8th	72	90	.444	27.0	Johnny Pesky, Billy Herman	883,276
1965	9th	62	100	.383	40.0	Billy Herman	652,201
1966	9th	72	90	.444	26.0	Billy Herman, Pete Runnels	811,172
1967	1st	92	70	.568	+1.0	Dick Williams	1,727,832
1968	4th	86	76	.531	17.0	Dick Williams	1,940,788
				East Division			
1969	3rd	87	75	.537	22.0	Dick Williams, Eddie Popowski	1,833,246
1970	3rd	87	75	.537	21.0	Eddie Kasko	1,595,278
1971	3rd	85	77	.525	18.0	Eddie Kasko	1,678,732
1972	2nd	85	70	.548	0.5	Eddie Kasko	1,441,718
1973	2nd	89	73	.549	8.0	Eddie Kasko	1,481,002
1974	3rd	84	78	.519	7.0	Darrell Johnson	1,556,411
1975	1st	95	65	.594	+4.5	Darrell Johnson	1,748,587
1976	3rd	83	79	.512	15.5	Darrell Johnson, Don Zimmer	1,895,846
1977	2nd (Tie)	97	64	.602	2.5	Don Zimmer	2,074,549
1978	2nd	99	64	.607	1.0	Don Zimmer	2,320,643
1979	3rd	91	69	.569	11.5	Don Zimmer	2,353,114
1980	4th	83	77	.519	19.0	Don Zimmer, Johnny Pesky	1,956,092
1981*	5th/ 2nd (Tie)	59	49	.546	4.0/1.5	Ralph Houk	1,060,379
1982	3rd	89	73	.549	6.0	Ralph Houk	1,950,124
1983	6th	78	84	.481	20.0	Ralph Houk	1,782,285
1984	4th	86	76	.531	18.0	Ralph Houk	1,661,618
1985	5th	81	81	.500	18.5	John McNamara	1,786,633
1986	1st	95	66	.590	+5.5	John McNamara	2,147,641
1987	5th	78	84	.481	20.0	John McNamara	2,231,551
1988	1st	89	73	.549	+1.0	John McNamara, Joe Morgan	2,464,851
1989	3rd	83	79	.512	6.0	Joe Morgan	2,510,012

1990	1st	88	74	.543	+2.0	Joe Morgan	2,528,986
1991	2nd (Tie)	84	78	.519	7.0	Joe Morgan	2,562,435
1992	7th	73	89	.451	23.0	Butch Hobson	2,468,574
1993	5th	80	82	.494	15.0	Butch Hobson	2,422,021
1994	4th	54	61	.470	17.0	Butch Hobson	1,775,818
1995	1st	86	58	.597	+7.0	Kevin Kennedy	2,164,410
1996	3rd	85	77	.525	7.0	Kevin Kennedy	2,315,231
1997	4th	78	84	.481	20.0	Jimy Williams	2,226,136
1998	2nd	92	70	.568	22.0	Jimy Williams	2,343,947
1999	2nd	94	68	.580	4.0	Jimy Williams	2,446,162
2000	2nd	85	77	.525	2.5	Jimy Williams	2,586,032
2001	2nd	82	79	.509	13.5	Jimy Williams, Joe Kerrigan	2,625,333
2002	2nd	93	69	.574	10.5	Grady Little	2,650,063
2003	2nd	95	67	.586	6.0	Grady Little	2,724,165
2004	2nd	98	64	.605	3.0	Terry Francona	2,837,304
2005	1st (Tie)	95	67	.586	—	Terry Francona	2,847,888
2006	3rd	86	76	.531	11.0	Terry Francona	2,967,508
2007	1st	96	66	.593	+2.0	Terry Francona	2,971,025
2008	2nd	95	67	.586	2.0	Terry Francona	3,048,250
2009	2nd	95	67	.586	8.0	Terry Francona	3,062,699
2010	3rd	89	73	.549	7.0	Terry Francona	3,046,445
2011	3rd	90	72	.556	7.0	Terry Francona	3,054,001
2012	5th	69	93	.426	26.0	John Farrell	3,043,003
2013	1st	97	65	.599	+5.5	John Farrell	2,833,333
2014	5th	71	91	.438	25.0	John Farrell	2,956,089
2015	5th	78	84	.481	15.0	John Farrell	2,880,694

*Split season.

Awards

Most Valuable Player

Tris Speaker, outfield, 1912
Jimmie Foxx, first base, 1938
Ted Williams, outfield, 1946
Ted Williams, outfield, 1949
Jackie Jensen, outfield, 1958
Carl Yastrzemski, outfield, 1967
Fred Lynn, outfield, 1975
Jim Rice, outfield, 1978
Roger Clemens, pitcher, 1986
Mo Vaughn, first base, 1995
Dustin Pedroia, second base, 2008

Rookie of the Year

Walt Dropo, first base, 1950
Don Schwall, pitcher, 1961
Carlton Fisk, catcher, 1972
Fred Lynn, outfield, 1975
Nomar Garciaparra, shortstop, 1997
Dustin Pedroia, second base, 2007

Cy Young

Jim Lonborg, 1967
Roger Clemens, 1986
Roger Clemens, 1987
Roger Clemens, 1991
Pedro Martinez, 1999
Pedro Martinez, 2000

Hall of Famers Who Played for the Red Sox

Luis Aparicio, shortstop, 1971–73
Wade Boggs, third base, 1982–92
Lou Boudreau, shortstop, 1951–52
Jesse Burkett, outfield, 1905
Orlando Cepeda, designated hitter, 1973
Jack Chesbro, pitcher, 1909
Jimmy Collins, third base, 1901–07
Joe Cronin, shortstop, 1935–45
Andre Dawson, outfielder, designated hitter, 1993–94
Bobby Doerr, second base, 1937–44 and 1946–51
Dennis Eckersley, pitcher, 1978–84 and 1998
Rick Ferrell, catcher, 1933–37
Carlton Fisk, catcher, 1969–80
Jimmie Foxx, first base, 1936–42
Lefty Grove, pitcher, 1934–41
Rickey Henderson, outfielder, 2002
Harry Hooper, outfield, 1909–20
Waite Hoyt, pitcher, 1919–20
Ferguson Jenkins, pitcher, 1976–77
George Kell, third base, 1952–54
Heinie Manush, outfield, 1936
Juan Marichal, pitcher, 1974
Pedro Martinez, pitcher, 1998–2004
Herb Pennock, pitcher, 1915–22
Tony Perez, first base, 1980–82
Jim Rice, outfielder, 1974–89
Red Ruffing, pitcher, 1924–30
Babe Ruth, pitcher and outfield, 1914–19
Tom Seaver, pitcher, 1986
Al Simmons, outfield, 1943
John Smoltz, pitcher, 2009
Tris Speaker, outfield, 1907–15
Ted Williams, outfield, 1939–42 and 1946–60
Carl Yastrzemski, outfield, 1961–83
Cy Young, pitcher, 1901–08

Retired Numbers

1 ..... Bobby Doerr
4 ..... Joe Cronin
6 ..... Johnny Pesky
8 ..... Carl Yastrzemski
9 ..... Ted Williams
14 ..... Jim Rice
26 ..... Wade Boggs
27 ..... Carlton Fisk
45 ..... Pedro Martinez

League Leaders, Batting

Batting Average, Season

Dale Alexander*, 1932 ..... .367
Jimmie Foxx, 1938 ..... .349
Ted Williams, 1941 ..... .406
Ted Williams, 1942 ..... .356
Ted Williams, 1947 ..... .343
Ted Williams, 1948 ..... .369
Billy Goodman, 1950 ..... .354
Ted Williams, 1957 ..... .388
Ted Williams, 1958 ..... .328
Pete Runnels, 1960 ..... .320
Pete Runnels, 1962 ..... .326
Carl Yastrzemski, 1963 ..... .321
Carl Yastrzemski, 1967 ..... .326
Carl Yastrzemski, 1968 ..... .301
Fred Lynn, 1979 ..... .333
Carney Lansford, 1981 ..... .336
Wade Boggs, 1983 ..... .361
Wade Boggs, 1985 ..... .368
Wade Boggs, 1986 ..... .357
Wade Boggs, 1987 ..... .363
Wade Boggs, 1988 ..... .366
Nomar Garciaparra, 1999 ..... .357
Nomar Garciaparra, 2000 ..... .372
Manny Ramirez, 2002 ..... .349
Bill Mueller, 2003 ..... .326
*.250 with Det. Tigers and .372 with Bost. Red Sox.

Home Runs, Season

Buck Freeman, 1903 13
Jake Stahl, 1910 10
Tris Speaker, 1912 ..... 10 (Tie)
Babe Ruth, 1918 ..... 11 (Tie)
Babe Ruth, 1919 29
Jimmie Foxx, 1939 35
Ted Williams, 1941 37
Ted Williams, 1942 36
Ted Williams, 1947 32
Ted Williams, 1949 43
Tony Conigliaro, 1965 32
Carl Yastrzemski, 1967 ..... 44 (Tie)
Jim Rice, 1977 39
Jim Rice, 1978 46
Dwight Evans, 1981 ..... 22 (Tie)
Jim Rice, 1983 39
Tony Armas, 1984 43
Manny Ramirez, 2004 43
David Ortiz, 2006 54

RBIs, Season

Babe Ruth, 1919 112
Jimmie Foxx, 1938 175
Ted Williams, 1939 145
Ted Williams, 1942 137
Ted Williams, 1947 114
Vern Stephens, 1949 ..... 159 (Tie)
Ted Williams, 1949 ..... 159 (Tie)
Walt Dropo, 1950 ..... 144 (Tie)
Vern Stephens, 1950 ..... 144 (Tie)
Jackie Jensen, 1955 ..... 116 (Tie)
Jackie Jensen, 1958 122
Jackie Jensen, 1959 112
Dick Stuart, 1963 118
Carl Yastrzemski, 1967 121
Ken Harrelson, 1968 109
Jim Rice, 1978 139
Jim Rice, 1983 ..... 126 (Tie)
Tony Armas, 1984 123
Mo Vaughn, 1995 ..... 126 (Tie)
David Ortiz, 2005 148
David Ortiz, 2006 137

Stolen Bases, Season

Buddy Myer, 1928 30
Billy Werber, 1934 40
Billy Werber, 1935 29
Ben Chapman*, 1937 ..... 35 (Tie)
Dom DiMaggio, 1950 15
Jackie Jensen, 1954 22
Tommy Harper, 1973 54
Jacoby Ellsbury, 2008 50
Jacoby Ellsbury, 2009 70
Jacoby Ellsbury, 2013 52
*8 with Wash. Senators and 27 with Bost. Red Sox.

Total Bases, Season

Buck Freeman, 1902 287
Buck Freeman, 1903 281
Tris Speaker, 1914 287
Babe Ruth, 1919 284
Jimmie Foxx, 1938 398
Ted Williams, 1939 344
Ted Williams, 1942 338
Ted Williams, 1946 343
Ted Williams, 1947 335
Ted Williams, 1949 368
Walt Dropo, 1950 326
Ted Williams, 1951 295
Dick Stuart, 1963 319
Carl Yastrzemski, 1967 360
Carl Yastrzemski, 1970 335
Reggie Smith, 1971 302
Jim Rice, 1977 382
Jim Rice, 1978 406
Jim Rice, 1979 369
Dwight Evans, 1981 215
Jim Rice, 1983 344
Tony Armas, 1984 339
David Ortiz, 2006 355
Jacoby Ellsbury, 2011 364

Most Hits, Season

Patsy Dougherty, 1903 195
Tris Speaker, 1914 193
Joe Vosmik, 1938 201
Doc Cramer, 1940 ..... 200 (Tie)
Johnny Pesky, 1942 205
Johnny Pesky, 1946 208
Johnny Pesky, 1947 207
Carl Yastrzemski, 1963 183
Carl Yastrzemski, 1967 189
Jim Rice, 1978 213
Wade Boggs, 1985 240
Nomar Garciaparra, 1997 209
Dustin Pedroia, 2008 ..... 213 (Tie)
Adrian Gonzalez, 2011 ..... 213 (tie)

Most Runs, Season

Patsy Dougherty, 1903 108
Babe Ruth, 1919 103
Ted Williams, 1940 134
Ted Williams, 1941 135
Ted Williams, 1942 141
Ted Williams, 1946 142
Ted Williams, 1947 125
Ted Williams, 1949 150
Dom DiMaggio, 1950 131
Dom DiMaggio, 1951 113
Carl Yastrzemski, 1967 112
Carl Yastrzemski, 1970 125
Carl Yastrzemski, 1974 93
Fred Lynn, 1975 103
Dwight Evans, 1984 121
Wade Boggs, 1988 128
Wade Boggs, 1989 ..... 113 (Tie)
Dustin Pedroia, 2008 118
Dustin Pedroia, 2009 115

Batting Feats

Triple Crown Winners

Ted Williams, 1942 (.356 BA, 35 HRs, 137 RBIs)
Ted Williams, 1947 (.343 BA, 32 HRs, 114 RBIs)
Carl Yastrzemski, 1967 (.326 BA, 44 HRs (Tie), 121 RBIs)

Hitting for the Cycle

Buck Freeman, July 21, 1903
Patsy Dougherty, July 29, 1903
Tris Speaker, June 9, 1912
Roy Carlyle, July 21, 1925
Moose Solters, Aug. 19, 1934
Joe Cronin, Aug. 2, 1940
Leon Culberson, July 3, 1943
Bobby Doerr, May 17, 1944
Bob Johnson, July 6, 1944
Ted Williams, July 21, 1946
Bobby Doerr, May 13, 1947
Lou Clinton, July 13, 1962
Carl Yastrzemski, May 14, 1965
Bob Watson, Sept. 15, 1979
Fred Lynn, May 13, 1980
Dwight Evans, June 28, 1984
Rich Gedman, Sept. 18, 1985
Mike Greenwell, Sept. 14, 1988
Scott Cooper, Apr. 12, 1994
John Valentin, June 6, 1996
Brock Holt, June 16, 2015

Six Hits in a Game

Jimmy Piersall, June 10, 1953
Pete Runnels, Aug. 30, 1960*
Jerry Remy, Sept. 3, 1981*
Nomar Garciaparra, June 21, 2003*
*Extra-inning game.

40 or More Home Runs, Season

54 ..... David Ortiz, 2006
50 ..... Jimmie Foxx, 1938
47 ..... David Ortiz, 2005
46 ..... Jim Rice, 1978
45 ..... Manny Ramirez, 2005
44 ..... Carl Yastrzemski, 1967
Mo Vaughn, 1996
43 ..... Ted Williams, 1949
Tony Armas, 1984
Manny Ramirez, 2004
42 ..... Dick Stuart, 1963
41 ..... Jimmie Foxx, 1936
Manny Ramirez, 2001
David Ortiz, 2004
40 ..... Rico Petrocelli, 1969
Carl Yastrzemski, 1969
Carl Yastrzemski, 1970
Mo Vaughn, 1998

League Leaders, Pitching

Triple Crown Winner

Cy Young, 1901 (33–10, 1.62 ERA, 150 SO)
Pedro Martinez, 1999 (23–4, 2.07 ERA, 313 SO)

Most Wins, Season

Cy Young, 1901 33
Cy Young, 1902 32
Cy Young, 1903 28
Smoky Joe Wood, 1912 34
Wes Ferrell, 1935 25
Tex Hughson, 1942 22
Mel Parnell, 1949 25
Frank Sullivan, 1955 18
Jim Lonborg, 1967 ..... 22 (Tie)
Roger Clemens, 1986 24
Roger Clemens, 1987 ..... 20 (Tie)
Curt Schilling, 2004 21
Josh Beckett, 2007 20

Most Strikeouts, Season

Cy Young, 1901 158
Tex Hughson, 1942 ..... 113 (Tie)
Jim Lonborg, 1967 246
Roger Clemens, 1988 291
Roger Clemens, 1991 241
Roger Clemens, 1996 257
Pedro Martinez, 1999 313
Pedro Martinez, 2000 284
Hideo Nomo, 2001 220
Pedro Martinez, 2002 239

Lowest ERA, Season

Dutch Leonard, 1914 ..... 1.00
Smoky Joe Wood, 1915 ..... 1.49
Babe Ruth, 1916 ..... 1.75
Lefty Grove, 1935 ..... 2.70
Lefty Grove, 1936 ..... 2.81
Lefty Grove, 1938 ..... 3.07
Lefty Grove, 1939 ..... 2.54
Mel Parnell, 1949 ..... 2.78
Luis Tiant, 1972 ..... 1.91
Roger Clemens, 1986 ..... 2.48
Roger Clemens, 1990 ..... 1.93
Roger Clemens, 1991 ..... 2.62
Roger Clemens, 1992 ..... 2.41
Pedro Martinez, 1999 ..... 2.07
Pedro Martinez, 2000 ..... 1.74
Pedro Martinez, 2002 ..... 2.26
Pedro Martinez, 2003 ..... 2.22

Most Saves, Season

Bill Campbell, 1977 31
Tom Gordon, 1998 46
Derek Lowe, 2000 ..... 42 (Tie)

Best Won–Lost Percentage, Season

Cy Young, 1903 ..... 28–9. .757
Jesse Tannehill, 1905 ..... 22–9. .710
Smoky Joe Wood, 1912 . 34–5. .872
Smoky Joe Wood, 1915 . 15–5. .750
Sad Sam Jones, 1918 ..... 16–5. .762
Lefty Grove, 1939 ..... 15–4. .789
Tex Hughson, 1944 ..... 18–5. .783
Dave Ferriss, 1946 ..... 25–6. .806
Jack Kramer, 1948 ..... 18–5. .783
Ellis Kinder, 1949 ..... 23–6. .793
Roger Clemens, 1986 ..... 24–4. .857
Roger Clemens, 1987 ..... 20–9. .690
Pedro Martinez, 1999 ..... 23–4. .852
Pedro Martinez, 2002 ..... 20–4. .833
Curt Schilling, 2004 ..... 21–6. .778

Pitching Feats

20 Wins, Season

Cy Young, 1901 33–10
Cy Young, 1902 32–11
Bill Dinneen, 1902 21–21
Cy Young, 1903 28–9
Bill Dinneen, 1903 21–13
Tom Hughes, 1903 20–7
Cy Young, 1904 26–16
Bill Dinneen, 1904 23–14
Jesse Tannehill, 1904 21–11
Jesse Tannehill, 1905 22–9
Cy Young, 1907 22–15
Cy Young, 1908 21–11
Smoky Joe Wood, 1911 23–17
Smoky Joe Wood, 1912 34–5
Hugh Bedient, 1912 20–9
Buck O'Brien, 1912 20–13
Ray Collins, 1914 20–13
Babe Ruth, 1916 23–12
Babe Ruth, 1917 24–13
Carl Mays, 1917 22–9
Carl Mays, 1918 21–13
Sad Sam Jones, 1921 23–16
Howard Ehmke, 1923 20–17
Wes Ferrell, 1935 25–14
Lefty Grove, 1935 20–12
Wes Ferrell, 1936 20–15
Tex Hughson, 1942 22–6
Dave Ferriss, 1945 21–10
Dave Ferriss, 1946 25–6
Tex Hughson, 1946 20–11
Mel Parnell, 1949 25–7
Ellis Kinder, 1949 23–6
Mel Parnell, 1953 21–8

Bill Monbouquette, 1963..... 20–10
Jim Lonborg, 1967..... 22–9
Luis Tiant, 1973..... 20–13
Luis Tiant, 1974..... 22–13
Luis Tiant, 1976..... 21–12
Dennis Eckersley, 1978..... 20–8
Roger Clemens, 1986..... 24–4
Roger Clemens, 1987..... 20–9
Roger Clemens, 1990..... 21–6
Pedro Martinez, 1999..... 23–4
Derek Lowe, 2002..... 21–8
Pedro Martinez, 2002..... 20–4
Curt Schilling, 2004..... 21–6
Josh Beckett, 2007..... 20–7

No-Hitters

Cy Young (vs. Phila. A's), May 5, 1904 (final: 3–0) (perfect game)
Jesse Tannehill (vs. Chi. White Sox), Aug. 17, 1904 (final: 6–0)
Bill Dinneen (vs. Chi. White Sox), Sept. 27, 1905 (final: 2–0)
Cy Young (vs. N.Y. Yankees), June 30, 1908 (final: 8–0)
Smoky Joe Wood (vs. St.L. Browns), July 29, 1911 (final: 5–0)
George Foster (vs. N.Y. Yankees), June 21, 1916 (final: 2–0)
Hub Leonard (vs. St.L. Browns), Aug. 30, 1916 (final: 4–0)
Babe Ruth and Ernie Shore (vs. Wash. Senators), June 23, 1917 (final: 4–0)
Hub Leonard (vs. Det. Tigers), June 3, 1918 (final: 5–0)
Ray Caldwell (vs. N.Y. Yankees), Sept. 10, 1919 (final: 3–0)
Howard Ehmke (vs. Phila. A's), Sept. 7, 1923 (final: 4–0)
Mel Parnell (vs. Chi. White Sox), July 14, 1956 (final: 4–0)
Earl Wilson (vs. L.A. Angels), June 26, 1962 (final: 2–0)
Bill Monbouquette (vs. Chi. White Sox), Aug. 1, 1962 (final: 1–0)
Dave Morehead (vs. Cle. Indians), Sept. 16, 1965 (final: 2–0)
Hideo Nomo (vs. Balt. Orioles), Apr. 4, 2001 (final: 3–0)
Derek Lowe (vs. T.B. Devil Rays), Apr. 27, 2002 (final: 10–0)
Clay Buchholz (vs. Balt. Orioles), Sept. 1, 2007 (final: 10–0)
Jon Lester (vs. K.C. Royals), May 19, 2008 (final 7–0)

No-Hitters Pitched Against

Ed Walsh, Chi. White Sox, Aug. 27, 1911 (final: 5–0)
George Mogridge, N.Y. Yankees, Apr. 24, 1917 (final: 2–1)
Walter Johnson, Wash. Senators, July 1, 1920 (final: 1–0)
Ted Lyons, Chi. White Sox, Aug. 21, 1926 (final: 6–0)
Bob Burke, Wash. Senators, Aug. 8, 1931 (final: 5–0)
Allie Reynolds, N.Y. Yankees, Sept. 28, 1951 (final: 8–0)
Jim Bunning, Det. Tigers, July 20, 1958 (final: 3–0)
Tom Phoebus, Balt. Orioles, Apr. 27, 1968 (final: 6–0)
Dave Righetti, N.Y. Yankees, July 4, 1983 (final: 4–0)
Chris Bosio, Sea. Mariners, Apr. 22, 1993 (final: 7–0)

Postseason Play

1903 World Series vs. Pitt. Pirates (NL), won 5 games to 3
1912 World Series vs. N.Y. Giants (NL), won 4 games to 3
1915 World Series vs. Phila. Phillies (NL), won 4 games to 1
1916 World Series vs. Bklyn. Dodgers (NL), won 4 games to 1
1918 World Series vs. Chi. Cubs (NL), won 4 games to 2
1946 World Series vs. St.L. Cardinals (NL), lost 4 games to 3
1948 Pennant Playoff Game vs. Cle. Indians, lost
1967 World Series vs. St.L. Cardinals (NL), lost 4 games to 3
1975 League Championship Series vs. Oak. A's, won 3 games to 0
World Series vs. Cin. Reds (NL), lost 4 games to 3
1978 East Division Playoff Game vs. N.Y. Yankees, lost
1986 League Championship Series vs. Cal. Angels, won 4 games to 3
World Series vs. N.Y. Mets (NL), lost 4 games to 3
1988 League Championship Series vs. Oak. A's, lost 4 games to 0
1990 League Championship Series vs. Oak. A's, lost 4 games to 0
1995 Division Series vs. Cle. Indians, lost 3 games to 0
1998 Division Series vs. Cle. Indians, lost 3 games to 1
1999 Division Series vs. Cle. Indians, won 3 games to 2
League Championship Series vs. N.Y. Yankees, lost 4 games to 1
2003 Division Series vs. Oak. A's, won 3 games to 2
League Championship Series vs. N.Y. Yankees, lost 4 games to 3
2004 Division Series vs. Ana. Angels, won 3 games to 0
League Championship Series vs. N.Y. Yankees, won 4 games to 3
World Series vs. St.L. Cardinals (NL), won 4 games to 0
2005 Division Series vs. Chi. White Sox, lost 3 games to 0
2007 Division Series vs. L.A. Angels, won 3 games to 0
League Championship Series vs. Cle. Indians, won 4 games to 3
World Series vs. Colo. Rockies (NL), won 4 games to 0
2008 Division Series vs. L.A. Angels, won 3 games to 1
League Championship Series vs. T.B. Rays, lost 4 games to 3
2009 Division Series vs. L.A. Angels, lost 3 games to 0
2013 Division Series vs. T.B. Rays, won 3 games to 1
League Championship Series vs Det. Tigers, won 4 games to 2
World Series vs. St.L. Cardinals (NL), won 4 games to 2

Chicago White Sox

Dates of Operation: 1901–present (115 years)

Overall Record: 9004 wins, 8797 losses (.505) (AL)

Stadiums: South Side Park (also known as White Stocking Park, 1901–03; White Sox Park, 1904–10), 1901–10; Comiskey Park (also known as White Sox Park, 1910–12, 1962–75), 1910–90; Milwaukee County Stadium, 1968–69; New Comiskey Park, 1991–2002; now U.S. Cellular Field, 2003–present (capacity: 40,615)

Other Name: White Stockings

Year-by-Year Finishes

Year	Finish	Wins	Losses	Percentage	Games Behind	Manager	Attendance
1901	1st	83	53	.610	+4.0	Clark Griffith	354,350
1902	4th	74	60	.552	8.0	Clark Griffith	337,898
1903	7th	60	77	.438	30.5	Nixey Callahan	286,183
1904	3rd	89	65	.578	6.0	Nixey Callahan, Fielder Jones	557,123
1905	2nd	92	60	.605	2.0	Fielder Jones	687,419
1906	1st	93	58	.616	+3.0	Fielder Jones	585,202
1907	3rd	87	64	.576	5.5	Fielder Jones	666,307
1908	3rd	88	64	.579	1.5	Fielder Jones	636,096
1909	4th	78	74	.513	20.0	Billy Sullivan	478,400
1910	6th	68	85	.444	35.5	Hugh Duffy	552,084
1911	4th	77	74	.510	24.0	Hugh Duffy	583,208
1912	4th	78	76	.506	28.0	Nixey Callahan	602,241
1913	5th	78	74	.513	17.5	Nixey Callahan	644,501
1914	6th (Tie)	70	84	.455	30.0	Nixey Callahan	469,290
1915	3rd	93	61	.604	9.5	Pants Rowland	539,461
1916	2nd	89	65	.578	2.0	Pants Rowland	679,923
1917	1st	100	54	.649	+9.0	Pants Rowland	684,521
1918	6th	57	67	.460	17.0	Pants Rowland	195,081
1919	1st	88	52	.629	+3.5	Kid Gleason	627,186
1920	2nd	96	58	.623	2.0	Kid Gleason	833,492
1921	7th	62	92	.403	36.5	Kid Gleason	543,650
1922	5th	77	77	.500	17.0	Kid Gleason	602,860
1923	7th	69	85	.448	30.0	Kid Gleason	573,778
1924	8th	66	87	.431	25.5	Johnny Evers	606,658
1925	5th	79	75	.513	18.5	Eddie Collins	832,231
1926	5th	81	72	.529	9.5	Eddie Collins	710,339
1927	5th	70	83	.458	29.5	Ray Schalk	614,423
1928	5th	72	82	.468	29.0	Ray Schalk, Lena Blackburne	494,152
1929	7th	59	93	.388	46.0	Lena Blackburne	426,795
1930	7th	62	92	.403	40.0	Donie Bush	406,123
1931	8th	56	97	.366	51.0	Donie Bush	403,550
1932	7th	49	102	.325	56.5	Lew Fonseca	233,198
1933	6th	67	83	.447	31.0	Lew Fonseca	397,789
1934	8th	53	99	.349	47.0	Lew Fonseca, Jimmy Dykes	236,559
1935	5th	74	78	.487	19.5	Jimmy Dykes	470,281
1936	3rd	81	70	.536	20.0	Jimmy Dykes	440,810
1937	3rd	86	68	.558	16.0	Jimmy Dykes	589,245
1938	6th	65	83	.439	32.0	Jimmy Dykes	338,278

1939	4th	85	69	.552	22.5	Jimmy Dykes	594,104
1940	4th (Tie)	82	72	.532	8.0	Jimmy Dykes	660,336
1941	3rd	77	77	.500	24.0	Jimmy Dykes	677,077
1942	6th	66	82	.446	34.0	Jimmy Dykes	425,734
1943	4th	82	72	.532	16.0	Jimmy Dykes	508,962
1944	7th	71	83	.461	18.0	Jimmy Dykes	563,539
1945	6th	71	78	.477	15.0	Jimmy Dykes	657,981
1946	5th	74	80	.481	30.0	Jimmy Dykes, Ted Lyons	983,403
1947	6th	70	84	.455	27.0	Ted Lyons	876,948
1948	8th	51	101	.336	44.5	Ted Lyons	777,844
1949	6th	63	91	.409	34.0	Jack Onslow	937,151
1950	6th	60	94	.390	38.0	Jack Onslow, Red Corriden	781,330
1951	4th	81	73	.526	17.0	Paul Richards	1,328,234
1952	3rd	81	73	.526	14.0	Paul Richards	1,231,675
1953	3rd	89	65	.578	11.5	Paul Richards	1,191,353
1954	3rd	94	60	.610	17.0	Paul Richards, Marty Marion	1,231,629
1955	3rd	91	63	.591	5.0	Marty Marion	1,175,684
1956	3rd	85	69	.552	12.0	Marty Marion	1,000,090
1957	2nd	90	64	.584	8.0	Al Lopez	1,135,668
1958	2nd	82	72	.532	10.0	Al Lopez	797,451
1959	1st	94	60	.610	+5.0	Al Lopez	1,423,144
1960	3rd	87	67	.565	10.0	Al Lopez	1,644,460
1961	4th	86	76	.531	23.0	Al Lopez	1,146,019
1962	5th	85	77	.525	11.0	Al Lopez	1,131,562
1963	2nd	94	68	.580	10.5	Al Lopez	1,158,848
1964	2nd	98	64	.605	1.0	Al Lopez	1,250,053
1965	2nd	95	67	.586	7.0	Al Lopez	1,130,519
1966	4th	83	79	.512	15.0	Eddie Stanky	990,016
1967	4th	89	73	.549	3.0	Eddie Stanky	985,634
1968	8th (Tie)	67	95	.414	36.0	Eddie Stanky, Al Lopez	803,775
				West Division			
1969	5th	68	94	.420	29.0	Al Lopez, Don Gutteridge	589,546
1970	6th	56	106	.346	42.0	Don Gutteridge, Chuck Tanner	495,355
1971	3rd	79	83	.488	22.5	Chuck Tanner	833,891
1972	2nd	87	67	.565	5.5	Chuck Tanner	1,177,318
1973	5th	77	85	.475	17.0	Chuck Tanner	1,302,527
1974	4th	80	80	.500	9.0	Chuck Tanner	1,149,596
1975	5th	75	86	.466	22.5	Chuck Tanner	750,802
1976	6th	64	97	.398	25.5	Paul Richards	914,945
1977	3rd	90	72	.556	12.0	Bob Lemon	1,657,135
1978	5th	71	90	.441	20.5	Bob Lemon, Larry Doby	1,491,100
1979	5th	73	87	.456	14.0	Don Kessinger, Tony La Russa	1,280,702
1980	5th	70	90	.438	26.0	Tony La Russa	1,200,365
1981*	3rd/6th	54	52	.509	2.5/7.0	Tony La Russa	946,651
1982	3rd	87	75	.537	6.0	Tony La Russa	1,567,787
1983	1st	99	63	.611	+20.0	Tony La Russa	2,132,821
1984	5th (Tie)	74	88	.457	10.0	Tony La Russa	2,136,988
1985	3rd	85	77	.525	6.0	Tony La Russa	1,669,888
1986	5th	72	90	.444	20.0	Tony La Russa, Jim Fregosi	1,424,313
1987	5th	77	85	.475	8.0	Jim Fregosi	1,208,060
1988	5th	71	90	.441	32.5	Jim Fregosi	1,115,749
1989	7th	69	92	.429	29.5	Jeff Torborg	1,045,651
1990	2nd	94	68	.580	9.0	Jeff Torborg	2,002,357

1991	2nd	87	75	.537	8.0	Jeff Torborg	2,934,154
1992	3rd	86	76	.531	10.0	Gene Lamont	2,681,156
1993	1st	94	68	.580	+8.0	Gene Lamont	2,581,091
				Central Division			
1994	1st	67	46	.593	+1.0	Gene Lamont	1,697,398
1995	3rd	68	76	.472	32.0	Gene Lamont, Terry Bevington	1,609,773
1996	2nd	85	77	.525	14.5	Terry Bevington	1,676,403
1997	2nd	80	81	.497	6.0	Terry Bevington	1,864,782
1998	2nd	80	82	.494	9.0	Jerry Manuel	1,391,146
1999	2nd	75	86	.466	21.5	Jerry Manuel	1,338,851
2000	1st	95	67	.586	+5.0	Jerry Manuel	1,947,799
2001	3rd	83	79	.512	8.0	Jerry Manuel	1,766,172
2002	2nd	81	81	.500	13.5	Jerry Manuel	1,676,804
2003	2nd	86	76	.531	4.0	Jerry Manuel	1,939,524
2004	2nd	83	79	.512	9.0	Ozzie Guillen	1,930,537
2005	1st	99	63	.611	+6.0	Ozzie Guillen	2,342,833
2006	3rd	90	72	.556	6.0	Ozzie Guillen	2,057,411
2007	4th	72	90	.444	24.5	Ozzie Guillen	2,684,395
2008	1st	89	74	.546	+1.0	Ozzie Guillen	2,501,103
2009	3rd	79	83	.488	7.5	Ozzie Guillen	2,284,164
2010	2nd	88	74	.543	6.0	Ozzie Guillen	2,194,378
2011	3rd	79	83	.488	16.0	Ozzie Guillen	2,001,117
2012	2nd	85	77	.525	3.0	Robin Ventura	1,965,955
2013	5th	63	99	.389	30.0	Robin Ventura	1,768,413
2014	4th	73	89	.451	17.0	Robin Ventura	1,650,821
2015	4th	76	86	.469	19.0	Robin Ventura	1,755,810

*Split season.

Awards

Most Valuable Player

Nellie Fox, second base, 1959
Dick Allen, first base, 1972
Frank Thomas, first base, 1993
Frank Thomas, first base, 1994

Rookie of the Year

Luis Aparicio, shortstop, 1956
Gary Peters, pitcher, 1963
Tommie Agee, outfield, 1966
Ron Kittle, outfield, 1983
Ozzie Guillen, shortstop, 1985
Jose Abreu, first base, 2014

Cy Young

Early Wynn, 1959
LaMarr Hoyt, 1983
Jack McDowell, 1993

Hall of Famers Who Played for the White Sox

Roberto Alomar, second base, 2003–04
Luis Aparicio, shortstop, 1956–62
Luke Appling, shortstop, 1930–43 and 1945–50
Chief Bender, pitcher, 1925
Steve Carlton, pitcher, 1986
Eddie Collins, second base, 1915–26
Jocko Conlan, outfield, 1934–35
George Davis, shortstop, 1902 and 1904–09
Larry Doby, outfield, 1956–57 and 1959
Johnny Evers, second base, 1922
Red Faber, pitcher, 1914–33
Carlton Fisk, catcher, 1981–93
Nellie Fox, second base, 1950–63
Goose Gossage, pitcher, 1972–76
Ken Griffey Jr., outfield, 2008
Clark Griffith, pitcher, 1901–02
Harry Hooper, outfield, 1921–25
George Kell, third base, 1954–56
Ted Lyons, pitcher, 1923–42 and 1946
Edd Roush, outfield, 1913
Red Ruffing, pitcher, 1947
Ron Santo, third base, 1974
Ray Schalk, catcher, 1912–28
Tom Seaver, pitcher, 1984–86
Al Simmons, outfield, 1933–35
Frank Thomas, first base and designated hitter, 1990–2005
Ed Walsh, pitcher, 1904–16
Hoyt Wilhelm, pitcher, 1963–68
Early Wynn, pitcher, 1958–62

Retired Numbers

2 ..... Nellie Fox
3 ..... Harold Baines
4 ..... Luke Appling
9 ..... Minnie Minoso
11 ..... Luis Aparicio
14 ..... Paul Konerko
16 ..... Ted Lyons
19 ..... Billy Pierce
35 ..... Frank Thomas
72 ..... Carlton Fisk

League Leaders, Batting

Batting Average, Season

Luke Appling, 1936 ..... .388
Luke Appling, 1943 ..... .328
Frank Thomas, 1997 ..... .347

Home Runs, Season

Braggo Roth*, 1915 7
Gus Zernial**, 1951 33
Bill Melton, 1971 33
Dick Allen, 1972 37
Dick Allen, 1974 32

*4 with Cle. Indians and 3 with Chi. White Sox.
**33 with Phila. A's and 0 with Chi. White Sox.

RBIs, Season

Gus Zernial*, 1951 129
Dick Allen, 1972 113
*125 with Phila. A's and 4 with Chi. White Sox.

Stolen Bases, Season

Frank Isbell, 1901 48
Patsy Dougherty, 1908 47
Eddie Collins, 1919 33
Eddie Collins, 1923 49
Eddie Collins, 1924 42
Johnny Mostil, 1925 43
Johnny Mostil, 1926 35
Minnie Minoso*, 1951 31
Minnie Minoso, 1952 22
Minnie Minoso, 1953 25
Jim Rivera, 1955 25
Luis Aparicio, 1956 21
Luis Aparicio, 1957 28
Luis Aparicio, 1958 29
Luis Aparicio, 1959 56
Luis Aparicio, 1960 51
Luis Aparicio, 1961 53
Luis Aparicio, 1962 31
Juan Pierre, 2010 68
*0 with Cle. Indians and 31 with Chi. White Sox.

Total Bases, Season

Joe Jackson, 1916 293
Minnie Minoso, 1954 304
Albert Belle, 1998 399

Most Hits, Season

Nellie Fox, 1952 192
Nellie Fox, 1954 ..... 201 (Tie)
Nellie Fox, 1957 196
Nellie Fox, 1958 187
Minnie Minoso, 1960 184
Lance Johnson, 1995 186

Most Runs, Season

Johnny Mostil, 1925 135
Frank Thomas, 1994 106

Batting Feats

Triple Crown Winners

[No player]

Hitting for the Cycle

Ray Schalk, June 27, 1922
Jack Brohamer, Sept. 24, 1977
Carlton Fisk, May 16, 1984
Chris Singleton, July 6, 1999
Jose Valentin, Apr. 27, 2000

Six Hits in a Game

Ray Radcliffe, July 18, 1936
Hank Steinbacher, June 22, 1938
Floyd Robinson, July 22, 1962
Lance Johnson, Sept. 23, 1995
Alex Rios, July 9, 2013

40 or More Home Runs, Season

49 ..... Albert Belle, 1998
44 ..... Jermaine Dye, 2006
43 ..... Frank Thomas, 2000
42 ..... Frank Thomas, 2003
Jim Thome, 2006
41 ..... Frank Thomas, 1993
Paul Konerko, 2004
Adam Dunn, 2012
40 ..... Frank Thomas, 1995
Frank Thomas, 1996
Paul Konerko, 2005

League Leaders, Pitching

Most Wins, Season

Doc White, 1907 ..... 27 (Tie)
Ed Walsh, 1908 40
Eddie Cicotte, 1917 28
Eddie Cicotte, 1919 29
Ted Lyons, 1925 ..... 21 (Tie)
Ted Lyons, 1927 ..... 22 (Tie)
Billy Pierce, 1957 ..... 20 (Tie)
Early Wynn, 1959 22
Gary Peters, 1964 ..... 20 (Tie)
Wilbur Wood, 1972 ..... 24 (Tie)
Wilbur Wood, 1973 24
LaMarr Hoyt, 1982 19
LaMarr Hoyt, 1983 24
Jack McDowell, 1993 22

Most Strikeouts, Season

Ed Walsh, 1908 269
Frank Smith, 1909 177
Ed Walsh, 1911 255
Billy Pierce, 1953 186
Early Wynn, 1958 179
Esteban Loaiza, 2003 207
Chris Sale, 2015 274

Lowest ERA, Season

Eddie Cicotte, 1917 ..... 1.53
Red Faber, 1921 ..... 2.47
Red Faber, 1922 ..... 2.80
Thornton Lee, 1941 ..... 2.37
Ted Lyons, 1942 ..... 2.10
Saul Rogovin*, 1951 ..... 2.78
Billy Pierce, 1955 ..... 1.97
Frank Baumann, 1960 ..... 2.68
Gary Peters, 1963 ..... 2.33
Gary Peters, 1966 ..... 1.98
Joe Horlen, 1967 ..... 2.06
*5.25 with Det. Tigers and 2.48 with Chi. White Sox.

Most Saves, Season

Terry Forster, 1974 24
Goose Gossage, 1975 26
Bobby Thigpen, 1990 57

Best Won–Lost Percentage, Season

Clark Griffith, 1901 ... 24–7 ..... .774
Ed Walsh, 1908 ..... 40–15 ..... .727
Eddie Cicotte, 1916 .. 15–7 ..... .682
Reb Russell, 1917 ..... 15–5 ..... .750
Eddie Cicotte, 1919 .. 29–7 ..... .806
Sandy Consuegra, 1954 ..... 16–3 ..... .842
Dick Donovan, 1957 ..... 16–6 .727 (Tie)
Bob Shaw, 1959 ..... 18–6 ..... .750
Ray Herbert, 1962 .... 20–9 ..... .690
Joe Horlen, 1967 ..... 19–7 ..... .731
Rich Dotson, 1983 .... 22–7 ..... .759
Jason Bere, 1994 ..... 12–2 ..... .857

Pitching Feats

20 Wins, Season

Clark Griffith, 1901 24–7
Roy Patterson, 1902 20–12
Frank Owen, 1904 21–15
Nick Altrock, 1905 24–12
Frank Owen, 1905 21–13
Frank Owen, 1906 22–13
Nick Altrock, 1906 20–13
Doc White, 1907 27–13
Ed Walsh, 1907 24–18
Frank Smith, 1907 23–10
Ed Walsh, 1908 40–15
Frank Smith, 1909 25–17
Ed Walsh, 1911 27–18
Ed Walsh, 1912 27–17
Reb Russell, 1913 22–16
Jim Scott, 1913 20–20
Jim Scott, 1915 24–11
Red Faber, 1915 24–14
Eddie Cicotte, 1917 28–12

Eddie Cicotte, 1919 29–7
Lefty Williams, 1919 23–11
Red Faber, 1920 23–13
Lefty Williams, 1920 22–14
Dickie Kerr, 1920 21–9
Eddie Cicotte, 1920 21–10
Red Faber, 1921 25–15
Red Faber, 1922 21–17
Sloppy Thurston, 1924 20–14
Ted Lyons, 1925 21–11
Ted Lyons, 1927 22–14
Ted Lyons, 1930 22–15
Vern Kennedy, 1936 21–9
Thornton Lee, 1941 22–11
Virgil Trucks, 1953 ..... 20–10*
Billy Pierce, 1956 20–9
Billy Pierce, 1957 20–12
Early Wynn, 1959 22–10
Ray Herbert, 1962 20–9
Gary Peters, 1964 20–8
Wilbur Wood, 1971 22–13
Wilbur Wood, 1972 24–17
Stan Bahnsen, 1972 21–16
Wilbur Wood, 1973 24–20
Jim Kaat, 1974 21–13
Wilbur Wood, 1974 20–19
Jim Kaat, 1975 20–14
LaMarr Hoyt, 1983 24–10
Rich Dotson, 1983 22–7
Jack McDowell, 1992 20–10
Jack McDowell, 1993 22–10
Esteban Loaiza, 2003 21–9

*15–6 with Chi. White Sox and 5–4 with St.L. Browns.

No-Hitters

Jimmy Callahan (vs. Det. Tigers), Sept. 20, 1902 (final: 3–0)
Frank Smith (vs. Det. Tigers), Sept. 6, 1905 (final: 15–0)
Frank Smith (vs. Phila. A's), Sept. 20, 1908 (final: 1–0)
Ed Walsh (vs. Bost. Red Sox), Aug. 27, 1911 (final: 5–0)
Joe Benz (vs. Cle. Indians), May 31, 1914 (final: 6–1)
Eddie Cicotte (vs. St.L. Browns), Apr. 14, 1917 (final: 11–0)
Charlie Robertson (vs. Det. Tigers), Apr. 30, 1922 (final: 2–0) (perfect game)
Ted Lyons (vs. Bost. Red Sox), Aug. 21, 1926 (final: 6–0)
Vern Kennedy (vs. St.L. Browns), Aug. 31, 1935 (final: 5–0)
Bill Dietrich (vs. St.L. Browns), June 1, 1937 (final: 8–0)
Bob Keegan (vs. Wash. Senators), Aug. 20, 1957 (final: 6–0)
Joe Horlen (vs. Det. Tigers), Sept. 10, 1967 (final: 6–0)
Blue Moon Odom and Francisco Barrios (vs. Oak. A's), July 28, 1976 (final: 6–0)
Joe Cowley (vs. Cal. Angels), Sept. 19, 1986 (final: 7–1)
Wilson Alvarez (vs. Balt. Orioles), Aug. 11, 1991 (final: 7–0)
Mark Buehrle (vs. Tex. Rangers), Apr. 18, 2007 (final: 6–0)
Mark Buehrle (vs. T.B. Rays), July 23, 2009 (final: 5–0) (perfect game)
Philip Humber (vs. Sea Mariners), Apr. 21, 2012 (final: 4–0) (perfect game)

No-Hitters Pitched Against

Jesse Tannehill, Bost. Red Sox, Aug. 17, 1904 (final: 6–0)
Bill Dinneen, Bost. Red Sox, Sept. 27, 1905 (final: 2–0)
Bob Rhoads, Cle. Indians, Sept. 18, 1908 (final: 2–0)
Addie Joss, Cle. Indians, Oct. 2, 1908 (final: 1–0) (perfect game)
Addie Joss, Cle. Indians, Apr. 20, 1910 (final: 1–0)
Ernie Koob, St.L. Browns, May 5, 1917 (final: 1–0)
Bob Groom, St.L. Browns, May 6, 1917 (final: 3–0)
Bob Feller, Cle. Indians, Apr. 16, 1940 (final: 1–0)
Mel Parnell, Bost. Red Sox, July 14, 1956 (final: 4–0)
Bill Monbouquette, Bost. Red Sox, Aug. 1, 1962 (final: 1–0)
Mike Warren, Oak. A's, Sept. 29, 1983 (final: 3–0)
Jack Morris, Det. Tigers, Apr. 7, 1984 (final: 4–0)
Bret Saberhagen, K.C. Royals, Aug. 26, 1991 (final: 7–0)
Francisco Liriano, Min. Twins, May 3, 2011 (final 1–0)

Postseason Play

1906 World Series vs. Chi. Cubs (NL), won 4 games to 2
1917 World Series vs. N.Y. Giants (NL), won 4 games to 2
1919 World Series vs. Cin. Reds (NL), lost 5 games to 3
1959 World Series vs. L.A. Dodgers (NL), lost 4 games to 2
1983 League Championship Series vs. Balt. Orioles, lost 3 games to 1
1993 League Championship Series vs. Tor. Blue Jays, lost 4 games to 2
2000 Division Series vs. Sea. Mariners, lost 3 games to 0
2005 Division Series vs. Bost. Red Sox, won 3 games to 0
League Championship Series vs. L.A. Angels, won 4 games to 1
World Series vs. Hous. Astros (NL), won 4 games to 0
2008 AL Central Playoff Game vs. Min. Twins, won
Division Series vs. T.B. Rays, lost 3 games to 1

Cleveland Indians

Dates of Operation: 1901–present (115 years)

Overall Record: 9097 wins, 8800 losses (.508)

Stadiums: League Park, 1901–09; League Park II (also called Dunn Field, 1916–27), 1910–32 and 1934–36; Cleveland Stadium (also known as Lakefront Stadium and Municipal Stadium, 1932–33, 1936–93), 1932–93; Progressive Field (formerly Jacobs Field, 1994–2007), 1994–present (capacity: 37,675)

Other Names: Blues, Broncos (or Bronchos), Molly Maguires, Naps

Year-by-Year Finishes

Year	Finish	Wins	Losses	Percentage	Games Behind	Manager	Attendance
1901	7th	54	82	.397	29.0	Jimmy McAleer	131,380
1902	5th	69	67	.507	14.0	Bill Armour	275,395
1903	3rd	77	63	.550	15.0	Bill Armour	311,280
1904	4th	86	65	.570	7.5	Bill Armour	264,749
1905	5th	76	78	.494	19.0	Nap Lajoie	316,306
1906	3rd	89	64	.582	5.0	Nap Lajoie	325,733
1907	4th	85	67	.559	8.0	Nap Lajoie	382,046
1908	2nd	90	64	.584	0.5	Nap Lajoie	422,242
1909	6th	71	82	.464	27.5	Nap Lajoie, Deacon McGuire	354,627
1910	5th	71	81	.467	32.0	Deacon McGuire	293,456
1911	3rd	80	73	.523	22.0	Deacon McGuire, George Stovall	406,296
1912	5th	75	78	.490	30.5	Harry Davis, Joe Birmingham	336,844
1913	3rd	86	66	.566	9.5	Joe Birmingham	541,000
1914	8th	51	102	.333	48.5	Joe Birmingham	185,997
1915	7th	57	95	.375	44.5	Joe Birmingham, Lee Fohl	159,285
1916	6th	77	77	.500	14.0	Lee Fohl	492,106
1917	3rd	88	66	.571	12.0	Lee Fohl	477,298
1918	2nd	73	54	.575	2.5	Lee Fohl	295,515
1919	2nd	84	55	.604	3.5	Lee Fohl, Tris Speaker	538,135
1920	1st	98	56	.636	+2.0	Tris Speaker	912,832
1921	2nd	94	60	.610	4.5	Tris Speaker	748,705
1922	4th	78	76	.506	16.0	Tris Speaker	528,145
1923	3rd	82	71	.536	16.5	Tris Speaker	558,856
1924	6th	67	86	.438	24.5	Tris Speaker	481,905
1925	6th	70	84	.455	27.5	Tris Speaker	419,005
1926	2nd	88	66	.571	3.0	Tris Speaker	627,426
1927	6th	66	87	.431	43.5	Jack McAllister	373,138
1928	7th	62	92	.403	39.0	Roger Peckinpaugh	375,907
1929	3rd	81	71	.533	24.0	Roger Peckinpaugh	536,210
1930	4th	81	73	.526	21.0	Roger Peckinpaugh	528,657
1931	4th	78	76	.506	30.0	Roger Peckinpaugh	483,027
1932	4th	87	65	.572	19.0	Roger Peckinpaugh	468,953
1933	4th	75	76	.497	23.5	Roger Peckinpaugh, Walter Johnson	387,936
1934	3rd	85	69	.552	16.0	Walter Johnson	391,338
1935	3rd	82	71	.536	12.0	Walter Johnson, Steve O'Neill	397,615
1936	5th	80	74	.519	22.5	Steve O'Neill	500,391
1937	4th	83	71	.539	19.0	Steve O'Neill	564,849
1938	3rd	86	66	.566	13.0	Ossie Vitt	652,006

1939	3rd	87	67	.565	20.5	Ossie Vitt	563,926
1940	2nd	89	65	.578	1.0	Ossie Vitt	902,576
1941	4th (Tie)	75	79	.487	26.0	Roger Peckinpaugh	745,948
1942	4th	75	79	.487	28.0	Lou Boudreau	459,447
1943	3rd	82	71	.536	15.5	Lou Boudreau	438,894
1944	5th (Tie)	72	82	.468	17.0	Lou Boudreau	475,272
1945	5th	73	72	.503	11.0	Lou Boudreau	558,182
1946	6th	68	86	.442	36.0	Lou Boudreau	1,057,289
1947	4th	80	74	.519	17.0	Lou Boudreau	1,521,978
1948	1st	97	58	.626	+1.0	Lou Boudreau	2,620,627
1949	3rd	89	65	.578	8.0	Lou Boudreau	2,233,771
1950	4th	92	62	.597	6.0	Lou Boudreau	1,727,464
1951	2nd	93	61	.604	5.0	Al Lopez	1,704,984
1952	2nd	93	61	.604	2.0	Al Lopez	1,444,607
1953	2nd	92	62	.597	8.5	Al Lopez	1,069,176
1954	1st	111	43	.721	+8.0	Al Lopez	1,335,472
1955	2nd	93	61	.604	3.0	Al Lopez	1,221,780
1956	2nd	88	66	.571	9.0	Al Lopez	865,467
1957	6th	76	77	.497	21.5	Kerby Farrell	722,256
1958	4th	77	76	.503	14.5	Bobby Bragan, Joe Gordon	663,805
1959	2nd	89	65	.578	5.0	Joe Gordon	1,497,976
1960	4th	76	78	.494	21.0	Joe Gordon, Jimmy Dykes	950,985
1961	5th	78	83	.484	30.5	Jimmy Dykes	725,547
1962	6th	80	82	.494	16.0	Mel McGaha	716,076
1963	5th (Tie)	79	83	.488	25.5	Birdie Tebbetts	562,507
1964	6th (Tie)	79	83	.488	20.0	Birdie Tebbetts	653,293
1965	5th	87	75	.537	15.0	Birdie Tebbetts	934,786
1966	5th	81	81	.500	17.0	Birdie Tebbetts, George Strickland	903,359
1967	8th	75	87	.463	17.0	Joe Adcock	662,980
1968	3rd	86	75	.534	16.5	Alvin Dark	857,994
				East Division			
1969	6th	62	99	.385	46.5	Alvin Dark	619,970
1970	5th	76	86	.469	32.0	Alvin Dark	729,752
1971	6th	60	102	.370	43.0	Alvin Dark, Johnny Lipon	591,361
1972	5th	72	84	.462	14.0	Ken Aspromonte	626,354
1973	6th	71	91	.438	26.0	Ken Aspromonte	615,107
1974	4th	77	85	.475	14.0	Ken Aspromonte	1,114,262
1975	4th	79	80	.497	15.5	Frank Robinson	977,039
1976	4th	81	78	.509	16.0	Frank Robinson	948,776
1977	5th	71	90	.441	28.5	Frank Robinson, Jeff Torborg	900,365
1978	6th	69	90	.434	29.0	Jeff Torborg	800,584
1979	6th	81	80	.503	22.0	Jeff Torborg, Dave Garcia	1,011,644
1980	6th	79	81	.494	23.0	Dave Garcia	1,033,827
1981*	6th/5th	52	51	.505	5.0/5.0	Dave Garcia	661,395
1982	6th (Tie)	78	84	.481	17.0	Dave Garcia	1,044,021
1983	7th	70	92	.432	28.0	Mike Ferraro, Pat Corrales	768,941
1984	6th	75	87	.463	29.0	Pat Corrales	734,079
1985	7th	60	102	.370	39.5	Pat Corrales	655,181
1986	5th	84	78	.519	11.5	Pat Corrales	1,471,805
1987	7th	61	101	.377	37.0	Pat Corrales, Doc Edwards	1,077,898
1988	6th	78	84	.481	11.0	Doc Edwards	1,411,610
1989	6th	73	89	.451	16.0	Doc Edwards, John Hart	1,285,542

1990	4th	77	85	.475	11.0	John McNamara	1,225,240
1991	7th	57	105	.352	34.0	John McNamara, Mike Hargrove	1,051,863
1992	4th (Tie)	76	86	.469	20.0	Mike Hargrove	1,224,274
1993	6th	76	86	.469	19.0	Mike Hargrove	2,177,908
				Central Division			
1994	2nd	66	47	.584	1.0	Mike Hargrove	1,995,174
1995	1st	100	44	.694	+30.0	Mike Hargrove	2,842,745
1996	1st	99	62	.615	+14.5	Mike Hargrove	3,318,174
1997	1st	86	75	.534	+6.0	Mike Hargrove	3,404,750
1998	1st	89	73	.549	+9.0	Mike Hargrove	3,467,299
1999	1st	97	65	.599	+21.5	Mike Hargrove	3,468,456
2000	2nd	90	72	.556	5.0	Charlie Manuel	3,456,278
2001	1st	91	71	.562	+6.0	Charlie Manuel	3,175,523
2002	3rd	74	88	.457	20.5	Charlie Manuel, Joel Skinner	2,616,940
2003	4th	68	94	.420	22.0	Eric Wedge	1,730,002
2004	3rd	80	82	.494	12.0	Eric Wedge	1,814,401
2005	2nd	93	69	.574	6.0	Eric Wedge	2,013,763
2006	4th	78	84	.481	18.0	Eric Wedge	1,997,995
2007	1st	96	66	.593	+8.5	Eric Wedge	2,275,916
2008	3rd	81	81	.500	7.5	Eric Wedge	2,169,760
2009	4th	65	97	.401	21.5	Eric Wedge	1,766,242
2010	4th	69	93	.416	25.0	Manny Acta	1,391,644
2011	2nd	80	82	.494	15.0	Manny Acta	1,840,835
2012	4th	68	94	.420	20.0	Manny Acta, Sandy Alomar	1,603,596
2013	2nd	92	70	.568	1.0	Terry Francona	1,572,926
2014	3rd	85	77	.525	5.0	Terry Francona	1,437,393
2015	3rd	81	80	.503	13.5	Terry Francona	1,388,905

*Split season.

Awards

Most Valuable Player

George H. Burns, first base, 1926
Lou Boudreau, shortstop, 1948
Al Rosen, third base, 1953

Rookie of the Year

Herb Score, pitcher, 1955
Chris Chambliss, first base, 1971
Joe Charboneau, outfield, 1980
Sandy Alomar Jr., catcher, 1990

Cy Young

Gaylord Perry, 1972
CC Sabathia, 2007
Cliff Lee, 2008
Corey Kluber, 2014

Hall of Famers Who Played for the Indians

Roberto Alomar, second base, 1999–2001
Earl Averill, outfield, 1929–39
Lou Boudreau, shortstop, 1938–50
Steve Carlton, pitcher, 1987
Stan Coveleski, pitcher, 1916–24
Larry Doby, outfield, 1947–55 and 1958
Dennis Eckersley, pitcher, 1975–77
Bob Feller, pitcher, 1936–41 and 1945–56
Elmer Flick, outfield, 1902–10
Joe Gordon, second base, 1947–50
Addie Joss, pitcher, 1902–10
Ralph Kiner, outfield, 1955
Nap Lajoie, second base, 1902–14
Bob Lemon, pitcher, 1941–42 and 1946–58
Al Lopez, catcher, 1947
Eddie Murray, designated hitter, 1994–96
Hal Newhouser, pitcher, 1954–55
Phil Niekro, pitcher, 1986–87
Satchel Paige, pitcher, 1948–49
Gaylord Perry, pitcher, 1972–75
Sam Rice, outfield, 1934
Frank Robinson, designated hitter, 1974–76
Joe Sewell, shortstop, 1920–30
Billy Southworth, outfield, 1913 and 1915
Tris Speaker, outfield, 1916–26
Hoyt Wilhelm, pitcher, 1957–58
Dave Winfield, designated hitter, 1995
Early Wynn, pitcher, 1949–57
Cy Young, pitcher, 1890–98 and 1909–11

Retired Numbers

3 .....Earl Averill
5 .....Lou Boudreau
14 .....Larry Doby
18 .....Mel Harder
19 .....Bob Feller
21 .....Bob Lemon
455.....The Fans (consecutive sellouts)

League Leaders, Batting

Batting Average, Season

Nap Lajoie, 1903 ..... .355
Nap Lajoie, 1904 ..... .381
Elmer Flick, 1905 ..... .308
Tris Speaker, 1916 ..... .386

Lew Fonseca, 1929 ..... .369
Lou Boudreau, 1944 ..... .327
Roberto Avila, 1954 ..... .341

Home Runs, Season

Braggo Roth*, 1915 7
Al Rosen, 1950 37
Larry Doby, 1952 32
Al Rosen, 1953 43
Larry Doby, 1954 32
Rocky Colavito, 1959 ..... 42 (Tie)
Albert Belle, 1995 50
*3 with Chi. White Sox and 4 with Cle. Indians.

RBIs, Season

Hal Trosky, 1936 162
Al Rosen, 1952 105
Al Rosen, 1953 145
Larry Doby, 1954 126
Rocky Colavito, 1965 108
Joe Carter, 1986 121
Albert Belle, 1993 129
Albert Belle, 1995 ..... 126 (Tie)
Albert Belle, 1996 148
Manny Ramirez, 1999 165

Stolen Bases, Season

Harry Bay, 1903 46
Harry Bay, 1904 ..... 42 (Tie)
Elmer Flick, 1904 ..... 42 (Tie)
Elmer Flick, 1906 ..... 39 (Tie)
George Case, 1946 28
Minnie Minoso*, 1951 31
Kenny Lofton, 1992 66
Kenny Lofton, 1993 70
Kenny Lofton, 1994 60
Kenny Lofton, 1995 54
Kenny Lofton, 1996 75
*31 with Chi. White Sox and 0 with Cle. Indians.

Total Bases, Season

Nap Lajoie, 1904 304
Nap Lajoie, 1910 304
Joe Jackson, 1912 331
Hal Trosky, 1936 405
Al Rosen, 1952 297
Al Rosen, 1953 367
Rocky Colavito, 1959 301
Albert Belle, 1994 294
Albert Belle, 1995 377

Most Hits, Season

Charlie Hickman*, 1902 194
Nap Lajoie, 1904 211
Nap Lajoie, 1906 214
Nap Lajoie, 1910 227
Joe Jackson, 1913 197
Tris Speaker, 1916 211
Charlie Jamieson, 1923 222
George Burns, 1926 ..... 216 (Tie)
Johnny Hodapp, 1930 225
Joe Vosmik, 1935 216
Earl Averill, 1936 232
Dale Mitchell, 1949 203
Kenny Lofton, 1994 160
*32 with Bost. Red Sox and 161 with Cle. Indians.

Most Runs, Season

Elmer Flick, 1906 98
Ray Chapman, 1918 84
Larry Doby, 1952 104
Al Rosen, 1953 115
Al Smith, 1955 123
Albert Belle, 1995 ..... 121 (Tie)
Roberto Alomar, 1999 138
Grady Sizemore, 2006 134

Batting Feats

Triple Crown Winners

[No player]

Hitting for the Cycle

Bill Bradley, Sept. 24, 1903
Earl Averill, Aug. 17, 1933
Odell Hale, July 12, 1938
Larry Doby, June 4, 1952
Tony Horton, July 2, 1970
Andre Thornton, Apr. 22, 1978
Travis Hafner, Aug. 14, 2003

Six Hits in a Game

Zaza Harvey, Apr. 25, 1902
Frank Brower, Aug. 7, 1923
George H. Burns, June 19, 1924
Johnny Burnett, July 10, 1932* (9 hits in game)
Bruce Campbell, July 2, 1936
Jim Fridley, Apr. 29, 1952
Jorge Orta, June 15, 1980
Carlos Baerga, Apr. 11, 1992*
Omar Vizquel, Aug. 31, 2004
*Extra-inning game.

40 or More Home Runs, Season

52 ..... Jim Thome, 2002
50 ..... Albert Belle, 1995
49 ..... Jim Thome, 2001
48 ..... Albert Belle, 1996
45 ..... Manny Ramirez, 1998
44 ..... Manny Ramirez, 1999
43 ..... Al Rosen, 1953
42 ..... Hal Trosky, 1936
Rocky Colavito, 1959
Travis Hafner, 2006
41 ..... Rocky Colavito, 1958
David Justice*, 2000
40 ..... Jim Thome, 1997
*20 with N.Y. Yankees and 21 with Cle. Indians.

League Leaders, Pitching

Triple Crown Winner

Bob Feller, 1940 (27–11, 2.61 ERA, 261 SO)

Most Wins, Season

Addie Joss, 1907 ..... 27 (Tie)
Jim Bagby Sr., 1920 31
George Uhle, 1923 26
George Uhle, 1926 27
Bob Feller, 1939 24
Bob Feller, 1940 27
Bob Feller, 1941 25
Bob Feller, 1946 ..... 26 (Tie)
Bob Feller, 1947 20
Bob Lemon, 1950 23
Bob Feller, 1951 22
Bob Lemon, 1954 ..... 23 (Tie)
Early Wynn, 1954 ..... 23 (Tie)
Bob Lemon, 1955 ..... 18 (Tie)
Jim Perry, 1960 ..... 18 (Tie)
Cliff Lee, 2008 22
Corey Kluber, 2014 ..... 18 (Tie)

Most Strikeouts, Season

Stan Coveleski, 1920 133
Bob Feller, 1938 240
Bob Feller, 1939 246
Bob Feller, 1940 261
Bob Feller, 1941 260
Allie Reynolds, 1943 151
Bob Feller, 1946 348
Bob Feller, 1947 196
Bob Feller, 1948 164
Bob Lemon, 1950 170
Herb Score, 1955 245
Herb Score, 1956 263
Early Wynn, 1957 184
Sam McDowell, 1965 325
Sam McDowell, 1966 225

Sam McDowell, 1968 283
Sam McDowell, 1969 279
Sam McDowell, 1970 304
Len Barker, 1980 187
Len Barker, 1981 127
Bert Blyleven*, 1985 206
*77 with Min. Twins and 129 with Cle. Indians.

Lowest ERA, Season

Stan Coveleski, 1923 ..... 2.76
Monte Pearson, 1933 ..... 2.33
Bob Feller, 1940 ..... 2.62
Gene Bearden, 1948 ..... 2.43
Early Wynn, 1950 ..... 3.20
Mike Garcia, 1954 ..... 2.64
Sam McDowell, 1965 ..... 2.18
Luis Tiant, 1968 ..... 1.60
Rick Sutcliffe, 1982 ..... 2.96
Kevin Millwood, 2005 ..... 2.64
Cliff Lee, 2008 ..... 2.54

Most Saves, Season

Jose Mesa, 1995 46
Bob Wickman, 2005 ..... 45 (Tie)
Joe Borowski, 2007 45

Best Won–Lost Percentage, Season

Bill Bernhard*, 1902 .... 18–5 ... .783
Jim Bagby, 1920 ..... 31–12 ... .721
George Uhle, 1926 .... 27–11 ... .711
Johnny Allen, 1937 ..... 15–1 ... .938
Bob Feller, 1951 ..... 22–8 ... .733
Jim Perry, 1960 ..... 18–10 ... .643
Sonny Siebert, 1966 .... 16–8 ... .667
Charles Nagy, 1996 .... 17–5 ... .773
Cliff Lee, 2005 ..... 18–5 ... .783
Cliff Lee, 2008 ..... 22–3 ... .880
*1–0 (1.000) with Phila. A's and 17–5 (.773) with Cle. Indians.

Pitching Feats

20 Wins, Season

Bill Bernhard, 1904 23–13
Addie Joss, 1905 20–12
Bob Rhoads, 1906 22–10
Addie Joss, 1906 21–9
Otto Hess, 1906 20–17
Addie Joss, 1907 27–10
Addie Joss, 1908 24–11
Vean Gregg, 1911 23–7
Vean Gregg, 1912 20–13
Cy Falkenberg, 1913 23–10
Vean Gregg, 1913 20–13
Jim Bagby, 1917 23–13
Stan Coveleski, 1918 22–13
Stan Coveleski, 1919 23–12
Jim Bagby, 1920 31–12
Stan Coveleski, 1920 24–14
Ray Caldwell, 1920 20–10
Stan Coveleski, 1921 23–13
George Uhle, 1922 22–16
George Uhle, 1923 26–16
Joe Shaute, 1924 20–17
George Uhle, 1926 27–11
Wes Ferrell, 1929 21–10
Wes Ferrell, 1930 25–13
Wes Ferrell, 1931 22–12
Wes Ferrell, 1932 23–13
Mel Harder, 1934 20–12
Mel Harder, 1935 22–11
Johnny Allen, 1936 20–10
Bob Feller, 1937 24–9
Bob Feller, 1940 27–11
Bob Feller, 1941 25–13
Bob Feller, 1946 26–15
Bob Feller, 1947 20–11
Gene Bearden, 1948 20–7
Bob Lemon, 1948 20–14
Bob Lemon, 1949 22–10
Bob Lemon, 1950 23–11
Bob Feller, 1951 22–8
Mike Garcia, 1951 20–13
Early Wynn, 1951 20–13
Early Wynn, 1952 23–12
Mike Garcia, 1952 22–11
Bob Lemon, 1952 22–11
Bob Lemon, 1953 21–15
Bob Lemon, 1954 23–7
Early Wynn, 1954 23–11
Herb Score, 1956 20–9
Early Wynn, 1956 20–9
Bob Lemon, 1956 20–14
Dick Donovan, 1962 20–10
Luis Tiant, 1968 21–9
Sam McDowell, 1970 20–12
Gaylord Perry, 1972 24–16
Gaylord Perry, 1974 21–13
Cliff Lee, 2008 22–3

No-Hitters

Bob Rhoads (vs. Chi. White Sox), Sept. 18, 1908 (final: 2–0)
Addie Joss (vs. Chi. White Sox), Oct. 2, 1908 (final: 1–0) (perfect game)
Addie Joss (vs. Chi. White Sox), Apr. 20, 1910 (final: 1–0)
Wes Ferrell (vs. St.L. Browns), Apr. 29, 1931 (final: 9–0)
Bob Feller (vs. Chi. White Sox), Apr. 16, 1940 (final: 1–0)
Bob Feller (vs. N.Y. Yankees), Apr. 30, 1946 (final: 1–0)
Don Black (vs. Phila. A's), July 10, 1947 (final: 3–0)
Bob Lemon (vs. Det. Tigers), June 30, 1948 (final: 2–0)
Bob Feller (vs. Det. Tigers), July 1, 1951 (final: 2–1)
Sonny Siebert (vs. Wash. Senators II), June 10, 1966 (final: 2–0)
Dick Bosman (vs. Oak. A's), July 19, 1974 (final: 4–0)
Dennis Eckersley (vs. Cal. Angels), May 30, 1977 (final: 1–0)
Len Barker (vs. Tor. Blue Jays), May 15, 1981 (final: 3–0) (perfect game)

No-Hitters Pitched Against

Chief Bender, Phila. A's, May 12, 1910 (final: 4–0)
Joe Benz, Chi. White Sox, May 31, 1914 (final: 6–1)
Joe Bush, Phila. A's, Aug. 26, 1916 (final: 5–0)
Monte Pearson, N.Y. Yankees, Aug. 27, 1938 (final: 13–0)
Allie Reynolds, N.Y. Yankees, July 12, 1951 (final: 1–0)
Dave Morehead, Bost. Red Sox, Sept. 16, 1965 (final: 2–0)
Dean Chance, Min. Twins, Aug. 25, 1967 (final: 2–1)
Jim Abbott, N.Y. Yankees, Sept. 4, 1993 (final: 4–0)
Ervin Santana, L.A. Angels, July 27, 2011 (final: 3–1)

Postseason Play

1920 World Series vs. Bklyn. Dodgers (NL), won 5 games to 2
1948 Pennant Playoff Game vs. Bost. Red Sox, won
World Series vs. Bost. Braves (NL), won 4 games to 2
1954 World Series vs. N.Y. Giants (NL), lost 4 games to 0

1995 Division Series vs. Bost. Red Sox, won 3 games to 0
League Championship Series vs. Sea. Mariners, won 4 games to 2
World Series vs. Atl. Braves (NL), lost 4 games to 2

1996 Division Series vs. Balt. Orioles, lost 3 games to 1

1997 Division Series vs. N.Y. Yankees, won 3 games to 2
League Championship Series vs. Balt. Orioles, won 4 games to 2
World Series vs. Fla. Marlins (NL), lost 4 games to 3

1998 Division Series vs. Bost. Red Sox, won 3 games to 1
League Championship Series vs. N.Y. Yankees, lost 4 games to 2

1999 Division Series vs. Bost. Red Sox, lost 3 games to 2

2001 Division Series vs. Sea. Mariners, lost 3 games to 2

2007 Division Series vs. N.Y. Yankees, won 3 games to 1
League Championship vs. Bost. Red Sox, lost 4 games to 3

2013 AL Wild Card Playoff Game vs T.B. Rays, lost

Detroit Tigers

Dates of Operation: 1901–present (115 years)

Overall Record: 9085 wins, 8806 losses (.507)

Stadiums: Bennett Park, 1901–11; Burns Park, 1901–02 (Sundays only); Tiger Stadium, 1912–1999 (also known as Navin Field, 1912–37, and Briggs Stadium, 1938–60); Comerica Park, 2000–present (capacity: 41,574)

Year-by-Year Finishes

Year	Finish	Wins	Losses	Percentage	Games Behind	Manager	Attendance
1901	3rd	74	61	.548	8.5	George Stallings	259,430
1902	7th	52	83	.385	30.5	Frank Dwyer	189,469
1903	5th	65	71	.478	25.0	Ed Barrow	224,523
1904	7th	62	90	.408	32.0	Ed Barrow, Bobby Lowe	177,796
1905	3rd	79	74	.516	15.5	Bill Armour	193,384
1906	6th	71	78	.477	21.0	Bill Armour	174,043
1907	1st	92	58	.613	+1.5	Hughie Jennings	297,079
1908	1st	90	63	.588	+0.5	Hughie Jennings	436,199
1909	1st	98	54	.645	+3.5	Hughie Jennings	490,490
1910	3rd	86	68	.558	18.0	Hughie Jennings	391,288
1911	2nd	89	65	.578	13.5	Hughie Jennings	484,988
1912	6th	69	84	.451	36.5	Hughie Jennings	402,870
1913	6th	66	87	.431	30.0	Hughie Jennings	398,502
1914	4th	80	73	.523	19.5	Hughie Jennings	416,225
1915	2nd	100	54	.649	2.5	Hughie Jennings	476,105
1916	3rd	87	67	.565	4.0	Hughie Jennings	616,772
1917	4th	78	75	.510	21.5	Hughie Jennings	457,289
1918	7th	55	71	.437	20.0	Hughie Jennings	203,719
1919	4th	80	60	.571	8.0	Hughie Jennings	643,805
1920	7th	61	93	.396	37.0	Hughie Jennings	579,650
1921	6th	71	82	.464	27.0	Ty Cobb	661,527
1922	3rd	79	75	.513	15.0	Ty Cobb	861,206
1923	2nd	83	71	.539	16.0	Ty Cobb	911,377
1924	3rd	86	68	.558	6.0	Ty Cobb	1,015,136
1925	4th	81	73	.526	16.5	Ty Cobb	820,766
1926	6th	79	75	.513	12.0	Ty Cobb	711,914
1927	4th	82	71	.536	27.5	George Moriarty	773,716
1928	6th	68	86	.442	33.0	George Moriarty	474,323
1929	6th	70	84	.455	36.0	Bucky Harris	869,318
1930	5th	75	79	.487	27.0	Bucky Harris	649,450
1931	7th	61	93	.396	47.0	Bucky Harris	434,056
1932	5th	76	75	.503	29.5	Bucky Harris	397,157
1933	5th	75	79	.487	25.0	Del Baker	320,972
1934	1st	101	53	.656	+7.0	Mickey Cochrane	919,161
1935	1st	93	58	.616	+3.0	Mickey Cochrane	1,034,929
1936	2nd	83	71	.539	19.5	Mickey Cochrane	875,948
1937	2nd	89	65	.578	13.0	Mickey Cochrane	1,072,276
1938	4th	84	70	.545	16.0	Mickey Cochrane, Del Baker	799,557
1939	5th	81	73	.526	26.5	Del Baker	836,279
1940	1st	90	64	.584	+1.0	Del Baker	1,112,693
1941	4th (Tie)	75	79	.487	26.0	Del Baker	684,915

1942	5th	73	81	.474	30.0	Del Baker	580,087
1943	5th	78	76	.506	20.0	Steve O'Neill	606,287
1944	2nd	88	66	.571	1.0	Steve O'Neill	923,176
1945	1st	88	65	.575	+1.5	Steve O'Neill	1,280,341
1946	2nd	92	62	.597	12.0	Steve O'Neill	1,722,590
1947	2nd	85	69	.552	12.0	Steve O'Neill	1,398,093
1948	5th	78	76	.506	18.5	Steve O'Neill	1,743,035
1949	4th	87	67	.565	10.0	Red Rolfe	1,821,204
1950	2nd	95	59	.617	3.0	Red Rolfe	1,951,474
1951	5th	73	81	.474	25.0	Red Rolfe	1,132,641
1952	8th	50	104	.325	45.0	Red Rolfe, Fred Hutchinson	1,026,846
1953	6th	60	94	.390	40.5	Fred Hutchinson	884,658
1954	5th	68	86	.442	43.0	Fred Hutchinson	1,079,847
1955	5th	79	75	.513	17.0	Bucky Harris	1,181,838
1956	5th	82	72	.532	15.0	Bucky Harris	1,051,182
1957	4th	78	76	.506	20.0	Jack Tighe	1,272,346
1958	5th	77	77	.500	15.0	Jack Tighe, Bill Norman	1,098,924
1959	4th	76	78	.494	18.0	Bill Norman, Jimmy Dykes	1,221,221
1960	6th	71	83	.461	26.0	Jimmy Dykes, Billy Hitchcock, Joe Gordon	1,167,669
1961	2nd	101	61	.623	8.0	Bob Scheffing	1,600,710
1962	4th	85	76	.528	10.5	Bob Scheffing	1,207,881
1963	5th (Tie)	79	83	.488	25.5	Bob Scheffing, Chuck Dressen	821,952
1964	4th	85	77	.525	14.0	Chuck Dressen	816,139
1965	4th	89	73	.549	13.0	Chuck Dressen, Bob Swift	1,029,645
1966	3rd	88	74	.543	10.0	Chuck Dressen, Bob Swift, Frank Skaff	1,124,293
1967	2nd (Tie)	91	71	.562	1.0	Mayo Smith	1,447,143
1968	1st	103	59	.636	+12.0	Mayo Smith	2,031,847
					East Division		
1969	2nd	90	72	.556	19.0	Mayo Smith	1,577,481
1970	4th	79	83	.488	29.0	Mayo Smith	1,501,293
1971	2nd	91	71	.562	12.0	Billy Martin	1,591,073
1972	1st	86	70	.551	+0.5	Billy Martin	1,892,386
1973	3rd	85	77	.525	12.0	Billy Martin, Joe Schultz	1,724,146
1974	6th	72	90	.444	19.0	Ralph Houk	1,243,080
1975	6th	57	102	.358	37.5	Ralph Houk	1,058,836
1976	5th	74	87	.460	24.0	Ralph Houk	1,467,020
1977	4th	74	88	.457	26.0	Ralph Houk	1,359,856
1978	5th	86	76	.531	13.5	Ralph Houk	1,714,893
1979	5th	85	76	.528	18.0	Les Moss, Dick Tracewski, Sparky Anderson	1,630,929
1980	5th	84	78	.519	19.0	Sparky Anderson	1,785,293
1981*	4th/2nd (Tie)	60	49	.550	3.5/1.5	Sparky Anderson	1,149,144
1982	4th	83	79	.512	12.0	Sparky Anderson	1,636,058
1983	2nd	92	70	.568	6.0	Sparky Anderson	1,829,636
1984	1st	104	58	.642	+15.0	Sparky Anderson	2,704,794
1985	3rd	84	77	.522	15.0	Sparky Anderson	2,286,609
1986	3rd	87	75	.537	8.5	Sparky Anderson	1,899,437
1987	1st	98	64	.605	+2.0	Sparky Anderson	2,061,830
1988	2nd	88	74	.543	1.0	Sparky Anderson	2,081,162
1989	7th	59	103	.364	30.0	Sparky Anderson	1,543,656

1990	3rd	79	83	.488	9.0	Sparky Anderson	1,495,785
1991	2nd	84	78	.519	7.0	Sparky Anderson	1,641,661
1992	6th	75	87	.463	21.0	Sparky Anderson	1,423,963
1993	3rd (Tie)	85	77	.525	10.0	Sparky Anderson	1,971,421
				Central Division			
1994	5th	53	62	.461	18.0	Sparky Anderson	1,184,783
1995	4th	60	84	.417	26.0	Sparky Anderson	1,180,979
1996	5th	53	109	.327	39.0	Buddy Bell	1,168,610
1997	3rd	79	83	.488	19.0	Buddy Bell	1,365,157
1998	5th	65	97	.401	24.0	Buddy Bell, Larry Parrish	1,409,391
1999	3rd	69	92	.429	27.5	Larry Parrish	2,026,441
2000	3rd	79	83	.488	16.0	Phil Garner	2,533,752
2001	4th	66	96	.407	25.0	Phil Garner	1,921,305
2002	4th	55	106	.342	39.0	Phil Garner, Luis Pujols	1,503,623
2003	5th	43	119	.265	47.0	Alan Trammell	1,368,245
2004	4th	72	90	.444	20.0	Alan Trammell	1,917,004
2005	4th	71	91	.438	28.0	Alan Trammell	2,024,485
2006	2nd	95	67	.586	1.0	Jim Leyland	2,595,937
2007	2nd	88	74	.543	8.5	Jim Leyland	3,047,139
2008	5th	74	88	.457	14.5	Jim Leyland	3,202,645
2009	2nd	86	77	.528	1.0	Jim Leyland	2,567,185
2010	3rd	81	81	.500	13.0	Jim Leyland	2,461,237
2011	1st	95	67	.586	+15.0	Jim Leyland	2,642,045
2012	1st	88	74	.543	+3.0	Jim Leyland	3,028,033
2013	1st	93	69	.574	+1.0	Jim Leyland	3,083,397
2014	1st	90	72	.556	+1.0	Brad Ausmus	2,917,209
2015	5th	74	87	.460	20.5	Brad Ausmus	2,726,048

*Split season.

Awards

Most Valuable Player

Ty Cobb, outfield, 1911
Mickey Cochrane, catcher, 1934
Hank Greenberg, first base, 1935
Charley Gehringer, second base, 1937
Hank Greenberg, outfield, 1940
Hal Newhouser, pitcher, 1944
Hal Newhouser, pitcher, 1945
Denny McLain, pitcher, 1968
Willie Hernandez, pitcher, 1984
Justin Verlander, pitcher, 2011
Miguel Cabrera, third base, 2012
Miguel Cabrera, third base, 2013

Rookie of the Year

Harvey Kuenn, shortstop, 1953
Mark Fidrych, pitcher, 1976
Lou Whitaker, second base, 1978
Justin Verlander, pitcher, 2006

Cy Young

Denny McLain, 1968
Denny McLain (co-winner), 1969
Willie Hernandez, 1984
Justin Verlander, 2011
Max Scherzer, 2013

Hall of Famers Who Played for the Tigers

Earl Averill, outfield, 1939–40
Jim Bunning, pitcher, 1955–63
Ty Cobb, outfield, 1905–26
Mickey Cochrane, catcher, 1934–37
Sam Crawford, outfield, 1903–17
Larry Doby, outfield, 1959
Charlie Gehringer, second base, 1924–42
Goose Goslin, outfield, 1934–37
Hank Greenberg, first base and outfield, 1930, 1933–41, and 1945–46
Bucky Harris, second base, 1929 and 1931
Harry Heilmann, outfield, 1914 and 1916–29
Waite Hoyt, pitcher, 1930–31
Hughie Jennings, infield, 1907, 1909, 1912, and 1918
Al Kaline, outfield, 1953–74
George Kell, third base, 1946–52
Heinie Manush, outfield, 1923–27
Eddie Mathews, third base, 1967–68
Hal Newhouser, pitcher, 1939–53
Al Simmons, outfield, 1936

Retired Numbers

— ..... Ty Cobb
— ..... Ernie Harwell
2 ..... Charlie Gehringer
5 ..... Hank Greenberg
6 ..... Al Kaline
11 ..... Sparky Anderson
16 ..... Hal Newhouser
23 ..... Willie Horton

League Leaders, Batting

Batting Average, Season

Ty Cobb, 1907 ..... .350
Ty Cobb, 1908 ..... .324
Ty Cobb, 1909 ..... .377
Ty Cobb, 1910 ..... .385
Ty Cobb, 1911 ..... .420
Ty Cobb, 1912 ..... .410
Ty Cobb, 1913 ..... .390
Ty Cobb, 1914 ..... .368

Ty Cobb, 1915 ..... .369
Ty Cobb, 1917 ..... .383
Ty Cobb, 1918 ..... .382
Ty Cobb, 1919 ..... .384
Harry Heilmann, 1921 ..... .394
Harry Heilmann, 1923 ..... .403
Harry Heilmann, 1925 ..... .393
Heinie Manush, 1926 ..... .378
Harry Heilmann, 1927 ..... .398
Dale Alexander*, 1932 ..... .367
Charlie Gehringer, 1937 ..... .371
George Kell, 1949 ..... .343
Al Kaline, 1955 ..... .340
Harvey Kuenn, 1959 ..... .353
Norm Cash, 1961 ..... .361
Maglio Ordonez, 2007 ..... .363
Miguel Cabrera, 2011 ..... .344
Miguel Cabrera, 2012 ..... .330
Miguel Cabrera, 2013 ..... .348
Miguel Cabrera, 2015 ..... .338

*.372 with Bost. Red Sox and .250 with Det. Tigers.

Home Runs, Season

Sam Crawford, 1908 7
Ty Cobb, 1909 9
Hank Greenberg, 1935 ..... 36 (Tie)
Hank Greenberg, 1938 58
Hank Greenberg, 1940 41
Rudy York, 1943 34
Hank Greenberg, 1946 44
Darrell Evans, 1985 40
Cecil Fielder, 1990 51
Cecil Fielder, 1991 44
Miguel Cabrera, 2008 ..... 37 (Tie)
Miguel Cabrera, 2012 44

RBIs, Season

Ty Cobb, 1907 116
Ty Cobb, 1908 101
Ty Cobb, 1909 115
Sam Crawford, 1910 115
Ty Cobb, 1911 144
Sam Crawford, 1914 112
Sam Crawford, 1915 116
Bobby Veach, 1917 115
Bobby Veach, 1918 ..... 74 (Tie)
Hank Greenberg, 1935 170
Hank Greenberg, 1937 183
Hank Greenberg, 1940 150
Rudy York, 1943 118
Hank Greenberg, 1946 127
Ray Boone, 1955 ..... 116 (Tie)
Cecil Fielder, 1990 132
Cecil Fielder, 1991 133
Cecil Fielder, 1992 124
Miguel Cabrera, 2010 126
Miguel Cabrera, 2012 139

Stolen Bases, Season

Ty Cobb, 1907 49
Ty Cobb, 1909 76
Ty Cobb, 1911 83
Ty Cobb, 1915 96
Ty Cobb, 1916 68
Ty Cobb, 1917 55
Charlie Gehringer, 1929 27
Marty McManus, 1930 23
Ron LeFlore, 1978 68
Brian Hunter, 1997 74
Brian Hunter*, 1999 44

*44 with Sea. Mariners and 0 with Det. Tigers.

Total Bases, Season

Ty Cobb, 1907 286
Ty Cobb, 1908 276
Ty Cobb, 1909 296
Ty Cobb, 1911 367
Sam Crawford, 1913 298
Ty Cobb, 1915 274
Ty Cobb, 1917 336
Hank Greenberg, 1935 389
Hank Greenberg, 1940 384
Rudy York, 1943 301
Al Kaline, 1955 321
Rocky Colavito, 1962 309
Cecil Fielder, 1990 339
Miguel Cabrera, 2008 ..... 331 (Tie)
Miguel Cabrera, 2012 377

Most Hits, Season

Ty Cobb, 1907 212
Ty Cobb, 1908 188
Ty Cobb, 1909 216
Ty Cobb, 1911 248
Ty Cobb, 1912 227
Ty Cobb, 1915 208
Ty Cobb, 1917 225
Ty Cobb, 1919 ..... 191 (Tie)
Bobby Veach, 1919 ..... 191 (Tie)
Harry Heilmann, 1921 237
Dale Alexander, 1929 ..... 215 (Tie)
Charlie Gehringer, 1929 ..... 215 (Tie)
Charlie Gehringer, 1934 214
Barney McCosky, 1940 ..... 200 (Tie)
Dick Wakefield, 1943 200
George Kell, 1950 218
George Kell, 1951 191
Harvey Kuenn, 1953 209
Harvey Kuenn, 1954 ..... 201 (Tie)
Al Kaline, 1955 200
Harvey Kuenn, 1956 196
Harvey Kuenn, 1959 198
Norm Cash, 1961 193

Most Runs, Season

Sam Crawford, 1907 102
Matty McIntyre, 1908 105
Ty Cobb, 1909 116
Ty Cobb, 1910 106
Ty Cobb, 1911 147
Ty Cobb, 1915 144
Ty Cobb, 1916 113
Donie Bush, 1917 112
Charlie Gehringer, 1929 131
Charlie Gehringer, 1935 134
Hank Greenberg, 1938 144
Eddie Yost, 1959 115
Dick McAuliffe, 1968 95
Ron LeFlore, 1978 126
Tony Phillips, 1992 114

Batting Feats

Triple Crown Winners

Ty Cobb, 1909 (.377 BA, 9 HRs, 115 RBIs)
Miguel Cabrera, 2012 (.330 BA, 44 HRs, 139 RBIs)

Hitting for the Cycle

Bobby Veach, Sept. 17, 1920
Fats Fothergill, Sept. 26, 1926
Gee Walker, Apr. 20, 1937
Charlie Gehringer, May 27, 1939
Vic Wertz, Sept. 14, 1947
George Kell, June 2, 1950
Hoot Evers, Sept. 7, 1950
Travis Fryman, July 28, 1993
Damion Easley, June 8, 2001
Carlos Guillen, Aug. 1, 2006

Six Hits in a Game

Doc Nance, July 13, 1901
Bobby Veach, Sept. 17, 1920*
Ty Cobb, May 5, 1925
George Kell, Sept. 20, 1946
Rocky Colavito, June 24, 1962* (7 hits in game)
Jim Northrup, Aug. 28, 1969*
Cesar Gutierrez, June 21, 1970* (7 hits in game)
Damion Easley, Aug. 8, 2001
Carlos Pena, May 27, 2004

*Extra-inning game.

40 or More Home Runs, Season

58 .....Hank Greenberg, 1938
51 .....Cecil Fielder, 1990
45 ..... Rocky Colavito, 1961
44 .....Hank Greenberg, 1946
Cecil Fielder, 1991
Miguel Cabrera, 2012
Miguel Cabrera, 2013
41 .....Hank Greenberg 1940
Norm Cash 1961
40 .....Hank Greenberg 1937
Darrell Evans, 1985

League Leaders, Pitching

Most Wins, Season

George Mullin, 1909.....29
Tommy Bridges, 1936.....23
Dizzy Trout, 1943.....20 (Tie)
Hal Newhouser, 1944.....29
Hal Newhouser, 1945.....25
Hal Newhouser, 1946.....26 (Tie)
Hal Newhouser, 1948.....21
Frank Lary, 1956.....21
Jim Bunning, 1957.....20 (Tie)
Earl Wilson, 1967.....22 (Tie)
Denny McLain, 1968.....31
Denny McLain, 1969.....24
Mickey Lolich, 1971.....25
Jack Morris, 1981.....14 (Tie)
Bill Gullickson, 1991.....20 (Tie)
Justin Verlander, 2009.....19 (Tie)
Justin Verlander, 2011.....24
Max Scherzer, 2013 21
Max Scherzer, 2014 ..... 18 (Tie)

Most Strikeouts, Season

Tommy Bridges, 1935.....163
Tommy Bridges, 1936.....175
Hal Newhouser, 1944.....187
Hal Newhouser, 1945.....212
Virgil Trucks, 1949.....153
Jim Bunning, 1959.....201
Jim Bunning, 1960.....201
Mickey Lolich, 1971.....308
Jack Morris, 1983.....232
Justin Verlander, 2009.....269
Justin Verlander, 2011.....250
Justin Verlander, 2012..... 239

Lowest ERA, Season

Dizzy Trout, 1944.....2.12
Hal Newhouser, 1945.....1.81
Hal Newhouser, 1946.....1.94
Hank Aguirre, 1962.....2.21
Mark Fidrych, 1976.....2.34
Justin Verlander, 2011.....2.40
Anibal Sanchez, 2013.....2.56
David Price*, 2015.....2.45
*2.30 with Tor. Blue Jays and 2.53 with Det. Tigers.

Most Saves, Season

John Hiller, 1973.....38
Todd Jones, 2000.....42 (Tie)
Jose Valverde, 2011.....49

Best Won-Lost Percentage, Season

Bill Donovan, 1907..... 25–4... .862
George Mullin, 1909.... 29–8... .784
Eldon Auker, 1935..... 18–7... .720
Schoolboy Rowe, 1940. 16–3... .842
Hal Newhouser, 1945.. 25–9... .735
Denny McLain, 1968.... 31–6... .838
Justin Verlander, 2009.. 18–6... .750
Justin Verlander, 2011.. 24–5... .828
Max Scherzer, 2013 .... 21–3... .875

Pitching Feats

Triple Crown Winner

Hal Newhouser, 1945 (25–9, 1.81 ERA, 212 SO)
Justin Verlander, 2011 (24–5, 2.40 ERA, 250 SO)

20 Wins, Season

Roscoe Miller, 1901..... 23–13
Ed Killian, 1905..... 23–13
George Mullin, 1905..... 21–20
George Mullin, 1906..... 21–18
Bill Donovan, 1907..... 25–4
Ed Killian, 1907..... 25–13
George Mullin, 1907..... 20–20
Ed Summers, 1908..... 24–12
George Mullin, 1909..... 29–8
Ed Willett, 1909..... 21–10
George Mullin, 1910..... 21–12
Harry Coveleski, 1914..... 22–12
Hooks Dauss, 1915..... 24–13
Harry Coveleski, 1915..... 22–13
Harry Coveleski, 1916..... 21–11
Hooks Dauss, 1919..... 21–9
Hooks Dauss, 1923..... 21–13
Schoolboy Rowe, 1934..... 24–8
Tommy Bridges, 1934..... 22–11
Tommy Bridges, 1935..... 21–10
Tommy Bridges, 1936..... 23–11
Bobo Newsom, 1939 .....20–11*
Bobo Newsom, 1940 21–5
Dizzy Trout, 1943..... 20–12
Hal Newhouser, 1944..... 29–9
Dizzy Trout, 1944..... 27–14
Hal Newhouser, 1945..... 25–9
Hal Newhouser, 1946..... 26–9
Hal Newhouser, 1948..... 21–12
Frank Lary, 1956..... 21–13
Billy Hoeft, 1956..... 20–14
Jim Bunning, 1957..... 20–8
Frank Lary, 1961..... 23–9
Denny McLain, 1966..... 20–14
Earl Wilson, 1967..... 22–11
Denny McLain, 1968..... 31–6
Denny McLain, 1969..... 24–9
Mickey Lolich, 1971..... 25–14
Joe Coleman, 1971..... 20–9
Mickey Lolich, 1972..... 22–14
Joe Coleman, 1973..... 23–15
Jack Morris, 1983..... 20–13
Jack Morris, 1986..... 21–8
Bill Gullickson, 1991..... 20–9
Justin Verlander, 2011..... 24–5
Max Scherzer, 2013 21–3
*17–10 with Det. Tigers and 3–1 with St.L. Browns.

No-Hitters

George Mullin (vs. St.L. Browns), July 4, 1912 (final: 7–0)
Virgil Trucks (vs. Wash. Senators), May 15, 1952 (final: 1–0)
Virgil Trucks (vs. N.Y. Yankees), Aug. 25, 1952 (final: 1–0)
Jim Bunning (vs. Bost. Red Sox), July 20, 1958 (final: 3–0)
Jack Morris (vs. Chi. White Sox), Apr. 7, 1984 (final: 4–0)
Justin Verlander (vs. Milw. Brewers), June 12, 2007 (final: 4–0)
Justin Verlander (vs. Tor. Blue Jays), May 7, 2011 (final: 9–0)

No-Hitters Pitched Against

Jimmy Callahan, Chi. White Sox, Sept. 20, 1902 (final: 3–0)
Frank Smith, Chi. White Sox, Sept. 6, 1905 (final: 15–0)
Earl Hamilton, St.L. Browns, Aug. 30, 1912 (final: 5–1)

Hub Leonard, Bost. Red Sox, June 3, 1918 (final: 5–0)
Charlie Robertson, Chi. White Sox, Apr. 30, 1922 (final: 2–0) (perfect game)
Bob Lemon, Cle. Indians, June 30, 1948 (final: 2–0)
Bob Feller, Cle. Indians, July 1, 1951 (final: 2–1)
Steve Barber and Stu Miller, Balt. Orioles, Apr. 30, 1967 (final: 1–2)
Joe Horlen, Chi. White Sox, Sept. 10, 1967 (final: 6–0)
Steve Busby, K.C. Royals, Apr. 27, 1973 (final: 3–0)
Nolan Ryan, Cal. Angels, July 15, 1973 (final: 6–0)
Randy Johnson, Sea. Mariners, June 2, 1990 (final: 2–0)
Dave Stieb, Tor. Blue Jays, Sept. 2, 1990 (final: 3–0)
Matt Garza, T.B. Rays, July 26, 2010 (final: 5–0)
Henderson Alvarez, Mia. Marlins, Sept. 29, 2013 (final: 1–0)

Postseason Play

1907 World Series vs. Chi. Cubs (NL), lost 4 games to 0, 1 tie
1908 World Series vs. Chi. Cubs (NL), lost 4 games to 1
1909 World Series vs. Pitt. Pirates (NL), lost 4 games to 3
1934 World Series vs. St.L. Cardinals (NL), lost 4 games to 3
1935 World Series vs. Chi. Cubs (NL), won 4 games to 2
1940 World Series vs. Cin. Reds (NL), lost 4 games to 3
1945 World Series vs. Chi. Cubs (NL), won 4 games to 3
1968 World Series vs. St.L. Cardinals (NL), won 4 games to 3
1972 League Championship Series vs. Oak. A's, lost 3 games to 2
1984 League Championship Series vs. K.C. Royals, won 3 games to 0
World Series vs. S.D. Padres (NL), won 4 games to 1
1987 League Championship Series vs. Min. Twins, lost 4 games to 1
2006 Division Series vs. N.Y. Yankees, won 3 games to 1
League Championship Series vs. Oak. A's, won 4 games to 0
World Series vs. St.L. Cardinals (NL), lost 4 games to 1
2009 AL Central Playoff Game vs. Min. Twins, lost
2011 Division Series vs. N.Y. Yankees, won 3 games to 2
2011 League Championship Series vs. Tex. Rangers, lost 4 games to 2
2012 Division Series vs. Oak. A's, won 3 games to 2
League Championship Series vs. N.Y. Yankees, won 4 games to 0
World Series vs. S.F. Giants (NL), lost 4 games to 0
2013 Division Series vs. Oak. A's, won 3 games to 2
League Championship Series vs. Bost. Red Sox, lost 4 games to 2
2014 Division Series vs. Balt. Orioles, lost 3 games to 0

Houston Astros

Dates of Operation: NL: 1962–2012 (51 years); AL: 2013-present (3 years)

Overall Record: NL: 3999, 4134 losses (.491); AL: 207 wins, 279 losses (.425); combined: 4206 wins, 4413 losses (.487)

Stadiums: Colt Stadium, 1962–64; The Astrodome, 1965–99; Minute Maid Park (formerly Enron Field, 2000–02, and Astros Field, 2002), 2000–present (capacity: 41,574)

Other Name: Colt .45s

Year-by-Year Finishes

Year	Finish	Wins	Losses	Percentage	Games Behind	Manager	Attendance
1962	8th	64	96	.400	36.5	Harry Craft	924,456
1963	9th	66	96	.407	33.0	Harry Craft	719,502
1964	9th	66	96	.407	27.0	Harry Craft, Luman Harris	725,773
1965	9th	65	97	.401	32.0	Luman Harris	2,151,470
1966	8th	72	90	.444	23.0	Grady Hatton	1,872,108
1967	9th	69	93	.426	32.5	Grady Hatton	1,348,303
1968	10th	72	90	.444	25.0	Grady Hatton, Harry Walker	1,312,887
				West Division			
1969	5th	81	81	.500	12.0	Harry Walker	1,442,995
1970	4th	79	83	.488	23.0	Harry Walker	1,253,444
1971	4th (Tie)	79	83	.488	11.0	Harry Walker	1,261,589
1972	2nd	84	69	.549	10.5	Harry Walker, Salty Parker, Leo Durocher	1,469,247
1973	4th	82	80	.506	17.0	Leo Durocher, Preston Gomez	1,394,004
1974	4th	81	81	.500	21.0	Preston Gomez	1,090,728
1975	6th	64	97	.398	43.5	Preston Gomez, Bill Virdon	858,002
1976	3rd	80	82	.494	22.0	Bill Virdon	886,146
1977	3rd	81	81	.500	17.0	Bill Virdon	1,109,560
1978	5th	74	88	.457	21.0	Bill Virdon	1,126,145
1979	2nd	89	73	.549	1.5	Bill Virdon	1,900,312
1980	1st	93	70	.571	+1.0	Bill Virdon	2,278,217
1981*	3rd/1st	61	49	.555	8.0/+1.5	Bill Virdon	1,321,282
1982	5th	77	85	.475	12.0	Bill Virdon, Bob Lillis	1,558,555
1983	3rd	85	77	.525	6.0	Bob Lillis	1,351,962
1984	2nd (Tie)	80	82	.494	12.0	Bob Lillis	1,229,862
1985	3rd (Tie)	83	79	.512	12.0	Bob Lillis	1,184,314
1986	1st	96	66	.593	+10.0	Hal Lanier	1,734,276
1987	3rd	76	86	.469	14.0	Hal Lanier	1,909,902
1988	5th	82	80	.506	12.5	Hal Lanier	1,933,505
1989	3rd	86	76	.531	6.0	Art Howe	1,834,908
1990	4th (Tie)	75	87	.463	16.0	Art Howe	1,310,927
1991	6th	65	97	.401	29.0	Art Howe	1,196,152
1992	4th	81	81	.500	17.0	Art Howe	1,211,412
1993	3rd	85	77	.525	19.0	Art Howe	2,084,546
				Central Division			
1994	2nd	66	49	.574	0.5	Terry Collins	1,561,136
1995	2nd	76	68	.528	9.0	Terry Collins	1,363,801
1996	2nd	82	80	.506	6.0	Terry Collins	1,975,888
1997	1st	84	78	.519	+5.0	Larry Dierker	2,046,781

1998	1st	102	60	.630	+12.5	Larry Dierker	2,450,451
1999	1st	97	65	.599	+1.5	Larry Dierker	2,706,017
2000	4th (Tie)	72	90	.444	23.0	Larry Dierker	3,056,139
2001	1st (Tie)	93	69	.574	—	Larry Dierker	2,904,280
2002	2nd	84	78	.519	13.0	Jimy Williams	2,517,407
2003	2nd	87	75	.537	1.0	Jimy Williams	2,454,241
2004	2nd	92	70	.568	13.0	Jimy Williams, Phil Garner	3,087,872
2005	2nd	89	73	.552	11.0	Phil Garner	2,804,760
2006	2nd	82	80	.506	1.5	Phil Garner	3,022,763
2007	4th	73	89	.451	12.0	Phil Garner, Cecil Cooper	3,020,405
2008	3rd	86	75	.534	11.0	Cecil Cooper	2,779,287
2009	5th	74	88	.457	17.0	Cecil Cooper, Dave Clark	2,521,076
2010	4th	76	86	.469	15.0	Brad Mills	2,331,490
2011	6th	56	106	.345	40.0	Brad Mills	2,067,016
American League Central Division							
2012	6th	55	107	.340	42.0	Brad Mills, Tony DeFrancesco	1,607,733
2013	5th	51	111	.315	45.0	Bo Porter	1,651,883
2014	4th	70	92	.432	28.0	Bo Porter, Tom Lawless	1,751,829
2015	2nd	86	76	.531	2.0	A.J. Hinch	2,153,585

*Split season.

Awards

Most Valuable Player

Jeff Bagwell, first base, 1994

Rookie of the Year

Jeff Bagwell, first base, 1991
Carlos Correa, shortstop, 2015

Cy Young

Mike Scott, 1986
Roger Clemens, 2004
Dallas Keuchel, 2015

Hall of Famers Who Played for the Astros

Craig Biggio, second base, 1988–2007
Nellie Fox, second base, 1964–65
Randy Johnson, pitcher, 1998
Eddie Mathews, third base, 1967
Joe Morgan, second base, 1963–71 and 1980
Robin Roberts, pitcher, 1965–66
Nolan Ryan, pitcher, 1980–88
Don Sutton, pitcher, 1981–82

Retired Numbers

5 ..... Jeff Bagwell
7 ..... Craig Biggio
24 ..... Jimmy Wynn
25 ..... Jose Cruz
32 ..... Jim Umbricht
33 ..... Mike Scott
34 ..... Nolan Ryan
40 ..... Don Wilson
49 ..... Larry Dierker

League Leaders, Batting

Batting Average, Season

Jose Altuve, 2014 ..... .341

Home Runs, Season

[No player]

RBIs, Season

Jeff Bagwell, 1994 116
Lance Berkman, 2002 128

Stolen Bases, Season

Craig Biggio, 1994 39
Michael Bourn, 2009 61
Michael Bourn, 2010 52
Jose Altuve, 2014 56
Jose Altuve, 2015 38

Total Bases, Season

Jeff Bagwell, 1994 300

Most Hits, Season

Jose Cruz, 1983 ..... 189 (Tie)
Jose Altuve, 2014 225
Jose Altuve, 2015 200

Most Runs, Season

Jeff Bagwell, 1994 104
Craig Biggio, 1995 123
Craig Biggio, 1997 146
Jeff Bagwell, 1999 143
Jeff Bagwell, 2000 152

Batting Feats

Triple Crown Winners

[No player]

Hitting for the Cycle

Cesar Cedeno, Aug. 2, 1972
Cesar Cedeno, Aug. 9, 1976
Bob Watson, June 24, 1977
Andujar Cedeno, Aug. 25, 1992
Jeff Bagwell, July 18, 2001
Craig Biggio, Apr. 8, 2002
Luke Scott, July 28, 2006
Brandon Barnes, July 19, 2013

Six Hits in a Game

Joe Morgan, July 8, 1965*

*Extra-inning game.

40 or More Home Runs, Season

47 ..... Jeff Bagwell, 2000
45 ..... Lance Berkman, 2006
44 ..... Richard Hidalgo, 2000
43 ..... Jeff Bagwell, 1997
42 ..... Jeff Bagwell, 1999
Lance Berkman, 2002

League Leaders, Pitching

Most Wins, Season

Joe Niekro, 1979.....21 (Tie)
Mike Scott, 1989.....20
Roy Oswalt, 2004.....20
Dallas Keuchel, 2015.....20

Most Strikeouts, Season

J.R. Richard, 1978.....303
J.R. Richard, 1979.....313
Mike Scott, 1986.....306
Nolan Ryan, 1987.....270
Nolan Ryan, 1988.....228

Lowest ERA, Season

J.R. Richard, 1979.....2.71
Nolan Ryan, 1981.....1.69
Mike Scott, 1986.....2.22
Nolan Ryan, 1987.....2.76
Danny Darwin, 1990.....2.21
Roger Clemens, 2005.....1.87
Roy Oswalt, 2006.....2.98

Most Saves, Season

Fred Gladding, 1969.....29
Jose Valverde, 2008.....44

Best Won–Lost Percentage, Season

Mark Portugal, 1993....18–4... .818
Mike Hampton, 1999...22–4... .846
Roger Clemens, 2004...18–4... .818

Pitching Feats

20 Wins, Season

Larry Dierker, 1969..... 20–13
J.R. Richard, 1976..... 20–15
Joe Niekro, 1979..... 21–11
Joe Niekro, 1980..... 20–12
Mike Scott, 1989..... 20–10
Mike Hampton, 1999..... 22–4
Jose Lima, 1999..... 21–10
Roy Oswalt, 2004..... 20–10
Roy Oswalt, 2005..... 20–12
Dallas Keuchel, 2015..... 20–8

No-Hitters

Don Nottebart (vs. Phila. Phillies), May 17, 1963 (final: 4–1)
Ken Johnson (vs. Cin. Reds), Apr. 23, 1964 (final: 0–1)
Don Wilson (vs. Atl. Braves), June 18, 1967 (final: 2–0)
Don Wilson (vs. Cin. Reds), May 1, 1969 (final: 4–0)
Larry Dierker (vs. Mont. Expos), July 9, 1976 (final: 6–0)
Ken Forsch (vs. Atl. Braves), Apr. 7, 1979 (final: 6–0)
Nolan Ryan (vs. L.A. Dodgers), Sept. 26, 1981 (final: 5–0)
Mike Scott (vs. S.F. Giants), Sept. 25, 1986 (final: 2–0)
Darryl Kile (vs. N.Y. Mets), Sept. 8, 1993 (final: 7–1)
Roy Oswalt, Pete Munro, Kirk Saarloos, Brad Lidge, Octavio Dotel, and Billy Wagner (vs. N.Y. Yankees, AL), June 11, 2003 (final: 8–0)
Mike Fiers (vs. L.A. Dodgers), Aug. 21, 2015 (final: 3–0)

No-Hitters Pitched Against

Juan Marichal, S.F. Giants, June 15, 1963 (final: 1–0)
Jim Maloney, Cin. Reds, Apr. 30, 1969 (final: 1–0)
Francisco Cordova and Ricardo Rincon, Pitt. Pirates, July 12, 1997 (final: 3–0)
Carlos Zambrano, Chi. Cubs, Sept. 14, 2008 (final: 5–0)
Matt Cain, S.F. Giants, June 13, 2012 (final: 10–0) (perfect game)

Postseason Play

1980 NL West Playoff Game vs. L.A. Dodgers, won
League Championship Series vs. Phila. Phillies, lost 3 games to 2
1981 First-Half Division Playoff Series vs. L.A. Dodgers, lost 3 games to 2
1986 League Championship Series vs. N.Y. Mets, lost 4 games to 2
1997 Division Series vs. Atl. Braves, lost 3 games to 0
1998 Division Series vs. S.D. Padres, lost 3 games to 1
1999 Division Series vs. Atl. Braves, lost 3 games to 1
2001 Division Series vs. Atl. Braves, lost 3 games to 0
2004 Division Series vs. Atl. Braves, won 3 games to 2
League Championship Series vs. St.L. Cardinals, lost 4 games to 3
2005 Division Series vs. Atl. Braves, won 3 games to 1
League Championship Series vs. St.L. Cardinals, won 4 games to 2
World Series vs. Chi. White Sox (AL), lost 4 games to 0
2015 AL Wild Card Playoff Game vs. N.Y. Yankees, won
Division Series vs. K.C. Royals, lost 3 games to 2

Kansas City Royals

Dates of Operation: 1969–present (47 years)

Overall Record: 3623 wins, 3852 losses (.484)

Stadiums: Municipal Stadium, 1969–72; Kauffman Stadium (formerly Royals Stadium, 1973–93) 1973–present (capacity: 37,903)

Year-by-Year Finishes

Year	Finish	Wins	Losses	Percentage	Games Behind	Manager	Attendance
					West Division		
1969	4th	69	93	.426	28.0	Joe Gordon	902,414
1970	4th (Tie)	65	97	.401	33.0	Charlie Metro, Bob Lemon	693,047
1971	2nd	85	76	.528	16.0	Bob Lemon	910,784
1972	4th	76	78	.494	16.5	Bob Lemon	707,656
1973	2nd	88	74	.543	6.0	Jack McKeon	1,345,341
1974	5th	77	85	.475	13.0	Jack McKeon	1,173,292
1975	2nd	91	71	.562	7.0	Jack McKeon, Whitey Herzog	1,151,836
1976	1st	90	72	.556	+2.5	Whitey Herzog	1,680,265
1977	1st	102	60	.630	+8.0	Whitey Herzog	1,852,603
1978	1st	92	70	.568	+5.0	Whitey Herzog	2,255,493
1979	2nd	85	77	.525	3.0	Whitey Herzog	2,261,845
1980	1st	97	65	.599	+14.0	Jim Frey	2,288,714
1981*	5th/1st	50	53	.485	12.0/+1.0	Jim Frey, Dick Howser	1,279,403
1982	2nd	90	72	.556	3.0	Dick Howser	2,284,464
1983	2nd	79	83	.488	20.0	Dick Howser	1,963,875
1984	1st	84	78	.519	+3.0	Dick Howser	1,810,018
1985	1st	91	71	.562	+1.0	Dick Howser	2,162,717
1986	3rd (Tie)	76	86	.469	16.0	Dick Howser, Mike Ferraro	2,320,794
1987	2nd	83	79	.512	2.0	Billy Gardner, John Wathan	2,392,471
1988	3rd	84	77	.522	19.5	John Wathan	2,350,181
1989	2nd	92	70	.568	7.0	John Wathan	2,477,700
1990	6th	75	86	.466	27.5	John Wathan	2,244,956
1991	6th	82	80	.506	13.0	John Wathan, Hal McRae	2,161,537
1992	5th (Tie)	72	90	.444	24.0	Hal McRae	1,867,689
1993	3rd	84	78	.519	10.0	Hal McRae	1,934,578
					Central Division		
1994	3rd	64	51	.557	4.0	Hal McRae	1,400,494
1995	2nd	70	74	.486	30.0	Bob Boone	1,233,530
1996	5th	75	86	.466	24.0	Bob Boone	1,435,997
1997	5th	67	94	.416	19.0	Bob Boone, Tony Muser	1,517,638
1998	3rd	72	89	.447	16.5	Tony Muser	1,494,875
1999	4th	64	97	.398	32.5	Tony Muser	1,506,068
2000	4th	77	85	.475	18.0	Tony Muser	1,677,915
2001	5th	65	97	.401	26.0	Tony Muser	1,536,371
2002	4th	62	100	.383	32.5	Tony Muser, Tony Pena	1,323,034
2003	3rd	83	79	.512	7.0	Tony Pena	1,779,895
2004	5th	58	104	.358	34.0	Tony Pena	1,661,478
2005	5th	56	106	.346	43.0	Tony Pena, Bob Schaefer, Buddy Bell	1,371,181

2006	5th	62	100	.383	34.0	Buddy Bell	1,372,638
2007	5th	69	93	.426	27.5	Buddy Bell	1,616,867
2008	4th	75	87	.463	13.5	Trey Hillman	1,578,922
2009	4th	65	97	.401	21.5	Trey Hillman	1,797,887
2010	5th	67	95	.414	27.0	Trey Hillman, Ned Yost	1,615,327
2011	4th	71	91	.438	24.0	Ned Yost	1,724,450
2012	3rd	72	90	.444	16.0	Ned Yost	1,739,859
2013	3rd	86	76	.531	7.0	Ned Yost	1,750,754
2014	2nd	89	73	.549	10.0	Ned Yost	1,956,482
2015	1st	95	67	.586	+12.0	Ned Yost	2,708,549

*Split season.

Awards

Most Valuable Player

George Brett, third base, 1980

Rookie of the Year

Lou Piniella, outfield, 1969
Bob Hamelin, designated hitter, 1994
Carlos Beltran, outfield, 1999
Angel Berroa, shortstop, 2003

Cy Young

Bret Saberhagen, 1985
Bret Saberhagen, 1989
David Cone, 1994
Zack Greinke, 2009

Hall of Famers Who Played for the Royals

George Brett, infield, 1973–93
Orlando Cepeda, designated hitter, 1974
Harmon Killebrew, designated hitter, 1975
Gaylord Perry, pitcher, 1983

Retired Numbers

5 ..... George Brett
10 ..... Dick Howser
20 ..... Frank White

League Leaders, Batting

Batting Average, Season

George Brett, 1976 ..... .333
George Brett, 1980 ..... .390
Willie Wilson, 1982 ..... .332
George Brett, 1990 ..... .329

Home Runs, Season

[No player]

RBIs, Season

Hal McRae, 1982 133

Stolen Bases, Season

Amos Otis, 1971 52
Freddie Patek, 1977 53
Willie Wilson, 1979 83
Johnny Damon, 2000 46

Total Bases, Season

George Brett, 1976 298

Most Hits, Season

George Brett, 1975 195
George Brett, 1976 215
George Brett, 1979 212
Willie Wilson, 1980 230
Kevin Seitzer, 1987 ..... 207 (Tie)

Most Runs, Season

Willie Wilson, 1980 133
Johnny Damon, 2000 136

Batting Feats

Triple Crown Winners

[No player]

Hitting for the Cycle

Freddie Patek, July 9, 1971
John Mayberry, Aug. 5, 1977
George Brett, May 28, 1979
Frank White, Sept. 26, 1979
Frank White, Aug. 3, 1982
George Brett, July 25, 1990

Six Hits in a Game

Bob Oliver, May 4, 1969
Kevin Seitzer, Aug. 2, 1987
Joe Randa, Sept. 9, 2004

40 or More Home Runs, Season

[No player]

League Leaders, Pitching

Most Wins, Season

Dennis Leonard, 1977 ..... 20 (Tie)
Bret Saberhagen, 1989 23

Most Strikeouts, Season

[No pitcher]

Lowest ERA, Season

Bret Saberhagen, 1989 ..... 2.16
Kevin Appier, 1993 ..... 2.56
Zack Greinke, 2009 ..... 2.16

Most Saves, Season

Dan Quisenberry, 1980 ..... 33 (Tie)
Dan Quisenberry, 1982 35
Dan Quisenberry, 1983 45
Dan Quisenberry, 1984 44
Dan Quisenberry, 1985 37
Jeff Montgomery, 1993 ..... 45 (Tie)
Greg Holland, 2014 46

Best Won–Lost Percentage, Season

Paul Splittorff, 1977 .. 16–6 ..... .727
Bret Saberhagen, 1981 . 23–6 ..... .793

Pitching Feats

20 Wins, Season

Paul Splittorff, 1973 20–11
Steve Busby, 1974 22–14
Dennis Leonard, 1977 20–12
Dennis Leonard, 1978 21–17
Dennis Leonard, 1980 20–11
Bret Saberhagen, 1985 20–6
Mark Gubicza, 1988 20–8
Bret Saberhagen, 1989 23–6

No-Hitters

Steve Busby (vs. Det. Tigers), Apr. 27, 1973 (final: 3–0)

Steve Busby (vs. Milw. Brewers), June 19, 1974 (final: 2–0)

Jim Colborn (vs. Tex. Rangers), May 14, 1977 (final: 6–0)

Bret Saberhagen (vs. Chi. White Sox), Aug. 26, 1991 (final: 7–0)

No-Hitters Pitched Against

Nolan Ryan, Cal. Angels, May 15, 1973 (final: 3–0)

Jon Lester, Bost. Red Sox, May 19, 2008 (final: 7–0)

Postseason Play

1976 League Championship Series vs. N.Y. Yankees, lost 3 games to 2

1977 League Championship Series vs. N.Y. Yankees, lost 3 games to 2

1978 League Championship Series vs. N.Y. Yankees, lost 3 games to 1

1980 League Championship Series vs. N.Y. Yankees, won 3 games to 0

World Series vs. Phila. Phillies (NL), lost 4 games to 2

1981 First-Half Division Playoff vs. Oak. A's, lost 3 games to 0

1984 League Championship Series vs. Det. Tigers, lost 3 games to 0

1985 League Championship Series vs. Tor. Blue Jays, won 4 games to 3

World Series vs. St.L. Cardinals (NL), won 4 games to 3

2014 AL Wild Card Playoff Game vs. Oak. A's, won

Division Series vs. L.A. Angels, won 3 games to 0

League Championship Series vs. Balt. Orioles, won 4 games to 0

World Series vs. S.F. Giants (NL), lost 4 games to 3

2015 Division Series vs. Hous. Astros, won 3 games to 2

League Championship Series vs. Tor. Blue Jays, won 4 games to 2

World Series vs. N.Y. Mets (NL), won 4 games to 1

Los Angeles Angels of Anaheim

Dates of Operation: 1961–present (55 years)

Overall Record: 4403 wins, 4377 losses (.501)

Stadiums: Wrigley Field, 1961; Chavez Ravine (a.k.a. Dodger Stadium), 1962–65; Angel Stadium of Anaheim (formerly Anaheim Stadium, 1996–97, Edison International Field 1998–2003), 1966–present (capacity: 45,957)

Other Names: Los Angeles Angels (1961–64), California Angels (1965–96), Anaheim Angels (1996–2004)

Year-by-Year Finishes

Year	Finish	Wins	Losses	Percentage	Games Behind	Manager	Attendance
1961	8th	70	91	.435	38.5	Bill Rigney	603,510
1962	3rd	86	76	.531	10.0	Bill Rigney	1,144,063
1963	9th	70	91	.435	34.0	Bill Rigney	821,015
1964	5th	82	80	.506	17.0	Bill Rigney	760,439
1965	7th	75	87	.463	27.0	Bill Rigney	566,727
1966	6th	80	82	.494	18.0	Bill Rigney	1,400,321
1967	5th	84	77	.522	7.5	Bill Rigney	1,317,713
1968	8th	67	95	.414	36.0	Bill Rigney	1,025,956
					West Division		
1969	3rd	71	91	.438	26.0	Bill Rigney, Lefty Phillips	758,388
1970	3rd	86	76	.531	12.0	Lefty Phillips	1,077,741
1971	4th	76	86	.469	25.5	Lefty Phillips	926,373
1972	5th	75	80	.484	18.0	Del Rice	744,190
1973	4th	79	83	.488	15.0	Bobby Winkles	1,058,206
1974	6th	68	94	.420	22.0	Bobby Winkles, Dick Williams	917,269
1975	6th	72	89	.447	25.5	Dick Williams	1,058,163
1976	4th (Tie)	76	86	.469	14.0	Dick Williams, Norm Sherry	1,006,774
1977	5th	74	88	.457	28.0	Norm Sherry, Dave Garcia	1,432,633
1978	2nd (Tie)	87	75	.537	5.0	Dave Garcia, Jim Fregosi	1,755,386
1979	1st	88	74	.543	+3.0	Jim Fregosi	2,523,575
1980	6th	65	95	.406	31.0	Jim Fregosi	2,297,327
1981*	4th/7th	51	59	.464	6.0/8.5	Jim Fregosi, Gene Mauch	1,441,545
1982	1st	93	69	.574	+3.0	Gene Mauch	2,807,360
1983	5th (Tie)	70	92	.432	29.0	John McNamara	2,555,016
1984	2nd (Tie)	81	81	.500	3.0	John McNamara	2,402,997
1985	2nd	90	72	.556	1.0	Gene Mauch	2,567,427
1986	1st	92	70	.568	+5.0	Gene Mauch	2,655,872
1987	6th (Tie)	75	87	.463	10.0	Gene Mauch	2,696,299
1988	4th	75	87	.463	29.0	Cookie Rojas	2,340,925
1989	3rd	91	71	.562	8.0	Doug Rader	2,647,291
1990	4th	80	82	.494	23.0	Doug Rader	2,555,688
1991	7th	81	81	.500	14.0	Doug Rader, Buck Rodgers	2,416,236
1992	5th (Tie)	72	90	.444	24.0	Buck Rodgers	2,065,444
1993	5th (Tie)	71	91	.438	23.0	Buck Rodgers	2,057,460
1994	4th	47	68	.409	5.5	Buck Rodgers, Marcel Lachemann	1,512,622
1995	2nd	78	67	.538	1.0	Marcel Lachemann	1,748,680
1996	4th	70	91	.435	19.5	Marcel Lachemann, John McNamara, Joe Maddon	1,820,521
1997	2nd	84	78	.519	6.0	Terry Collins	1,767,330
1998	2nd	85	77	.525	3.0	Terry Collins	2,519,210

1999	4th	70	92	.432	25.0	Terry Collins, Joe Maddon	2,253,123
2000	3rd	82	80	.506	9.5	Mike Scioscia	2,066,977
2001	3rd	75	87	.463	41.0	Mike Scioscia	2,000,917
2002	2nd	99	63	.611	4.0	Mike Scioscia	2,305,565
2003	3rd	77	85	.475	19.0	Mike Scioscia	3,061,094
2004	1st	92	70	.568	+1.0	Mike Scioscia	3,375,677
2005	1st	95	67	.586	+7.0	Mike Scioscia	3,404,686
2006	2nd	89	73	.649	4.0	Mike Scioscia	3,406,790
2007	1st	94	68	.580	+6.5	Mike Scioscia	3,365,632
2008	1st	100	62	.617	+21.0	Mike Scioscia	3,336,744
2009	1st	97	65	.599	+10.0	Mike Scioscia	3,240,386
2010	3rd	80	82	.494	10.0	Mike Scioscia	3,250,814
2011	2nd	86	76	.531	10.0	Mike Scioscia	3,166,321
2012	3rd	89	73	.549	5.0	Mike Scioscia	3,061,770
2013	3rd	78	84	.481	18.0	Mike Scioscia	3,019,505
2014	1st	98	64	.605	+10.0	Mike Scioscia	3,095,935
2015	3rd	85	77	.525	3.0	Mike Scioscia	3,012,765

*Split season.

Awards

Most Valuable Player

Don Baylor, outfield, 1979
Vladimir Guererro, outfield, 2004
Mike Trout, outfield, 2014

Rookie of the Year

Tim Salmon, outfield, 1993
Mike Trout, outfield, 2012

Cy Young

Dean Chance, 1964
Bartolo Colon, 2005

Hall of Famers Who Played for the Angels

Rod Carew, infield, 1979–85
Rickey Henderson, outfield, 1997
Reggie Jackson, designated hitter and outfield, 1982–86
Eddie Murray, designated hitter, 1997
Frank Robinson, designated hitter, 1973–74
Nolan Ryan, pitcher, 1972–79
Don Sutton, pitcher, 1985–87
Hoyt Wilhelm, pitcher, 1969
Dave Winfield, outfield and designated hitter, 1990–91

Retired Numbers

11 ..... Jim Fregosi
26 ..... Gene Autry
29 ..... Rod Carew
30 ..... Nolan Ryan
50 ..... Jimmy Reese

League Leaders, Batting

Batting Average, Season

Alex Johnson, 1970 ..... .329

Home Runs, Season

Bobby Grinch, 1981 ..... 22 (Tie)
Reggie Jackson, 1982 ..... 39 (Tie)
Troy Glaus, 2000 47

RBIs, Season

Don Baylor, 1979 139
Mike Trout, 2014 111

Stolen Bases, Season

Mickey Rivers, 1975 70
Chone Figgins, 2005 62
Mike Trout, 2012 49

Total Bases, Season

Vladimir Guerrero, 2004 366
Mike Trout, 2014 338

Most Hits, Season

Darin Erstad, 2000 240

Most Runs, Season

Albie Pearson, 1962 115
Don Baylor, 1979 120
Vladimir Guerrero, 2004 124
Mike Trout, 2012 129
Mike Trout, 2013 109
Mike Trout, 2014 115

Batting Feats

Triple Crown Winners

[No player]

Hitting for the Cycle

Jim Fregosi, July 28, 1964
Jim Fregosi, May 20, 1968
Dan Ford, Aug. 10, 1979
Dave Winfield, June 24, 1991
Jeff DaVanon, Aug. 25, 2004
Chone Figgins, Sept. 16, 2006
Mike Trout, May 21, 2013

Six Hits in a Game

Garret Anderson, Sept. 27, 1996*
*Extra-inning game.

40 or More Home Runs, Season

47 ..... Troy Glaus, 2000
41 ..... Troy Glaus, 2001

League Leaders, Pitching

Most Wins, Season

Dean Chance, 1964 ..... 20 (Tie)
Bartolo Colon, 2005 21
Jered Weaver, 2012 ..... 20 (Tie)
Jered Weaver, 2014 ..... 18 (Tie)

Most Strikeouts, Season

Nolan Ryan, 1972 329
Nolan Ryan, 1973 383
Nolan Ryan, 1974 367
Frank Tanana, 1975 269
Nolan Ryan, 1976 327

Nolan Ryan, 1977 341
Nolan Ryan, 1978 260
Nolan Ryan, 1979 223
Jered Weaver, 2010 233

Lowest ERA, Season

Dean Chance, 1964 ..... 1.65
Frank Tanana, 1977 ..... 2.54
John Lackey, 2007 ..... 3.01

Most Saves, Season

Bryan Harvey, 1991 46
Francisco Rodriguez, 2005 ..... 45 (Tie)
Francisco Rodriguez, 2006 47
Francisco Rodriguez, 2007 62
Brian Fuentes, 2008 48

Best Won–Lost Percentage, Season

Jered Weaver, 2012....20–5...800 (Tie)
Matt Shoemaker, 2014....16–4.....800

Pitching Feats

20 Wins, Season

Dean Chance, 1964 20–9
Clyde Wright, 1970 22–12
Andy Messersmith, 1971 20–13
Nolan Ryan, 1973 21–16
Bill Singer, 1973 20–14
Nolan Ryan, 1974 22–16
Bartolo Colon, 2005 21–8
Jered Weaver, 2012 20–5

No-Hitters

Bo Belinsky (vs. Balt. Orioles), May 5, 1962 (final: 2–0)
Clyde Wright (vs. Oak. A's), July 3, 1970 (final: 4–0)
Nolan Ryan (vs. K.C. Royals), May 15, 1973 (final: 3–0)
Nolan Ryan (vs. Det. Tigers), July 15, 1973 (final: 6–0)
Nolan Ryan (vs. Min. Twins), Sept. 28, 1974 (final: 4–0)
Nolan Ryan (vs. Balt. Orioles), June 1, 1975 (final: 1–0)
Mike Witt (vs. Tex. Rangers), Sept. 30, 1984 (final: 1–0) (perfect game)
Mark Langston and Mike Witt (vs. Sea. Mariners), Apr. 11, 1990 (final: 1–0)
Jered Weaver (vs. Min. Twins), May 2, 2012 (final: 9–0)

No-Hitters Pitched Against

Earl Wilson, Bost. Red Sox, June 26, 1962 (final: 2–0)
Vida Blue, Glenn Abbott, Paul Lindblad, and Rollie Fingers, Oak. A's, Sept. 28, 1975 (final: 5–0)
Dennis Eckersley, Cle. Indians, May 30, 1977 (final: 1–0)
Bert Blyleven, Tex. Rangers, Sept. 22, 1977 (final: 6–0)
Joe Cowley, Chi. White Sox, Sept. 19, 1986 (final: 7–1)
Kenny Rogers, Tex. Rangers, July 28, 1994 (final: 4–0) (perfect game)
Eric Milton, Min. Twins, Sept. 11, 1999 (final: 7–0)

Postseason

1979 League Championship Series vs. Balt. Orioles, lost 3 games to 1
1982 League Championship Series vs. Milw. Brewers, lost 3 games to 2
1986 League Championship Series vs. Bost. Red Sox, lost 4 games to 3
1995 AL West Playoff Game vs. Sea. Mariners, lost
2002 Division Series vs. N.Y. Yankees, won 3 games to 1
League Championship Series vs. Min. Twins, won 4 games to 1
World Series vs. S.F. Giants (NL), won 4 games to 3
2004 Division Series vs. Bost. Red Sox, lost 3 games to 0
2005 Division Series vs. N.Y. Yankees, won 3 games to 2
League Championship Series vs. Chi. White Sox, lost 4 games to 1
2007 Division Series vs. Bost. Red Sox, lost 3 games to 0
2008 Division Series vs. Bost. Red Sox, lost 3 games to 1
2009 Division Series vs. Bost. Red Sox, won 3 games to 0
League Championship Series vs. N.Y. Yankees, lost 4 games to 2
2014 Division Series vs. K.C. Royals, lost 3 games to 0

Minnesota Twins

Dates of Operation: 1961–present (55 years)
Overall Record: 4357 wins, 4414 losses (.496)
Stadiums: Metropolitan Stadium, 1961–81; Hubert H. Humphrey Metrodome (also known as The Metrodome), 1982–2009; Target Field, 2010–present (capacity: 39,021)

Year-by-Year Finishes

Year	Finish	Wins	Losses	Percentage	Games Behind	Manager	Attendance
1961	7th	70	90	.438	38.0	Cookie Lavagetto, Sam Mele	1,256,723
1962	2nd	91	71	.562	5.0	Sam Mele	1,433,116
1963	3rd	91	70	.565	13.0	Sam Mele	1,406,652
1964	6th (Tie)	79	83	.488	20.0	Sam Mele	1,207,514
1965	1st	102	60	.630	+7.0	Sam Mele	1,463,258
1966	2nd	89	73	.549	9.0	Sam Mele	1,259,374
1967	2nd (Tie)	91	71	.562	1.0	Sam Mele, Cal Ermer	1,483,547
1968	7th	79	83	.488	24.0	Cal Ermer	1,143,257
				West Division			
1969	1st	97	65	.599	+9.0	Billy Martin	1,349,328
1970	1st	98	64	.605	+9.0	Bill Rigney	1,261,887
1971	5th	74	86	.463	26.5	Bill Rigney	940,858
1972	3rd	77	77	.500	15.5	Bill Rigney, Frank Quilici	797,901
1973	3rd	81	81	.500	13.0	Frank Quilici	907,499
1974	3rd	82	80	.506	8.0	Frank Quilici	662,401
1975	4th	76	83	.478	20.5	Frank Quilici	737,156
1976	3rd	85	77	.525	5.0	Gene Mauch	715,394
1977	4th	84	77	.522	17.5	Gene Mauch	1,162,727
1978	4th	73	89	.451	19.0	Gene Mauch	787,878
1979	4th	82	80	.506	6.0	Gene Mauch	1,070,521
1980	3rd	77	84	.478	19.5	Gene Mauch, Johnny Goryl	769,206
1981*	7th/4th	41	68	.376	18.0/6.0	Johnny Goryl, Billy Gardner	469,090
1982	7th	60	102	.370	33.0	Billy Gardner	921,186
1983	5th (Tie)	70	92	.432	29.0	Billy Gardner	858,939
1984	2nd (Tie)	81	81	.500	3.0	Billy Gardner	1,598,422
1985	4th (Tie)	77	85	.475	14.0	Billy Gardner, Ray Miller	1,651,814
1986	6th	71	91	.438	21.0	Ray Miller, Tom Kelly	1,255,453
1987	1st	85	77	.525	+2.0	Tom Kelly	2,081,976
1988	2nd	91	71	.562	13.0	Tom Kelly	3,030,672
1989	5th	80	82	.494	19.0	Tom Kelly	2,277,438
1990	7th	74	88	.457	29.0	Tom Kelly	1,751,584
1991	1st	95	67	.586	+8.0	Tom Kelly	2,293,842
1992	2nd	90	72	.556	6.0	Tom Kelly	2,482,428
1993	5th (Tie)	71	91	.438	23.0	Tom Kelly	2,048,673
				Central Division			
1994	4th	53	60	.469	14.0	Tom Kelly	1,398,565
1995	5th	56	88	.389	44.0	Tom Kelly	1,057,667
1996	4th	78	84	.481	21.5	Tom Kelly	1,437,352
1997	4th	68	94	.420	18.5	Tom Kelly	1,411,064
1998	4th	70	92	.432	19.0	Tom Kelly	1,165,980
1999	5th	63	97	.394	33.0	Tom Kelly	1,202,829
2000	5th	69	93	.426	26.0	Tom Kelly	1,059,715

2001	2nd	85	77	.525	6.0	Tom Kelly	1,782,926
2002	1st	94	67	.584	+13.5	Ron Gardenhire	1,924,473
2003	1st	90	72	.556	+4.0	Ron Gardenhire	1,946,011
2004	1st	92	70	.568	+9.0	Ron Gardenhire	1,911,418
2005	3rd	83	79	.512	16.0	Ron Gardenhire	2,034,243
2006	1st	96	66	.593	+1.0	Ron Gardenhire	2,285,018
2007	3rd	79	83	.488	17.5	Ron Gardenhire	2,296,347
2008	2nd	88	75	.540	1.0	Ron Gardenhire	2,302,431
2009	1st	87	76	.534	+1.0	Ron Gardenhire	2,416,237
2010	1st	94	68	.580	+6.0	Ron Gardenhire	3,223,640
2011	5th	63	99	.389	32.0	Ron Gardenhire	3,168,116
2012	5th	66	96	.407	22.0	Ron Gardenhire	2,776,354
2013	4th	66	96	.407	27.0	Ron Gardenhire	2,477,644
2014	5th	70	92	.432	20.0	Ron Gardenhire	2,250,606
2015	2nd	83	79	.512	12.0	Paul Molitor	2,220,054

*Split season.

Awards

Most Valuable Player

Zoilo Versalles, shortstop, 1965
Harmon Killebrew, infield, 1969
Rod Carew, first base, 1977
Justin Morneau, first base, 2006
Joe Mauer, catcher, 2009

Rookie of the Year

Tony Oliva, outfield, 1964
Rod Carew, second base, 1967
John Castino (co-winner), third base, 1979
Chuck Knoblauch, second base, 1991
Marty Cordova, outfield, 1995

Cy Young

Jim Perry, 1970
Frank Viola, 1988
Johan Santana, 2004
Johan Santana, 2006

Hall of Famers Who Played for the Twins

Rod Carew, infield, 1967–78
Steve Carlton, pitcher, 1987–88
Harmon Killebrew, infield and outfield, 1961–74
Paul Molitor, shortstop, second base, designated hitter, 1996–98
Kirby Puckett, outfield, 1984–95
Dave Winfield, designated hitter, 1993–94

Retired Numbers

3 ..... Harmon Killebrew
6 ..... Tony Oliva
10 ..... Tom Kelly
14 ..... Kent Hrbek
28 ..... Bert Blyleven
29 ..... Rod Carew
34 ..... Kirby Puckett

League Leaders, Batting

Batting Average, Season

Tony Oliva, 1964 ..... .323
Tony Oliva, 1965 ..... .321
Rod Carew, 1969 ..... .332
Tony Oliva, 1971 ..... .337
Rod Carew, 1972 ..... .318
Rod Carew, 1973 ..... .350
Rod Carew, 1974 ..... .364
Rod Carew, 1975 ..... .359
Rod Carew, 1977 ..... .388
Rod Carew, 1978 ..... .333
Kirby Puckett, 1989 ..... .339
Joe Mauer, 2006 ..... .347
Joe Mauer, 2008 ..... .328
Joe Mauer, 2009 ..... .365

Home Runs, Season

Harmon Killebrew, 1962 48
Harmon Killebrew, 1963 45
Harmon Killebrew, 1964 49
Harmon Killebrew, 1967 ..... 44 (Tie)
Harmon Killebrew, 1969 49

RBIs, Season

Harmon Killebrew, 1962 126
Harmon Killebrew, 1969 140
Harmon Killebrew, 1971 119
Larry Hisle, 1977 119
Kirby Puckett, 1994 112

Stolen Bases, Season

[No player]

Total Bases, Season

Tony Oliva, 1964 374
Zoilo Versalles, 1965 308
Kirby Puckett, 1988 358
Kirby Puckett, 1992 313

Most Hits, Season

Tony Oliva, 1964 217
Tony Oliva, 1965 185
Tony Oliva, 1966 191
Tony Oliva, 1969 197
Tony Oliva, 1970 204
Cesar Tovar, 1971 204
Rod Carew, 1973 203
Rod Carew, 1974 218
Rod Carew, 1977 239
Kirby Puckett, 1987 ..... 207 (Tie)
Kirby Puckett, 1988 234
Kirby Puckett, 1989 215
Kirby Puckett, 1992 210
Paul Molitor, 1996 225

Most Runs, Season

Bob Allison, 1963 99
Tony Oliva, 1964 109
Zoilo Versalles, 1965 126
Rod Carew, 1977 128

Batting Feats

Triple Crown Winners

[No player]

Hitting for the Cycle

Rod Carew, May 20, 1970
Cesar Tovar, Sept. 19, 1972
Larry Hisle, June 4, 1976
Lyman Bostock, July 24, 1976

Mike Cubbage, July 27, 1978
Gary Ward, Sept. 18, 1980
Kirby Puckett, Aug. 1, 1986
Carlos Gomez, May 7, 2008
Jason Kubel, Apr. 17, 2009
Michael Cuddyer, May 22, 2009

Six Hits in a Game

Kirby Puckett, Aug. 30, 1987
Kirby Puckett, May 23, 1991*
*Extra-inning game.

40 or More Home Runs, Season

49 ..... Harmon Killebrew, 1964
Harmon Killebrew, 1969
48 ..... Harmon Killebrew, 1962
46 ..... Harmon Killebrew, 1961
45 ..... Harmon Killebrew, 1963
44 ..... Harmon Killebrew, 1967
41 ..... Harmon Killebrew, 1970

League Leaders, Pitching

Most Wins, Season

Mudcat Grant, 1965 21
Jim Kaat, 1966 25
Jim Perry, 1970 24
Gaylord Perry, 1972 ..... 24 (Tie)
Frank Viola, 1988 24
Scott Erickson, 1991 ..... 20 (Tie)
Johan Santana, 2006 ..... 19 (Tie)

Most Strikeouts, Season

Camilo Pascual, 1961 221
Camilo Pascual, 1962 206
Camilo Pascual, 1963 202
Bert Blyleven*, 1985 206
Johan Santana, 2004 265
Johan Santana, 2005 238
Johan Santana, 2006 245
*129 with Cle. Indians and 77 with Min. Twins.

Lowest ERA, Season

Allan Anderson, 1988 ..... 2.45
Johan Santana, 2004 ..... 2.61
Johan Santana, 2006 ..... 2.77

Most Saves, Season

Ron Perranoski, 1969 31
Ron Perranoski, 1970 34
Mike Marshall, 1979 32
Eddie Guardado, 2002 45

Best Won–Lost Percentage, Season

Mudcat Grant, 1965... 21–7..... .750
Bill Campbell, 1976.... 17–5..... .773
Frank Viola, 1988 ..... 24–7..... .774
Scott Erickson, 1991 ... 20–8..... .714
Johan Santana, 2003.. 12–3..... .800
Francisco Liriano, 2006 12–3..... .800

Pitching Feats

Triple Crown Winner

Johan Santana, 2006 (19–6, 2.77 ERA, 245 SO)

20 Wins, Season

Camilo Pascual, 1962 20–11
Camilo Pascual, 1963 21–9
Mudcat Grant, 1965 21–7
Jim Kaat, 1966 25–13
Dean Chance, 1967 20–14
Jim Perry, 1969 20–6
Dave Boswell, 1969 20–12
Jim Perry, 1970 24–12
Bert Blyleven, 1973 20–17
Dave Goltz, 1977 20–11
Jerry Koosman, 1979 20–13
Frank Viola, 1988 24–7
Scott Erickson, 1991 20–8
Brad Radke, 1997 20–10
Johan Santana, 2004 20–6

No-Hitters

Jack Kralick (vs. K.C. A's), Aug. 26, 1962 (final: 1–0)
Dean Chance (vs. Cle. Indians), Aug. 25, 1967 (final: 2–1)
Scott Erickson (vs. Milw. Brewers), Apr. 27, 1994 (final: 6–0)
Eric Milton (vs. Ana. Angels), Sept. 11, 1999 (final: 7–0)
Francisco Liriano (vs. Cle. Indians), May 3, 2011 (final 1–0)

No-Hitters Pitched Against

Catfish Hunter, Oak. A's, May 8, 1968 (final: 4–0) (perfect game)
Vida Blue, Oak. A's, Sept. 21, 1970 (final: 6–0)
Nolan Ryan, Cal. Angels, Sept. 28, 1974 (final: 4–0)
David Wells, N.Y. Yankees, May 17, 1998 (final: 4–0) (perfect game)
Jered Weaver, L.A. Angels, May 2, 2012 (final: 4–0)

Postseason Play

1965 World Series vs. L.A. Dodgers (NL), lost 4 games to 3
1969 Championship Series vs. Balt. Orioles, lost 3 games to 0
1970 Championship Series vs. Balt. Orioles, lost 3 games to 0
1987 Championship Series vs. Det. Tigers, won 3 games to 1
World Series vs. St.L. Cardinals (NL), won 4 games to 3
1991 Championship Series vs. Tor. Blue Jays, won 4 games to 1
World Series vs. Atl. Braves (NL), won 4 games to 3
2002 Division Series vs. Oak. A's, won 3 games to 2
Championship Series vs. Ana. Angels, lost 4 games to 1
2003 Division Series vs. N.Y. Yankees, lost 3 games to 1
2004 Division Series vs. N.Y. Yankees, lost 3 games to 1
2006 Division Series vs. Oak. A's, lost 3 games to 0
2008 AL Central Playoff Game vs. Chi White Sox, lost
2009 AL Central Playoff Game vs. Det. Tigers, won
Division Series vs. N.Y. Yankees, lost 3 games to 0
2010 Division Series vs. N.Y. Yankees, lost 3 games to 0

New York Yankees

Dates of Operation: (as the Baltimore Orioles) 1901–02 (2 years)
Overall Record: 118 wins, 153 losses (.435)
Stadium: Oriole Park, Baltimore, 1901–02

Dates of Operation: (as the New York Yankees) 1903–present (113 years)
Overall Record: 10,000 wins, 7570 losses (.578)
Stadiums: Hilltop Park, 1903–12; Polo Grounds, 1912, 1913–22; Harrison Field, 1918 (Sundays only); Yankee Stadium, 1923–73, 1976–2008; Shea Stadium, 1974–75; Yankee Stadium II, 2009–present (capacity: 49,642)
Other Name: Hilltoppers, Highlanders

Year-by-Year Finishes

Year	Finish	Wins	Losses	Percentage	Games Behind	Manager	Attendance
					Balt. Orioles		
1901	5th	68	65	.511	13.5	John McGraw	141,952
1902	8th	50	88	.362	34.0	John McGraw, Wilbert Robinson	174,606
					N.Y. Yankees		
1903	4th	72	62	.537	17.0	Clark Griffith	211,808
1904	2nd	92	59	.609	1.5	Clark Griffith	438,919
1905	6th	71	78	.477	21.5	Clark Griffith	309,100
1906	2nd	90	61	.596	3.0	Clark Griffith	434,709
1907	5th	70	78	.473	21.0	Clark Griffith	350,020
1908	8th	51	103	.331	39.5	Clark Griffith, Kid Elberfeld	305,500
1909	5th	74	77	.490	23.5	George Stallings	501,000
1910	2nd	88	63	.583	14.5	George Stallings, Hal Chase	355,857
1911	6th	76	76	.500	25.5	Hal Chase	302,444
1912	8th	50	102	.329	55.0	Harry Wolverton	242,194
1913	7th	57	94	.377	38.0	Frank Chance	357,551
1914	6th (Tie)	70	84	.455	30.0	Frank Chance, Roger Peckinpaugh	359,477
1915	5th	69	83	.454	32.5	Bill Donovan	256,035
1916	4th	80	74	.519	11.0	Bill Donovan	469,211
1917	6th	71	82	.464	28.5	Bill Donovan	330,294
1918	4th	60	63	.488	13.5	Miller Huggins	282,047
1919	3rd	80	59	.576	7.5	Miller Huggins	619,164
1920	3rd	95	59	.617	3.0	Miller Huggins	1,289,422
1921	1st	98	55	.641	+4.5	Miller Huggins	1,230,696
1922	1st	94	60	.610	+1.0	Miller Huggins	1,026,134
1923	1st	98	54	.645	+16.0	Miller Huggins	1,007,066
1924	2nd	89	63	.586	2.0	Miller Huggins	1,053,533
1925	7th	69	85	.448	30.0	Miller Huggins	697,267
1926	1st	91	63	.591	+3.0	Miller Huggins	1,027,095
1927	1st	110	44	.714	+19.0	Miller Huggins	1,164,015
1928	1st	101	53	.656	+2.5	Miller Huggins	1,072,132
1929	2nd	88	66	.571	18.0	Miller Huggins, Art Fletcher	960,148
1930	3rd	86	68	.558	16.0	Bob Shawkey	1,169,230
1931	2nd	94	59	.614	13.5	Joe McCarthy	912,437
1932	1st	107	47	.695	+13.0	Joe McCarthy	962,320

1933	2nd	91	59	.607	7.0	Joe McCarthy	728,014
1934	2nd	94	60	.610	7.0	Joe McCarthy	854,682
1935	2nd	89	60	.597	3.0	Joe McCarthy	657,508
1936	1st	102	51	.667	+19.5	Joe McCarthy	976,913
1937	1st	102	52	.662	+13.0	Joe McCarthy	998,148
1938	1st	99	53	.651	+9.5	Joe McCarthy	970,916
1939	1st	106	45	.702	+17.0	Joe McCarthy	859,785
1940	3rd	88	66	.571	2.0	Joe McCarthy	988,975
1941	1st	101	53	.656	+17.0	Joe McCarthy	964,722
1942	1st	103	51	.669	+9.0	Joe McCarthy	988,251
1943	1st	98	56	.636	+13.5	Joe McCarthy	645,006
1944	3rd	83	71	.539	6.0	Joe McCarthy	822,864
1945	4th	81	71	.533	6.5	Joe McCarthy	881,846
1946	3rd	87	67	.565	17.0	Joe McCarthy, Bill Dickey, Johnny Neun	2,265,512
1947	1st	97	57	.630	+12.0	Bucky Harris	2,178,937
1948	3rd	94	60	.610	2.5	Bucky Harris	2,373,901
1949	1st	97	57	.630	+1.0	Casey Stengel	2,281,676
1950	1st	98	56	.636	+3.0	Casey Stengel	2,081,380
1951	1st	98	56	.636	+5.0	Casey Stengel	1,950,107
1952	1st	95	59	.617	+2.0	Casey Stengel	1,629,665
1953	1st	99	52	.656	+8.5	Casey Stengel	1,537,811
1954	2nd	103	51	.669	8.0	Casey Stengel	1,475,171
1955	1st	96	58	.623	+3.0	Casey Stengel	1,490,138
1956	1st	97	57	.630	+9.0	Casey Stengel	1,491,784
1957	1st	98	56	.636	+8.0	Casey Stengel	1,497,134
1958	1st	92	62	.597	+10.0	Casey Stengel	1,428,438
1959	3rd	79	75	.513	15.0	Casey Stengel	1,552,030
1960	1st	97	57	.630	+8.0	Casey Stengel	1,627,349
1961	1st	109	53	.673	+8.0	Ralph Houk	1,747,725
1962	1st	96	66	.593	+5.0	Ralph Houk	1,493,574
1963	1st	104	57	.646	+10.5	Ralph Houk	1,308,920
1964	1st	99	63	.611	+1.0	Yogi Berra	1,305,638
1965	6th	77	85	.475	25.0	Johnny Keane	1,213,552
1966	10th	70	89	.440	26.5	Johnny Keane, Ralph Houk	1,124,648
1967	9th	72	90	.444	20.0	Ralph Houk	1,259,514
1968	5th	83	79	.512	20.0	Ralph Houk	1,185,666
				East Division			
1969	5th	80	81	.497	28.5	Ralph Houk	1,067,996
1970	2nd	93	69	.574	15.0	Ralph Houk	1,136,879
1971	4th	82	80	.506	21.0	Ralph Houk	1,070,771
1972	4th	79	76	.510	6.5	Ralph Houk	966,328
1973	4th	80	82	.494	17.0	Ralph Houk	1,262,103
1974	2nd	89	73	.549	2.0	Bill Virdon	1,273,075
1975	3rd	83	77	.519	12.0	Bill Virdon, Billy Martin	1,288,048
1976	1st	97	62	.610	+10.5	Billy Martin	2,012,434
1977	1st	100	62	.617	+2.5	Billy Martin	2,103,092
1978	1st	100	63	.613	+1.0	Billy Martin, Dick Howser, Bob Lemon	2,335,871
1979	4th	89	71	.556	13.5	Bob Lemon, Billy Martin	2,537,765
1980	1st	103	59	.636	+3.0	Dick Howser	2,627,417
1981*	1st/6th	59	48	.551	+2.0/5.0	Gene Michael, Bob Lemon	1,614,533
1982	5th	79	83	.488	16.0	Bob Lemon, Gene Michael, Clyde King	2,041,219

1983	3rd	91	71	.562	7.0	Billy Martin	2,257,976
1984	3rd	87	75	.537	17.0	Yogi Berra	1,821,815
1985	2nd	97	64	.602	2.0	Yogi Berra, Billy Martin	2,214,587
1986	2nd	90	72	.556	5.5	Lou Piniella	2,268,030
1987	4th	89	73	.549	9.0	Lou Piniella	2,427,672
1988	5th	85	76	.528	3.5	Billy Martin, Lou Piniella	2,633,701
1989	5th	74	87	.460	14.5	Dallas Green, Bucky Dent	2,170,485
1990	7th	67	95	.414	21.0	Bucky Dent, Stump Merrill	2,006,436
1991	5th	71	91	.438	20.0	Stump Merrill	1,863,733
1992	4th (Tie)	76	86	.469	20.0	Buck Showalter	1,748,733
1993	2nd	88	74	.543	7.0	Buck Showalter	2,416,965
1994	1st	70	43	.619	+6.5	Buck Showalter	1,675,556
1995	2nd	79	65	.549	7.0	Buck Showalter	1,705,263
1996	1st	92	70	.568	+4.0	Joe Torre	2,250,877
1997	2nd	96	66	.593	2.0	Joe Torre	2,580,325
1998	1st	114	48	.704	+22.0	Joe Torre	2,949,734
1999	1st	98	64	.605	+4.0	Joe Torre	3,292,736
2000	1st	87	74	.540	+2.5	Joe Torre	3,227,657
2001	1st	95	65	.594	+13.5	Joe Torre	3,264,777
2002	1st	103	58	.640	+10.5	Joe Torre	3,461,644
2003	1st	101	61	.623	+6.0	Joe Torre	3,465,600
2004	1st	101	61	.623	+3.0	Joe Torre	3,775,292
2005	1st (Tie)	95	67	.585	—	Joe Torre	4,090,692
2006	1st	97	65	.599	+10.0	Joe Torre	4,243,780
2007	2nd	94	68	.580	2.0	Joe Torre	4,271,083
2008	3rd	89	73	.549	8.0	Joe Girardi	4,298,655
2009	1st	103	59	.636	+8.0	Joe Girardi	3,719,358
2010	2nd	95	67	.586	1.0	Joe Girardi	3,765,807
2011	1st	97	65	.599	+6.0	Joe Girardi	3,653,680
2012	1st	95	67	.586	+2.0	Joe Girardi	3,542,406
2013	3rd	85	77	.525	12.0	Joe Girardi	3,279,589
2014	2nd	84	78	.519	12.0	Joe Girardi	3,401,624
2015	2nd	87	75	.537	6.0	Joe Girardi	3,193,795

*Split season.

Awards

Most Valuable Player

Babe Ruth, outfield, 1923
Lou Gehrig, first base, 1927
Lou Gehrig, first base, 1936
Joe DiMaggio, outfield, 1939
Joe DiMaggio, outfield, 1941
Joe Gordon, second base, 1942
Spud Chandler, pitcher, 1943
Joe DiMaggio, outfield, 1947
Phil Rizzuto, shortstop, 1950
Yogi Berra, catcher, 1951
Yogi Berra, catcher, 1954
Yogi Berra, catcher, 1955
Mickey Mantle, outfield, 1956
Mickey Mantle, outfield, 1957
Roger Maris, outfield, 1960
Roger Maris, outfield, 1961
Mickey Mantle, outfield, 1962
Elston Howard, catcher, 1963
Thurman Munson, catcher, 1976
Don Mattingly, first base, 1985
Alex Rodriguez, third base, 2005
Alex Rodriguez, third base, 2007

Rookie of the Year

Gil McDougald, infield, 1951
Bob Grim, pitcher, 1954
Tony Kubek, infield, 1957
Tom Tresh, shortstop and outfield, 1962
Stan Bahnsen, pitcher, 1968
Thurman Munson, catcher, 1970
Dave Righetti, pitcher, 1981
Derek Jeter, shortstop, 1996

Cy Young

Bob Turley, 1958
Whitey Ford, 1961
Sparky Lyle, 1977
Ron Guidry, 1978
Roger Clemens, 2001

Hall of Famers Who Played for the Yankees

Home Run Baker, third base, 1916–19 and 1921–22
Yogi Berra, catcher and outfield, 1946–63 and 1965
Wade Boggs, third base, 1993–97
Frank Chance, first base, 1913–14
Jack Chesbro, pitcher, 1903–09
Earle Combs, outfield, 1924–35
Stan Coveleski, pitcher, 1928

Bobby Cox, third base, 1968–69
Bill Dickey, catcher, 1928–43 and 1946
Joe DiMaggio, outfield, 1936–42 and 1946–51
Leo Durocher, shortstop, 1925 and 1928–29
Whitey Ford, pitcher, 1950 and 1953–67
Lou Gehrig, first base, 1923–39
Lefty Gomez, pitcher, 1930–42
Joe Gordon, second base, 1938–43 and 1946
Goose Gossage, pitcher, 1978–83 and 1989
Clark Griffith, pitcher, 1903–07
Burleigh Grimes, pitcher, 1934
Rickey Henderson, outfield, 1985–89
Waite Hoyt, pitcher, 1921–30
Catfish Hunter, pitcher, 1975–79
Reggie Jackson, outfield, 1977–81
Randy Johnson, pitcher, 2005–06
Wee Willie Keeler, outfield, 1903–09
Tony Lazzeri, second base, 1926–37
Mickey Mantle, outfield, 1951–68
Bill McKechnie, infield, 1913
Johnny Mize, first base and pinch hitter, 1949–53
Phil Niekro, pitcher, 1984–85
Herb Pennock, pitcher, 1923–33
Gaylord Perry, pitcher, 1980
Branch Rickey, outfield and catcher, 1907
Phil Rizzuto, shortstop, 1941–42 and 1946–56
Red Ruffing, pitcher, 1930–42 and 1945–46
Babe Ruth, outfield, 1920–34
Joe Sewell, third base, 1931–33
Enos Slaughter, outfield, 1954–55 and 1956–59
Dazzy Vance, pitcher, 1915
Paul Waner, pinch hitter, 1944–45
Dave Winfield, outfield, 1981–90

Retired Numbers

1 ..... Billy Martin
3 ..... Babe Ruth
4 ..... Lou Gehrig
5 ..... Joe DiMaggio
6 ..... Joe Torre
7 ..... Mickey Mantle
8 ..... Yogi Berra
8 ..... Bill Dickey
9 ..... Roger Maris
10 ..... Phil Rizzuto
15 ..... Thurman Munson
16 ..... Whitey Ford
20 ..... Jorge Posada
23 ..... Don Mattingly
32 ..... Elston Howard
37 ..... Casey Stengel
42 ..... Mariano Rivera
44 ..... Reggie Jackson
46 ..... Andy Pettitte
49 ..... Ron Guidry
51 ..... Bernie Williams

League Leaders, Batting

Batting Average, Season

Babe Ruth, 1924 ..... .378
Lou Gehrig, 1934 ..... .363
Joe DiMaggio, 1939 ..... .381
Joe DiMaggio, 1940 ..... .352
Snuffy Stirnweiss, 1945 ..... .309
Mickey Mantle, 1956 ..... .353
Don Mattingly, 1984 ..... .343
Paul O'Neill, 1994 ..... .359
Bernie Williams, 1998 ..... .339

Home Runs, Season

Wally Pipp, 1916 12
Wally Pipp, 1917 9
Babe Ruth, 1920 54
Babe Ruth, 1921 59
Babe Ruth, 1923 41
Babe Ruth, 1924 46
Bob Meusel, 1925 33
Babe Ruth, 1926 47
Babe Ruth, 1927 60
Babe Ruth, 1928 54
Babe Ruth, 1929 46
Babe Ruth, 1930 49
Babe Ruth, 1931 ..... 46 (Tie)
Lou Gehrig, 1931 ..... 46 (Tie)
Lou Gehrig, 1934 49
Lou Gehrig, 1936 49
Joe DiMaggio, 1937 46
Nick Etten, 1944 22
Joe DiMaggio, 1948 39
Mickey Mantle, 1955 37
Mickey Mantle, 1956 52
Mickey Mantle, 1958 42
Mickey Mantle, 1960 40
Roger Maris, 1961 61
Graig Nettles, 1976 32
Reggie Jackson, 1980 ..... 41 (Tie)
Alex Rodriguez, 2005 48
Alex Rodriguez, 2007 54
Mark Teixeira, 2009 ..... 39 (Tie)

RBIs, Season

Wally Pipp, 1916 99
Babe Ruth, 1920 137
Babe Ruth, 1921 171
Babe Ruth, 1923 131
Bob Meusel, 1925 138
Babe Ruth, 1926 145
Lou Gehrig, 1927 175
Lou Gehrig, 1928 ..... 142 (Tie)
Babe Ruth, 1928 ..... 142 (Tie)
Lou Gehrig, 1930 174
Lou Gehrig, 1931 184
Lou Gehrig, 1934 165
Joe DiMaggio, 1941 125
Nick Etten, 1945 111
Joe DiMaggio, 1948 155
Mickey Mantle, 1956 130
Roger Maris, 1960 112
Roger Maris, 1961 142
Reggie Jackson, 1973 117
Don Mattingly, 1985 145
Alex Rodriguez, 2007 156
Mark Teixeira, 2009 122
Curtis Granderson, 2011 119

Stolen Bases, Season

Fritz Maisel, 1914 74
Ben Chapman, 1931 61
Ben Chapman, 1932 38
Ben Chapman, 1933 27
Frankie Crosetti, 1938 27
Snuffy Stirnweiss, 1944 55
Snuffy Stirnweiss, 1945 33
Rickey Henderson, 1985 80
Rickey Henderson, 1986 87
Rickey Henderson, 1988 93
Rickey Henderson*, 1989 77
Alfonso Soriano, 2002 41
*52 with Oak. A's and 25 with N.Y. Yankees.

Total Bases, Season

Babe Ruth, 1921 457
Babe Ruth, 1923 399
Babe Ruth, 1924 391
Babe Ruth, 1926 365
Lou Gehrig, 1927 447
Babe Ruth, 1928 380
Lou Gehrig, 1930 419
Lou Gehrig, 1931 410
Lou Gehrig, 1934 409
Joe DiMaggio, 1937 418
Joe DiMaggio, 1941 348
Johnny Lindell, 1944 297
Snuffy Stirnweiss, 1945 301
Joe DiMaggio, 1948 355
Mickey Mantle, 1956 376

Mickey Mantle, 1958 307
Mickey Mantle, 1960 294
Roger Maris, 1961 366
Bobby Murcer, 1972 314
Don Mattingly, 1985 370
Don Mattingly, 1986 388
Alex Rodriguez, 2007 376
Mark Teixeira, 2009 344

Most Hits, Season

Earle Combs, 1927 231
Lou Gehrig, 1931 211
Red Rolfe, 1939 213
Snuffy Stirnweiss, 1944 205
Snuffy Stirnweiss, 1945 195
Bobby Richardson, 1962 209
Don Mattingly, 1984 207
Don Mattingly, 1986 238
Derek Jeter, 1999 219
Alfonso Soriano, 2002 209
Derek Jeter, 2012 216

Most Runs, Season

Patsy Dougherty*, 1904 113
Babe Ruth, 1920 158
Babe Ruth, 1921 177
Babe Ruth, 1923 151
Babe Ruth, 1924 143
Babe Ruth, 1926 139
Babe Ruth, 1927 158
Babe Ruth, 1928 163
Lou Gehrig, 1931 163
Lou Gehrig, 1933 138
Lou Gehrig, 1935 125
Lou Gehrig, 1936 167
Joe DiMaggio, 1937 151
Red Rolfe, 1939 139
Snuffy Stirnweiss, 1944 125
Snuffy Stirnweiss, 1945 107
Tommy Henrich, 1948 138
Mickey Mantle, 1954 129
Mickey Mantle, 1956 132
Mickey Mantle, 1957 121
Mickey Mantle, 1958 127
Mickey Mantle, 1960 119
Mickey Mantle, 1961 ..... 132 (Tie)
Roger Maris, 1961 ..... 132 (Tie)
Bobby Murcer, 1972 102
Roy White, 1976 104
Rickey Henderson, 1985 146
Rickey Henderson, 1986 130
Rickey Henderson**, 1989 .. 113 (Tie)
Derek Jeter, 1998 127
Alfonso Soriano, 2002 128
Alex Rodriguez, 2005 124
Alex Rodriguez, 2007 143
Mark Teixeira, 2010 113
Curtis Granderson, 2011 136

*33 with Bost. Red Sox and 80 with N.Y. Yankees.
**72 with Oak. A's and 41 with N.Y. Yankees.

Batting Feats

Triple Crown Winners

Lou Gehrig, 1934 (.363 BA, 49 HRs, 165 RBIs)
Mickey Mantle, 1956 (.353 BA, 52 HRs, 130 RBIs)

Hitting for the Cycle

Bert Daniels, July 25, 1912
Bob Meusel, May 7, 1921
Bob Meusel, July 3, 1922
Bob Meusel, July 26, 1928
Tony Lazzeri, June 3, 1932
Lou Gehrig, June 25, 1934
Joe DiMaggio, July 9, 1937
Lou Gehrig, Aug. 1, 1937
Buddy Rosar, July 19, 1940
Joe Gordon, Sept. 8, 1940
Joe DiMaggio, May 20, 1948
Mickey Mantle, July 23, 1957
Bobby Murcer, Aug. 29, 1972
Tony Fernandez, Sept. 3, 1995
Johnny Damon, June 7, 2008
Melky Cabrera, Aug. 2, 2009

Six Hits in a Game

Mike Donlin, June 24, 1901 (Balt. Orioles)
Jimmy Williams, Aug. 25, 1902 (Balt. Orioles)
Myril Hoag, June 6, 1934
Gerald Williams, May 1, 1996*

*Extra-inning game.

40 or More Home Runs, Season

61 ..... Roger Maris, 1961
60 ..... Babe Ruth, 1927
59 ..... Babe Ruth, 1921
54 ..... Babe Ruth, 1920
Babe Ruth, 1928
Mickey Mantle, 1961
Alex Rodriguez, 2005
52 ..... Mickey Mantle, 1956
49 ..... Babe Ruth, 1930
Lou Gehrig, 1934
Lou Gehrig, 1936
48 ..... Alex Rodriguez, 2007
47 ..... Babe Ruth, 1926
Lou Gehrig, 1927
46 ..... Babe Ruth, 1924
Babe Ruth, 1929
Lou Gehrig, 1931
Babe Ruth, 1931
Joe DiMaggio, 1937
44 ..... Tino Martinez, 1997
43 ..... Curtis Granderson, 2012
42 ..... Mickey Mantle, 1958
41 ..... Babe Ruth, 1923
Lou Gehrig, 1930
Babe Ruth, 1932
Reggie Jackson, 1980
David Justice*, 2000
Jason Giambi, 2002
Jason Giambi, 2003
Curtis Granderson, 2011
40 ..... Mickey Mantle, 1960

*20 with Cle. Indians and 21 with N.Y. Yankees.

League Leaders, Pitching

Most Wins, Season

Jack Chesbro, 1904 41
Al Orth, 1906 27
Carl Mays, 1921 ..... 27 (Tie)
Waite Hoyt, 1927 ..... 22 (Tie)
George Pipgras, 1928 ..... 24 (Tie)
Lefty Gomez, 1934 26
Lefty Gomez, 1937 21
Red Ruffing, 1938 21
Spud Chandler, 1943 ..... 20 (Tie)
Whitey Ford, 1955 ..... 18 (Tie)
Bob Turley, 1958 21
Whitey Ford, 1961 25
Ralph Terry, 1962 23
Whitey Ford, 1963 24
Ron Guidry, 1978 25
Ron Guidry, 1985 22
Jimmy Key, 1994 17
Andy Pettitte, 1996 21
David Cone, 1998 ..... 20 (Tie)
Chien-Ming Wang, 2006 19
CC Sabathia, 2009 ..... 19 (Tie)
CC Sabathia, 2010 21

Most Strikeouts, Season

Red Ruffing, 1932 190
Lefty Gomez, 1933 163
Lefty Gomez, 1934 158
Lefty Gomez, 1937 194
Vic Rashi, 1951 164
Allie Reynolds, 1952 160
Al Downing, 1964 217

Lowest ERA, Season

Bob Shawkey, 1920 ..... 2.45
Wiley Moore, 1927 ..... 2.28
Lefty Gomez, 1934 ..... 2.33
Lefty Gomez, 1937 ..... 2.33
Spud Chandler, 1943 ..... 1.64
Spud Chandler, 1947 ..... 2.46
Allie Reynolds, 1952 ..... 2.07
Eddie Lopat, 1953 ..... 2.43
Whitey Ford, 1956 ..... 2.47
Bobby Shantz, 1957 ..... 2.45
Whitey Ford, 1958 ..... 2.01
Ron Guidry, 1978 ..... 1.74
Ron Guidry, 1979 ..... 2.78
Rudy May, 1980 ..... 2.47

Most Saves, Season

Sparky Lyle, 1972 35
Sparky Lyle, 1976 23
Goose Gossage, 1978 27
Goose Gossage, 1980 ..... 33 (Tie)
Dave Righetti, 1986 46
John Wetteland, 1996 43
Mariano Rivera, 1999 45
Mariano Rivera, 2001 50
Mariano Rivera, 2004 53

Best Won–Lost Percentage, Season

Jack Chesbro, 1904 ... 41–13 ... .759
Carl Mays, 1921 ..... 27–9 ... .750
Joe Bush, 1922 ..... 26–7 ... .788
Herb Pennock, 1923 .... 19–6 ... .760
Waite Hoyt, 1927 ..... 22–7 ... .759
Johnny Allen, 1932 ..... 17–4 ... .810
Lefty Gomez, 1934 ..... 26–5 ... .839
Monte Pearson, 1936 ... 19–7 ... .731
Red Ruffing, 1938 ..... 21–7 ... .750
Lefty Gomez, 1941 ..... 15–5 ... .750
Tiny Bonham, 1942 ..... 21–5 ... .808
Spud Chandler, 1943 ... 20–4 ... .833
Allie Reynolds, 1947 .... 19–8 ... .704
Vic Raschi, 1950 ..... 21–8 ... .724
Eddie Lopat, 1953 ..... 16–4 ... .800
Tommy Byrne, 1955 ..... 16–5 ... .762
Whitey Ford, 1956 ..... 19–6 ... .760
Tom Sturdivant, 1957 ... 16–6 ... .727 (Tie)
Bob Turley, 1958 ..... 21–7 ... .750
Whitey Ford, 1961 ..... 25–4 ... .862
Whitey Ford, 1963 ..... 24–7 ... .774
Ron Guidry, 1978 ..... 25–3 ... .893
Ron Guidry, 1985 ..... 22–6 ... .786
Jimmy Key, 1993 ..... 18–6 ... .750
David Wells, 1998 ..... 18–4 ... .818
Roger Clemens, 2001 ... 20–3 ... .870
Nathan Eovaldi, 2015 .. 14–3 .... .824

Pitching Feats

Triple Crown Winner

Lefty Gomez, 1934 (26–5, 2.33 ERA, 158 SO)
Lefty Gomez, 1935 (21–11, 2.33 ERA, 194 SO)

20 Wins, Season

Joe McGinnity, 1901 ..... 26–21 (Balt. Orioles)
Jack Chesbro, 1903 21–15
Jack Chesbro, 1904 41–13
Jack Powell, 1904 23–19
Al Orth, 1906 27–17
Jack Chesbro, 1906 24–16
Russ Ford, 1910 26–6
Russ Ford, 1911 22–11
Bob Shawkey, 1916 24–14
Bob Shawkey, 1919 20–13
Carl Mays, 1920 26–11
Bob Shawkey, 1920 20–13
Carl Mays, 1921 27–9
Joe Bush, 1922 26–7
Bob Shawkey, 1922 20–12
Sad Sam Jones, 1923 21–8
Herb Pennock, 1924 21–9
Herb Pennock, 1927 23–11
Waite Hoyt, 1927 22–7
George Pipgras, 1928 24–13
Waite Hoyt, 1928 23–7
Lefty Gomez, 1931 21–9
Lefty Gomez, 1932 24–7
Lefty Gomez, 1934 26–5
Red Ruffing, 1936 20–12
Lefty Gomez, 1937 21–11
Red Ruffing, 1937 20–7
Red Ruffing, 1938 21–7
Red Ruffing, 1939 21–7
Tiny Bonham, 1942 21–5
Spud Chandler, 1943 20–4
Spud Chandler, 1946 20–8
Vic Raschi, 1949 21–10
Vic Raschi, 1950 21–8
Ed Lopat, 1951 21–9
Vic Raschi, 1951 21–10
Allie Reynolds, 1952 20–8
Bob Grim, 1954 20–6
Bob Turley, 1958 21–7
Whitey Ford, 1961 25–4
Ralph Terry, 1962 23–12
Whitey Ford, 1963 24–7
Jim Bouton, 1963 21–7
Mel Stottlemyre, 1965 20–9
Mel Stottlemyre, 1968 21–12
Mel Stottlemyre, 1969 20–14
Fritz Peterson, 1970 20–11
Catfish Hunter, 1975 23–14
Ron Guidry, 1978 25–3
Ed Figueroa, 1978 20–9
Tommy John, 1979 21–9
Tommy John, 1980 22–9
Ron Guidry, 1983 21–9
Ron Guidry, 1985 22–6
Andy Pettitte, 1996 21–8
David Cone, 1998 20–7
Roger Clemens, 2001 20–3
Andy Pettitte, 2003 21–8
Mike Mussina, 2008 20–9
CC Sabathia, 2010 21–7

No-Hitters

George Mogridge (vs. Bost. Red Sox), Apr. 24, 1917 (final: 2–1)
Sam Jones (vs. Phila. A's), Sept. 4, 1923 (final: 4–0)
Monte Pearson (vs. Cle. Indians), Aug. 27, 1938 (final: 13–0)
Allie Reynolds (vs. Cle. Indians), July 12, 1951 (final: 1–0)
Allie Reynolds (vs. Bost. Red Sox), Sept. 28, 1951 (final: 8–0)
Don Larsen (vs. Bklyn. Dodgers, NL), Oct. 8, 1956 (final: 2–0) (World Series, perfect game)
Dave Righetti (vs. Bost. Red Sox), July 4, 1983 (final: 4–0)
Jim Abbott (vs. Cle. Indians), Sept. 4, 1993 (final: 4–0)
Dwight Gooden (vs. Sea. Mariners), May 14, 1996 (final: 2–0)
David Wells (vs. Min. Twins), May 17, 1998 (final: 4–0) (perfect game)
David Cone (vs. Mont. Expos, NL), July 18, 1999 (final: 6–0) (perfect game)

No-Hitters Pitched Against

Cy Young, Bost. Red Sox, June 30, 1908 (final: 8–0)
George Foster, Bost. Red Sox, June 21, 1916 (final: 2–0)
Ray Caldwell, Bost. Red Sox, Sept. 10, 1919 (final: 3–0)
Bob Feller, Cle. Indians, Apr. 30, 1946 (final: 1–0)
Virgil Trucks, Det. Tigers, Aug. 25, 1952 (final: 1–0)

Hoyt Wilhelm, Balt. Orioles, Sept. 2, 1958 (final: 1–0)

Roy Oswalt, Pete Munro, Kirk Saarloos, Brad Lidge, Octavio Dotel, and Billy Wagner, Hous. Astros (NL), June 11, 2003 (final: 8–0)

Postseason Play

1921 World Series vs. N.Y. Giants (NL), lost 5 games to 3

1922 World Series vs. N.Y. Giants (NL), lost 4 games to 0, 1 tie

1923 World Series vs. N.Y. Giants (NL), won 4 games to 2

1926 World Series vs. St.L. Cardinals (NL), lost 4 games to 3

1927 World Series vs. Pitt. Pirates (NL), won 4 games to 0

1928 World Series vs. St.L. Cardinals (NL), won 4 games to 0

1932 World Series vs. Chi. Cubs (NL), won 4 games to 0

1936 World Series vs. N.Y. Giants (NL), won 4 games to 2

1937 World Series vs. N.Y. Giants (NL), won 4 games to 1

1938 World Series vs. Chi. Cubs (NL), won 4 games to 0

1939 World Series vs. Cin. Reds (NL), won 4 games to 0

1941 World Series vs. Bklyn. Dodgers (NL), won 4 games to 1

1942 World Series vs. St.L. Cardinals (NL), lost 4 games to 1

1943 World Series vs. St.L. Cardinals (NL), won 4 games to 1

1947 World Series vs. Bklyn. Dodgers (NL), won 4 games to 3

1949 World Series vs. Bklyn. Dodgers (NL), won 4 games to 1

1950 World Series vs. Phila. Phillies (NL), won 4 games to 0

1951 World Series vs. N.Y. Giants (NL), won 4 games to 2

1952 World Series vs. Bklyn. Dodgers (NL), won 4 games to 3

1953 World Series vs. Bklyn. Dodgers (NL), won 4 games to 2

1955 World Series vs. Bklyn. Dodgers (NL), lost 4 games to 3

1956 World Series vs. Bklyn. Dodgers (NL), won 4 games to 3

1957 World Series vs. Milw. Braves (NL), lost 4 games to 3

1958 World Series vs. Milw. Braves (NL), won 4 games to 3

1960 World Series vs. Pitt. Pirates (NL), lost 4 games to 3

1961 World Series vs. Cin. Reds (NL), won 4 games to 1

1962 World Series vs. S.F. Giants (NL), won 4 games to 3

1963 World Series vs. L.A. Dodgers (NL), lost 4 games to 0

1964 World Series vs. St.L. Cardinals (NL), lost 4 games to 3

1976 League Championship Series vs. K.C. Royals, won 3 games to 2
World Series vs. Cin. Reds (NL), lost 4 games to 0

1977 League Championship Series vs. K.C. Royals, won 3 games to 2
World Series vs. L.A. Dodgers (NL), won 4 games to 2

1978 Pennant Playoff Game vs. Bost. Red Sox, won
League Championship Series vs. K.C. Royals, won 3 games to 1
World Series vs. L.A. Dodgers (NL), won 4 games to 2

1980 League Championship Series vs. K.C. Royals, lost 3 games to 0

1981 Second-Half Division Playoff vs. Milw. Brewers, won 3 games to 2
League Championship Series vs. Oak. A's, won 3 games to 0
World Series vs. L.A. Dodgers (NL), lost 4 games to 2

1995 Division Series vs. Sea. Mariners, lost 3 games to 2

1996 Division Series vs. Tex. Rangers, won 3 games to 1
League Championship Series vs. Balt. Orioles, won 4 games to 1
World Series vs. Atl. Braves (NL), won 4 games to 2

1997 Division Series vs. Cle. Indians, lost 3 games to 2

1998 Division Series vs. Tex. Rangers, won 3 games to 0
League Championship Series vs. Cle. Indians, won 4 games to 2
World Series vs. S.D. Padres (NL), won 4 games to 0

1999 Division Series vs. Tex. Rangers, won 3 games to 0
League Championship Series vs. Bost. Red Sox, won 4 games to 1
World Series vs. Atl. Braves (NL), won 4 games to 0

2000 Division Series vs. Oak. A's, won 3 games to 2
League Championship Series vs. Sea. Mariners, won 4 games to 2
World Series vs. N.Y. Mets (NL), won 4 games to 1

2001 Division Series vs. Oak. A's, won 3 games to 2
League Championship Series vs. Sea. Mariners, won 4 games to 1
World Series vs. Ariz. D'backs (NL), lost 4 games to 3

2002 Division Series vs. Ana. Angels, lost 3 games to 1

2003 Division Series vs. Min. Twins, won 3 games to 1
League Championship Series vs. Bost. Red Sox, won 4 games to 3
World Series vs. Fla. Marlins (NL), lost 4 games to 2

2004 Division Series vs. Min. Twins, won 3 games to 1
League Championship Series vs. Bost. Red Sox, lost 4 games to 3

2005 Division Series vs. L.A. Angels, lost 3 games to 2

2006 Division Series vs. Det. Tigers, lost 3 games to 1

2007 Division Series vs. Cle. Indians, lost 3 games to 1

2009 Division Series vs. Min. Twins, won 3 games to 0
League Championship Series vs. L.A. Angels, won 4 games to 2
World Series vs. Phila. Phillies (NL), won 4 games to 2

2010 Division Series vs. Min. Twins, won 3 games to 0
League Championship Series vs. Tex. Rangers, lost 4 games to 2

2011 Division Series vs. Det. Tigers, lost 3 games to 2

2012 Division Series vs. Balt. Orioles, won 3 games to 2
League Championship Series vs. Det. Tigers, lost 4 games to 0

2015 AL Wild Card Playoff Game vs. Hous. Astros, lost

Oakland Athletics (formerly the Kansas City Athletics)

Dates of Operation: (as the Philadelphia Athletics) 1901–1954
Overall Record: 3886 wins, 4248 losses
Stadium: Columbia Park (1901–1908), Shibe Park, Park (1909–1954)
Other Name: A's

Dates of Operation: (as the Kansas City Athletics) 1955–67 (13 years)
Overall Record: 829 wins, 1224 losses (.404)
Stadium: Municipal Stadium, 1955–67
Other Name: A's

Dates of Operation: (as the Oakland Athletics) 1968–present (48 years)
Overall Record: 3975 wins, 3670 losses (.519)
Stadium: O.co Coliseum (also known as Overstock.com Coliseum) (formerly UMax Coliseum, 1997–98, Network Associates Coliseum, 1998–2004, and McAfee Coliseum, 2004–008, Oakland–Alameda County Coliseum, 2008–11), 1968–present (capacity: 35,067)
Other Name: A's

Year-by-Year Finishes

Year	Finish	Wins	Losses	Percentage	Games Behind	Manager	Attendance
					K.C. Athletics		
1955	6th	63	91	.409	33.0	Lou Boudreau	1,393,054
1956	8th	52	102	.338	45.0	Lou Boudreau	1,015,154
1957	7th	59	94	.386	38.5	Lou Boudreau, Harry Craft	901,067
1958	7th	73	81	.474	19.0	Harry Craft	925,090
1959	7th	66	88	.429	28.0	Harry Craft	963,683
1960	8th	58	96	.377	39.0	Bob Elliott	774,944
1961	9th (Tie)	61	100	.379	47.5	Joe Gordon, Hank Bauer	683,817
1962	9th	72	90	.444	24.0	Hank Bauer	635,675
1963	8th	73	89	.451	31.5	Ed Lopat	762,364
1964	10th	57	105	.352	42.0	Ed Lopat, Mel McGaha	642,478
1965	10th	59	103	.364	43.0	Mel McGaha, Haywood Sullivan	528,344
1966	7th	74	86	.463	23.0	Alvin Dark	773,929
1967	10th	62	99	.385	29.5	Alvin Dark, Luke Appling	726,639
					Oak. Athletics		
1968	6th	82	80	.506	21.0	Bob Kennedy	837,466
					West Division		
1969	2nd	88	74	.543	9.0	Hank Bauer, John McNamara	778,232
1970	2nd	89	73	.549	9.0	John McNamara	778,355
1971	1st	101	60	.627	+16.0	Dick Williams	914,993
1972	1st	93	62	.600	+5.5	Dick Williams	921,323
1973	1st	94	68	.580	+6.0	Dick Williams	1,000,763
1974	1st	90	72	.556	+5.0	Alvin Dark	845,693
1975	1st	98	64	.605	+7.0	Alvin Dark	1,075,518
1976	2nd	87	74	.540	2.5	Chuck Tanner	780,593
1977	7th	63	98	.391	38.5	Jack McKeon, Bobby Winkles	495,599
1978	6th	69	93	.426	23.0	Bobby Winkles, Jack McKeon	526,999
1979	7th	54	108	.333	34.0	Jim Marshall	306,763
1980	2nd	83	79	.512	14.0	Billy Martin	842,259
1981*	1st/2nd	64	45	.587	+1.5/1.0	Billy Martin	1,304,054
1982	5th	68	94	.420	25.0	Billy Martin	1,735,489
1983	4th	74	88	.457	25.0	Steve Boros	1,294,941

1984	4th	77	85	.475	7.0	Steve Boros, Jackie Moore	1,353,281
1985	4th (Tie)	77	85	.475	14.0	Jackie Moore	1,334,599
1986	3rd (Tie)	76	86	.469	16.0	Jackie Moore, Tony La Russa	1,314,646
1987	3rd	81	81	.500	4.0	Tony La Russa	1,678,921
1988	1st	104	58	.642	+13.0	Tony La Russa	2,287,335
1989	1st	99	63	.611	+7.0	Tony La Russa	2,667,225
1990	1st	103	59	.636	+9.0	Tony La Russa	2,900,217
1991	4th	84	78	.519	11.0	Tony La Russa	2,713,493
1992	1st	96	66	.593	+6.0	Tony La Russa	2,494,160
1993	7th	68	94	.420	26.0	Tony La Russa	2,035,025
1994	2nd	51	63	.447	1.0	Tony La Russa	1,242,692
1995	4th	67	77	.465	11.5	Tony La Russa	1,174,310
1996	3rd	78	84	.481	12.0	Art Howe	1,148,380
1997	4th	65	97	.401	25.0	Art Howe	1,264,218
1998	4th	74	88	.457	14.0	Art Howe	1,232,339
1999	2nd	87	75	.537	8.0	Art Howe	1,434,610
2000	1st	91	70	.565	+0.5	Art Howe	1,728,888
2001	2nd	102	60	.630	14.0	Art Howe	2,133,277
2002	1st	103	59	.636	+4.0	Art Howe	2,169,811
2003	1st	96	66	.593	+3.0	Ken Macha	2,216,596
2004	2nd	91	71	.562	1.0	Ken Macha	2,201,516
2005	2nd	88	74	.543	7.0	Ken Macha	2,109,118
2006	1st	93	69	.574	+4.0	Ken Macha	1,976,625
2007	3rd	76	86	.469	18.0	Bob Geren	1,921,834
2008	3rd	75	86	.466	24.5	Bob Geren	1,665,256
2009	4th	75	87	.463	22.0	Bob Geren	1,408,783
2010	2nd	81	81	.500	9.0	Bob Geren	1,418,391
2011	3rd	74	88	.457	22.0	Bob Geren, Bob Melvin	1,476,791
2012	1st	94	68	.580	+1.0	Bob Melvin	1,679,013
2013	1st	96	66	.593	+5.5	Bob Melvin	1,809,302
2014	2nd	88	74	.543	10.0	Bob Melvin	2,003,628
2015	5th	68	94	.420	20.0	Bob Melvin	1,768,175

*Split season.

Awards

Most Valuable Player

Vida Blue, pitcher, 1971
Reggie Jackson, outfield, 1973
Jose Canseco, outfield, 1988
Rickey Henderson, outfield, 1990
Dennis Eckersley, pitcher, 1992
Jason Giambi, first base, 2000
Miguel Tejada, shortstop, 2002

Rookie of the Year

Jose Canseco, outfield, 1986
Mark McGwire, first base, 1987
Walt Weiss, shortstop, 1988
Ben Grieve, outfield, 1998
Bobby Crosby, shortstop, 2004
Huston Street, pitcher, 2005
Andrew Bailey, pitcher, 2009

Cy Young

Vida Blue, 1971
Catfish Hunter, 1974
Bob Welch, 1990
Dennis Eckersley, 1992
Barry Zito, 2002

Hall of Famers Who Played for the Athletics

Dennis Eckersley, pitcher, 1987–95
Rollie Fingers, pitcher, 1968–76
Goose Gossage, pitcher, 1992–93
Rickey Henderson, outfield, 1979–84, 1989–93, 1994–95, and 1998
Catfish Hunter, pitcher, 1965–74
Reggie Jackson, outfield, 1967–75 and 1987
Tony La Russa, second base and shortstop, 1963 (K.C.) and 1968–71
Willie McCovey, designated hitter, 1976
Joe Morgan, second base, 1984
Satchel Paige, pitcher, 1965 (K.C.)
Mike Piazza, designated hitter, 2007
Enos Slaughter, outfield, 1955–56 (K.C.)
Don Sutton, pitcher, 1985
Frank Thomas, first base and designated hitter, 2006 and 2008

Retired Numbers

9 ..... Reggie Jackson
24 ..... Rickey Henderson
27 ..... Catfish Hunter
34 ..... Rollie Fingers
43 ..... Dennis Eckersley

League Leaders, Batting

Batting Average, Season

[No player]

Home Runs, Season

Reggie Jackson, 1973 32
Reggie Jackson, 1975 ..... 36 (Tie)
Tony Armas, 1981 ..... 22 (Tie)
Mark McGwire, 1987 49
Jose Canseco, 1988 42
Jose Canseco, 1991 ..... 44 (Tie)
Mark McGwire, 1996 52

RBIs, Season

Jose Canseco, 1988 124

Stolen Bases, Season

Bert Campaneris, 1965 (K.C.) 51
Bert Campaneris, 1966 (K.C.) 52

Bert Campaneris, 1967 (K.C.).....55
Bert Campaneris, 1968.....62
Bert Campaneris, 1970.....42
Bert Campaneris, 1972.....52
Billy North, 1974.....54
Billy North, 1976.....75
Rickey Henderson, 1980.....100
Rickey Henderson, 1981.....56
Rickey Henderson, 1982.....130
Rickey Henderson, 1983.....108
Rickey Henderson, 1984.....66
Rickey Henderson*, 1989.....77
Rickey Henderson, 1990.....65
Rickey Henderson, 1991.....58
Rickey Henderson, 1998.....66
Coco Crisp, 2011.....49 (Tie)
*25 with N.Y. Yankees and 52 with Oak. A's.

Total Bases, Season
Sal Bando, 1973.....295 (Tie)
Joe Rudi, 1974.....287

Most Hits, Season
Bert Campaneris, 1968.....177
Joe Rudi, 1972.....181
Rickey Henderson, 1981.....135

Most Runs, Season
Reggie Jackson, 1969.....123
Reggie Jackson, 1973.....99
Rickey Henderson, 1981.....89
Rickey Henderson*, 1989....113 (Tie)
Rickey Henderson, 1990.....119
*41 with N.Y. Yankees and 72 with Oak. A's.

Batting Feats

Triple Crown Winners
[No player]

Hitting for the Cycle
Tony Phillips, May 16, 1986
Mike Blowers, May 18, 1998
Eric Chavez, June 21, 2000
Miguel Tejada, Sept. 29, 2001
Eric Byrnes, June 29, 2003
Mark Ellis, June 4, 2007

Six Hits in a Game
Joe DeMaestri, July 8, 1955* (K.C.)
*Extra-inning game.

40 or More Home Runs, Season
52.....Mark McGwire, 1996
49.....Mark McGwire, 1987
47.....Reggie Jackson, 1969
44.....Jose Canseco, 1991
43.....Jason Giambi, 2000
42.....Jose Canseco, 1988
Mark McGwire, 1992

League Leaders, Pitching

Most Wins, Season
Catfish Hunter, 1974.....25 (Tie)
Catfish Hunter, 1975.....23 (Tie)
Steve McCatty, 1981.....14 (Tie)
Dave Stewart, 1987.....20 (Tie)
Bob Welch, 1990.....27

Most Strikeouts, Season
[No pitcher]

Lowest ERA, Season
Diego Segui, 1970.....2.56
Vida Blue, 1971.....1.82
Catfish Hunter, 1974.....2.49
Steve McCatty, 1981.....2.32
Steve Ontiveros, 1994.....2.65

Most Saves, Season
Dennis Eckersley, 1988.....45
Dennis Eckersley, 1992.....51
Keith Foulke, 2003.....43

Best Won–Lost Percentage, Season
Catfish Hunter, 1972...21–7.... .750
Catfish Hunter, 1973...21–5.... .808
Bob Welch, 1982.....27–6.... .818
Tim Hudson, 2000.....20–6.... .769

Pitching Feats

20 Wins, Season
Vida Blue, 1971.....24–8
Catfish Hunter, 1971.....21–11
Catfish Hunter, 1972.....21–7
Catfish Hunter, 1973.....21–5
Ken Holtzman, 1973.....21–13
Vida Blue, 1973.....20–9
Catfish Hunter, 1974.....25–12
Vida Blue, 1975.....22–11
Mike Norris, 1980.....22–9
Dave Stewart, 1987.....20–13
Dave Stewart, 1988.....21–12
Dave Stewart, 1989.....21–9
Bob Welch, 1990.....27–6
Dave Stewart, 1990.....22–11
Tim Hudson, 2000.....20–6
Mark Mulder, 2001.....21–8
Barry Zito, 2002.....23–5

No-Hitters
Catfish Hunter (vs. Min. Twins), May 8, 1968 (final: 4–0) (perfect game)
Vida Blue (vs. Min. Twins), Sept. 21, 1970 (final: 6–0)
Vida Blue, Glenn Abbott, Paul Lindblad, and Rollie Fingers (vs. Cal. Angels), Sept. 28, 1975 (final: 5–0)
Mike Warren (vs. Chi. White Sox), Sept. 29, 1983 (final: 3–0)
Dave Stewart (vs. Tor. Blue Jays), June 29, 1990 (final: 5–0)
Dallas Braden (v.s. T.B. Rays), May 9, 2010 (final: 4–0) (perfect game)

No-Hitters Pitched Against
Jack Kralick, Min. Twins (vs. K.C.), Aug. 26, 1962 (final: 1–0)
Jim Palmer, Balt. Orioles, Aug. 13, 1969 (final: 8–0)
Clyde Wright, Cal. Angels, July 3, 1970 (final: 4–0)
Jim Bibby, Tex. Rangers, July 30, 1973 (final: 6–0)
Dick Bosman, Cle. Indians, July 19, 1974 (final: 4–0)
Blue Moon Odom and Francisco Barrios, Chi. White Sox, July 28, 1976 (final: 6–0)
Nolan Ryan, Tex. Rangers, June 11, 1990 (final: 5–0)
Bob Milacki, Mike Flanagan, Mark Williamson, and Gregg Olson, Balt. Orioles, July 13, 1991 (final: 2–0)

Postseason Play

1971 League Championship Series vs. Balt. Orioles, lost 3 games to 0
1972 League Championship Series vs. Det. Tigers, won 3 games to 2
World Series vs. Cin. Reds (NL), won 4 games to 3
1973 League Championship Series vs. Balt. Orioles, won 3 games to 2
World Series vs. N.Y. Mets (NL), won 4 games to 3
1974 League Championship Series vs. Balt. Orioles, won 3 games to 1

World Series vs. L.A. Dodgers (NL), won 4 games to 1

1975 League Championship Series vs. Bost. Red Sox, lost 3 games to 0

1981 First-Half Pennant Playoff vs. K.C. Royals, won 3 games to 0

League Championship Series vs. N.Y. Yankees, lost 3 games to 0

1988 League Championship Series vs. Bost. Red Sox, won 4 games to 0

World Series vs. L.A. Dodgers (NL), lost 4 games to 1

1989 League Championship Series vs. Tor. Blue Jays, won 4 games to 1

World Series vs. S.F. Giants (NL), won 4 games to 0

1990 League Championship Series vs. Bost. Red Sox, won 4 games to 0

World Series vs. Cin. Reds (NL), lost 4 games to 0

1992 League Championship Series vs. Tor. Blue Jays, lost 4 games to 2

2000 Division Series vs. N.Y. Yankees, lost 3 games to 2

2001 Division Series vs. N.Y. Yankees, lost 3 games to 2

2002 Division Series vs. Min. Twins, lost 3 games to 2

2003 Division Series vs. Bost. Red Sox, lost 3 games to 2

2006 Division Series vs. Min. Twins, won 3 games to 0

League Championship Series vs. Det. Tigers, lost 4 games to 0

2012 Division Series vs. Det. Tigers, lost 3 games to 2

2013 Division Series vs. Det. Tigers, lost 3 games to 2

2014 AL Wild Card Playoff Game vs. K.C. Royals, lost

Seattle Mariners

Dates of Operation: 1977–present (39 years)
Overall Record: 2898 wins, 3295 losses (.467)
Stadiums: Kingdome, 1977–99; Safeco Field (also known as King County Stadium), 1999–present (capacity: 47,574)

Year-by-Year Finishes

Year	Finish	Wins	Losses	Percentage	Games Behind	Manager	Attendance
					West Division		
1977	6th	64	98	.395	38.0	Darrell Johnson	1,338,511
1978	7th	56	104	.350	35.0	Darrell Johnson	877,440
1979	6th	67	95	.414	21.0	Darrell Johnson	844,447
1980	7th	59	103	.364	38.0	Darrell Johnson, Maury Wills	836,204
1981*	6th/5th	44	65	.404	14.5/6.5	Maury Wills, Rene Lachemann	636,276
1982	4th	76	86	.469	17.0	Rene Lachemann	1,070,404
1983	7th	60	102	.370	39.0	Rene Lachemann, Del Crandall	813,537
1984	5th (Tie)	74	88	.457	10.0	Del Crandall, Chuck Cottier	870,372
1985	6th	74	88	.457	17.0	Chuck Cottier	1,128,696
1986	7th	67	95	.414	25.0	Chuck Cottier, Marty Martinez, Dick Williams	1,029,045
1987	4th	78	84	.481	7.0	Dick Williams	1,134,255
1988	7th	68	93	.422	35.5	Dick Williams, Jim Snyder	1,022,398
1989	6th	73	89	.451	26.0	Jim Lefebvre	1,298,443
1990	5th	77	85	.475	26.0	Jim Lefebvre	1,509,727
1991	5th	83	79	.512	12.0	Jim Lefebvre	2,147,905
1992	7th	64	98	.395	32.0	Bill Plummer	1,651,398
1993	4th	82	80	.506	12.0	Lou Piniella	2,051,853
1994	3rd	49	63	.438	2.0	Lou Piniella	1,104,206
1995	1st	79	66	.545	+1.0	Lou Piniella	1,643,203
1996	2nd	85	76	.528	4.5	Lou Piniella	2,732,850
1997	1st	90	72	.556	+6.0	Lou Piniella	3,192,237
1998	3rd	76	85	.472	11.5	Lou Piniella	2,644,166
1999	3rd	79	83	.488	16.0	Lou Piniella	2,916,346
2000	2nd	91	71	.562	0.5	Lou Piniella	3,148,317
2001	1st	116	46	.716	+14.0	Lou Piniella	3,507,975
2002	3rd	93	69	.574	10.0	Lou Piniella	3,540,482
2003	2nd	93	69	.574	3.0	Bob Melvin	3,268,509
2004	4th	63	99	.389	29.0	Bob Melvin	2,940,731
2005	4th	69	93	.426	26.0	Mike Hargrove	2,725,549
2006	4th	78	84	.481	15.0	Mike Hargrove	2,481,375
2007	2nd	88	75	.540	6.5	Mike Hargrove, John McLaren	2,672,485
2008	4th	61	101	.377	39.0	John McLaren, Jim Riggleman	2,329,702
2009	3rd	85	77	.525	12.0	Don Wakamatsu	2,195,284
2010	4th	61	101	.377	29.0	Don Wakamatsu, Darren Brown	2,085,630
2011	4th	67	95	.414	29.0	Eric Wedge	1,939,421
2012	4th	75	87	.463	19.0	Eric Wedge	1,721,920
2013	4th	71	91	.438	25.0	Eric Wedge	1,761,546
2014	3rd	87	75	.537	11.0	Lloyd McClendon	2,064,334
2015	4th	76	86	.469	12.0	Lloyd McClendon	2,193,581

*Split season.

Awards

Most Valuable Player
Ken Griffey Jr., outfield, 1997
Ichiro Suzuki, outfield, 2001
Ichiro Suzuki, outfield, 2002

Rookie of the Year
Alvin Davis, first base, 1984
Kazuhiro Sasaki, pitcher, 2000
Ichiro Suzuki, outfield, 2001

Cy Young
Randy Johnson, 1995
Felix Hernandez, 2010

Hall of Famers Who Played for the Mariners
Goose Gossage, pitcher, 1994
Ken Griffey Jr., outfield and designated hitter, 1989–99 and 2009–10
Randy Johnson, pitcher, 1989–98
Gaylord Perry, pitcher, 1982–83

Retired Numbers
24 ..... Ken Griffey Jr.

League Leaders, Batting

Batting Average, Season
Edgar Martinez, 1992 ..... .343
Edgar Martinez, 1995 ..... .356
Alex Rodriguez, 1996 ..... .358
Ichiro Suzuki, 2001 ..... .350
Ichiro Suzuki, 2004 ..... .372

Home Runs, Season
Ken Griffey Jr., 1994 40
Ken Griffey Jr., 1997 56
Ken Griffey Jr., 1998 56
Ken Griffey Jr., 1999 48

RBIs, Season
Ken Griffey Jr., 1997 147
Edgar Martinez, 2000 145
Bret Boone, 2001 141

Stolen Bases, Season
Harold Reynolds, 1987 60
Brian Hunter*, 1999 44
Ichiro Suzuki, 2001 56
*0 with Det. Tigers and 44 with Sea. Mariners.

Total Bases, Season
Ken Griffey Jr., 1993 359
Alex Rodriguez, 1996 379
Ken Griffey Jr., 1997 393

Most Hits, Season
Alex Rodriguez, 1998 213
Ichiro Suzuki, 2001 242
Ichiro Suzuki, 2004 262
Ichiro Suzuki, 2006 224
Ichiro Suzuki, 2007 238
Ichiro Suzuki, 2008 ..... 213 (Tie)
Ichiro Suzuki, 2009 225
Ichiro Suzuki, 2010 214

Most Runs, Season
Edgar Martinez, 1995 ..... 121 (Tie)
Alex Rodriguez, 1996 141
Ken Griffey Jr., 1997 125

Batting Feats

Triple Crown Winners
[No player]

Hitting for the Cycle
Jay Buhner, July 23, 1993
Alex Rodriguez, June 5, 1997
John Olerud, June 16, 2001
Adrian Beltre, Sept. 1, 2008

Six Hits in a Game
Raul Ibanez, Sept. 22, 2004

40 or More Home Runs, Season
56 ..... Ken Griffey Jr., 1997
Ken Griffey Jr., 1998
49 ..... Ken Griffey Jr., 1996
48 ..... Ken Griffey Jr., 1999
45 ..... Ken Griffey Jr., 1993
44 ..... Jay Buhner, 1996
42 ..... Alex Rodriguez, 1998
Alex Rodriguez, 1999
41 ..... Alex Rodriguez, 2000
40 ..... Ken Griffey Jr., 1994
Jay Buhner, 1995
Jay Buhner, 1997

League Leaders, Pitching

Most Wins, Season
Felix Hernandez, 2009 ..... 19 (Tie)

Most Strikeouts, Season
Floyd Bannister, 1982 209
Mark Langston, 1984 204
Mark Langston, 1986 245
Mark Langston, 1987 262
Randy Johnson, 1992 241
Randy Johnson, 1993 308
Randy Johnson, 1994 204
Randy Johnson, 1995 294

Lowest ERA, Season
Randy Johnson, 1995 ..... 2.48
Freddy Garcia, 2001 ..... 3.05
Felix Hernandez, 2010 ..... 2.27
Felix Hernandez, 2014 ..... 2.14

Most Saves, Season
[No pitcher]

Best Won–Lost Percentage, Season
Randy Johnson, 1995 ... 18–2 .. .900
Randy Johnson, 1997 ... 20–4 .. .833
Felix Hernandez, 2009 ... 19–5 ... .792

Pitching Feats

20 Wins, Season
Randy Johnson, 1997 20–4
Jamie Moyer, 2001 20–6
Jamie Moyer, 2003 21–7

No-Hitters
Randy Johnson (vs. Det. Tigers), June 2, 1990 (final: 2–0)
Chris Bosio (vs. Bost. Red Sox), Apr. 22, 1993 (final: 7–0)
Kevin Millwood, Charlie Furbush, Stephen Pryor, Lucas Luetge, Brandon League, Tom Wilhelmsen (vs. L.A. Dodgers), June 8, 2012 (final: 1–0)
Felix Hernandez (vs. T.B. Rays), Aug. 15, 2012 (final: 1–0) (perfect game)
Hisashi Iwakuma (vs. Balt. Orioles), Aug. 12, 2015 (final: 3–0)

No-Hitters Pitched Against
Mark Langston and Mike Witt, Cal. Angels, Apr. 11, 1990 (final: 1–0)
Dwight Gooden, N.Y. Yankees, May 14, 1996 (final: 2–0)
Philip Humber, Chi. White Sox, Apr. 21, 2012 (final: 4–0) (perfect game)

Postseason Play

1995 Division Playoff Game vs. Cal. Angels, won
Division Series vs. N.Y. Yankees, won 3 games to 2
League Championship Series vs. Cle. Indians, lost 4 games to 2
1997 Division Series vs. Balt. Orioles, lost 3 games to 1
2000 Division Series vs. Chi. White Sox, won 3 games to 0
League Championship Series vs. N.Y. Yankees, lost 4 games to 2
2001 Division Series vs. Cle. Indians, won 3 games to 2
League Championship Series vs. N.Y. Yankees, lost 4 games to 1

Tampa Bay Rays

Dates of Operation: 1998–present (18 years)
Overall Record: 1352 wins, 1562 losses (.463)
Stadium: Tropicana Field, 1998–present (capacity: 31,042)
Other Name: Devil Rays

Year-by-Year Finishes

Year	Finish	Wins	Losses	Percentage	Games Behind	Manager	Attendance
					East Division		
1998	5th	63	99	.389	51.0	Larry Rothschild	2,261,158
1999	5th	69	93	.426	29.0	Larry Rothschild	1,562,827
2000	5th	69	92	.429	18.0	Larry Rothschild	1,549,052
2001	5th	62	100	.383	34.0	Larry Rothschild, Hal McRae	1,227,673
2002	5th	55	106	.342	48.0	Hal McRae	1,065,762
2003	5th	63	99	.389	38.0	Lou Piniella	1,058,695
2004	4th	70	91	.435	30.0	Lou Piniella	1,275,011
2005	5th	67	95	.414	28.0	Lou Piniella	1,152,793
2006	5th	61	101	.377	36.0	Joe Maddon	1,370,963
2007	5th	66	96	.407	30.0	Joe Maddon	1,387,603
2008	1st	97	65	.599	+2.0	Joe Maddon	1,780,791
2009	3rd	84	78	.519	19.0	Joe Maddon	1,874,962
2010	1st	96	66	.593	+1.0	Joe Maddon	1,864,999
2011	2nd	91	71	.562	6.0	Joe Maddon	1,529,188
2012	3rd	90	72	.556	5.0	Joe Maddon	1,559,681
2013	2nd	92	71	.564	5.5	Joe Maddon	1,510,300
2014	4th	77	85	.475	19.0	Joe Maddon	1,446,464
2015	4th	80	82	.494	13.0	Kevin Cash	1,287,054

Awards

Most Valuable Player
[No player]

Rookie of the Year
Evan Longoria, third base, 2008
Jeremy Hellickson, pitcher, 2011
Wil Myers, outfield, 2013

Cy Young
David Price, 2012

Hall of Famer Who Played for the Rays
Wade Boggs, third base, 1998–99

Retired Numbers
12 ..... Wade Boggs
66 ..... Don Zimmer

League Leaders, Batting

Batting Average, Season
[No player]

Home Runs, Season
Carlos Pena, 2009 ..... 39 (Tie)

RBIs, Season
[No player]

Stolen Bases, Season
Carl Crawford, 2003 55
Carl Crawford, 2004 59
Carl Crawford, 2006 58
Carl Crawford, 2007 ..... 50 (Tie)

Total Bases, Season
[No player]

Most Hits, Season
[No player]

Most Runs, Season
[No player]

Batting Feats

Triple Crown Winners
[No player]

Hitting for the Cycle
Melvin Upton, Oct. 2, 2009

Six Hits in a Game
[No player]

40 or More Home Runs, Season
46 ..... Carlos Pena, 2007

League Leaders, Pitching

Most Wins, Season

David Price, 2012.....20 (Tie)

Most Strikeouts, Season

Scott Kazmir, 2007.....239

David Price, 2014.....271

Lowest ERA, Season

David Price, 2012.....2.56

Most Saves, Season

Rafael Soriano, 2010.....45

Brad Boxberger, 2015.....41

Pitching Feats

Best Won–Lost Percentage, Season

David Price, 2012 .... 20–5 .... .800 (Tie)

20 Wins, Season

David Price, 2012 20–5

No-Hitters

Matt Garza (vs. Det. Tigers), July 26, 2010 (final 5–0)

No-Hitters Pitched Against

Derek Lowe, Bost. Red Sox, Apr. 27, 2002 (final: 10–0)

Mark Buehrle, Chi. White Sox, July 23, 2009 (final: 5–0) (perfect game)

Dallas Braden, Oak. A's, May 9, 2010 (final: 4–0) (perfect game)

Edwin Jackson, Ariz. D'backs (NL), June 25, 2010 (final 1–0)

Felix Hernandez, Sea. Mariners, Aug. 15, 2015 (final:1–0) (perfect game)

Postseason Play

2008 Division Series vs. Chi. White Sox, won 3 games to 1
League Championship Series vs. Bost. Red Sox, won 4 games to 3
World Series vs. Phila. Phillies (NL), lost 4 games to 1

2010 Division Series vs. Tex. Rangers, lost 3 games to 2

2011 Division Series vs. Tex. Rangers, lost 3 games to 1

2013 AL Wild Card tiebreaker Game vs. Tex. Rangers, won
AL Wild Card Playoff Game vs. Cle. Indians, won
Division Series vs. Bost. Red Sox, lost 3 games to 1

Texas Rangers

Dates of Operation: 1972–present (44 years)

Overall Record: 3442 wins, 3550 losses (.492)

Stadiums: Arlington Stadium, 1972–93; Globe Life Park in Arlington (formerly The Ballpark in Arlington, 1994–2004, and Ameriquest Field in Arlington, 2004–06, and Rangers Ballpark in Arlington, 2007–13), 1994–present (capacity: 48,114)

Year-by-Year Finishes

Year	Finish	Wins	Losses	Percentage	Games Behind	Manager	Attendance
					West Division		
1972	6th	54	100	.351	38.5	Ted Williams	662,974
1973	6th	57	105	.352	37.0	Whitey Herzog, Del Wilber, Billy Martin	686,085
1974	2nd	84	76	.525	5.0	Billy Martin	1,193,902
1975	3rd	79	83	.488	19.0	Billy Martin, Frank Lucchesi	1,127,924
1976	4th (Tie)	76	86	.469	14.0	Frank Lucchesi	1,164,982
1977	2nd	94	68	.580	8.0	Frank Lucchesi, Eddie Stanky, Connie Ryan, Billy Hunter	1,250,722
1978	2nd (Tie)	87	75	.537	5.0	Billy Hunter, Pat Corrales	1,447,963
1979	3rd	83	79	.512	5.0	Pat Corrales	1,519,671
1980	4th (Tie)	76	85	.472	20.5	Pat Corrales	1,198,175
1981*	2nd/3rd	57	48	.543	1.5/4.5	Don Zimmer	850,076
1982	6th	64	98	.395	29.0	Don Zimmer, Darrell Johnson	1,154,432
1983	3rd	77	85	.475	22.0	Doug Rader	1,363,469
1984	7th	69	92	.429	14.5	Doug Rader	1,102,471
1985	7th	62	99	.385	28.5	Doug Rader, Bobby Valentine	1,112,497
1986	2nd	87	75	.537	5.0	Bobby Valentine	1,692,002
1987	6th (Tie)	75	87	.463	10.0	Bobby Valentine	1,763,053
1988	6th	70	91	.435	33.5	Bobby Valentine	1,581,901
1989	4th (Tie)	83	79	.512	16.0	Bobby Valentine	2,043,993
1990	3rd	83	79	.512	20.0	Bobby Valentine	2,057,911
1991	3rd	85	77	.525	10.0	Bobby Valentine	2,297,720
1992	4th (Tie)	77	85	.475	19.0	Bobby Valentine, Toby Harrah	2,198,231
1993	2nd	86	76	.531	8.0	Kevin Kennedy	2,244,616
1994	1st	52	62	.456	+1.0	Kevin Kennedy	2,503,198
1995	3rd	74	70	.514	4.5	Johnny Oates	1,985,910
1996	1st	90	72	.556	+4.5	Johnny Oates	2,889,020
1997	3rd	77	85	.475	13.0	Johnny Oates	2,945,228
1998	1st	88	74	.543	+3.0	Johnny Oates	2,927,409
1999	1st	95	67	.586	+8.0	Johnny Oates	2,771,469
2000	4th (Tie)	71	91	.438	20.5	Johnny Oates	2,800,147
2001	4th (Tie)	73	89	.451	43.0	Johnny Oates, Jerry Narron	2,831,111
2002	4th (Tie)	72	90	.444	31.0	Jerry Narron	2,352,447
2003	4th	71	91	.438	25.0	Buck Showalter	2,094,394
2004	3rd	89	73	.549	3.0	Buck Showalter	2,513,685
2005	3rd	79	83	.488	16.0	Buck Showalter	2,525,221
2006	3rd	80	82	.494	13.0	Buck Showalter	2,388,757
2007	4th	75	87	.463	19.0	Ron Washington	2,353,862
2008	2nd	79	83	.488	21.0	Ron Washington	1,945,677
2009	2nd	87	75	.537	10.0	Ron Washington	2,156,016
2010	1st	90	72	.556	+9.0	Ron Washington	2,505,171
2011	1st	96	65	.593	+10.0	Ron Washington	2,946,949
2012	2nd	93	69	.574	1.0	Ron Washington	3,460,280
2013	2nd	91	72	.558	5.5	Ron Washington	3,178,273
2014	5th	67	95	.414	31.0	Ron Washington, Tim Bogar	2,718,733
2015	1st	88	74	.543	+2.0	Jeff Banister	2,491,875

*Split season.

Awards

Most Valuable Player
Jeff Burroughs, outfield, 1974
Juan Gonzalez, outfield, 1996
Juan Gonzalez, outfield, 1998
Ivan Rodriguez, catcher, 1999
Alex Rodriguez, shortstop, 2003
Josh Hamilton, outfield, 2010

Rookie of the Year
Mike Hargrove, first base, 1974
Neftali Feliz, pitcher, 2010

Cy Young
[No pitcher]

Hall of Famers Who Played for the Rangers
Goose Gossage, picher, 1993
Ferguson Jenkins, pitcher, 1974–75 and 1978–81
Gaylord Perry, pitcher, 1975–77 and 1980
Nolan Ryan, pitcher, 1989–93

Retired Numbers
26 ..... Johnny Oates
34 ..... Nolan Ryan

League Leaders, Batting

Batting Average, Season
Julio Franco, 1991 ..... .341
Michael Young, 2005 ..... .331
Josh Hamilton, 2010 ..... .359

Home Runs, Season
Juan Gonzalez, 1992 43
Juan Gonzalez, 1993 46
Alex Rodriguez, 2001 52
Alex Rodriguez, 2002 57
Alex Rodriguez, 2003 47

RBIs, Season
Jeff Burroughs, 1974 118
Ruben Sierra, 1989 119
Juan Gonzalez, 1998 157
Alex Rodriguez, 2002 142
Josh Hamilton, 2008 130

Stolen Bases, Season
[No player]

Total Bases, Season
Ruben Sierra, 1989 344
Alex Rodriguez, 2001 393
Alex Rodriguez, 2002 389
Mark Teixeira, 2005 370
Josh Hamilton, 2008 ..... 331 (Tie)

Most Hits, Season
Rafael Palmeiro, 1990 191
Michael Young, 2005 221
Michael Young, 2011 ..... 213 (Tie)
Adrian Beltre, 2013 199

Most Runs, Season
Rafael Palmeiro, 1993 124
Alex Rodriguez, 2001 133
Alex Rodriguez, 2003 124

Batting Feats

Triple Crown Winners
[No player]

Hitting for the Cycle
Oddibe McDowell, July 23, 1985
Mark Teixeira, Aug. 17, 2004
Gary Matthews Jr., Sept. 13, 2006
Ian Kinsler, Apr. 15, 2005
Bengie Molina, July 16, 2010
Adrian Beltre, Aug. 24, 2012
Alex Rios, Sept. 23, 2013
Adrian Beltre, Aug. 3, 2015
Shin-Soo Choo, July 21, 2015

Six Hits in a Game
Alfonso Soriano, May 8, 2004
Ian Kinsler, Apr. 15, 2005

40 or More Home Runs, Season
57 ..... Alex Rodriguez, 2002
52 ..... Alex Rodriguez, 2001
47 ..... Juan Gonzalez, 1996
Rafael Palmeiro, 1999
Rafael Palmeiro, 2001
Alex Rodriguez, 2003
46 ..... Juan Gonzalez, 1993
45 ..... Juan Gonzalez, 1998
43 ..... Juan Gonzalez, 1992
Rafael Palmeiro, 2002
Mark Teixeira, 2005
Josh Hamilton, 2012
42 ..... Juan Gonzalez, 1997

League Leaders, Pitching

Most Wins, Season
Ferguson Jenkins, 1974 ..... 25 (Tie)
Kevin Brown, 1992 ..... 21 (Tie)
Rick Helling, 1998 ..... 20 (Tie)

Most Strikeouts, Season
Nolan Ryan, 1989 301
Nolan Ryan, 1990 232
Yu Darvish, 2013 277

Lowest ERA, Season
Rick Honeycutt, 1983 ..... 2.42

Most Saves, Season
Jeff Russell, 1989 38

Best Won–Lost Percentage, Season
Tommy Hunter, 2010 ..... .765

Pitching Feats

20 Wins, Season
Ferguson Jenkins, 1974 25–12
Kevin Brown, 1992 21–11
Rich Helling, 1998 20–7

No-Hitters
Jim Bibby (vs. Oak. A's), July 30, 1973 (final: 6–0)
Bert Blyleven (vs. Cal. Angels), Sept. 22, 1977 (final: 6–0)
Nolan Ryan (vs. Oak. A's), June 11, 1990 (final: 5–0)
Nolan Ryan (vs. Tor. Blue Jays), May 1, 1991 (final: 3–0)
Kenny Rogers (vs. Cal. Angels), July 28, 1994 (final: 4–0) (perfect game)

No-Hitters Pitched Against
Jim Colborn, K.C. Royals, May 14, 1977 (final: 6–0)
Mike Witt, Cal. Angels, Sept. 30, 1984 (final: 1–0) (perfect game)
Mark Buehrle, Chi. White Sox, Apr. 18, 2007 (final: 6–0)

Postseason Play

1996 Division Series vs. N.Y. Yankees, lost 3 games to 1
1999 Division Series vs. N.Y. Yankees, lost 3 games to 0
1998 Division Series vs. N.Y. Yankees, lost 3 games to 0
2010 Division Series vs. T.B. Rays, won 3 games to 2
League Championship Series vs. N.Y. Yankees, won 4 games to 2
World Series vs. S. F. Giants (NL), lost 4 games to 1
2011 Division Series vs. T.B. Rays, won 3 games to 1
League Championship Series vs. Det. Tigers, won 4 games to 2
World Series vs. St.L. Cardinals (NL) lost 4 games to 3
2012 AL Wild Card Playoff Game vs. Balt. Orioles, lost
2013 AL Wild Card tiebreaker Game vs. T.B. Rays, lost
2015 Division Series vs. Tor. Blue Jays, lost 3 games to 2

Toronto Blue Jays

Dates of Operation: 1977–present (39 years)

Overall Record: 3078 wins, 3115 losses (.497)

Stadiums: Exhibition Stadium (1977–82), 1977–89; Rogers Centre (formerly Skydome, 1989–2004), 1989–present (capacity: 49,282)

Year-by-Year Finishes

Year	Finish	Wins	Losses	Percentage	Games Behind	Manager	Attendance
					East Division		
1977	7th	54	107	.335	45.5	Roy Hartsfield	1,701,052
1978	7th	59	102	.366	40.0	Roy Hartsfield	1,562,585
1979	7th	53	109	.327	50.5	Roy Hartsfield	1,431,651
1980	7th	67	95	.414	36.0	Bobby Mattick	1,400,327
1981*	7th/7th	37	69	.349	19.0/7.5	Bobby Mattick	755,083
1982	6th (Tie)	78	84	.481	17.0	Bobby Cox	1,275,978
1983	4th	89	73	.549	9.0	Bobby Cox	1,930,415
1984	2nd	89	73	.549	15.0	Bobby Cox	2,110,009
1985	1st	99	62	.615	+2.0	Bobby Cox	2,468,925
1986	4th	86	76	.531	9.5	Jimy Williams	2,455,477
1987	2nd	96	66	.593	2.0	Jimy Williams	2,778,429
1988	3rd (Tie)	87	75	.537	2.0	Jimy Williams	2,595,175
1989	1st	89	73	.549	+2.0	Jimy Williams, Cito Gaston	3,375,883
1990	2nd	86	76	.531	2.0	Cito Gaston	3,885,284
1991	1st	91	71	.562	+7.0	Cito Gaston	4,001,527
1992	1st	96	66	.593	+4.0	Cito Gaston	4,028,318
1993	1st	95	67	.586	+7.0	Cito Gaston	4,057,947
1994	3rd	55	60	.478	16.0	Cito Gaston	2,907,933
1995	5th	56	88	.389	30.0	Cito Gaston	2,826,483
1996	4th	74	88	.457	18.0	Cito Gaston	2,559,573
1997	5th	76	86	.469	22.0	Cito Gaston, Mel Queen	2,589,297
1998	3rd	88	74	.543	26.0	Tim Johnson	2,454,183
1999	3rd	84	78	.519	14.0	Jim Fregosi	2,163,464
2000	3rd	83	79	.512	4.5	Jim Fregosi	1,819,886
2001	3rd	80	82	.494	16.0	Buck Martinez	1,915,438
2002	3rd	78	84	.481	25.5	Buck Martinez, Carlos Tosca	1,636,904
2003	3rd	86	76	.531	15.0	Carlos Tosca	1,799,458
2004	5th	67	94	.416	33.5	Carlos Tosca, John Gibbons	1,900,041
2005	3rd	80	82	.494	15.0	John Gibbons	2,014,987
2006	2nd	87	75	.537	10.0	John Gibbons	2,302,212
2007	3rd	83	79	.512	13.0	John Gibbons	2,360,648
2008	4th	86	76	.531	11.0	John Gibbons, Cito Gaston	2,399,786
2009	4th	75	87	.463	28.0	Cito Gaston	1,876,129
2010	4th	85	77	.525	11.0	Cito Gaston	1,495,482
2011	4th	81	81	.500	16.0	John Farrell	1,818,103
2012	4th	73	89	.451	22.0	John Farrell	2,099,663
2013	5th	74	88	.457	23.0	John Gibbons	2,536,562
2014	3rd	83	79	.512	13.0	John Gibbons	2,375,525
2015	1st	93	69	.574	+6.0	John Gibbons	2,794,891

*Split season.

Awards

Most Valuable Player
George Bell, outfield, 1987
Josh Donaldson, third base, 2015

Rookie of the Year
Alfredo Griffin (co-winner), shortstop, 1979
Eric Hinske, third base, 2002

Cy Young
Pat Hentgen, 1996
Roger Clemens, 1997
Roger Clemens, 1998
Roy Halladay, 2003

Hall of Famers Who Played for the Blue Jays
Roberto Alomar, second base, 1991–95
Rickey Henderson, outfield, 1993
Paul Molitor, designated hitter, 1993–95
Phil Niekro, pitcher, 1987
Frank Thomas, first base and designated hitter, 2007–08
Dave Winfield, designated hitter, 1992

Retired Numbers
12 ..... Roberto Alomar

League Leaders, Batting

Batting Average, Season
John Olerud, 1993 ..... .363

Home Runs, Season
Jesse Barfield, 1986 40
Fred McGriff, 1989 36
Jose Bautista, 2010 54
Jose Bautista, 2011 43

RBIs, Season
George Bell, 1987 134
Carlos Delgado, 2003 145
Josh Donaldson, 2015 123

Stolen Bases, Season
[No player]

Total Bases, Season
George Bell, 1987 369
Shawn Green, 1999 361
Carlos Delgado, 2000 378
Vernon Wells, 2003 373
Jose Bautista, 2010 351
Josh Donaldson, 2015 352

Most Hits, Season
Paul Molitor, 1993 211
Vernon Wells, 2003 215

Most Runs, Season
Josh Donaldson, 2015 122

Batting Feats

Triple Crown Winners
[No player]

Hitting for the Cycle
Kelly Gruber, Apr. 16, 1989
Jeff Frye, Aug. 17, 2001

Six Hits in a Game
Frank Catalanotto, May 1, 2004

40 or More Home Runs, Season
54 ..... Jose Bautista, 2010
47 ..... George Bell, 1987
46 ..... Jose Canseco, 1998
44 ..... Carlos Delgado, 1999
43 ..... Jose Bautista, 2011
42 ..... Shawn Green, 1999
Carlos Delgado, 2003
Edwin Encarnacion, 2012
41 ..... Tony Batista, 2000
Carlos Delgado, 2000
40 ..... Jesse Barfield, 1986

League Leaders, Pitching

Most Wins, Season
Jack Morris, 1992 ..... 21 (Tie)
Roger Clemens, 1997 21
Roger Clemens, 1998 ..... 20 (Tie)

Most Strikeouts, Season
Roger Clemens, 1997 292
Roger Clemens, 1998 271
A.J. Burnett, 2008 231

Lowest ERA, Season
Dave Stieb, 1985 ..... 2.48
Jimmy Key, 1987 ..... 2.76
Juan Guzman, 1996 ..... 2.93
Roger Clemens, 1997 ..... 2.05
Roger Clemens, 1998 ..... 2.65
David Price, 2015 ..... 2.45*
*2.53 with Det. Tigers and 2.30 with Tor. Blue Jays.

Most Saves, Season
Tom Heinke, 1987 34
Duane Ward, 1993 ..... 45 (Tie)

Best Won–Lost Percentage, Season
Doyle Alexander, 1984... 17–6. .739
Roy Halladay, 2003 ..... 22–7. .759

Pitching Feats

Triple Crown Winner
Roger Clemens, 1997 (21–7, 2.05 ERA, 292 SO)
Roger Clemens, 1998 (20–6, 2.65 ERA, 271 SO)

20 Wins, Season
Jack Morris, 1992 21–6
Pat Hentgen, 1996 20–10
Roger Clemens, 1997 21–7
Roger Clemens, 1998 20–6
David Wells, 2000 20–8
Roy Halladay, 2003 22–7
Roy Halladay, 2008 20–11

No-Hitters
Dave Stieb (vs. Det. Tigers), Sept. 2, 1990 (final: 3–0)

No-Hitters Pitched Against
Len Barker, Cle. Indians, May 15, 1981 (final: 3–0) (perfect game)
Dave Stewart, Oak. A's, June 29, 1990 (final: 5–0)
Nolan Ryan, Tex. Rangers, May 1, 1991 (final: 3–0)
Justin Verlander, Det. Tigers, May 7, 2011 (final: 9–0)

Postseason Play

1985 League Championship Series vs. K.C. Royals, lost 4 games to 3
1989 League Championship Series vs. Oak. A's, lost 4 games to 1
1991 League Championship Series vs. Min. Twins, lost 4 games to 1
1992 League Championship Series vs. Oak. A's, won 4 games to 2
World Series vs. Atl. Braves (NL), won 4 games to 2
1993 League Championship Series vs. Chi. White Sox, won 4 games to 2
World Series vs. Phila. Phillies (NL), won 4 games to 2
2015 Division Series vs. Tex. Rangers, won 3 games to 2
League Championship Series vs. K.C. Royals, lost 4 games to 2

NATIONAL LEAGUE

Arizona Diamondbacks

Dates of Operation: 1998–present (18 years)
Overall Record: 1434 wins, 1482 losses (.491)
Stadium: Chase Field (formerly Bank One Ballpark (The BOB), 1998–2005) 1998–present (capacity: 48,519)
Other Name: D'backs

Year-by-Year Finishes

Year	Finish	Wins	Losses	Percentage	Games Behind	Manager	Attendance
					West Division		
1998	5th	65	97	.401	33.0	Buck Showalter	3,600,412
1999	1st	100	62	.617	+14.0	Buck Showalter	3,019,654
2000	3rd	85	77	.525	12.0	Buck Showalter	2,942,516
2001	1st	92	70	.556	+2.0	Bob Brenly	2,740,554
2002	1st	98	64	.605	+2.5	Bob Brenly	3,200,725
2003	3rd	84	78	.519	16.5	Bob Brenly	2,805,542
2004	5th	51	111	.315	42.0	Bob Brenly, Al Pedrique	2,519,560
2005	2nd	77	85	.465	5.0	Bob Melvin	2,058,718
2006	4th	76	86	.469	12.0	Bob Melvin	2,092,189
2007	1st	90	72	.556	+0.5	Bob Melvin	2,325,414
2008	2nd	82	80	.506	2.0	Bob Melvin	2,509,924
2009	5th	70	92	.432	25.0	Bob Melvin, A. J. Hinch	2,129,183
2010	5th	65	97	.401	27.0	A.J. Hinch, Kirk Gibson	2,056,697
2011	1st	94	68	.580	+8.0	Kirk Gibson	2,105,432
2012	3rd	81	81	.500	13.0	Kirk Gibson	2,177,617
2013	2nd	81	81	.500	11.0	Kirk Gibson	2,134,895
2014	5th	64	98	.395	30.0	Kirk Gibson, Alan Trammell	2,073,730
2015	3rd	79	83	.488	13.0	Chip Hale	2,080,145

Awards

Most Valuable Player
[No player]

Rookie of the Year
[No player]

Cy Young
Randy Johnson, 1999
Randy Johnson, 2000
Randy Johnson, 2001
Randy Johnson, 2002
Brandon Webb, 2006

Hall of Famers Who Played for the Diamondbacks
Roberto Alomar, second base, 2004
Randy Johnson, pitcher, 1999–2004

Retired Numbers
20 ..... Luis Gonzalez
51 ..... Randy Johnson

League Leaders, Batting

Batting Average, Season
[No player]

Home Runs, Season
Paul Goldschmidt, 2013.....36 (Tie)

RBIs, Season
Paul Goldschmidt, 2013 125

Stolen Bases, Season
Tony Womack, 1999 72

Total Bases, Season
Paul Goldschmidt, 2013 332

Most Hits, Season
Luis Gonzalez, 1999 206

Most Runs, Season
[No player]

Batting Feats

Triple Crown Winners
[No player]

Hitting for the Cycle
Luis Gonzalez, July 5, 2000
Greg Colbrunn, Sept. 18, 2002
Stephen Drew, Sept. 1, 2008
Kelly Johnson, July 13, 2010
Aaron Hill, June 18, 2012
Aaron Hill, June 29, 2012

Six Hits in a Game
[No player]

40 or More Home Runs, Season
57 ..... Luis Gonzalez, 2001
44 ..... Mark Reynolds, 2009
40 ..... Adam Dunn*, 2008
*32 for Cin. Reds and 8 for Ariz. D'backs.

League Leaders, Pitching

Most Wins, Season
Randy Johnson, 2002 24
Brandon Webb, 2006 ..... 16 (Tie)
Brandon Webb, 2008 22
Ian Kennedy, 2011 ..... 21 (Tie)

Most Strikeouts, Season
Randy Johnson, 1999 364
Randy Johnson, 2000 347
Randy Johnson, 2001 372
Randy Johnson, 2002 334
Randy Johnson, 2004 290

Lowest ERA, Season
Randy Johnson, 1999 ..... 2.48
Randy Johnson, 2001 ..... 2.49
Randy Johnson, 2002 ..... 2.32

Most Saves, Season
Jose Valverde, 2007 47

Best Won–Lost Percentage, Season
Randy Johnson, 2000 ... 19–7 ... .731
Curt Schilling, 2001 ..... 22–6 ... .786
Randy Johnson, 2002 ... 24–5 ... .828
Ian Kennedy, 2011 ..... 21–4 ... .840

Pitching Feats

Triple Crown Winner
Randy Johnson, 2002 (24–5, 2.32 ERA, 334 SO)

20 Wins, Season
Curt Schilling, 2001 22–6
Randy Johnson, 2001 21–6
Randy Johnson, 2002 24–5
Curt Schilling, 2002 23–7
Brandon Webb, 2008 22–7
Ian Kennedy, 2011 21–4

No-Hitters
Randy Johnson (vs. Atl. Braves), May 18, 2004 (final: 2–0) (perfect game)
Edwin Jackson (vs. T.B. Rays), June 25, 2010 (final: 1–0)

No-Hitters Pitched Against
Jose Jimenez, St.L. Cardinals, June 25, 1999 (final: 1–0)
Anibal Sanchez, Fla. Marlins, Sept. 6, 2006 (final: 2–0)

Postseason Play

1999 Division Series vs. N.Y. Mets, lost 3 games to 1
2001 Division Series vs. St.L. Cardinals, won 3 games to 2
League Championship Series vs. Atl. Braves, won 4 games to 1
World Series vs. N.Y. Yankees (AL), won 4 games to 3
2002 Division Series vs. St.L. Cardinals, lost 3 games to 2
2007 Division Series vs. Chi. Cubs, won 3 games to 0
League Championship Series vs. Colo. Rockies, lost 4 games to 0
2011 Division Series vs. Milw. Brewers, lost 3 games to 2

Atlanta Braves (formerly the Milwaukee Braves)

Dates of Operation: (as the Milwaukee Braves) 1953–65 (13 years)
Overall Record: 1146 wins, 890 losses (.563)
Stadium: Milwaukee County Stadium, 1953–65 (capacity: 44,091)

Dates of Operation: (as the Atlanta Braves) 1966–present (50 years)
Overall Record: 4106 wins, 3851 losses (.516)
Stadiums: Atlanta–Fulton County Stadium, 1966–96; Turner Field, 1997–2016 (capacity: 49,586); SunTrust Park, 2017– (capacity: 41,500)

Year-by-Year Finishes

Year	Finish	Wins	Losses	Percentage	Games Behind	Manager	Attendance
					Milw. Braves		
1953	2nd	92	62	.597	13.0	Charlie Grimm	1,826,397
1954	3rd	89	65	.578	8.0	Charlie Grimm	2,131,388
1955	2nd	85	69	.552	13.5	Charlie Grimm	2,005,836
1956	2nd	92	62	.597	1.0	Charlie Grimm, Fred Haney	2,046,331
1957	1st	95	59	.617	+8.0	Fred Haney	2,215,404
1958	1st	92	62	.597	+8.0	Fred Haney	1,971,101
1959	2nd	86	70	.551	2.0	Fred Haney	1,749,112
1960	2nd	88	66	.571	7.0	Chuck Dressen	1,497,799
1961	4th	83	71	.539	10.0	Chuck Dressen, Birdie Tebbetts	1,101,441
1962	5th	86	76	.531	15.5	Birdie Tebbetts	766,921
1963	6th	84	78	.519	15.0	Bobby Bragan	773,018
1964	5th	88	74	.543	5.0	Bobby Bragan	910,911
1965	5th	86	76	.531	11.0	Bobby Bragan	555,584
					Atl. Braves		
1966	5th	85	77	.525	10.0	Bobby Bragan, Billy Hitchcock	1,539,801
1967	7th	77	85	.475	24.5	Billy Hitchcock, Ken Silvestri	1,389,222
1968	5th	81	81	.500	16.0	Lum Harris	1,126,540
					West Division		
1969	1st	93	69	.574	+3.0	Lum Harris	1,458,320
1970	5th	76	86	.469	26.0	Lum Harris	1,078,848
1971	3rd	82	80	.506	8.0	Lum Harris	1,006,320
1972	4th	70	84	.455	25.0	Lum Harris, Eddie Mathews	752,973
1973	5th	76	85	.472	22.5	Eddie Mathews	800,655
1974	3rd	88	74	.543	14.0	Eddie Mathews, Clyde King	981,085
1975	5th	67	94	.416	40.5	Clyde King, Connie Ryan	534,672
1976	6th	70	92	.432	32.0	Dave Bristol	818,179
1977	6th	61	101	.377	37.0	Dave Bristol, Ted Turner	872,464
1978	6th	69	93	.426	26.0	Bobby Cox	904,494
1979	6th	66	94	.413	23.5	Bobby Cox	769,465
1980	4th	81	80	.503	11.0	Bobby Cox	1,048,411
1981*	4th/5th	50	56	.472	9.5/7.5	Bobby Cox	535,418
1982	1st	89	73	.549	+1.0	Joe Torre	1,801,985
1983	2nd	88	74	.543	3.0	Joe Torre	2,119,935
1984	2nd (Tie)	80	82	.494	12.0	Joe Torre	1,724,892
1985	5th	66	96	.407	29.0	Eddie Haas, Bobby Wine	1,350,137
1986	6th	72	89	.447	23.5	Chuck Tanner	1,387,181
1987	5th	69	92	.429	20.5	Chuck Tanner	1,217,402

1988	6th	54	106	.338	39.5	Chuck Tanner, Russ Nixon	848,089
1989	6th	63	97	.394	28.0	Russ Nixon	984,930
1990	6th	65	97	.401	26.0	Russ Nixon, Bobby Cox	980,129
1991	1st	94	68	.580	+1.0	Bobby Cox	2,140,217
1992	1st	98	64	.605	+8.0	Bobby Cox	3,077,400
1993	1st	104	58	.642	+1.0	Bobby Cox	3,884,725
				East Division			
1994	2nd	68	46	.596	6.0	Bobby Cox	2,539,240
1995	1st	90	54	.625	+21.0	Bobby Cox	2,561,831
1996	1st	96	66	.593	+8.0	Bobby Cox	2,901,242
1997	1st	101	61	.623	+9.0	Bobby Cox	3,464,488
1998	1st	106	56	.654	+18.0	Bobby Cox	3,361,350
1999	1st	103	59	.636	+6.5	Bobby Cox	3,284,897
2000	1st	95	67	.586	+1.0	Bobby Cox	3,234,301
2001	1st	88	74	.543	+2.0	Bobby Cox	2,823,494
2002	1st	101	59	.631	+19.0	Bobby Cox	2,603,482
2003	1st	101	61	.623	+10.0	Bobby Cox	2,401,104
2004	1st	96	66	.593	+10.0	Bobby Cox	2,322,565
2005	1st	90	72	.556	+2.0	Bobby Cox	2,521,167
2006	3rd	79	83	.488	18.0	Bobby Cox	2,550,524
2007	3rd	84	78	.519	5.0	Bobby Cox	2,745,210
2008	4th	72	90	.444	20.0	Bobby Cox	2,532,834
2009	3rd	86	76	.531	7.0	Bobby Cox	2,373,631
2010	2nd	91	71	.562	6.0	Bobby Cox	2,510,119
2011	2nd	89	73	.549	13.0	Fredi Gonzalez	2,372,940
2012	2nd	94	68	.580	4.0	Fredi Gonzalez	2,420,171
2013	1st	96	66	.593	+10.0	Fredi Gonzalez	2,548,679
2014	2nd	79	83	.488	17.0	Fredi Gonzalez	2,354,305
2015	4th	67	95	.141	23.0	Fredi Gonzalez	2,001,392

*Split season.

Awards

Most Valuable Player

Hank Aaron, outfield, 1957 (Milw.)
Dale Murphy, outfield, 1982
Dale Murphy, outfield, 1983
Terry Pendleton, third base, 1991
Chipper Jones, third base, 1999

Rookie of the Year

Bob Horner, third base, 1978
David Justice, outfield, 1990
Rafael Furcal, second base and shortstop, 2000
Craig Kimbrel, pitcher, 2011

Cy Young

Warren Spahn, 1957 (Milw.)
Tom Glavine, 1991
Greg Maddux, 1993
Greg Maddux, 1994
Greg Maddux, 1995
John Smoltz, 1996
Tom Glavine, 1998

Hall of Famers Who Played for the Braves

Hank Aaron, outfield, 1954–65 (Milw.) and 1966–74 (Atl.)
Orlando Cepeda, first base, 1969–72
Tom Glavine, pitcher, 1987–2002 and 2008
Tony La Russa, second base, 1971
Greg Maddux, pitcher, 1993–2003
Eddie Mathews, third base, 1953–65 (Milw.) and 1966 (Atl.)
Phil Niekro, pitcher, 1964–65 (Milw.) and 1966–83 (Atl.)
Gaylord Perry, pitcher, 1981
Red Schoendienst, infield, 1957–60 (Milw.)
Enos Slaughter, outfield, 1959 (Milw.)
John Smoltz, pitcher, 1988–2008
Warren Spahn, pitcher, 1953–64 (Milw.)
Bruce Sutter, pitcher, 1985–88
Joe Torre, catcher and first base, 1960–65 (Milw.) and 1966–68 (Atl.)
Hoyt Wilhelm, pitcher, 1969–70, 1971

Retired Numbers

3 ..... Dale Murphy
6 ..... Bobby Cox
10 ..... Chipper Jones
21 ..... Warren Spahn
29 ..... John Smoltz
31 ..... Greg Maddux
35 ..... Phil Niekro
41 ..... Eddie Mathews
44 ..... Hank Aaron
47 ..... Tom Glavine

League Leaders, Batting

Batting Average, Season

Hank Aaron, 1956 (Milw.) ..... .328
Hank Aaron, 1959 (Milw.) ..... .355
Rico Carty, 1970 ..... .366
Ralph Garr, 1974 ..... .353
Terry Pendleton, 1991 ..... .319
Chipper Jones, 2008 ..... .364

Home Runs, Season

Eddie Mathews, 1953 (Milw.) 47
Hank Aaron, 1957 (Milw.) 44
Eddie Mathews, 1959 (Milw.) 46
Hank Aaron, 1963 (Milw.) 44
Hank Aaron, 1966 44
Hank Aaron, 1967 39
Dale Murphy, 1984 ..... 36 (Tie)

Dale Murphy, 1985 37
Andruw Jones, 2005 51

RBIs, Season

Hank Aaron, 1957 (Milw.) 132
Hank Aaron, 1960 (Milw.) 126
Hank Aaron, 1963 (Milw.) 130
Hank Aaron, 1966 127
Dale Murphy, 1982 ..... 109 (Tie)
Dale Murphy, 1983 121
Andruw Jones, 2005 128

Stolen Bases, Season

Bill Bruton, 1953 (Milw.) 26
Bill Bruton, 1954 (Milw.) 34
Bill Bruton, 1955 (Milw.) 25
Michael Bourn*, 2011 61
*39 with Hous. Astros and 22 with Atl. Braves.

Total Bases, Season

Hank Aaron, 1956 (Milw.) 340
Hank Aaron, 1957 (Milw.) 369
Hank Aaron, 1959 (Milw.) 400
Hank Aaron, 1960 (Milw.) 334
Hank Aaron, 1961 (Milw.) 358
Hank Aaron, 1963 (Milw.) 370
Felipe Alou, 1966 355
Hank Aaron, 1967 344
Hank Aaron, 1969 332
Dale Murphy, 1984 332
Terry Pendleton, 1991 ..... 303 (Tie)

Most Hits, Season

Hank Aaron, 1956 (Milw.) 200
Red Schoendienst*, 1957 (Milw.) . 200
Hank Aaron, 1959 (Milw.) 223
Felipe Alou, 1966 218
Felipe Alou, 1968 ..... 210 (Tie)
Ralph Garr, 1974 214
Terry Pendleton, 1991 187
Terry Pendleton, 1992 ..... 199 (Tie)
*78 with N.Y. Giants and 122 with Milw. Braves.

Most Runs, Season

Hank Aaron, 1957 (Milw.) 118
Bill Bruton, 1960 (Milw.) 112
Hank Aaron, 1963 (Milw.) 121
Felipe Alou, 1966 122
Hank Aaron, 1967 ..... 113 (Tie)
Dale Murphy, 1985 118

Batting Feats

Triple Crown Winners

[No player]

Hitting for the Cycle

Albert Hall, Sept. 23, 1987
Mark Kotsay, Aug. 14, 2008

Six Hits in a Game

Felix Milan, July 6, 1970
Willie Harris, July 21, 2007

40 or More Home Runs, Season

51 ..... Andruw Jones, 2005
47 ..... Eddie Mathews, 1953 (Milw.)
Hank Aaron, 1971
46 ..... Eddie Mathews, 1959 (Milw.)
45 ..... Hank Aaron, 1962 (Milw.)
Chipper Jones, 1999
44 ..... Hank Aaron, 1957 (Milw.)
Hank Aaron, 1963 (Milw.)
Hank Aaron, 1966
Hank Aaron, 1969
Dale Murphy, 1987
Andres Galarraga, 1998
43 ..... Davey Johnson, 1973
Javy Lopez, 2003
41 ..... Eddie Mathews, 1955 (Milw.)
Darrell Evans, 1973
Jeff Burroughs, 1977
Andruw Jones, 2006
40 ..... Eddie Mathews, 1954 (Milw.)
Hank Aaron, 1960 (Milw.)
Hank Aaron, 1973
David Justice, 1993

League Leaders, Pitching

Most Wins, Season

Warren Spahn, 1957 (Milw.) 21
Warren Spahn, 1958 (Milw.) . 22 (Tie)
Lew Burdette, 1959 (Milw.) .... 21 (Tie)
Warren Spahn, 1959 (Milw.) . 21 (Tie)
Warren Spahn, 1960 (Milw.) . 21 (Tie)
Warren Spahn, 1961 (Milw.) . 21 (Tie)
Phil Niekro, 1974 ..... 20 (Tie)
Phil Niekro, 1979 ..... 21 (Tie)
Tom Glavine, 1991 ..... 20 (Tie)
Tom Glavine, 1992 ..... 20 (Tie)
Tom Glavine, 1993 ..... 22 (Tie)
Greg Maddux, 1994 ..... 16 (Tie)
Greg Maddux, 1995 19
John Smoltz, 1996 24
Denny Neagle, 1997 20
Tom Glavine, 1998 20
John Smoltz, 2006 ..... 16 (Tie)

Most Strikeouts, Season

Phil Niekro, 1977 262
John Smoltz, 1992 215
John Smoltz, 1996 276

Lowest ERA, Season

Warren Spahn, 1953 (Milw.) 2.10
Lew Burdette, 1956 (Milw.) 2.71
Warren Spahn, 1961 (Milw.) 3.01
Phil Niekro, 1967 ..... 1.87
Buzz Capra, 1974 ..... 2.28
Greg Maddux, 1993 ..... 2.36
Greg Maddux, 1994 ..... 1.56
Greg Maddux, 1995 ..... 1.63
Greg Maddux, 1998 ..... 2.22

Most Saves, Season

John Smoltz, 2002 55
Craig Kimbrel, 2011 ..... 46 (Tie)
Craig Kimbrel, 2012 42
Craig Kimbrel, 2013 50
Craig Kimbrel, 2014 47

Best Won–Lost Percentage, Season

Bob Buhl, 1957 (Milw.). 18–7 ... .720
Warren Spahn, 1958
(Milw.) ..... 22–11 .667 (Tie)
Lew Burdette, 1958
(Milw.) ..... 20–10 .667 (Tie)
Phil Niekro, 1982 ..... 17–4 ... .810
Greg Maddux, 1995 .... 19–2 ... .905
John Smoltz, 1996 ..... 24–8 ... .750
Greg Maddux, 1997 .... 19–4 ... .826
John Smoltz, 1998 ..... 17–3 ... .850
Russ Ortiz, 2003 ..... 21–7 ... .750
Jorge Sosa, 2005 ..... 13–3 ... .813
Chuck James, 2006 ..... 11–4 ... .733

Pitching Feats

20 Wins, Season

Warren Spahn, 1953 (Milw.) 23–7
Warren Spahn, 1954 (Milw.) .. 21–12
Warren Spahn, 1956 (Milw.) .. 20–11
Warren Spahn, 1957 (Milw.) .. 21–11
Warren Spahn, 1958 (Milw.) .. 22–11
Lew Burdette, 1958 (Milw.) 20–10
Lew Burdette, 1959 (Milw.) 21–15
Warren Spahn, 1959 (Milw.) .. 21–15
Warren Spahn, 1960 (Milw.) .. 21–10
Warren Spahn, 1961 (Milw.) .. 21–13
Warren Spahn, 1963 (Milw.) 23–7
Tony Cloninger, 1965 (Milw.) .. 24–11
Phil Niekro, 1969 23–13
Phil Niekro, 1974 20–13
Phil Niekro, 1979 21–20

Tom Glavine, 1991 20–11
Tom Glavine, 1992 20–8
Tom Glavine, 1993 22–6
Greg Maddux, 1993 20–10
John Smoltz, 1996 24–8
Denny Neagle, 1997..... 20–5
Tom Glavine, 1998 20–6
Tom Glavine, 2000 21–9
Russ Ortiz, 2003..... 21–7

No-Hitters

Jim Wilson (vs. Phila. Phillies), June 12, 1954 (final: 2–0) (Milw.)

Lew Burdette (vs. Phila. Phillies), Aug. 18, 1960 (final: 1–0) (Milw.)

Warren Spahn (vs. Phila. Phillies), Sept. 15, 1960 (final: 4–0) (Milw.)

Warren Spahn (vs. S.F. Giants), Apr. 28, 1961 (final: 1–0) (Milw.)

Phil Niekro (vs. S.D. Padres), Aug. 5, 1973 (final: 9–0)

Kent Mercker, Mark Wohlers, and Alejandro Pena (vs. S.D. Padres), Sept. 11, 1991 (final: 1–0)

Kent Mercker (vs. L.A. Dodgers), Apr. 8, 1994 (final: 6–0)

No-Hitters Pitched Against

Don Wilson, Hous. Astros, June 18, 1967 (final: 2–0)

Ken Holtzman, Chi. Cubs, Aug. 19, 1969 (final: 3–0)

John Montefusco, S.F. Giants, Sept. 29, 1976 (final: 9–0)

Ken Forsch, Hous. Astros, Apr. 7, 1979 (final: 6–0)

Randy Johnson, Ariz. D'backs, May 18, 2004 (final: 2–0) (perfect game)

Ubaldo Jimenez, Colo. Rockies, Apr. 17, 2010 (final: 4–0)

Cole Hamels, Jake Diekman, Ken Giles, Jonathan Papelbon, Phila. Phillies, Sept. 1, 2014 (final: 7–0)

Postseason Play

1957 World Series vs. N.Y. Yankees (AL), won 4 games to 3 (Milw.)

1958 World Series vs. N.Y. Yankees (AL), lost 4 games to 3 (Milw.)

1959 Pennant Playoff Series vs. L.A. Dodgers, lost 2 games to 0 (Milw.)

1969 League Championship Series vs. N.Y. Mets, lost 3 games to 0

1982 League Championship Series vs. St.L. Cardinals, lost 3 games to 0

1991 League Championship Series vs. Pitt. Pirates, won 4 games to 3
World Series vs. Min. Twins (AL), lost 4 games to 3

1992 League Championship Series vs. Pitt. Pirates, won 4 games to 3
World Series vs. Tor. Blue Jays (AL), lost 4 games to 2

1993 League Championship Series vs. Phila. Phillies, lost 4 games to 2

1995 Division Series vs. Colo. Rockies, won 3 games to 1
League Championship Series vs. Cin. Reds, won 4 games to 0
World Series vs. Cle. Indians (AL), won 4 games to 2

1996 Division Series vs. L.A. Dodgers, won 3 games to 0
League Championship Series vs. St.L. Cardinals, won 4 games to 3
World Series vs. N.Y. Yankees (AL), lost 4 games to 2

1997 Division Series vs. Hous. Astros, won 3 games to 0
League Championship Series vs. Fla. Marlins, lost 4 games to 2

1998 Division Series vs. Chi. Cubs, won 3 games to 0
League Championship Series vs. S.D. Padres, lost 4 games to 2

1999 Division Series vs. Hous. Astros, won 3 games to 1
League Championship Series vs. N.Y. Mets, won 4 games to 2
World Series vs. N.Y. Yankees (AL), lost 4 games to 0

2000 Division Series vs. St.L. Cardinals, lost 3 games to 0

2001 Division Series vs. Hous. Astros, won 3 games to 0
League Championship Series vs. Ariz. D'backs, lost 4 games to 1

2002 Division Series vs. S.F. Giants, lost 3 games to 1

2003 Division Series vs. Chi. Cubs, lost 3 games to 2

2004 Division Series vs. Hous. Astros, lost 3 games to 2

2005 Division Series vs. Hous. Astros, lost 3 games to 1

2010 Division Series vs. S. F. Giants, lost 3 games to 1

2012 NL Wild Card Playoff Game vs. St.L. Cardinals, lost

2013 Division Series vs. L.A. Dodgers, lost 3 games to 1

Chicago Cubs

Dates of Operation: 1876–present (140 years)

Overall Record: 10608 wins, 10130 losses (.511)

Stadiums: 23rd Street Grounds, 1876–77; Lakefront Park, 1878–84; West Side Park, 1885–92; South Side Park, 1891–93 and 1897; New West Side Park (also called West Side Grounds), 1893–1915; Comiskey Park, 1918 (World Series only); Wrigley Field (formerly Weeghman Field), 1916–present (capacity: 42,495)

Other Names: Broncos, Colts, Cowboys, Orphans, White Stockings

Year-by-Year Finishes

Year	Finish	Wins	Losses	Percentage	Games Behind	Manager	Attendance
1876	1st	52	14	.788	+6.0	A. G. Spalding	not available
1877	5th	26	33	.441	15.5	A. G. Spalding	not available
1878	4th	30	30	.500	11.0	Robert Ferguson	not available
1879	3rd (Tie)	44	32	.579	10.0	Cap Anson	not available
1880	1st	67	17	.798	+15.0	Cap Anson	not available
1881	1st	56	28	.667	+9.0	Cap Anson	not available
1882	1st	55	29	.655	+3.0	Cap Anson	not available
1883	2nd	59	29	.602	4.0	Cap Anson	not available
1884	4th (Tie)	62	50	.554	22.0	Cap Anson	not available
1885	1st	87	25	.776	+2.0	Cap Anson	not available
1886	1st	90	34	.725	+2.5	Cap Anson	not available
1887	3rd	71	50	.587	6.5	Cap Anson	not available
1888	2nd	77	58	.578	9.0	Cap Anson	not available
1889	3rd	67	65	.508	19.0	Cap Anson	not available
1890	2nd	83	53	.610	6.5	Cap Anson	not available
1891	2nd	82	53	.607	3.5	Cap Anson	not available
1892	7th	70	76	.479	40.0	Cap Anson	not available
1893	9th	57	71	.445	28.0	Cap Anson	not available
1894	8th	57	75	.432	34.0	Cap Anson	not available
1895	4th	72	58	.554	15.0	Cap Anson	not available
1896	5th	71	57	.555	18.5	Cap Anson	not available
1897	9th	59	73	.447	34.0	Cap Anson	not available
1898	4th	85	65	.567	17.5	Tom Burns	not available
1899	8th	75	73	.507	22.0	Tom Burns	not available
1900	5th (Tie)	65	75	.464	19.0	Tom Loftus	not available
1901	6th	53	86	.381	37.0	Tom Loftus	205,071
1902	5th	68	69	.496	34.0	Frank Selee	263,700
1903	3rd	82	56	.594	8.0	Frank Selee	386,205
1904	2nd	93	60	.608	13.0	Frank Selee	439,100
1905	3rd	92	61	.601	13.0	Frank Selee, Frank Chance	509,900
1906	1st	116	36	.763	+20.0	Frank Chance	654,300
1907	1st	107	45	.704	+17.0	Frank Chance	422,550
1908	1st	99	55	.643	+1.0	Frank Chance	665,325
1909	2nd	104	49	.680	6.5	Frank Chance	633,480
1910	1st	104	50	.675	+13.0	Frank Chance	526,152
1911	2nd	92	62	.597	7.5	Frank Chance	576,000
1912	3rd	91	59	.607	11.5	Frank Chance	514,000

1913	3rd	88	65	.575	13.5	Johnny Evers	419,000
1914	4th	78	76	.506	16.5	Hank O'Day	202,516
1915	4th	73	80	.477	17.5	Roger Bresnahan	217,058
1916	5th	67	86	.438	26.5	Joe Tinker	453,685
1917	5th	74	80	.481	24.0	Fred Mitchell	360,218
1918	1st	84	45	.651	+10.5	Fred Mitchell	337,256
1919	3rd	75	65	.536	21.0	Fred Mitchell	424,430
1920	5th (Tie)	75	79	.487	18.0	Fred Mitchell	480,783
1921	7th	64	89	.418	30.0	Johnny Evers, Bill Killefer	410,107
1922	5th	80	74	.519	13.0	Bill Killefer	542,283
1923	4th	83	71	.539	12.5	Bill Killefer	703,705
1924	5th	81	72	.529	12.0	Bill Killefer	716,922
1925	8th	68	86	.442	27.5	Bill Killefer, Rabbit Maranville, George Gibson	622,610
1926	4th	82	72	.532	7.0	Joe McCarthy	885,063
1927	4th	85	68	.556	8.5	Joe McCarthy	1,159,168
1928	3rd	91	63	.591	4.0	Joe McCarthy	1,143,740
1929	1st	98	54	.645	+10.5	Joe McCarthy	1,485,166
1930	2nd	90	64	.584	2.0	Joe McCarthy, Rogers Hornsby	1,463,624
1931	3rd	84	70	.545	17.0	Rogers Hornsby	1,086,422
1932	1st	90	64	.584	+4.0	Rogers Hornsby, Charlie Grimm	974,688
1933	3rd	86	68	.558	6.0	Charlie Grimm	594,112
1934	3rd	86	65	.570	8.0	Charlie Grimm	707,525
1935	1st	100	54	.649	+4.0	Charlie Grimm	692,604
1936	2nd (Tie)	87	67	.565	5.0	Charlie Grimm	699,370
1937	2nd	93	61	.604	3.0	Charlie Grimm	895,020
1938	1st	89	63	.586	+2.0	Charlie Grimm, Gabby Hartnett	951,640
1939	4th	84	70	.545	13.0	Gabby Hartnett	726,663
1940	5th	75	79	.487	25.5	Gabby Hartnett	534,878
1941	6th	70	84	.455	30.0	Jimmy Wilson	545,159
1942	6th	68	86	.442	38.0	Jimmy Wilson	590,872
1943	5th	74	79	.484	30.5	Jimmy Wilson	508,247
1944	4th	75	79	.487	30.0	Jimmy Wilson, Charlie Grimm	640,110
1945	1st	98	56	.636	+3.0	Charlie Grimm	1,036,386
1946	3rd	82	71	.536	14.5	Charlie Grimm	1,342,970
1947	6th	69	85	.448	25.0	Charlie Grimm	1,364,039
1948	8th	64	90	.416	27.5	Charlie Grimm	1,237,792
1949	8th	61	93	.396	36.0	Charlie Grimm, Frankie Frisch	1,143,139
1950	7th	64	89	.418	26.5	Frankie Frisch	1,165,944
1951	8th	62	92	.403	34.5	Frankie Frisch, Phil Cavarretta	894,415
1952	5th	77	77	.500	19.5	Phil Cavarretta	1,024,826
1953	7th	65	89	.422	40.0	Phil Cavarretta	763,658
1954	7th	64	90	.416	33.0	Stan Hack	748,183
1955	6th	72	81	.471	26.0	Stan Hack	875,800
1956	8th	60	94	.390	33.0	Stan Hack	720,118
1957	7th (Tie)	62	92	.403	33.0	Bob Scheffing	670,629
1958	5th (Tie)	72	82	.468	20.0	Bob Scheffing	979,904
1959	5th (Tie)	74	80	.481	13.0	Bob Scheffing	858,255
1960	7th	60	94	.390	35.0	Charlie Grimm, Lou Boudreau	809,770
1961	7th	64	90	.416	29.0	Vedie Himsl, Harry Craft, Elvin Tappe, Lou Klein	673,057
1962	9th	59	103	.364	42.5	Charlie Metro, Elvin Tappe, Lou Klein	609,802
1963	7th	82	80	.506	17.0	Bob Kennedy	979,551

1964	8th	76	86	.469	17.0	Bob Kennedy	751,647
1965	8th	72	90	.444	25.0	Bob Kennedy, Lou Klein	641,361
1966	10th	59	103	.364	36.0	Leo Durocher	635,891
1967	3rd	87	74	.540	14.0	Leo Durocher	977,226
1968	3rd	84	78	.519	13.0	Leo Durocher	1,043,409
				East Division			
1969	2nd	92	70	.568	8.0	Leo Durocher	1,674,993
1970	2nd	84	78	.519	5.0	Leo Durocher	1,642,705
1971	3rd (Tie)	83	79	.512	14.0	Leo Durocher	1,653,007
1972	2nd	85	70	.548	11.0	Leo Durocher, Whitey Lockman	1,299,163
1973	5th	77	84	.478	5.0	Whitey Lockman	1,351,705
1974	6th	66	96	.407	22.0	Whitey Lockman, Jim Marshall	1,015,378
1975	5th (Tie)	75	87	.463	17.5	Jim Marshall	1,034,819
1976	4th	75	87	.463	26.0	Jim Marshall	1,026,217
1977	4th	81	81	.500	20.0	Herman Franks	1,439,834
1978	3rd	79	83	.488	11.0	Herman Franks	1,525,311
1979	5th	80	82	.494	18.0	Herman Franks, Joe Amalfitano	1,648,587
1980	6th	64	98	.395	27.0	Preston Gomez, Joe Amalfitano	1,206,776
1981*	6th/5th	38	65	.369	17.5/6.0	Joe Amalfitano	565,637
1982	5th	73	89	.451	19.0	Lee Elia	1,249,278
1983	5th	71	91	.438	19.0	Lee Elia, Charlie Fox	1,479,717
1984	1st	96	65	.596	+6.5	Jim Frey	2,107,655
1985	4th	77	84	.478	23.5	Jim Frey	2,161,534
1986	5th	70	90	.438	37.0	Jim Frey, John Vukovich, Gene Michael	1,859,102
1987	6th	76	85	.472	18.5	Gene Michael, Frank Lucchesi	2,035,130
1988	4th	77	85	.475	24.0	Don Zimmer	2,089,034
1989	1st	93	69	.574	+6.0	Don Zimmer	2,491,942
1990	4th	77	85	.475	18.0	Don Zimmer	2,243,791
1991	4th	77	83	.481	20.0	Don Zimmer, Joe Altobelli, Jim Essian	2,314,250
1992	4th	78	84	.481	18.0	Jim Lefebvre	2,126,720
1993	4th	84	78	.519	13.0	Jim Lefebvre	2,653,763
				Central Division			
1994	5th	49	64	.434	16.5	Tom Trebelhorn	1,845,208
1995	3rd	73	71	.570	12.0	Jim Riggleman	1,918,265
1996	4th	76	86	.469	12.0	Jim Riggleman	2,219,110
1997	5th	68	94	.420	16.0	Jim Riggleman	2,190,308
1998	2nd	90	73	.552	12.5	Jim Riggleman	2,623,000
1999	6th	67	95	.414	30.0	Jim Riggleman	2,813,854
2000	6th	65	97	.401	30.0	Don Baylor	2,789,511
2001	3rd	88	74	.543	5.0	Don Baylor	2,779,456
2002	5th	67	95	.414	30.0	Don Baylor, Bruce Kimm	2,693,071
2003	1st	88	74	.543	+1.0	Dusty Baker	2,962,630
2004	3rd	89	73	.549	16.0	Dusty Baker	3,170,184
2005	4th	79	83	.488	21.0	Dusty Baker	3,099,992
2006	6th	66	96	.407	17.5	Dusty Baker	3,123,215
2007	1st	85	77	.525	+2.0	Lou Piniella	3,123,215
2008	1st	97	64	.602	+7.5	Lou Piniella	3,300,200
2009	2nd	83	78	.516	7.5	Lou Piniella	3,168,859
2010	5th	75	87	.463	16.0	Lou Piniella, Mike Quade	3,062,973
2011	5th	71	91	.438	25.0	Mike Quade	3,017,966
2012	5th	61	101	.377	36.0	Dale Sveum	2,882,756
2013	5th	66	96	.407	31.0	Dale Sveum	2,642,682
2014	5th	73	89	.451	17.0	Rick Renteria	2,652,113
2015	3rd	97	65	.599	3.0	Joe Maddon	2,959,812

*Split season.

Awards

Most Valuable Player

Frank Schulte, outfield, 1911
Rogers Hornsby, second base, 1929
Gabby Hartnett, catcher, 1935
Phil Cavarretta, first base, 1945
Hank Sauer, outfield, 1952
Ernie Banks, shortstop, 1958
Ernie Banks, shortstop, 1959
Ryne Sandberg, second base, 1984
Andre Dawson, outfield, 1987
Sammy Sosa, outfield, 1998

Rookie of the Year

Billy Williams, outfield, 1961
Ken Hubbs, second base, 1962
Jerome Walton, outfield, 1989
Kerry Wood, pitcher, 1998
Geovany Soto, catcher, 2008
Kris Bryant, third base, 2015

Cy Young

Ferguson Jenkins, 1971
Bruce Sutter, 1979
Rick Sutcliffe, 1984
Greg Maddux, 1992
Jake Arrieta, 2015

Hall of Famers Who Played for the Cubs

Grover C. Alexander, pitcher, 1918–26
Cap Anson, first base, 1876–97
Richie Ashburn, outfield, 1960–61
Ernie Banks, shortstop, 1953–71
Roger Bresnahan, catcher, 1900 and 1913–15
Lou Brock, outfield, 1961–64
Three Finger Brown, pitcher, 1904–12 and 1916
Frank Chance, first base, 1898–1912
John Clarkson, pitcher, 1884–87
Kiki Cuyler, outfield, 1928–35
Andre Dawson, outfield, 1987–92
Dizzy Dean, pitcher, 1938–41
Hugh Duffy, outfield, 1888–89
Dennis Eckersley, pitcher, 1984–86
Johnny Evers, second base, 1902–13
Jimmie Foxx, first base, 1942 and 1944
Goose Gossage, pitcher, 1988
Clark Griffith, pitcher, 1893–1900
Burleigh Grimes, pitcher, 1932–33
Gabby Hartnett, catcher, 1922–40
Billy Herman, second base, 1931–41
Rogers Hornsby, second base, 1929–32
Monte Irvin, outfield, 1956
Ferguson Jenkins, pitcher, 1966–73 and 1982–83
George Kelly, first base, 1930
King Kelly, outfield, 1880–86
Ralph Kiner, outfield, 1953–54
Chuck Klein, outfield, 1934–36
Tony La Russa, shortstop, 1973
Tony Lazzeri, second base, 1938
Fred Lindstrom, outfield, 1935
Greg Maddux, pitcher, 1986–92 and 2004–06
Rabbit Maranville, shortstop, 1925
Robin Roberts, pitcher, 1966
Ryne Sandberg, second base, 1982–94, 1996–97
Ron Santo, third base, 1960–73
Al Spalding, pitcher, 1876–78
Bruce Sutter, pitcher, 1976–88
Joe Tinker, shortstop, 1902–12 and 1916
Rube Waddell, pitcher, 1901
Hoyt Wilhelm, pitcher, 1970
Billy Williams, outfield, 1959–74
Hack Wilson, outfield, 1926–31

Retired Numbers

10 ..... Ron Santo
14 ..... Ernie Banks
23 ..... Ryne Sandberg
26 ..... Billy Williams
31 ..... Ferguson Jenkins
31 ..... Greg Maddux

League Leaders, Batting (Post-1900)

Batting Average, Season

Heinie Zimmerman, 1912 ..... .372
Phil Cavarretta, 1945 ..... .355
Billy Williams, 1972 ..... .333
Bill Madlock, 1975 ..... .354
Bill Madlock, 1976 ..... .339
Bill Buckner, 1980 ..... .324
Derrek Lee, 2005 ..... .335

Home Runs, Season

Frank Schulte, 1910 ..... 10 (Tie)
Frank Schulte, 1911 21
Heinie Zimmerman, 1912 14
Cy Williams, 1916 ..... 12 (Tie)
Hack Wilson, 1926 21
Hack Wilson, 1927 ..... 30 (Tie)
Hack Wilson, 1928 ..... 31 (Tie)
Hack Wilson, 1930 56
Bill Nicholson, 1943 29
Bill Nicholson, 1944 33
Hank Sauer, 1952 ..... 37 (Tie)
Ernie Banks, 1958 47
Ernie Banks, 1960 41
Dave Kingman, 1979 48
Andre Dawson, 1987 49
Ryne Sandberg, 1990 40
Sammy Sosa, 2000 50
Sammy Sosa, 2002 49

RBIs, Season

Harry Steinfeldt, 1906 83
Frank Schulte, 1911 121
Heinie Zimmerman, 1912 98
Heinie Zimmerman*, 1916 83
Fred Merkle, 1918 71
Hack Wilson, 1929 159
Hack Wilson, 1930 191
Bill Nicholson, 1943 128
Bill Nicholson, 1944 122
Hank Sauer, 1952 121
Ernie Banks, 1958 129
Ernie Banks, 1959 143
Andre Dawson, 1987 137
Sammy Sosa, 1998 158
Sammy Sosa, 2001 160

*19 with N.Y. Giants and 64 with Chi. Cubs.

Stolen Bases, Season

Frank Chance, 1903 ..... 67 (Tie)
Billy Maloney, 1905 ..... 59 (Tie)
Frank Chance, 1906 57
Kiki Cuyler, 1928 37
Kiki Cuyler, 1929 43
Kiki Cuyler, 1930 37
Augie Galan, 1935 22
Augie Galan, 1937 23
Stan Hack, 1938 16
Stan Hack, 1939 ..... 17 (Tie)

Total Bases, Season

Frank Schulte, 1911 308
Heinie Zimmerman, 1912 318
Charlie Hollocher, 1918 202
Rogers Hornsby, 1929 409
Bill Nicholson, 1944 317
Ernie Banks, 1958 379
Billy Williams, 1968 321
Billy Williams, 1970 373
Billy Williams, 1972 348
Andre Dawson, 1987 353
Ryne Sandberg, 1990 344
Sammy Sosa, 1998 416

Sammy Sosa, 1999 397
Sammy Sosa, 2001 425

Most Hits, Season

Harry Steinfeldt, 1906 176
Heinie Zimmerman, 1912 207
Charlie Hollocher, 1918 161
Billy Herman, 1935 227
Stan Hack, 1940 ..... 191 (Tie)
Stan Hack, 1941 186
Phil Cavarretta, 1944 ..... 197 (Tie)
Billy Williams, 1970 ..... 205 (Tie)
Derrek Lee, 2005 199
Juan Pierre, 2006 204
Starlin Castro, 2011 207

Most Runs, Season

Frank Chance, 1906 ..... 103 (Tie)
Jimmy Sheckard, 1911 121
Tommy Leach, 1913 ..... 99 (Tie)
Rogers Hornsby, 1929 156
Augie Galan, 1935 133
Bill Nicholson, 1944 116
Glenn Beckert, 1968 98
Billy Williams, 1970 137
Ivan DeJesus, 1978 104
Ryne Sandberg, 1984 114
Ryne Sandberg, 1989 ..... 104 (Tie)
Ryne Sandberg, 1990 116
Sammy Sosa, 1998 134
Sammy Sosa, 2001 146
Sammy Sosa, 2002 122

Batting Feats

Triple Crown Winners

Heinie Zimmerman, 1912 (.372 BA, 14 HRs, 98 RBIs)

Hitting for the Cycle

Jimmy Ryan, July 28, 1888
Jimmy Ryan, July 1, 1891
Hack Wilson, June 23, 1930
Babe Herman, Sept. 30, 1933
Roy Smalley, June 28, 1950
Lee Walls, July 2, 1957
Billy Williams, July 17, 1966
Randy Hundley, Aug. 11, 1966
Ivan DeJesus, Apr. 22, 1980
Andre Dawson, Apr. 29, 1987
Mark Grace, May 9, 1993

Six Hits in a Game (Post-1900)

Frank Demaree, July 5, 1937*
Don Kessinger, July 17, 1971*
Bill Madlock, July 26, 1975*
Jose Cardenal, May 2, 1976*
Sammy Sosa, July 2, 1993
*Extra-inning game.

40 or More Home Runs, Season

66 ..... Sammy Sosa, 1998
64 ..... Sammy Sosa, 2001
63 ..... Sammy Sosa, 1999
56 ..... Hack Wilson, 1930
50 ..... Sammy Sosa, 2000
49 ..... Andre Dawson, 1987
Sammy Sosa, 2002
48 ..... Dave Kingman, 1979
47 ..... Ernie Banks, 1958
46 ..... Derrek Lee, 2005
45 ..... Ernie Banks, 1959
44 ..... Ernie Banks, 1955
43 ..... Ernie Banks, 1957
42 ..... Billy Williams, 1970
41 ..... Hank Sauer, 1954
Ernie Banks, 1960
40 ..... Ryne Sandberg, 1990
Sammy Sosa, 1996
Sammy Sosa, 2003

League Leaders, Pitching (Post-1900)

Most Wins, Season

Three Finger Brown, 1909 27
Larry Cheney, 1912 ..... 26 (Tie)
Hippo Vaughn, 1918 22
Grover C. Alexander, 1920 27
Charlie Root, 1927 26
Pat Malone, 1929 22
Pat Malone, 1930 ..... 20 (Tie)
Lon Warneke, 1932 22
Bill Lee, 1938 22
Larry Jackson, 1964 24
Ferguson Jenkins, 1971 24
Rick Sutcliffe, 1987 18
Greg Maddux, 1992 ..... 20 (Tie)
Carlos Zambrano, 2006 ..... 16 (Tie)
Jake Arrieta, 2015 22

Most Strikeouts, Season

Fred Beebe*, 1906 171
Orval Overall, 1909 205
Hippo Vaughn, 1918 148
Hippo Vaughn, 1919 141
Grover C. Alexander, 1920 173
Pat Malone, 1929 166
Clay Bryant, 1938 135
Claude Passeau**, 1939 ..... 137 (Tie)
Johnny Schmitz, 1946 135
Sam Jones, 1955 198
Sam Jones, 1956 176
Ferguson Jenkins, 1969 273
Kerry Wood, 2003 266
*116 with St.L. Cardinals and 55 with Chi. Cubs.
**29 with Phila. Phillies and 108 with Chi. Cubs.

Lowest ERA, Season

Hippo Vaughn, 1918 ..... 1.74
Grover C. Alexander, 1919 ..... 1.72
Grover C. Alexander, 1920 ..... 1.91
Lon Warneke, 1932 ..... 2.37
Bill Lee, 1938 ..... 2.66
Hank Borowy, 1945 ..... 2.13

Most Saves, Season

Bruce Sutter, 1979 37
Bruce Sutter, 1980 28
Lee Smith, 1983 29
Randy Myers, 1993 53
Randy Myers, 1995 38

Best Won–Lost Percentage, Season

Ed Reulbach, 1906 ..... 19–4 ... .826
Ed Reulbach, 1907 ..... 17–4 ... .810
Ed Reulbach, 1908 ..... 24–7 ... .774
King Cole, 1910 ..... 20–4 ... .833
Bert Humphries, 1913 ... 16–4 ... .800
Claude Hendrix, 1918 .. 20–7 ... .741
Charlie Root, 1929 ..... 19–6 ... .760
Lon Warneke, 1932 ..... 22–6 ... .786
Bill Lee, 1935 ..... 20–6 ... .769
Bill Lee, 1938 ..... 22–9 ... .710
Rick Sutcliffe, 1984 ..... 16–1 ... .941
Mike Bielecki, 1989 ..... 18–7 ... .720

Pitching Feats

Triple Crown Winner

Hippo Vaughn, 1918 (22–10, 1.74 ERA, 148 SO)
Grover C. Alexander, 1920 (27–14, 1.91 ERA, 173 SO)

20 Wins, Season

Jack Taylor, 1902 22–10
Jack Taylor, 1903 21–14
Jake Weimer, 1903 20–8
Jake Weimer, 1904 20–14
Three Finger Brown, 1906 26–6
Jack Pfiester, 1906 20–8
Jack Taylor, 1906 ..... 20–12*
Orval Overall, 1907 23–8
Three Finger Brown, 1907 20–6

Three Finger Brown, 1908..... 29–9
Ed Reulbach, 1908 24–7
Three Finger Brown, 1909..... 27–9
Orval Overall, 1909..... 20–11
Three Finger Brown, 1910..... 25–14
King Cole, 1910..... 20–4
Three Finger Brown, 1911..... 21–11
Larry Cheney, 1912 26–10
Larry Cheney, 1913 21–14
Hippo Vaughn, 1914 21–13
Larry Cheney, 1914 20–18
Hippo Vaughn, 1915 20–12
Hippo Vaughn, 1917 23–13
Hippo Vaughn, 1918 22–10
Claude Hendrix, 1918..... 20–7
Hippo Vaughn, 1919 21–14
Grover C. Alexander, 1920 27–14
Grover C. Alexander, 1923 22–12
Charlie Root, 1927 26–15
Pat Malone, 1929..... 22–10
Pat Malone, 1930..... 20–9
Lon Warneke, 1932 22–6
Guy Bush, 1933 20–12
Lon Warneke, 1934 22–10
Bill Lee, 1935..... 20–6
Lon Warneke, 1935 20–13
Bill Lee, 1938..... 22–9
Claude Passeau, 1940..... 20–13
Hank Wyse, 1945 22–10
Hank Borowy, 1945.....21–7**
Dick Ellsworth, 1953 22–10
Larry Jackson, 1964 24–11
Ferguson Jenkins, 1967..... 20–13
Ferguson Jenkins, 1968..... 20–15
Ferguson Jenkins, 1969..... 21–15
Bill Hands, 1969..... 20–14
Ferguson Jenkins, 1970..... 22–16
Ferguson Jenkins, 1971..... 24–13
Ferguson Jenkins, 1972..... 20–12
Rick Reuschel, 1977 20–10
Rick Sutcliffe, 1984 .....20–6***
Greg Maddux, 1992..... 20–11
Jon Lieber, 2001..... 20–6
Jake Arrieta, 2015 22–6

*8–9 with St.L. Cardinals and 12–3 with Chi. Cubs.
**10–5 with N.Y. Yankees and 11–2 with Chi. Cubs.
***4–5 with Cle. Indians and 16–1 with Chi. Cubs.

No-Hitters

Jimmy Lavender (vs. N.Y. Giants), Aug. 31, 1915 (final: 2–0)
Sam Jones (vs. Pitt. Pirates), May 12, 1955 (final: 4–0)
Don Cardwell (vs. St.L. Cardinals), May 15, 1960 (final: 4–0)
Ken Holtzman (vs. Atl. Braves), Aug. 19, 1969 (final: 3–0)
Ken Holtzman (vs. Cin. Reds), June 3, 1971 (final: 1–0)
Burt Hooton (vs. Phila. Phillies), Apr. 16, 1972 (final: 4–0)
Milt Pappas (vs. S.D. Padres), Sept. 2, 1972 (final: 8–0)
Carlos Zambrano (vs. Hous. Astros), Sept. 14, 2008 (final: 5–0)
Jake Arrieta (vs. L.A. Dodgers), Aug. 30, 2015 (final: 2–0)

No-Hitters Pitched Against

Chick Fraser, Phila. Phillies, Sept. 18, 1903 (final: 10–0)
Christy Mathewson, N.Y. Giants, June 13, 1905 (final: 1–0)
Jim Toney, Cin. Reds, May 2, 1917 (final: 1–0) (10 innings)
Carl Erskine, Bklyn. Dodgers, June 19, 1952 (final: 5–0)
Jim Maloney, Cin. Reds, Aug. 9, 1965 (final: 1–0) (10 innings)
Sandy Koufax, L.A. Dodgers, Sept. 9, 1965 (final: 1–0) (perfect game)
Cole Hamels, Phila. Phillies, July 25, 2015 (final: 5–0)

Postseason Play

1906 World Series vs. Chi. White Sox (AL), lost 4 games to 2
1907 World Series vs. Det. Tigers (AL), won 4 games to 0, 1 tie
1908 Pennant Playoff Game vs. N.Y. Giants, won
World Series vs. Det. Tigers (AL), won 4 games to 1
1910 World Series vs. Phila. A's (AL), lost 4 games to 1
1918 World Series vs. Bost. Red Sox (AL), lost 4 games to 2
1929 World Series vs. Phila. A's (AL), lost 4 games to 1
1932 World Series vs. N.Y. Yankees (AL), lost 4 games to 0
1935 World Series vs. Det. Tigers (AL), lost 4 games to 2
1938 World Series vs. N.Y. Yankees (AL), lost 4 games to 0
1945 World Series vs. Det. Tigers (AL), lost 4 games to 3
1984 League Championship Series vs. S.D. Padres, lost 3 games to 2
1989 League Championship Series vs. S.F. Giants, lost 4 games to 1
1998 NL Wild Card Playoff Game vs. S.F. Giants, won
Division Series vs. Atl. Braves, lost 3 games to 0
2003 Division Series vs. Atl. Braves, won 3 games to 2
League Championship Series vs. Fla. Marlins, lost 4 games to 3
2007 Division Series vs. Ariz. D'backs, lost 3 games to 0
2008 Division Series vs. L.A. Dodgers, lost 3 games to 0
2015 NL Wild Card Playoff Game vs. Pitt. Pirates, won
Division Series vs. St.L. Cardinals, won 3 games to 1
League Championship Series vs. N.Y. Mets, lost 4 games to 0

Cincinnati Reds

Dates of Operation: 1876–80; 1890–present (131 years)

Overall Record: 9772 wins, 9627 losses (.503)

Stadiums: Avenue Grounds, 1876–79; Bank Street Grounds, 1880; League Park, 1890–92; Redland Field, 1892–1901; Palace of the Fans, 1902–11; Redland Field (also known as Crosley Field), 1912–70; Riverfront Stadium (also known as Cinergy Field, 1996–2002), 1970–2002; Great American Ball Park, 2003–present (capacity: 42,319)

Other Names: Red Stockings, Redlegs

Year-by-Year Finishes

Year	Finish	Wins	Losses	Percentage	Games Behind	Manager	Attendance
1876	8th	9	56	.138	42.5	Charlie Gould	not available
1877	6th	15	42	.263	25.5	Lip Pike, Bob Addy	not available
1878	2nd	37	23	.617	4.0	Cal McVey	not available
1879	5th	43	37	.538	14.0	Deacon White, Cal McVey	not available
1880	8th	21	59	.263	44.0	John Clapp	not available
1890	4th	78	55	.586	10.0	Tom Loftus	not available
1891	7th	56	81	.409	30.5	Tom Loftus	not available
1892	5th	82	68	.547	20.0	Charles Comiskey	not available
1893	6th	65	63	.508	20.0	Charles Comiskey	not available
1894	10th	54	75	.419	35.5	Charles Comiskey	not available
1895	8th	66	64	.508	21.0	Buck Ewing	not available
1896	3rd	77	50	.606	12.0	Buck Ewing	not available
1897	4th	76	56	.576	17.0	Buck Ewing	not available
1898	3rd	92	60	.605	11.5	Buck Ewing	not available
1899	6th	83	67	.553	15.0	Buck Ewing	not available
1900	7th	62	77	.446	21.5	Robert Allen	not available
1901	8th	52	87	.374	38.0	Bid McPhee	205,728
1902	4th	70	70	.500	33.5	Bid McPhee, Frank Bancroft, Joe Kelley	217,300
1903	4th	74	65	.532	16.5	Joe Kelley	351,680
1904	3rd	88	65	.575	18.0	Joe Kelley	391,915
1905	5th	79	74	.516	26.0	Joe Kelley	313,927
1906	6th	64	87	.424	51.5	Ned Hanlon	330,056
1907	6th	66	87	.431	41.5	Ned Hanlon	317,500
1908	5th	73	81	.474	26.0	John Ganzel	399,200
1909	4th	77	76	.503	33.5	Clark Griffith	424,643
1910	5th	75	79	.487	29.0	Clark Griffith	380,622
1911	6th	70	83	.458	29.0	Clark Griffith	300,000
1912	4th	75	78	.490	29.0	Hank O'Day	344,000
1913	7th	64	89	.418	37.5	Joe Tinker	258,000
1914	8th	60	94	.390	34.5	Buck Herzog	100,791
1915	7th	71	83	.461	20.0	Buck Herzog	218,878
1916	7th (Tie)	60	93	.392	33.5	Buck Herzog, Christy Mathewson	255,846
1917	4th	78	76	.506	20.0	Christy Mathewson	269,056
1918	3rd	68	60	.531	15.5	Christy Mathewson, Heinie Groh	163,009
1919	1st	96	44	.686	+9.0	Pat Moran	532,501
1920	3rd	82	71	.536	10.5	Pat Moran	568,107
1921	6th	70	83	.458	24.0	Pat Moran	311,227

1922	2nd	86	68	.558	7.0	Pat Moran	493,754
1923	2nd	91	63	.591	4.5	Pat Moran	575,063
1924	4th	83	70	.542	10.0	Jack Hendricks	437,707
1925	3rd	80	73	.523	15.0	Jack Hendricks	464,920
1926	2nd	87	67	.565	2.0	Jack Hendricks	672,987
1927	5th	75	78	.490	18.5	Jack Hendricks	442,164
1928	5th	78	74	.513	16.0	Jack Hendricks	490,490
1929	7th	66	88	.429	33.0	Jack Hendricks	295,040
1930	7th	59	95	.383	33.0	Dan Howley	386,727
1931	8th	58	96	.377	43.0	Dan Howley	263,316
1932	8th	60	94	.390	30.0	Dan Howley	356,950
1933	8th	58	94	.382	33.0	Donie Bush	218,281
1934	8th	52	99	.344	42.0	Bob O'Farrell, Chuck Dressen	206,773
1935	6th	68	85	.444	31.5	Chuck Dressen	448,247
1936	5th	74	80	.481	18.0	Chuck Dressen	466,245
1937	8th	56	98	.364	40.0	Chuck Dressen, Bobby Wallace	411,221
1938	4th	82	68	.547	6.0	Bill McKechnie	706,756
1939	1st	97	57	.630	+4.5	Bill McKechnie	981,443
1940	1st	100	53	.654	+12.0	Bill McKechnie	850,180
1941	3rd	88	66	.571	12.0	Bill McKechnie	643,513
1942	4th	76	76	.500	29.0	Bill McKechnie	427,031
1943	2nd	87	67	.565	18.0	Bill McKechnie	379,122
1944	3rd	89	65	.578	16.0	Bill McKechnie	409,567
1945	7th	61	93	.396	37.0	Bill McKechnie	290,070
1946	6th	67	87	.435	30.0	Bill McKechnie	715,751
1947	5th	73	81	.474	21.0	Johnny Neun	899,975
1948	7th	64	89	.418	27.0	Johnny Neun, Bucky Walters	823,386
1949	7th	62	92	.403	35.0	Bucky Walters	707,782
1950	6th	66	87	.431	24.5	Luke Sewell	538,794
1951	6th	68	86	.442	28.5	Luke Sewell	588,268
1952	6th	69	85	.448	27.5	Luke Sewell, Rogers Hornsby	604,197
1953	6th	68	86	.442	37.0	Rogers Hornsby, Buster Mills	548,086
1954	5th	74	80	.481	23.0	Birdie Tebbetts	704,167
1955	5th	75	79	.487	23.5	Birdie Tebbetts	693,662
1956	3rd	91	63	.591	2.0	Birdie Tebbetts	1,125,928
1957	4th	80	74	.519	15.0	Birdie Tebbetts	1,070,850
1958	4th	76	78	.494	16.0	Birdie Tebbetts, Jimmy Dykes	788,582
1959	5th (Tie)	74	80	.481	13.0	Mayo Smith, Fred Hutchinson	801,289
1960	6th	67	87	.435	28.0	Fred Hutchinson	663,486
1961	1st	93	61	.604	+4.0	Fred Hutchinson	1,117,603
1962	3rd	98	64	.605	3.5	Fred Hutchinson	982,085
1963	5th	86	76	.531	13.0	Fred Hutchinson	858,805
1964	2nd (Tie)	92	70	.568	1.0	Fred Hutchinson, Dick Sisler	862,466
1965	4th	89	73	.549	8.0	Dick Sisler	1,047,824
1966	7th	76	84	.475	18.0	Don Heffner, Dave Bristol	742,958
1967	4th	87	75	.537	14.5	Dave Bristol	958,300
1968	4th	83	79	.512	14.0	Dave Bristol	733,354
				West Division			
1969	3rd	89	73	.549	4.0	Dave Bristol	987,991
1970	1st	102	60	.630	+14.5	Sparky Anderson	1,803,568
1971	4th (Tie)	79	83	.488	11.0	Sparky Anderson	1,501,122
1972	1st	95	59	.617	+10.5	Sparky Anderson	1,611,459
1973	1st	99	63	.611	+3.5	Sparky Anderson	2,017,601

1974	2nd	98	64	.605	4.0	Sparky Anderson	2,164,307
1975	1st	108	54	.667	+20.0	Sparky Anderson	2,315,603
1976	1st	102	60	.630	+10.0	Sparky Anderson	2,629,708
1977	2nd	88	74	.543	10.0	Sparky Anderson	2,519,670
1978	2nd	92	69	.571	2.5	Sparky Anderson	2,532,497
1979	1st	90	71	.559	+1.5	John McNamara	2,356,933
1980	3rd	89	73	.549	3.5	John McNamara	2,022,450
1981*	2nd/2nd	66	42	.611	0.5/1.5	John McNamara	1,093,730
1982	6th	61	101	.377	28.0	John McNamara, Russ Nixon	1,326,528
1983	6th	74	88	.457	17.0	Russ Nixon	1,190,419
1984	5th	70	92	.432	22.0	Vern Rapp, Pete Rose	1,275,887
1985	2nd	89	72	.553	5.5	Pete Rose	1,834,619
1986	2nd	86	76	.531	10.0	Pete Rose	1,692,432
1987	2nd	84	78	.519	6.0	Pete Rose	2,185,205
1988	2nd	87	74	.540	7.0	Pete Rose	2,072,528
1989	5th	75	87	.463	17.0	Pete Rose, Tommy Helms	1,979,320
1990	1st	91	71	.562	+5.0	Lou Piniella	2,400,892
1991	5th	74	88	.457	20.0	Lou Piniella	2,372,377
1992	2nd	90	72	.556	8.0	Lou Piniella	2,315,946
1993	5th	73	89	.451	31.0	Tony Perez, Davey Johnson	2,453,232
				Central Division			
1994	1st	66	48	.579	+0.5	Davey Johnson	1,897,681
1995	1st	85	59	.590	+9.0	Davey Johnson	1,837,649
1996	3rd	81	81	.500	7.0	Ray Knight	1,861,428
1997	3rd	76	86	.469	8.0	Ray Knight, Jack McKeon	1,785,788
1998	4th	77	85	.475	25.0	Jack McKeon	1,793,679
1999	2nd	96	67	.589	1.5	Jack McKeon	2,061,222
2000	2nd	85	77	.525	10.0	Jack McKeon	2,577,351
2001	5th	66	96	.407	27.0	Bob Boone	1,882,732
2002	3rd	78	84	.481	19.0	Bob Boone	1,855,973
2003	5th	69	93	.426	19.0	Bob Boone, Dave Miley	2,355,259
2004	4th	76	86	.469	29.0	Dave Miley	2,287,250
2005	5th	73	89	.451	27.0	Dave Miley, Jerry Narron	1,943,068
2006	3rd	80	82	.494	3.5	Jerry Narron	2,134,633
2007	5th	72	90	.444	13.0	Jerry Narron, Pete Mackanin	2,058,632
2008	5th	74	88	.457	23.5	Dusty Baker	2,058,632
2009	4th	78	84	.481	13.0	Dusty Baker	1,747,919
2010	1st	91	71	.562	+5.0	Dusty Baker	2,060,550
2011	3rd	79	83	.488	17.0	Dusty Baker	2,213,588
2012	1st	97	65	.599	+9.0	Dusty Baker	2,347,251
2013	3rd	90	72	.556	7.0	Dusty Baker	2,492,101
2014	4th	76	86	.469	14.0	Bryan Price	2,476,664
2015	5th	64	98	.395	36.0	Bryan Price	2,419,506

*Split season.

Awards

Most Valuable Player

Ernie Lombardi, catcher, 1938
Bucky Walters, pitcher, 1939
Frank McCormick, first base, 1940
Frank Robinson, outfield, 1961
Johnny Bench, catcher, 1970
Johnny Bench, catcher, 1972
Pete Rose, outfield, 1973
Joe Morgan, second base, 1975
Joe Morgan, second base, 1976
George Foster, outfield, 1977
Barry Larkin, shortstop, 1995
Joey Votto, first baseman, 2010

Rookie of the Year

Frank Robinson, outfield, 1956
Pete Rose, second base, 1963
Tommy Helms, third base, 1966
Johnny Bench, catcher, 1968
Pat Zachry, pitcher, 1976 (co-winner)
Chris Sabo, third base, 1988
Scott Williamson, pitcher, 1999

Cy Young
[No pitcher]

Hall of Famers Who Played for the Reds
Jake Beckley, first base, 1897–1903
Johnny Bench, catcher, 1967–83
Jim Bottomley, first base, 1933–35
Three Finger Brown, pitcher, 1913
Sam Crawford, outfield, 1899–1902
Candy Cummings, pitcher, 1877
Kiki Cuyler, outfield, 1935–37
Leo Durocher, shortstop, 1930–33
Ken Griffey Jr., outfield, 2000–08
Clark Griffith, pitcher, 1909–10
Chick Hafey, outfield, 1932–35 and 1937
Jesse Haines, pitcher, 1918
Harry Heilmann, outfield, 1930–31
Miller Huggins, second base, 1904–09
Joe Kelley, outfield, 1902–06
George Kelly, first base, 1927–30
King Kelly, outfield, 1878–79
Barry Larkin, shortstop, 1986–2004
Ernie Lombardi, catcher, 1932–41
Rube Marquard, pitcher, 1921
Christy Mathewson, pitcher, 1916
Bill McKechnie, second base, 1916–17
Joe Morgan, second base, 1972–79
Tony Perez, first base, 1964–76 and 1984–86
Old Hoss Radbourn, pitcher, 1891
Eppa Rixey, pitcher, 1921–33
Frank Robinson, outfield, 1956–65
Edd Roush, outfield, 1916–26, 1931
Amos Rusie, pitcher, 1901
Tom Seaver, pitcher, 1977–82
Al Simmons, outfield, 1939
Joe Tinker, shortstop, 1913
Dazzy Vance, pitcher, 1934
Lloyd Waner, outfield, 1941

Retired Numbers
1 ..... Fred Hutchinson
5 ..... Willard Hershberger
5 ..... Johnny Bench
8 ..... Joe Morgan
10 ..... Sparky Anderson
11 ..... Barry Larkin
13 ..... Dave Concepcion
14 ..... Pete Rose
18 ..... Ted Kluszewski
20 ..... Frank Robinson
24 ..... Tony Perez

League Leaders, Batting (Post-1900)

Batting Average, Season
Cy Seymour, 1905 ..... .377
Hal Chase, 1916 ..... .339
Edd Roush, 1917 ..... .341
Edd Roush, 1919 ..... .321
Bubbles Hargrave, 1926 ..... .353
Ernie Lombardi, 1938 ..... .342
Pete Rose, 1968 ..... .335
Pete Rose, 1969 ..... .348
Pete Rose, 1973 ..... .338

Home Runs, Season
Sam Crawford, 1901 16
Fred Odwell, 1905 9
Ted Kluszewski, 1954 49
Johnny Bench, 1970 45
Johnny Bench, 1972 40
George Foster, 1977 52
George Foster, 1978 40

RBIs, Season
Frank McCormick, 1939 128
Ted Kluszewski, 1954 141
Deron Johnson, 1965 130
Johnny Bench, 1970 148
Johnny Bench, 1972 125
Johnny Bench, 1974 129
George Foster, 1976 121
George Foster, 1977 149
George Foster, 1978 120
Dave Parker, 1985 125

Stolen Bases, Season
Jimmy Barrett, 1900 46
Bob Bescher, 1909 54
Bob Bescher, 1910 70
Bob Bescher, 1911 81
Bob Bescher, 1912 67
Lonny Frey, 1940 22
Bobby Tolan, 1970 57

Total Bases, Season
Sam Crawford, 1902 256
Cy Seymour, 1905 325
Johnny Bench, 1974 315
George Foster, 1977 388
Dave Parker, 1985 350
Dave Parker, 1986 304

Most Hits, Season
Cy Seymour, 1905 219
Hal Chase, 1916 184
Heinie Groh, 1917 182
Frank McCormick, 1938 209
Frank McCormick, 1939 209
Frank McCormick, 1940 ..... 191 (Tie)
Ted Kluszewski, 1955 192
Vada Pinson, 1961 208
Vada Pinson, 1963 204
Pete Rose, 1965 209
Pete Rose, 1968 ..... 210 (Tie)
Pete Rose, 1970 205
Pete Rose, 1972 198
Pete Rose, 1973 230
Pete Rose, 1976 215

Most Runs, Season
Bob Bescher, 1912 120
Heinie Groh, 1918 88
Billy Werber, 1939 115
Frank Robinson, 1956 122
Vada Pinson, 1959 131
Frank Robinson, 1962 134
Tommy Harper, 1965 126
Pete Rose, 1969 ..... 120 (Tie)
Joe Morgan, 1972 122
Pete Rose, 1974 110
Pete Rose, 1975 112
Pete Rose, 1976 130
George Foster, 1977 124

Batting Feats

Triple Crown Winners
[No player]

Hitting for the Cycle
John Reilly, Aug. 6, 1890
Tom Parrott, Sept. 28, 1894
Mike Mitchell, Aug. 19, 1911
Heinie Groh, July 5, 1915
Harry Craft, June 8, 1940
Frank Robinson, May 2, 1959
Eric Davis, June 2, 1989

Six Hits in a Game (Post-1900)
Tony Cuccinello, Aug. 13, 1931
Ernie Lombardi, May 9, 1937
Walker Cooper, July 6, 1949

40 or More Home Runs, Season

52 ..... George Foster, 1977
49 ..... Ted Kluszewski, 1954
47 ..... Ted Kluszewski, 1955
46 ..... Adam Dunn, 2004
45 ..... Johnny Bench, 1970
Greg Vaughn, 1999
40 ..... Ted Kluszewski, 1953
Wally Post, 1955
Tony Perez, 1970
Johnny Bench, 1972
George Foster, 1978
Ken Griffey Jr., 2000
Adam Dunn, 2005
Adam Dunn, 2006
Adam Dunn, 2007
Adam Dunn*, 2008

*8 with Ariz. D'backs and 32 with Cin. Reds.

League Leaders, Pitching (Post-1900)

Most Wins, Season

Eppa Rixey, 1922 25
Dolf Luque, 1923 27
Pete Donohue, 1926 ..... 20 (Tie)
Bucky Walters, 1939 27
Bucky Walters, 1940 22
Elmer Riddle, 1943 ..... 21 (Tie)
Bucky Walters, 1944 23
Ewell Blackwell, 1947 22
Joey Jay, 1961 ..... 21 (Tie)
Tom Seaver, 1981 14
Danny Jackson, 1988 ..... 23 (Tie)
Aaron Harang, 2006 ..... 16 (Tie)

Most Strikeouts, Season

Noodles Hahn, 1901 233
Bucky Walters, 1939 ..... 137 (Tie)
Johnny Vander Meer, 1941 202
Johnny Vander Meer, 1942 186
Johnny Vander Meer, 1943 174
Ewell Blackwell, 1947 193
Jose Rijo, 1993 227
Aaron Harang, 2006 216
Johnny Cueto, 2014 ..... 242 (Tie)

Lowest ERA, Season

Dolf Luque, 1923 ..... 1.93
Dolf Luque, 1925 ..... 2.63
Bucky Walters, 1939 ..... 2.29
Bucky Walters, 1940 ..... 2.48
Elmer Riddle, 1941 ..... 2.24
Ed Heusser, 1944 ..... 2.38

Most Saves, Season

Wayne Granger, 1970 35
Clay Carroll, 1972 37
Rawly Eastwick, 1975 ..... 22 (Tie)
Rawly Eastwick, 1977 26
John Franco, 1988 39
Jeff Brantley, 1996 44
Jeff Shaw, 1997 42

Best Won–Lost Percentage, Season

Dutch Ruether, 1919 ..... 19–6 ... .760
Pete Donohue, 1922 ..... 18–9 ... .667
Dolf Luque, 1923 ..... 27–8 ... .771
Paul Derringer, 1939 ..... 25–7 ... .781
Elmer Riddle, 1941 ..... 19–4 ... .826
Bob Purkey, 1962 ..... 23–5 ... .821
Don Gullett, 1971 ..... 16–6 ... .727
Gary Nolan, 1972 ..... 15–5 ... .750
Don Gullett, 1975 ..... 15–4 ... .789
Tom Seaver, 1979 ..... 16–6 ... .727
Tom Seaver, 1981 ..... 14–2 ... .875
Jose Rijo, 1991 ..... 15–6 ... .714

Pitching Feats

Triple Crown Winner

Bucky Walters, 1939 (27–11, 2.29 ERA, 137 SO)

20 Wins, Season

Noodles Hahn, 1901 22–19
Noodles Hahn, 1902 22–12
Noodles Hahn, 1903 22–12
Jack Harper, 1904 23–9
Bob Ewing, 1905 20–11
Jake Weimer, 1906 20–14
George Suggs, 1910 20–12
Fred Toney, 1917 24–16
Pete Schneider, 1917 20–19
Slim Sallee, 1919 21–7
Eppa Rixey, 1922 25–13
Dolf Luque, 1923 27–8
Pete Donohue, 1923 21–15
Eppa Rixey, 1923 20–15
Carl Mays, 1924 20–9
Eppa Rixey, 1925 21–11
Pete Donohue, 1925 21–14
Pete Donohue, 1926 20–14
Paul Derringer, 1935 22–13
Paul Derringer, 1938 21–14
Bucky Walters, 1939 27–11
Paul Derringer, 1939 25–7
Bucky Walters, 1940 22–10
Paul Derringer, 1940 20–12
Elmer Riddle, 1943 21–11
Bucky Walters, 1944 23–8
Ewell Blackwell, 1947 22–8
Joey Jay, 1961 21–10
Bob Purkey, 1962 23–5
Joey Jay, 1962 21–14
Jim Maloney, 1963 23–7
Sammy Ellis, 1965 22–10
Jim Maloney, 1965 20–9
Jeff Merritt, 1970 20–12
Tom Seaver*, 1977 21–6
Tom Browning, 1985 20–9
Danny Jackson, 1988 23–8
Johnny Cueto, 2014 20–9

*7–3 with N.Y. Mets and 14–3 with Cin. Reds.

No-Hitters

Jim Toney (vs. Chi. Cubs), May 2, 1917 (final: 1–0) (10 innings)
Hod Eller (vs. St.L. Cardinals), May 11, 1919 (final: 6–0)
Johnny Vander Meer (vs. Bost. Braves), June 11, 1938 (final: 3–0)
Johnny Vander Meer (vs. Bklyn. Dodgers), June 15, 1938 (final: 6–0)
Clyde Shoun (vs. Bost. Braves), May 15, 1944 (final: 1–0)
Ewell Blackwell (vs. Bost. Braves), June 18, 1947 (final: 6–0)
Jim Maloney (vs. Chi. Cubs), Aug. 9, 1965 (final: 1–0) (10 innings)
George Culver (vs. Phila. Phillies), July 29, 1968 (final: 6–1)
Jim Maloney (vs. Hous. Astros), Apr. 30, 1969 (final: 1–0)
Tom Seaver (vs. St.L. Cardinals), June 16, 1978 (final: 4–0)
Tom Browning (vs. L.A. Dodgers), Sept. 16, 1988 (final: 1–0) (perfect game)
Homer Bailey (vs. Pitt. Pirates), Sept. 28, 2012 (final: 1–0)
Homer Bailey (vs. S.F. Giants), July 2, 2013 (final: 3–0)

No-Hitters Pitched Against

Fred Pfeffer, Bost. Doves, May 8, 1907 (final: 6–0)
Tex Carleton, Bklyn. Dodgers, Apr. 30, 1940 (final: 3–0)
Lon Warneke, St.L. Cardinals, Aug. 30, 1941 (final: 2–0)
Ken Johnson, Hous. Colt .45s, Apr. 23, 1964 (final: 0–1)
Don Wilson, Hous. Astros, May 1, 1969 (final: 4–0)

Ken Holtzman, Chi. Cubs, June 3, 1971 (final: 1–0)

Rick Wise, Phila. Phillies, June 23, 1971 (final: 4–0)

Roy Halladay, Phila. Phillies, Oct. 6, 2010 (final: 4–0) (Postseason game)

Postseason Play

1919 World Series vs. Chi. White Sox (AL), won 5 games to 3

1939 World Series vs. N.Y. Yankees (AL), lost 4 games to 0

1940 World Series vs. Det. Tigers (AL), won 4 games to 3

1961 World Series vs. N.Y. Yankees (AL), lost 4 games to 1

1970 League Championship Series vs. Pitt. Pirates, won 3 games to 0
World Series vs. Balt. Orioles (AL), lost 4 games to 1

1972 League Championship Series vs. Pitt. Pirates, won 3 games to 2
World Series vs. Oak. A's (AL), lost 4 games to 3

1973 League Championship Series vs. N.Y. Mets, lost 3 games to 2

1975 League Championship Series vs. Pitt. Pirates, won 3 games to 0
World Series vs. Bost. Red Sox (AL), won 4 games to 3

1976 League Championship Series vs. Phila. Phillies, won 3 games to 0
World Series vs. N.Y. Yankees (AL), won 4 games to 0

1979 League Championship Series vs. Pitt. Pirates, lost 3 games to 0

1990 League Championship Series vs. Pitt. Pirates, won 4 games to 2
World Series vs. Oak. A's (AL), won 4 games to 0

1995 Division Series vs. L.A. Dodgers, won 3 games to 0
League Championship Series vs. Atl. Braves, lost 4 games to 0

1999 NL Wild Card Playoff Game vs. N.Y. Mets, lost

2010 Division Series vs. Phila. Phillies, lost 3 games to 0

2012 Division Series vs. S.F. Giants, lost 3 games to 2

2013 NL Wild Card Playoff Game vs. Pitt. Pirates, lost

Colorado Rockies

Dates of Operation: 1993–present (23 years)
Overall Record: 1709 wins, 1955 losses (.466)
Stadiums: Mile High Stadium, 1993–94; Coors Field, 1995–present (capacity: 50,398)

Year-by-Year Finishes

Year	Finish	Wins	Losses	Percentage	Games Behind	Manager	Attendance
					West Division		
1993	6th	67	95	.414	37.0	Don Baylor	4,483,350
1994	3rd	53	64	.453	6.5	Don Baylor	3,281,511
1995	2nd	77	67	.535	1.0	Don Baylor	3,390,037
1996	3rd	83	79	.512	8.0	Don Baylor	3,891,014
1997	3rd	83	79	.512	7.0	Don Baylor	3,888,453
1998	4th	77	85	.475	21.0	Don Baylor	3,789,347
1999	5th	72	90	.444	28.0	Jim Leyland	3,481,065
2000	4th	82	80	.506	15.0	Buddy Bell	3,285,710
2001	5th	73	89	.451	19.0	Buddy Bell	3,159,385
2002	4th	73	89	.451	25.0	Buddy Bell, Clint Hurdle	2,737,918
2003	4th	74	88	.457	26.5	Clint Hurdle	2,334,085
2004	4th	68	94	.420	25.0	Clint Hurdle	2,338,069
2005	5th	67	95	.414	15.0	Clint Hurdle	1,914,389
2006	4th	76	86	.469	12.0	Clint Hurdle	2,104,362
2007	2nd	90	73	.552	5.5	Clint Hurdle	2,376,250
2008	3rd	74	88	.457	10.0	Clint Hurdle	2,650,218
2009	2nd	92	70	.568	3.0	Clint Hurdle, Jim Tracy	2,665,080
2010	3rd	83	79	.512	9.0	Jim Tracy	2,875,245
2011	4th	73	84	.451	21.0	Jim Tracy	2,909,777
2012	5th	64	98	.395	30.0	Jim Tracy	2,630,458
2013	5th	74	88	.457	18.0	Walt Weiss	2,793,828
2014	4th	66	96	.407	28.0	Walt Weiss	2,680,329
2015	5th	68	94	.420	24.0	Walt Weiss	2,506,789

Awards

Most Valuable Player
Larry Walker, outfield, 1997

Rookie of the Year
Jason Jennings, pitcher, 2002

Cy Young
[No pitcher]

Hall of Famers Who Played for the Rockies
[No player]

Retired Numbers
17 ..... Todd Helton

League Leaders, Batting

Batting Average, Season
Andres Galarraga, 1993 ..... .370
Larry Walker, 1998 ..... .363
Larry Walker, 1999 ..... .379
Todd Helton, 2000 ..... .372
Larry Walker, 2001 ..... .350
Matt Holliday, 2007 ..... .340
Carlos Gonzalez, 2010 ..... .336
Michael Cuddyer, 2013 ..... .331
Justin Morneau, 2014 ..... .319

Home Runs, Season
Dante Bichette, 1995 40
Andres Galarraga, 1996 47
Larry Walker, 1997 49
Nolan Arenado, 2015 ..... 42 (Tie)

RBIs, Season
Dante Bichette, 1995 128
Andres Galarraga, 1996 150
Andres Galarraga, 1997 140
Todd Helton, 2000 147
Preston Wilson, 2003 141
Vinny Castilla, 2004 131
Matt Holliday, 2007 137
Nolan Arenado, 2015 130

Stolen Bases, Season
Eric Young, 1996 53
Juan Pierre, 2001 ..... 46 (Tie)
Willy Taveras, 2007 68
Eric Young Jr.*, 2013 46

*38 with N.Y. Mets and 8 with Colo. Rockies.

Total Bases, Season

Dante Bichette, 1995 359
Ellis Burks, 1996 392
Larry Walker, 1997 409
Todd Helton, 2000 405
Matt Holliday, 2007 386
Carlos Gonzalez, 2010 351
Nolan Arenado, 2015 354

Most Hits, Season

Dante Bichette, 1995 ..... 197 (Tie)
Dante Bichette, 1998 219
Todd Helton, 2000 216
Matt Holliday, 2007 216
Carlos Gonzalez, 2010 197

Most Runs, Season

Ellis Burks, 1996 142

Batting Feats

Triple Crown Winners

[No player]

Hitting for the Cycle

Dante Bichette, June 10, 1998
Neifi Perez, July 25, 1998
Todd Helton, June 19, 1999
Mike Lansing, June 18, 2000
Troy Tulowitzki, Aug. 10, 2009
Carlos Gonzalez, July 31, 2010
Michael Cuddyer, Aug. 17, 2014

Six Hits in a Game

Andres Galarraga, July 3, 1995
Charlie Blackmon, Apr. 4, 2014

40 or More Home Runs, Season

49 ..... Larry Walker, 1997
Todd Helton, 2001
47 ..... Andres Galarraga, 1996
46 ..... Vinny Castilla, 1998
42 ..... Todd Helton, 2000
Nolan Arenado, 2015
41 ..... Andres Galarraga, 1997
40 ..... Dante Bichette, 1995
Ellis Burks, 1996
Vinny Castilla, 1996
Vinny Castilla, 1997

League Leaders, Pitching

Most Wins, Season

[No pitcher]

Most Strikeouts, Season

[No pitcher]

Lowest ERA, Season

[No pitcher]

Most Saves, Season

[No pitcher]

Best Won–Lost Percentage, Season

Marvin Freeman, 1994 . 10–2 ... .833
Ubaldo Jimenez, 2010 .. 19–8 ... .704

Pitching Feats

20 Wins, Season

[No pitcher]

No-Hitters

Ubaldo Jimenez (vs. Atl. Braves), Apr. 17, 2010 (final: 4–0)

No-Hitters Pitched Against

Al Leiter, Fla. Marlins, May 11, 1996 (final: 11–0)
Hideo Nomo, L.A. Dodgers, Sept. 17, 1996 (final: 9–0)
Clayton Kershaw, L.A. Dodgers, June 18, 2014 (final: 8–0)

Postseason Play

1995 Division Series vs. Atl. Braves, lost 3 games to 1
NL Wild Card Playoff Game vs. S.D. Padres, won
2007 Division Series vs. Phila. Phillies, won 3 games to 0
League Championship Series vs. Ariz. D'backs, won 4 games to 0
World Series vs. Bost. Red Sox (AL), lost 4 games to 0
2009 Division Series vs. Phila. Phillies, lost 3 games to 0

Los Angeles Dodgers

Dates of Operation: 1958–present (58 years)
Overall Record: 4957 wins, 4282 losses (.536)
Stadiums: L.A. Memorial Coliseum, 1958–61; Dodger Stadium (also known as Chavez Ravine), 1962–present (capacity: 56,000)

Year-by-Year Finishes

Year	Finish	Wins	Losses	Percentage	Games Behind	Manager	Attendance
1958	7th	71	83	.461	21.0	Walter Alston	1,845,556
1959	1st	88	68	.564	+2.0	Walter Alston	2,071,045
1960	4th	82	72	.532	13.0	Walter Alston	2,253,887
1961	2nd	89	65	.578	4.0	Walter Alston	1,804,250
1962	2nd	102	63	.618	1.0	Walter Alston	2,755,184
1963	1st	99	63	.611	+6.0	Walter Alston	2,538,602
1964	6th (Tie)	80	82	.494	13.0	Walter Alston	2,228,751
1965	1st	97	65	.599	+2.0	Walter Alston	2,553,577
1966	1st	95	67	.586	+1.5	Walter Alston	2,617,029
1967	8th	73	89	.451	28.5	Walter Alston	1,664,362
1968	7th	76	86	.469	21.0	Walter Alston	1,581,093
					West Division		
1969	4th	85	77	.525	8.0	Walter Alston	1,784,527
1970	2nd	87	74	.540	14.5	Walter Alston	1,697,142
1971	2nd	89	73	.549	1.0	Walter Alston	2,064,594
1972	3rd	85	70	.548	10.5	Walter Alston	1,860,858
1973	2nd	95	66	.590	3.5	Walter Alston	2,136,192
1974	1st	102	60	.630	+4.0	Walter Alston	2,632,474
1975	2nd	88	74	.543	20.0	Walter Alston	2,539,349
1976	2nd	92	70	.568	10.0	Walter Alston, Tommy Lasorda	2,386,301
1977	1st	98	64	.605	+10.0	Tommy Lasorda	2,955,087
1978	1st	95	67	.586	+2.5	Tommy Lasorda	3,347,845
1979	3rd	79	83	.488	11.5	Tommy Lasorda	2,860,954
1980	2nd	92	71	.564	1.0	Tommy Lasorda	3,249,287
1981*	1st/4th	63	47	.573	+0.5/6.0	Tommy Lasorda	2,381,292
1982	2nd	88	74	.543	1.0	Tommy Lasorda	3,608,881
1983	1st	91	71	.562	+3.0	Tommy Lasorda	3,510,313
1984	4th	79	83	.488	13.0	Tommy Lasorda	3,134,824
1985	1st	95	67	.586	+5.5	Tommy Lasorda	3,264,593
1986	5th	73	89	.451	23.0	Tommy Lasorda	3,023,208
1987	4th	73	89	.451	17.0	Tommy Lasorda	2,797,409
1988	1st	94	67	.584	+7.0	Tommy Lasorda	2,980,262
1989	4th	77	83	.481	14.0	Tommy Lasorda	2,944,653
1990	2nd	86	76	.531	5.0	Tommy Lasorda	3,002,396
1991	2nd	93	69	.574	1.0	Tommy Lasorda	3,348,170
1992	6th	63	99	.389	35.0	Tommy Lasorda	2,473,266
1993	4th	81	81	.500	23.0	Tommy Lasorda	3,170,392
1994	1st	58	56	.509	+3.5	Tommy Lasorda	2,279,355
1995	1st	78	66	.542	+1.0	Tommy Lasorda	2,766,251
1996	2nd	90	72	.556	1.0	Tommy Lasorda, Bill Russell	3,188,454
1997	2nd	88	74	.543	2.0	Bill Russell	3,319,504
1998	3rd	83	79	.512	15.0	Bill Russell, Glenn Hoffman	3,089,201
1999	3rd	77	85	.475	23.0	Davey Johnson	3,095,346
2000	2nd	86	76	.531	11.0	Davey Johnson	3,010,819

2001	3rd	86	76	.531	6.0	Jim Tracy	3,017,502
2002	3rd	92	70	.568	6.0	Jim Tracy	3,131,077
2003	2nd	85	77	.525	10.5	Jim Tracy	3,138,626
2004	1st	93	69	.574	+2.0	Jim Tracy	3,488,283
2005	4th	71	91	.438	11.0	Jim Tracy	3,603,646
2006	1st	88	74	.543	+11.5	Grady Little	3,758,545
2007	4th	82	80	.506	8.0	Grady Little	3,857,036
2008	1st	84	78	.519	+2.0	Joe Torre	3,730,553
2009	1st	95	67	.586	+3.0	Joe Torre	3,761,669
2010	4th	80	82	.494	12.0	Joe Torre	3,562,310
2011	3rd	82	79	.509	11.5	Don Mattingly	2,935,139
2012	2nd	86	76	.531	8.0	Don Mattingly	3,324,246
2013	1st	92	70	.568	+11.0	Don Mattingly	3,743,527
2014	1st	94	68	.580	+6.0	Don Mattingly	3,782,337
2015	1st	92	70	.568	+8.0	Don Mattingly	3,764,815

*Split season.

Awards

Most Valuable Player

Maury Wills, shortstop, 1962
Sandy Koufax, pitcher, 1963
Steve Garvey, first base, 1974
Kirk Gibson, outfield, 1988
Clayton Kershaw, pitcher, 2014

Rookie of the Year

Frank Howard, outfield, 1960
Jim Lefebvre, second base, 1965
Ted Sizemore, second base, 1969
Rick Sutcliffe, pitcher, 1979
Steve Howe, pitcher, 1980
Fernando Valenzuela, pitcher, 1981
Steve Sax, second base, 1982
Eric Karros, first base, 1992
Mike Piazza, catcher, 1993
Raul Mondesi, outfield, 1994
Hideo Nomo, pitcher, 1995
Todd Hollandsworth, outfield, 1996

Cy Young

Don Drysdale, 1962
Sandy Koufax, 1963
Sandy Koufax, 1965
Sandy Koufax, 1966
Mike Marshall, 1974
Fernando Valenzuela, 1981
Orel Hershiser, 1988
Eric Gagne, 2003
Clayton Kershaw, 2011
Clayton Kershaw, 2013
Clayton Kershaw, 2014

Hall of Famers Who Played for the Los Angeles Dodgers

Jim Bunning, pitcher, 1969
Gary Carter, catcher, 1991
Don Drysdale, pitcher, 1958–69
Rickey Henderson, outfield, 2003
Sandy Koufax, pitcher, 1958–66
Greg Maddux, pitcher, 2006 and 2008
Juan Marichal, pitcher, 1975
Pedro Martinez, pitcher, 1992–93
Eddie Murray, first base, 1989–91 and 1997
Mike Piazza, catcher, 1992–98
Pee Wee Reese, shortstop, 1958
Frank Robinson, outfield, 1972
Duke Snider, outfield, 1958–62
Don Sutton, pitcher, 1966–80 and 1988
Hoyt Wilhelm, pitcher, 1971–72

Retired Numbers

1 ..... Pee Wee Reese
2 ..... Tommy Lasorda
4 ..... Duke Snider
19 ..... Jim Gilliam
20 ..... Don Sutton
24 ..... Walter Alston
32 ..... Sandy Koufax
39 ..... Roy Campanella
42 ..... Jackie Robinson
53 ..... Don Drysdale

League Leaders, Batting

Batting Average, Season

Tommy Davis, 1962 ..... .346
Tommy Davis, 1963 ..... .326

Home Runs, Season

Adrian Beltre, 2004 48
Matt Kemp, 2011 39

RBIs, Season

Tommy Davis, 1962 153
Matt Kemp, 2011 125
Adrian Gonzalez, 2014 116

Stolen Bases, Season

Maury Wills, 1960 50
Maury Wills, 1961 35
Maury Wills, 1962 104
Maury Wills, 1963 40
Maury Wills, 1964 53
Maury Wills, 1965 94
Davey Lopes, 1975 77
Davey Lopes, 1976 63
Dee Gordon, 2014 64

Total Bases, Season

Matt Kemp, 2011 353

Most Hits, Season

Tommy Davis, 1962 230
Steve Garvey, 1978 202
Steve Garvey, 1980 200

Most Runs, Season

Brett Butler, 1990 112
Matt Kemp, 2011 115

Batting Feats

Triple Crown Winners

[No player]

Hitting for the Cycle

Wes Parker, May 7, 1970
Orlando Hudson, Apr. 13, 2009

Six Hits in a Game

Willie Davis, May 24, 1973*
Paul LoDuca, May 28, 2001*
Shawn Green, May 23, 2002

*Extra-inning game.

40 or More Home Runs, Season

49 ..... Shawn Green, 2001
48 ..... Adrian Beltre, 2004
43 ..... Gary Sheffield, 2000
42 ..... Shawn Green, 2002
40 ..... Mike Piazza, 1997

League Leaders, Pitching

Most Wins, Season

Don Drysdale, 1962 25
Sandy Koufax, 1963 ..... 25 (Tie)
Sandy Koufax, 1965 26
Sandy Koufax, 1966 27
Andy Messersmith, 1974 ..... 20 (Tie)
Fernando Valenzuela, 1986 21
Orel Hershiser, 1988 ..... 23 (Tie)
Derek Lowe, 2006 ..... 16 (Tie)
Clayton Kershaw, 2011 ..... 21 (Tie)
Clayton Kershaw, 2014 21

Most Strikeouts, Season

Don Drysdale, 1959 242
Don Drysdale, 1960 246
Sandy Koufax, 1961 269
Don Drysdale, 1962 232
Sandy Koufax, 1963 306
Sandy Koufax, 1965 382
Sandy Koufax, 1966 317
Fernando Valenzuela, 1981 180
Hideo Nomo, 1995 236
Clayton Kershaw, 2011 248
Clayton Kershaw, 2013 232
Clayton Kershaw, 2015 301

Lowest ERA, Season

Sandy Koufax, 1962 ..... 2.54
Sandy Koufax, 1963 ..... 1.88
Sandy Koufax, 1964 ..... 1.74
Sandy Koufax, 1965 ..... 2.04
Sandy Koufax, 1966 ..... 1.73
Don Sutton, 1980 ..... 2.21
Alejandro Pena, 1984 ..... 2.48
Kevin Brown, 2000 ..... 2.58
Clayton Kershaw, 2011 ..... 2.28
Clayton Kershaw, 2012 ..... 2.53
Clayton Kershaw, 2013 ..... 1.83
Clayton Kershaw, 2014 ..... 1.77
Zack Greinke, 2015 ..... 1.66

Most Saves, Season

Mike Marshall, 1974 21
Todd Worrell, 1996 ..... 44 (Tie)
Eric Gagne, 2003 55

Best Won–Lost Percentage, Season

Johnny Podres, 1961 ..... 18–5 . .783
Ron Perranoski, 1963 ..... 17–3 . .842
Sandy Koufax, 1964 ..... 19–5 . .792
Sandy Koufax, 1965 ..... 26–8 . .765
Tommy John, 1973 ..... 16–7 . .696
Andy Messersmith, 1974. 20–6 . .769
Orel Hershiser, 1985 ..... 19–3 . .864
Brad Penny, 2007 ..... 16–4 . .800
Zack Greinke, 2013 ..... 15–4 .789
Clayon Kershaw, 2014 ... 21–3 .875
Zack Greinke, 2015 ..... 19–3 .864

Pitching Feats

Triple Crown Winner

Sandy Koufax, 1963 (25–5, 1.88 ERA, 306 SO)
Sandy Koufax, 1964 (26–8, 2.04 ERA, 382 SO)
Sandy Koufax, 1965 (27–9 1.73 ERA, 317 SO)
Clayton Kershaw, 2011 (21–5, 2.28 ERA, 248 SO)

20 Wins, Season

Don Drysdale, 1962 25–9
Sandy Koufax, 1963 25–5
Sandy Koufax, 1965 26–8
Don Drysdale, 1965 23–12
Sandy Koufax, 1966 27–9
Bill Singer, 1969 20–12
Claude Osteen, 1969 20–15
Al Downing, 1971 20–9
Claude Osteen, 1972 20–11
Andy Messersmith, 1974 20–6
Don Sutton, 1976 21–10
Tommy John, 1977 20–7
Fernando Valenzuela, 1986 21–11
Orel Hershiser, 1988 23–8
Ramon Martinez, 1990 20–6
Clayton Kershaw, 2011 21–5
Clayton Kershaw, 2014 21–3

No-Hitters

Sandy Koufax (vs. N.Y. Mets), June 30, 1962 (final: 5–0)
Sandy Koufax (vs. S.F. Giants), May 11, 1963 (final: 8–0)
Sandy Koufax (vs. Phila. Phillies), June 4, 1964 (final: 3–0)
Sandy Koufax (vs. Chi. Cubs), Sept. 9, 1965 (final: 1–0) (perfect game)
Bill Singer (vs. Phila. Phillies), July 20, 1970 (final: 5–0)
Jerry Reuss (vs. S.F. Giants), June 27, 1980 (final: 8–0)
Fernando Valenzuela (vs. St.L. Cardinals), June 29, 1990 (final: 6–0)
Kevin Gross (vs. S.F. Giants), Aug. 17, 1992 (final: 2–0)
Ramon Martinez (vs. Fla. Marlins), July 14, 1995 (final: 7–0)
Hideo Nomo (vs. Colo. Rockies), Sept. 17, 1996 (final: 9–0)
Josh Beckett (vs. Phila. Phillies), May 25, 2014 (final: 6–0)
Clayton Kershaw (vs. Colo. Rockies), June 18, 2014 (final: 8–0)

No-Hitters Pitched Against

John Candelaria, Pitt. Pirates, Aug. 9, 1976 (final: 2–0)
Nolan Ryan, Hous. Astros, Sept. 26, 1981 (final: 5–0)
Tom Browning, Cin. Reds, Sept. 16, 1988 (final: 1–0) (perfect game)
Dennis Martinez, Mont. Expos, July 28, 1991 (final: 2–0) (perfect game)
Kent Mercker, Atl. Braves, Apr. 8, 1994 (final: 6–0)
Kevin Millwood, Charlie Furbush, Stephen Pryor, Lucas Luetge, Brandon League, Tom Wilhelmsen, Sea. Mariners, June 8, 2012 (final: 1–0)
Mike Fiers, Hous. Astros, Aug. 21, 2015 (final: 3–0)
Jake Arrieta, Chi. Cubs, Aug. 30, 2015 (final: 2–0)

Postseason Play

1959 Pennant Playoff Series vs. Milw. Braves, won 2 games to 0
World Series vs. Chi. White Sox (AL), won 4 games to 2
1962 Pennant Playoff Series vs. S.F. Giants, lost 2 games to 1
1963 World Series vs. N.Y. Yankees (AL), won 4 games to 0
1965 World Series vs. Min. Twins (AL), won 4 games to 3
1966 World Series vs. Balt. Orioles (AL), lost 4 games to 0
1974 League Championship Series vs. Pitt. Pirates, won 3 games to 1
World Series vs. Oak. A's (AL) lost 4 games to 1

1977 League Championship Series vs. Phila. Phillies, won 3 games to 1
World Series vs. N.Y. Yankees (AL), lost 4 games to 2

1978 League Championship Series vs. Phila. Phillies, won 3 games to 1
World Series vs. N.Y. Yankees (AL), lost 4 games to 2

1980 NL West Playoff Game vs. Hous. Astros, lost

1981 First-Half Division Playoff Series vs. Hous. Astros, won 3 games to 2
League Championship Series vs. Mont. Expos, won 3 games to 2
World Series vs. N.Y. Yankees (AL), won 4 games to 2

1983 League Championship Series vs. Phila. Phillies, lost 3 games to 1

1985 League Championship Series vs. St.L. Cardinals, lost 4 games to 2

1988 League Championship Series vs. N.Y. Mets, won 4 games to 3
World Series vs. Oak. A's (AL), won 4 games to 1

1995 Division Series vs. Cin. Reds, lost 3 games to 0

1996 Division Series vs. Atl. Braves, lost 3 games to 0

2004 Division Series vs. St.L. Cardinals, lost 3 games to 1

2006 Division Series vs. N.Y. Mets, lost 3 games to 0

2008 Division Series vs. Chi. Cubs, won 3 games to 0
League Championship Series vs. Phila. Phillies lost 4 games to 1

2009 Division Series vs. St.L. Cardinals, won 3 games to 0
League Championship Series vs. Phila. Phillies, lost 4 games to 1

2013 Division Series vs. Atl. Braves, won 3 games to 1
League Championship Series vs. St.L. Cardinals, lost 4 games to 2

2014 Division Series vs. St.L. Cardinals, lost 3 games to 1

2015 Division Series vs. N.Y. Mets, lost 3 games to 2

Miami Marlins

Dates of Operation: 1993–present (23 years)
Overall Record: 1714 wins, 1944 losses (.468)
Stadium: Sun Life Stadium, 1993–2011; Marlins Park, 2012–present (capacity: 36,742)
Other Name: Florida Marlins (1993–2011)

Year-by-Year Finishes

Year	Finish	Wins	Losses	Percentage	Games Behind	Manager	Attendance
					East Division		
1993	6th	64	98	.395	33.0	Rene Lachemann	3,064,847
1994	5th	51	64	.443	23.5	Rene Lachemann	1,937,467
1995	4th	67	76	.469	22.5	Rene Lachemann	1,700,466
1996	3rd	80	82	.494	16.0	Rene Lachemann, John Boles	1,746,767
1997	2nd	92	70	.586	9.0	Jim Leyland	2,364,387
1998	5th	54	108	.333	52.0	Jim Leyland	1,750,395
1999	5th	64	98	.395	39.0	John Boles	1,369,421
2000	3rd	79	82	.491	15.5	John Boles	1,218,326
2001	4th	76	86	.469	12.0	John Boles, Tony Perez	1,261,220
2002	4th	79	83	.488	23.0	Jeff Torborg	813,111
2003	2nd	91	71	.562	10.0	Jeff Torborg, Jack McKeon	1,303,215
2004	3rd	83	79	.512	13.0	Jack McKeon	1,723,105
2005	3rd (Tie)	83	79	.512	7.0	Jack McKeon	1,852,608
2006	4th	78	84	.481	19.0	Joe Girardi	1,164,134
2007	5th	71	91	.438	18.0	Fredi Gonzalez	1,370,511
2008	3rd	84	77	.522	7.5	Fredi Gonzalez	1,335,075
2009	2nd	87	75	.537	6.0	Fredi Gonzalez	1,464,109
2010	3rd	80	82	.494	17.0	Fredi Gonzalez, Edwin Rodriguez	1,524,894
2011	5th	72	90	.444	30.0	Edwin Rodriguez, Brandon Hyde, Jack McKeon	1,477,462
2012	5th	69	93	.426	29.0	Ozzie Guillen	2,219,444
2013	5th	62	100	.383	34.0	Mike Redmond	1,586,322
2014	4th	77	85	.475	19.0	Mike Redmond	1,732,283
2015	3rd	71	91	.438	19.0	Mike Redmond, Dan Jennings	1,752,235

Awards

Most Valuable Player
[No player]

Rookie of the Year
Dontrelle Willis, pitcher, 2003
Hanley Ramirez, shortstop, 2006
Chris Coghlan, outfield, 2009
Jose Fernandez, pitcher, 2013

Cy Young
[No pitcher]

Hall of Famers Who Played for the Marlins
Andre Dawson, outfield, 1995–1996
Mike Piazza, catcher, 1998

Retired Numbers
[None]

League Leaders, Batting

Batting Average, Season
Hanley Ramirez, 2009 ..... .342
Dee Gordon, 2015 ..... .333

Home Runs, Season
Giancarlo Stanton, 2014 37

RBIs, Season
[No player]

Stolen Bases, Season
Chuck Carr, 1993 58
Quilvio Veras, 1995 56
Luis Castillo, 2000 62
Luis Castillo, 2002 48
Juan Pierre, 2003 65
Dee Gordon, 2015 58

Total Bases, Season
Giancarlo Stanton, 2014 299

Most Hits, Season
Juan Pierre, 2004 221
Dee Gordon, 2015 205

Most Runs, Season
Hanley Ramirez, 2008 125

Batting Feats

Triple Crown Winners

[No player]

Hitting for the Cycle

[No player]

Six Hits in a Game

[No player]

40 or More Home Runs, Season

42 .....Gary Sheffield, 1996

League Leaders, Pitching

Most Wins, Season

Dontrelle Willis, 2005 22

Most Strikeouts, Season

[No pitcher]

Lowest ERA, Season

Kevin Brown, 1996 .....1.89

Josh Johnson, 2010.....2.30

Most Saves, Season

Antonio Alfonseca, 2000 45

Armando Benitez, 2004.....47 (Tie)

Best Won–Lost Percentage, Season

[No pitcher]

Pitching Feats

20 Wins, Season

Dontrelle Willis, 2005 22–10

No-Hitters

Al Leiter (vs. Colo. Rockies), May 11, 1996 (final: 11–0)

Kevin Brown (vs. S.F. Giants), June 10, 1997 (final: 9–0)

A.J. Burnett (vs. S.D. Padres), May 12, 2001 (final: 3–0)

Anibal Sanchez (vs. Ariz. D'backs), Sept. 6, 2006 (final: 2–0)

Henderson Alvarez (vs. Det. Tigers), Sept. 29, 2013 (final: 1–0)

No-Hitters Pitched Against

Ramon Martinez, L.A. Dodgers, July 14, 1995 (final: 7–0)

Roy Halladay, Phila. Phillies, May 29, 2010 (final: 1–0) (perfect game)

Jordan Zimmermann, Wash. Nationals, Sept. 28, 2014 (final: 1–0)

Postseason Play

1997 Division Series vs. S.F. Giants, won 3 games to 0
League Championship Series vs. Atl. Braves, won 4 games to 2
World Series vs. Cle. Indians (AL), won 4 games to 3

2003 Division Series vs. S.F. Giants, won 3 games to 1
League Championship Series vs. Chi. Cubs, won 4 games to 3
World Series vs. N.Y. Yankees (AL), won 4 games to 2

Milwaukee Brewers (formerly the Seattle Pilots)

Dates of Operation: (as the Seattle Pilots) 1969 (1 year)
Overall Record: 64 wins, 98 losses (.395)
Stadium: Sick's Stadium, 1969

Dates of Operation: (as the Milwaukee Brewers) AL: 1970–97 (28 years); NL: 1998–present (12 years)
Overall Record: AL: 2136 wins, 2269 losses (.485); NL: 1196 wins, 1394 losses (.461); combined: 3332 wins, 3663 losses (.476)
Stadiums: Milwaukee County Stadium, 1970–2000; Miller Park, 2001–present (capacity: 41,900)

Year-by-Year Finishes

Year	Finish	Wins	Losses	Percentage	Games Behind	Manager	Attendance
				American League West Division			
				Sea. Pilots			
1969	6th	64	98	.395	33.0	Joe Schultz	677,944
				Milw. Brewers			
1970	4th	65	97	.401	33.0	Dave Bristol	933,690
1971	6th	69	92	.429	32.0	Dave Bristol	731,531
				American League East Division			
1972	6th	65	91	.417	21.0	Dave Bristol, Del Crandall	600,440
1973	5th	74	88	.457	23.0	Del Crandall	1,092,158
1974	5th	76	86	.469	15.0	Del Crandall	955,741
1975	5th	68	94	.420	28.0	Del Crandall	1,213,357
1976	6th	66	95	.410	32.0	Alex Grammas	1,012,164
1977	6th	67	95	.414	33.0	Alex Grammas	1,114,938
1978	3rd	93	69	.574	6.5	George Bamberger	1,601,406
1979	2nd	95	66	.590	8.0	George Bamberger	1,918,343
1980	3rd	86	76	.531	17.0	George Bamberger, Buck Rodgers	1,857,408
1981*	3rd/1st	62	47	.569	3.0/+1.5	Buck Rodgers	878,432
1982	1st	95	67	.586	+1.0	Buck Rodgers, Harvey Kuenn	1,978,896
1983	5th	87	75	.537	11.0	Harvey Kuenn	2,397,131
1984	7th	67	94	.416	36.5	Rene Lachemann	1,608,509
1985	6th	71	90	.441	28.0	George Bamberger	1,360,265
1986	6th	77	84	.478	18.0	George Bamberger, Tom Trebelhorn	1,265,041
1987	3rd	91	71	.562	7.0	Tom Trebelhorn	1,909,244
1988	3rd (Tie)	87	75	.537	2.0	Tom Trebelhorn	1,923,238
1989	4th	81	81	.500	8.0	Tom Trebelhorn	1,970,735
1990	6th	74	88	.457	14.0	Tom Trebelhorn	1,752,900
1991	4th	83	79	.512	8.0	Tom Trebelhorn	1,478,729
1992	2nd	92	70	.568	4.0	Phil Garner	1,857,314
1993	7th	69	93	.426	26.0	Phil Garner	1,688,080
				Central Division			
1994	5th	53	62	.461	15.0	Phil Garner	1,268,399
1995	4th	65	79	.451	35.0	Phil Garner	1,087,560
1996	3rd	80	82	.494	19.5	Phil Garner	1,327,155
1997	3rd	78	83	.484	8.0	Phil Garner	1,444,027

National League Central Division

1998	5th	74	88	.457	28.0	Phil Garner	1,811,548
1999	5th	74	87	.460	22.5	Phil Garner, Jim Lefebvre	1,701,796
2000	3rd	73	89	.451	22.0	Davey Lopes	1,573,621
2001	4th	68	94	.420	25.0	Davey Lopes	2,811,041
2002	6th	56	106	.346	41.0	Davey Lopes, Jerry Royster	1,969,693
2003	6th	68	94	.420	20.0	Ned Yost	1,700,354
2004	6th	67	94	.416	37.5	Ned Yost	2,062,382
2005	3rd	81	81	.500	19.0	Ned Yost	2,211,023
2006	4th	75	87	.463	8.5	Ned Yost	2,335,643
2007	2nd	83	79	.512	2.0	Ned Yost	2,869,144
2008	2nd	90	72	.556	7.5	Ned Yost, Dale Sveum	3,068,458
2009	3rd	80	82	.494	11.0	Ken Macha	3,037,451
2010	3rd	77	85	.475	14.0	Ken Macha	2,776,531
2011	1st	96	66	.593	+6.0	Ron Roenicke	3,071,373
2012	3rd	83	79	.512	14.0	Ron Roenicke	2,831,385
2013	4th	74	88	.457	23.0	Ron Roenicke	2,531,105
2014	3rd	82	80	.506	8.0	Ron Roenicke	2,797,384
2015	4th	68	94	.420	32.0	Ron Roenicke, Craig Counsell	2,542,558

*Split season.

Awards

Most Valuable Player

Rollie Fingers, pitcher, 1981
Robin Yount, shortstop, 1982
Robin Yount, outfield, 1989
Ryan Braun, outfield, 2011

Rookie of the Year

Pat Listach, shortstop, 1992
Ryan Braun, third base, 2007

Cy Young

Rollie Fingers, 1981
Pete Vuckovich, 1982

Hall of Famers Who Played for the Brewers

Hank Aaron, designated hitter, 1975–76
Rollie Fingers, pitcher, 1981–82 and 1984–85
Paul Molitor, infield and designated hitter, 1978–92
Don Sutton, pitcher, 1982–84
Robin Yount, shortstop and outfield, 1974–93

Retired Numbers

1 ..... Bud Selig
4 ..... Paul Molitor
19 ..... Robin Yount
34 ..... Rollie Fingers
44 ..... Hank Aaron

League Leaders, Batting

Batting Average, Season

[No player]

Home Runs, Season

George Scott, 1975 (AL) ..... 36 (Tie)
Gorman Thomas, 1979 (AL) 45
Ben Oglivie, 1980 (AL) ..... 41 (Tie)
Gorman Thomas, 1982 (AL) .... 39 (Tie)
Prince Fielder, 2007 (NL) 50
Ryan Braun, 2012 (NL) 41

RBIs, Season

George Scott, 1975 (AL) 109
Cecil Cooper, 1980 (AL) 122
Cecil Cooper, 1983 (AL) 126
Prince Fielder, 2009 (NL) ..... 141 (Tie)

Stolen Bases, Season

Tommy Harper, 1969 (Sea. Pilots) .. 73
Scott Podsednik, 2004 (NL) 70

Total Bases, Season

Dave May, 1973 (AL) ..... 295 (Tie)
George Scott, 1973 (AL) ..... 295 (Tie)
George Scott, 1975 (AL) 318
Cecil Cooper, 1980 (AL) 335
Robin Yount, 1982 (AL) 367
Ryan Braun, 2012 (NL) 356

Most Hits, Season

Robin Yount, 1982 (AL) 210
Paul Molitor, 1991 (AL) 216
Ryan Braun, 2009 (NL) 203

Most Runs, Season

Paul Molitor, 1982 (AL) 136
Paul Molitor, 1987 (AL) 114
Paul Molitor, 1991 (AL) 133
Ryan Braun, 2012 (NL) 108

Batting Feats

Triple Crown Winners

[No player]

Hitting for the Cycle

Mike Hegan, Sept. 3 1976 (AL)
Charlie Moore, Oct. 1, 1980 (AL)
Robin Yount, June 12, 1988 (AL)
Paul Molitor, May 15, 1991 (AL)
Chad Moeller, Apr. 27, 2004 (NL)
Jody Gerut, May 8, 2010 (NL)
George Kottaras, Sept. 3, 2011 (NL)

Six Hits in a Game

Johnny Briggs, Aug. 4, 1973 (AL)
Kevin Reimer, Aug. 24, 1993 (AL)
Jean Segura, May 28, 2013 (NL)

40 or More Home Runs, Season

50 ..... Prince Fielder, 2009 (NL)
46 ..... Prince Fielder, 2007 (NL)
45 .....Gorman Thomas, 1979 (AL)
Richie Sexson, 2001 (NL)
Richie Sexson, 2003 (NL)
41 ..... Ben Oglivie, 1980 (AL)
Ryan Braun, 2012 (NL)

League Leaders, Pitching

Most Wins, Season

Pete Vuckovich, 1981 (AL).....14 (Tie)

Most Strikeouts, Season

[No pitcher]

Lowest ERA, Season

[No pitcher]

Most Saves, Season

Ken Sanders, 1971 (AL).....31
Rollie Fingers, 1981 (AL).....28
John Axford, 2011 (NL) .....46 (Tie)

Best Won–Lost Percentage, Season

Mike Caldwell, 1979 (AL)...16–6 .727
Pete Vuckovich, 1981 (AL)..14–4 .778
Pete Vuckovich, 1982 (AL)..18–6 .750

Pitching Feats

20 Wins, Season

Jim Colborn, 1973 (AL)..... 20–12
Mike Caldwell, 1978 (AL) 22–9
Ted Higuera, 1986 (AL) 20–11

No-Hitters

Juan Nieves (AL) (vs. Balt. Orioles, AL), Apr. 15, 1987 (final: 7–0)

No-Hitters Pitched Against

Steve Busby, K.C. Royals (AL), June 19, 1974 (final: 2–0)
Scott Erickson, Min. Twins (AL), Apr. 27, 1994 (final: 6–0)
Justin Verlander, Det. Tigers (AL), June 12, 2007 (final: 6–0)

Postseason Play

1981 (AL) Second-Half Pennant Playoff Series vs. N.Y. Yankees, lost 3 games to 2
1982 (AL) League Championship Series vs. Cal. Angels, won 3 games to 2
World Series vs. St.L. Cardinals (NL), lost 4 games to 3
2008 (NL) Division Series vs. Phila. Phillies, lost 3 games to 1
2011 (NL) Division Series vs. Ariz. D'backs, won 3 games to 2
(NL) League Championship Series vs. St.L. Cardinals, lost 4 games to 2

New York Mets

Dates of Operation: 1962–present (54 years)
Overall Record: 4128 wins, 4499 losses (.478)
Stadiums: Polo Grounds, 1962–63; Shea Stadium, 1964–2008; Citi Field, 2009–present (capacity: 41,922)

Year-by-Year Finishes

Year	Finish	Wins	Losses	Percentage	Games Behind	Manager	Attendance
1962	10th	40	120	.250	60.5	Casey Stengel	922,530
1963	10th	51	111	.315	48.0	Casey Stengel	1,080,108
1964	10th	53	109	.327	40.0	Casey Stengel	1,732,597
1965	10th	50	112	.309	47.0	Casey Stengel, Wes Westrum	1,768,389
1966	9th	66	95	.410	28.5	Wes Westrum	1,932,693
1967	10th	61	101	.377	40.5	Wes Westrum, Salty Parker	1,565,492
1968	9th	73	89	.451	24.0	Gil Hodges	1,781,657
					East Division		
1969	1st	100	62	.617	+8.0	Gil Hodges	2,175,373
1970	3rd	83	79	.512	6.0	Gil Hodges	2,697,479
1971	3rd (Tie)	83	79	.512	14.0	Gil Hodges	2,266,680
1972	3rd	83	73	.532	13.5	Yogi Berra	2,134,185
1973	1st	82	79	.509	+1.5	Yogi Berra	1,912,390
1974	5th	71	91	.438	17.0	Yogi Berra	1,722,209
1975	3rd (Tie)	82	80	.506	10.5	Yogi Berra, Roy McMillan	1,730,566
1976	3rd	86	76	.531	15.0	Joe Frazier	1,468,754
1977	6th	64	98	.395	37.0	Joe Frazier, Joe Torre	1,066,825
1978	6th	66	96	.407	24.0	Joe Torre	1,007,328
1979	6th	63	99	.389	35.0	Joe Torre	788,905
1980	5th	67	95	.414	24.0	Joe Torre	1,192,073
1981*	5th/4th	41	62	.398	15.0/5.5	Joe Torre	704,244
1982	6th	65	97	.401	27.0	George Bamberger	1,323,036
1983	6th	68	94	.420	22.0	George Bamberger, Frank Howard	1,112,774
1984	2nd	90	72	.556	6.5	Davey Johnson	1,842,695
1985	2nd	98	64	.605	3.0	Davey Johnson	2,761,601
1986	1st	108	54	.667	+21.5	Davey Johnson	2,767,601
1987	2nd	92	70	.568	3.0	Davey Johnson	3,034,129
1988	1st	100	60	.625	+15.0	Davey Johnson	3,055,445
1989	2nd	87	75	.537	6.0	Davey Johnson	2,918,710
1990	2nd	91	71	.562	4.0	Davey Johnson, Bud Harrelson	2,732,745
1991	5th	77	84	.478	20.5	Bud Harrelson, Mike Cubbage	2,284,484
1992	5th	72	90	.444	24.0	Jeff Torborg	1,779,534
1993	7th	59	103	.364	38.0	Jeff Torborg, Dallas Green	1,873,183
1994	3rd	55	58	.487	18.5	Dallas Green	1,151,471
1995	2nd (Tie)	69	75	.479	21.0	Dallas Green	1,273,183
1996	4th	71	91	.438	25.0	Dallas Green, Bobby Valentine	1,588,323
1997	3rd	88	74	.543	13.0	Bobby Valentine	1,766,174
1998	2nd	88	74	.543	18.0	Bobby Valentine	2,287,942
1999	2nd	97	66	.595	6.5	Bobby Valentine	2,725,668
2000	2nd	94	68	.580	1.0	Bobby Valentine	2,800,221
2001	3rd	82	80	.506	6.0	Bobby Valentine	2,658,279
2002	5th	75	86	.466	26.5	Bobby Valentine	2,804,838
2003	5th	66	95	.410	34.5	Art Howe	2,140,599
2004	4th	71	91	.438	25.0	Art Howe	2,318,321

2005	3rd	83	79	.512	7.0	Willie Randolph	2,829,931
2006	1st	97	65	.599	+12.0	Willie Randolph	3,379,535
2007	2nd	88	74	.543	1.0	Willie Randolph	3,853,949
2008	2nd	89	73	.549	3.0	Willie Randolph, Jerry Manuel	4,042,047
2009	4th	70	92	.432	23.0	Jerry Manuel	3,154,262
2010	4th	79	83	.488	18.0	Jerry Manuel	2,559,738
2011	4th	77	85	.475	25.0	Terry Collins	2,352,596
2012	4th	74	88	.457	24.0	Terry Collins	2,242,803
2013	3rd	74	88	.457	22.0	Terry Collins	2,135,657
2014	2nd	79	83	.488	17.0	Terry Collins	2,148,808
2015	1st	90	72	.556	+7.0	Terry Collins	2,569,753

*Split season.

Awards

Most Valuable Player

R.A. Dickey, pitcher, 2012

Rookie of the Year

Tom Seaver, pitcher, 1967
Jon Matlack, pitcher, 1972
Darryl Strawberry, outfield, 1983
Dwight Gooden, pitcher, 1984
Jacob deGrom, pitcher, 2014

Cy Young

Tom Seaver, 1969
Tom Seaver, 1973
Tom Seaver, 1975
Dwight Gooden, 1985
R.A. Dickey, 2012

Hall of Famers Who Played for the Mets

Roberto Alomar, second base, 2002–03
Tom Glavine, pitcher, 2003–07
Richie Ashburn, outfield, 1962
Yogi Berra, catcher, 1965
Gary Carter, catcher, 1985–89
Tom Glavine, pitcher, 2003–07
Rickey Henderson, outfield, 1999–2000
Pedro Martinez, pitcher, 2005–08
Willie Mays, outfield, 1972–73
Eddie Murray, first base, 1992–93
Mike Piazza, catcher and first base, 1998–2005
Nolan Ryan, pitcher, 1966 and 1968–71
Tom Seaver, pitcher, 1967–77 and 1983
Duke Snider, outfield, 1963
Warren Spahn, pitcher, 1965
Joe Torre, first base and third base, 1975–77

Retired Numbers

14 ..... Gil Hodges
31 ..... Mike Piazza
37 ..... Casey Stengel
41 ..... Tom Seaver

League Leaders, Batting

Batting Average, Season

Jose Reyes, 2011 ..... .337

Home Runs, Season

Dave Kingman, 1982 37
Darryl Strawberry, 1988 39
Howard Johnson, 1991 38

RBIs, Season

Howard Johnson, 1991 117

Stolen Bases, Season

Jose Reyes, 2005 60
Jose Reyes, 2006 64
Jose Reyes, 2007 78
Eric Young, 2013 ..... 46*

*8 with Colo. Rockies and 38 with N.Y. Mets.

Total Bases, Season

[No player]

Most Hits, Season

Lance Johnson, 1996 227
Jose Reyes, 2008 204

Most Runs, Season

Howard Johnson, 1989 ..... 104 (Tie)

Batting Feats

Triple Crown Winners

[No player]

Hitting for the Cycle

Jim Hickman, Aug. 7, 1963
Tommie Agee, July 6, 1970
Mike Phillips, June 25, 1976
Keith Hernandez, July 4, 1985
Kevin McReynolds, Aug. 1, 1989
Alex Ochoa, July 3, 1996
John Olerud, Sept. 11, 1997
Eric Valent, July 29, 2004
Jose Reyes, June 21, 2006
Scott Hairston, Apr. 27, 2012

Six Hits in a Game

Edgardo Alfonzo, Aug. 30, 1999

40 or More Home Runs, Season

41 ..... Todd Hundley, 1996
Carlos Beltran, 2006
40 ..... Mike Piazza, 1999

League Leaders, Pitching

Most Wins, Season

Tom Seaver, 1969 25
Tom Seaver, 1975 22
Dwight Gooden, 1985 24

Most Strikeouts, Season

Tom Seaver, 1970 283
Tom Seaver, 1971 289
Tom Seaver, 1973 251
Tom Seaver, 1975 243
Tom Seaver, 1976 235
Dwight Gooden, 1984 276
Dwight Gooden, 1985 268
David Cone, 1990 233
David Cone, 1991 241
R.A. Dickey, 2012 230

Lowest ERA, Season

Tom Seaver, 1970 ..... 2.81
Tom Seaver, 1971 ..... 1.76
Tom Seaver, 1973 ..... 2.08
Craig Swan, 1978 ..... 2.43

Dwight Gooden, 1985 ..... 1.53
Johan Santana, 2008 ..... 2.53

Most Saves, Season

John Franco, 1990 33
John Franco, 1994 30

Best Won–Lost Percentage, Season

Tom Seaver, 1969 ..... 25–7 ... .781
Bob Ojeda, 1986 ..... 18–5 ... .783
Dwight Gooden, 1987 .. 15–7 ... .682
David Cone, 1988 ..... 20–3 ... .870

Pitching Feats

Triple Crown Winner

Dwight Gooden, 1985 (24–4, 1.53 ERA, 268 SO)

20 Wins, Season

Tom Seaver, 1969 25–7
Tom Seaver, 1971 20–10
Tom Seaver, 1972 21–12
Tom Seaver, 1975 22–9
Jerry Koosman, 1976 21–10
Dwight Gooden, 1985 24–4
David Cone, 1988 20–3
Frank Viola, 1990 20–12
R.A. Dickey, 2012 20–6

No-Hitters

Johan Santana (vs. St.L. Cardinals), June 1, 2012 (final: 8–0)

No-Hitters Pitched Against

Sandy Koufax, L.A. Dodgers, June 30, 1962 (final: 5–0)
Jim Bunning, Phila. Phillies, June 21, 1964 (final: 6–0) (perfect game)
Bob Moose, Pitt. Pirates, Sept. 20, 1969 (final: 4–0)
Bill Stoneman, Mont. Expos, Oct. 2, 1972 (final: 7–0)
Ed Halicki, S.F. Giants, Aug. 24, 1975 (final: 6–0)
Darryl Kile, Hous. Astros, Sept. 8, 1993 (final: 7–1)
Chris Heston, S.F. Giants, June 9, 2015 (final: 5–0)
Max Scherzer, Wash. Nationals, Oct. 3, 2015 (final: 2–0)

Postseason Play

1969 League Championship Series vs. Atl. Braves, won 3 games to 0
World Series vs. Balt. Orioles (AL), won 4 games to 1
1973 League Championship Series vs. Cin. Reds, won 3 games to 2
World Series vs. Oak. A's (AL), lost 4 games to 3
1986 League Championship Series vs. Hous. Astros, won 4 games to 2
World Series vs. Bost. Red Sox (AL), won 4 games to 3
1988 League Championship Series vs. L.A. Dodgers, lost 4 games to 3
1999 NL Wild Card Playoff Game vs. Cin. Reds, won
Division Series vs. Ariz. D'backs, won 3 games to 1
League Championship Series vs. Atl. Braves, lost 4 games to 2
2000 Division Series vs. S.F. Giants, won 3 games to 1
League Championship Series vs. St.L. Cardinals, won 4 games to 1
World Series vs. N.Y. Yankees (AL), lost 4 games to 1
2006 Division Series vs. L.A. Dodgers, won 3 games to 0
League Championship Series vs. St.L. Cardinals, lost 4 games to 3
2015 Division Series vs. L.A. Dodgers, won 3 games to 2
League Championship Series vs. Chi. Cubs, won 4 games to 0
World Series vs. K.C. Royals (AL), lost 4 games to 1

Philadelphia Phillies

Dates of Operation: 1876, 1883–present (134 years)

Overall Record: 9541 wins, 10,696 losses (.471)

Stadiums: Jefferson Street Grounds, 1876; Recreation Park, 1883–86; Huntington Grounds, 1887–94; University of Pennsylvania Athletic Field, 1894; Baker Bowl, 1895–1938; Columbia Park, 1903; Shibe Park (also known as Connie Mack Stadium), 1927; 1938–70; Veterans Stadium, 1971–2003; Citizens Bank Park, 2004–present (capacity: 43,651)

Other Names: Quakers, Live Wires, Blue Jays

Year-by-Year Finishes

Year	Finish	Wins	Losses	Percentage	Games Behind	Manager	Attendance
1876	7th	14	45	.237	34.5	Al Wright	not available
1883	8th	17	81	.173	46.0	Robert Ferguson	not available
1884	6th	39	73	.348	45.0	Harry Wright	not available
1885	3rd	56	54	.509	30.0	Harry Wright	not available
1886	4th	71	43	.622	19.0	Harry Wright	not available
1887	2nd	75	48	.610	3.5	Harry Wright	not available
1888	3rd	69	61	.531	15.5	Harry Wright	not available
1889	4th	63	64	.496	20.5	Harry Wright	not available
1890	3rd	78	54	.591	9.5	Harry Wright	not available
1891	4th	68	69	.496	18.5	Harry Wright	not available
1892	4th	87	66	.569	16.5	Harry Wright	not available
1893	4th	72	57	.558	13.5	Harry Wright	not available
1894	4th	71	56	.559	17.5	Arthur Irwin	not available
1895	3rd	78	53	.595	9.5	Arthur Irwin	not available
1896	8th	62	68	.477	28.5	William Nash	not available
1897	10th	55	77	.417	38.0	George Stallings	not available
1898	6th	78	71	.523	24.0	George Stallings, Bill Shettsline	not available
1899	3rd	94	58	.618	5.0	Bill Shettsline	not available
1900	3rd	75	63	.543	8.0	Bill Shettsline	not available
1901	2nd	83	57	.593	7.5	Bill Shettsline	234,937
1902	7th	56	81	.409	46.0	Bill Shettsline	112,066
1903	7th	49	86	.363	39.5	Chief Zimmer	151,729
1904	8th	52	100	.342	53.5	Hugh Duffy	140,771
1905	4th	83	69	.546	21.5	Hugh Duffy	317,932
1906	4th	71	82	.464	45.5	Hugh Duffy	294,680
1907	3rd	83	64	.565	21.5	Bill Murray	341,216
1908	4th	83	71	.539	16.0	Bill Murray	420,660
1909	5th	74	79	.484	36.5	Bill Murray	303,177
1910	4th	78	75	.510	25.5	Red Dooin	296,597
1911	4th	79	73	.520	19.5	Red Dooin	416,000
1912	5th	73	79	.480	30.5	Red Dooin	250,000
1913	2nd	88	63	.583	12.5	Red Dooin	470,000
1914	6th	74	80	.481	20.5	Red Dooin	138,474
1915	1st	90	62	.592	+7.0	Pat Moran	449,898
1916	2nd	91	62	.595	2.5	Pat Moran	515,365
1917	2nd	87	65	.572	10.0	Pat Moran	354,428
1918	6th	55	68	.447	26.0	Pat Moran	122,266
1919	8th	47	90	.343	47.5	Jack Coombs, Gavvy Cravath	240,424

1920	8th	62	91	.405	30.5	Gavvy Cravath	330,998
1921	8th	51	103	.331	43.5	Bill Donovan, Kaiser Wilhelm	273,961
1922	7th	57	96	.373	35.5	Kaiser Wilhelm	232,471
1923	8th	50	104	.325	45.5	Art Fletcher	228,168
1924	7th	55	96	.364	37.0	Art Fletcher	299,818
1925	6th (Tie)	68	85	.444	27.0	Art Fletcher	304,905
1926	8th	58	93	.384	29.5	Art Fletcher	240,600
1927	8th	51	103	.331	43.0	Stuffy McInnis	305,420
1928	8th	43	109	.283	51.0	Burt Shotton	182,168
1929	5th	71	82	.464	27.5	Burt Shotton	281,200
1930	8th	52	102	.338	40.0	Burt Shotton	299,007
1931	6th	66	88	.429	35.0	Burt Shotton	284,849
1932	4th	78	76	.506	12.0	Burt Shotton	268,914
1933	7th	60	92	.395	31.0	Burt Shotton	156,421
1934	7th	56	93	.376	37.0	Jimmie Wilson	169,885
1935	7th	64	89	.418	35.5	Jimmie Wilson	205,470
1936	8th	54	100	.351	38.0	Jimmie Wilson	249,219
1937	7th	61	92	.399	34.5	Jimmie Wilson	212,790
1938	8th	45	105	.300	43.0	Jimmie Wilson, Hans Lobert	166,111
1939	8th	45	106	.298	50.5	Doc Prothro	277,973
1940	8th	50	103	.327	50.0	Doc Prothro	207,177
1941	8th	43	111	.279	57.0	Doc Prothro	231,401
1942	8th	42	109	.278	62.5	Hans Lobert	230,183
1943	7th	64	90	.416	41.0	Bucky Harris, Fred Fitzsimmons	466,975
1944	8th	61	92	.399	43.5	Fred Fitzsimmons	369,586
1945	8th	46	108	.299	52.0	Fred Fitzsimmons, Ben Chapman	285,057
1946	5th	69	85	.448	28.0	Ben Chapman	1,045,247
1947	7th (Tie)	62	92	.403	32.0	Ben Chapman	907,332
1948	6th	66	88	.429	25.5	Ben Chapman, Dusty Cooke, Eddie Sawyer	767,429
1949	3rd	81	73	.526	16.0	Eddie Sawyer	819,698
1950	1st	91	63	.591	+2.0	Eddie Sawyer	1,217,035
1951	5th	73	81	.474	23.5	Eddie Sawyer	937,658
1952	4th	87	67	.565	9.5	Eddie Sawyer, Steve O'Neill	775,417
1953	3rd (Tie)	83	71	.539	22.0	Steve O'Neill	853,644
1954	4th	75	79	.487	22.0	Steve O'Neill, Terry Moore	738,991
1955	4th	77	77	.500	21.5	Mayo Smith	922,886
1956	5th	71	83	.461	22.0	Mayo Smith	934,798
1957	5th	77	77	.500	19.0	Mayo Smith	1,146,230
1958	8th	69	85	.448	23.0	Mayo Smith, Eddie Sawyer	931,110
1959	8th	64	90	.416	23.0	Eddie Sawyer	802,815
1960	8th	59	95	.383	36.0	Eddie Sawyer, Andy Cohen, Gene Mauch	862,205
1961	8th	47	107	.305	46.0	Gene Mauch	590,039
1962	7th	81	80	.503	20.0	Gene Mauch	762,034
1963	4th	87	75	.537	12.0	Gene Mauch	907,141
1964	2nd (Tie)	92	70	.568	1.0	Gene Mauch	1,425,891
1965	6th	85	76	.528	11.5	Gene Mauch	1,166,376
1966	4th	87	75	.537	8.0	Gene Mauch	1,108,201
1967	5th	82	80	.506	19.5	Gene Mauch	828,888
1968	7th (Tie)	76	86	.469	21.0	Gene Mauch, George Myatt, Bob Skinner	664,546

East Division

1969	5th	63	99	.389	37.0	Bob Skinner, George Myatt	519,414
1970	5th	73	88	.453	15.5	Frank Lucchesi	708,247
1971	6th	67	95	.414	30.0	Frank Lucchesi	1,511,223
1972	6th	59	97	.378	37.5	Frank Lucchesi, Paul Owens	1,343,329
1973	6th	71	91	.438	11.5	Danny Ozark	1,475,934
1974	3rd	80	82	.494	8.0	Danny Ozark	1,808,648
1975	2nd	86	76	.531	6.5	Danny Ozark	1,909,233
1976	1st	101	61	.623	+9.0	Danny Ozark	2,480,150
1977	1st	101	61	.623	+5.0	Danny Ozark	2,700,070
1978	1st	90	72	.556	+1.5	Danny Ozark	2,583,389
1979	4th	84	78	.519	14.0	Danny Ozark, Dallas Green	2,775,011
1980	1st	91	71	.562	+1.0	Dallas Green	2,651,650
1981*	1st/3rd	59	48	.551	+1.5/4.5	Dallas Green	1,638,752
1982	2nd	89	73	.549	3.0	Pat Corrales	2,376,394
1983	1st	90	72	.556	+6.0	Pat Corrales, Paul Owens	2,128,339
1984	4th	81	81	.500	15.5	Paul Owens	2,062,693
1985	5th	75	87	.463	26.0	John Felske	1,830,350
1986	2nd	86	75	.534	21.5	John Felske	1,933,335
1987	4th (Tie)	80	82	.494	15.0	John Felske, Lee Elia	2,100,110
1988	6th	65	96	.404	35.5	Lee Elia, John Vukovich	1,990,041
1989	6th	67	95	.414	26.0	Nick Leyva	1,861,985
1990	4th (Tie)	77	85	.475	18.0	Nick Leyva	1,992,484
1991	3rd	78	84	.481	20.0	Nick Leyva, Jim Fregosi	2,050,012
1992	6th	70	92	.432	26.0	Jim Fregosi	1,927,448
1993	1st	97	65	.599	+3.0	Jim Fregosi	3,137,674
1994	4th	54	61	.470	20.5	Jim Fregosi	2,290,971
1995	2nd (Tie)	69	75	.479	21.0	Jim Fregosi	2,043,598
1996	5th	67	95	.414	29.0	Jim Fregosi	1,801,677
1997	5th	68	94	.420	33.0	Terry Francona	1,490,638
1998	3rd	75	87	.463	31.0	Terry Francona	1,715,702
1999	3rd	77	85	.475	26.0	Terry Francona	1,825,337
2000	5th	65	97	.401	30.0	Terry Francona	1,612,769
2001	2nd	86	76	.531	2.0	Larry Bowa	1,782,460
2002	3rd	80	81	.497	21.5	Larry Bowa	1,618,141
2003	3rd	86	76	.531	15.0	Larry Bowa	2,259,940
2004	2nd	86	76	.531	10.0	Larry Bowa, Gary Varsho	3,250,092
2005	2nd	88	74	.543	2.0	Charlie Manuel	2,665,304
2006	2nd	85	77	.525	12.0	Charlie Manuel	2,701,815
2007	1st	89	73	.549	+1.0	Charlie Manuel	3,108,325
2008	1st	92	70	.568	+3.0	Charlie Manuel	3,422,583
2009	1st	93	69	.574	+6.0	Charlie Manuel	3,600,693
2010	1st	97	65	.599	+6.0	Charlie Manuel	3,377,322
2011	1st	102	60	.630	+13.0	Charlie Manuel	3,680,718
2012	3rd	81	81	.500	17.0	Charlie Manuel	3,565,718
2013	4th	73	89	.451	23.0	Charlie Manuel, Ryne Sandberg	3,012,403
2014	5th	73	89	.451	23.0	Ryne Sandberg	2,423,852
2015	5th	63	99	.389	27.0	Ryne Sandberg, Pete Mackanin	1,831,080

*Split season.

Awards

Most Valuable Player

Chuck Klein, outfield, 1932
Jim Konstanty, pitcher, 1950
Mike Schmidt, third base, 1980
Mike Schmidt, third base, 1981
Mike Schmidt, third base, 1986
Ryan Howard, first base, 2006
Jimmy Rollins, shortstop, 2007

Rookie of the Year

Jack Sanford, pitcher, 1957
Dick Allen, third base, 1964
Scott Rolen, third base, 1997
Ryan Howard, first base, 2005

Cy Young

Steve Carlton, 1972
Steve Carlton, 1977
Steve Carlton, 1980
Steve Carlton, 1982
John Denny, 1983
Steve Bedrosian, 1987
Roy Halladay, 2010

Hall of Famers Who Played for the Phillies

Grover C. Alexander, pitcher, 1911–17 and 1930
Richie Ashburn, outfield, 1948–59
Dave Bancroft, shortstop, 1915–20
Chief Bender, pitcher, 1916–17
Dan Brouthers, first base, 1896
Jim Bunning, pitcher, 1964–67 and 1970–71
Steve Carlton, pitcher, 1972–86
Roger Connor, first base, 1892
Ed Delahanty, outfield, 1888–89 and 1891–1901
Hugh Duffy, outfield, 1904–06
Johnny Evers, second base, 1917
Elmer Flick, outfield, 1898–1901
Jimmie Foxx, first base, 1945
Billy Hamilton, outfield, 1890–95
Ferguson Jenkins, pitcher, 1965–66
Hughie Jennings, infield, 1901–02
Tim Keefe, pitcher, 1891–93
Chuck Klein, outfield, 1928–33, 1936–39, and 1940–44
Nap Lajoie, second base and first base, 1896–1900
Pedro Martinez, pitcher, 2009
Tommy McCarthy, outfield, 1886–87
Joe Morgan, second base, 1983
Kid Nichols, pitcher, 1905–06
Tony Perez, first base, 1983
Eppa Rixey, pitcher, 1912–17 and 1919–20
Robin Roberts, pitcher, 1948–61
Ryne Sandberg, shortstop, 1981
Mike Schmidt, third base, 1972–89
Casey Stengel, outfield, 1920–21
Sam Thompson, outfield, 1889–98
Lloyd Waner, outfield, 1942
Hack Wilson, outfield, 1934

Retired Numbers

PA.....Grover C. Alexander
HK.....Harry Kalas
CK.....Chuck Klein
1.....Richie Ashburn
14.....Jim Bunning
20.....Mike Schmidt
32.....Steve Carlton
36.....Robin Roberts

League Leaders, Batting (Post-1900)

Batting Average, Season

Sherry Magee, 1910..... .331
Lefty O'Doul, 1929..... .398
Chuck Klein, 1933..... .368
Harry Walker*, 1947..... .363
Richie Ashburn, 1955..... .338
Richie Ashburn, 1958..... .350

*.200 with St.L. Cardinals and .371 with Phila. Phillies.

Home Runs, Season

Gavvy Cravath, 1913.....19
Gavvy Cravath, 1914.....19
Gavvy Cravath, 1915.....24
Gavvy Cravath, 1917.....12 (Tie)
Gavvy Cravath, 1918.....8
Gavvy Cravath, 1919.....12
Cy Williams, 1920.....15
Cy Williams, 1923.....41
Cy Williams, 1927.....30 (Tie)
Chuck Klein, 1929.....43
Chuck Klein, 1931.....31
Chuck Klein, 1932.....38 (Tie)
Chuck Klein, 1933.....28
Mike Schmidt, 1974.....36
Mike Schmidt, 1975.....38
Mike Schmidt, 1976.....38
Mike Schmidt, 1980.....48
Mike Schmidt, 1981.....31
Mike Schmidt, 1983.....40
Mike Schmidt, 1984.....36 (Tie)
Mike Schmidt, 1986.....37
Jim Thome, 2003.....47
Ryan Howard, 2006.....58
Ryan Howard, 2008.....48

RBIs, Season

Sherry Magee, 1910.....116
Gavvy Cravath, 1913.....118
Sherry Magee, 1914.....101
Gavvy Cravath, 1915.....118
Chuck Klein, 1931.....121
Don Hurst, 1932.....143
Chuck Klein, 1933.....120
Del Ennis, 1950.....126
Greg Luzinski, 1975.....120
Mike Schmidt, 1980.....121
Mike Schmidt, 1981.....91
Mike Schmidt, 1984.....106 (Tie)
Mike Schmidt, 1986.....119
Darren Daulton, 1992.....109
Ryan Howard, 2006.....149
Ryan Howard, 2008.....146
Ryan Howard, 2009.....141 (Tie)

Stolen Bases, Season

Chuck Klein, 1932.....20
Danny Murtaugh, 1941.....18
Richie Ashburn, 1948.....32
Jimmy Rollins, 2001.....46 (Tie)

Total Bases, Season

Elmer Flick, 1900.....305
Sherry Magee, 1910.....263
Gavvy Cravath, 1913.....298
Sherry Magee, 1914.....277
Gavvy Cravath, 1915.....266
Chuck Klein, 1930.....445
Chuck Klein, 1931.....347
Chuck Klein, 1932.....420
Chuck Klein, 1933.....365
Dick Allen, 1964.....352
Greg Luzinski, 1975.....322
Mike Schmidt, 1976.....306
Mike Schmidt, 1980.....342
Mike Schmidt, 1981.....228
Ryan Howard, 2006.....383

Most Hits, Season

Gavvy Cravath, 1913.....179
Sherry Magee, 1914.....171
Lefty O'Doul, 1929.....254
Chuck Klein, 1932.....226
Chuck Klein, 1933.....223
Richie Ashburn, 1951.....221
Richie Ashburn, 1953.....205
Richie Ashburn, 1958.....215
Dave Cash, 1975.....213
Pete Rose, 1981.....140
Lenny Dykstra, 1990.....192 (Tie)
Lenny Dykstra, 1993.....194
Ben Revere, 2014.....184 (Tie)

Most Runs, Season

Roy Thomas, 1900.....131
Sherry Magee, 1910.....110
Gavvy Cravath, 1915.....89
Chuck Klein, 1930.....158
Chuck Klein, 1931.....121 (Tie)

Chuck Klein, 1932 152
Dick Allen, 1964..... 125
Mike Schmidt, 1981 78
Van Hayes, 1986..... 107 (Tie)
Lenny Dykstra, 1993..... 143
Chase Utley, 2006..... 131
Jimmy Rollins, 2007 139

Batting Feats

Triple Crown Winners

Chuck Klein, 1933 (.368 BA, 28 HRs, 120 RBIs)

Hitting for the Cycle

Lave Cross, Apr. 24, 1894
Sam Thompson, Aug. 17, 1894
Cy Williams, Aug. 5, 1927
Chuck Klein, July 1, 1931
Chuck Klein, May 26, 1933
Johnny Callison, June 27, 1963
Gregg Jefferies, Aug. 25, 1995
David Bell, June 28, 2004

Six Hits in a Game (Post-1900)

Connie Ryan, Apr. 16, 1953

40 or More Home Runs, Season

58 ..... Ryan Howard, 2006
48 ..... Mike Schmidt, 1980
Ryan Howard, 2008
47 ..... Jim Thome, 2003
Ryan Howard, 2007
45 ..... Mike Schmidt, 1979
Ryan Howard, 2009
43 ..... Chuck Klein, 1929
42 ..... Jim Thome, 2004
41 ..... Cy Williams, 1923
40 ..... Chuck Klein, 1930
Dick Allen, 1966
Mike Schmidt, 1983

League Leaders, Pitching (Post-1900)

Most Wins, Season

Grover C. Alexander, 1911 28
Tom Seaton, 1913 27
Grover C. Alexander, 1914 ... 27 (Tie)
Grover C. Alexander, 1915 31
Grover C. Alexander, 1916 33
Grover C. Alexander, 1917 30
Jumbo Elliott, 1931 ..... 19 (Tie)
Robin Roberts, 1952..... 28
Robin Roberts, 1953..... 23 (Tie)
Robin Roberts, 1954..... 23
Robin Roberts, 1955..... 23
Steve Carlton, 1972..... 27
Steve Carlton, 1977..... 23
Steve Carlton, 1980..... 24
Steve Carlton, 1982..... 23
John Denny, 1983..... 19
Roy Halladay, 2011..... 19

Most Strikeouts, Season

Grover C. Alexander, 1912 195
Tom Seaton, 1913 165
Grover C. Alexander, 1914 214
Grover C. Alexander, 1915 241
Grover C. Alexander, 1916 167
Grover C. Alexander, 1917 200
Kirby Higbe, 1940..... 137
Robin Roberts, 1953..... 198
Robin Roberts, 1954..... 185
Jack Sanford, 1957..... 188
Jim Bunning, 1967 253
Steve Carlton, 1972 310
Steve Carlton, 1974 240
Steve Carlton, 1980 286
Steve Carlton, 1982 286
Steve Carlton, 1983 275
Curt Schilling, 1997 319
Curt Schilling, 1998 300

Lowest ERA, Season

Grover C. Alexander, 1915 ..... 1.22
Grover C. Alexander, 1916 ..... 1.55
Grover C. Alexander, 1917 ..... 1.83
Steve Carlton, 1972..... 1.98

Most Saves, Season

Steve Bedrosian, 1987..... 40

Best Won–Lost Percentage, Season

Grover C. Alexander, 1915 ..... 31–10 ... .756
Steve Carlton, 1976 ..... 20–7 ... .741
John Denny, 1983..... 19–6 ... .760

Pitching Feats

Triple Crown Winner

Grover C. Alexander, 1915 (31–10, 1.22 ERA, 241 SO)
Grover C. Alexander, 1916 (33–12, 1.55 ERA, 167 SO)
Steve Carlton, 1972 (27–10, 1.97 ERA, 310 SO)

20 Wins, Season

Al Orth, 1901 20–12
Frank Donahue, 1901..... 20–13
Togie Pittinger, 1905..... 23–14
Tully Sparks, 1907 22–8
George McQuillan, 1908..... 23–17
Earl Moore, 1910 22–15
Grover C. Alexander, 1911 28–13
Tom Seaton, 1913 27–12
Grover C. Alexander, 1913 22–8
Grover C. Alexander, 1914 27–15
Erskine Mayer, 1914..... 21–19
Grover C. Alexander, 1915 31–10
Erskine Mayer, 1915..... 21–15
Grover C. Alexander, 1916 33–12
Eppa Rixey, 1916..... 22–10
Grover C. Alexander, 1917 30–13
Robin Roberts, 1950..... 20–11
Robin Roberts, 1951..... 21–15
Robin Roberts, 1952..... 28–7
Robin Roberts, 1953..... 23–16
Robin Roberts, 1954..... 23–15
Robin Roberts, 1955..... 23–14
Chris Short, 1966 20–10
Steve Carlton, 1972 27–10
Steve Carlton, 1976 20–7
Steve Carlton, 1977 23–10
Steve Carlton, 1980 24–9
Steve Carlton, 1982 23–11
Roy Halladay, 2010..... 21–10

No-Hitters

Chick Fraser (vs. Chi. Cubs), Sept. 18, 1903 (final: 10–0)
John Lush (vs. Bklyn. Dodgers), May 1, 1906 (final: 1–0)
Jim Bunning (vs. N.Y. Mets), June 21, 1964 (final: 6–0) (perfect game)
Rick Wise (vs. Cin. Reds), June 23, 1971 (final: 4–0)
Terry Mulholland (vs. S.F. Giants), Aug. 15, 1990 (final: 6–0)
Tommy Greene (vs. Mont. Expos), May 23, 1991 (final: 2–0)
Kevin Millwood (vs. S.F. Giants), Apr. 27, 2003 (final: 1–0)
Roy Halladay (vs. Fla. Marins), May 29, 2010 (final: 1–0) (Perfect Game)
Roy Halladay (vs. Cin. Reds), Oct. 6, 2010 (final: 4–0) (Postseason Game)
Cole Hamels, Jake Diekman, Ken Giles, Jonathan Papelbon (vs. Atl. Braves), Sept. 1, 2014 (final: 7–0)
Cole Hamels (vs. Chi. Cubs), July 25, 2015 (final: 5–0)

No-Hitters Pitched Against

Hooks Wiltse, N.Y. Giants, Sept. 5, 1908 (final: 1–0) (10 innings)

Jeff Tesereau, N.Y. Giants, Sept. 6, 1912 (final: 3–0)

George Davis, Bost. Braves, Sept. 9, 1914 (final: 7–0)

Jesse Barnes, N.Y. Giants, May 7, 1922 (final: 6–0)

Dazzy Vance, Bklyn. Dodgers, Sept. 13, 1925 (final: 10–1)

Jim Wilson, Milw. Braves, June 12, 1954 (final: 2–0)

Sal Maglie, Bklyn. Dodgers, Sept. 25, 1956 (final: 5–0)

Lew Burdette, Milw. Braves, Aug. 18, 1960 (final: 1–0)

Warren Spahn, Milw. Braves, Sept. 15, 1960 (final: 4–0)

Don Nottebart, Hous. Astros, May 17, 1963 (final: 4–1)

Sandy Koufax, L.A. Dodgers, June 4, 1964 (final: 3–0)

George Culver, Cin. Reds, July 29, 1968 (final: 6–1)

Bill Stoneman, Mont. Expos, Apr. 17, 1969 (final: 7–0)

Bill Singer, L.A. Dodgers, July 20, 1970 (final: 5–0)

Burt Hooton, Chi. Cubs, Apr. 16, 1972 (final: 4–0)

Bob Forsch, St.L. Cardinals, Apr. 16, 1978 (final: 5–0)

Josh Beckett, L.A. Dodgers, May 25, 2014 (final: 6–0)

Postseason Play

1915 World Series vs. Bost. Red Sox (AL), lost 4 games to 1

1950 World Series vs. N.Y. Yankees (AL), lost 4 games to 0

1976 League Championship Series vs. Cin. Reds, lost 3 games to 0

1977 League Championship Series vs. L.A. Dodgers, lost 3 games to 1

1978 League Championship Series vs. L.A. Dodgers, lost 3 games to 1

1980 League Championship Series vs. Hous. Astros, won 3 games to 2
World Series vs. K.C. Royals (AL), won 4 games to 2

1981 First-Half Division Playoff Series vs. Mont. Expos, lost 3 games to 2

1983 League Championship Series vs. L.A. Dodgers, won 3 games to 1
World Series vs. Balt. Orioles (AL), lost 4 games to 1

1993 League Championship Series vs. Atl. Braves, won 4 games to 2
World Series vs. Tor. Blue Jays (AL), lost 4 games to 2

2007 Division Series vs. Colo. Rockies, lost 3 games to 0

2008 Division Series vs. Milw. Brewers, won 3 games to 1
League Championship vs. L.A. Dodgers, won 4 games to 1
World Series vs. T.B. Rays (AL), won 4 games to 1

2009 Division Series vs. Colo. Rockies, won 3 games to 1
League Championship Series vs. L.A. Dodgers, won 4 games to 1
World Series vs. N.Y. Yankees (AL), lost 4 games to 2

2010 Division Series vs. Cin. Reds, won 3 games to 0
League Championship Series vs. S.F. Giants, lost 4 games to 2

2011 Division Series vs. St.L. Cardinals, lost 3 games to 2

Pittsburgh Pirates

Dates of Operation: 1887–present (129 years)
Overall Record: 10,005 wins, 9767 losses (.506)
Stadiums: Recreation Park, 1887–90; Exposition Park, 1891–1909; Forbes Field, 1909–70; Three Rivers Stadium, 1970–2000; PNC Park, 2001–present (capacity: 38,362)
Other Names: Alleghenys, Innocents

Year-by-Year Finishes

Year	Finish	Wins	Losses	Percentage	Games Behind	Manager	Attendance
1887	6th	55	69	.444	24.0	Horace Phillips	not available
1888	6th	66	68	.493	19.5	Horace Phillips	not available
1889	5th	61	71	.462	25.0	Horace Phillips, Fred Dunlap, Ned Hanlon	not available
1890	8th	23	113	.169	66.5	Guy Hecker	not available
1891	8th	55	80	.407	30.5	Ned Hanlon, Bill McGunnigle	not available
1892	6th	80	73	.523	23.5	Tom Burns, Al Buckenberger	not available
1893	2nd	81	48	.628	4.5	Al Buckenberger	not available
1894	7th	65	65	.500	25.0	Al Buckenberger, Connie Mack	not available
1895	7th	71	61	.538	17.0	Connie Mack	not available
1896	6th	66	63	.512	24.0	Connie Mack	not available
1897	8th	60	71	.458	32.5	Patrick Donovan	not available
1898	8th	72	76	.486	29.5	Bill Watkins	not available
1899	7th	76	73	.510	15.5	Bill Watkins, Patsy Donovan	not available
1900	2nd	79	60	.568	4.5	Fred Clarke	not available
1901	1st	90	49	.647	+7.5	Fred Clarke	251,955
1902	1st	103	36	.741	+27.5	Fred Clarke	243,826
1903	1st	91	49	.650	+6.5	Fred Clarke	326,855
1904	4th	87	66	.569	19.0	Fred Clarke	340,615
1905	2nd	96	57	.627	9.0	Fred Clarke	369,124
1906	3rd	93	60	.608	23.5	Fred Clarke	394,877
1907	2nd	91	63	.591	17.0	Fred Clarke	319,506
1908	2nd (Tie)	98	56	.636	1.0	Fred Clarke	382,444
1909	1st	110	42	.724	+6.5	Fred Clarke	534,950
1910	3rd	86	67	.562	17.5	Fred Clarke	436,586
1911	3rd	85	69	.552	14.5	Fred Clarke	432,000
1912	2nd	93	58	.616	10.0	Fred Clarke	384,000
1913	4th	78	71	.523	21.5	Fred Clarke	296,000
1914	7th	69	85	.448	25.5	Fred Clarke	139,620
1915	5th	73	81	.474	18.0	Fred Clarke	225,743
1916	6th	65	89	.422	29.0	Jimmy Callahan	289,132
1917	8th	51	103	.331	47.0	Jimmy Callahan, Honus Wagner, Hugo Bezdek	192,807
1918	4th	65	60	.520	17.0	Hugo Bezdek	213,610
1919	4th	71	68	.511	24.5	Hugo Bezdek	276,810
1920	4th	79	75	.513	14.0	George Gibson	429,037
1921	2nd	90	63	.588	4.0	George Gibson	701,567
1922	3rd (Tie)	85	69	.552	8.0	George Gibson, Bill McKechnie	523,675
1923	3rd	87	67	.565	8.5	Bill McKechnie	611,082
1924	3rd	90	63	.588	3.0	Bill McKechnie	736,883

1925	1st	95	58	.621	+8.5	Bill McKechnie	804,354
1926	3rd	84	69	.549	4.5	Bill McKechnie	798,542
1927	1st	94	60	.610	+1.5	Donie Bush	869,720
1928	4th	85	67	.559	9.0	Donie Bush	495,070
1929	2nd	88	65	.575	10.5	Donie Bush, Jewel Ens	491,377
1930	5th	80	74	.519	12.0	Jewel Ens	357,795
1931	5th	75	79	.487	26.0	Jewel Ens	260,392
1932	2nd	86	68	.558	4.0	George Gibson	287,262
1933	2nd	87	67	.565	5.0	George Gibson	288,747
1934	5th	74	76	.493	19.5	George Gibson, Pie Traynor	322,622
1935	4th	86	67	.562	13.5	Pie Traynor	352,885
1936	4th	84	70	.545	8.0	Pie Traynor	372,524
1937	3rd	86	68	.558	10.0	Pie Traynor	459,679
1938	2nd	86	64	.573	2.0	Pie Traynor	641,033
1939	6th	68	85	.444	28.5	Pie Traynor	376,734
1940	4th	78	76	.506	22.5	Frankie Frisch	507,934
1941	4th	81	73	.526	19.0	Frankie Frisch	482,241
1942	5th	66	81	.449	36.5	Frankie Frisch	448,897
1943	4th	80	74	.519	25.0	Frankie Frisch	604,278
1944	2nd	90	63	.588	14.5	Frankie Frisch	498,740
1945	4th	82	72	.532	16.0	Frankie Frisch	604,694
1946	7th	63	91	.409	34.0	Frankie Frisch, Spud Davis	749,962
1947	7th (Tie)	62	92	.403	32.0	Billy Herman, Bill Burwell	1,283,531
1948	4th	83	71	.539	8.5	Billy Meyer	1,517,021
1949	6th	71	83	.461	26.0	Billy Meyer	1,499,435
1950	8th	57	96	.373	33.5	Billy Meyer	1,166,267
1951	7th	64	90	.416	32.5	Billy Meyer	980,590
1952	8th	42	112	.273	54.5	Billy Meyer	686,673
1953	8th	50	104	.325	55.0	Fred Haney	572,757
1954	8th	53	101	.344	44.0	Fred Haney	475,494
1955	8th	60	94	.390	38.5	Fred Haney	469,397
1956	7th	66	88	.429	27.0	Bobby Bragan	949,878
1957	7th (Tie)	62	92	.403	33.0	Bobby Bragan, Danny Murtaugh	850,732
1958	2nd	84	70	.545	8.0	Danny Murtaugh	1,311,988
1959	4th	78	76	.506	9.0	Danny Murtaugh	1,359,917
1960	1st	95	59	.617	+7.0	Danny Murtaugh	1,705,828
1961	6th	75	79	.487	18.0	Danny Murtaugh	1,199,128
1962	4th	93	68	.578	8.0	Danny Murtaugh	1,090,648
1963	8th	74	88	.457	25.0	Danny Murtaugh	783,648
1964	6th (Tie)	80	82	.494	13.0	Danny Murtaugh	759,496
1965	3rd	90	72	.556	7.0	Harry Walker	909,279
1966	3rd	92	70	.568	3.0	Harry Walker	1,196,618
1967	6th	81	81	.500	20.5	Harry Walker, Danny Murtaugh	907,012
1968	6th	80	82	.494	17.0	Larry Shepard	693,485
				East Division			
1969	3rd	88	74	.543	12.0	Larry Shepard, Alex Grammas	769,369
1970	1st	89	73	.549	+5.0	Danny Murtaugh	1,341,947
1971	1st	97	65	.599	+7.0	Danny Murtaugh	1,501,132
1972	1st	96	59	.619	+11.0	Bill Virdon	1,427,460
1973	3rd	80	82	.494	2.5	Bill Virdon, Danny Murtaugh	1,319,913
1974	1st	88	74	.543	+1.5	Danny Murtaugh	1,110,552

1975	1st	92	69	.571	+6.5	Danny Murtaugh	1,270,018
1976	2nd	92	70	.568	9.0	Danny Murtaugh	1,025,945
1977	2nd	96	66	.593	5.0	Chuck Tanner	1,237,349
1978	2nd	88	73	.547	1.5	Chuck Tanner	964,106
1979	1st	98	64	.605	+2.0	Chuck Tanner	1,435,454
1980	3rd	83	79	.512	8.0	Chuck Tanner	1,646,757
1981*	4th/6th	46	56	.451	5.5/9.5	Chuck Tanner	541,789
1982	4th	84	78	.519	8.0	Chuck Tanner	1,024,106
1983	2nd	84	78	.519	6.0	Chuck Tanner	1,225,916
1984	6th	75	87	.463	21.5	Chuck Tanner	773,500
1985	6th	57	104	.354	43.5	Chuck Tanner	735,900
1986	6th	64	98	.395	44.0	Jim Leyland	1,000,917
1987	4th (Tie)	80	82	.494	15.0	Jim Leyland	1,161,193
1988	2nd	85	75	.531	15.0	Jim Leyland	1,866,713
1989	5th	74	88	.457	19.0	Jim Leyland	1,374,141
1990	1st	95	67	.586	+4.0	Jim Leyland	2,049,908
1991	1st	98	64	.605	+14.0	Jim Leyland	2,065,302
1992	1st	96	66	.593	+9.0	Jim Leyland	1,829,395
1993	5th	75	87	.463	22.0	Jim Leyland	1,650,593
				Central Division			
1994	3rd (Tie)	53	61	.465	13.0	Jim Leyland	1,222,520
1995	5th	58	86	.403	27.0	Jim Leyland	905,517
1996	5th	73	89	.451	15.0	Jim Leyland	1,332,150
1997	2nd	79	83	.488	5.0	Gene Lamont	1,657,022
1998	6th	69	93	.426	33.0	Gene Lamont	1,560,950
1999	3rd	78	83	.484	18.5	Gene Lamont	1,638,023
2000	5th	69	93	.426	26.0	Gene Lamont	1,748,908
2001	6th	62	100	.383	31.0	Lloyd McClendon	2,436,126
2002	4th	72	89	.447	24.5	Lloyd McClendon	1,784,993
2003	4th	75	87	.463	13.0	Lloyd McClendon	1,636,751
2004	5th	72	89	.447	32.5	Lloyd McClendon	1,583,031
2005	6th	67	95	.414	33.0	Lloyd McClendon, Pete Mackanin	1,817, 245
2006	5th	67	95	.414	16.5	Jim Tracy	1,861,549
2007	6th	68	94	.420	17.0	Jim Tracy	1,749,142
2008	6th	67	95	.414	30.5	John Russell	1,609,076
2009	6th	62	99	.385	28.5	John Russell	1,577,853
2010	6th	57	105	.352	34.0	John Russell	1,613,399
2011	4th	72	90	.444	24.0	Clint Hurdle	1,940,429
2012	4th	79	83	.488	18.0	Clint Hurdle	2,091,918
2013	2nd	94	68	.580	2.0	Clint Hurdle	2,256,862
2014	2nd	88	74	.543	3.0	Clint Hurdle	2,442,564
2015	2nd	98	64	.605	2.0	Clint Hurdle	2,498,596

*Split season.

Awards

Most Valuable Player

Paul Waner, outfield, 1927
Dick Groat, shortstop, 1960
Roberto Clemente, outfield, 1966
Dave Parker, outfield, 1978
Willie Stargell (co-winner), first base, 1979
Barry Bonds, outfield, 1990
Barry Bonds, outfield, 1992
Andrew McCutchen, outfield, 2013

Rookie of the Year

Jason Bay, outfield, 2004

Cy Young

Vernon Law, 1960
Doug Drabek, 1990

Hall of Famers Who Played for the Pirates

Jake Beckley, first base, 1888–89 and 1891–96
Jim Bunning, pitcher, 1968–69
Max Carey, outfield, 1910–26
Jack Chesbro, pitcher, 1899–1902
Fred Clarke, outfield, 1900–11 and 1913–15
Roberto Clemente, outfield, 1955–72
Joe Cronin, infield, 1926–27
Kiki Cuyler, outfield, 1921–27
Pud Galvin, pitcher, 1887–89 and 1891–92

Goose Gossage, pitcher, 1977
Hank Greenberg, first base, 1947
Burleigh Grimes, pitcher, 1916–17, 1928–29, and 1934
Billy Herman, second base, 1947
Waite Hoyt, pitcher, 1933–37
Joe Kelley, outfield, 1891–92
George Kelly, first base, 1917
Ralph Kiner, outfield, 1946–53
Chuck Klein, outfield, 1939
Fred Lindstrom, outfield, 1933–34
Al Lopez, catcher, 1940–46
Connie Mack, catcher, 1891–96
Heinie Manush, outfield, 1938–39
Rabbit Maranville, shortstop, 1921–24
Bill Mazeroski, second base, 1956–72
Bill McKechnie, infield, 1907, 1910–12, 1918, and 1920
Billy Southworth, outfield, 1918–20
Willie Stargell, outfield and first base, 1962–82
Casey Stengel, outfield, 1918–19
Pie Traynor, third base, 1920–35 and 1937
Dazzy Vance, pitcher, 1915
Arky Vaughan, shortstop, 1932–41
Rube Waddell, pitcher, 1900–01
Honus Wagner, shortstop, 1900–17
Lloyd Waner, outfield, 1927–41 and 1944–45
Paul Waner, outfield, 1926–40
Vic Willis, pitcher, 1906–09

Retired Numbers

1 ..... Billy Meyer
4 ..... Ralph Kiner
8 ..... Willie Stargell
9 ..... Bill Mazeroski
11 ..... Paul Waner
20 ..... Pie Traynor
21 ..... Roberto Clemente
33 ..... Honus Wagner
40 ..... Danny Murtaugh

League Leaders, Batting (Post-1900)

Batting Average, Season

Honus Wagner, 1900 ..... .381
Ginger Beaumont, 1902 ..... .357
Honus Wagner, 1903 ..... .355
Honus Wagner, 1904 ..... .349
Honus Wagner, 1906 ..... .339
Honus Wagner, 1907 ..... .350
Honus Wagner, 1908 ..... .354
Honus Wagner, 1909 ..... .339
Honus Wagner, 1911 ..... .334
Paul Waner, 1927 ..... .380
Paul Waner, 1934 ..... .362
Arky Vaughan, 1935 ..... .385
Paul Waner, 1936 ..... .373
Debs Garms, 1940 ..... .355
Dick Groat, 1960 ..... .325
Roberto Clemente, 1961 ..... .351
Roberto Clemente, 1964 ..... .339
Roberto Clemente, 1965 ..... .329
Matty Alou, 1966 ..... .342
Roberto Clemente, 1967 ..... .357
Dave Parker, 1977 ..... .338
Dave Parker, 1978 ..... .334
Bill Madlock, 1981 ..... .341
Bill Madlock, 1983 ..... .323
Freddy Sanchez, 2006 ..... .344

Home Runs, Season

Tommy Leach, 1902 6
Ralph Kiner, 1946 23
Ralph Kiner, 1947 ..... 51 (Tie)
Ralph Kiner, 1948 ..... 40 (Tie)
Ralph Kiner, 1949 54
Ralph Kiner, 1950 47
Ralph Kiner, 1951 42
Ralph Kiner, 1952 ..... 37 (Tie)
Willie Stargell, 1971 48
Willie Stargell, 1973 44
Pedro Alvarez, 2013 ..... 36 (Tie)

RBIs, Season

Honus Wagner, 1907 91
Honus Wagner, 1908 106
Honus Wagner, 1909 102
Paul Waner, 1927 131
Ralph Kiner, 1949 127
Willie Stargell, 1973 119

Stolen Bases, Season

Honus Wagner, 1901 48
Honus Wagner, 1902 43
Honus Wagner, 1904 53
Honus Wagner, 1907 61
Honus Wagner, 1908 53
Max Carey, 1913 61
Max Carey, 1915 36
Max Carey, 1916 63
Max Carey, 1917 46
Max Carey, 1918 58
Max Carey, 1920 52
Max Carey, 1922 51
Max Carey, 1923 51
Max Carey, 1924 49
Max Carey, 1925 46
Kiki Cuyler, 1926 35
Lee Handley, 1939 ..... 17 (Tie)
Johnny Barrett, 1944 28
Frank Tavaras, 1977 70
Omar Moreno, 1978 71
Omar Moreno, 1979 77
Tony Womack, 1997 60
Tony Womack, 1998 58

Total Bases, Season

Ginger Beaumont, 1903 272
Honus Wagner, 1904 255
Honus Wagner, 1906 237
Honus Wagner, 1907 264
Honus Wagner, 1908 308
Honus Wagner, 1909 242
Paul Waner, 1927 342
Ralph Kiner, 1947 361
Dave Parker, 1978 340

Most Hits, Season

Ginger Beaumont, 1902 194
Ginger Beaumont, 1903 209
Ginger Beaumont, 1904 185
Honus Wagner, 1908 201
Bobby Byrne, 1910 ..... 178 (Tie)
Honus Wagner, 1910 ..... 178 (Tie)
Paul Waner, 1927 237
Lloyd Waner, 1931 214
Paul Waner, 1934 217
Roberto Clemente, 1964 ..... 211 (Tie)
Roberto Clemente, 1967 209
Matty Alou, 1969 231
Dave Parker, 1977 215
Andy Van Slyke, 1992 ..... 199 (Tie)
Andrew McCutchen, 2012 194

Most Runs, Season

Honus Wagner, 1902 105
Ginger Beaumont, 1903 137
Honus Wagner, 1906 ..... 103 (Tie)
Tommy Leach, 1909 126
Max Carey, 1913 ..... 99 (Tie)
Kiki Cuyler, 1925 144
Kiki Cuyler, 1926 113
Lloyd Waner, 1927 ..... 133 (Tie)
Paul Waner, 1928 142

Paul Waner, 1934 122
Arky Vaughan, 1936 122
Arky Vaughan, 1940 113
Ralph Kiner, 1951 ..... 124 (Tie)
Barry Bonds, 1992 109

Batting Feats

Triple Crown Winners

[No player]

Hitting for the Cycle

Fred Carroll, May 2, 1887
Fred Clarke, July 23, 1901
Fred Clarke, May 7, 1903
Chief Wilson, July 3, 1910
Honus Wagner, Aug. 22, 1912
Dave Robertson, Aug. 30, 1921
Pie Traynor, July 7, 1923
Kiki Cuyler, June 4, 1925
Max Carey, June 20, 1925
Arky Vaughan, June 24, 1933
Arky Vaughan, July 19, 1939
Bob Elliott, July 15, 1945
Bill Salkeld, Aug. 4, 1945
Wally Westlake, July 30, 1948
Wally Westlake, June 14, 1949
Ralph Kiner, June 25, 1950
Gus Bell, June 4, 1951
Willie Stargell, July 22, 1964
Richie Zisk, June 9, 1974
Mike Easler, June 12, 1980
Gary Redus, Aug. 25, 1989
Jason Kendall, May 19, 2000
Daryle Ward, May 27, 2004

Six Hits in a Game (Post-1900)

Carson Bigbee, Aug. 22, 1917*
Max Carey, July 7, 1922*
Johnny Gooch, July 7, 1922*
Kiki Cuyler, Aug. 9, 1924
Paul Waner, Aug. 26, 1926
Lloyd Waner, June 15, 1929
Johnny Hopp, May 14, 1950
Dick Groat, May 13, 1960
Rennie Stennett, Sept. 16, 1975
(7 hits in game)
Wally Backman, Apr. 27, 1990
Freddy Sanchez, May 25, 2009
*Extra-inning game.

40 or More Home Runs, Season

54 ..... Ralph Kiner, 1949
51 ..... Ralph Kiner, 1947
48 ..... Willie Stargell, 1971
47 ..... Ralph Kiner, 1950
44 ..... Willie Stargell, 1973
42 ..... Ralph Kiner, 1951
40 ..... Ralph Kiner, 1948

League Leaders, Pitching (Post-1900)

Most Wins, Season

Jack Chesbro, 1902 28
Wilbur Cooper, 1921 ..... 22 (Tie)
Roy Kremer, 1926 ..... 20 (Tie)
Lee Meadows, 1926 ..... 20 (Tie)
Burleigh Grimes, 1928 ..... 25 (Tie)
Ray Kremer, 1930 ..... 20 (Tie)
Heinie Meine, 1931 ..... 19 (Tie)
Rip Sewell, 1943 ..... 21 (Tie)
Bob Friend, 1958 ..... 22 (Tie)
Doug Drabek, 1990 22
John Smiley, 1991 ..... 20 (Tie)

Most Strikeouts, Season

Rube Waddell, 1900 133
Preacher Roe, 1945 148
Bob Veale, 1964 250

Lowest ERA, Season

Ray Kremer, 1926 ..... 2.61
Ray Kremer, 1927 ..... 2.47
Cy Blanton, 1935 ..... 2.59
Bob Friend, 1955 ..... 2.84
John Candelaria, 1977 ..... 2.34

Most Saves, Season

Dave Giusti, 1971 30
Mark Melancon, 2015 51

Best Won–Lost Percentage, Season

Jack Chesbro, 1901 ..... 21–9 ... .700
Jack Chesbro, 1902 ..... 28–6 ... .824
Sam Leever, 1903 ..... 25–7 ... .781
Sam Leever, 1905 ..... 20–5 ... .800
Howie Camnitz, 1909 .. 25–6 ... .806 (Tie)
Claude Hendrix, 1912 .. 24–9 ... .727
Emil Yde, 1924 ..... 16–3 ... .842
Ray Kremer, 1926 ..... 20–6 ... .769
Roy Face, 1959 ..... 18–1 ... .947
Steve Blass, 1968 ..... 18–6 ... .750
John Candelaria, 1977 . 20–5 ... .800
Jim Bibby, 1980 ..... 19–6 ... .760
Doug Drabek, 1990 ..... 22–6 ... .786
John Smiley, 1991 ..... 20–8 ... .714 (Tie)

Pitching Feats

20 Wins, Season

Jesse Tannehill, 1900 20–7
Deacon Phillippe, 1901 22–12
Jack Chesbro, 1901 21–9
Jack Chesbro, 1902 28–6
Jesse Tannehill, 1902 20–6
Deacon Phillippe, 1902 20–9
Sam Leever, 1903 25–7
Deacon Phillippe, 1903 25–9
Patsy Flaherty*, 1904 21–11
Sam Leever, 1905 20–5
Deacon Phillippe, 1905 20–13
Vic Willis, 1906 23–13
Sam Leever, 1906 22–7
Vic Willis, 1907 21–11
Lefty Leifield, 1907 20–16
Nick Maddox, 1908 23–8
Vic Willis, 1908 23–11
Howie Camnitz, 1909 25–6
Vic Willis, 1909 22–11
Babe Adams, 1911 22–12
Howie Camnitz, 1911 20–15
Claude Hendrix, 1912 24–9
Howie Camnitz, 1912 22–12
Babe Adams, 1913 21–10
Al Mamaux, 1915 21–8
Al Mamaux, 1916 21–15
Wilbur Cooper, 1920 24–15
Wilbur Cooper, 1921 22–14
Wilbur Cooper, 1922 23–14
Johnny Morrison, 1923 25–13
Wilbur Cooper, 1924 20–14
Ray Kremer, 1926 20–6
Lee Meadows, 1926 20–9
Carmen Hill, 1927 22–11
Burleigh Grimes, 1928 25–14
Ray Kremer, 1930 20–12
Rip Sewell, 1943 21–9
Rip Sewell, 1944 21–12
Murry Dickson, 1951 20–16
Bob Friend, 1958 22–14
Vernon Law, 1960 20–9
John Candelaria, 1977 20–5
Doug Drabek, 1990 22–6
John Smiley, 1991 20–8
*2–2 with Chi. White Sox and 19–9 with Pitt. Pirates.

No-Hitters

Nick Maddox (vs. Bklyn. Dodgers), Sept. 29, 1907 (final: 2–1)

Cliff Chambers (vs. Bost. Braves), May 6, 1951 (final: 3–0)

Bob Moose (vs. N.Y. Mets), Sept. 20, 1969 (final: 4–0)

Dock Ellis (vs. S.D. Padres), June 12, 1970 (final: 2–0)

John Candelaria (vs. L.A. Dodgers), Aug. 9, 1976 (final: 2–0)

Francisco Cordova and Ricardo Rincon (vs. Hous. Astros), July 12, 1997 (final: 3–0)

No-Hitters Pitched Against

Tom Hughes, Bost. Braves, June 16, 1916 (final: 2–0)

Carl Hubbell, N.Y. Giants, May 8, 1929 (final: 11–0)

Sam Jones, Chi. Cubs, May 12, 1955 (final: 4–0)

Bob Gibson, St.L. Cardinals, Aug. 14, 1971 (final: 11–0)

Homer Bailey, Cin. Reds, Sept. 28, 2012 (final: 1–0)

Max Scherzer, Wash. Nationals, June 20, 2015 (final: 6–0)

Postseason Play

1903 World Series vs. Bost. Red Sox (AL), lost 5 games to 3

1909 World Series vs. Det. Tigers (AL), won 4 games to 3

1925 World Series vs. Wash. Senators (AL), won 4 games to 3

1927 World Series vs. N.Y. Yankees (AL), lost 4 games to 0

1960 World Series vs. N.Y. Yankees (AL), won 4 games to 3

1970 League Championship Series vs. Cin. Reds, lost 3 games to 0

1971 League Championship Series vs. S.F. Giants, won 3 games to 1
World Series vs. Balt. Orioles (AL), won 4 games to 3

1972 League Championship Series vs. Cin. Reds, lost 3 games to 2

1974 League Championship Series vs. L.A. Dodgers, lost 3 games to 1

1975 League Championship Series vs. Cin. Reds, lost 3 games to 0

1979 League Championship Series vs. Cin. Reds, won 3 games to 0
World Series vs. Balt. Orioles (AL), won 4 games to 3

1990 League Championship Series vs. Cin. Reds, lost 4 games to 2

1991 League Championship Series vs. Atl. Braves, lost 4 games to 3

1992 League Championship Series vs. Atl. Braves, lost 4 games to 3

2013 NL Wild Card Playoff Game vs. Cin. Reds, won
Division Series vs. St.L. Cardinals, lost 3 games to 2

2014 NL Wild Card Playoff Game vs. S.F. Giants, lost

2015 NL Wild Card Playoff Game vs. Chi. Cubs, lost

St. Louis Cardinals

Dates of Operation: 1876–77, 1885–86, 1892–present (128 years)

Overall Record: 9942 wins, 9533 losses (.510)

Stadiums: Lucas Park, 1876; Sportsman's Park, 1876–77; Palace Park of America and Vandeventer Lot, 1885–86; Sportsman's Park II (also known as Robison Field and League Park, 1899–1911; Cardinal Field, 1918–20), 1892–1920; Sportsman's Park V (also known as Busch Stadium, 1954–66), 1920–66; Busch Memorial Stadium II, 1966–2005; Busch Stadium III, 2006–present (capacity: 43,975)

Other Names: Browns, Perfectos

Year-by-Year Finishes

Year	Finish	Wins	Losses	Percentage	Games Behind	Manager	Attendance
1876	2nd	45	19	.703	6.0	Herman Hehlman	not available
1877	4th	28	32	.467	32.0	John Lucas, George McManus	not available
1885	8th	36	72	.333	49.0	Henry Lucas	not available
1886	6th	43	79	.352	46.0	Gus Schmelz	not available
1892	11th	56	94	.373	46.0	Chris Von der Ahe	not available
1893	10th	57	75	.432	29.0	Bill Watkins	not available
1894	9th	56	76	.424	35.0	George Miller	not available
1895	11th	39	92	.298	48.5	Al Buckenberger, Joe Quinn, Lew Phelan, Chris Von der Ahe	not available
1896	11th	40	90	.308	50.5	Harry Diddledock, Arlie Latham, Chris Von der Ahe, Roger Conner, Tommy Dowd	not available
1897	12th	29	102	.221	63.5	Tommy Dowd, Hugh Nicol, Bill Hallman, Chris Von der Ahe	not available
1898	12th	39	111	.260	63.5	Tim Hurst	not available
1899	5th	83	66	.557	9.5	Patsy Tebeau	not available
1900	5th (Tie)	65	75	.464	19.0	Patsy Tebeau, Louie Heilbroner	not available
1901	4th	76	64	.543	14.5	Patsy Donovan	379,988
1902	6th	56	78	.418	44.5	Patsy Donovan	226,417
1903	8th	43	94	.314	46.5	Patsy Donovan	226,538
1904	5th	75	79	.487	31.5	Kid Nichols	386,750
1905	6th	58	96	.377	47.5	Kid Nichols, Jimmy Burke, Matt Robison	292,800
1906	7th	52	98	.347	63.0	John McCloskey	283,770
1907	8th	52	101	.340	55.5	John McCloskey	185,377
1908	8th	49	105	.318	50.0	John McCloskey	205,129
1909	7th	54	98	.355	56.0	Roger Bresnahan	299,982
1910	7th	63	90	.412	40.5	Roger Bresnahan	355,668
1911	5th	75	74	.503	22.0	Roger Bresnahan	447,768
1912	6th	63	90	.412	41.0	Roger Bresnahan	241,759
1913	8th	51	99	.340	49.0	Miller Huggins	203,531
1914	3rd	81	72	.529	13.0	Miller Huggins	256,099
1915	6th	72	81	.471	18.5	Miller Huggins	252,666
1916	7th (Tie)	60	93	.392	33.5	Miller Huggins	224,308
1917	3rd	82	70	.539	15.0	Miller Huggins	288,491
1918	8th	51	78	.395	33.0	Jack Hendricks	110,599

1919	7th	54	83	.394	40.5	Branch Rickey	167,059
1920	5th (Tie)	75	79	.487	18.0	Branch Rickey	326,836
1921	3rd	87	66	.569	7.0	Branch Rickey	384,773
1922	3rd (Tie)	85	69	.552	8.0	Branch Rickey	536,998
1923	5th	79	74	.516	16.0	Branch Rickey	338,551
1924	6th	65	89	.422	28.5	Branch Rickey	272,885
1925	4th	77	76	.503	18.0	Branch Rickey, Rogers Hornsby	404,959
1926	1st	89	65	.578	+2.0	Rogers Hornsby	668,428
1927	2nd	92	61	.601	1.5	Bob O'Farrell	749,340
1928	1st	95	59	.617	+2.0	Bill McKechnie	761,574
1929	4th	78	74	.513	20.0	Bill McKechnie, Billy Southworth	399,887
1930	1st	92	62	.597	+2.0	Gabby Street	508,501
1931	1st	101	53	.656	+13.0	Gabby Street	608,535
1932	6th (Tie)	72	82	.468	18.0	Gabby Street	279,219
1933	5th	82	71	.536	9.5	Gabby Street, Frankie Frisch	256,171
1934	1st	95	58	.621	+2.0	Frankie Frisch	325,056
1935	2nd	96	58	.623	4.0	Frankie Frisch	506,084
1936	2nd (Tie)	87	67	.565	5.0	Frankie Frisch	448,078
1937	4th	81	73	.526	15.0	Frankie Frisch	430,811
1938	6th	71	80	.470	17.5	Frankie Frisch, Mike Gonzalez	291,418
1939	2nd	92	61	.601	4.5	Ray Blades	400,245
1940	3rd	84	69	.549	16.0	Ray Blades, Mike Gonzalez, Billy Southworth	324,078
1941	2nd	97	56	.634	2.5	Billy Southworth	633,645
1942	1st	106	48	.688	+2.0	Billy Southworth	553,552
1943	1st	105	49	.682	+18.0	Billy Southworth	517,135
1944	1st	105	49	.682	+14.5	Billy Southworth	461,968
1945	2nd	95	59	.617	3.0	Billy Southworth	594,630
1946	1st	98	58	.628	+2.0	Eddie Dyer	1,061,807
1947	2nd	89	65	.578	5.0	Eddie Dyer	1,247,913
1948	2nd	85	69	.552	6.5	Eddie Dyer	1,111,440
1949	2nd	96	58	.623	1.0	Eddie Dyer	1,430,676
1950	5th	78	75	.510	12.5	Eddie Dyer	1,093,411
1951	3rd	81	73	.526	15.5	Marty Marion	1,013,429
1952	3rd	88	66	.571	8.5	Eddie Stanky	913,113
1953	3rd (Tie)	83	71	.539	22.0	Eddie Stanky	880,242
1954	6th	72	82	.468	25.0	Eddie Stanky	1,039,698
1955	7th	68	86	.442	30.5	Eddie Stanky, Harry Walker	849,130
1956	4th	76	78	.494	17.0	Fred Hutchinson	1,029,773
1957	2nd	87	67	.565	8.0	Fred Hutchinson	1,183,575
1958	5th (Tie)	72	82	.468	20.0	Fred Hutchinson, Stan Hack	1,063,730
1959	7th	71	83	.461	16.0	Solly Hemus	929,953
1960	3rd	86	68	.558	9.0	Solly Hemus	1,096,632
1961	5th	80	74	.519	13.0	Solly Hemus, Johnny Keane	855,305
1962	6th	84	78	.519	17.5	Johnny Keane	953,895
1963	2nd	93	69	.574	6.0	Johnny Keane	1,170,546
1964	1st	93	69	.574	+1.0	Johnny Keane	1,143,294
1965	7th	80	81	.497	16.5	Red Schoendienst	1,241,201
1966	6th	83	79	.512	12.0	Red Schoendienst	1,712,980
1967	1st	101	60	.627	+10.5	Red Schoendienst	2,090,145
1968	1st	97	65	.599	+9.0	Red Schoendienst	2,011,167

				East Division			
1969	4th	87	75	.537	13.0	Red Schoendienst	1,682,783
1970	4th	76	86	.469	13.0	Red Schoendienst	1,629,736
1971	2nd	90	72	.556	7.0	Red Schoendienst	1,604,671
1972	4th	75	81	.481	21.5	Red Schoendienst	1,196,894
1973	2nd	81	81	.500	1.5	Red Schoendienst	1,574,046
1974	2nd	86	75	.534	1.5	Red Schoendienst	1,838,413
1975	3rd (Tie)	82	80	.506	10.5	Red Schoendienst	1,695,270
1976	5th	72	90	.444	29.0	Red Schoendienst	1,207,079
1977	3rd	83	79	.512	18.0	Vern Rapp	1,659,287
1978	5th	69	93	.426	21.0	Vern Rapp, Jack Krol, Ken Boyer	1,278,215
1979	3rd	86	76	.531	12.0	Ken Boyer	1,627,256
1980	4th	74	88	.457	17.0	Ken Boyer, Jack Krol, Whitey Herzog, Red Schoendienst	1,385,147
1981*	2nd/2nd	59	43	.578	1.5/0.5	Whitey Herzog	1,010,247
1982	1st	92	70	.568	+3.0	Whitey Herzog	2,111,906
1983	4th	79	83	.488	11.0	Whitey Herzog	2,317,914
1984	3rd	84	78	.519	12.5	Whitey Herzog	2,037,448
1985	1st	101	61	.623	+3.0	Whitey Herzog	2,637,563
1986	3rd	79	82	.491	28.5	Whitey Herzog	2,471,974
1987	1st	95	67	.586	+3.0	Whitey Herzog	3,072,122
1988	5th	76	86	.469	25.0	Whitey Herzog	2,892,799
1989	3rd	86	76	.531	7.0	Whitey Herzog	3,080,980
1990	6th	70	92	.432	25.0	Whitey Herzog, Red Schoendienst, Joe Torre	2,573,225
1991	2nd	84	78	.519	14.0	Joe Torre	2,448,699
1992	3rd	83	79	.512	13.0	Joe Torre	2,418,483
1993	3rd	87	75	.537	10.0	Joe Torre	2,844,328
				Central Division			
1994	3rd (Tie)	53	61	.465	13.0	Joe Torre	1,866,544
1995	4th	62	81	.434	22.5	Joe Torre, Mike Jorgensen	1,756,727
1996	1st	88	74	.543	+6.0	Tony La Russa	2,654,718
1997	4th	73	89	.451	11.0	Tony La Russa	2,634,014
1998	3rd	83	79	.512	19.0	Tony La Russa	3,194,092
1999	4th	75	86	.466	21.5	Tony La Russa	3,225,334
2000	1st	95	67	.586	+10.0	Tony La Russa	3,336,493
2001	1st (Tie)	93	69	.574	—	Tony La Russa	3,113,091
2002	1st	97	65	.599	+13.0	Tony La Russa	3,011,756
2003	3rd	85	77	.525	3.0	Tony La Russa	2,910,386
2004	1st	105	57	.648	+13.0	Tony La Russa	3,048,427
2005	1st	100	62	.617	+11.0	Tony La Russa	3,538,988
2006	1st	83	78	.516	+1.5	Tony La Russa	3,407,114
2007	3rd	78	84	.481	7.0	Tony La Russa	3,552,180
2008	4th	86	76	.531	11.5	Tony La Russa	3,430,660
2009	1st	91	71	.562	+7.5	Tony La Russa	3,343,252
2010	2nd	86	76	.531	5.0	Tony La Russa	3,301,218
2011	2nd	90	72	.556	6.0	Tony La Russa	3,093,954
2012	2nd	88	74	.543	9.0	Mike Matheny	3,262,109
2013	1st	97	65	.599	+3.0	Mike Matheny	3,369,769
2014	1st	90	72	.556	+2.0	Mike Matheny	3,540,649
2015	1st	100	62	.617	+2.0	Mike Matheny	3,520,889

*Split season.

Awards

Most Valuable Player

Rogers Hornsby, second base, 1925
Bob O'Farrell, catcher, 1926
Jim Bottomley, first base, 1928
Frankie Frisch, second base, 1931
Dizzy Dean, pitcher, 1934
Joe Medwick, outfield, 1937
Mort Cooper, pitcher, 1942
Stan Musial, outfield, 1943
Marty Marion, shortstop, 1944
Stan Musial, first base and outfield, 1946
Stan Musial, outfield, 1948
Ken Boyer, third base, 1964
Orlando Cepeda, first base, 1967
Bob Gibson, pitcher, 1968
Joe Torre, third base, 1971
Keith Hernandez (co-winner), first base, 1979
Willie McGee, outfield, 1985
Albert Pujols, first base, 2005
Albert Pujols, first base, 2008
Albert Pujols, first base, 2009

Rookie of the Year

Wally Moon, outfield, 1954
Bill Virdon, outfield, 1955
Bake McBride, outfield, 1974
Vince Coleman, outfield, 1985
Todd Worrell, pitcher, 1986
Albert Pujols, outfield, 2001

Cy Young

Bob Gibson, 1968
Bob Gibson, 1970
Chris Carpenter, 2005

Hall of Famers Who Played for the Cardinals

Grover C. Alexander, pitcher, 1926–29
Walter Alston, first base, 1936
Jake Beckley, first base, 1904–07
Jim Bottomley, first base, 1922–32
Roger Bresnahan, catcher, 1909–12
Lou Brock, outfield, 1964–79
Three Finger Brown, pitcher, 1903
Jesse Burkett, outfield, 1899–1901
Steve Carlton, pitcher, 1965–71
Orlando Cepeda, first base, 1966–68
Roger Connor, first base, 1894–97
Dizzy Dean, pitcher, 1930 and 1932–37
Leo Durocher, shortstop, 1933–37
Dennis Eckersley, pitcher, 1996–97
Frankie Frisch, second base, 1927–37
Pud Galvin, pitcher, 1892
Bob Gibson, pitcher, 1959–75
Burleigh Grimes, pitcher, 1930–31 and 1933–34
Chick Hafey, outfield, 1924–31
Jesse Haines, pitcher, 1920–37
Rogers Hornsby, second base, 1915–26 and 1933
Miller Huggins, second base, 1910–16
Rabbit Maranville, shortstop, 1927–28
John McGraw, third base, 1900
Joe Medwick, outfield, 1932–40 and 1947–48
Johnny Mize, first base, 1936–41
Stan Musial, outfield and first base, 1941–44 and 1946–63
Kid Nichols, pitcher, 1904–05
Wilbert Robinson, catcher, 1900
Red Schoendienst, second base, 1945–56 and 1961–63
Enos Slaughter, outfield, 1938–42 and 1946–53
Ozzie Smith, shortstop, 1982–96
John Smoltz, pitcher, 2009
Billy Southworth, outfield, 1926–27, 1929
Bruce Sutter, pitcher, 1981–84
Joe Torre, catcher, first base, third base, 1969–74
Dazzy Vance, pitcher, 1933–34
Bobby Wallace, shortstop, 1899–1901 and 1917–18
Hoyt Wilhelm, pitcher, 1957
Vic Willis, pitcher, 1910
Cy Young, pitcher, 1899–1900

Retired Numbers

JB ..... Jack Buck
RH ..... Rogers Hornsby
1 ..... Ozzie Smith
2 ..... Red Schoendienst
6 ..... Stan Musial
9 ..... Enos Slaughter
10 ..... Tony La Russa
14 ..... Ken Boyer
17 ..... Dizzy Dean
20 ..... Lou Brock
24 ..... Whitey Herzog
42 ..... Bruce Sutter
45 ..... Bob Gibson
85 ..... August Busch Jr.

League Leaders, Batting (Post-1900)

Batting Average, Season

Jesse Burkett, 1901 ..... .382
Rogers Hornsby, 1920 ..... .370
Rogers Hornsby, 1921 ..... .397
Rogers Hornsby, 1922 ..... .401
Rogers Hornsby, 1923 ..... .384
Rogers Hornsby, 1924 ..... .424
Rogers Hornsby, 1925 ..... .403
Chick Hafey, 1931 ..... .349
Joe Medwick, 1937 ..... .374
Johnny Mize, 1939 ..... .349
Stan Musial, 1943 ..... .357
Stan Musial, 1946 ..... .365
Harry Walker*, 1947 ..... .363
Stan Musial, 1948 ..... .376
Stan Musial, 1950 ..... .346
Stan Musial, 1951 ..... .355
Stan Musial, 1952 ..... .336
Stan Musial, 1957 ..... .351
Joe Torre, 1971 ..... .363
Keith Hernandez, 1979 ..... .344
Willie McGee, 1985 ..... .353
Willie McGee, 1990 ..... .335
Albert Pujols, 2003 ..... .359

*.371 with Phila. Phillies and .200 with St.L. Cardinals.

Home Runs, Season

Rogers Hornsby, 1922 42
Rogers Hornsby, 1925 39
Jim Bottomley, 1928 31
Rip Collins, 1934 ..... 35 (Tie)
Joe Medwick, 1937 ..... 31 (Tie)
Johnny Mize, 1939 28
Johnny Mize, 1940 43
Mark McGwire, 1988 70
Mark McGwire, 1999 65
Albert Pujols, 2009 47
Albert Pujols, 2010 42

RBIs, Season

Rogers Hornsby, 1920 ..... 94 (Tie)
Rogers Hornsby, 1921 126
Rogers Hornsby, 1922 152
Rogers Hornsby, 1925 143
Jim Bottomley, 1926 120
Jim Bottomley, 1928 136
Joe Medwick, 1936 138
Joe Medwick, 1937 154
Joe Medwick, 1938 122
Johnny Mize, 1940 137

Enos Slaughter, 1946 130
Stan Musial, 1948 131
Stan Musial, 1956 109
Ken Boyer, 1964 119
Joe Torre, 1971 137
Mark McGwire, 1999 147
Albert Pujols, 2010 118

Stolen Bases, Season

Frankie Frisch, 1927 48
Frankie Frisch, 1931 28
Pepper Martin, 1933 26
Pepper Martin, 1934 23
Pepper Martin, 1936 23
Red Schoendienst, 1945 26
Lou Brock, 1966 74
Lou Brock, 1967 52
Lou Brock, 1968 62
Lou Brock, 1969 53
Lou Brock, 1971 64
Lou Brock, 1972 63
Lou Brock, 1973 70
Lou Brock, 1974 118
Vince Coleman, 1985 110
Vince Coleman, 1986 107
Vince Coleman, 1987 109
Vince Coleman, 1988 81
Vince Coleman, 1989 65
Vince Coleman, 1990 77

Total Bases, Season

Jesse Burkett, 1901 313
Rogers Hornsby, 1917 253
Rogers Hornsby, 1920 329
Rogers Hornsby, 1921 378
Rogers Hornsby, 1922 450
Rogers Hornsby, 1924 373
Rogers Hornsby, 1925 381
Jim Bottomley, 1926 305
Jim Bottomley, 1928 362
Rip Collins, 1934 369
Joe Medwick, 1935 365
Joe Medwick, 1936 367
Joe Medwick, 1937 406
Johnny Mize, 1938 326
Johnny Mize, 1939 353
Johnny Mize, 1940 368
Enos Slaughter, 1942 292
Stan Musial, 1943 347
Stan Musial, 1946 366
Stan Musial, 1948 429
Stan Musial, 1949 382
Stan Musial, 1951 355
Stan Musial, 1952 311
Joe Torre, 1971 352
Albert Pujols, 2003 394
Albert Pujols, 2004 389
Albert Pujols, 2008 342
Albert Pujols, 2009 374

Most Hits, Season

Jesse Burkett, 1901 228
Rogers Hornsby, 1920 218
Rogers Hornsby, 1921 235
Rogers Hornsby, 1922 250
Rogers Hornsby, 1924 227
Jim Bottomley, 1925 227
Joe Medwick, 1936 223
Joe Medwick, 1937 237
Enos Slaughter, 1942 188
Stan Musial, 1943 220
Stan Musial, 1944 ..... 197 (Tie)
Stan Musial, 1946 228
Stan Musial, 1948 230
Stan Musial, 1949 207
Stan Musial, 1952 194
Curt Flood, 1964 ..... 211 (Tie)
Joe Torre, 1971 230
Garry Templeton, 1979 211
Willie McGee, 1985 216
Albert Pujols, 2003 212
Matt Carpenter, 2013 199

Most Runs, Season

Jesse Burkett, 1901 139
Rogers Hornsby, 1921 131
Rogers Hornsby, 1922 141
Rogers Hornsby, 1924 ..... 121 (Tie)
Pepper Martin, 1933 122
Joe Medwick, 1937 111
Stan Musial, 1946 124
Stan Musial, 1948 135
Stan Musial, 1951 ..... 124 (Tie)
Stan Musial, 1952 ..... 105 (Tie)
Solly Hemus, 1952 ..... 105 (Tie)
Stan Musial, 1954 ..... 120 (Tie)
Lou Brock, 1967 ..... 113 (Tie)
Lou Brock, 1971 126
Keith Hernandez, 1979 116
Keith Hernandez, 1980 111
Lonnie Smith, 1982 120
Albert Pujols, 2003 137
Albert Pujols, 2004 133
Albert Pujols, 2005 129
Albert Pujols, 2009 124
Albert Pujols, 2010 115
Matt Carpenter, 2013 126

Batting Feats

Triple Crown Winners

Rogers Hornsby, 1922 (.401 BA, 42 HRs, 152 RBIs)
Rogers Hornsby, 1925 (.403 BA, 39 HRs, 143 RBIs)
Joe Medwick, 1937 (.374 BA, 31 HRs, 153 RBIs)

Hitting for the Cycle

Fred Dunlap, May 24, 1886
Tip O'Neil, Apr. 30, 1887
Tip O'Neil, May 7, 1887
Tommy Dowd, Aug. 16, 1895
Cliff Heathcote, July 13, 1918
Jim Bottomley, July 15, 1927
Chick Hafey, Aug. 21, 1930
Pepper Martin, May 5, 1933
Joe Medwick, June 29, 1935
Johnny Mize, July 13, 1940
Stan Musial, July 24, 1949
Bill White, Aug. 14, 1960
Ken Boyer, Sept. 14, 1961
Ken Boyer, June 16, 1964
Joe Torre, June 27, 1973
Lou Brock, May 27, 1975
Willie McGee, June 23, 1984
Ray Lankford, Sept. 15, 1991
John Mabry, May 18, 1996
Mark Grudzielanek, Apr. 27, 2005

Six Hits in a Game (Post-1900)

Jim Bottomley, Sept. 16, 1924
Jim Bottomley, Aug. 5, 1931
Terry Moore, Sept. 5, 1935

40 or More Home Runs, Season

70 ..... Mark McGwire, 1998
65 ..... Mark McGwire, 1999
49 ..... Albert Pujols, 2006
47 ..... Albert Pujols, 2009
46 ..... Albert Pujols, 2004
43 ..... Johnny Mize, 1940
Albert Pujols, 2003
42 ..... Rogers Hornsby, 1922
Jim Edmonds, 2000
Jim Edmonds, 2004
Albert Pujols, 2010
41 ..... Albert Pujols, 2005

League Leaders, Pitching (Post-1900)

Most Wins, Season

Flint Rhem, 1926 ..... 20 (Tie)
Bill Hallahan, 1931 ..... 19 (Tie)
Dizzy Dean, 1934 30
Dizzy Dean, 1935 28
Mort Cooper, 1942 22
Mort Cooper, 1943 ..... 21 (Tie)
Red Barrett*, 1945 23
Howie Pollet, 1946 21
Ernie Broglio, 1960 ..... 21 (Tie)
Bob Gibson, 1970 ..... 23 (Tie)
Joaquin Andujar, 1984 20
Adam Wainwright, 2009 19
Adam Wainwright, 2013 ..... 19 (Tie)

*2 with Bost. Beaneaters and 21 with St.L. Cardinals.

Most Strikeouts, Season

Fred Beebe*, 1906 171
Bill Hallahan, 1930 177
Bill Hallahan, 1931 159
Dizzy Dean, 1932 191
Dizzy Dean, 1933 199
Dizzy Dean, 1934 195
Dizzy Dean, 1935 182
Harry Brecheen, 1948 149
Sam Jones, 1958 225
Bob Gibson, 1968 268
Jose DeLeon, 1989 201

*2 with Bost. Beaneaters and 21 with St.L. Cardinals

Lowest ERA, Season

Bill Doak, 1914 ..... 1.72
Bill Doak, 1921 ..... 2.58
Mort Cooper, 1942 ..... 1.77
Howie Pollet, 1943 ..... 1.75
Howie Pollet, 1946 ..... 2.10
Harry Brecheen, 1948 ..... 2.24
Bob Gibson, 1968 ..... 1.12
John Denny, 1976 ..... 2.52
Joe Magrane, 1988 ..... 2.18
Chris Carpenter, 2009 ..... 2.24

Most Saves, Season

Al Hrabosky, 1976 ..... 22 (Tie)
Bruce Sutter, 1981 25
Bruce Sutter, 1982 36
Bruce Sutter, 1984 45
Todd Worrell, 1986 36
Lee Smith, 1991 47
Lee Smith, 1992 43
Jason Isringhausen, 2004 ..... 47 (Tie)

Best Won-Lost Percentage, Season

Bill Doak, 1921 ..... 15–6 ... .714
Willie Sherdel, 1925 .... 15–6 ... .714
Paul Derringer, 1931 .... 18–8 ... .692
Dizzy Dean, 1934 ..... 30–7 ... .811
Mort Cooper, 1943 ..... 21–8 ... .724
Ted Wilks, 1944 ..... 17–4 ... .810
Harry Brecheen, 1945 .. 15–4 ... .789
Murry Dickson, 1946 .... 15–6 ... .714
Harry Brecheen, 1948 .. 20–7 ... .741
Ernie Broglio, 1960 ..... 21–9 ... .700
Dick Hughes, 1967 ..... 16–6 ... .727
Bob Gibson, 1970 ..... 23–7 ... .767
Bob Tewksbury, 1992 ... 16–5 ... .762
Chris Carpenter, 2009 .. 17–4 ... .810
Kyle Lohse, 2012 ..... 16–3 ... .842

Pitching Feats

20 Wins, Season

Cy Young, 1900 20–18
Jack Harper, 1901 20–12
Bob Wicker*, 1903 20–9
Kid Nichols, 1904 21–13
Jack Taylor, 1904 20–19
Bob Harmon, 1911 23–16
Bill Doak, 1920 20–12
Jesse Haines, 1923 20–13
Flint Rhem, 1926 20–7
Jesse Haines, 1927 24–10
Grover C. Alexander, 1927 21–10
Bill Sherdel, 1928 21–10
Jesse Haines, 1928 20–8
Dizzy Dean, 1933 20–18
Dizzy Dean, 1934 30–7
Dizzy Dean, 1935 28–12
Dizzy Dean, 1936 24–13
Curt Davis, 1939 22–16
Mort Cooper, 1942 22–7
Johnny Beazley, 1942 21–6
Mort Cooper, 1943 21–8
Mort Cooper, 1944 22–7
Red Barrett**, 1945 23–12
Howie Pollet, 1946 21–10
Howie Pollet, 1949 20–9
Harvey Haddix, 1953 20–9
Ernie Broglio, 1960 21–9
Ray Sadecki, 1964 20–11
Bob Gibson, 1965 20–12
Bob Gibson, 1966 21–12
Bob Gibson, 1968 22–9
Bob Gibson, 1969 20–13
Bob Gibson, 1970 23–7
Steve Carlton, 1971 20–9
Bob Forsch, 1977 20–7
Joaquin Andujar, 1984 20–14
John Tudor, 1985 21–8
Joaquin Andujar, 1985 21–12
Darryl Kile, 2000 20–9
Matt Morris, 2001 22–8
Chris Carpenter, 2005 21–5
Adam Wainwright, 2010 20–11
Adam Wainwright, 2014 20–9

*0–0 with Chi. Cubs and 20–9 with St.L. Cardinals.
**2–3 with Bost. Braves and 21–9 with St.L. Cardinals.

No-Hitters

Jesse Haines (vs. Bost. Braves), July 17, 1924 (final: 5–0)
Paul Dean (vs. Bklyn. Dodgers), Sept. 21, 1934 (final: 3–0)
Lon Warneke (vs. Cin. Reds), Aug. 30, 1941 (final: 2–0)
Ray Washburn (vs. S.F. Giants), Sept. 18, 1968 (final: 2–0)
Bob Gibson (vs. Pitt. Pirates), Aug. 14, 1971 (final: 11–0)
Bob Forsch (vs. Phila. Phillies), Apr. 16, 978 (final: 5–0)
Bob Forsch (vs. Mont. Expos), Sept. 26, 1983 (final: 3–0)
Jose Jimenez (vs. Ariz. D'backs), June 25, 1999 (final: 1–0)
Bud Smith (vs. S.D. Padres), Sept. 3, 2001 (final: 4–0)

No-Hitters Pitched Against

Christy Mathewson, N.Y. Giants, July 15, 1901 (final: 4–0)
Mal Eason, Bklyn. Dodgers, July 20, 1906 (final: 2–0)
Hod Eller, Cin. Reds, May 11, 1919 (final: 6–0)
Don Cardwell, Chi. Cubs, May 15, 1960 (final: 4–0)
Gaylord Perry, S.F. Giants, Sept. 17, 1968 (final: 1–0)
Tom Seaver, Cin. Reds, June 16, 1978 (final: 4–0)
Fernando Valenzuela, L.A. Dodgers, June 29, 1990 (final: 6–0)
Johan Santana, N.Y. Mets, June 1, 2012 (final: 8–0)

Postseason Play

1926 World Series vs. N.Y. Yankees (AL), won 4 games to 3
1928 World Series vs. N.Y. Yankees (AL), lost 4 games to 0
1930 World Series vs. Phila. A's (AL), lost 4 games to 2
1931 World Series vs. Phila. A's (AL), won 4 games to 3
1934 World Series vs. Det. Tigers (AL), won 4 games to 3
1942 World Series vs. N.Y. Yankees (AL), won 4 games to 1
1943 World Series vs. N.Y. Yankees (AL), lost 4 games to 1
1944 World Series vs. St.L. Browns (AL), won 4 games to 2
1946 Pennant Playoff Series vs. Bklyn. Dodgers, won 2 games to 0
World Series vs. Bost. Red Sox (AL), won 4 games to 3
1964 World Series vs. N.Y. Yankees (AL), won 4 games to 3
1967 World Series vs. Bost. Red Sox (AL), won 4 games to 3
1968 World Series vs. Det. Tigers (AL), lost 4 games to 3
1982 League Championship Series vs. Atl. Braves, won 3 games to 0
World Series vs. Milw. Brewers (AL), won 4 games to 3
1985 League Championship Series vs. L.A. Dodgers, won 4 games to 2
World Series vs. K.C. Royals (AL), lost 4 games to 3
1987 League Championship Series vs. S.F. Giants, won 4 games to 3
World Series vs. Min. Twins (AL), lost 4 games to 3
1996 Division Series vs. S.D. Padres, won 3 games to 0
League Championship Series vs. Atl. Braves, lost 4 games to 3
2000 Division Series vs. Atl. Braves, won 3 games to 0
League Championship Series vs. N.Y. Mets, lost 4 games to 1
2001 Division Series vs. Ariz. D'backs, lost 3 games to 2
2002 Division Series vs. Ariz. D'backs, won 3 games to 0
League Championship Series vs. S.F. Giants, lost 4 games to 1
2004 Division Series vs. L.A. Dodgers, won 3 games to 1
League Championship Series vs. Hous. Astros, won 4 games to 3
World Series vs. Bost. Red Sox (AL), lost 4 games to 0
2005 Division Series vs. S.D. Padres, won 3 games to 0
League Championship Series vs. Hous. Astros, lost 4 games to 2
2006 Division Series vs. S.D. Padres, won 3 games to 1
League Championship Series vs. N.Y. Mets, won 4 games to 3
World Series vs. Det. Tigers (AL), won 4 games to 1
2009 Division Series vs. L.A. Dodgers, lost 3 games to 0
2011 Division Series vs. Phila. Phillies, won 3 games to 2
League Championship Series vs. Milw. Brewers, won 4 games to 2
World Series vs. Tex. Rangers (AL), won 4 games to 3
2012 NL Wild Card Playoff Game vs. Atl. Braves, won
Division Series vs. Wash. Nationals, won 3 games to 2
League Championship Series vs. S.F. Giants, lost 4 games to 3
2013 Division Series vs. Pitt. Pirates, won 3 games to 2
League Championship Series vs. L.A. Dodgers, won 4 games to 2
World Series vs. Bost. Red Sox (AL), lost 4 games to 2
2014 Division Series to L.A. Dodgers, won 3 games to 1
League Championship Series vs. S.F. Giants, lost 4 games to 1
2015 Division Series vs. Chi. Cubs, lost 3 games to 1

San Diego Padres

Dates of Operation: 1969–present (47 years)

Overall Record: 3472 wins, 4016 losses (.463)

Stadiums: Qualcomm Stadium at Jack Murphy Field (also known as San Diego Stadium, 1967–79; San Diego–Jack Murphy Stadium, 1980; Jack Murphy Stadium, 1981–97), 1969–2003; Petco Park, 2004–present (capacity: 41,164)

Year-by-Year Finishes

Year	Finish	Wins	Losses	Percentage	Games Behind	Manager	Attendance
					West Division		
1969	6th	52	110	.321	41.0	Preston Gomez	512,970
1970	6th	63	99	.389	39.0	Preston Gomez	643,679
1971	6th	61	100	.379	28.5	Preston Gomez	557,513
1972	6th	58	95	.379	36.5	Preston Gomez, Don Zimmer	644,273
1973	6th	60	102	.370	39.0	Don Zimmer	611,826
1974	6th	60	102	.370	42.0	John McNamara	1,075,399
1975	4th	71	91	.438	37.0	John McNamara	1,281,747
1976	5th	73	89	.451	29.0	John McNamara	1,458,478
1977	5th	69	93	.426	29.0	John McNamara, Bob Skinner, Alvin Dark	1,376,269
1978	4th	84	78	.519	11.0	Roger Craig	1,670,107
1979	5th	68	93	.422	22.0	Roger Craig	1,456,967
1980	6th	73	89	.451	19.5	Jerry Coleman	1,139,026
1981*	6th/6th	41	69	.373	12.5/15.5	Frank Howard	519,161
1982	4th	81	81	.500	8.0	Dick Williams	1,607,516
1983	4th	81	81	.500	10.0	Dick Williams	1,539,815
1984	1st	92	70	.568	+12.0	Dick Williams	1,983,904
1985	3rd (Tie)	83	79	.512	12.0	Dick Williams	2,210,352
1986	4th	74	88	.457	22.0	Steve Boros	1,805,716
1987	6th	65	97	.401	25.0	Larry Bowa	1,454,061
1988	3rd	83	78	.516	11.0	Larry Bowa, Jack McKeon	1,506,896
1989	2nd	89	73	.549	3.0	Jack McKeon	2,009,031
1990	4th (Tie)	75	87	.463	16.0	Jack McKeon, Greg Riddoch	1,856,396
1991	3rd	84	78	.519	10.0	Greg Riddoch	1,804,289
1992	3rd	82	80	.506	16.0	Greg Riddoch, Jim Riggleman	1,722,102
1993	7th	61	101	.377	43.0	Jim Riggleman	1,375,432
1994	4th	47	70	.402	12.5	Jim Riggleman	953,857
1995	3rd	70	74	.486	8.0	Bruce Bochy	1,041,805
1996	1st	91	71	.562	+1.0	Bruce Bochy	2,187,886
1997	4th	76	86	.469	14.0	Bruce Bochy	2,089,333
1998	1st	98	64	.605	+9.5	Bruce Bochy	2,555,901
1999	4th	74	88	.457	26.0	Bruce Bochy	2,523,538
2000	5th	76	86	.469	21.0	Bruce Bochy	2,423,149
2001	4th	79	83	.488	13.0	Bruce Bochy	2,377,969
2002	5th	66	96	.407	32.0	Bruce Bochy	2,220,416
2003	5th	64	98	.395	36.5	Bruce Bochy	2,030,084
2004	3rd	87	75	.537	6.0	Bruce Bochy	3,016,752
2005	1st	82	80	.506	+5.0	Bruce Bochy	2,869,787
2006	1st (Tie)	88	74	.543	—	Bruce Bochy	2,659,754
2007	3rd	89	74	.546	1.5	Bud Black	2,790,074
2008	5th	63	99	.389	21.0	Bud Black	2,427,535
2009	4th	75	87	.463	20.0	Bud Black	1,922,603
2010	2nd	90	72	.556	2.0	Bud Black	2,131,774

2011	5th	71	91	.438	23.0	Bud Black	2,143,018
2012	4th	76	86	.469	18.0	Bud Black	2,123,721
2013	3rd	76	86	.469	16.0	Bud Black	2,166,691
2014	3rd	77	85	.475	17.0	Bud Black	2,195,373
2015	4th	74	88	.457	18.0	Bud Black, Dave Roberts, Pat Murphy	2,459,742

*Split season.

Awards

Most Valuable Player
Ken Caminiti, third base, 1996

Rookie of the Year
Butch Metzger (cowinner), pitcher, 1976
Benito Santiago, catcher, 1987

Cy Young
Randy Jones, 1976
Gaylord Perry, 1978
Mark Davis, 1989
Jake Peavy, 2007

Hall of Famers Who Played for the Padres
Rollie Fingers, pitcher, 1977–80
Goose Gossage, pitcher, 1984–87
Tony Gwynn, outfield, 1982–2001
Rickey Henderson, outfield, 1996–2001
Greg Maddux, pitcher, 2007–08
Willie McCovey, first base, 1974–76
Gaylord Perry, pitcher, 1978–79
Mike Piazza, catcher, 2006
Ozzie Smith, shortstop, 1978–81
Dave Winfield, outfield, 1973–80

Retired Numbers
JC ..... Jerry Coleman
RK ..... Ray Kroc
6 ..... Steve Garvey
19 ..... Tony Gwynn
31 ..... Dave Winfield
35 ..... Randy Jones
51 ..... Trevor Hoffman

League Leaders, Batting

Batting Average, Season
Tony Gwynn, 1984 ..... .351
Tony Gwynn, 1987 ..... .370
Tony Gwynn, 1988 ..... .313
Tony Gwynn, 1989 ..... .336
Gary Sheffield, 1992 ..... .330
Tony Gwynn, 1994 ..... .394
Tony Gwynn, 1995 ..... .368
Tony Gwynn, 1996 ..... .353
Tony Gwynn, 1997 ..... .372

Home Runs, Season
Fred McGriff, 1992 35

RBIs, Season
Dave Winfield, 1979 118
Chase Headley, 2012 115

Stolen Bases, Season
Everth Cabrera, 2012 44

Total Bases, Season
Dave Winfield, 1979 333
Gary Sheffield, 1992 323

Most Hits, Season
Tony Gwynn, 1984 213
Tony Gwynn, 1986 211
Tony Gwynn, 1987 218
Tony Gwynn, 1989 203
Tony Gwynn, 1994 165
Tony Gwynn, 1995 ..... 197 (Tie)
Tony Gwynn, 1997 220

Most Runs, Season
Tony Gwynn, 1986 ..... 107 (Tie)

Batting Feats

Triple Crown Winners
[No player]

Hitting for the Cycle
Matt Kemp, Aug. 14, 2015

Six Hits in a Game
Gene Richards, July 26, 1977*
Jim Lefebvre, Sept. 13, 1982*
Tony Gwynn, Aug. 4, 1993*
Adrian Gonzalez, Aug. 11, 2009
*Extra-inning game.

40 or More Home Runs, Season
50 ..... Greg Vaughn, 1998
41 ..... Phil Nevin, 2001
40 ..... Ken Caminiti, 1996
Adrian Gonzalez, 2009

League Leaders, Pitching

Most Wins, Season
Randy Jones, 1976 22
Gaylord Perry, 1978 21
Jake Peavy, 2007 19

Most Strikeouts, Season
Andy Benes, 1994 189
Jake Peavy, 2005 216
Jake Peavy, 2007 240

Lowest ERA, Season
Randy Jones, 1975 ..... 2.24
Jake Peavy, 2004 ..... 2.27
Jake Peavy, 2007 ..... 2.54

Most Saves, Season
Rollie Fingers, 1977 35
Rollie Fingers, 1978 37
Mark Davis, 1989 44
Trevor Hoffman, 1998 53
Trevor Hoffman, 2006 46
Heath Bell, 2009 42

Best Won–Lost Percentage, Season
Gaylord Perry, 1978 .... 21–6 ... .778

Pitching Feats

Triple Crown Winner
Jake Peavy, 2007 (19–6, 2.54 ERA, 240 SO)

20 Wins, Season
Randy Jones, 1975 20–12
Randy Jones, 1976 22–14
Gaylord Perry, 1978 21–6

No-Hitters
[No pitcher]

No-Hitters Pitched Against
Dock Ellis, Pitt. Pirates, June 12, 1970 (final: 2–0)
Milt Pappas, Chi. Cubs, Sept. 2, 1972 (final: 8–0)
Phil Niekro, Atl. Braves, Aug. 5, 1973 (final: 9–0)

Kent Mercker, Mark Wohlers, and Alejandro Pena, Atl. Braves, Sept. 11, 1991 (final: 1–0)
A.J. Burnett, Fla. Marlins, May 12, 2001 (final: 3–0)
Bud Smith, St.L. Cardinals, Sept. 3, 2001 (final: 4–0)
Jonathan Sanchez, S.F. Giants, July 10, 2009 (final: 8–0)
Tim Lincecum, S.F. Giants, July 13, 2013 (final: 9–0)
Tim Lincecum, S.F. Giants, June 25, 2014 (final: 4–0)

Postseason Play

1984 League Championship Series vs. Chi. Cubs, won 3 games to 2
World Series vs. Det. Tigers (AL), lost 4 games to 1
1996 Division Series vs. St.L. Cardinals, lost 3 games to 0
1998 Division Series vs. Hous. Astros, won 3 games to 1
League Championship Series vs. Atl. Braves, won 4 games to 2
World Series vs. N.Y. Yankees (AL), lost 4 games to 0
2005 Division Series vs. St.L. Cardinals, lost 3 games to 0
2006 Division Series vs. St.L. Cardinals, lost 3 games to 1
2007 NL Wild Card Playoff Game vs. Colo. Rockies, lost

San Francisco Giants

Dates of Operation: 1958–present (58 years)
Overall Record: 4797 wins, 4442 losses (.519)
Stadiums: Seals Stadium, 1958–59; Candlestick Park (also known as 3Com Park, 1996–99), 1960–2000; AT&T Park (formerly Pacific Bell Park, or Pac Bell, 2000–02; and SBC Park, 2003–05), 2000–present (capacity: 41,915)

Year-by-Year Finishes

Year	Finish	Wins	Losses	Percentage	Games Behind	Manager	Attendance
1958	3rd	80	74	.519	12.0	Bill Rigney	1,272,625
1959	3rd	83	71	.539	4.0	Bill Rigney	1,422,130
1960	5th	79	75	.513	16.0	Bill Rigney, Tom Sheehan	1,795,356
1961	3rd	85	69	.552	8.0	Alvin Dark	1,390,679
1962	1st	103	62	.624	+1.0	Alvin Dark	1,592,594
1963	3rd	88	74	.543	11.0	Alvin Dark	1,571,306
1964	4th	90	72	.556	3.0	Alvin Dark	1,504,364
1965	2nd	95	67	.586	2.0	Herman Franks	1,546,075
1966	2nd	93	68	.578	1.5	Herman Franks	1,657,192
1967	2nd	91	71	.562	10.5	Herman Franks	1,242,480
1968	2nd	88	74	.543	9.0	Herman Franks	837,220
					West Division		
1969	2nd	90	72	.556	3.0	Clyde King	873,603
1970	3rd	86	76	.531	16.0	Clyde King, Charlie Fox	740,720
1971	1st	90	72	.556	+1.0	Charlie Fox	1,106,043
1972	5th	69	86	.445	26.5	Charlie Fox	647,744
1973	3rd	88	74	.543	11.0	Charlie Fox	834,193
1974	5th	72	90	.444	30.0	Charlie Fox, Wes Westrum	519,987
1975	3rd	80	81	.497	27.5	Wes Westrum	522,919
1976	4th	74	88	.457	28.0	Bill Rigney	626,868
1977	4th	75	87	.463	23.0	Joe Altobelli	700,056
1978	3rd	89	73	.549	6.0	Joe Altobelli	1,740,477
1979	4th	71	91	.438	19.5	Joe Altobelli, Dave Bristol	1,456,402
1980	5th	75	86	.466	17.0	Dave Bristol	1,096,115
1981*	5th/3rd	56	55	.505	10.0/3.5	Frank Robinson	632,274
1982	3rd	87	75	.537	2.0	Frank Robinson	1,200,948
1983	5th	79	83	.488	12.0	Frank Robinson	1,251,530
1984	6th	66	96	.407	26.0	Frank Robinson, Danny Ozark	1,001,545
1985	6th	62	100	.383	33.0	Jim Davenport, Roger Craig	818,697
1986	3rd	83	79	.512	13.0	Roger Craig	1,528,748
1987	1st	90	72	.556	+6.0	Roger Craig	1,917,168
1988	4th	83	79	.512	11.5	Roger Craig	1,785,297
1989	1st	92	70	.568	+3.0	Roger Craig	2,059,701
1990	3rd	85	77	.525	6.0	Roger Craig	1,975,528
1991	4th	75	87	.463	19.0	Roger Craig	1,737,478
1992	5th	72	90	.444	26.0	Roger Craig	1,561,987
1993	2nd	103	59	.636	1.0	Dusty Baker	2,606,354
1994	2nd	55	60	.478	3.5	Dusty Baker	1,704,608
1995	4th	67	77	.465	11.0	Dusty Baker	1,241,500
1996	4th	68	94	.420	23.0	Dusty Baker	1,413,922
1997	1st	90	72	.556	+2.0	Dusty Baker	1,690,869
1998	2nd	89	74	.546	9.5	Dusty Baker	1,925,634
1999	2nd	86	76	.531	14.0	Dusty Baker	2,078,399

2000	1st	97	65	.599	+11.0	Dusty Baker	3,315,330
2001	2nd	90	72	.556	2.0	Dusty Baker	3,277,244
2002	2nd	95	66	.590	2.5	Dusty Baker	3,253,205
2003	1st	100	61	.621	+15.5	Felipe Alou	3,264,898
2004	2nd	91	71	.562	2.0	Felipe Alou	3,256,858
2005	3rd	75	87	.463	7.0	Felipe Alou	3,223,217
2006	3rd	76	85	.472	11.5	Felipe Alou	3,129,785
2007	5th	71	91	.438	19.0	Bruce Bochy	3,223,217
2008	4th	72	90	.444	12.0	Bruce Bochy	2,863,837
2009	3rd	88	74	.543	7.0	Bruce Bochy	2,861,113
2010	1st	92	70	.568	+2.0	Bruce Bochy	3,037,443
2011	2nd	86	76	.531	8.0	Bruce Bochy	3,387,303
2012	1st	94	68	.580	+8.0	Bruce Bochy	3,377,371
2013	3rd	76	86	.469	16.0	Bruce Bochy	3,369,106
2014	2nd	88	74	.543	6.0	Bruce Bochy	3,368,697
2015	2nd	84	78	.519	8.0	Bruce Bochy	3,375,882

*Split season.

Awards

Most Valuable Player

Willie Mays, outfield, 1965
Willie McCovey, first base, 1969
Kevin Mitchell, outfield, 1989
Barry Bonds, outfield, 1993
Jeff Kent, second base, 2000
Barry Bonds, outfield, 2001
Barry Bonds, outfield, 2002
Barry Bonds, outfield, 2003
Barry Bonds, outfield, 2004

Rookie of the Year

Orlando Cepeda, first base, 1958
Willie McCovey, first base, 1959
Gary Matthews, outfield, 1973
John Montefusco, pitcher, 1975
Buster Posey, catcher, 2010

Cy Young

Mike McCormick, 1967
Tim Lincecum, 2008
Tim Lincecum, 2009

Hall of Famers Who Played for the San Francisco Giants

Steve Carlton, pitcher, 1986
Gary Carter, catcher, 1990
Orlando Cepeda, first base, 1958–66
Goose Gossage, pitcher, 1989
Randy Johnson, pitcher, 2009
Juan Marichal, pitcher, 1960–73
Willie Mays, outfield, 1958–72
Willie McCovey, first base and outfield, 1959–73 and 1977–80
Joe Morgan, second base, 1981–82
Gaylord Perry, pitcher, 1962–71
Duke Snider, outfield, 1964
Warren Spahn, pitcher, 1965

Retired Numbers

CM ..... Christy Mathewson
JM..... John McGraw
RH ..... Russ Hodges
LS ..... Lon Simmons
3 ..... Bill Terry
4 ..... Mel Ott
11 ..... Carl Hubbell
20 ..... Monte Irvin
24 ..... Willie Mays
27 ..... Juan Marichal
30 ..... Orlando Cepeda
36 ..... Gaylord Perry
44 ..... Willie McCovey

League Leaders, Batting

Batting Average, Season

Barry Bonds, 2002..... .370
Barry Bonds, 2004..... .363
Buster Posey, 2012 ..... .336

Home Runs, Season

Orlando Cepeda, 1961 46
Willie Mays, 1962.....49
Willie McCovey, 1963 .....44 (Tie)
Willie Mays, 1964.....47
Willie Mays, 1965.....52
Willie McCovey, 1968 36
Willie McCovey, 1969 45
Kevin Mitchell, 1989 47
Barry Bonds, 1993.....46
Matt Williams, 1994 43
Barry Bonds, 2001 73

RBIs, Season

Orlando Cepeda, 1961 142
Orlando Cepeda, 1967.....111
Willie McCovey, 1968 105
Willie McCovey, 1969 126
Will Clark, 1988 109
Kevin Mitchell, 1989 125
Matt Williams, 1990 122
Barry Bonds, 1993.....123

Stolen Bases, Season

Willie Mays, 1958.....31
Willie Mays, 1959.....27

Total Bases, Season

Willie Mays, 1962.....382
Willie Mays, 1965.....360
Bobby Bonds, 1973 341
Kevin Mitchell, 1989 345
Will Clark, 1991 .....303 (Tie)
Barry Bonds, 1993.....365

Most Hits, Season

Willie Mays, 1960.....190
Brett Butler, 1990.....192 (Tie)
Rich Aurilia, 2001.....206

Most Runs, Season

Willie Mays, 1958.....121
Willie Mays, 1961.....129
Bobby Bonds, 1969 .....120 (Tie)
Bobby Bonds, 1973 131
Brett Butler, 1988.....109
Will Clark, 1989 .....104 (Tie)

Batting Feats

Triple Crown Winners

[No player]

Hitting for the Cycle

Jim Ray Hart, July 8, 1970
Dave Kingman, Apr. 16, 1972
Jeffrey Leonard, June 27, 1985
Candy Maldonado, May 4, 1987
Chris Speier, July 9, 1988
Robby Thompson, Apr. 22, 1991
Jeff Kent, May 3, 1999
Randy Winn, Aug. 15, 2005
Fred Lewis, May 13, 2007
Pablo Sandoval, Sept. 15, 2011

Six Hits in a Game

Jesus Alou, July 10, 1964
Mike Benjamin, June 14, 1995*
Randy Winn, Aug. 15, 2005
Fred Lewis, May 13, 2007
*Extra-inning game.

40 or More Home Runs, Season

73 ..... Barry Bonds, 2001
52 ..... Willie Mays, 1965
49 ..... Willie Mays, 1962
Barry Bonds, 2000
47 ..... Willie Mays, 1964
Kevin Mitchell, 1989
46 ..... Orlando Cepeda, 1961
Barry Bonds, 1993
Barry Bonds, 2002
45 ..... Willie McCovey, 1969
Barry Bonds, 2003
Barry Bonds, 2004
44 ..... Willie McCovey, 1963
43 ..... Matt Williams, 1994
42 ..... Barry Bonds, 1996
40 ..... Willie Mays, 1961
Barry Bonds, 1997

League Leaders, Pitching

Most Wins, Season

Sam Jones, 1959 ..... 21 (Tie)
Juan Marichal, 1963 ..... 25 (Tie)
Mike McCormick, 1967 22
Juan Marichal, 1968 26
Gaylord Perry, 1970 ..... 23 (Tie)
Ron Bryant, 1973 24
John Burnett, 1993 ..... 22 (Tie)

Most Strikeouts, Season

Tim Lincecum, 2008 265
Tim Lincecum, 2009 261
Tim Lincecum, 2010 231

Lowest ERA, Season

Stu Miller, 1958 ..... 2.47
Sam Jones, 1959 ..... 2.82
Mike McCormick, 1960 ..... 2.70
Juan Marichal, 1969 ..... 2.10
Atlee Hammaker, 1983 ..... 2.25
Scott Garrelts, 1989 ..... 2.28
Bill Swift, 1992 ..... 2.08
Jason Schmidt, 2003 ..... 2.34

Most Saves, Season

Rob Nen, 2001 45
Brian Wilson, 2010 48

Best Won–Lost Percentage, Season

Juan Marichal, 1966 .... 25–6 ... .806
Jason Schmidt, 2003 .... 17–5 ... .773
Tim Lincecum, 2008 ..... 18–5 ... .783

Pitching Feats

20 Wins, Season

Sam Jones, 1959 21–15
Jack Sanford, 1962 24–7
Juan Marichal, 1963 25–8
Juan Marichal, 1964 21–8
Juan Marichal, 1965 22–13
Juan Marichal, 1966 25–6
Gaylord Perry, 1966 21–8
Mike McCormick, 1967 22–10
Juan Marichal, 1968 26–9
Juan Marichal, 1969 21–11
Gaylord Perry, 1970 23–13
Ron Bryant, 1973 24–12
Mike Krukow, 1986 20–9
John Burkett, 1993 22–7
Bill Swift, 1993 21–8

No-Hitters

Juan Marichal (vs. Hous. Astros), June 15, 1963 (final: 1–0)
Gaylord Perry (vs. St.L. Cardinals), Sept. 17, 1968 (final: 1–0)
Ed Halicki (vs. N.Y. Mets), Aug. 24, 1975 (final: 6–0)
John Montefusco (vs. Atl. Braves), Sept. 29, 1976 (final: 9–0)
Jonathan Sanchez (vs. S.D. Padres), July 10, 2009 (final 8–0)
Matt Cain (vs. Hous. Astros), June 13, 2012 (final: 10–0) (perfect game)
Tim Lincecum (vs. S.D. Padres), July 13, 2013 (final: 9–0)
Tim Lincecum (vs. S.D. Padres), June 25, 2014 (final: 4–0)
Chris Heston (vs. N.Y. Mets), June 9, 2015 (final: 5–0)

No-Hitters Pitched Against

Warren Spahn, Milw. Braves, Apr. 28, 1961 (final: 1–0)
Sandy Koufax, L.A. Dodgers, May 11, 1963 (final: 8–0)
Ray Washburn, St.L. Cardinals, Sept. 18, 1968 (final: 2–0)
Jerry Reuss, L.A. Dodgers, June 27, 1980 (final: 8–0)
Charlie Lea, Mont. Expos, May 10, 1981 (final: 4–0)
Mike Scott, Hous. Astros, Sept. 25, 1986 (final: 2–0)
Terry Mulholland, Phila. Phillies, Aug. 15, 1990 (final: 6–0)
Kevin Gross, L.A. Dodgers, Aug. 17, 1992 (final: 2–0)
Kevin Brown, Fla. Marlins, June 10, 1997 (final: 9–0)
Kevin Millwood, Phila. Phillies, Apr. 27, 2003 (final: 1–0)
Homer Bailey, Cin. Reds, July 2, 2013 (final: 3–0)

Postseason Play

1962 Pennant Playoff Series vs. L.A. Dodgers, won 2 games to 1
World Series vs. N.Y. Yankees (AL), lost 4 games to 3
1971 League Championship Series vs. Pitt. Pirates, lost 3 games to 1
1987 League Championship Series vs. St.L. Cardinals, lost 4 games to 3
1989 League Championship Series vs. Chi. Cubs, won 4 games to 1
World Series vs. Oak. A's (AL), lost 4 games to 0
1997 Division Series vs. Fla. Marlins, lost 3 games to 0
1998 NL Wild Card Playoff Game vs. Chi. Cubs, lost
2000 Division Series vs. N.Y. Mets, lost 3 games to 1
2002 Division Series vs. Atl. Braves, won 3 games to 1
League Championship Series vs. St.L. Cardinals, won 4 games to 1
World Series vs. Ana. Angels (AL), lost 4 games to 3
2003 Division Series vs. Fla. Marlins, lost 3 games to 1
2010 Division Series vs. Atl. Braves, won 3 games to 1
League Championship Series vs. Phila. Phillies, won 4 games to 2
World Series vs. Tex. Rangers (AL), won 4 games to 1
2012 Division Series vs. Cin. Reds, won 3 games to 2
League Championship Series vs. St.L. Cardinals, won 4 games to 3
World Series vs. Det. Tigers (AL), won 4 games to 0
2014 NL Wild Card Playoff Game vs. Pitt. Pirates, won
Division Series vs. Wash. Nationals, won 3 games to 1
League Championship Series vs. St.L. Cardinals, won 4 games to 1
World Series vs. K.C. Royals (AL), won 4 games to 3

Washington Nationals (formerly the Montreal Expos)

Dates of Operation: (as the Montreal Expos) 1969–2004 (36 years)
Overall Record: 2755 wins, 2943 losses (.484)
Stadiums: Jerry Park, 1969–76; Olympic Stadium, 1977–2004 (capacity: 46,500); Estadio Hiram Bithorn, San Juan, Puerto Rico (part of 2003 and 2004 seasons) (capacity: 18,000)

Dates of Operation: (as the Washington Nationals) 2005–present (11 years)
Overall Record: 855 wins, 925 losses (.480)
Stadiums: RFK Stadium, 2005–07; Nationals Park, 2008–present (capacity: 41,888)

Year-by-Year Finishes

Year	Finish	Wins	Losses	Percentage	Games Behind	Manager	Attendance
					Mont. Expos		
					East Division		
1969	6th	52	110	.321	48.0	Gene Mauch	1,212,608
1970	6th	73	89	.451	16.0	Gene Mauch	1,424,683
1971	5th	71	90	.441	25.5	Gene Mauch	1,290,963
1972	5th	70	86	.449	26.5	Gene Mauch	1,142,145
1973	4th	79	83	.488	3.5	Gene Mauch	1,246,863
1974	4th	79	82	.491	8.5	Gene Mauch	1,019,134
1975	5th (Tie)	75	87	.463	17.5	Gene Mauch	908,292
1976	6th	55	107	.340	46.0	Karl Kuehl, Charlie Fox	646,704
1977	5th	75	87	.463	26.0	Dick Williams	1,433,757
1978	4th	76	86	.469	14.0	Dick Williams	1,427,007
1979	2nd	95	65	.594	2.0	Dick Williams	2,102,173
1980	2nd	90	72	.556	1.0	Dick Williams	2,208,175
1981*	3rd/1st	60	48	.556	4.0/+0.5	Dick Williams, Jim Fanning	1,534,564
1982	3rd	86	76	.531	6.0	Jim Fanning	2,318,292
1983	3rd	82	80	.506	8.0	Bill Virdon	2,320,651
1984	5th	78	83	.484	18.0	Bill Virdon, Jim Fanning	1,606,531
1985	3rd	84	77	.522	16.5	Buck Rodgers	1,502,494
1986	4th	78	83	.484	29.5	Buck Rodgers	1,128,981
1987	3rd	91	71	.562	4.0	Buck Rodgers	1,850,324
1988	3rd	81	81	.500	20.0	Buck Rodgers	1,478,659
1989	4th	81	81	.500	12.0	Buck Rodgers	1,783,533
1990	3rd	85	77	.525	10.0	Buck Rodgers	1,373,087
1991	6th	71	90	.441	26.5	Buck Rodgers, Tom Runnells	934,742
1992	2nd	87	75	.537	9.0	Tom Runnells, Felipe Alou	1,669,077
1993	2nd	94	68	.580	3.0	Felipe Alou	1,641,437
1994	1st	74	40	.649	+6.0	Felipe Alou	1,276,250
1995	5th	66	78	.458	24.0	Felipe Alou	1,309,618
1996	2nd	88	74	.543	8.0	Felipe Alou	1,616,709
1997	4th	78	84	.481	23.0	Felipe Alou	1,497,609
1998	4th	65	97	.401	41.0	Felipe Alou	914,717
1999	4th	68	94	.420	35.0	Felipe Alou	773,277
2000	4th	67	95	.414	28.0	Felipe Alou	926,263
2001	5th	68	94	.420	20.0	Felipe Alou, Jeff Torborg	609,473
2002	2nd	83	79	.512	19.0	Frank Robinson	732,901
2003	4th	83	79	.512	18.0	Frank Robinson	1,025,639
2004	5th	67	95	.414	29.0	Frank Robinson	748,550
					Wash. Nationals		
2005	5th	81	81	.500	9.0	Frank Robinson	2,731,993
2006	5th	71	91	.438	26.0	Frank Robinson	2,153,058

2007	4th	73	89	.451	16.0	Manny Acta	1,961,606
2008	5th	59	102	.366	32.5	Manny Acta	2,320,400
2009	5th	59	103	.364	34.0	Manny Acta, Jim Riggleman	1,817,226
2010	5th	69	93	.425	28.0	Jim Riggleman	1,828,065
2011	3rd	80	81	.497	21.5	Jim Riggleman, Davey Johnson	1,940,478
2012	1st	98	64	.605	+4.0	Davey Johnson	2,370,794
2013	2nd	86	76	.531	10.0	Davey Johnson	2,652,422
2014	1st	96	66	.597	+17.0	Matt Williams	2,579,389
2015	2nd	83	79	.512	7.0	Matt Williams	2,619,843

*Split season.

Awards

Most Valuable Player

Bryce Harper, outfield, 2015

Rookie of the Year

Carl Morton, pitcher, 1970 (Mont.)
Andre Dawson, outfield, 1977 (Mont.)
Bryce Harper, outfield, 2012

Cy Young

Pedro Martinez, 1997 (Mont.)

Hall of Famers Who Played for the Expos

Gary Carter, catcher, 1974–84 and 1992
Andre Dawson, outfield, 1976–86
Randy Johnson, pitcher, 1988–89
Pedro Martinez, pitcher, 1994–97
Tony Perez, first base, 1977–79

Retired Numbers (Mont.)

CB ..... Charles Bronfman
8 ..... Gary Carter
10 ..... Rusty Staub
10 ..... Andre Dawson
20 ..... Monte Irvin
30 ..... Tim Raines

League Leaders, Batting

Batting Average, Season

Al Oliver, 1982 (Mont.) ..... .331
Tim Raines, 1986 (Mont.) ..... .334

Home Runs, Season

Bryce Harper, 2015 ..... 42 (Tie)

RBIs, Season

Al Oliver, 1982 (Mont.) ..... 109 (Tie)
Gary Carter, 1984 (Mont.) ... 106 (Tie)

Stolen Bases, Season

Ron LeFlore, 1980 (Mont.) 97
Tim Raines, 1981 (Mont.) 71
Tim Raines, 1982 (Mont.) 78
Tim Raines, 1983 (Mont.) 90
Tim Raines, 1984 (Mont.) 75
Marquis Grissom, 1991 (Mont.) 76
Marquis Grissom, 1992 (Mont.) 78

Total Bases, Season

Al Oliver, 1982 (Mont.) 317
Andre Dawson, 1983 (Mont.) 341
Andres Galarraga, 1988 (Mont.) . 329
Vladimir Guererro, 2002 (Mont.) .. 364

Most Hits, Season

Al Oliver, 1982 (Mont.) 204
Andre Dawson, 1983 (Mont.) 189 (Tie)
Andres Galarraga, 1988 (Mont.) . 184
Vladimir Guerrero, 2002 (Mont.) .. 206
Denard Span, 2014 ..... 184 (Tie)

Most Runs, Season

Tim Raines, 1983 (Mont.) 133
Tim Raines, 1987 (Mont.) 123
Anthony Rendon, 2014 111
Bryce Harper, 2015 118

Batting Feats

Triple Crown Winners

[No player]

Hitting for the Cycle

Tim Foli, Apr. 22, 1976 (Mont.)
Chris Speier, July 20, 1978 (Mont.)
Tim Raines, Aug. 16, 1987 (Mont.)
Rondell White, June 11, 1995 (Mont.)
Brad Wilkerson, June 24, 2003 (Mont.)
Vladimir Guerrero, Sept. 14, 2003 (Mont.)

Six Hits in a Game

Rondell White, June 11, 1995* (Mont.)
Brad Wilkerson, Apr. 6, 2005
Cristian Guzman, Aug. 28, 2008

*Extra-inning game.

40 or More Home Runs, Season

46 ..... Alfonso Soriano, 2006
44 ... Vladimir Guerrero, 2000 (Mont.)
42 ... Vladimir Guerrero, 1999 (Mont.)
Bryce Harper, 2015

League Leaders, Pitching

Most Wins, Season

Ken Hill, 1994 (Mont.) ..... 16 (Tie)
Gio Gonzalez, 2012 21
Jordan Zimmerman, 2013 ..... 19 (Tie)

Most Strikeouts, Season

Stephen Strausburg, 2014 .... 242 (Tie)

Lowest ERA, Season

Steve Rogers, 1982 (Mont.) 2.40
Dennis Martinez, 1991 (Mont.) ... 2.39
Pedro Martinez, 1997 (Mont.) 1.90

Most Saves, Season

Mike Marshall, 1973 (Mont.) 31
Jeff Reardon, 1985 (Mont.) 41
Ugueth Urbina, 1999 (Mont.) 41
Chad Cordero, 2005 47

Best Won-Lost Percentage, Season

[No pitcher]

Pitching Feats

20 Wins, Season

Ross Grimsley, 1978 (Mont.) ... 20–11
Bartolo Colon*, 2002 (Mont.) 20–8
Gio Gonzalez, 2012 21–8

*10–4 with Cle. Indians (AL) and 10–4 with Mont. Expos.

No-Hitters

Bill Stoneman (vs. Phila. Phillies), Apr. 17, 1969 (final: 7–0) (Mont.)
Bill Stoneman (vs. N.Y. Mets), Oct. 2,

1972 (final: 7–0) (Mont.)
Charlie Lea (vs. S.F. Giants), May 10, 1981 (final: 4–0) (Mont.)
Dennis Martinez (Mont.) (vs. L.A. Dodgers), July 28, 1991 (final: 2–0) (perfect game) (Mont.)
Jordan Zimmermann (vs. Mia. Marlins), Sept. 28, 2014 (final: 1–0)
Max Scherzer (vs. Pitt. Pirates), June 20, 2015 (final: 6–0)
Max Scherzer (vs. N.Y. Mets), Oct. 3, 2015 (final: 2–0)

No-Hitters Pitched Against

Larry Dierker, Hous. Astros, July 9, 1976 (final: 6–0) (Mont.)
Bob Forsch, St.L. Cardinals, Sept. 26, 1983 (final: 3–0) (Mont.)
Tommy Greene, Phila. Phillies, May 23, 1991 (final: 2–0) (Mont.)
David Cone, N.Y. Yankees (AL), July 18, 1999 (final: 6–0) (perfect game) (Mont.)

Postseason Play

1981 Second-Half Division Playoff Series vs. Phila. Phillies, won 3 games to 2 (Mont.)
League Championship Series vs. L.A. Dodgers, lost 3 games to 2 (Mont.)
2012 Division Series vs. St.L. Cardinals, lost 3 games to 2
2014 Division Series vs. S.F. Giants, lost 3 games to 1

FRANCHISES NO LONGER IN EXISTENCE

Boston Braves

Dates of Operation: 1876–1952 (77 years)
Overall Record: 5118 wins, 5598 losses (.478)
Stadiums: South End Grounds, 1876–93 and 1895–1914; Congress Street Grounds, 1894; Fenway Park, 1914–15 and 1946; Braves Field, 1915–52 (capacity: 44,500)
Other Names: Red Stockings, Red Caps, Beaneaters, Nationals, Doves, Rustlers, Bees

Year-by-Year Finishes

Year	Finish	Wins	Losses	Percentage	Games Behind	Manager	Attendance
1876	4th	39	31	.557	15.0	Harry Wright	not available
1877	1st	42	18	.700	+7.0	Harry Wright	not available
1878	1st	41	19	.683	+4.0	Harry Wright	not available
1879	2nd	49	29	.628	6.0	Harry Wright	not available
1880	6th	40	44	.476	27.0	Harry Wright	not available
1881	6th	38	45	.458	17.5	Harry Wright	not available
1882	3rd (Tie)	45	39	.536	10.0	John Morrill	not available
1883	1st	63	35	.643	+4.0	Jack Burdock, John Morrill	not available
1884	2nd	73	38	.658	10.5	John Morrill	not available
1885	5th	48	66	.410	31.0	John Morrill	not available
1886	5th	56	61	.478	30.5	John Morrill	not available
1887	5th	61	60	.504	16.5	John Morrill	not available
1888	4th	70	64	.522	15.5	John Morrill	not available
1889	2nd	83	45	.648	1.0	Jim Hart	not available
1890	5th	76	57	.571	12.0	Frank Selee	not available
1891	1st	87	51	.630	+3.5	Frank Selee	not available
1892	1st	102	48	.680	+9.5	Frank Selee	not available
1893	1st	86	44	.662	+4.5	Frank Selee	not available
1894	3rd	83	49	.629	8.0	Frank Selee	not available
1895	5th (Tie)	71	60	.542	16.5	Frank Selee	not available
1896	4th	74	57	.565	17.0	Frank Selee	not available
1897	1st	93	39	.705	+2.0	Frank Selee	not available
1898	1st	102	47	.685	+6.0	Frank Selee	not available
1899	2nd	95	57	.625	4.0	Frank Selee	not available
1900	4th	66	72	.478	17.0	Frank Selee	not available
1901	5th	69	69	.500	20.5	Frank Selee	146,502
1902	3rd	73	64	.533	29.0	Al Buckenberger	116,960
1903	6th	58	80	.420	32.0	Al Buckenberger	143,155
1904	7th	55	98	.359	51.0	Al Buckenberger	140,694
1905	7th	51	103	.331	54.5	Fred Tenney	150,003

1906	8th	49	102	.325	66.5	Fred Tenney	143,280
1907	7th	58	90	.392	47.0	Fred Tenney	203,221
1908	6th	63	91	.409	36.0	Joe Kelley	253,750
1909	8th	45	108	.294	65.5	Fred Bowerman, Harry Smith	195,188
1910	8th	53	100	.346	50.5	Fred Lake	149,027
1911	8th	44	107	.291	54.0	Fred Tenney	96,000
1912	8th	52	101	.340	52.0	Johnny Kling	121,000
1913	5th	69	82	.457	31.5	George Stallings	208,000
1914	1st	94	59	.614	+10.5	George Stallings	382,913
1915	2nd	83	69	.546	7.0	George Stallings	376,283
1916	3rd	89	63	.586	4.0	George Stallings	313,495
1917	6th	72	81	.471	25.5	George Stallings	174,253
1918	7th	53	71	.427	28.5	George Stallings	84,938
1919	6th	57	82	.410	38.5	George Stallings	167,401
1920	7th	62	90	.408	30.0	George Stallings	162,483
1921	4th	79	74	.516	15.0	Fred Mitchell	318,627
1922	8th	53	100	.346	39.5	Fred Mitchell	167,965
1923	7th	54	100	.351	41.5	Fred Mitchell	227,802
1924	8th	53	100	.346	40.0	Dave Bancroft	177,478
1925	5th	70	83	.458	25.0	Dave Bancroft	313,528
1926	7th	66	86	.434	22.0	Dave Bancroft	303,598
1927	7th	60	94	.390	34.0	Dave Bancroft	288,685
1928	7th	50	103	.327	44.5	Jack Slattery, Rogers Hornsby	227,001
1929	8th	56	98	.364	43.0	Judge Emil Fuchs	372,351
1930	6th	70	84	.455	22.0	Bill McKechnie	464,835
1931	7th	64	90	.416	37.0	Bill McKechnie	515,005
1932	5th	77	77	.500	13.0	Bill McKechnie	507,606
1933	4th	83	71	.539	9.0	Bill McKechnie	517,803
1934	4th	78	73	.517	16.0	Bill McKechnie	303,205
1935	8th	38	115	.248	61.5	Bill McKechnie	232,754
1936	6th	71	83	.461	21.0	Bill McKechnie	340,585
1937	5th	79	73	.520	16.0	Bill McKechnie	385,339
1938	5th	77	75	.507	12.0	Casey Stengel	341,149
1939	7th	63	88	.417	32.5	Casey Stengel	285,994
1940	7th	65	87	.428	34.5	Casey Stengel	241,616
1941	7th	62	92	.403	38.0	Casey Stengel	263,680
1942	7th	59	89	.399	44.0	Casey Stengel	285,322
1943	6th	68	85	.444	36.5	Casey Stengel	271,289
1944	6th	65	89	.422	40.0	Bob Coleman	208,691
1945	6th	67	85	.441	30.0	Bob Coleman, Del Bissonette	374,178
1946	4th	81	72	.529	15.5	Billy Southworth	969,673
1947	3rd	86	68	.558	8.0	Billy Southworth	1,277,361
1948	1st	91	62	.595	+6.5	Billy Southworth	1,455,439
1949	4th	75	79	.487	22.0	Billy Southworth	1,081,795
1950	4th	83	71	.539	8.0	Billy Southworth	944,391
1951	4th	76	78	.494	20.5	Billy Southworth, Tommy Holmes	487,475
1952	7th	64	89	.418	32.0	Tommy Holmes, Charlie Grimm	281,278

Awards

Most Valuable Player
Johnny Evers, second base, 1914
Bob Elliott, third base, 1947

Rookie of the Year
Alvin Dark, shortstop, 1948
Sam Jethroe, outfield, 1950

Cy Young
[No pitcher]

Hall of Famers Who Played for the Boston Braves
Earl Averill, outfield, 1941
Dave Bancroft, shortstop, 1924–27
Dan Brouthers, first base, 1889
John Clarkson, pitcher, 1888–92
Hugh Duffy, outfield, 1892–1900
Johnny Evers, second base, 1914–17
Burleigh Grimes, pitcher, 1930
Billy Hamilton, outfield, 1896–1901
Billy Herman, second base, 1946
Rogers Hornsby, second base, 1928
Joe Kelley, outfield, 1891 and 1908
King Kelly, outfield and catcher, 1887–90
Ernie Lombardi, catcher, 1942
Al Lopez, catcher, 1936–40
Rabbit Maranville, shortstop, 1912–20 and 1929–35
Rube Marquard, pitcher, 1922–25
Eddie Mathews, third base, 1952
Tommy McCarthy, outfield and infield, 1885 and 1892–95
Bill McKechnie, infield, 1913
Joe Medwick, outfield, 1945
Kid Nichols, pitcher, 1890–1901
Jim O'Rourke, outfield and infield, 1876–78
Old Hoss Radbourn, pitcher, 1886–89
Babe Ruth, outfield, 1935
Al Simmons, outfield, 1939
George Sisler, first base, 1928–30
Billy Southworth, outfield, 1921–23
Warren Spahn, pitcher, 1942 and 1946–52
Casey Stengel, outfield, 1924–25
Ed Walsh, pitcher, 1917
Lloyd Waner, outfield, 1941
Paul Waner, outfield, 1941–42
Vic Willis, pitcher, 1898–1905
Cy Young, pitcher, 1911

Retired Numbers
[None]

League Leaders, Batting (Post-1900)

Batting Average, Season
Rogers Hornsby, 1928 ..... .387
Ernie Lombardi, 1942 ..... .330

Home Runs, Season
Herman Long, 1900 12
Dave Brain, 1907 10
Fred Beck, 1910 ..... 10 (Tie)
Wally Berger, 1935 34
Tommy Holmes, 1945 28

RBIs, Season
Wally Berger, 1935 130

Stolen Bases, Season
Sam Jethroe, 1950 35
Sam Jethroe, 1951 35

Total Bases, Season
Tommy Holmes, 1945 367

Most Hits, Season
Ginger Beaumont, 1907 187
Doc Miller, 1911 192
Eddie Brown, 1926 201
Tommy Holmes, 1945 224
Tommy Holmes, 1947 191

Most Runs, Season
Earl Torgeson, 1950 120

Batting Feats

Triple Crown Winners
[No player]

Hitting for the Cycle
Herman Long, May 9, 1896
Duff Colley, June 20, 1904
John Bates, Apr. 26, 1907
Bill Collins, Oct. 6, 1910

Six Hits in a Game
Sam Wise, June 20, 1883
King Kelly, Aug. 27, 1887
Bobby Lowe, June 11, 1891
Fred Tenney, May 31, 1897
Chick Stahl, May 31, 1899

40 or More Home Runs, Season
[No player]

League Leaders, Pitching (Post-1900)

Most Wins, Season
Dick Rudolph, 1914 ..... 27 (Tie)
Johnny Sain, 1948 24
Warren Spahn, 1949 21
Warren Spahn, 1950 21
Warren Spahn, 1953 ..... 23 (Tie)

Most Strikeouts, Season
Vic Willis, 1902 226
Warren Spahn, 1949 151
Warren Spahn, 1950 191
Warren Spahn, 1951 ..... 164 (Tie)
Warren Spahn, 1952 183

Lowest ERA, Season
Jim Turner, 1937 ..... 2.38
Warren Spahn, 1947 ..... 2.33
Chet Nichols, 1951 ..... 2.88

Most Saves, Season
[No pitcher]

Best Won–Lost Percentage, Season
Bill James, 1914 ..... 26–7 ... .788
Tom Hughes, 1916 ..... 16–3 ... .842
Ben Cantwell, 1933 ... 20–10 ... .667

Pitching Feats

Triple Crown Winner
Tommy Bond, 1877 (40–17, 2.11 ERA, 170 SO)
John Clarkson, 1889 (49–19, 2.73 ERA, 284 SO)

20 Wins, Season (1900–52)
Bill Dinneen, 1900 21–15
Vic Willis, 1901 20–17
Togie Pittinger, 1902 27–16
Vic Willis, 1902 27–20
Irv Young, 1905 20–21
Bill James, 1914 26–7
Dick Rudolph, 1914 26–10
Dick Rudolph, 1915 22–19
Joe Oeschger, 1921 20–14
Ben Cantwell, 1933 20–10
Lou Fette, 1937 20–10
Jim Turner, 1937 20–11
Johnny Sain, 1946 20–14
Warren Spahn, 1947 21–10
Johnny Sain, 1947 21–12
Johnny Sain, 1948 24–15
Warren Spahn, 1948 20–7
Warren Spahn, 1949 21–14
Warren Spahn, 1950 21–17

Johnny Sain, 1950 20–13
Warren Spahn, 1951 22–14

No-Hitters

Fred Pfeffer (vs. Cin. Reds), May 8, 1907 (final: 6–0)
George Davis (vs. Phila. Phillies), Sept. 9, 1914 (final: 7–0)
Tom Hughes (vs. Pitt. Pirates), June 16, 1916 (final: 2–0)
Jim Tobin (vs. Bklyn. Dodgers), Apr. 27, 1944 (final: 2–0)
Vern Bickford (vs. Bklyn. Dodgers), Aug. 11, 1950 (final: 7–0)

No-Hitters Pitched Against

Nap Rucker, Bklyn. Dodgers, Sept. 5, 1908 (final: 6–0)
Jesse Haines, St.L. Cardinals, July 17, 1924 (final: 5–0)
Johnny Vander Meer, Cin. Reds, June 11, 1938 (final: 3–0)
Clyde Shoun, Cin. Reds, May 15, 1944 (final: 1–0)
Ed Head, Bklyn. Dodgers, Apr. 23, 1946 (final: 5–0)
Ewell Blackwell, Cin. Reds, June 18, 1947 (final: 6–0)
Cliff Chambers, Pitt. Pirates, May 6, 1951 (final: 3–0)

Postseason Play

1914 World Series vs. Phila. A's (AL), won 4 games to 0
1948 World Series vs. Cle. Indians (AL), lost 4 games to 2

Brooklyn Dodgers

Dates of Operation: 1890–1957 (68 years)

Overall Record: 5214 wins, 4926 losses (.514)

Stadiums: Washington Park II, 1890; Eastern Park, 1891–97; West N.Y. Field Club Grounds, 1898; Washington Park III, 1898–1912; Ebbets Field, 1913–57; Roosevelt Stadium (Jersey City, NJ) 1956–57 (capacity: 31,903)

Other Names: Bridegrooms, Superbas, Trolley Dodgers, Robins

Year-by-Year Finishes

Year	Finish	Wins	Losses	Percentage	Games Behind	Manager	Attendance
1890	1st	86	43	.667	+6.5	Bill McGunnigle	not available
1891	6th	61	76	.445	25.5	Monte Ward	not available
1892	3rd	95	59	.617	9.0	Monte Ward	not available
1893	6th	65	63	.508	20.0	Dave Foutz	not available
1894	5th	70	61	.534	25.5	Dave Foutz	not available
1895	5th	71	60	.542	16.5	Dave Foutz	not available
1896	9th	57	73	.443	33.0	Dave Foutz	not available
1897	6th	61	71	.462	32.0	Billy Barnie	not available
1898	10th	54	91	.372	46.0	Billy Barnie, Mike Griffin, Charlie Ebbets	not available
1899	1st	88	42	.677	+4.0	Ned Hanlon	not available
1900	1st	82	54	.603	+4.5	Ned Hanlon	not available
1901	3rd	79	57	.581	9.5	Ned Hanlon	198,200
1902	2nd	75	63	.543	27.5	Ned Hanlon	199,868
1903	5th	70	66	.515	19.0	Ned Hanlon	224,670
1904	6th	56	97	.366	50.0	Ned Hanlon	214,600
1905	8th	48	104	.316	56.5	Ned Hanlon	227,924
1906	5th	66	86	.434	50.0	Patsy Donovan	277,400
1907	5th	65	83	.439	40.0	Patsy Donovan	312,500
1908	7th	53	101	.344	46.0	Patsy Donovan	275,600
1909	6th	55	98	.359	55.5	Harry Lumley	321,300
1910	6th	64	90	.416	40.0	Bill Dahlen	279,321
1911	7th	64	86	.427	33.5	Bill Dahlen	269,000
1912	7th	58	95	.379	46.0	Bill Dahlen	243,000
1913	6th	65	84	.436	34.5	Bill Dahlen	347,000
1914	5th	75	79	.487	19.5	Wilbert Robinson	122,671
1915	3rd	80	72	.526	10.0	Wilbert Robinson	279,766
1916	1st	94	60	.610	+2.5	Wilbert Robinson	447,747
1917	7th	70	81	.464	26.5	Wilbert Robinson	221,619
1918	5th	57	69	.452	25.5	Wilbert Robinson	83,831
1919	5th	69	71	.493	27.0	Wilbert Robinson	360,721
1920	1st	93	61	.604	+7.0	Wilbert Robinson	808,722
1921	5th	77	75	.507	16.5	Wilbert Robinson	613,245
1922	6th	76	78	.494	17.0	Wilbert Robinson	498,865
1923	6th	76	78	.494	19.5	Wilbert Robinson	564,666
1924	2nd	92	62	.597	1.5	Wilbert Robinson	818,883
1925	6th (Tie)	68	85	.444	27.0	Wilbert Robinson	659,435
1926	6th	71	82	.464	17.5	Wilbert Robinson	650,819
1927	6th	65	88	.425	28.5	Wilbert Robinson	637,230
1928	6th	77	76	.503	17.5	Wilbert Robinson	664,863

1929	6th	70	83	.458	28.5	Wilbert Robinson	731,886
1930	4th	86	68	.558	6.0	Wilbert Robinson	1,097,339
1931	4th	79	73	.520	21.0	Wilbert Robinson	753,133
1932	3rd	81	73	.526	9.0	Max Carey	681,827
1933	6th	65	88	.425	26.5	Max Carey	526,815
1934	6th	71	81	.467	23.5	Casey Stengel	434,188
1935	5th	70	83	.458	29.5	Casey Stengel	470,517
1936	7th	67	87	.435	25.0	Casey Stengel	489,618
1937	6th	62	91	.405	33.5	Burleigh Grimes	482,481
1938	7th	69	80	.463	18.5	Burleigh Grimes	663,087
1939	3rd	84	69	.549	12.5	Leo Durocher	955,668
1940	2nd	88	65	.575	12.0	Leo Durocher	975,978
1941	1st	100	54	.649	+2.5	Leo Durocher	1,214,910
1942	2nd	104	50	.675	2.0	Leo Durocher	1,037,765
1943	3rd	81	72	.529	23.5	Leo Durocher	661,739
1944	7th	63	91	.409	42.0	Leo Durocher	605,905
1945	3rd	87	67	.565	11.0	Leo Durocher	1,059,220
1946	2nd	96	60	.616	2.0	Leo Durocher	1,796,824
1947	1st	94	60	.610	+5.0	Burt Shotton	1,807,526
1948	3rd	84	70	.545	7.5	Leo Durocher, Burt Shotton	1,398,967
1949	1st	97	57	.630	+1.0	Burt Shotton	1,633,747
1950	2nd	89	65	.578	2.0	Burt Shotton	1,185,896
1951	2nd	97	60	.618	1.0	Chuck Dressen	1,282,628
1952	1st	96	57	.627	+4.5	Chuck Dressen	1,088,704
1953	1st	105	49	.682	+13.0	Chuck Dressen	1,163,419
1954	2nd	92	62	.597	5.0	Walter Alston	1,020,531
1955	1st	98	55	.641	+13.5	Walter Alston	1,033,589
1956	1st	93	61	.604	+1.0	Walter Alston	1,213,562
1957	3rd	84	70	.545	11.0	Walter Alston	1,028,258

Awards

Most Valuable Player

Jake Daubert, first base, 1913
Dazzy Vance, pitcher, 1924
Dolph Camilli, first base, 1941
Jackie Robinson, second base, 1949
Roy Campanella, catcher, 1951
Roy Campanella, catcher, 1953
Roy Campanella, catcher, 1955
Don Newcombe, pitcher, 1956

Rookie of the Year

Jackie Robinson, first base, 1947
Don Newcombe, pitcher, 1949
Joe Black, pitcher, 1952
Junior Gilliam, second base, 1953

Cy Young

Don Newcombe, 1956

Hall of Famers Who Played for the Brooklyn Dodgers

Dave Bancroft, shortstop, 1928–29
Dan Brouthers, first base, 1892–93
Roy Campanella, catcher, 1948–57
Max Carey, outfield, 1926–29
Kiki Cuyler, outfield, 1938
Don Drysdale, pitcher, 1956–57
Leo Durocher, shortstop, 1938–41, 1943, and 1945
Burleigh Grimes, pitcher, 1918–26
Billy Herman, second base, 1941–43 and 1946
Waite Hoyt, pitcher, 1932 and 1937–38
Hughie Jennings, infield, 1899–1900
Willie Keeler, outfield, 1893 and 1899–1902
Joe Kelley, outfield, 1899–1901
George Kelly, first base, 1932
Sandy Koufax, pitcher, 1955–57
Tony Lazzeri, second base, 1939
Fred Lindstrom, third base, 1936
Ernie Lombardi, catcher, 1931
Al Lopez, catcher, 1928 and 1930–35
Heinie Manush, outfield, 1937–38
Rabbit Maranville, shortstop, 1926
Rube Marquard, pitcher, 1915–20
Tommy McCarthy, outfield and infield, 1896
Joe McGinnity, pitcher, 1900
Joe Medwick, outfield, 1940–43 and 1946
Pee Wee Reese, shortstop, 1940–42 and 1946–57
Jackie Robinson, infield, 1947–56

Duke Snider, outfield, 1947–57
Casey Stengel, outfield, 1912–17
Dazzy Vance, pitcher, 1922–32 and 1935
Arky Vaughan, infield, 1942–43 and 1947–48
Paul Waner, outfield, 1941 and 1943–44
John Montgomery Ward, infield and pitcher, 1890–92
Zack Wheat, outfield, 1909–26
Hack Wilson, outfield, 1932–34

Retired Numbers

[None]

League Leaders, Batting (Post-1900)

Batting Average, Season

Jake Daubert, 1913 ..... .350
Jake Daubert, 1914 ..... .329
Zack Wheat, 1918 ..... .335
Lefty O'Doul, 1932 ..... .368
Pete Reiser, 1941 ..... .343
Dixie Walker, 1944 ..... .357
Jackie Robinson, 1949 ..... .342
Carl Furillo, 1953 ..... .344

Home Runs, Season

Jimmy Sheckard, 1903 9
Harry Lumley, 1904 9
Tim Jordan, 1906 12
Tim Jordan, 1908 12
Jack Fournier, 1924 27
Dolph Camilli, 1941 34
Duke Snider, 1956 43

RBIs, Season

Hy Myers, 1919 72
Dolph Camilli, 1941 120
Dixie Walker, 1945 124
Roy Campanella, 1953 142
Duke Snider, 1955 136

Stolen Bases, Season

Jimmy Sheckard, 1903 67
Pete Reiser, 1942 20
Arky Vaughan, 1943 20
Pete Reiser, 1946 34
Jackie Robinson, 1947 29
Jackie Robinson, 1949 37
Pee Wee Reese, 1952 30

Total Bases, Season

Zack Wheat, 1916 262
Hy Myers, 1919 223
Pete Reiser, 1941 299
Duke Snider, 1950 343
Duke Snider, 1953 370
Duke Snider, 1954 378

Most Hits, Season

Willie Keeler, 1900 208
Ivy Olson, 1919 164
Duke Snider, 1950 199

Most Runs, Season

Pete Reiser, 1941 117
Arky Vaughan, 1943 112
Eddie Stanky, 1945 128
Pee Wee Reese, 1949 132
Duke Snider, 1953 132
Duke Snider, 1954 ..... 120 (Tie)
Duke Snider, 1955 126

Batting Feats

Triple Crown Winners

[No player]

Hitting for the Cycle

Tom Burns, Aug. 1, 1890
Jimmy Johnston, May 25, 1922
Babe Herman, May 18, 1931
Babe Herman, July 24, 1931
Dixie Walker, Sept. 2, 1944
Jackie Robinson, Aug. 29, 1948
Gil Hodges, June 25, 1949

Six Hits in a Game

George Cutshaw, Aug. 9, 1915
Jack Fournier, June 29, 1923
Hank DeBerry, June 23, 1929*
Wally Gilbert, May 30, 1931
Cookie Lavagetto, Sept. 23, 1939
*Extra-inning game.

40 or More Home Runs, Season

43 ..... Duke Snider, 1956
42 ..... Duke Snider, 1953
Gil Hodges, 1954
Duke Snider, 1955
41 ..... Roy Campanella, 1953
40 ..... Gil Hodges, 1951
Duke Snider, 1954
Duke Snider, 1957

League Leaders, Pitching (Post-1900)

Most Wins, Season

Bill Donovan, 1901 25
Burleigh Grimes, 1921 ..... 22 (Tie)
Dazzy Vance, 1924 28
Dazzy Vance, 1925 22
Kirby Higbe, 1941 ..... 22 (Tie)
Whit Wyatt, 1941 ..... 22 (Tie)
Don Newcombe, 1956 27

Most Strikeouts, Season

Burleigh Grimes, 1921 136
Dazzy Vance, 1922 134
Dazzy Vance, 1923 197
Dazzy Vance, 1924 262
Dazzy Vance, 1925 221
Dazzy Vance, 1926 140
Dazzy Vance, 1927 184
Dazzy Vance, 1928 200
Van Lingle Mungo, 1936 238
Don Newcombe, 1951 ..... 164 (Tie)

Lowest ERA, Season

Dazzy Vance, 1924 ..... 2.16
Dazzy Vance, 1928 ..... 2.09
Dazzy Vance, 1930 ..... 2.61
Johnny Podres, 1957 ..... 2.66

Most Saves, Season

[No pitcher]

Best Won–Lost Percentage, Season

Joe McGinnity, 1900 ..... 29–9 . .763
Burleigh Grimes, 1920 ... 23–11 . .676
Freddie Fitzsimmons, 1940 . 16–2 . .889
Larry French, 1942 ..... 15–4 . .789
Preacher Roe, 1949 ..... 15–6 . .714
Preacher Roe, 1951 ..... 22–3 . .880
Carl Erskine, 1953 ..... 20–6 . .769
Don Newcombe, 1955 ... 20–5 . .800
Don Newcombe, 1956 ... 27–7 . .794

Pitching Feats

Triple Crown Winner

Dazzy Vance, 1924 (28–6, 2.16 ERA, 262 SO)

20 Wins, Season (1900–57)

Joe McGinnity, 1900 29–9
William Kennedy, 1900 22–15
Bill Dinneen, 1901 25–15
Henry Schmidt, 1903 22–13

Nap Rucker, 1911 22–18
Jeff Pfeffer, 1914 23–12
Jeff Pfeffer, 1916 25–11
Burleigh Grimes, 1920 23–11
Burleigh Grimes, 1921 22–13
Dutch Ruether, 1922..... 21–12
Burleigh Grimes, 1923 21–18
Dazzy Vance, 1924..... 28–6
Burleigh Grimes, 1924 22–13
Dazzy Vance, 1925..... 22–9
Dazzy Vance, 1928..... 22–10
Watty Clark, 1932..... 20–12
Luke Hamlin, 1939..... 20–13
Kirby Higbe, 1941..... 22–9
Whit Wyatt, 1941 22–10
Ralph Branca, 1947..... 21–12
Preacher Roe, 1951 22–3
Don Newcombe, 1951 20–9
Carl Erskine, 1953..... 20–6
Don Newcombe, 1955 20–5
Don Newcombe, 1956 27–7

No-Hitters

Mal Eason (vs. St.L. Cardinals), July 20, 1906 (final: 2–0)
Nap Rucker (vs. Bost. Doves), Sept. 5, 1908 (final: 6–0)
Dazzy Vance (vs. Phila. Phillies), Sept. 13, 925 (final: 10–1)
Tex Carleton (vs. Cin. Reds), Apr. 30, 1940 (final: 3–0)
Ed Head (vs. Bost. Braves), Apr. 23, 1946 (final: 5–0)
Rex Barney (vs. N.Y. Giants), Sept. 9, 1948 (final: 2–0)
Carl Erskine (vs. Chi. Cubs), June 19, 1952 (final: 5–0)
Carl Erskine (vs. N.Y. Giants), May 12, 1956 (final: 3–0)
Sal Maglie (vs. Phila. Phillies), Sept. 25, 1956 (final: 5–0)

No-Hitters Pitched Against

John Lush, Phila. Phillies, May 1, 1906 (final: 1–0)
Nick Maddox, Pitt. Pirates, Sept. 29, 1907 (final: 2–1)
Rube Marquard, N.Y. Giants, Apr. 15, 1915 (final: 2–0)
Paul Dean, St.L. Cardinals, Sept. 21, 1934 (final: 3–0)
Johnny Vander Meer, Cin. Reds, June 15, 1938 (final: 6–0)
Jim Tobin, Bost. Braves, Apr. 27, 1944 (final: 2–0)
Vern Bickford, Bost. Braves, Aug. 11, 1950 (final: 7–0)

Postseason Play

1916 World Series vs. Bost. Red Sox (AL), lost 4 games to 1
1920 World Series vs. Cle. Indians (AL), lost 5 games to 2
1941 World Series vs. N.Y. Yankees (AL), lost 4 games to 1
1946 Pennant Playoff Series vs. St.L. Cardinals, lost 2 games to 0
1947 World Series vs. N.Y. Yankees (AL), lost 4 games to 3
1949 World Series vs. N.Y. Yankees (AL), lost 4 games to 1
1951 Pennant Playoff Series vs. N.Y. Giants, lost 2 games to 1
1952 World Series vs. N.Y. Yankees (AL), lost 4 games to 3
1953 World Series vs. N.Y. Yankees (AL), lost 4 games to 2
1955 World Series vs. N.Y. Yankees (AL), won 4 games to 3
1956 World Series vs. N.Y. Yankees (AL), lost 4 games to 3

New York Giants

Dates of Operation: 1876, 1883–1957 (76 years)

Overall Record: 6088 wins, 4933 losses (.552)

Stadiums: Polo Grounds I, 1876, 1883–88; Oakland Park, 1889; St. George Cricket Grounds, 1889; Polo Grounds III, 1889–90; Harrison Field, 1890–99 and 1918 (Sundays only); Polo Grounds IV, 1891–1911; Hilltop Park, 1911; Polo Grounds V, 1911–57 (capacity: 55,137)

Other Names: Maroons, Gothams

Year-by-Year Finishes

Year	Finish	Wins	Losses	Percentage	Games Behind	Manager	Attendance
1876	6th	21	35	.375	26.0	Bill Cammeyer	not available
1883	6th	46	50	.479	16.0	John Clapp	not available
1884	4th (Tie)	62	50	.544	22.0	James Price, Monte Ward	not available
1885	2nd	85	27	.758	2.0	Jim Mutrie	not available
1886	3rd	75	44	.630	12.5	Jim Mutrie	not available
1887	4th	68	55	.553	10.5	Jim Mutrie	not available
1888	1st	84	47	.641	+9.0	Jim Mutrie	not available
1889	1st	83	43	.659	+1.0	Jim Mutrie	not available
1890	6th	63	68	.481	24.0	Jim Mutrie	not available
1891	3rd	71	61	.538	13.0	Jim Mutrie	not available
1892	8th	71	80	.470	31.5	Pat Powers	not available
1893	5th	68	64	.515	19.0	Monte Ward	not available
1894	2nd	88	44	.667	3.0	Monte Ward	not available
1895	9th	66	65	.504	21.5	George Davis, Jack Doyle, Harvey Watkins	not available
1896	7th	64	67	.489	37.0	Arthur Irwin, Bill Joyce	not available
1897	3rd	83	48	.634	9.5	Bill Joyce	not available
1898	7th	77	73	.513	25.5	Bill Joyce, Cap Anson	not available
1899	10th	60	86	.411	26.0	John Day, Fred Hoey	not available
1900	8th	60	78	.435	23.0	Buck Ewing, George Davis	not available
1901	7th	52	85	.380	37.0	George Davis	297,650
1902	8th	48	88	.353	53.5	Horace Fogel, Heinie Smith, John McGraw	302,875
1903	2nd	84	55	.604	6.5	John McGraw	579,530
1904	1st	106	47	.693	+13.0	John McGraw	609,826
1905	1st	105	48	.686	+9.0	John McGraw	552,700
1906	2nd	96	56	.632	20.0	John McGraw	402,850
1907	4th	82	71	.536	25.5	John McGraw	538,350
1908	2nd (Tie)	98	56	.636	1.0	John McGraw	910,000
1909	3rd	92	61	.601	18.5	John McGraw	783,700
1910	2nd	91	63	.591	13.0	John McGraw	511,785
1911	1st	99	54	.647	+7.5	John McGraw	675,000
1912	1st	103	48	.682	+10.0	John McGraw	638,000
1913	1st	101	51	.664	+12.5	John McGraw	630,000
1914	2nd	84	70	.545	10.5	John McGraw	364,313
1915	8th	69	83	.454	21.0	John McGraw	391,850
1916	4th	86	66	.566	7.0	John McGraw	552,056
1917	1st	98	56	.636	+10.0	John McGraw	500,264
1918	2nd	71	53	.573	10.5	John McGraw	256,618
1919	2nd	87	53	.621	9.0	John McGraw	708,857

1920	2nd	86	68	.558	7.0	John McGraw	929,609
1921	1st	94	59	.614	+4.0	John McGraw	773,477
1922	1st	93	61	.604	+7.0	John McGraw	945,809
1923	1st	95	58	.621	+4.5	John McGraw	820,780
1924	1st	93	60	.608	+1.5	John McGraw	844,068
1925	2nd	86	66	.566	8.5	John McGraw	778,993
1926	5th	74	77	.490	13.5	John McGraw	700,362
1927	3rd	92	62	.597	2.0	John McGraw	858,190
1928	2nd	93	61	.604	2.0	John McGraw	916,191
1929	3rd	84	67	.556	13.5	John McGraw	868,806
1930	3rd	87	67	.565	5.0	John McGraw	868,714
1931	2nd	87	65	.572	13.0	John McGraw	812,163
1932	6th (Tie)	72	82	.468	18.0	John McGraw, Bill Terry	484,868
1933	1st	91	61	.599	+5.0	Bill Terry	604,471
1934	2nd	93	60	.608	2.0	Bill Terry	730,851
1935	3rd	91	62	.595	8.5	Bill Terry	748,748
1936	1st	92	62	.597	+5.0	Bill Terry	837,952
1937	1st	95	57	.625	+3.0	Bill Terry	926,887
1938	3rd	83	67	.553	5.0	Bill Terry	799,633
1939	5th	77	74	.510	18.5	Bill Terry	702,457
1940	6th (Tie)	72	80	.474	27.5	Bill Terry	747,852
1941	5th	74	79	.484	25.5	Bill Terry	763,098
1942	3rd	85	67	.559	20.0	Mel Ott	779,621
1943	8th	55	98	.359	49.5	Mel Ott	466,095
1944	5th	67	87	.435	38.0	Mel Ott	674,083
1945	5th	78	74	.513	19.0	Mel Ott	1,016,468
1946	8th	61	93	.396	36.0	Mel Ott	1,219,873
1947	4th	81	73	.526	13.0	Mel Ott	1,600,793
1948	5th	78	76	.506	13.5	Mel Ott, Leo Durocher	1,459,269
1949	5th	73	81	.474	24.0	Leo Durocher	1,218,446
1950	3rd	86	68	.558	5.0	Leo Durocher	1,008,876
1951	1st	98	59	.624	+1.0	Leo Durocher	1,059,539
1952	2nd	92	62	.597	4.5	Leo Durocher	984,940
1953	5th	70	84	.455	35.0	Leo Durocher	811,518
1954	1st	97	57	.630	+5.0	Leo Durocher	1,155,067
1955	3rd	80	74	.519	18.5	Leo Durocher	824,112
1956	6th	67	87	.435	26.0	Bill Rigney	629,179
1957	6th	69	85	.448	26.0	Bill Rigney	653,923

Awards

Most Valuable Player

Larry Doyle, second base, 1912
Carl Hubbell, pitcher, 1933
Carl Hubbell, pitcher, 1936
Willie Mays, outfield, 1954

Rookie of the Year

Willie Mays, outfield, 1951

Cy Young

[No pitcher]

Hall of Famers Who Played for the New York Giants

Dave Bancroft, shortstop, 1920–23 and 1930
Jake Beckley, first base, 1896–97
Roger Bresnahan, catcher, 1902–08
Dan Brouthers, first base, 1904
Jesse Burkett, outfield, 1890
Roger Connor, first base, 1883–89, 1891, and 1893–94
George Davis, outfield and infield, 1893–1901 and 1903
Buck Ewing, catcher and infield, 1883–89 and 1891–92
Frankie Frisch, second base, 1919–26
Burleigh Grimes, pitcher, 1927
Gabby Hartnett, catcher, 1941
Waite Hoyt, pitcher, 1918 and 1932
Monte Irvin, outfield, 1949–55

Travis Jackson, shortstop, 1922–36
Tim Keefe, pitcher, 1885–91
Willie Keeler, outfield, 1892–93 and 1910
George Kelly, first base, 1915–17 and 1919–26
King Kelly, catcher and infield, 1893
Tony Lazzeri, second base, 1939
Fred Lindstrom, third base, 1924–32
Ernie Lombardi, catcher, 1943–47
Rube Marquard, pitcher, 1908–15
Christy Mathewson, pitcher, 1900–16
Willie Mays, outfield, 1951–52 and 1954–57
Joe McGinnity, pitcher, 1902–08
John McGraw, infield, 1902–06
Bill McKechnie, third base, 1916
Joe Medwick, outfield, 1943–45
Johnny Mize, first base, 1942 and 1946–49
Jim O'Rourke, catcher, outfield, and infield, 1885–89, 1904
Mel Ott, outfield, 1926–47
Edd Roush, outfield, 1916 and 1927–29
Amos Rusie, pitcher, 1890–95 and 1897–98
Ray Schalk, catcher, 1929
Red Schoendienst, second base, 1956–57
Billy Southworth, outfield, 1924–26
Casey Stengel, outfield, 1921–23
Bill Terry, first base, 1923–36
Monte Ward, infield and pitcher, 1883–89
Mickey Welch, pitcher, 1883–92
Hoyt Wilhelm, pitcher, 1952–56
Hack Wilson, outfield, 1923–25
Ross Youngs, outfield, 1917–26

Retired Numbers

[None]

League Leaders, Batting (Post-1900)

Batting Average, Season

Larry Doyle, 1915 ..... .320
Bill Terry, 1930 ..... .401
Willie Mays, 1954 ..... .345

Home Runs, Season

Red Murray, 1909 7
Dave Robertson, 1916 ..... 12 (Tie)
Dave Robertson, 1917 ..... 12 (Tie)
George Kelly, 1921 23
Mel Ott, 1932 ..... 38 (Tie)
Mel Ott, 1934 ..... 35 (Tie)
Mel Ott, 1936 33
Mel Ott, 1937 ..... 31 (Tie)
Mel Ott, 1938 ..... 36 (Tie)
Mel Ott, 1942 30
Johnny Mize, 1947 ..... 51 (Tie)
Johnny Mize, 1948 ..... 40 (Tie)
Willie Mays, 1955 51

RBIs, Season

Heinie Zimmerman*, 1916 83
Heinie Zimmerman, 1917 102
George Kelly, 1920 ..... 94 (Tie)
Irish Meusel, 1923 125
George Kelly, 1924 136
Mel Ott, 1934 135
Johnny Mize, 1942 110
Johnny Mize, 1947 138
Monte Irvin, 1951 121
*64 with Chi. Cubs and 19 with N.Y. Giants.

Stolen Bases, Season

Art Devlin, 1905 ..... 59 (Tie)
George J. Burns, 1914 62
George J. Burns, 1919 40
Frankie Frisch, 1921 49
Willie Mays, 1956 40
Willie Mays, 1957 38

Total Bases, Season

Frankie Frisch, 1923 311
Willie Mays, 1955 382

Most Hits, Season

Larry Doyle, 1909 172
Larry Doyle, 1915 189
Frankie Frisch, 1923 223
Fred Lindstrom, 1928 231
Bill Terry, 1930 254
Don Mueller, 1954 212

Most Runs, Season

George Browne, 1904 99
Mike Donlin, 1905 124
Spike Shannon, 1907 104
Fred Tenney, 1908 101
George J. Burns, 1914 100
George J. Burns, 1916 105
George J. Burns, 1917 103
George J. Burns, 1919 86
George J. Burns, 1920 115
Ross Youngs, 1923 121
Frankie Frisch, 1924 ..... 121 (Tie)
Rogers Hornsby, 1927 ..... 133 (Tie)
Bill Terry, 1931 ..... 121 (Tie)
Mel Ott, 1938 116
Mel Ott, 1942 118
Johnny Mize, 1947 137

Batting Feats

Triple Crown Winners

[No player]

Hitting for the Cycle

Dave Orr, June 12, 1885
Dave Orr, Aug. 10, 1887
Mike Tiernan, Aug. 25, 1888
Mike Tiernan, Aug. 28, 1890
Sam Mertes, Oct. 4, 1904
Chief Meyers, June 10, 1912
George J. Burns, Sept. 17, 1920
Dave Bancroft, June 1, 1921
Ross Youngs, Apr. 29, 1922
Bill Terry, May 29, 1928
Mel Ott, May 16, 1929
Fred Lindstrom, May 8, 1930
Sam Leslie, May 24, 1936
Harry Danning, June 15, 1940
Don Mueller, July 11, 1954

Six Hits in a Game

Kip Selbach, June 9, 1901
Dave Bancroft, June 28, 1920
Frankie Frisch, Sept. 10, 1924

40 or More Home Runs, Season

51 ..... Johnny Mize, 1947
Willie Mays, 1955
42 ..... Mel Ott, 1929
41 ..... Willie Mays, 1954
40 ..... Johnny Mize, 1948

League Leaders, Pitching (Post-1900)

Most Wins, Season

Joe McGinnity, 1900 29
Joe McGinnity, 1903 31

Joe McGinnity, 1904 35
Christy Mathewson, 1905 31
Joe McGinnity, 1906 27
Christy Mathewson, 1907 24
Christy Mathewson, 1908 37
Christy Mathewson, 1910 27
Rube Marquard, 1912 ..... 26 (Tie)
Jesse Barnes, 1919 25
Larry Benton, 1928 ..... 25 (Tie)
Carl Hubbell, 1933 23
Carl Hubbell, 1936 26
Carl Hubbell, 1937 22
Larry Jansen, 1951 ..... 23 (Tie)
Sal Maglie, 1951 ..... 23 (Tie)

Most Strikeouts, Season

Christy Mathewson, 1903 267
Christy Mathewson, 1904 212
Christy Mathewson, 1905 206
Christy Mathewson, 1907 178
Christy Mathewson, 1908 259
Christy Mathewson, 1910 190
Rube Marquard, 1911 237
Carl Hubbell, 1937 159
Bill Voiselle, 1944 161

Lowest ERA, Season

Jeff Tesreau, 1912 ..... 1.96
Christy Mathewson, 1913 ..... 2.06
Rosy Ryan, 1922 ..... 3.00
Bill Walker, 1929 ..... 3.08
Bill Walker, 1931 ..... 2.26
Carl Hubbell, 1933 ..... 1.66
Carl Hubbell, 1934 ..... 2.30
Carl Hubbell, 1936 ..... 2.31
Dave Koslo, 1949 ..... 2.50
Jim Hearn*, 1950 ..... 2.49
Hoyt Wilhelm, 1952 ..... 2.43
Johnny Antonelli, 1954 ..... 2.29
*10.00 with St.L. Cardinals and 1.94 with N.Y. Giants.

Most Saves, Season

[No pitcher]

Best Won–Lost Percentage, Season

Joe McGinnity, 1904 .... 35–8 ... .814
Christy Mathewson, 1909 ..... 25–6 ..... .806 (Tie)
Rube Marquard, 1911 .. 24–7 ... .774
Ferdie Schupp, 1917 .... 21–7 ... .750
Larry Benton*, 1927 ..... 17–7 ... .708
Larry Benton, 1928 ..... 25–9 ... .735
Freddie Fitzsimmons, 1930 ..... 19–7 ..... .731
Carl Hubbell, 1936 ..... 26–6 ... .813
Carl Hubbell, 1937 ..... 22–8 ... .733
Larry Jansen, 1947 ..... 21–5 ... .808
Sal Maglie, 1950 ..... 18–4 ... .818
Hoyt Wilhelm, 1952 ..... 15–3 ... .833
Johnny Antonelli, 1954 . 21–7 ... .750
*.667 with Bost. Braves and .722 with N.Y. Giants.

Pitching Feats

Triple Crown Winner

Tim Keefe, 1888 (35–12, 1.74 ERA, 335 SO)
Amos Rusie, 1894 (36–13, 2.78 ERA, 195 SO)
Christy Mathewson, 1905 (31–9, 1.28 ERA, 206 SO)
Christy Mathewson, 1908 (37–11, 1.43 ERA, 259 SO)

20 Wins, Season (1900–57)

Christy Mathewson, 1901 20–17
Joe McGinnity*, 1902 21–18
Joe McGinnity, 1903 31–20
Christy Mathewson, 1903 30–13
Joe McGinnity, 1904 35–8
Christy Mathewson, 1904 33–12
Dummy Taylor, 1904 21–15
Christy Mathewson, 1905 31–9
Red Ames, 1905 22–8
Joe McGinnity, 1905 21–15
Joe McGinnity, 1906 27–12
Christy Mathewson, 1906 22–12
Christy Mathewson, 1907 24–12
Christy Mathewson, 1908 37–11
Hooks Wiltse, 1908 23–14
Christy Mathewson, 1909 25–6
Hooks Wiltse, 1909 20–11
Christy Mathewson, 1910 27–9
Christy Mathewson, 1911 26–13
Rube Marquard, 1911 24–7
Rube Marquard, 1912 26–11
Christy Mathewson, 1912 23–12
Christy Mathewson, 1913 25–11
Rube Marquard, 1913 23–10
Jeff Tesreau, 1913 22–13
Jeff Tesreau, 1914 26–10
Christy Mathewson, 1914 24–13
Ferdie Schupp, 1917 21–7
Jesse Barnes, 1919 25–9
Fred Toney, 1920 21–11
Art Nehf, 1920 21–12
Jesse Barnes, 1920 20–15
Art Nehf, 1921 20–10
Larry Benton, 1928 25–9
Freddie Fitzsimmons, 1928 20–9
Carl Hubbell, 1933 23–12
Hal Schumacher, 1934 23–10
Carl Hubbell, 1934 21–12
Carl Hubbell, 1935 23–12
Carl Hubbell, 1936 26–6
Carl Hubbell, 1937 22–8
Cliff Melton, 1937 20–9
Bill Voiselle, 1944 21–16
Larry Jansen, 1947 21–5
Sal Maglie, 1951 23–6
Larry Jansen, 1951 23–11
Johnny Antonelli, 1954 21–7
Johnny Antonelli, 1956 20–13
*13–10 with Balt. Orioles (AL) and 8–8 with N.Y. Giants.

No-Hitters

Christy Mathewson (vs. St.L. Cardinals), July 15, 1901 (final: 4–0)
Christy Mathewson (vs. Chi. Cubs), June 13, 1905 (final: 1–0)
Hooks Wiltse (vs. Phila. Phillies), Sept. 5, 1908 (final: 1–0) (10 innings)
Jeff Tesreau (vs. Phila. Phillies), Sept. 6, 1912 (final: 3–0)
Rube Marquard (vs. Bklyn. Dodgers), Apr. 15, 1915 (final: 2–0)
Jesse Barnes (vs. Phila. Phillies), May 7, 1922 (final: 6–0)
Carl Hubbell (vs. Pitt. Pirates), May 8, 1929 (final: 11–0)

No-Hitters Pitched Against

Bob Wicker, Chi. Cubs, June 11, 1904 (final: 1–0) (allowed hit in 10th and won in 12th)
Jimmy Lavender, Chi. Cubs, Aug. 31, 1915 (final: 2–0)
Rex Barney, Bklyn. Dodgers, Sept. 9, 1948 (final: 2–0)
Carl Erskine, Bklyn. Dodgers, May 12, 1956 (final: 3–0)

Postseason Play

1905 World Series vs. Phila. A's (AL), won 4 games to 1

1908 Pennant Playoff Game vs. Chi. Cubs (NL), lost

1911 World Series vs. Phila. A's (AL), lost 4 games to 2

1912 World Series vs. Bost. Red Sox (AL), lost 4 games to 3

1913 World Series vs. Phila. A's (AL), lost 4 games to 1

1917 World Series vs. Chi. White Sox (AL), lost 4 games to 2

1921 World Series vs. N.Y. Yankees (AL), won 5 games to 3

1922 World Series vs. N.Y. Yankees (AL), won 4 games to 0

1923 World Series vs. N.Y. Yankees (AL), lost 4 games to 2

1924 World Series vs. Wash. Senators (AL), lost 4 games to 3

1933 World Series vs. Wash. Senators (AL), won 4 games to 1

1936 World Series vs. N.Y. Yankees (AL), lost 4 games to 2

1937 World Series vs. N.Y. Yankees (AL), lost 4 games to 1

1951 Pennant Playoff Series vs. Bklyn. Dodgers (NL), won 2 games to 1

World Series vs. N.Y. Yankees (AL), lost 4 games to 2

1954 World Series vs. Cle. Indians (AL), won 4 games to 0

Philadelphia Athletics

Dates of Operation: 1901–54 (54 years)
Overall Record: 3886 wins, 4248 losses (.478)
Stadiums: Columbia Park, 1901–08; Shibe Park (also known as Connie Mack Stadium), 1909–54 (capacity: 33,000)
Other Name: A's

Year-by-Year Finishes

Year	Finish	Wins	Losses	Percentage	Games Behind	Manager	Attendance
1901	4th	74	62	.544	9.0	Connie Mack	206,329
1902	1st	83	53	.610	+5.0	Connie Mack	442,473
1903	2nd	75	60	.556	14.5	Connie Mack	420,078
1904	5th	81	70	.536	12.5	Connie Mack	512,294
1905	1st	92	56	.622	+2.0	Connie Mack	554,576
1906	4th	78	67	.538	12.0	Connie Mack	489,129
1907	2nd	88	57	.607	1.5	Connie Mack	625,581
1908	6th	68	85	.444	22.0	Connie Mack	455,062
1909	2nd	95	58	.621	3.5	Connie Mack	674,915
1910	1st	102	48	.680	+14.5	Connie Mack	588,905
1911	1st	101	50	.669	+13.5	Connie Mack	605,749
1912	3rd	90	62	.592	15.0	Connie Mack	517,653
1913	1st	96	57	.627	+6.5	Connie Mack	571,896
1914	1st	99	53	.651	+8.5	Connie Mack	346,641
1915	8th	43	109	.283	58.5	Connie Mack	146,223
1916	8th	36	117	.235	54.5	Connie Mack	184,471
1917	8th	55	98	.359	44.5	Connie Mack	221,432
1918	8th	52	76	.406	24.0	Connie Mack	177,926
1919	8th	36	104	.257	52.0	Connie Mack	225,209
1920	8th	48	106	.312	50.0	Connie Mack	287,888
1921	8th	53	100	.346	45.0	Connie Mack	344,430
1922	7th	65	89	.422	29.0	Connie Mack	425,356
1923	6th	69	83	.454	29.0	Connie Mack	534,122
1924	5th	71	81	.467	20.0	Connie Mack	531,992
1925	2nd	88	64	.579	8.5	Connie Mack	869,703
1926	3rd	83	67	.553	6.0	Connie Mack	714,308
1927	2nd	91	63	.591	19.0	Connie Mack	605,529
1928	2nd	98	55	.641	2.5	Connie Mack	689,756
1929	1st	104	46	.693	+18.0	Connie Mack	839,176
1930	1st	102	52	.662	+8.0	Connie Mack	721,663
1931	1st	107	45	.704	+13.5	Connie Mack	627,464
1932	2nd	94	60	.610	13.0	Connie Mack	405,500
1933	3rd	79	72	.523	19.5	Connie Mack	297,138
1934	5th	68	82	.453	31.0	Connie Mack	305,847
1935	8th	58	91	.389	34.0	Connie Mack	233,173
1936	8th	53	100	.346	49.0	Connie Mack	285,173
1937	7th	54	97	.358	46.5	Connie Mack	430,733
1938	8th	53	99	.349	46.0	Connie Mack	385,357
1939	7th	55	97	.362	51.5	Connie Mack	395,022
1940	8th	54	100	.351	36.0	Connie Mack	432,145
1941	8th	64	90	.416	37.0	Connie Mack	528,894

1942	8th	55	99	.357	48.0	Connie Mack	423,487
1943	8th	49	105	.318	49.0	Connie Mack	376,735
1944	5th (Tie)	72	82	.468	17.0	Connie Mack	505,322
1945	8th	52	98	.347	34.5	Connie Mack	462,631
1946	8th	49	105	.318	55.0	Connie Mack	621,793
1947	5th	78	76	.506	19.0	Connie Mack	911,566
1948	4th	84	70	.545	12.5	Connie Mack	945,076
1949	5th	81	73	.526	16.0	Connie Mack	816,514
1950	8th	52	102	.338	46.0	Connie Mack	309,805
1951	6th	70	84	.455	28.0	Jimmy Dykes	465,469
1952	4th	79	75	.513	16.0	Jimmy Dykes	627,100
1953	7th	59	95	.383	41.5	Jimmy Dykes	362,113
1954	8th	51	103	.331	60.0	Eddie Joost	304,666

Awards

Most Valuable Player

Eddie Collins, second base, 1914
Mickey Cochrane, catcher, 1928
Lefty Grove, pitcher, 1931
Jimmie Foxx, first base, 1932
Jimmie Foxx, first base, 1933
Bobby Shantz, pitcher, 1952

Rookie of the Year

Harry Byrd, pitcher, 1952

Cy Young

[No pitcher]

Hall of Famers Who Played for the Philadelphia Athletics

Home Run Baker, third base, 1908–14
Chief Bender, pitcher, 1903–14
Ty Cobb, outfield, 1927–28
Mickey Cochrane, catcher, 1925–33
Eddie Collins, second base, 1906–14 and 1927–30
Jimmy Collins, third base, 1907–08
Stan Coveleski, pitcher, 1912
Jimmie Foxx, catcher, third base, and first base, 1925–35
Waite Hoyt, pitcher, 1931
George Kell, third base, 1943–46
Nap Lajoie, second base, 1901–02, 1915–16
Herb Pennock, pitcher, 1912–15
Eddie Plank, pitcher, 1901–14
Al Simmons, outfield, 1924–32, 1940–41, and 1944
Tris Speaker, outfield, 1928
Rube Waddell, pitcher, 1902–07
Zack Wheat, outfield, 1927

Retired Numbers

[None]

League Leaders, Batting

Batting Average, Season

Nap Lajoie, 1901 ..... .426
Al Simmons, 1930 ..... .381
Al Simmons, 1931 ..... .390
Jimmie Foxx, 1933 ..... .356
Ferris Fain, 1951 ..... .344
Ferris Fain, 1952 ..... .327

Home Runs, Season

Nap Lajoie, 1901 14
Socks Seybold, 1902 16
Harry Davis, 1904 10
Harry Davis, 1905 8
Harry Davis, 1906 12
Harry Davis, 1907 8
Home Run Baker, 1911 11
Home Run Baker, 1912 ..... 10 (Tie)
Home Run Baker, 1913 12
Home Run Baker, 1914 9
Tilly Walker, 1918 ..... 11 (Tie)
Jimmie Foxx, 1932 58
Jimmie Foxx, 1933 48
Jimmie Foxx, 1935 ..... 36 (Tie)
Gus Zernial*, 1951 33
*0 with Chi. White Sox and 33 with Phila. A's.

RBIs, Season

Home Run Baker, 1912 133
Home Run Baker, 1913 126
George H. Burns, 1918 ..... 74 (Tie)
Al Simmons, 1929 157
Jimmie Foxx, 1932 169
Jimmie Foxx, 1933 163
Gus Zernial*, 1951 129
*4 with Chi. White Sox and 125 with Phila. A's.

Stolen Bases, Season

Topsy Hartsel, 1902 54
Danny Hoffman, 1905 46
Eddie Collins, 1910 81
Billy Werber, 1937 ..... 35 (Tie)

Total Bases, Season

Nap Lajoie, 1901 345
George H. Burns, 1918 236
Al Simmons, 1925 392
Al Simmons, 1929 373
Jimmie Foxx, 1932 438
Jimmie Foxx, 1933 403

Most Hits, Season

Nap Lajoie, 1901 229
George H. Burns, 1918 178
Al Simmons, 1925 253
Al Simmons, 1932 216

Most Runs, Season

Nap Lajoie, 1901 145
Dave Fultz, 1902 110
Harry Davis, 1905 92
Eddie Collins, 1912 137

Eddie Collins, 1913 125
Eddie Collins, 1914 122
Al Simmons, 1930 152
Jimmie Foxx, 1932 151

Batting Feats

Triple Crown Winners

Nap Lajoie, 1901 (.426 BA, 14 HRs, 125 RBIs)

Hitting for the Cycle

Harry Davis, July 10, 1901
Nap Lajoie, July 30, 1901
Danny Murphy, Aug. 25, 1910
Home Run Baker, July 3, 1911
Mickey Cochrane, July 22, 1932
Mickey Cochrane, Aug. 2, 1933
Pinky Higgins, Aug. 6, 1933
Jimmie Foxx, Aug. 14, 1933
Doc Cramer, June 10, 1934
Sam Chapman, May 5, 1939
Elmer Valo, Aug. 2, 1950

Six Hits in a Game

Danny Murphy, July 8, 1902
Jimmie Foxx, May 30, 1930*
Doc Cramer, June 20, 1932
Jimmie Foxx, July 10, 1932*
Bob Johnson, June 16, 1934*
Doc Cramer, July 13, 1935
*Extra-inning game.

40 or More Home Runs, Season

58 ..... Jimmie Foxx, 1932
48 ..... Jimmie Foxx, 1933
44 ..... Jimmie Foxx, 1934
42 ..... Gus Zernial, 1953

League Leaders, Pitching

Most Wins, Season

Rube Waddell, 1905 27
Jack Coombs, 1910 31
Jack Coombs, 1911 28
Ed Rommel, 1922 27
Ed Rommel, 1925 ..... 21 (Tie)
Lefty Grove, 1928 ..... 24 (Tie)
George Earnshaw, 1929 24
Lefty Grove, 1930 28
Lefty Grove, 1931 31
Lefty Grove, 1933 ..... 24 (Tie)
Bobby Shantz, 1952 24

Most Strikeouts, Season

Rube Waddell, 1902 210
Rube Waddell, 1903 301
Rube Waddell, 1904 349
Rube Waddell, 1905 286
Rube Waddell, 1906 203
Rube Waddell, 1907 226
Lefty Grove, 1925 116
Lefty Grove, 1926 194
Lefty Grove, 1927 174
Lefty Grove, 1928 183
Lefty Grove, 1929 170
Lefty Grove, 1930 209
Lefty Grove, 1931 175

Lowest ERA, Season

Lefty Grove, 1926 ..... 2.51
Lefty Grove, 1929 ..... 2.81
Lefty Grove, 1930 ..... 2.54
Lefty Grove, 1931 ..... 2.06
Lefty Grove, 1932 ..... 2.84

Most Saves, Season

[No pitcher]

Best Won–Lost Percentage, Season

Eddie Plank, 1906 ..... 19–8 ... .760
Chief Bender, 1910 ..... 23–5 ... .821
Chief Bender, 1911 ..... 17–9 ... .773
Chief Bender, 1914 ..... 17–3 ... .850
Lefty Grove, 1929 ..... 20–6 ... .769
Lefty Grove, 1930 ..... 28–5 ... .848
Lefty Grove, 1931 ..... 31–4 ... .886
Lefty Grove, 1933 ..... 24–8 ... .750
Bobby Shantz, 1952 .... 24–7 ... .774

Pitching Feats

Triple Crown Winner

Rube Waddell, 1905 (27–10, 1.48 ERA, 287 SO)
Lefty Grove, 1930 (28–5, 2.54 ERA, 209 SO)
Lefty Grove, 1931 (31–4, 2.06 ERA, 175 SO)

20 Wins, Season

Chick Fraser, 1901 22–16
Rube Waddell, 1902 23–7
Eddie Plank, 1902 20–15
Eddie Plank, 1903 23–16
Rube Waddell, 1903 21–16
Eddie Plank, 1904 26–17
Rube Waddell, 1904 25–19
Rube Waddell, 1905 26–11
Eddie Plank, 1905 25–12
Eddie Plank, 1907 24–16
Jimmy Dygert, 1907 20–9
Jack Coombs, 1910 31–9
Chief Bender, 1910 23–5
Jack Coombs, 1911 28–12
Eddie Plank, 1911 22–8
Eddie Plank, 1912 26–6
Jack Coombs, 1912 21–10
Chief Bender, 1913 21–10
Scott Perry, 1918 21–19
Eddie Rommel, 1922 27–13
Eddie Rommel, 1925 21–10
Lefty Grove, 1927 20–13
Lefty Grove, 1928 24–8
George Earnshaw, 1929 24–8
Lefty Grove, 1929 20–6
Lefty Grove, 1930 28–5
George Earnshaw, 1930 22–13
Lefty Grove, 1931 31–4
George Earnshaw, 1931 21–7
Rube Walberg, 1931 20–12
Lefty Grove, 1932 25–10
Lefty Grove, 1933 24–8
Alex Kellner, 1949 20–12
Bobby Shantz, 1952 24–7

No-Hitters

Weldon Henley (vs. St.L. Browns), July 22, 1905 (final: 6–0)
Chief Bender (vs. Cle. Indians), May 12, 1910 (final: 4–0)
Joe Bush (vs. Cle. Indians), Aug. 26, 1916 (final: 5–0)
Dick Fowler (vs. St.L. Browns), Sept. 9, 1945 (final: 1–0)
Bill McCahan (vs. Wash. Senators), Sept. 3, 1947 (final: 3–0)

No-Hitters Pitched Against

Cy Young, Bost. Red Sox, May 5, 1904 (final: 3–0) (perfect game)
Frank Smith, Chi. White Sox, Sept. 20, 1908 (final: 1–0)
Sam Jones, N.Y. Yankees, Sept. 4, 1923 (final: 4–0)
Howard Ehmke, Bost. Red Sox, Sept. 7, 1923 (final: 4–0)
Don Black, Cle. Indians, July 10, 1947 (final: 3–0)
Bobo Holloman, St.L. Browns, May 6, 1953 (final: 6–0)

Postseason Play

1905 World Series vs. N.Y. Giants (NL), lost 4 games to 1

1910 World Series vs. Chi. Cubs (NL), won 4 games to 1

1911 World Series vs. N.Y. Giants (NL), won 4 games to 2

1913 World Series vs. N.Y. Giants (NL), won 4 games to 1

1914 World Series vs. Bost. Braves (NL), lost 4 games to 0

1929 World Series vs. Chi. Cubs (NL), won 4 games to 1

1930 World Series vs. St.L. Cardinals (NL), won 4 games to 3

1931 World Series vs. St.L. Cardinals (NL), lost 4 games to 2

St. Louis Browns

Date of Operation: (as the Milwaukee Brewers) 1901 (1 year)
Overall Record: 48 wins, 89 losses (.350)
Stadium: Lloyd Street Park, 1901

Dates of Operation: (as the St. Louis Browns) 1902–53 (52 years)
Overall Record: 3414 wins, 4465 losses (.433)
Stadiums: Sportsman's Park IV, 1902–08; Sportsman's Park V, 1909–53 (capacity: 30,500)

Year-by-Year Finishes

Year	Finish	Wins	Losses	Percentage	Games Behind	Manager	Attendance
					Milw. Brewers		
1901	8th	48	89	.350	35.5	Hugh Duffy	139,034
					St.L. Browns		
1902	2nd	78	58	.574	5.0	Jimmy McAleer	272,283
1903	6th	65	74	.468	26.5	Jimmy McAleer	380,405
1904	6th	65	87	.428	29.0	Jimmy McAleer	318,108
1905	8th	54	99	.353	40.5	Jimmy McAleer	339,112
1906	5th	76	73	.510	16.0	Jimmy McAleer	389,157
1907	6th	69	83	.454	24.0	Jimmy McAleer	419,025
1908	4th	83	69	.546	6.5	Jimmy McAleer	618,947
1909	7th	61	89	.407	36.0	Jimmy McAleer	366,274
1910	8th	47	107	.305	57.0	Jack O'Connor	249,889
1911	8th	45	107	.296	56.5	Bobby Wallace	207,984
1912	7th	53	101	.344	53.0	Bobby Wallace, George Stovall	214,070
1913	8th	57	96	.373	39.0	George Stovall, Branch Rickey	250,330
1914	5th	71	82	.464	28.5	Branch Rickey	244,714
1915	6th	63	91	.409	39.5	Branch Rickey	150,358
1916	5th	79	75	.513	12.0	Fielder Jones	335,740
1917	7th	57	97	.370	43.0	Fielder Jones	210,486
1918	5th	58	64	.475	15.0	Fielder Jones, Jimmy Austin, Jimmy Burke	122,076
1919	5th	67	72	.482	20.5	Jimmy Burke	349,350
1920	4th	76	77	.497	21.5	Jimmy Burke	419,311
1921	3rd	81	73	.526	17.5	Lee Fohl	355,978
1922	2nd	93	61	.604	1.0	Lee Fohl	712,918
1923	5th	74	78	.487	24.0	Lee Fohl, Jimmy Austin	430,296
1924	4th	74	78	.487	17.0	George Sisler	533,349
1925	3rd	82	71	.536	15.0	George Sisler	462,898
1926	7th	62	92	.403	29.0	George Sisler	283,986
1927	7th	59	94	.386	50.5	Dan Howley	247,879
1928	3rd	82	72	.532	19.0	Dan Howley	339,497
1929	4th	79	73	.520	26.0	Dan Howley	280,697
1930	6th	64	90	.416	38.0	Bill Killefer	152,088
1931	5th	63	91	.409	45.0	Bill Killefer	179,126
1932	6th	63	91	.409	44.0	Bill Killefer	112,558
1933	8th	55	96	.364	43.5	Bill Killefer, Allen Sothoron, Rogers Hornsby	88,113

1934	6th	67	85	.441	33.0	Rogers Hornsby	115,305
1935	7th	65	87	.428	28.5	Rogers Hornsby	80,922
1936	7th	57	95	.375	44.5	Rogers Hornsby	93,267
1937	8th	46	108	.299	56.0	Rogers Hornsby, Jim Bottomley	123,121
1938	7th	55	97	.362	44.0	Gabby Street	130,417
1939	8th	43	111	.279	64.5	Fred Haney	109,159
1940	6th	67	87	.435	23.0	Fred Haney	239,591
1941	6th (Tie)	70	84	.455	31.0	Fred Haney, Luke Sewell	176,240
1942	3rd	82	69	.543	19.5	Luke Sewell	255,617
1943	6th	72	80	.474	25.0	Luke Sewell	214,392
1944	1st	89	65	.578	+1.0	Luke Sewell	508,644
1945	3rd	81	70	.536	6.0	Luke Sewell	482,986
1946	7th	66	88	.429	38.0	Luke Sewell, Zack Taylor	526,435
1947	8th	59	95	.383	38.0	Muddy Ruel	320,474
1948	6th	59	94	.386	37.0	Zack Taylor	335,546
1949	7th	53	101	.344	44.0	Zack Taylor	270,936
1950	7th	58	96	.377	40.0	Zack Taylor	247,131
1951	8th	52	102	.338	46.0	Zack Taylor	293,790
1952	7th	64	90	.416	31.0	Rogers Hornsby, Marty Marion	518,796
1953	8th	54	100	.351	46.5	Marty Marion	297,238

Awards

Most Valuable Player

George Sisler, first base, 1922

Rookie of the Year

Roy Sievers, outfield, 1949

Cy Young

[No pitcher]

Hall of Famers Who Played for the St. Louis Browns

Jim Bottomley, first base, 1936–37
Jesse Burkett, outfield, 1902–04
Rick Ferrell, catcher, 1929–33 and 1941–43
Goose Goslin, outfield, 1930–32
Heinie Manush, outfield, 1928–30
Satchel Paige, pitcher, 1951–53
Eddie Plank, pitcher, 1916–17
Branch Rickey, catcher, 1905–06 and 1914
George Sisler, first base, 1915–22 and 1924–27
Rube Waddell, pitcher, 1908–10
Bobby Wallace, shortstop, 1902–16

Retired Numbers

[None]

League Leaders, Batting

Batting Average, Season

George Stone, 1906 ..... .358
George Sisler, 1920..... .407
George Sisler, 1922..... .420

Home Runs, Season

Ken Williams, 1922 39
Vern Stephens, 1945 24

RBIs, Season

Ken Williams, 1922 155
Vern Stephens, 1944 109

Stolen Bases, Season

George Sisler, 1918.....45
George Sisler, 1921.....35
George Sisler, 1922.....51
George Sisler, 1927.....27
Lyn Lary, 1936 37
Bob Dillinger, 1947.....34
Bob Dillinger, 1948.....28
Bob Dillinger, 1949.....20

Total Bases, Season

George Stone, 1905 260
George Stone, 1906 288
George Sisler, 1920.....399
Ken Williams, 1922 367

Most Hits, Season

George Stone, 1905 187
George Sisler, 1920.....257
George Sisler, 1922.....246
Heinie Manush, 1928.....241
Beau Bell, 1937.....218
Rip Radcliff, 1940.....200 (Tie)
Bob Dillinger, 1948.....207

Most Runs, Season

George Sisler, 1922.....134

Batting Feats

Triple Crown Winners

[No player]

Hitting for the Cycle

George Sisler, Aug. 8, 1920
George Sisler, Aug. 13, 1921
Baby Doll Jacobson, Apr. 17, 1924
Oscar Mellilo, May 23, 1929
George McQuinn, July 19, 1941

Six Hits in a Game

George Sisler, Aug. 9, 1921*
Sammy West, Apr. 13, 1933*
*Extra-inning game.

40 or More Home Runs, Season
[No player]

League Leaders, Pitching

Most Wins, Season
Urban Shocker, 1921 ..... 27 (Tie)

Most Strikeouts, Season
Urban Shocker, 1922 149

Lowest ERA, Season
[No pitcher]

Most Saves, Season
[No pitcher]

Best Won–Lost Percentage, Season
General Crowder, 1928 . 21–5.... .808

Pitching Feats

20 Wins, Season (1901–53)
Frank Donahue, 1902..... 22–11
Jack Powell, 1902..... 22–17
Willie Sudhoff, 1903..... 21–15
Allen Sothoron, 1919 21–11
Urban Shocker, 1920..... 20–10
Urban Shocker, 1921 27–12
Urban Shocker, 1922..... 24–17
Urban Shocker, 1923..... 20–12
General Crowder, 1928 21–5
Sam Gray, 1928..... 20–12
Lefty Stewart, 1930 20–12
Bobo Newsom, 1938 20–16
Ned Garver, 1951..... 20–12

No-Hitters
Earl Hamilton (vs. Det. Tigers), Aug. 30, 1912 (final: 5–1)
Ernie Koob (vs. Chi. White Sox), May 5, 1917 (final: 1–0)
Bob Groom (vs. Chi. White Sox), May 6, 1917 (final: 3–0)
Bobo Newsom (vs. Bost. Red Sox), Sept. 18, 1934 (final: 1–2) (lost in 10th)
Bobo Holloman (vs. Phila. A's), May 6, 1953 (final: 6–0)

No-Hitters Pitched Against
Weldon Henley, Phila. A's, July 22, 1905 (final: 6–0)
Smoky Joe Wood, Bost. Red Sox, July 29, 1911 (final: 5–0)
George Mullin, Det. Tigers, July 4, 1912 (final: 7–0)
Hub Leonard, Bost. Red Sox, Aug. 30, 1916 (final: 4–0)
Eddie Cicotte, Chi. White Sox, Apr. 14, 1917 (final: 11–0)
Wes Ferrell, Cle. Indians, Apr. 29, 1931 (final: 9–0)
Vern Kennedy, Chi. White Sox, Aug. 31, 1935 (final: 5–0)
Bill Dietrich, Chi. White Sox, June 1, 1937 (final: 8–0)
Dick Fowler, Phila. A's, Sept. 9, 1945 (final: 1–0)

Postseason Play

1944 World Series vs. St.L. Cardinals (NL), lost 4 games to 2

Washington Senators

Dates of Operation: (as the Washington Senators) 1901–60 (60 years)
Overall Record: 4223 wins, 4864 losses (.465)
Stadiums: American League Park I, 1901–03; American League Park II, 1904–10; Griffith Stadium (also known as National Park, 1911–21; Clark Griffith Park, 1922), 1911–60
Other Name: Nationals

Dates of Operation: (as the Washington Senators II) 1961–71 (11 years)
Overall Record: 740 wins, 1032 losses (.418)
Stadiums: Griffith Stadium, 1961; Robert F. Kennedy (RFK) Stadium, 1962–71
Other Name: Nats

Year-by-Year Finishes

Year	Finish	Wins	Losses	Percentage	Games Behind	Manager	Attendance
					Wash. Senators		
1901	6th	61	72	.459	20.5	Jimmy Manning	161,661
1902	6th	61	75	.449	22.0	Tom Loftus	188,158
1903	8th	43	94	.314	47.5	Tom Loftus	128,878
1904	8th	38	113	.252	55.5	Patsy Donovan	131,744
1905	7th	64	87	.424	29.5	Jake Stahl	252,027
1906	7th	55	95	.367	37.5	Jake Stahl	129,903
1907	8th	49	102	.325	43.5	Joe Cantillon	221,929
1908	7th	67	85	.441	22.5	Joe Cantillon	264,252
1909	8th	42	110	.276	56.0	Joe Cantillon	205,199
1910	7th	66	85	.437	36.5	Jimmy McAleer	254,591
1911	7th	64	90	.416	38.5	Jimmy McAleer	244,884
1912	2nd	91	61	.599	14.0	Clark Griffith	350,663
1913	2nd	90	64	.584	6.5	Clark Griffith	325,831
1914	3rd	81	73	.526	19.0	Clark Griffith	243,888
1915	4th	85	68	.556	17.0	Clark Griffith	167,332
1916	7th	76	77	.497	14.5	Clark Griffith	177,265
1917	5th	74	79	.484	25.5	Clark Griffith	89,682
1918	3rd	72	56	.563	4.0	Clark Griffith	182,122
1919	7th	56	84	.400	32.0	Clark Griffith	234,096
1920	6th	68	84	.447	29.0	Clark Griffith	359,260
1921	4th	80	73	.523	18.0	George McBride	456,069
1922	6th	69	85	.448	25.0	Clyde Milan	458,552
1923	4th	75	78	.490	23.5	Donie Bush	357,406
1924	1st	92	62	.597	+2.0	Bucky Harris	534,310
1925	1st	96	55	.636	+8.5	Bucky Harris	817,199
1926	4th	81	69	.540	8.0	Bucky Harris	551,580
1927	3rd	85	69	.552	25.0	Bucky Harris	528,976
1928	4th	75	79	.487	26.0	Bucky Harris	378,501
1929	5th	71	81	.467	34.0	Walter Johnson	355,506
1930	2nd	94	60	.610	8.0	Walter Johnson	614,474
1931	3rd	92	62	.597	16.0	Walter Johnson	492,657
1932	3rd	93	61	.604	14.0	Walter Johnson	371,396
1933	1st	99	53	.651	+7.0	Joe Cronin	437,533
1934	7th	66	86	.434	34.0	Joe Cronin	330,374

1935	6th	67	86	.438	27.0	Bucky Harris	255,011
1936	4th	82	71	.536	20.0	Bucky Harris	379,525
1937	6th	73	80	.477	28.5	Bucky Harris	397,799
1938	5th	75	76	.497	23.5	Bucky Harris	522,694
1939	6th	65	87	.428	41.5	Bucky Harris	339,257
1940	7th	64	90	.416	26.0	Bucky Harris	381,241
1941	6th (Tie)	70	84	.455	31.0	Bucky Harris	415,663
1942	7th	62	89	.411	39.5	Bucky Harris	403,493
1943	2nd	84	69	.549	13.5	Ossie Bluege	574,694
1944	8th	64	90	.416	25.0	Ossie Bluege	525,235
1945	2nd	87	67	.565	1.5	Ossie Bluege	652,660
1946	4th	76	78	.494	28.0	Ossie Bluege	1,027,216
1947	7th	64	90	.416	33.0	Ossie Bluege	850,758
1948	7th	56	97	.366	40.0	Joe Kuhel	795,254
1949	8th	50	104	.325	47.0	Joe Kuhel	770,745
1950	5th	67	87	.435	31.0	Bucky Harris	699,697
1951	7th	62	92	.403	36.0	Bucky Harris	695,167
1952	5th	78	76	.506	17.0	Bucky Harris	699,457
1953	5th	76	76	.500	23.5	Bucky Harris	595,594
1954	6th	66	88	.429	45.0	Bucky Harris	503,542
1955	8th	53	101	.344	43.0	Chuck Dressen	425,238
1956	7th	59	95	.383	38.0	Chuck Dressen	431,647
1957	8th	55	99	.357	43.0	Chuck Dressen, Cookie Lavagetto	457,079
1958	8th	61	93	.396	31.0	Cookie Lavagetto	475,288
1959	8th	63	91	.409	31.0	Cookie Lavagetto	615,372
1960	5th	73	81	.474	24.0	Cookie Lavagetto	743,404
				Wash. Senators II			
1961	9th (Tie)	61	100	.379	47.5	Mickey Vernon	597,287
1962	10th	60	101	.373	35.5	Mickey Vernon	729,775
1963	10th	56	106	.346	48.5	Mickey Vernon, Gil Hodges	535,604
1964	9th	62	100	.383	37.0	Gil Hodges	600,106
1965	8th	70	92	.432	32.0	Gil Hodges	560,083
1966	8th	71	88	.447	25.5	Gil Hodges	576,260
1967	6th (Tie)	76	85	.472	15.5	Gil Hodges	770,863
1968	10th	65	96	.404	37.5	Jim Lemon	546,661
				East Division			
1969	4th	86	76	.531	23.0	Ted Williams	918,106
1970	6th	70	92	.432	38.0	Ted Williams	824,789
1971	5th	63	96	.396	38.5	Ted Williams	655,156

Awards

Most Valuable Player

Walter Johnson, pitcher, 1913
Walter Johnson, pitcher, 1924
Roger Peckinpaugh, shortstop, 1925

Rookie of the Year

Albie Pearson, outfield, 1958
Bob Allison, outfield, 1959

Cy Young

[No pitcher]

Hall of Famers Who Played for the Senators

Stan Coveleski, pitcher, 1925–27
Joe Cronin, shortstop, 1928–34
Ed Delahanty, first base and outfield, 1902–03
Rick Ferrell, catcher, 1937–41, 1944–45, and 1947
Lefty Gomez, pitcher, 1943
Goose Goslin, outfield, 1921–30, 1933, and 1938
Bucky Harris, second base, 1919–28
Walter Johnson, pitcher, 1907–27
Harmon Killebrew, third base and first base, 1956–60

Heinie Manush, outfield, 1930–35
Sam Rice, outfield, 1915–33
Al Simmons, outfield, 1937–38
Early Wynn, pitcher, 1939, 1941–44, and 1946–48

Retired Numbers
[None]

League Leaders, Batting

Batting Average, Season
Ed Delahanty, 1902 ..... .376
Goose Goslin, 1928 ..... .379
Buddy Myer, 1935 ..... .349
Mickey Vernon, 1946 ..... .353
Mickey Vernon, 1953 ..... .337

Home Runs, Season
Roy Sievers, 1957 42
Harmon Killebrew, 1959 ..... 42 (Tie)
Frank Howard, 1968 (Senators II) .. 44
Frank Howard, 1970 (Senators II) .. 44

RBIs, Season
Goose Goslin, 1924 129
Roy Sievers, 1957 114
Frank Howard, 1970 (Senators II) 126

Stolen Bases, Season
John Anderson, 1906 ..... 39 (Tie)
Clyde Milan, 1912 88
Clyde Milan, 1913 75
Sam Rice, 1920 63
Ben Chapman*, 1937 ..... 35 (Tie)
George Case, 1939 51
George Case, 1940 35
George Case, 1941 33
George Case, 1942 44
George Case, 1943 61
*27 with Bost. Red Sox and 8 with Wash. Senators.

Total Bases, Season
Roy Sievers, 1957 331
Frank Howard, 1968 (Senators II) 330
Frank Howard, 1969 (Senators II) 340

Most Hits, Season
Sam Rice, 1924 216
Sam Rice, 1926 ..... 216 (Tie)
Heinie Manush, 1933 221
Cecil Travis, 1941 218

Most Runs, Season
George Case, 1943 102

Batting Feats

Triple Crown Winners
[No player]

Hitting for the Cycle
Otis Clymer, Oct. 2, 1908
Goose Goslin, Aug. 28, 1924
Joe Cronin, Sept. 2, 1929
Mickey Vernon, May 19, 1946
Jim King, May 26, 1964 (Senators II)

Six Hits in a Game
George Myatt, May 1, 1944
Stan Spence, June 1, 1944

40 or More Home Runs, Season
48 .. Frank Howard, 1969 (Senators II)
44 .. Frank Howard, 1968 (Senators II)
Frank Howard, 1970 (Senators II)
42 ..... Roy Sievers, 1957
Harmon Killebrew, 1959

League Leaders, Pitching

Most Wins, Season
Walter Johnson, 1913 36
Walter Johnson, 1914 28
Walter Johnson, 1915 27
Walter Johnson, 1916 25
Walter Johnson, 1918 23
Walter Johnson, 1924 23
General Crowder, 1932 26
General Crowder, 1933 ..... 24 (Tie)
Bob Porterfield, 1953 22

Most Strikeouts, Season
Walter Johnson, 1910 313
Walter Johnson, 1912 303
Walter Johnson, 1913 243
Walter Johnson, 1914 225
Walter Johnson, 1915 203
Walter Johnson, 1916 228
Walter Johnson, 1917 188
Walter Johnson, 1918 162
Walter Johnson, 1919 147
Walter Johnson, 1921 143
Walter Johnson, 1923 130
Walter Johnson, 1924 158
Bobo Newsom, 1942 ..... 113 (Tie)

Lowest ERA, Season
Walter Johnson, 1913 ..... 1.14
Walter Johnson, 1918 ..... 1.27
Walter Johnson, 1919 ..... 1.49
Walter Johnson, 1924 ..... 2.72
Stan Coveleski, 1925 ..... 2.84
Garland Braxton, 1928 ..... 2.52
Dick Donovan, 1961 (Senators II) . 2.40
Dick Bosman, 1969 (Senators II) . 2.19

Most Saves, Season
[No pitcher]

Best Won–Lost Percentage, Season
Walter Johnson, 1913 .. 36–7 ... .837
Walter Johnson, 1924 .. 23–7 ... .767
Stan Coveleski, 1925 ... 20–5 ... .800

Pitching Feats

Triple Crown Winner
Walter Johnson, 1913 (36–7, 1.14 ERA, 243 SO)
Walter Johnson, 1918 (23–13, 1.27 ERA, 162 SO)
Walter Johnson, 1924 (23–7, 2.72 ERA, 158 SO)

20 Wins, Season
Walter Johnson, 1910 25–17
Walter Johnson, 1911 25–13
Walter Johnson, 1912 33–12
Bob Groom, 1912 24–13
Walter Johnson, 1913 36–7
Walter Johnson, 1914 28–18
Walter Johnson, 1915 27–13
Walter Johnson, 1916 25–20
Walter Johnson, 1917 23–16
Walter Johnson, 1918 23–13
Walter Johnson, 1919 20–14
Walter Johnson, 1924 23–7
Stan Coveleski, 1925 20–5
Walter Johnson, 1925 20–7
General Crowder, 1932 26–13
Monte Weaver, 1932 22–10
General Crowder, 1933 24–15
Earl Whitehill, 1933 22–8
Dutch Leonard, 1939 20–8
Roger Wolff, 1945 20–10
Bob Porterfield, 1953 22–10

No-Hitters
Walter Johnson (vs. Bost. Red Sox), July 1, 1920 (final: 1–0)
Bob Burke (vs. Bost. Red Sox), Aug. 8, 1931 (final: 5–0)

No-Hitters Pitched Against

Ernie Shore, Bost. Red Sox, June 23, 1917 (final: 4–0) (perfect game)

Bill McCahan, Phila. A's, Sept. 3, 1947 (final: 3–0)

Virgil Trucks, Det. Tigers, May 15, 1952 (final: 1–0)

Bob Keegan, Chi. White Sox, Aug. 20, 1957 (final: 6–0)

Sonny Siebert, Cle. Indians, June 10, 1966 (final: 2–0) (Senators II)

Postseason Play

1924 World Series vs. N.Y. Giants (NL), won 4 games to 3

1925 World Series vs. Pitt. Pirates (NL), lost 4 games to 3

1933 World Series vs. N.Y. Giants (NL), lost 4 games to 1